Modern Real Estate Practice in New York

Edith Lank
Third Edition

For Salespersons & Brokers

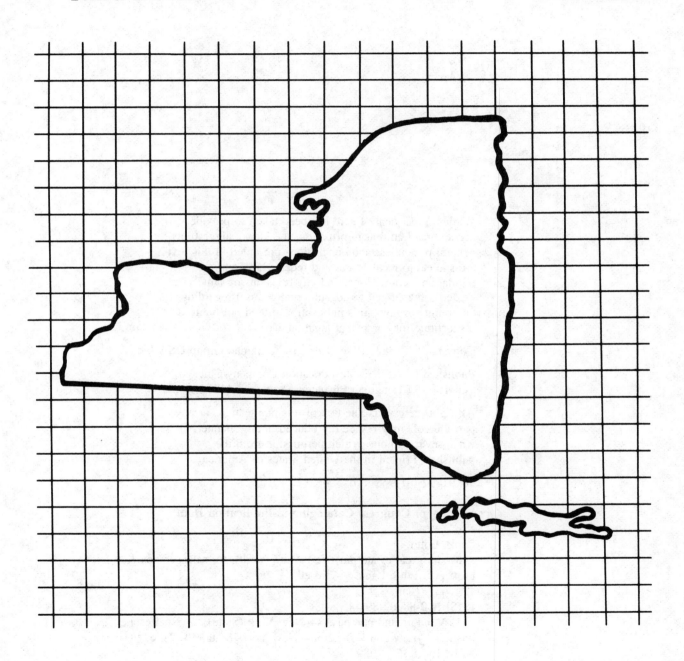

REAL ESTATE EDUCATION COMPANY
® a division of Longman Financial Services Institute, Inc.

While a great deal of care has been taken to provide
accurate and current information, the ideas, suggestions,
general principles, and conclusions presented in this text
are subject to local, state, and federal laws and
regulations, court cases, and any revisions of same. The
reader is thus urged to consult legal counsel regarding
any points of law—this publication should not be used as
a substitute for competent legal advice.

Library of Congress Cataloging-in-Publication Data

Lank, Edith.
  Modern real estate practice in New York : for salespersons &
brokers. / Edith Lank. — 3rd ed.
    p.   cm.
  ISBN 0-88462-891-4
  1. Vendors and purchasers—New York (State) 2. Real estate
business—Law and legislation—New York (State) I. Title.
KFN5166.L36 1989
346.74704'37—dc20
[347.4706437]   89-10921
                      CIP

Sponsoring Editor: Margaret M. Maloney
Project Editor: Ronald J. Liszkowski

Real Estate Education Company Series

Bellairs, Helsel & Caldwell	Modern Real Estate Practice in Pennsylvania, 5th Edition
Coit	Introduction to Real Estate Law, 3rd Edition
Cyr & Sobeck	Real Estate Brokerage: A Success Guide, 2nd Edition
Deickler	New York Real Estate Exam Guide
Fournier	How to Use the HP-18C in Real Estate
Floyd	Real Estate Principles, 2nd Edition, Revised
Friedman & Henszey	Protecting Your Sales Commission: Professional Liability in Real Estate
Gaddy & Hart	Real Estate Fundamentals, 3rd Edition
Gaines & Coleman	Basic Real Estate Math, 3rd Edition
Galaty, Allaway & Kyle	Modern Real Estate Practice, 11th Edition
Gibson, Karp & Klayman	Real Estate Law, 2nd Edition
Greynolds & Aronofsky	Practical Real Estate Financial Analysis: Using The HP-12C Calculator
Kyle	Property Management, 3rd Edition
Lank	Modern Real Estate Practice in New York, 3rd Edition
Lank	The Complete Homebuyer's Kit
Lank	The Complete Homeseller's Kit
Martin & Jackson	New Jersey Supplement for Modern Real Estate Practice, 5th Edition
Mettling & Cortesi	Modern Residential Financing Methods: Tools of the Trade, 2nd Edition
Pivar	Classified Secrets, 2nd Edition
Pivar	Power Real Estate Listing, 2nd Edition
Pivar	Power Real Estate Selling, 2nd Edition
Pivar	Real Estate Ethics, 2nd Edition
Pivar	Real Estate Guide for the Licensing Exam (ASI), 2nd Edition
Developed by Real Estate Education Company in conjunction with Grubb & Ellis Company	Successful Industrial Real Estate Brokerage, 3rd Edition Successful Leasing & Selling of Office Property, 3rd Edition Successful Leasing & Selling of Retail Property, 3rd Edition
Reilly	Agency Relationships in Real Estate
Reilly	Language of Real Estate, 3rd Edition
Reilly & Vitousek	Questions & Answers to Help You Pass the Real Estate Exam, 3rd Edition
Rosenauer	Effective Real Estate Sales and Marketing, 2nd Edition

Contents

7   Real Estate Financing 102

8   License Law and Ethics 126

9   Valuation and Listing Proceedures 156

10   Human Rights and Fair Housing 174

Preface

This third edition of *Modern Real Estate Practice in New York* is dedicated to the many thousands of real estate students and instructors whose enthusiastic acceptance has made it the best-selling real estate textbook in the Empire State. Once again, many valuable suggestions for the new edition have come from those who are using the book.

The text provides basic material for the standard salesperson's course in Part One and state-mandated topics for the broker's course in Part Two. It has been updated throughout, with particular attention to recent changes in financing, license law, human rights, construction and investment strategies.

The book was originally adapted from the classic text, *Modern Real Estate Practice* by Galaty, Allaway and Kyle, which has sold more than a million copies since it was first published in 1959.

Thanks are due to the instructors who responded to a call for suggestions, and to the reviewers who offered valuable assistance in the development of this third edition: Beverly L. Deickler, Esquire; Judith J. Deickler, GRI, real estate consultant; Thomas Thomassian, PACE University, Pratt College and Bernard Baruch College and Chris E. Wittstruck, Esquire, Saint John's University.

Special contributions to earlier editions came from Charles E. Davies; Thomas DeCelle, Judith J. Deickler, Peter Karl, III; Leon Katzen, Esq.; William Lange, Jr.; George Lasch, John Mataraza; James Myers, Esq.; and Dorothy Tymon.

The author is particularly grateful to Maureen Glasheen, Esq., Gail Bates, William Stavola, Willard Roff and Joseph Amello of the New York Department of State; Charles M. Staro, Georgianne Bailey and Mark Morano of the New York State Association of REALTORS®; Bonnie May and Thomas R. Viola of the State Division of Housing and Community Renewal; Liz Johnson and Jeff Lubar with the National Association of REALTORS®; Eileen Taus and P. Gilbert Mercurio of the Westchester County Board of REALTORS®; Robert Elwell, Robert Wilson and John Piper of the Greater Rochester Association of REALTORS®; bankers Rose Bernstein and Gaye Greene; and Longman Financial Services Publishing's Robert Kyle and Anita Constant, who first sponsored this book; Margaret Maloney, development editor; Ronald J. Liszkowski, project editor; and Esther Vail, indexer.

Valuable help has also come from attorneys Abraham Berkowitz, Donald Friedman, Harold Geringer, David Henehan, Benjamin Henszey, Ezra Katzen, James Loeb, Joseph M. O'Donnell, Louis Ryen, Karen Schaefer, Sally Smith and Christine Van Benschoten. Among REALTORS® who offered suggestions and assistance are Ronald Baroody, Thomas Carozza, John Cyr, Barry Deickler, Ruth De Roo, Thomas Galvin, Harold Kahn, Norman Lank, William Lester, Robert Michaels, Joan Sobeck, Thomas Wills, III and Rex Vail. Special assistance came from John Alberts, Professor Kenneth Beckerink, Cindy Faire, Jim Foley, John Keaton, Eli Kimels, Nicholas Morabito and Larry Rockefeller.

For permission to use forms and figures, thanks go to Julius Blumberg, Inc.; National Association of REALTORS® Economics and Research Division; New York Board of Title Underwriters; New York Department of State, Greater Rochester Association of REALTORS®, Inc.; Professional Publishing Corporation and the Westchester Multiple Listing System, Inc.

Instructors are encouraged to write the publisher on school letterheads for the complimentary Instructors Manual that accompanies this textbook. The author would also like to recommend to them the National Real Estate Educators Association, 230 N. Michigan Ave., Suite 1200, Chicago, Illinois, 60601. The association offers workshops, publications and conferences, and has local chapters in New York.

Part of the fascination of the real estate field is the way it changes and adapts to new economic and social conditions. The author always enjoys discussing new information, suggestions and criticism with students and instructors who write or telephone:

Edith Lank
240 Hemingway Drive
Rochester, NY 14620
716-473-4973

About the Author   Edith Lank has been a licensed broker in New York for more than 20 years and has taught real estate at St. John Fisher College. Her award-winning weekly column on real estate, distributed by the Los Angeles Times Syndicate, has appeared in newspapers in Buffalo, Rochester, Syracuse, Schenectady, Amsterdam, Elmira, Brooklyn, Binghamton, Kingston, Ithaca, Middletown, Westchester and Rockland counties and Long Island, as well as in 100 other newpapers around the country.

She appears weekly on public radio and has hosted her own television and radio shows. She is a frequent speaker at Boards of REALTORS® functions and has published six books on real estate. Her work has been honored by the Monroe County Bar Association, Women in Communication, local and national associations of REALTORS®, the National Association of Real Estate Editors, the Real Estate Educators Association, and Governor Mario Cuomo. A graduate of Penn Yan Academy and Syracuse University, she is a member of Phi Beta Kappa.

Part One

Real Estate Salesperson

1

What is Real Estate?

Overview

Tens of thousands of men and women in New York State work in some aspect of the real estate industry as brokers, salespersons, appraisers, builders, developers, lawyers or property managers. They aid buyers, sellers and investors in making decisions that involve billions of dollars in property each year. But what exactly is real estate? This chapter will discuss the nature of land, real estate, and real and personal property and will introduce you to the many facets of the real estate industry.

Real Estate Transactions

The purchase of *real estate* differs markedly from the purchase of *personal property*, like groceries, automobiles or television sets. *Even the simplest of real estate transactions brings into play a body of complex laws.*

Real property has often been described as a **bundle of legal rights.** When a person purchases a parcel of real estate, he or she is actually buying the rights previously held by the seller. These *rights of ownership (see* Figure 1.1) include the right to *possession,* the right to *control the property* within the framework of the law, the right of *enjoyment* (to use the property in any legal manner), the right of *exclusion* (to keep others from entering or occupying the property), and the right of *disposition* or *alienation* (to be able to sell or otherwise convey the property). Within these ownership rights are included further rights to *devise* (leave by will) mortgage, encumber, cultivate, explore, lease, license, dedicate, give away, abandon, share, trade or exchange the property.

Figure 1.1
Bundle of Legal Rights

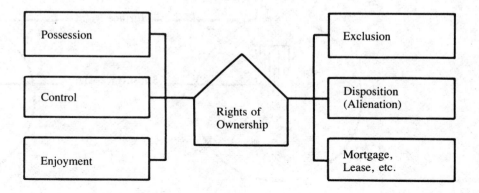

Land, Real Estate, and Real Property

The words *land, real estate* and *real property* often are used to describe the same commodity. There are, however, important differences in their technical meanings.

Land

The term *land* refers to more than just the surface of the earth; it includes the underlying soil and things permanently attached to the land by nature, such as trees and water. Land ownership also includes possession and control of the minerals and substances below the earth's surface together with the airspace above the land up to infinity.

Thus **land** is defined as *the earth's surface extending downward to the center of the earth and upward to infinity, including things permanently attached by nature, such as trees and water* (*see* Figure 1.2).

A specific tract of land is commonly referred to as a **parcel,** which can be of any size but has specific boundaries.

Real Estate

The term *real estate* is broader than the term *land* and includes also all man-made permanent improvements. The word **improvement** includes buildings erected on the land as well as streets, utilities, sewers and other man-made additions to the property.

Real estate, therefore, is defined as *the earth's surface extending downward to the center of the earth and upward into space, including all things permanently attached to it by nature or by people* (*see* Figure 1.2).

**Figure 1.2
Land/Real Estate**

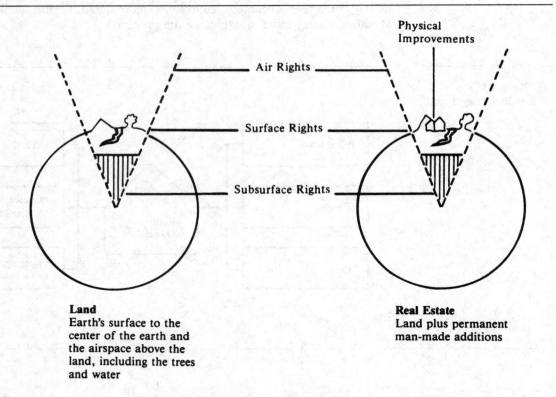

Land
Earth's surface to the center of the earth and the airspace above the land, including the trees and water

Real Estate
Land plus permanent man-made additions

Real Property

The term *real property* is broader still and includes that *bundle of legal rights of ownership.*

Thus **real property** is defined as *the earth's surface extending downward to the center of the earth and upward into space, including all things permanently attached to it by nature or by man, as well as the interests, benefits and rights inherent in the ownership of real estate* (*see* Figure 1.3).

In everyday usage, the term *real estate* or *realty* is commonly used for *real property.*

Figure 1.3
Real Property

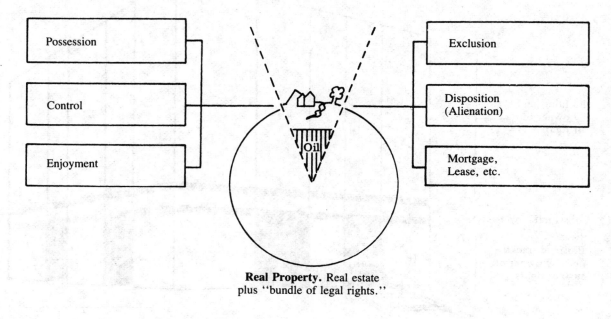

Real Property. Real estate
plus "bundle of legal rights."

Subsurface rights, the rights to the natural resources lying below the earth's surface, may be owned separately.

A landowner, for example, may sell to an oil company his or her rights to any oil and gas found in the land. The landowner could then sell the land to a purchaser and in the sale reserve the rights to all coal that may be found in the land. After these sales, three parties have ownership interests in this real estate: (1) the oil company owns all oil and gas, (2) the seller owns all coal and (3) the new landowner owns the rights to all the rest of the real estate.

Mineral rights may also be leased, and much of the farmland in southwestern New York State is subject to oil and gas leases.

Air rights. The rights to use the air above the land may be sold or leased independently of the land itself. Such **air rights** are an increasingly important part of real estate, particularly in large cities, where air rights over railroads have been purchased to construct huge office buildings like the Pan-Am Building in New York City. For the construction of such a building, the developer must purchase not only the air rights above the land but also numerous small portions of the actual land in order to construct the building's foundation supports, called *caissons* (*see* Figure 1.4).

Until the development of airplanes, a property's air rights were considered to be unlimited. Today, however, the courts permit reasonable interference with these rights by aircraft, as long as the owner's right to use and occupy the land is not unduly lessened. Governments and airport authorities often purchase air rights adjacent to an airport to provide glide patterns for air traffic. With the continuing

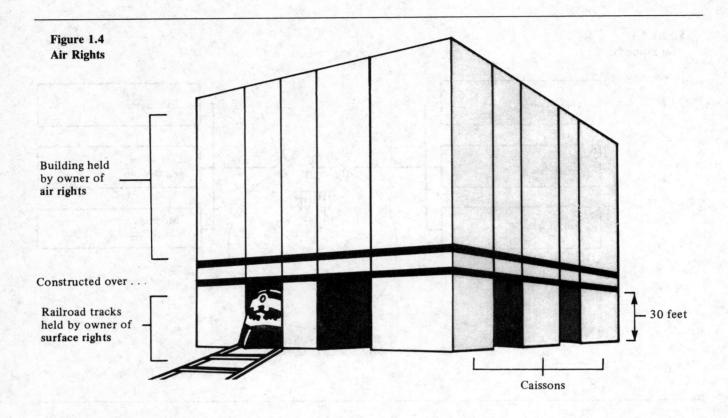

**Figure 1.4
Air Rights**

Building held
by owner of
air rights

Constructed over . . .

Railroad tracks
held by owner of
surface rights

30 feet

Caissons

development of solar power, air rights—more specifically, rights to sun and light—
may be redefined by the courts. They may consider tall buildings that block sun-
light from smaller buildings to be interfering with the smaller buildings' rights
to solar energy.

In summary, the rights in one parcel of real property may be owned by many
people: (1) an owner of the surface rights, (2) an owner of the subsurface mineral rights, (3) an owner of the subsurface gas and oil rights and (4) an owner of
the air rights.

Riparian rights are the owner's rights in land bordering a river. In New York,
persons owning land bordering navigable streams own the property to the high-
water mark; the riverbed belongs to the state. Persons owning land bordering nonnavigable streams own the land to the midpoint of the stream (*see* Figure 1.5).

Closely related to riparian rights are the **littoral rights** of owners whose land borders on large, navigable lakes and oceans. Owners with littoral rights may enjoy unrestricted use of available waters but own the land adjacent to the water
only up to the mean high-water mark (*see* Figure 1.6). All land below this point
is owned by the government. Riparian and littoral rights are appurtenant (attached) to the land and cannot be sold separately or retained when the land is
sold.

Where land adjoins streams or rivers, an owner is entitled to all *accretions,* or
increases in the land resulting from the deposit of soil by the natural action of

Figure 1.5
Riparian Rights

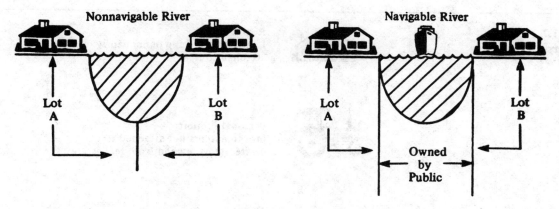

the water. An owner may also lose land through gradual *erosion*, or through *avulsion* due to a sudden change in the channel of a stream.

Real Property versus Personal Property

Everything that can be owned may be classified as either real or personal property. Real estate has already been defined as a part of the earth including the permanent additions or growing things attached to it, the airspace above it and the minerals below it.

Personal property is *all property that does not fit the definition of real estate*. Thus, personal property has the unique characteristic of being *movable*. Items of personal property, also referred to as **chattels**, *movables* or *personalty*, include

Figure 1.6
Littoral Rights

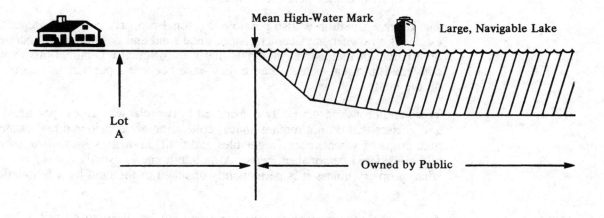

such tangibles as refrigerators, drapes, clothing, money, bonds and bank accounts (*see* Figure 1.7.)

Figure 1.7
Real versus Personal
Property

Real Estate
Land and anything permanently
attached to it

Personal Property
Movable items not attached to real
estate; items severed from real estate

Fixture
Item of personal property converted to
real estate by attaching it to the real
estate with the intention that it become
permanently a part thereof

Trade Fixture
Item of personal property attached to
real estate that is owned by a tenant
and is used in a business; legally
removable by tenant

The distinction between personal and real property is of great importance to the real estate practitioner. Buyers and sellers must be guided to clear written agreements about what "goes with" property being sold. The distinction also is significant with regard to taxation when property is sold: Personal property may be subject to sales tax, real property to transfer tax.

It is possible to change an item of real estate to personal property. A growing tree is real estate, but if the owner cuts down the tree and thereby severs it from the earth, it becomes personal property.

The reverse situation is also possible. Personal property can be changed to real estate. If an owner buys cement, stones and sand and constructs a concrete walk on a parcel of real estate, materials that were originally personal property are converted into real estate because they have become a permanent improvement on the land.

Trees and crops are generally considered in two classes. Trees, perennial bushes and grasses that do not require annual cultivation are considered real estate. Annual crops of wheat, corn, vegetables and fruit, known as *emblements,* are generally considered personal property. A mobile home is usually considered personal property unless it is permanently attached to the land by a foundation.

Fixtures

An article that was once personal property but has been so affixed to land or to a building that the law construes it to be a part of the real estate is a **fixture.**

Examples of fixtures are heating plants, elevator equipment, radiators, kitchen cabinets, light fixtures and plumbing fixtures. Almost any item that has been added as *a permanent part* of a building is considered a fixture.

Trade fixtures. An article owned by a tenant and attached to a rented space for use in conducting a business is a **trade fixture.** Examples of trade fixtures are bowling alleys, store shelves, bars and restaurant equipment. Agricultural fixtures such as chicken coops and toolsheds also are included in this definition (*see* Figure 1.7). Trade fixtures must be removed on or before the last day the property is rented. Trade fixtures that are not removed become the real property of the landlord.

Trade fixtures differ from other fixtures in the following ways:

1. Fixtures belong to the owner of the real estate but trade fixtures are usually owned and installed by a tenant for his or her business use.
2. Fixtures are considered a permanent part of a building but trade fixtures are removable. (The tenant must, however, restore the property to its original condition—repairing holes left by bolts, for example.)
3. Fixtures are legally considered real estate but trade fixtures are legally considered to be personal property.

Legal tests of a fixture. Courts apply four basic tests to determine whether an article is a fixture (and therefore a part of the real estate) or removable personal property. These tests are based on: (1) the adaptation of the article to the real estate, (2) the method of annexation of the item, (3) the intention and relationship of the parties and (4) the existence of an agreement.

Although these tests seem simple, there is no uniformity in court decisions regarding what constitutes a fixture. Articles that appear to be permanently affixed sometimes have been held by the courts to be personal property, while items that do not appear to be permanently attached have been held to be fixtures. The front door key, although not attached, is clearly a fixture that belongs with a house.

Real Estate Law

Buying real estate is usually the biggest financial transaction of a person's life. At the center of this important and sensitive transaction there is generally a real estate **broker.** A real estate **salesperson** works on behalf of the broker. The broker and the salesperson generally represent the seller and seek a buyer for the property. After they have found a prospective buyer, they bring the parties together. Then both seller and buyer look to the broker and their respective lawyers to guide and facilitate the transfer of the real estate from one party to the other.

Certain specific areas of law are important to the real estate practitioner. These include the *law of contracts,* the *real property law,* the *law of agency* (which covers the obligations of a broker to the person who engages his or her services) and the *real estate license law,* all of which will be discussed in this text.

A person engaged in the real estate business need not be an expert on real estate law but should have a knowledge and understanding of basic principles. A real estate practitioner must be able to recognize technical legal problems and should appreciate the necessity of referring such problems to a competent attorney. *An* **attorney** *is a person trained and licensed to represent another person in court, to prepare documents defining or transferring rights in property or to give advice or counsel on matters of law.* Brokers and salespeople must be aware of their limitations in such areas.

Extreme care should be taken in handling all phases of a real estate transaction. Carelessness in handling the documents connected with a real estate sale can result in expensive legal contests. In many such cases costly court actions could have been avoided if the parties handling negotiations had exercised greater care and employed competent legal counsel.

Real estate license laws. Because real estate brokers and salespeople are engaged in the business of handling other people's real estate and money, the need for regulation of their activities has long been recognized. New York first required licensing in 1922. The license laws of the various states are similar in many respects but differ in details. Under these laws a person must obtain a license in order to engage in the real estate business. The applicant must possess certain personal and educational qualifications and must pass an examination to prove adequate knowledge of the business. In addition, in order to qualify for license renewal and continue in business, the licensee must meet continuing education requirements and follow certain prescribed standards of conduct in the operation of business. Chapter 8 describes in detail New York's license laws and the required standards.

Real Estate—A Business of Many Specializations

Some people think of the real estate business as made up only of brokers and salespeople. Today's real estate industry, however, employs scores of well-trained, knowledgeable individuals in other areas. Modern real estate practice provides many specializations for people who want to serve the community and earn a better-than-average income. The specializations that make up the real estate business include brokerage, appraisal, property management, financing, property development, counseling, education, syndication, law and insurance. To be truly competent a real estate licensee must possess at least a basic knowledge of all phases of the business.

Brokerage. The bringing together of people interested in making a real estate transaction is *brokerage*. Typically, the broker acts as an *agent;* that is, he or she negotiates the sale, purchase or rental of property on behalf of others for a fee or commission. The agent's commission is generally a percentage of the amount involved in the transaction. It usually is paid by the seller. Brokerage is discussed further in Chapter 2.

Appraisal. The process of estimating the value of a parcel of real estate is *appraisal.* Although brokers must have some understanding of valuation as part of their training, an appraisal specialist generally is employed when property is financed or sold by court order and large sums of money are involved. The appraiser must have sound judgment, experience and a detailed knowledge of the methods of valuation. Appraisal is covered in Chapter 16.

Property management. A real estate agent who operates a property for its owner is involved in *property management.* The property manager may be responsible for soliciting tenants, collecting rents, altering or constructing new space for tenants, ordering repairs and generally maintaining the property. The manager's basic responsibility is to protect the owner's investment and maximize the owner's return on the investment. Property management is discussed in Chapter 21.

Financing. The business of providing the funds necessary to complete real estate transactions is *financing*. Most transactions are financed by means of a mortgage loan in which the property is pledged as security for the payment of the loan. However, there are other methods of financing real estate in addition to mortgages. Real estate financing is examined in Chapter 7.

Property development. *Property development* includes the work of *subdividers* who purchase raw land, divide it into lots, build roads and install sewers; the skills of *developers* who improve the building lots with houses and other buildings and sell the improved real estate, either themselves or through brokerage firms; and the work of *builders* and *architects* who plan and construct the houses and other buildings. Property development is discussed in Chapter 18.

Counseling. Providing competent, independent advice and guidance on a variety of real estate problems is known as *counseling*. A counselor attempts to furnish the client with direction in choosing among alternative courses of action.

Education. Both the real estate licensee and the consumer can learn more about the complexities of the real estate business through *education*. Colleges, schools, real estate organizations and continuing education programs conduct courses and seminars in all areas of the business. New York State requires that courses for licensure or continuing education credit be taught by instructors with five years' experience in the subjects being taught.

Syndication. *Syndication* is the bringing together of groups of investors for large ventures. In New York State sale of syndications requires a special securities license.

Insurance. *Insurance* is sometimes included among the major services of the real estate business. In many real estate offices the real estate broker is also an insurance broker; however, *insurance brokerage is a separate business that requires a separate state license.*

Uses of Real Property

Just as there are many areas of specialization within the real estate industry, so too are there many different types of property in which to specialize (*see* Figure 1.8). According to its use, real estate can be classified generally into one of the following categories:

- **Residential**—all property used for housing, from acreage to small city lots, both single-family and multifamily, in urban, suburban and rural areas.
- **Commercial**—business property, including offices, shopping centers, stores, executive offices, theaters, hotels and parking facilities.
- **Industrial**—warehouses, factories, land in industrial districts and research facilities.
- **Agricultural**—farms, timberland, pasture land, ranches and orchards.
- **Special purpose**—churches, schools, cemeteries and government-held lands.

The market for each of these types of properties can be further subdivided into: the *sale market*, which involves the transfer of title, and the *rental market*, which involves the transfer of space on a rental basis.

Figure 1.8
Uses of Real Property

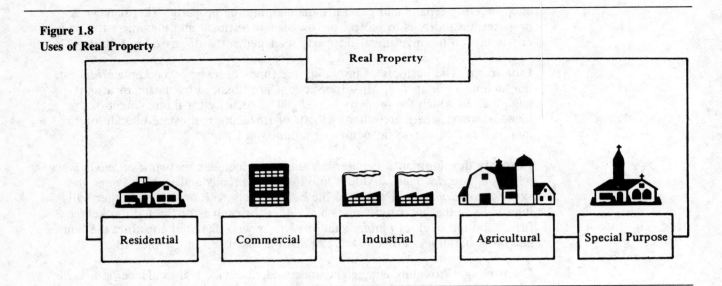

In theory, a real estate person or firm can perform all services and handle all five classes of property. This is rarely done, however, except in small towns. Most real estate firms tend to specialize to some degree, especially in urban areas. The vast majority perform two or more services for two or more types of property. One firm may provide brokerage and management services for residential property only; another firm may perform all services but specialize in industrial or commercial property.

Summary

Even the simplest real estate transactions involve a complex body of laws. When a person purchases real estate, he or she is purchasing not only the land itself but also the *legal rights* to use the land in certain ways that formerly were held by the seller.

Although most people think of *land* as the surface of the earth, the definition of this word really applies not only to the *earth's surface* but also to the *mineral deposits under the earth* and the *air above it*. The term *real estate* expands this definition to include *all man-made improvements attached to the land. Real property* is the term used to describe real estate plus the *bundle of legal rights* associated with its ownership.

The same parcel of real estate may be owned and controlled by different parties, one owning the *surface rights,* one owning the *air rights* and another owning the *subsurface rights.*

Ownership of land encompasses not only the land itself but also the right to use the water on or adjacent to it. The doctrine of *riparian rights* gives the owner of land adjacent to nonnavigable water ownership of the stream to its midpoint. *Littoral rights* are held by owners of land bordering large lakes and oceans and include rights to use of the water and ownership of the land up to the high-water mark.

All property that does not fit the definition of real estate is classified as *personal property,* or *chattels.* When articles of personal property are permanently affixed to land, they may become *fixtures* and as such are considered a part of the real estate. However, personal property attached to real estate by a tenant for a business purpose is classified as a *trade fixture* and remains personal property.

The real estate business is a dynamic industry employing hundreds of thousands of men and women. Every state and Canadian province has some type of *licensing requirement* for real estate brokers and salespeople. Although selling is the most widely recognized activity of the real estate business, the industry also involves other services like *appraisal, property management, property development, counseling, property financing, education, law, syndication* and *insurance*.

Real property can be classified according to its general use as either *residential, commercial, industrial, agricultural* or *special purpose*. Although many brokers deal with more than one type of real property, they usually specialize to some degree.

Questions

1. Real property is often referred to as a *bundle of legal rights*. Which of the following is *not* among these rights?

    a. Right of exclusion
    b. Right to use the property for private purposes, legal or otherwise
    c. Right of enjoyment
    d. Right to sell or otherwise convey the property

2. The definition of *land* does *not* include:

    a. minerals in the earth.
    b. the air above the ground up to infinity.
    c. trees.
    d. buildings.

3. A specific tract of land is known as a:

    a. bundle.   c. chattel.
    b. parcel.   d. littoral.

4. Dell Hicks, owner of a large farm in Livingston County, may lease to a gas-drilling company his:

    a. riparian rights.   c. air rights.
    b. subsurface rights.   d. littoral rights.

5. Man-made, permanent additions to land are called:

    a. chattels.   c. improvements.
    b. parcels.   d. trade fixtures.

6. When a building is to be constructed over land owned by another, the builder purchases the landowner's:

    a. riparian rights.   c. air rights.
    b. subsurface rights.   d. littoral rights.

7. Molly Malone owns land along the Mohawk River and as such has certain:

    a. riparian rights.   c. air rights
    b. subsurface rights.   d. littoral rights.

8. Which of the following items would *not* be a part of real estate?

    a. Fences   c. Farm equipment
    b. Permanent buildings   d. Growing trees

9. Steve Jackson is a tenant in a small house under a one-year lease. Two months into the rental period, Jackson installs awnings over the building's front windows to keep the sun away from some delicate hanging plants. Which of the following is true?

    a. Jackson must remove the awnings before the rental period is over.
    b. Because of their permanent nature, the awnings are considered to be personal property.
    c. Jackson may not remove the awnings.
    d. The awnings are removable trade fixtures.

10. When the Hair Zoo moved in, the hairdresser installed three shampoo basins, four large plate-glass mirrors and custom work-station counters. Just before the expiration of the lease, the hairdresser has the right to remove:

    a. everything but the shampoo basins because they are attached to the plumbing.
    b. only the mirrors, and then only if holes in the walls are repaired.
    c. all of the items mentioned above.
    d. nothing because all the items became fixtures when they were attached.

11. Legal tests for a fixture do *not* include:

    a. annexation.   c. accretion.
    b. adaptation.   d. intention.

12. Fred and Celia Evers are building a new enclosed front porch to their home. The lumber dealer with whom they are contracting has just unloaded in front of their house a truckload of lumber that will be used to build the porch. At this point, the lumber is considered:

    a. a chattel.   c. a fixture.
    b. real estate.   d. a trade fixture.

13. When the Evers' new front porch is completed, the lumber that the dealer originally delivered will be considered:

    a. a chattel.   c. a fixture.
    b. real estate.   d. a trade fixture.

14. Which of the following refers to a different type of property from the other three?

    a. Chattels   c. Realty
    b. Movables   d. Personal property

15. New York's real estate license laws:
    a. are uniform with those in the 49 other states.
    b. authorize the licensee to practice law only as it pertains to real estate.
    c. include a continuing education requirement for license renewal.
    d. protect the public by requiring the prospective broker to post a bond.

16. The bringing together of people interested in making a real estate transaction is known as:
    a. appraisal.   c. cooperation.
    b. brokerage.   d. development.

17. Harry Wales buys farmland outside New York City, splits it into lots, and sells it to homebuilders. He is acting as a:
    a. broker.   c. manager.
    b. developer.   d. subdivider.

18. Special-purpose real estate includes:
    a. apartment houses.   c. factories.
    b. churches.   d. shopping plazas.

19. Property that is part of the commercial market includes:
    a. office buildings for lease.
    b. apartments for rent.
    c. churches.
    d. factories.

20. Peter Dickinson is a real estate broker in a large Upstate city. Chances are his real estate firm:
    a. performs most or all of the various real estate specializations.
    b. deals only in farm property.
    c. deals only in insurance.
    d. performs two or more of the various real estate specializations for at least two types of property.

2

Law of Agency

Key Terms

Agency coupled with an interest	Kickbacks
Agent	Latent defects
Antitrust laws	Law of agency
Broker	Listing agreement
Buyer's broker	Meeting of the minds
Client	Power of attorney
Commission	Principal
Customer	Procuring cause of sale
Dual agency	Puffing
Employee	Ready, willing and able buyer
Fiduciary	Salesperson
Fiduciary relationship	Special agent
Fraud	Subagent
General agent	Universal agent
Independent contractors	

Overview

Real estate brokers (and the salespersons assisting them) bring together buyers and sellers. Real estate brokerage today is a complex operation involving strictly defined legal relationships. The broker generally acts as the agent of the seller. This chapter will discuss the laws governing agency and also will examine the nature of the real estate brokerage business.

Brokerage Defined	The business of bringing buyers and sellers together in the marketplace is *brokerage*. In the real estate business a **broker** is defined as a person who is licensed to assist others in real estate transactions and *to charge a fee* for services. Working on behalf of and licensed to represent the broker is the real estate **salesperson.**

The **principal** who employs the broker may be a seller, a prospective buyer, an owner who wishes to lease his or her property or a person seeking property to rent. The real estate broker acts as the **agent** of the principal, who usually compensates the broker with a **commission.** This commission depends on the broker's successfully performing the service for which he or she was employed, which is generally to procure a prospective purchaser, seller, lessor or lessee who is ready, willing and able to complete the contract. The principal is also known as the **client.** In the usual real estate transaction the seller is the client, to whom specific duties are owed; the buyer is merely the agent's **customer,** to whom the agent owes only fair and trustworthy treatment.

Agency	The role of a broker as the agent of his or her principal is a **fiduciary relationship** that falls within the requirements of the **law of agency.** The fiduciary relationship is one of trust and confidence in which an agent is responsible for the money and/or property of others. It requires putting the principal's interest above all others', including the broker's own interest. The agent is also known as a **fiduciary.**
Types of Agencies	An agent may be classified as a universal agent, general agent, or special agent based on his or her authority.

A **universal agent** is empowered to represent the principal in *all matters* that can be delegated. The universal agent has the power to enter into *any* contract (such as the selling and buying of property) on behalf of the principal without prior permission. This type of agency is created by a written document known as a **power of attorney,** which grants the agent unlimited authority in the principal's financial and other matters.

A **general agent** is empowered to represent the principal in a *specific range of matters*. The general agent may bind the principal to any contracts within the scope of his or her authority. This type of agency is also created by a power of attorney that stipulates the specific areas of authority in which the agent may act.

A **special agent** is authorized to represent the principal in *one specific transaction or business activity only*. A real estate broker is generally a special agent hired by a seller *to find a ready, willing and able buyer* for the seller's property. As a special agent, the broker is *not authorized* to sell the property or to bind the principal to any contract.

An **agency coupled with an interest** is an agency relationship in which the agent has some interest in the property being sold. Such an agency *cannot be revoked* *by the principal, nor can it be terminated upon the principal's death.* For example, a broker might supply the financing for a condominium development provided the developer agrees to give the broker the exclusive right to sell the completed condo units. Because this is an agency coupled with an interest, the developer would not be able to revoke the listing agreement after the broker provided the financing.

Creation of Agency

The special agency relationship between broker and seller is generally created by an employment contract, commonly referred to as a **listing agreement.**

In New York State a written listing agreement is required only if it is for a period of one year or more. Oral agreements of agency for a shorter period of time are binding. Most brokers, however, require that all agreements be in writing and signed by the principal. The possibilities of misunderstanding and the difficulty of proving an oral agreement make it risky to rely on an oral listing.

Termination of Agency

An agency between a principal and an agent may be terminated at any time, except in the case of an agency coupled with an interest. An agency may be terminated for any of the following reasons:

- Death or incompetency of either party.
- Destruction or condemnation of the property.
- Expiration of the terms of the agency.
- Mutual agreement to terminate the agency.
- Renunciation by the agent or revocation by the principal.
- Bankruptcy of either party.
- Completion or fulfillment of the purpose for which the agency was created.

Since an amendment to New York State law in 1975, agency does not automatically terminate upon the incompetency of the principal; the power-of-attorney document contains wording that determines the matter.

In New York the principal acting in good faith always has the power to cancel a listing at any time but may be answerable to the broker for damages if he or she cancels before the agency's expiration.

Buyer as Principal

Usually, a real estate broker is hired by a seller to locate a buyer for the seller's real property. In some cases, however, a broker may be hired by a potential buyer to find a parcel of real estate for purchase.

A prospective purchaser seeking commercial or industrial property is particularly likely to hire a broker for this reason. In this situation the broker and the buyer usually will draw up an agreement commonly referred to as a finder's agreement. This document sets forth in detail the nature of the property desired and the amount of the broker's compensation.

In recent years more sophisticated home buyers, who realize that the usual agent is supposed to put the seller's interests first, have started employing their own **buyer's broker.** The broker who is working for the buyer must, of course, make the exact situation known to all parties. A buyer's broker may be paid with a retainer, a flat fee, a percentage of the purchase price, or an hourly fee.

Agent's Responsibilities to Principal

An agent has a *fiduciary relationship* with his or her principal, that is, a relationship of trust and confidence between employer and employee. This confidential relationship carries with it certain duties that the broker must perform—the duties of *notice, obedience, care, accounting,* and *loyalty,* easily remembered as the word NO-CAL (see Figure 2.1).

Figure 2.1
Agent's Responsibilities

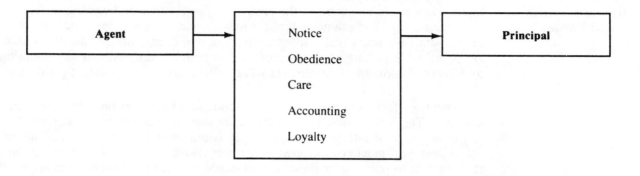

Notice. It is the broker's duty to pass on to the principal all facts or information the broker obtains that could affect the principal's business or decisions. In certain instances the broker may be held liable for damages for failure to disclose such information. The broker must volunteer pertinent information whether or not the client asks.

Obedience. The broker is obligated to obey the principal's instructions. The broker is not, however, required to obey unlawful or unethical instructions—violating human rights laws, for example, or lying to buyers about the condition of the property.

Care. The broker must exercise a reasonable degree of care while transacting business entrusted to him or her by the principal. The broker is liable to the principal for any loss resulting from negligence or carelessness.

Accounting. The broker must be able to report the status of all funds entrusted to him or her. Real estate license laws require brokers to give duplicate originals of all documents to all parties affected by them and to keep copies of such documents on file for three years. In addition, the license laws require the broker to deposit all funds entrusted to him or her immediately in a special trust, or escrow, account. It is illegal for the broker to commingle (mix) such monies with personal funds or to retain any interest they earn.

Loyalty. An agent must always place a principal's interests above those of other persons, including the agent's own interests. Thus an agent cannot disclose such information as the principal's financial condition, the fact that the principal (if the seller) will accept a price lower than the listing price or any confidential facts that might harm the principal's bargaining position. A buyer's broker, on the other hand, would not reveal the buyer's readiness to pay more if necessary.

New York forbids brokers or salespersons from buying property listed with them for themselves or for accounts in which they have a personal interest, without first notifying the principal of such interest. By law neither brokers nor salespersons may sell property in which they have a personal interest without informing the purchaser of that interest. It is prudent to make such a disclosure in writing as part of the purchase contract.

Agent's Responsibilities to Third Parties

In dealing with a buyer, a broker, as an agent of the seller, must exercise extreme caution and be aware of the laws and ethical considerations that affect this relationship. For example, brokers must be careful about the statements they or their staff members make about a parcel of real estate. Statements of opinion are permissible as long as they are offered as opinions and without any intention to deceive. Making such statements when selling real estate is called **puffing.**

Statements of fact, however, must be accurate and questions must be answered honestly. The broker must be alert to ensure that none of his or her statements can in any way be interpreted as involving **fraud,** which encompasses all deceitful or dishonest practices intended to harm or take advantage of another person. If a contract to purchase real estate is obtained as a result of misstatements made by a broker or his or her salespersons, the contract may be disaffirmed or renounced by the purchaser. In such a case the broker will lose a commission. If either party suffers loss because of a broker's misrepresentations, the broker can be held liable for damages. Fraud is discussed in detail in Chapter 14.

Brokers and salespersons should be aware that the courts have ruled that a seller is responsible for revealing to a buyer any hidden or **latent defects** in a building. *A latent defect is one that is not discoverable by ordinary inspection.* As an agent of the seller, a broker is likewise responsible for disclosing such *hidden defects.* Buyers have been able to either rescind the sales contract or receive damages in such instances. Examples include a house built over a ditch that was filled with decaying timber; a buried drain tile that caused water to accumulate; or a driveway built partly on adjoining property. New York courts have not completely ruled in this area, but it is increasingly risky for sellers or brokers to rely on the old legal principal of *caveat emptor* (let the buyer beware).

Dual agency. In dealing with buyers, the broker must be careful of any situation that might be considered a **dual agency.** Sometimes a broker may have the opportunity to receive compensation from both the buyer and seller in a transaction. An agent cannot, however, give first loyalty to two or more principals in the same transaction. Thus real estate license laws prohibit a broker from representing and collecting compensation from both parties to a transaction without their prior knowledge and consent.

Before entering into a listing agreement a licensee should fully explain to a seller/principal the nature of the agency relationship and the provisions of the document that creates it. Also, to avoid potential problems arising from misunderstanding under the usual agency arrangement in which the seller is principal, a licensee should inform each buyer/customer that he or she represents the seller and owes the seller 100-percent loyalty. Giving this information, however, does not relieve the licensee from dealing fairly and honestly with the buyer/customer.

Nature of the Brokerage Business

A broker has the right to reject agency contracts that in his or her judgment violate the ethics or high standards of the office. After a brokerage relationship has been established, however, the broker owes that person, the principal, the duty to exercise care, skill and integrity in carrying out instructions.

Broker-Salesperson Relationship

A person licensed to perform any real estate activities on behalf of a licensed real estate broker is known as a real estate salesperson. *The salesperson is responsible to the broker under whom he or she is licensed.* A salesperson can carry out only those responsibilities assigned by that broker.

A broker is licensed to act as the principal's agent and thus can collect a commission for performing his or her assigned duties. A salesperson, on the other hand, has no authority to make contracts or receive compensation directly from a principal. The broker is fully responsible for the actions of all salespeople licensed under him or her. *All of a salesperson's activities must be performed in the name of his or her supervising broker.*

The salesperson functions as an **agent** of the broker and **subagent** of the principal (usually the seller). So do cooperating brokers who choose to work on the broker's listings. In a multiple listing cooperative sale, *both* listing broker and selling broker have a fiduciary relationship with the *seller* unless the buyers have specifically retained their own agent.

It is therefore inaccurate to refer to the buyer as one's client except when the broker has been retained by that buyer. The salesperson who says "I have a client who wants to look at your house" is in danger of forgetting that while one may be working *with* the buyer, one is working *for* the seller. It's easier to remember the fiduciary duties—and where first loyalty lies—if the salesperson makes a habit of saying "I have a customer," "I am working with a prospective buyer" or "I'd like to bring over a prospect for your house."

Independent contractor versus employee. Salespersons are engaged by brokers as either employees or independent contractors. The agreement between a broker and a salesperson should be set down in a written contract that defines the obligations and responsibilities of the relationship. The independent contractor relationship is discussed in detail in Chapter 13.

The employer-employee relationship allows a broker to exercise certain *controls* over salespeople who are employees. The broker can require an **employee** to adhere to regulations such as working hours, office routine and dress standards. As an employer a broker is required by the federal government to withhold social security tax and income tax from wages paid to employees. He or she also is required to pay unemployment compensation tax on wages as defined by state and federal laws. A broker may provide employees with such benefits as health insurance.

Most salespersons, however, act as **independent contractors.** An independent contractor assumes responsibility for paying his or her own income and social security taxes and must provide his or her own health insurance if such coverage is desired. An independent contractor receives nothing from his or her broker that could be construed as an employee benefit (*see* Figure 2.2).

The Internal Revenue Service has provided "safe harbor" guidelines under which independent contractor status will not be challenged where the associate is licensed, has fluctuating income based on commissions, and works under a written contract specifying independent contractor status.

Figure 2.2
Employee versus
Independent Contractor

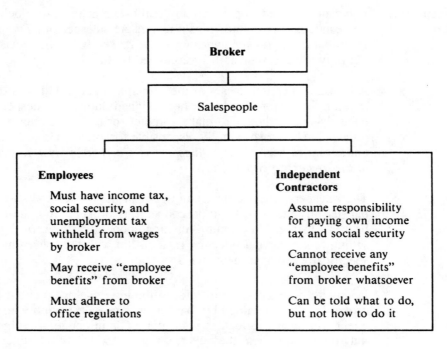

Broker's Compensation

The broker's compensation is specified in the listing agreement, management agreement or other contract with the principal and is subject to negotiation between the parties. Compensation usually is computed as a *percentage of the total amount of money involved* but could be a flat fee. The commission or fee is usually considered to be earned when the broker has accomplished the work for which he or she was hired. Unless there is an agreement to the contrary, after a seller accepts an offer from a ready, willing and able buyer, the seller technically is liable for the broker's commission regardless of whether the buyer completes the purchase. **A ready, willing and able buyer** is one who is *prepared to buy on the seller's terms, is financially capable and is ready to take positive steps toward consummation of the transaction.*

A broker who has produced a buyer who is ready, willing and able to meet the listing terms is usually still entitled to a commission if the transaction is *not* consummated for any of the following reasons:

• The owner changes his or her mind and refuses to sell.
• There are defects in the owner's title that are not corrected.
• The owner commits fraud with respect to the transaction.
• The owner is unable to deliver possession within a reasonable time.
• The owner insists on terms not in the listing (for example, the right to restrict the use of the property).
• The owner and the buyer agree to cancel the transaction.

In other words, *a broker generally is due a commission if a sale is not consummated because of the principal's default.*

The broker is entitled to a fee if he or she is the **procuring cause of sale,** produces a ready, willing and able buyer or brings about a **meeting of the minds.** Where several brokers disagree as to which one brought about a sale, the one with the best claim to be the procuring cause is that broker who brought the parties into agreement, as evidenced by the sales contract. A meeting of the minds is said to have taken place when the parties are in agreement on price, down payment and financing method (*see* Figure 2.3).

Figure 2.3
Broker's Compensation

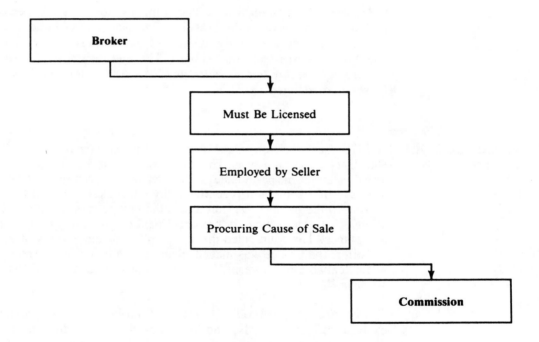

It is customary in New York that the broker wait to collect the commission until transfer of title (final settlement, closing of the sale) even though the fee is actually earned earlier.

New York allows a broker who fears avoidance of commission to file an affidavit of entitlement or, in some cases, a lien (financial claim) against property. The process is detailed in Chapter 24.

The rate of a broker's commission is *negotiable in every case,* although a particular firm may have its own independent policy of standard rates or fees. Any attempt, no matter how subtle, to impose uniform commission rates with competing firms would be a clear violation of state and federal antitrust laws (which will be discussed later in this chapter).

New York's license laws make it illegal for a broker to share a commission with anyone who is not licensed as a salesperson or broker. This has been construed to include any form of gift or compensation—for instance, giving a TV to a friend for providing a valuable lead or paying finder's fees and portions of the commission. **Kickbacks,** the return of part of the commission as gifts or money to buyers or sellers, are also prohibited.

Occasionally, a broker may agree during final negotiations to discount the previously agreed-on commission "to help make the deal." Because the broker's concession could be construed as a kickback to the seller, it is customary in many areas for a substitute listing contract to be drawn up at that point, reflecting the new lower rate of commission or the flat fee involved.

Salesperson's compensation. The compensation of a salesperson is set by a mutual agreement between the broker and salesperson. A broker may agree to pay a salary or, more commonly, a share of the commissions from transactions originated by a salesperson (the "split"). *The salesperson may never accept compensation from any buyer, seller or broker except the one broker with whom he or she is associated.*

Duncan and Hill Decision

A 1978 court decision, *Duncan and Hill v. the Department of State,* involved a Rochester real estate firm. The court considered the question: To what extent can a real estate agent participate in the preparation of a real estate offer and counteroffer? In a complaint precipitated by the broker's refusal to return a $200 deposit to the prospective purchaser, the charge was made that the broker, not being an attorney, illegally prepared legal documents: an offer, counteroffer and acceptance. The court ruled that by inserting detailed terms of the mortgage into the offer, the broker was indeed illegally practicing law. Among the terms cited were "callable in 10 years," "prepayment privileges" and "standard default in 10 days."

The court cautioned brokers to refrain from inserting any provision that requires exercise of legal expertise and to confine themselves to a general description of the property, price to be paid and mortgaging to be secured. The court also said that brokers may readily protect themselves from the charge of unlawful practice of law by inserting in the document that it is subject to the approval of the respective attorneys for the parties.

Antitrust Laws

The real estate industry is subject to federal and state **antitrust laws.** The most common antitrust violations that can occur in the real estate business are price fixing and allocation of customers or markets.

Illegal *price fixing* occurs when brokers conspire to set prices for the services they perform (sales commissions, management rates) rather than let those prices be established through competition in the open market.

Real estate licensees must be scrupulously careful to dissociate themselves immediately from the slightest discussion of commission rates with any member of a *competing* firm. In the past a number of New York brokers and real estate boards have suffered from charges under antitrust laws.

Allocation of customers or markets involves an agreement between brokers to divide their markets and refrain from competing with each other's business. Allocations may take place on a geographic basis with brokers agreeing to specific territories within which they will operate exclusively. The division may also take place along other lines; for example, two brokers may agree that one will handle only residential properties less than $100,000 in value, while another will handle residential properties more than $100,000 in value.

Individual firms may establish their own fee schedules and allocate sales territories between salespersons. Violations occur only when competing firms agree to act together in these matters.

The penalties for such acts are severe. Under the Sherman Antitrust Act people who fix prices or allocate markets may be found guilty of a misdemeanor, punishable by a maximum $100,000 fine and three years in prison. In a civil suit a person who has suffered a loss because of the antitrust activities of a guilty party may recover triple the value of the actual damages plus attorney's fees and costs.

Summary

Real estate brokerage is the bringing together, for a fee or commission, of people who wish to buy, sell, exchange or lease real estate.

Real estate brokerage is governed by the *law of agency*. A real estate broker is the *agent,* hired by either a buyer or a seller of real estate to sell or find a particular parcel of real estate. The person who hires the broker is the *principal* or *client.* The principal and the agent have a *fiduciary relationship* under which the agent owes the principal the duties of notice, obedience, care, accounting, and loyalty.

The broker's compensation in a real estate sale generally takes the form of a *commission,* which is often a percentage of the real estate's selling price. The broker is considered to have earned a commission when he or she procures a *ready, willing and able buyer* for a seller or brings about a *meeting of the minds*.

A broker may use salespeople to assist in this work. The salesperson works as a subagent on the broker's behalf as either an *employee* or an *independent contractor.* The salesperson is the broker's agent and the seller's *subagent* (or rarely, if specifically retained as such, the buyer's subagent).

Many of the general operations of a real estate brokerage are regulated by the real estate license laws. In addition, state and federal *antitrust laws* prohibit brokers from conspiring to fix prices or allocate customers or markets.

Questions

1. The legal relationship between broker and seller is generally a(n):

   a. special agency.
   b. general agency.
   c. ostensible agency.
   d. universal agency.

2. The real estate broker usually is hired as an agent through the document known as a:

   a. listing agreement.
   b. finder's agreement.
   c. meeting of the minds.
   d. procuring contract.

3. The statement "a broker must be employed to recover a commission for his or her services" means the:

   a. broker must work in a real estate office.
   b. seller must have made an agreement to pay a commission to the broker for selling the property.
   c. broker must have asked the seller the price of the property and then found a ready, willing and able buyer.
   d. broker must have a salesperson employed in the office.

4. Any listing agreement in New York State must be in writing if:

   a. the broker intends to collect a commission.
   b. it is for a period of more than one year.
   c. the broker produced a buyer ready, willing and able.
   d. the property was previously listed with another broker.

5. A listing may be terminated when either broker or principal:

   a. gets married.
   b. goes bankrupt.
   c. overfinances other property.
   d. becomes 21 years of age.

6. When retained by the seller, the broker owes a prospective buyer:

   a. obedience to lawful instructions.
   b. confidentiality about the buyer's financial situation.
   c. honest straightforward treatment.
   d. first loyalty.

7. The salesperson who sincerely tries to represent both buyer and seller is in danger of falling into:

   a. fraud.
   b. puffing.
   c. dual agency.
   d. general agency.

8. A seller who wishes to cancel a listing agreement in New York:

   a. must cite a legally acceptable reason.
   b. may not cancel without the agent's consent.
   c. may be held liable for money and time expended by the broker.
   d. may not sell the property for six months after.

9. A broker is entitled to collect a commission from both the seller and the buyer when:

   a. the broker holds a state license.
   b. the buyer and the seller are related.
   c. both parties know about and agree to such a transaction.
   d. both parties have attorneys.

10. Miss Mollie's father bought the house in 1940 for $4,500. She asks Bob Broker to list it and instructs him to see if he can get as much as $85,000 "because she's heard houses have gone up in value." Bob knows the property might bring $125,000. Bob should:

    a. take the listing as instructed, knowing he can produce a prompt, trouble-free sale for Miss Mollie.
    b. buy the house himself for the full $85,000, making sure his purchase contract reveals that he is a licensed broker.
    c. buy the house only through his cousin, who has a different last name, in order to avoid a breach of fiduciary duty.
    d. tell Miss Mollie that he believes the house is worth much more.

11. An example of a latent defect would be a:

    a. large crack in the dining room ceiling.
    b. roof with warped shingles.
    c. used car–lot next door.
    d. malfunctioning septic tank.

12. An independent contractor may be paid:
    a. regular draw against earnings.
    b. reimbursed car expenses.
    c. commissions on sales.
    d. two-week vacations each year.

13. Commissions usually are earned when:
    a. the buyer makes a purchase offer.
    b. the seller accepts the buyer's offer without conditions.
    c. a new mortgage has been promised by the lender.
    d. title to the property transfers.

14. Even if a proposed transaction does not go through, the broker sometimes may collect a commission where the:
    a. buyer turned out to be financially unable.
    b. seller refused to do repairs required by the lender.
    c. seller simply backed out.
    d. lender did not appraise the house for the sales price.

15. A meeting of the minds occurs when the:
    a. seller signs a listing agreement.
    b. buyer is introduced to the seller.
    c. buyer and seller agree on price and terms of sale.
    d. final closing (settlement) of the transaction takes place.

16. Commission rates are set by:
    a. state law.
    b. local custom.
    c. the broker.
    d. agreement between seller and broker.

17. Henry Householder lists his house with Larry Lister. Henry offers a bonus commission of $500 to the salesperson who brings a good buyer before Thanksgiving. Sam Salesman, who is associated with the cooperating firm of Olive Otherbroker, effects the sale on November 1. Sam may collect that bonus from:
    a. Henry.   c. Olive.
    b. Larry.   d. no one.

18. In the situation described in question 17, Olive was acting as agent for:
    a. Henry.   c. the buyer.
    b. Sam.   d. no one.

19. The Duncan and Hill decision warned real estate licensees against:
    a. drawing up legal documents.
    b. entering into dual agency.
    c. committing fraud.
    d. puffing.

20. At a booth in the neighborhood coffee shop, Bob Broker is seated with his friendly rival, Olive Otherbroker. Olive says, "Did you hear about that firm that's charging a flat fee for selling property? Do you think they'll make it?" Bob's proper response is to:
    a. explain to Olive that flat fees are allowed by law, just as commissions are.
    b. assure Olive that his commission rates are not going to change.
    c. caution Olive about the dangers of discussing commission rates with competing firms.
    d. say "good-bye" immediately and walk out.

Appendix: Excerpts from New York State's Study Booklet for Brokers

SUMMARY OF THE LAW OF AGENCY RELATING TO REAL ESTATE BROKERAGE

Authorization—employment. The foundation of an agency is an authorization or contract of employment, the terms of which may be either expressed or implied. The law of New York State does not require that an authorization must be in writing unless, by its terms, it is not to be performed within one year, in which event a written contract is required to be signed by the party to be bound. . . .

Duration and termination of broker's employment. It should be noted that a principal has the unquestionable power to cancel the authority or agency given by the principal to a broker. Where the authority is for a fixed time, the principal is answerable for damages for the cancellation of the broker's authority prior to the expiration date whereas where the authority is for an unspecified time, the principal acting in good faith, may cancel the broker's authority at will. . . . Authority . . . is terminable upon the occurrence of any of the following events: (a) when the object has not been performed during the specified period or, where the period of authority is unspecified, the object has not been performed or accomplished within a reasonable time, (b) death or insanity of a broker or principal, (c) bankruptcy of either, (d) destruction of the subject matter, (e) broker's fraudulent conduct for own benefit or (f) sale by another broker if the authority is for an unspecified time.

Dual employment. A broker may be employed by both the seller and buyer of real estate, neither of whom can avoid payment of compensation if he or she knew and consented that the broker also represented the other party.

When commissions are earned. A broker is not entitled to a commission until the buyer and seller agree, not only as to the respective price, but as to the terms of the transaction and all other points material thereto. A broker may not be entitled to commission where, although the broker introduced the purchaser to the seller, the broker did not bring them to an agreement and the transaction was subsequently negotiated by another broker.

The terms essential to effect a meeting of minds are: (1) Price; (2) Amount of Cash; (3) Duration of Mortgages; (4) Rate of Interest; and (5) Amortization. Having rendered the services described in these two transactions, the broker's right to the commissions is undisturbed even though the transaction was not consummated by the principals.

Commission rates. The commission or compensation of a real estate broker is not regulated by statute; nor is it legally fixed by the regulations of the real estate board in a particular community, as many suppose. The broker and the employer may agree upon any reasonable rate of compensation, or the method or time of payment thereof, that is mutually acceptable.

Conflicting commission claims: "procuring cause." Where an owner employs a number of brokers to negotiate a transaction, the broker whose services are the procuring cause of the sale or lease is entitled to compensation; usually this means the broker who first induces the customer to agree to the owner's terms. The broker who actually negotiates a sale or lease may be entitled to compensation, notwithstanding the fact that the owner has erroneously paid a full commission on the same transaction to another broker.

"Ready, willing and able." The words "ready" and "willing" are synonymously used to mean that the broker's customer is prepared to enter into a contract with the broker's principal on his/her terms. The word "able" refers to the customer's financial ability to buy. Where the principals entered into a written contract they are both treated as being mutually satisfied of each other's ability to perform.

Commissions payable. Unless otherwise provided in the authorization, a broker's commission is due and payable when it has been earned. A broker employed to negotiate a sale of real property, for instance, earns a commission when the broker produces a purchaser who is ready, able and willing to buy on the seller's terms. The broker is entitled to a commission if the broker brings the client and the customer together and, after mutual bargaining, they come to an agreement; even at a price and on terms materially different from those specified in the authorization.

Deferment of payment of commissions. The original commission agreement between a broker and employer may contemplate that the commission will be earned by the broker only if and when title passes to the buyer.

Default by owner. In order to deprive a broker of a commission, an owner cannot, in bad faith, terminate a broker's employment and make a sale or lease directly. A broker is entitled to compensation where the owner refuses to sign a contract of sale on the terms the owner originally proposed or where, because of some defect, the title to the property is unmarketable, or where the owner is guilty of misrepresentation or mistake as to size of property or is guilty of a misstatement of the amount of rentals. . . .

Default by buyer. A broker is not entitled to a commission unless the buyer is ready and able to comply with the terms of the agreement to buy or lease. If a contract is entered into between a buyer and seller, the broker's right to commission is not affected by the buyer's . . . refusal or failure to perform.

Duty to owners. An agent is bound, not only to good faith, but to reasonable diligence and such skill as is generally possessed by persons of ordinary capacity in the same business. A broker may not profit by deceiving the owner.

If a broker submits any offer of purchase to the owner, the broker is duty bound to reveal any other better offers that have been made. If a broker fails to do so, the broker cannot recover commissions. A broker must disclose higher offers even if the higher offer has less cash. A broker is not entitled to any commission where the broker induced the owner to accept less than the asking price after the buyer has indicated a willingness to pay the asking price. A broker cannot claim commissions where the broker has induced the owner to accept less than the asking price knowing the property is of special value to the buyer. A broker is duty bound to reveal any facts in the broker's possession concerning the buyer's intention to resell at an increased price.

A broker cannot take a position which is not in the best interest of an owner. Hence, a broker employed to sell cannot purchase for himself or herself without a full disclosure of the broker's interest. A broker cannot sell the owner's property to a corporation or partnership in which the broker is interested without similar disclosure.

Duty to buyers. Brokers should guard against inaccuracies in their representations to buyers. If a misstatement is made as to a matter of fact by a broker, it may have the most serious consequences, both to the broker and to the owner. Such a misrepresentation, if it is material and intentional, may be fraudulent and may justify a refusal by a buyer to take title and afford the owner a defense to the broker's claim for a commission. It is not the duty of the broker to verify all representations made by the owner. Nonetheless, if the broker knows or has reason to know that the owner has made misrepresentations, or has failed to disclose material defects, then the broker is under a duty not to perpetuate such misrepresentations.

Deposit money. A real estate broker, by reason of the nature of the broker's work, is in a position to come into possession of funds belonging to others. The question often arises as to whom such money belongs and what disposition should be made of the funds by the broker. A real estate broker who is duly authorized to manage real property is authorized to collect rents. With relation to such moneys, there is never any question but that the money belongs to the owner and must be kept in a separate bank account and must be duly accounted for to the broker's client.

However, where a real estate broker has been employed by an owner to find a buyer, it is customary for the broker to take a deposit from the prospective buyer, issue a receipt and have the prospective purchaser execute an offer to buy subject to acceptance by the owner. . . . Experience has demonstrated that brokers may become involved in difficulties and may place their licenses in jeopardy when they do not take time to learn their responsibilities with relation to other people's money. Brokers should be thoroughly familiar with the law of agency and the rules applicable to deposits to avoid the pitfalls encountered in the handling of funds belonging to third persons.

3

Real Estate Instruments: Estates and Interests

Key Terms

Beneficiary	License
Common elements	Liens
Condominium	Life estate
Convey	Limited partnership
Conveyance	Lis pendens
Cooperative	Partition
Co-ownership	Partnership
Corporation	Party wall
Deed restrictions	Qualified fee
Easement	Remainder interest
Easement appurtenant	Reversionary interest
Easement by necessity	Right of survivorship
Easement in gross	Severalty
Easement by prescription	Sole proprietorship
Encroachment	Syndicate
Encumbrance	Tacking
Estate in land	Tenancy by the entirety
Fee simple	Tenant in common
Fee on condition	Title
Freehold estates	Trust
General partnership	Trustee
Homestead	Trustor
Interest	Undivided interest
Joint tenancy	Usage encumbrances
Leasehold estates	

Overview

Ownership of a parcel of real estate is not necessarily absolute. An owner may or may not be able to pass property on to heirs. Sometimes ownership may exist only as long as property is used for one specific purpose. In addition other persons may possess certain interests in one's real estate.

Purchasers must consider many different forms of ownership before they take title to a parcel of real estate. The choice of ownership form will affect such matters as the owner's legal right to sell without the consent of others, right to choose heirs and the future rights of creditors. This chapter will discuss various interests in real estate and the basic forms of real estate ownership.

| Estates in Land | The amount and kind of **interest** that a person has in real property ownership is an **estate in land.** Estates in land are divided into two major classifications: (1) freehold estates and (2) leasehold estates (those involving tenants). |

Freehold estates *are estates of indeterminable length,* such as those existing for a lifetime or forever. The freehold estates recognized in New York are: (1) fee simple, (2) qualified (determinable) fee, (3) fee on condition and (4) life estates.

The first three of these estates continue for an indefinite period and are inheritable by the heirs of the owner; the fourth ends upon the death of the person on whose life it is based.

Leasehold estates are *estates for a fixed term of years.* They are classified as:

Estate for years: Commonly established by a lease, written or (if for a period of less than one year) oral, an estate for years gives the tenant possession of the property for a specific period of time. No notice is necessary from either party to end the tenancy at the expiration of the term.

Periodic estate, estate at will, estate at sufferance: These leasehold estates are covered at length in Chapter 22. Each lasts for an indefinite length of time. If the premises are let on a month-to-month tenancy, New York State law requires 30 days' notice to terminate, from the day the rent is due, typically the first day of the month.

Various estates and interests are illustrated in Figure 3.1.

Fee Simple Estate

An estate in **fee simple** is the *highest type of interest in real estate recognized by law.* A fee simple estate is one in which the holder is entitled to all rights in the property. There is no time limit on its existence—it is said to run forever. It is complete ownership. Upon the death of its owner the estate passes to heirs. The terms *fee, fee simple* and *fee simple absolute* are basically the same. New York law provides that grants of real property **convey** (transfer) fee simple ownership unless the terms of the grant show a clear intention to convey a lesser estate.

Qualified Fee Estate

In New York a **qualified fee,** also known as a *determinable fee* or *fee on limitation,* is an estate in land that terminates *automatically* on the occurrence or non-occurrence of a specified event. The words "while," "until" and "so long as" generally signify the **conveyance** (gift or sale) of a qualified fee estate. For example, Smith conveys 1,000 acres to the Jones Foundation "so long as it is maintained as a wildlife preserve and used for no other purpose." Five years later the Jones Foundation decides to build its corporate headquarters on this land. **Title** (ownership) to the land *automatically* reverts to Smith or to Smith's heirs. This future interest is called a *possibility of reverter.*

Figure 3.1
Estates and Interests in
Real Estate

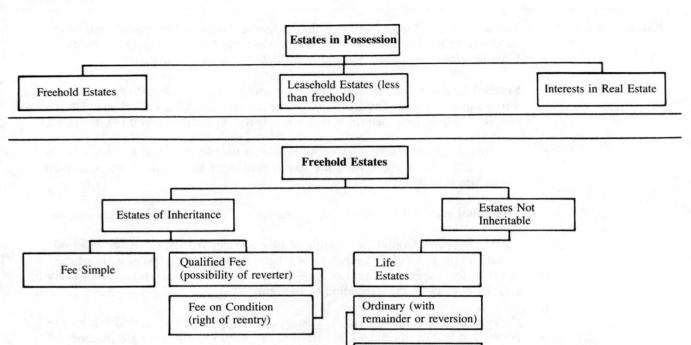

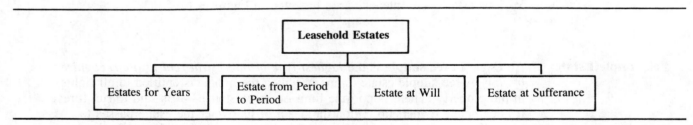

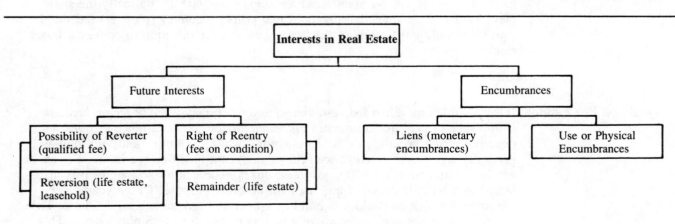

Fee on Condition

A **fee on condition** differs from a qualified fee in that the occurrence or nonoccurrence of a specified condition *may* terminate the estate created by the grant. The occurrence of such a condition creates a *right of reacquisition* for the grantor but is not automatic. Thus, if Smith conveyed land to the Jones Foundation, "provided it be used solely as a wildlife preserve," Jones's use of the land as its corporate headquarters would create a *right* for Smith or Smith's heirs to recover title to the land. Title would remain with Jones, however, until Smith filed suit in court to recover it.

Life Estates

A **life estate** is *limited to the life of some designated person.* The owner does not have the right to pass ownership to heirs because the ordinary life estate ends with the death of the owner. Life estates may be *ordinary* or *pur autre vie.*

An *ordinary* life estate lasts as long as the life tenant is alive. *A* may leave property to *B,* who will be complete owner in fee simple for the rest of his or her life. *B* does not, however, have the right to leave the property to anyone at death. A life estate *pur autre vie* (for another life) lasts as long as some third person is alive. Mrs. *A* might, for example, leave her home to neighbor *B,* to be owned by *B* "as long as my cat, Felix, is alive and living in the home." *B* (or even *B*'s heirs) would be complete owner of the property, but only until the cat's death.

Remainder and reversion. The owner creating a life interest provides for the eventual disposal of the property. After the death of the life tenant, the property may return to the original owner or pass to some third party.

1. **Remainder interest:** Mr. *A* may leave the family homestead to the second Mrs. *A* for her lifetime with the provision that it pass, at her death, to the son of his first marriage, *A, Jr.* During Mrs. *A*'s lifetime, *A, Jr.* owns a *remainder interest* and is known as a *remainderman.*
2. **Reversionary interest:** Mr. *A* may give his home to poor relative *B* for *B*'s lifetime with the provision that at *B*'s death, ownership reverts to *A* (or, if *A* has died, to *A*'s heirs). During B's lifetime, Mr. *A* owns a *reversionary interest (see* Figure 3.2). A life tenant's interest in real property is true ownership. The life tenant cannot, however, perform any acts that would permanently injure the land or property. Such injury to real estate is known in legal terms as *waste.*

Figure 3.2
Life Estate

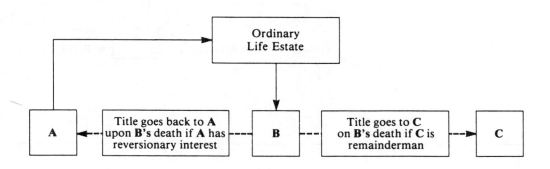

A life tenant is entitled to all income and profits arising from the property. A life interest may be sold, leased, mortgaged or given away, but it always will terminate (end) upon the death of the person against whose life the estate is measured.

A husband's life estate in the real estate of his deceased wife is called *curtesy*. *Dower* is the life estate that a wife has in the real estate of her deceased husband. New York law no longer recognizes dower and curtesy as legal life estates. Brokers should be alert, however, to possible rights of dower and curtesy in property owned by couples married before September 1, 1930.

Homestead

In New York **homestead** is not an estate but rather the right to protection of a principal residence against certain creditors' claims, particularly in bankruptcy. The homestead exemption protects up to $10,000 of a homeowner's equity from the court-ordered sale of his or her home to satisfy *unsecured* debts. An unsecured debt is one in which there is no collateral—the person's home has not been given as security for payment of the loan. A charge account or personal loan would be an example of an unsecured debt. A mortgage is a *secured* debt.

Encumbrances

An **encumbrance** is a right or interest held by a party who is not the owner of the property. Encumbrances may be divided into two general classifications:

- **liens,** financial claims against the property; and
- **usage encumbrances,** restrictions, easements, licenses and encroachments (*see* Figure 3.3).

Figure 3.3
Encumbrances

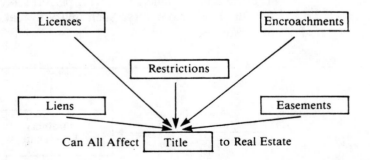

Liens

A financial claim against property that provides security for a debt or obligation of the property owner is a *lien*. If the obligation is not repaid, the lienholder, or creditor, has the right to have it paid out of the property usually from the proceeds of a court sale.

Real estate taxes (discussed at more length in Chapter 25) have first claim against the proceeds of such a sale. *Judgments* are court orders to pay a debt, for example, an outstanding hospital bill. They may be filed against any real estate owned by the debtor in the county where the judgment was obtained or in any county in the state.

Mechanics' liens are placed against a specific property by workers or suppliers who have not been paid for labor or materials used in construction or repairs. A claim for a mechanic's lien must be placed within four months of the completion of the work on a single dwelling and eight months on other buildings. A mechanic's lien is valid for one year and may be renewed. A **lis pendens** gives notice that a mechanic's lien may be filed. Liens will be discussed in detail in Chapter 24.

Deed Restrictions

Private agreements that affect the use of land are **deed restrictions** *and covenants.* They usually are imposed by an owner of real estate when he or she sells the property and they are included in the seller's deed to the buyer. Deed restrictions typically would be imposed by a developer or subdivider to maintain specific standards in a subdivision. Deed restrictions are discussed further in Chapter 6.

Easements

A right acquired by one party to use the land of another party for a special purpose is an **easement**. Easements are discussed in detail in Chapter 24.

Easement appurtenant. The permanent right to use another's land for the benefit of an adjoining parcel is an **easement appurtenant**. In Figure 3.4, for example, *B* has the right to cross *A*'s land to reach the lake. The easement was granted (given) by *A* and is owned by *B*. An easement appurtenant *runs with the land*, so that if *B* sells the property to *C*, *C* acquires the same right-of-way over *A*'s land. If *A* sells to *D*, *B* still owns the easement. Easements appurtenant involve two parcels of land.

Easement in gross; by necessity; by prescription. A simple right to use the land of another is an **easement in gross**. In Figure 3.4, the power company owns an easement in gross on the boundary line of both lots. In certain cases, if the only access to a parcel is through another's property, the owner may acquire an **easement by necessity** in order to reach his or her land. In Figure 3.4, *A* owns an easement by necessity, from the road across *B*'s land. Under specific circumstances, one may acquire the right to *use* another's property by doing so for a period of ten years, creating an **easement by prescription. Tacking** allows consecutive owners to accumulate the ten years' usage. (A similar process, *adverse possession,* sometimes allows the user to acquire *ownership*; *see* Chapter 23.)

Party walls. A wall shared by two buildings and constructed on the boundary line between two owners' lots is shared by the owners. Each owns his or her side of the **party wall** and an easement right in the other half.

Creating an easement. Easements commonly are created by written agreement between the parties establishing the easement right. Methods of creating easements by prescription and terminating easements are discussed in Chapter 24.

Figure 3.4.
Easements

The owner of Lot A has an **easement by necessity** across Lot B to gain access to his property from the paved road. The owner of Lot B has an **easement appurtenant** across Lot A so that Lot B's owner may reach the lake. The utility company has an **easement in gross** across both parcels of land for its electric power lines.

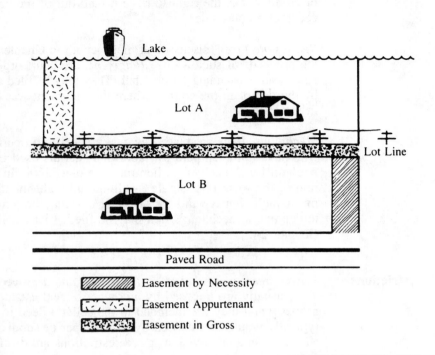

Lake

Lot A

Lot Line

Lot B

Paved Road

///////// Easement by Necessity

Easement Appurtenant

Easement in Gross

Licenses

A privilege to enter the land of another for a specific purpose is a **license.** It is not a permanent right and may be withdrawn. Examples of license include permission to park in a neighbor's driveway and permission to erect a billboard.

Encroachments

When a building (or some portion of it), fence, driveway or any other installation illegally *extends beyond the land of its owner* and covers some land of an adjoining owner or a street or alley, an **encroachment** arises. Encroachments usually are disclosed by either a physical inspection of the property or a survey. A survey shows the location of all improvements on a property and whether any improvements extend over the lot lines. If a building encroaches on neighboring land, the neighbor may be able to recover damages or secure removal of the portion of the building that encroaches. Encroachments of long standing (for a ten-year period) may give rise to easements by prescription.

For encroachments of six inches or less by the wall of a building, the encroacher receives an easement by prescription unless the offended neighbor seeks removal within one year or damages within two years.

Forms of Ownership

A fee simple estate in land may be held (1) in **severalty,** where title is held by one owner, (2) in **co-ownership,** where title is held by two or more persons or (3) in **trust,** where title is held by a third person for the benefit of another.

The form by which property is owned is important to the real estate broker's work for two reasons: (1) *the form of ownership existing when a property is sold determines who must sign the various documents involved* (listing contract, acceptance of offer to purchase, sales contract and deed) and (2) *the purchaser must determine in what form he or she wishes to take title.* When questions about these forms are raised, the real estate broker should recommend that the parties seek legal advice.

Co-Ownership

When title to one parcel of real estate is vested in two or more persons or organizations, those parties are said to be *co-owners* or *concurrent owners* of the property. New York recognizes (1) tenancy in common, (2) joint tenancy and (3) tenancy by the entirety.

Tenancy in Common

A **tenant in common** owns an **undivided interest.** Although a tenant in common may hold, say, a one-half or one-third interest in a property, it is impossible to distinguish physically which specific half or third of the property is owned. The deed creating a tenancy in common may or may not state the fractional interest held by each co-owner. If no fractions are stated and two people hold title to the property, each has an undivided one-half interest.

The second important characteristic of a tenancy in common is that *each owner* can sell, convey, mortgage or transfer that interest *without the consent* of the other co-owners. Upon the death of a co-owner, his or her interest passes to chosen heirs or devisees (*see* Figure 3.5).

**Figure 3.5
Tenancy in Common**

A and B are tenants in common.

A	B
$^1/_2$	$^1/_2$

B dies and wills his interest to C and D equally.

A	C	D
$^1/_2$	$^1/_4$	$^1/_4$

Tenants in common have the right of partition as explained below; either could force a sale.

In New York a conveyance to two or more persons not married to each other creates a tenancy in common unless otherwise stated in the deed. Property inherited by two or more persons is owned by them as tenants in common, unless a will stated otherwise.

Joint Tenancy

The basis of **joint tenancy** is *unity of ownership.* The property is owned by a group made up of two or more people. The death of one of the joint tenants simply means there is one fewer person in the group. The remaining joint tenants receive the share owned by the deceased tenant, by **right of survivorship** (*see* Figure 3.6). In contrast to a tenant in common, no joint tenant has the right to devise the property by will.

Figure 3.6
Joint Tenancy with
Right of Survivorship

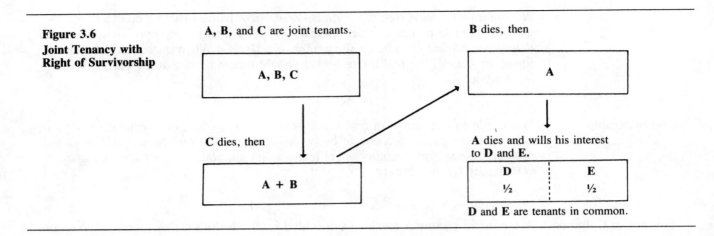

As each successive joint tenant dies, the surviving joint tenants acquire the interest of the deceased joint tenant. Only the last survivor may dispose of the property by will.

Creating joint tenancies. To create a joint tenancy in New York, language in the deed must expressly state that title is to be taken in that form of ownership. Acquisition of property by two more executors, trustees or guardians creates in them a joint tenancy.

Four unities are required to create a joint tenancy:

1. Unity of *time*—all joint tenants acquire their interest at the same time.
2. Unity of *title*—all joint tenants acquire their interest by the same deed.
3. Unity of *interest*—all joint tenants hold equal ownership interests.
4. Unity of *possession*—all joint tenants hold an undivided interest in the property.

These four unities are present when title is acquired by *one deed, executed and delivered at one time and conveying equal interests to all the owners who hold undivided possession of the property as joint tenants.*

Terminating joint tenancies. A joint tenancy is destroyed when any one of the essential unities of joint tenancy is terminated. Thus while a joint tenant is free to convey his or her interest in the jointly held property, doing so will destroy the unity of interest and, in turn, the joint tenancy. For example, if, *A, B* and *C* hold title as joint tenants and *A* sells her interest to *D*, then *D* will own an undivided one-third interest as a tenant in common with *B* and *C*, who will continue to own their undivided two-thirds interest as joint tenants (*see* Figure 3.7).

Figure 3.7
Combination of
Tenancies

A, B and C are joint tenants.

A, B, C

A sells her interest to D.

D 1/3	B + C 2/3

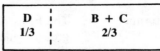

D becomes a tenant in common
with **B** and **C** as joint tenants.

If *D* died, one-third interest would go to *D*'s heir. If *B* died, *C* would own two-thirds.

Joint tenancies also may be terminated by operation of law, as in bankruptcy or foreclosure sale proceedings.

Termination of Co-Ownership by Partition Suit

Tenants in common or joint tenants may file in court a suit to **partition** the land. The right of partition is a legal way to dissolve a co-ownership when the parties do not voluntarily agree to its termination. If the court determines that the land cannot actually be divided into parts, it will order the real estate sold and divide the proceeds of the sale among the co-owners according to their fractional interests. Such a forced sale, however, may not yield full market value.

Tenancy by the Entirety

A **tenancy by the entirety** is a *special joint tenancy between husband and wife.* The distinguishing characteristics of this tenancy are: (1) the owners must be husband and wife when they receive the property, (2) the owners have rights of survivorship and (3) there is no right to partition.

In New York a conveyance to a man and a woman who are legally married to each other creates in them a tenancy by the entirety unless the deed expressly states otherwise. When a couple becomes divorced, the tenancy by the entirety is broken and they immediately become tenants in common. (Tenancy by the entirety is not used in all states.)

Community Property Rights

The concept of community property originated in Spanish law rather than English common law and was adopted by eight of the western and southwestern states. New York is not a community property state.

Trusts

Property owners may provide for their own financial care and/or that of their families by establishing trusts. Such trusts may be created by agreement during a property owner's lifetime (living trust), or established by will after his or her death (testamentary trust).

The individual creating a trust, the **trustor,** makes an agreement with a **trustee** (usually a corporate trustee) by which the individual conveys assets to the trustee with the understanding that the trustee will assume certain duties. These duties include the care and investment of the trust assets to produce income. After payment of operating expenses and trustee's fees, this income is paid or used for the benefit of a **beneficiary.** These trusts may continue for the lifetimes of the beneficiaries or the assets can be distributed when the beneficiaries reach certain predetermined ages.

Ownership of Real Estate by Business Organizations

Ownership by a business organization makes it possible for many people to hold an interest in the same parcel of real estate. There are various ways in which investors may be organized to finance a real estate project. Some provide for the real estate to be owned by the entity itself; others provide for direct ownership of the real estate by the investors. Business organizations may be categorized as:

(1) partnerships, (2) corporations or (3) syndicates. The purchase or sale of real estate by any business organization involves complex legal questions, and legal counsel usually is required.

All of the following types of business organizations are contrasted with **sole proprietorship,** which is a business owned by one individual.

Partnerships

An association of two or more people to carry on a business as co-owners and share in the business's profits and losses is a **partnership.** Partnerships are classified as general and limited. In a **general partnership** all partners participate to some extent in the operation and management of the business and may be held personally liable for business losses and obligations. A **limited partnership** includes general partners as well as limited, or silent, partners. The business is run by the general partner or partners. The limited partners do not participate and each can be held liable for the business's losses *only* to the extent of his or her investment. The limited partnership is a popular method of organizing investors in a real estate project.

Corporations

A **corporation** is an artificial person or legal entity created under the laws of the state from which it receives its charter. Because the corporation is a legal entity, real estate ownership by a corporation is an *ownership in severalty*. A corporation is managed and operated by its *board of directors*. Some charters permit a corporation to purchase real estate for any purpose; others limit such purchases to land that is needed to fulfill the entity's corporate purpose.

As a legal entity, a corporation exists until it is formally dissolved. The death of one of the officers or directors does not affect title to property that is owned by the corporation.

Individuals participate, or invest, in a corporation by purchasing stock. Because stock is *personal property,* stockholders do not have a direct ownership interest in real estate owned by a corporation. Each stockholder's liability for the corporation's losses usually is limited to the amount of his or her investment.

Syndicates

Generally, a **syndicate** is a *joining together of two or more people or firms in order to carry out one or more business projects*. A syndicate is not in itself a legal entity. It may be organized into a number of ownership forms, including co-ownership (tenancy in common, joint tenancy), partnership, trust or corporation. A *joint venture* is an organization of two or more people or firms to carry out a *single project*. A joint venture lasts for a limited time and is not intended to establish a permanent relationship. More will be said about these organizations in Chapter 17.

The real estate practitioner who organizes or sells a real estate venture involving investors who expect to benefit without active participation should be alert for special registration or licensing required for syndication activity.

Cooperative and Condominium Ownership

In the past few decades apartment dwellers have turned to arrangements under which they own their living space. Cooperative ownership was the first to develop; condominium ownership appeared more recently.

Cooperative Ownership

Under the usual **cooperative** arrangement, title to land and building is held by a *corporation*. Tenants buy stock in the corporation and in return receive proprietary leases to their apartments. As stockholders they exercise control over the administration of the building through an elected board of directors. Barring any violation of antidiscrimination laws, tenants often can approve or disapprove of prospective purchasers of the apartment leases. Tenants contribute monthly fees to cover maintenance costs, the corporation's property taxes and overall mortgage on the building.

The corporation, however, is vulnerable to financial problems. If other tenants cannot pay their monthly charges, the owner-occupant may lose out in the event of a forced sale of the property. Cooperative ownership typically is found in and around New York City more than in other parts of the state.

Condominium Ownership

The **condominium** form of occupant ownership has gained increasing popularity in recent years. The occupant-owner of each apartment holds a *fee simple title* to his or her apartment and a percentage of the indivisible parts of the building and land, known as the **common elements.** The individual unit owners in a condominium own these common elements together as *tenants in common,* but with *no right to partition.*

The condominium form of ownership is often used for apartment buildings. These may range from freestanding high-rise buildings to town-house arrangements. The common elements include such items as the land, walls, hallways, elevators, stairways and roof. Lawns and recreational facilities such as swimming pools, clubhouses, tennis courts and golf courses also may be considered common elements. In addition, condominium ownership is sometimes used for commercial property, office buildings or multiuse buildings that contain offices and shops as well as residential units.

Ownership. A condominium unit is *owned in fee simple.* The owner receives a separate tax bill and may mortgage the individual living unit.

Default in the payment of taxes or a mortgage loan by one unit owner may result in a foreclosure sale of that owner's unit but does not affect the ownership of the other unit owners. A condominium unit may be owned in severalty or in any form of co-ownership.

Operation and administration. The condominium property is administered by an association of unit owners according to the bylaws set forth in the declaration. The association may be governed by a board of directors or other official entity. It may manage the property on its own or it may engage a professional property manager to perform this function. Owners pay monthly charges for maintenance.

Town-house ownership is a hybrid form. The town-house occupant owns the land directly beneath his or her unit, and the living unit including roof and basement, in fee simple. Sometimes a small lawn or patio is individually owned also. A town-house owner also becomes a member of a homeowners' association, which owns the common elements.

Time-sharing is a variation of condominium ownership in which the buyer receives the right to use a living unit, usually in a resort area, for a specific portion of a year. The buyer might own an undivided one-twelfth interest together with a right to use the facility for one month of the year.

New York State regulations on the formation and administration of condominiums and cooperatives will be discussed at length in Chapter 20.

Summary

An *estate* is the amount and kind of interest a person holds in land. *Freehold estates* are estates of indeterminate length. Less-than-freehold estates are those for which the length can be accurately determined. These are called *leasehold estates* and they concern landlords and tenants.

Freehold estates are further divided into fee estates and life estates. Estates of inheritance include *fee simple* and *qualified fee* estates. Life estates can be granted for the life of the new owner or for the life of some third party (*pur autre vie*). At the end of the life estate, ownership can go back to the original owner (*reverter*), or pass to a designated third party (*remainder*). In New York, the old matrimonial estates of curtesy and dower were abolished in 1930. Homestead in New York is not an estate but a right to partial exemption of the equity in a residence from seizure for unsecured debts, as in bankruptcy.

Encumbrances against real estate may be in the form of liens, deed restrictions, easements, licenses, and encroachments.

Liens are financial claims against a parcel of real property.

An *easement* is the permanent right acquired by one person to use another's real estate. *Easements appurtenant* involve two separately owned tracts. An *easement in gross* is a right such as that granted to utility companies to maintain poles, wires and pipelines.

A *license* is permission to enter another's property for a specific purpose. A license usually is created orally, is of a temporary nature and can be revoked.

An *encroachment* is physical intrusion of some improvement upon another's land.

Sole ownership or *ownership in severalty* indicates that title is held by one person or entity.

There are three ways in which title to real estate can be held at the same time by more than one person, with each having an undivided interest. Under *tenancy in common* an individual owner may sell his or her interest and has the right to leave the share to any designated heirs. When two or more persons not married to each other hold title to real estate, they own it as tenants in common unless their deed specifically states some other intention. *Joint tenancy* involves two or more owners with the right of survivorship. Upon the death of one owner, that person's share passes to the remaining co-owner or co-owners. The intention of the parties to establish joint tenancy with right of survivorship must be clearly stated in their deed, and four *unities* must exist. Both tenants in common and joint tenants have the right to force a sale by partition. *Tenancy by the entirety* is a special joint tenancy for property acquired jointly by husband and wife. Unless their deed specifically states that they wish to own the property as tenants in common, they will own it by the entirety. Both must sign a deed for complete title to pass to a purchaser, and neither can force a sale by partition. Divorce changes their ownership to tenancy in common.

Real estate ownership also may be held in *trust*. In creating a trust, title to the property involved is conveyed to a *trustee,* who administers it for the benefit of a *beneficiary*.

Various types of business organizations may own real estate. A *corporation* is a legal entity and holds title to real estate in severalty. A *partnership* may own real estate in its own name. A *syndicate* is an association of two more people or firms to make an investment. Many syndicates are *joint ventures* and are organized for only a single project. A syndicate may be organized as a co-ownership, trust, corporation or partnership.

With *cooperative ownership,* title to the property, usually an apartment building, is held by a corporation that pays taxes, principal and interest on the building's mortgage, and operating expenses. The purchaser of an apartment receives shares in the corporation and a long-term lease to the living unit, and pays monthly charges to cover a share of expenses.

Under *condominium ownership* each occupant-owner holds fee simple title to his or her apartment unit plus a share of the common elements. Each owner receives an individual tax bill and may mortgage the unit as desired. Expenses for operating the building are collected by an owners' association through monthly assessments. In *town-house ownership* each occupant also owns the land directly below the unit.

Questions

1. The most complete ownership recognized by law is a(n):
   - a. life estate.
   - b. fee simple estate.
   - c. leasehold estate.
   - d. estate at will.

2. Herbert Kramer devises a parcel of land to New York University "so long as it is used for an experimental farm." Two years after Kramer's death the university begins to build a cafeteria on the land. In this case:
   - a. Kramer's heirs automatically become owners.
   - b. Kramer's heirs are joint tenants with the university.
   - c. Kramer's heirs own the land but the university owns the cafeteria.
   - d. Kramer's heirs have no claim on the land.

3. Which one of the following best describes a life estate?
   - a. An estate conveyed to A for the life of Z, and upon Z's death to B
   - b. An estate held by A and B in joint tenancy with right of survivorship
   - c. An estate upon condition
   - d. An estate given by law to a husband

4. Matilda inherited her cousin's house, but it is hers only as long as the dog, Skippy, is alive and well and living in the house. When Skippy dies, the house is to go to her cousin's son. The cousin's son is a:
   - a. beneficiary.
   - b. remainderman.
   - c. life tenant.
   - d. limited partner.

5. When a homeowner who is entitled by state law to a homestead exemption is sued by his or her creditors, then the creditors:
   - a. can have the court sell the home and apply the full proceeds of the sale to the debts.
   - b. have no right to have the debtor's home sold.
   - c. can order the debtor to sell the home to pay them.
   - d. can have a court sale and apply the sale proceeds, in excess of $10,000, to the debts.

6. Encumbrances include:
   - a. encroachments.
   - b. liens.
   - c. easements.
   - d. all of the above.

7. Deed restrictions are created by a:
   - a. seller.
   - b. buyer.
   - c. neighborhood association.
   - d. governmental agency.

8. In certain circumstances the owner of landlocked property can go to court and request a permanent right to go over a neighbor's land for access, in the form of an:
   - a. easement in gross.
   - b. estate for life.
   - c. encroachment.
   - d. easement by necessity.

9. Mary buys a house and automatically receives the same right the seller had to use a party wall. Mary owns an:
   - a. estate at sufferance.
   - b. emblement.
   - c. encroachment.
   - d. easement.

10. The right to run a power line across the back of someone's property is an example of an easement:
    - a. in gross.
    - b. by prescription.
    - c. by necessity.
    - d. in common.

11. John owns a small country house and gives a neighboring farmer permission to plant crops on the two acres around his house. John changes his mind and decides to put in a lawn. He may withdraw the permission because the farmer had only a(n):
    - a. estate at sufferance.
    - b. easement by necessity.
    - c. license.
    - d. life estate.

12. A license is an example of a(n):
    - a. easement.
    - b. encroachment.
    - c. encumbrance.
    - d. restriction.

13. Ownership of real property by one person is called ownership in:
    - a. trust.
    - b. severalty.
    - c. entirety.
    - d. condominium.

14. A parcel of real estate was purchased by Howard Evers and Tinker Chance. Evers paid one-third of the cost and Chance paid the balance. The seller's deed received at the closing conveyed the property "to Howard Evers and Tinker Chance," without further explanation. Thus Evers and Chance are:
    a. joint tenants.
    b. tenants in common, each owning a one-half undivided interest.
    c. tenants in common, with Evers owning an undivided one-third interest.
    d. general partners in a joint venture.

15. If property is held by two or more owners as tenants in common, upon the death of one owner the ownership of his or her share will pass to the:
    a. remaining owner or owners.
    b. heirs or whomever is designated under the deceased owner's will.
    c. surviving owner and/or his or her heirs.
    d. deceased owner's surviving spouse.

16. The right of survivorship is closely associated with a:
    a. corporation.   c. trust.
    b. cooperative.   d. joint tenancy.

17. In New York a deed conveying property to a married couple, such as: to "Frank Peters and Marcia Peters, husband and wife," creates a:
    a. joint tenancy.
    b. tenancy by the entirety.
    c. tenancy in common.
    d. periodic tenancy.

18. Which of the following statements applies equally to joint tenants and tenants by the entireties?
    a. There is no right to file a partition suit.
    b. The survivor becomes complete owner.
    c. Sale of one share creates a tenancy in common.
    d. A deed must state the type of tenancy desired.

19. Henry's will provides that the local bank will receive his real estate and administer it for the benefit of his children until they reach the age of 18. Henry has established a:
    a. life estate.   c. testamentary trust.
    b. joint venture.   d. tenancy in common.

20. An artificial person created by legal means is known as a:
    a. trust.   c. limited partnership.
    b. corporation.   d. joint tenancy.

21. A syndicate formed to carry out a single business project is commonly known as a:
    a. joint venture.   c. limited partnership.
    b. corporation.   d. joint tenancy.

22. Dorothy bought an apartment in Manhattan and received shares in a corporation and a proprietary lease to her unit. Her building is organized as a:
    a. cooperative.   c. joint venture.
    b. condominium.   d. syndicate.

23. Residents of a building commonly reserve the right to approve or disapprove of potential buyers in which form of joint ownership?
    a. Cooperative   c. Joint venture
    b. Condominium   d. Tenancy in common

24. A condominium is a form of:
    a. apartment building. c. living unit.
    b. co-ownership.   d. cooperative.

25. Townhouse ownership differs from condominium arrangements because the occupant also owns in fee simple:
    a. shares in a corporation.
    b. a proprietary lease.
    c. the land directly under the living unit.
    d. part of the golf course.

4

Real Estate Instruments: Deeds and Mortgages

Key Terms

Acceleration clause
Acknowledgment
Alienation clause
Attorney-in-fact
Bargain and sale deed
Bargain and sale deed with covenant
Benchmarks
Bond
Consideration
Covenants
Datum
Deed
Default
Deficiency judgment
Delivery and acceptance
Estoppel certificate
Foreclosure
Grantee/Grantor
Granting clause
Habendum clause

Legal description
Lessee/Lessor
Lien theory
Metes and bounds
Monuments
Mortgage
Mortgagee/Mortgagor
Note
Plat of subdivision
Point (place) of beginning
Quitclaim deed
Rectangular (government) survey system
Reduction certificate
Satisfaction of mortgage
Sections
Seisin
Title
Title theory
Warranty deed

Overview

This chapter will discuss deeds—the documents used to transfer ownership of real property—and mortgages—the documents used to pledge real property as security for debts. Because "the big house at the corner of Oak and Main" is insufficient identification for these important instruments, the standard system of legal descriptions also will be discussed.

Legal Descriptions

A deed is the instrument that conveys title to real property, the document that transfers ownership. One of the essential elements of a valid deed is an adequate description of the *land* being conveyed (the deed does not usually describe improvements on the land). A **legal description** is an *exact way of describing real estate in a contract, deed, mortgage or other document that will be accepted by a court of law.*

Land can be described by three methods: by metes and bounds, by government survey or by reference to a plat (map) filed in the county clerk's office in the county where the land is located. In New York a legal description may combine different descriptive methods.

Legal descriptions should not be changed, altered or combined without adequate information from a competent authority such as a surveyor or title attorney. Legal descriptions always should include the name of the county and state in which the land is located.

Street address and property tax account number, while helpful for quick reference to what is being described, are not usually acceptable as legal descriptions.

Metes and Bounds

A **metes-and-bounds description** makes use of the boundaries and measurements of the land in question. Such a description starts at a definitely designated point called the **point (place) of beginning** (POB) and proceeds clockwise around the boundaries of the tract by reference to measurements and directions. A metes-and-bounds description always ends at the point where it began (the POB).

A tract of land located in the City of Elmira, County of Chemung, State of New York, described as follows: Beginning at the intersection of the east line of Jones Road and the south line of Skull Drive; thence east along the south line of Skull Drive 200 feet; thence south 15° east 216.5 feet, more or less, to the center thread of Red Skull Creek; thence northwesterly along the center line of said creek to its intersection with the east line of Jones Road; thence north 105 feet, more or less, along the east line of Jones Road to the place of beginning.

Figure 4.1
Metes-and-Bounds Tract

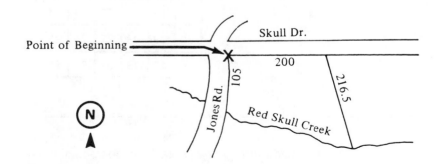

In a metes-and-bounds description **monuments** are fixed objects used to establish real estate boundaries. In the past, natural objects such as stones, large trees, lakes, streams and intersections of major streets or highways, as well as man-made markers placed by surveyors, were commonly used as monuments. Today man-made markers are the more common monuments because it is recognized that natural objects may change or be removed. An example of a metes-and-bounds description of a parcel of land (pictured in Figure 4.1) appeared on page 47.

Metes-and-bounds descriptions are used everywhere, from rural, undeveloped areas to Manhattan, with street intersections as monuments.

Rectangular (Government) Survey System

The **rectangular survey system,** sometimes called the *government survey method,* was established by Congress in 1785, soon after the federal government was organized. The system was developed as a standard method of describing all lands conveyed to or acquired by the federal government, including the extensive area of the Northwest Territory. It is seldom used in New York State.

The rectangular survey system is based on sets of two intersecting lines: principal meridians and base lines. The *principal meridians* are north and south lines and the *base lines* are east and west lines. Both are exactly located by reference to degrees of longitude and latitude.

Townships. Using these meridians and base lines, land is surveyed into six-mile square *townships*, each with identifying reference numbers. Each township contains 36 square miles.

Sections. A township is further divided into 36 numbered **sections.** Sections are numbered 1 through 36, as shown in Figure 4.2. Section 1 is always in the northeast, or upper right-hand, corner.

**Figure 4.2
Sections in a
Township**

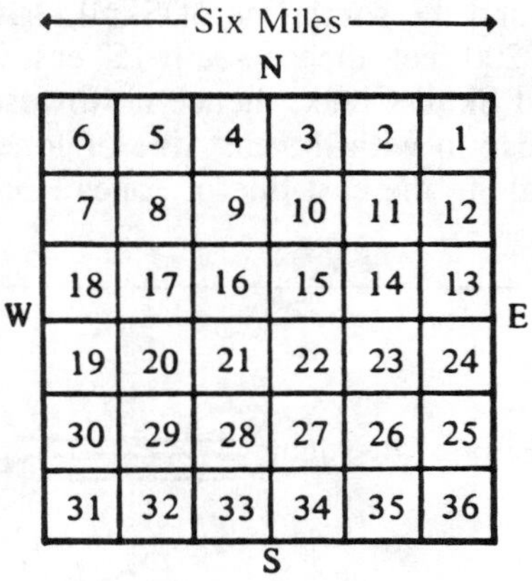

As illustrated in Figure 4.3, each section contains one square mile, or *640 acres*, and is divided into *quarters* for reference purposes. One could refer to the southeast quarter, which is a 160-acre tract; this would be abbreviated as SE¼. Quarter

Figure 4.3
A Section

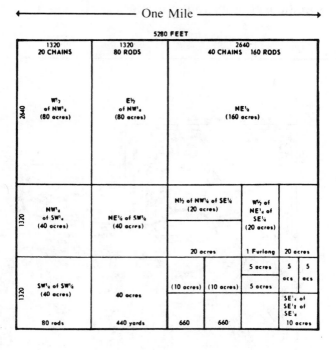

sections can be divided into quarters or halves, and such parts can be further divided by quarters. The SE¼ of SE¼ of SE¼ of Section 1 would be a ten-acre square in the lower right-hand corner of Section 1.

Recorded Plat of Subdivision

The third method of land description is by *lot and map number* referring to a **plat of subdivision** filed with the clerk of the county where the land is located.

The first step in subdividing land is the preparation of a *plat (map) of survey* by a licensed surveyor or engineer, as illustrated in Figure 4.4. On this plat the land is divided into blocks and lots, and streets or access roads for public use are indicated. The lots are assigned numbers or letters. Lot sizes and street details must be indicated. When properly signed and approved, the subdivision plat may be recorded in the county in which the land is located; it thereby becomes part of the legal description. In describing a lot from a recorded subdivision plat, the lot number, name or number of the subdivision plat, and name of the county and state are used. For example:

> THAT TRACT OR PARCEL OF LAND, situate in the Town of Brighton, County of Monroe, and State of New York, known and designated as Lot No. 58 of the Elmwood Heights Tract. Said Lot is situated on Hemingway Drive and is of the dimensions shown on a map of Elmwood Heights filed in the Monroe County Clerk's Office in Liber 125 of Maps at page 95.

The word *liber* is Latin for *book*. Sometimes a *reel* number is used, referring to a specific reel of microfilm records.

Figure 4.4
Subdivision Plat Map

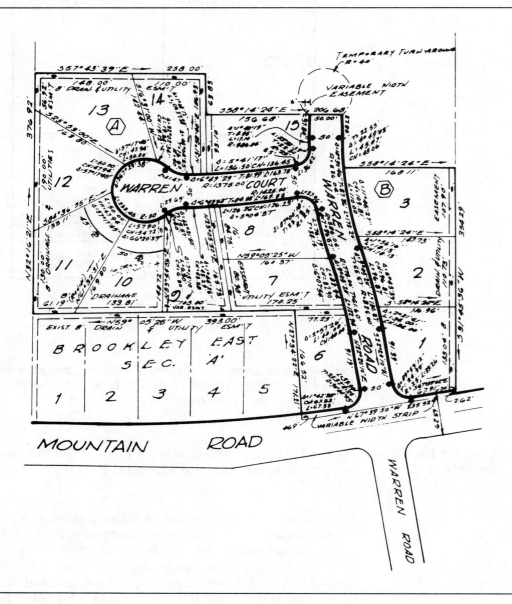

Preparation and Use of a Survey

A licensed surveyor is trained and authorized to locate a given parcel of land and to determine its legal description. The surveyor does this by preparing a *survey*, which sets forth the legal description of the property. A survey map shows the location and dimensions of the parcel and the location, size and shape of buildings located on the lot. Surveys may be required for conveying a portion of a given tract of land, placing a mortgage loan, showing the location of new construction, locating roads and highways and determining the legal description of the land on which a particular building is located.

Measuring Elevations

Air Lots

The owner of a parcel of land may subdivide the air above the land into *air lots.* This type of description is found in titles to tall buildings located on air rights. In preparing a subdivision plat for condominium use, a surveyor describes each condominium unit by reference to the elevation of the floors and ceilings above the city datum.

Datum

A point, line or surface from which elevations are measured or indicated is a **datum,** defined by the United States Geological Survey as the mean sea level at New York harbor. A datum is of special significance to surveyors in determining the height of structures, establishing the grade of streets and similar situations. Many large cities have established a local official datum.

Benchmarks. To aid surveyors, permanent reference points called **benchmarks** have been established throughout the United States (*see* Figure 4.5). Local benchmarks simplify surveyors' work because measurements may be based on them rather than on the basic benchmark, which may be miles away.

**Figure 4.5
Benchmark**

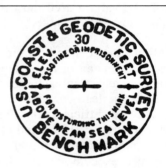

Condominium Descriptions

A sufficient description of condominium property to be conveyed must include: (1) a description of the land on which the building and improvements are located; (2) a designation of the unit conveyed as listed in the declaration, filed in accordance with the *New York Condominium Act;* and (3) a description of the common interest conveyed with the unit.

Deeds

A **deed** is a *written instrument by which an owner of real estate intentionally conveys his or her right, title or interest in a parcel of real estate.* All deeds must be in writing, in accordance with the requirements of the statute of frauds. The owner (who sells or gives the land) is referred to as the **grantor,** and the new owner (who acquires the title) is called the **grantee.** A deed is *executed* (signed) by the grantor.

Requirements for a Valid Conveyance

Although the formal requirements for a valid deed are not uniform in all states, certain requirements are basic. These are:

1. a *grantor* having the legal capacity to execute (sign) the deed;
2. a *grantee* named with reasonable certainty, so that he or she can be identified;
3. a recital of *consideration*;
4. a *granting clause* (words of conveyance);
5. a *habendum clause* (to define ownership in deed);
6. designation of any *limitations* on the conveyance of a full fee simple estate;
7. an *adequate description* of the property conveyed;
8. *exceptions and reservations* affecting the title;
9. the *signature of the grantor, acknowledgment;* and
10. *delivery* of the deed and *acceptance* by the grantee to pass title.

Grantor. In New York both grantee and grantor must be identified by residence if the deed is to be recorded.

In New York a person must be of sound mind and have reached the age of 18 in order to effect a valid conveyance. A contract executed by an incompetent or a minor is *voidable* by the courts; that is, it may be set aside in a lawsuit conducted by a representative of the incompetent or minor. A minor may disaffirm a contract upon reaching the age of 18. A minor who is married may convey property used as a home as if he or she had reached the age of 18. A grantor generally is held to have sufficient mental capacity to execute a deed if he or she is capable of understanding the action.

Grantee. To be valid a deed must name a grantee and do so in such a way that he or she is readily identifiable.

Consideration. In order to be valid all deeds must contain a clause acknowledging the grantor's receipt of a consideration. **Consideration** is defined as something of value given in an exchange. The amount of consideration must be stated in dollars. When a deed conveys real estate as a gift to a relative, "love and affection" may be sufficient consideration. It is customary to recite a *nominal* consideration such as "$10.00 and other good and valuable consideration." The full dollar amount of consideration seldom is set forth in the deed, except when the instrument is executed by an administrator, an executor or trustee, or pursuant to court order.

Granting clause (words of conveyance). A deed must contain words in the **granting clause** that state the grantor's intention to convey the property. Depending on the type of deed and the obligations agreed to by the grantor, the wording generally is either "convey and warrant," "grant," "grant, bargain and sell" or "remise, release and quitclaim."

If more than one grantee is involved, the granting clause should cover the creation of their specific rights in the property. The clause might state, for example, that the grantees will take title as joint tenants or tenants in common. This is especially important because specific wording is necessary to create a joint tenancy.

Deeds that convey the entire fee simple interest of the grantor usually contain wording such as "to Jacqueline Smith and to her heirs and assigns forever." If the grantor is conveying less than his or her complete interest, such as a life estate to property, the wording must indicate this limitation. A deed creating a life estate would convey property "to Jacqueline Smith for the duration of her natural life."

Habendum clause. When it is necessary to define or explain the ownership to be enjoyed by the grantee, a **habendum clause** follows the granting clause. The habendum clause begins with the words "to have and to hold." Its provisions must agree with those set down in the granting clause.

Description of real estate. For a deed to be valid it must contain an adequate description of the real estate conveyed. Land is considered adequately described if a competent surveyor can locate the property from the description used.

Exceptions and reservations. A grantor may reserve some right in the land for his or her own use (an easement, for instance). A grantor also may place certain restrictions on a grantee's use of the property. A developer, for example, can restrict the number of houses that may be built on a one-acre lot in a subdivision. Such restrictions may be stated in the deed or contained in a previously recorded document (such as the subdivider's master deed) that is expressly cited in the deed.

Signature of grantor. To be valid a deed must be signed by *all grantors* named in the deed. New York permits a grantor's signature to be signed by an attorney-in-fact acting under a power of attorney (specific written authority). An **attorney-in-fact** is any person who has been given power of attorney to execute and sign legal instruments for a grantor. In such cases it usually is necessary for the power of attorney to be recorded in the county where the property is located. Because the power of attorney terminates upon the death of the person granting such authority, adequate evidence must be submitted that the grantor is alive at the time the attorney-in-fact signs the deed.

Acknowledgment. An **acknowledgment** is a declaration made by a person who is signing a document before a *notary public* or authorized public officer. This acknowledgment usually states that the person signing the deed or other document is known to the officer or has produced sufficient identification. The acknowledgment provides evidence that the signature is genuine.

Although an acknowledgment is usually made before a notary public, it can also be taken by a judge, justice of the peace or other qualified person (*see* Chapter 4 Appendix).

Although an acknowledgment is not required to make a deed valid, in New York all deeds, mortgages and similar documents must be acknowledged before they can be recorded. Each document must be signed before a notary public or other authorized public official or before a witness, who must attest to the validity of the grantor's signature. The signature of the witness would then be acknowledged before an authorized public official.

From a purely practical point of view a deed that is not acknowledged is not a satisfactory instrument. Although an unrecorded deed is valid between the grantor and the grantee, it does not protect against claims by subsequent innocent purchasers. To help assure good title a grantee should always require acknowledgment of the grantor's signature on a deed, so that it may be recorded. Further requirements before a deed may be recorded are detailed in Chapter 11.

Delivery and acceptance. Before a transfer of title by conveyance can take effect, there must be an actual **delivery** of the deed by the grantor and either actual or implied **acceptance** by the grantee. *Title is said to pass when a deed is* *delivered.* The effective date of the transfer of title from the grantor to the grantee is the date of delivery of the deed itself.

In England during the Middle Ages, when few people were literate, transfer of title occurred in the following manner: Seller took buyer into the field in question and they walked the boundaries together ("beating the bounds"). Then the seller reached down, took up a clod of earth to represent the whole field, and handed it to the buyer. At the moment when the buyer seized the clod, he became owner of the land. Today a document is used instead of a clod of earth, but title still transfers at the moment of delivery and acceptance, and the owner is still said to be *seized* of the property. The Latin word **seisin** still denotes ownership and control.

Execution of Corporate Deeds

Under the law a corporation is considered to be a legal entity. Some basic rules must be followed when corporations are to convey real estate:

1. A corporation can convey real estate only upon a proper resolution passed by its *board of directors*. If all or a substantial portion of a corporation's real estate is being conveyed, it is also usually required that a resolution authorizing the sale be secured from the *stockholders*.
2. *Deeds to real estate can be signed only by an authorized officer.* The authority of the officer must be granted by a resolution properly passed by the board of directors.
3. The corporate *seal* need not be affixed to the conveyance unless the acknowledgment mentions the seal.

Rules pertaining to religious corporations and not-for-profit corporations vary widely. Because the legal requirements must be followed explicitly it is advisable to consult an attorney for all corporate conveyances.

Types of Deeds

The most common forms of deed in New York are:

1. full covenant and warranty deed;
2. bargain and sale deed with covenant against grantor's acts;
3. bargain and sale deed without covenant against grantor's acts;
4. quitclaim deed;
5. executor's deed; and
6. referee's deed.

Warranty deeds. For a purchaser of real estate, a **full covenant and warranty deed** (shown in Figure 4.6) provides the *greatest protection* of any deed. It is referred to as a warranty deed because the grantor is legally bound by certain **covenants** or warranties. The warranties usually are written into the deed itself. The basic warranties are:

1. *Covenant of seisin:* The grantor warrants that he or she is the owner of the property and has the right to convey title to it. The grantee may recover damages up to the full purchase price if this covenant is broken.
2. *Covenant against encumbrances:* The grantor warrants that the property is free from any liens or encumbrances except those specifically stated in the deed. If this covenant is breached, the grantee may sue for expenses to remove the encumbrance or receive compensation..

Figure 4.6
Full Covenant and
Warranty Deed

Standard N.Y. B.T.U. Form 8003 — 8-53 — Warranty Deed With Full Covenants — Individual or Corporation. (single sheet)

35-3100-021
Form 31-21

THIS INDENTURE, made the   day of   , nineteen hundred and

BETWEEN

party of the first part, and

party of the second part,

WITNESSETH, that the party of the first part, in consideration of Ten Dollars and other valuable consideration paid by the party of the second part, does hereby grant and release unto the party of the second part, the heirs or successors and assigns of the party of the second part forever,

ALL that certain plot, piece or parcel of land, with the buildings and improvements thereon erected, situate, lying and being in the

TOGETHER with all right, title and interest, if any, of the party of the first part of, in and to any streets and roads abutting the above-described premises to the center lines thereof; TOGETHER with the appurtenances and all the estate and rights of the party of the first part in and to said premises; TO HAVE AND TO HOLD the premises herein granted unto the party of the second part, the heirs or successors and assigns of the party of the second part forever.

AND the party of the first part, in compliance with Section 13 of the Lien Law, covenants that the party of the first part will receive the consideration for this conveyance and will hold the right to receive such consideration as a trust fund to be applied first for the purpose of paying the costs of the improvement and will apply the same first to the payment of the cost of the improvement before using any part of the total of the same for any other purpose.

AND the party of the first part covenants as follows: that said party of the first part is seized of the said premises in fee simple, and has good right to convey the same; that the party of the second part shall quietly enjoy the said premises; that the said premises are free from incumbrances, except as aforesaid; that the party of the first part will execute or procure any further necessary assurance of the title to said premises; and that said party of the first part will forever warrant the title to said premises.

The word "party" shall be construed as if it read "parties" whenever the sense of this indenture so requires.

IN WITNESS WHEREOF, the party of the first part has duly executed this deed the day and year first above written.

IN PRESENCE OF:

Forms may be purchased from Julius Blumberg, Inc., New York, NY 10013, or any of its dealers. Reproduction prohibited.

3. *Covenant of quiet enjoyment:* The grantor guarantees that the grantee's title is good against third parties who might bring court actions to establish superior title to the property. If the grantee's title is found to be inferior, the grantor is liable for damages.
4. *Covenant of further assurance:* The grantor promises to obtain and deliver any instrument needed in order to make the title good.
5. *Covenant of warranty forever:* The grantor guarantees that if at any time in the future the title fails, he or she will compensate the grantee for the loss sustained.

These covenants in a warranty deed are not limited to matters that occurred during the time the grantor owned the property; they extend back to all previous owners.

In addition, a deed in New York usually contains a *lien covenant,* stating that in accordance with Section 13 of the lien law, the seller holds the proceeds of the sale in trust against unpaid improvements to the property.

In New York State the seller need not deliver a full covenant and warranty deed unless the purchase agreement stipulates it. In many Upstate areas the warranty deed is the one most commonly used.

Bargain and sale deed without covenant. A **bargain and sale deed without covenant** contains no warranties. It does, however, *imply* that the grantor holds title to the property. The grantee has little legal recourse if defects later appear in the title. The bargain and sale deed without covenant is used in foreclosure and tax sales and as a *referee's deed.*

Bargain and sale deed with covenant against grantor's acts. A covenant may be added under which grantors covenant that they have done nothing to encumber the property while it was in their possession. This deed often is used by fiduciaries: executors, trustees and corporations. The grantors are willing to warrant about the time they owned the property but not about previous owners.

The bargain and sale deed with covenant (against grantor's acts) often is used in real estate transactions in the New York City area; the buyer may look to title insurance for protection in the event of future title problems. In most other states, this deed is known as a special warranty deed.

Figure 4.7 illustrates the wording of granting clauses on various types of deeds.

Quitclaim deeds. A **quitclaim deed** provides the grantee with the least protection of any deed. It carries no covenant or warranties and conveys only such interest, if any, as the grantor may have when the deed is delivered. By a quitclaim deed the grantor only "remises, releases and quitclaims" his or her interest in the property to the grantee.

If the grantor has no interest in the property the grantee will acquire nothing, nor will he or she acquire any claim against the grantor. A quitclaim deed can convey title as effectively as a warranty deed if the grantor has good title when he or she delivers the deed, but it provides no guarantees.

A quitclaim deed commonly is used for simple transfers within a family and for property transferred during divorce settlements. It also can be used to clear a

Figure 4.7
Types of Deeds

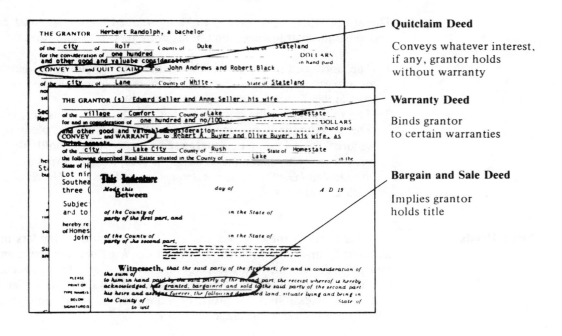

Mortgages

cloud on a title when persons who may or may not have some claim to property are asked to "sign off."

Executor's and referee's deeds. An *executor's deed* is a bargain and sale deed with covenant; a *referee's deed* contains no covenants or warranties although it does *imply* seisin (ownership). One characteristic of such instruments is that the *full consideration* (sales price) usually is stated in the deed. This is done because the deed is executed pursuant to a court order; and because the court has authorized the sale of the property for a given amount of consideration, this amount should be *exactly* stated in the document.

Mortgages

United States Mortgage Law

Some states recognize a lender as the owner of mortgaged land. These states are called **title theory** states. Connecticut, for example, is a title theory state.

New York, however, interprets a mortgage purely as a lien on real property and is called a **lien theory** state. If a mortgagor defaults, the lender is required to foreclose the lien (generally through a court action), offer the property for sale and apply the funds received from the sale to reduce or pay off the debt.

Mortgage Loan Instruments

By itself a mortgage is a pledge of property given by a borrower to a lender to secure a loan. Because a pledge of security is not legally effective unless there is a debt to secure, a note is also required. *Both documents must be executed in order to create an enforceable mortgage loan.*

Therefore, when a property is to be mortgaged the owner must execute, or sign, two separate instruments (sometimes combined into one form):

1. The **note,** or the **bond,** which is similar to a note, is evidence of the promise, or agreement, to repay the debt. The mortgagor executes one or more promissory notes to total the amount of the debt.
2. The **mortgage** is the document that creates the lien as *security* for the debt. The **mortgagor** is the one who does the mortgaging, pledging real estate as security for a loan. The **mortgagee** accepts, takes, holds the mortgage and gives money in exchange. To help in keeping the terms straight, it is useful to note that *bOrrOwer,* like *mOrtgagOr,* contains two *O*s; *lEndEr* and *mortgagEE* each contain two *E*s.

Trust Deeds

In some areas of the country, and in certain situations, lenders prefer to use a three-party instrument known as a *trust deed,* or *deed of trust,* rather than a mortgage document. A trust deed conveys the real estate as security for the loan to a third party, called the *trustee.* In case of default, the lender with a trust deed can gain possession of the property more promptly and more simply than a lender who forecloses on a mortgage.

Provisions of the Note or Bond

The promissory note (or bond) executed by a borrower (known as the *maker* or *payor*) states the amount of the debt, the time and method of payment, and the rate of interest, if any. The bond, like the mortgage, should be signed by all parties who have an interest in the property. Figure 4.8 is an example of a note and mortgage commonly used in some areas of New York State.

Provisions of the Mortgage Document

The mortgage document refers to the terms of the note and clearly establishes that the land is security for the debt. It identifies the lender as well as the borrower and it includes an accurate legal description of the property. It should be signed by all parties who have an interest in the real estate. It also sets forth the obligations of the borrower and the rights of the lender. The essentials of a valid mortgage are listed in the excerpts from the New York State study booklet in the Appendix to this chapter.

Duties of the Mortgagor

The borrower's obligations usually include the following:

* paying the debt in accordance with the terms of the note;
* paying all real estate taxes on the property given as security;
* maintaining adequate insurance to protect the lender if the property is destroyed or damaged by fire, windstorm or other hazard;
* obtaining lender's authorization before making any major alterations on the property;
* maintaining the property in good repair at all times; and
* obtaining lender's authorization before placing a second mortgage (junior lien) against the property.

Figure 4.8
Sample Note and Mortgage

P 666—Note and Mortgage, short form, plain English format, 11-78

CONSULT YOUR LAWYER BEFORE SIGNING THIS FORM—THIS FORM SHOULD BE USED BY LAWYERS ONLY.

NOTE AND MORTGAGE

$.. Date..

Parties — Mortgagor

Mortgagee
Address

Promise to pay principal amount (debt) interest payments — Mortgagor promises to pay to Mortgagee or order the sum of dollars ($ with interest at the rate of % per year from the date above until the debt is paid in full.
Mortgagor will pay the debt as follows:

Application of payments — The Mortgagee will apply each payment first to interest charges and then to repayment of the debt.

Address for payment — Payment shall be made at Mortgagee's address above or at any other address Mortgagee directs.

Additional promises and agreements of the Mortgagor:

Transfer of rights in the Property — 1. The Mortgagor hereby mortgages to the Mortgagee the Property described in this Note and Mortgage. Mortgagor can lose the Property for failure to keep the promises in this Note and Mortgage.

Property Mortgaged — 2. The Property mortgaged (the "Property") is All

Future advances — 3. The Mortgagee may make advances in the future to the Mortgagor or future owners of the Property. In addition to the above Debt this Note and Mortgage is intended to secure any more debts now or in the future owed by the Mortgagor to the Mortgagee. The principal amount of the above Debt shall be the maximum amount of debt secured by this Note and Mortgage. Mortgagee is not obligated to make future advances.

**Figure 4.8
(continued)**

Insurance 4. Mortgagor will keep the buildings on the Property insured against loss by fire and other risks included in the standard form of extended coverage insurance. The amount shall be approved by Mortgagee, but shall not exceed full replacement value of the buildings. Mortgagor will assign and deliver the policies to Mortgagee. The policies shall contain the standard New York Mortgage clause in the name of Mortgagee. If Mortgagor fails to keep the buildings insured Mortgagee may obtain the insurance. Within 30 days after notice and demand, Mortgagor must insure the Property against war risk and any other risk reasonably required by Mortgagee.

Maintenance 5. Mortgagor will keep the Property in reasonably good repair.

No sale or alteration 6. The Mortgagor may not, without the consent of Mortgagee, (a) alter, demolish or remove the buildings and improvements on the Property, or (b) sell the Property or any part of it.

Taxes, etc. 7. Mortgagor will pay all taxes, assessments, sewer rents or water rates within 30 days after they are due. Mortgagor must show receipts for these payments within 10 days of Mortgagee's demand for them.

Mortgagee's right to cure 8. Mortgagor authorizes Mortgagee to make payments necessary to correct a default of Mortgagor under Paragraphs 4 and 7 of this Mortgage. Payments made by Mortgagee together with interest at the rate provided in this Note and Mortgage from the date paid until the date of repayment shall be added to the Debt and secured by this Mortgage. Mortgagor shall repay Mortgagee with interest within 10 days after demand.

Statement of the amount due 9. Within five days after request in person or within ten days after request by mail, Mortgagor shall give to Mortgagee a signed statement of the amount due on this Note and Mortgage and whether there are any offsets or defenses against the Debt.

Title 10. Mortgagor warrants the title to the Property. Mortgagor is responsible for any costs or losses of the Mortgagee if an interest in the Property is claimed by others.

Lien law section 13 11. Mortgagor will receive the advances secured by this Note and Mortgage and will hold the right to receive the advances as a trust fund. The advances will be applied first for the purpose of paying the cost of improvement. Mortgagor will apply the advances first to the payment to the cost of improvement before using any part of the total of the advances for any other purpose.

Default, when full amount of debt due immediately 12. Mortgagee may declare the full amount of the Debt to be due and payable immediately for any default. The following are defaults:

  (a) Mortgagor fails to make any payment required by this Note and Mortgage within 15 days of its due date;
  (b) Mortgagor fails to keep any other promise or agreement in this Note and Mortgage within the time set forth, or if no time is set forth, within a reasonable time after notice is given that Mortgagor is in Default.

Sale 13. If Mortgagor defaults under this Note and Mortgage and the Property is to be sold at a foreclosure sale, the Property may be sold in one parcel.

Receiver 14. If Mortgagee sues to foreclose the Note and Mortgage, Mortgagee shall have the right to have a receiver appointed to take control of the Property.

Payment of rent and eviction after Default 15. If there is a Default under this Note and Mortgage, Mortgagor must pay monthly in advance to Mortgagee, or to a receiver who may be appointed to take control of the Property, the fair rental for the use and occupancy of the part of the Property that is in the possession of the Mortgagor. If Mortgagor does not pay the rent when due, Mortgagor will vacate and surrender the Property to Mortgagee or to the receiver. Mortgagor may be evicted by summary proceedings or other court proceedings.

Applicable law 16. Mortgagee shall have all the rights set forth in Section 254 of the New York Real Property Law in addition to Mortgagee's rights set forth in this Note and Mortgage, even if the rights are different from each other.

No oral changes 17. This Note and Mortgage may not be changed or ended orally.

Notices 18. Notices, demands or requests may be in writing and may be delivered in person or sent by mail.

Who is bound 19. If there are more than one Mortgagor each shall be separately liable. The words "Mortgagor" and "Mortgagee" shall include their heirs, executors, administrators, successors and assigns. If there are more than one Mortgagor or Mortgagee the words "Mortgagor" and "Mortgagee" used in this Mortgage includes them.

Signatures Mortgagor has signed this Note and Mortgage as of the date at the top of the first page.

WITNESS   MORTGAGOR...

Note and Mortgage

TO

Dated,   19

STATE OF NEW YORK

County of

RECORDED ON THE

...........day of....................................,19.......
        at............o'clock..........M.
in Liber....................of Mortgages
at Page....................and examined

CLERK

STATE OF NEW YORK, COUNTY OF   ss.:
        On   19   , before me personally came   to me known, who, being by me duly sworn, did depose and say that deponent resides at No.
deponent is   of   the corporation described in and which executed, the foregoing instrument; deponent knows the seal of said corporation; that the seal affixed to said instrument is such corporate seal; that it was so affixed by order of the Board of Directors of said corporation; deponent signed deponent's name thereto by like order.

STATE OF NEW YORK, COUNTY OF   ss.:
        On   19   , before me personally came
to me known to be the individual   described in, and who executed the foregoing instrument, and acknowledged that   he executed the same.

Failure to meet any of these obligations can result in a borrower's **default** on the note. When this happens the mortgage usually provides for a grace period (30 days, for example) during which the borrower can meet the obligation and cure the default. If he or she does not do so, the lender has the right to foreclose the mortgage and collect on the note. The most frequent cause of default is the borrower's failure to pay monthly installments.

Most mortgages contain a late-payment clause. For one- to six-family owner-occupied residences, New York allows a late-payment penalty 15 days after payment is due. An individual may charge a 2 percent penalty; a lending institution, 4 percent on government-backed mortgages, 5 percent on conventional loans.

Provisions for Default

A mortgage may include an **acceleration clause** to assist the lender in a foreclosure. If a borrower defaults the lender has the right to accelerate the maturity of the debt—to declare the *entire* debt due and owing *immediately*.

Other clauses in a mortgage enable the lender to take care of the property in the event of the borrower's negligence or default. If the borrower does not pay taxes or insurance premiums or make necessary repairs on the property, the lender may step in and do so to protect his or her security (the real estate). Any money advanced by the lender to cure such defaults is either added to the unpaid debt or declared immediately due and owing from the borrower.

Assignment of the Mortgage

A note or bond is usually a *negotiable instrument;* as such it may be sold to a third party, or assignee. An **estoppel certificate** executed by the borrower will verify the amount owed and interest rate. Upon payment in full, or satisfaction of the debt, the assignee is required to execute the satisfaction, or release, of mortgage. In the event of a foreclosure the assignee (not the original mortgagee) files the suit.

Recording Mortgages

The mortgage document must be recorded in the recorder's office of the county in which the real estate is located. This gives notice to the world of the borrower's obligations and establishes the lien's priority over future mortgages or other liens.

First and Second Mortgages

Mortgages and other liens normally have priority in the order in which they have been recorded. A mortgage on land that has no prior mortgage lien on it is a *first mortgage*. When the owner of this land later executes another mortgage for additional funds the new mortgage becomes a *second mortgage,* or *junior lien,* when recorded. The first mortgage has prior claim to the value of the land pledged as security.

The priority of mortgage liens may be changed by the execution of a *subordination agreement* in which the first lender subordinates his or her lien to that of the second lender. To be valid such an agreement must be signed by both lenders.

Satisfaction of the Mortgage Lien

When all mortgage loan payments have been made and the note paid in full the mortgagor wants the public record to show that the debt has been paid and the mortgage lien satisfied. When the note has been fully paid the mortgagee is usually required to execute a *release of mortgage,* or **satisfaction of mortgage.**

This document reconveys to the mortgagor all interest in the real estate that was conveyed to the mortgagee by the original recorded mortgage document. By having this release entered in the public record the owner shows that the mortgage lien has been removed from his or her property. Neglecting to do so can lead to irritating legal problems in later years.

Buying Subject to or Assuming a Seller's Mortgage

Anyone who purchases real estate that has an assumable mortgage on it may take the property *subject to* the mortgage or may *assume* it and *agree to pay* the debt. This technical distinction becomes important if the buyer defaults and the mortgage is foreclosed.

When the property is sold *subject to* the mortgage the purchaser is not personally obligated to pay the debt in full. The new owner has bought the real estate knowing that he or she must make the loan payments and that, upon default, the lender will foreclose and the property will be sold by court order to pay the debt. But if the sale does not pay off the entire debt, the new owner is not liable for the difference.

In contrast, when the new owner not only purchases the property subject to the mortgage but *assumes and agrees to pay* the debt, then he or she becomes personally obligated for the payment of the *debt*. If the mortgage is foreclosed in such a case and the court sale does not bring enough money to pay the debt in full, a deficiency judgment against both the assumer and the original borrower can be obtained for the unpaid balance.

When a mortgage is being assumed or paid off, the borrower will want a statement from the mortgagee detailing the amount currently due. This **reduction certificate** is often—and wrongly—referred to as an estoppel certificate.

Alienation clause. Frequently when a real estate loan is made, the lender wishes to prevent some future purchaser of the property from being able to assume that loan, particularly at its old rate of interest. For this reason some lenders include an **alienation clause** (also known as a *resale clause* or *due-on-sale clause*) in the note. An alienation clause provides that upon the sale of the property, the lender has the choice of either declaring the entire debt to be immediately due and owing or permitting the buyer to assume the loan.

In New York a mortgage is assumable unless the document contains a specific alienation clause.

Foreclosure

When a borrower defaults in making payments or fulfilling any of the obligations set forth in the mortgage, the lender can enforce his or her rights through a **foreclosure,** a legal procedure whereby the property pledged as security is sold to satisfy the debt. The foreclosure procedure passes title to a purchaser at a *foreclosure sale*. Property thus sold is *free of the mortgage and all junior liens* but subject to any prior liens.

Methods of Foreclosure

There are two general types of foreclosure proceedings—judicial and strict foreclosure. Strict foreclosure rarely is used; judicial foreclosure is the procedure followed in the majority of cases. In a *judicial foreclosure,* upon a borrower's default the lender may *accelerate* the due date of all remaining monthly payments. The lender's attorney can then file a suit to foreclose the lien. The property is ordered sold. A public sale is advertised and held and the real estate is sold to the highest bidder. The borrower has the right to redeem the property until the moment of sale by producing full payment including back interest and costs incurred in the foreclosure proceedings. In New York, however, the defaulting borrower does not have the right to redeem the property after the foreclosure sale.

The purchaser at a foreclosure sale receives a referee's deed. The referee is appointed by the court and executes the deed by virtue of the authorization given by the court.

Deed in Lieu of Foreclosure

An alternative to foreclosure would be for the lender to accept a *deed in lieu of foreclosure* from the borrower. This is sometimes known as a *friendly foreclosure* because it is by agreement rather than by civil action. The major disadvantage to this manner of default settlement is that the mortgagee takes the real estate subject to all junior liens, while foreclosure eliminates all such liens.

Deficiency Judgment

If the foreclosure sale does not produce sufficient cash to pay the loan balance in full after deducting expenses and accrued unpaid interest, the mortgagee may be entitled to seek a *personal judgment* against the signer of the note for the unpaid balance. Such a judgment is called a **deficiency judgment.** It may be obtained against any endorsers or guarantors of the note and any owners of the mortgaged property who may have assumed the debt by written agreement. If, on the other hand, there are any surplus proceeds from the foreclosure sale after the debt is paid off and expenses are deducted, they are paid to the borrower.

Other Real Estate Instruments

Among other important instruments used in the practice of real estate are listing agreements, which will be discussed in detail in Chapter 9; leases, the subject of Chapter 22; purchase and sale contracts, option agreements and land contracts, which will be treated in Chapter 5.

Leases

Through a lease the owner of property, the **lessor,** allows some other person to use it in exchange for periodic payments. The tenant, or **lessee,** has a leasehold estate. Four different types of tenancy are discussed in Chapter 22.

In New York, leases for a period of one year or less need not be written. Leases for a period of three years or more may, if properly acknowledged, be entered into the public records. Leases may be assigned or sublet unless the lease expressly prohibits the tenant from doing so. If the building contains four or more residential units, subletting may not usually be prohibited in this state, subject to landlord's reasonable approval of the subtenants.

Unless the lease states otherwise, it *survives a sale;* it is still valid after any transfer of title.

A *net lease* is one in which the tenant pays all or part of expenses: utilities, insurance, property taxes, maintenance.

Summary   Documents affecting or conveying interests in real estate must contain a *legal description* that accurately identifies the property involved. There are three methods of describing land in the United States: (1) metes and bounds, (2) rectangular (government) survey and (3) recorded plat of subdivision.

In a *metes-and-bounds description,* the actual location of *monuments* is the most important consideration. When property is being described by metes and bounds the description always must enclose a tract of land; the boundary line must end at the point at which it started.

The *rectangular survey system* is not used in New York. It involves surveys based on principal meridians. Land is surveyed into squares 36 miles in area, called *townships.* Townships are divided into 36 *sections* of one square mile each. Each square mile contains 640 acres.

Land can be subdivided into lots by means of a *recorded plat of subdivision.* An approved plat of survey giving the size, location and designation of lots, and specifying the location and size of streets to be dedicated for public use is filed for record in the recorder's office of the county in which the land is located.

A survey prepared by a surveyor is the usual method of certifying the legal description of a certain parcel of land. Surveys customarily are required when a mortgage or new construction is involved.

Air lots, condominium descriptions, and other measurements of vertical elevations may be computed from the United States Geological Survey *datum,* which is the mean sea level in New York harbor. Most large cities have established local survey datums for surveying within the area. The elevations from these datums are further supplemented by reference points, called *benchmarks.*

The voluntary transfer of an owner's title is made by a *deed,* executed (signed) by the owner as *grantor* to the purchaser or donee as *grantee.*

Among the most common requirements for a valid deed are: a grantor with legal capacity to contract, a readily identifiable grantee, a granting clause, a legal description of the property, a recital of consideration, exceptions and reservations on the title and the signature of the grantor. In addition the deed should be acknowledged before a notary public or other officer in order to provide evidence that the signature is genuine and to allow recording. Title to the property passes when the grantor delivers a deed to the grantee and it is accepted.

The obligation of a grantor is determined by the form of the deed. A *general warranty deed* provides the greatest protection of any deed by binding the grantor to certain covenants or warranties. A *bargain and sale deed* carries with it no warranties but implies that the grantor holds title to the property. A *bargain and sale deed with covenant* warrants only that the real estate has not been encumbered by the grantor. A *quitclaim deed* carries with it no warranties whatsoever and conveys only the interest, *if any,* the grantor possesses in the property.

Mortgage loans provide the principal sources of financing for real estate operations. Mortgage loans involve a borrower, called the *mortgagor,* and a lender, the *mortgagee.*

The borrower is required to execute a *note* agreeing to repay the debt and a *mortgage* placing a lien on the real estate to secure his or her note. This is recorded in the public record in order to give notice to the world of the lender's interest. Payment in full of the note by its terms entitles the borrower to a *satisfaction,* or *release,* which is recorded to clear the lien from the public records. Default by the borrower may result in *acceleration* of payments and a *foreclosure* sale. If the sale proceeds fail to clear the debt the mortgagee may seek a deficiency judgment against the borrower. A subsequent owner who *assumes* the loan is also personally responsible and liable to a deficiency judgment; one who *takes* the property *subject to* the mortgage is not.

Questions

1. Monuments, angles and distances are used in which type of legal description?
   a. Plat
   b. Government survey
   c. Metes and bounds
   d. Tape location map

2. According to the accompanying plat map, which of the following lots has the most frontage on Manassas Lane?
   a. Lot 10, Block B   c. Lot 8, Block A
   b. Lot 11, Block B   d. Lot 1, Block A

3. On the plat, how many lots have easements?
   a. One   c. Three
   b. Two   d. Four

4. A person legally authorized to locate land and give a legal description of it is a(n):
   a. assessor.   c. abstractor.
   b. surveyor.   d. recorder.

5. It is essential that every deed be signed by the:
   a. grantor.   c. grantor and grantee.
   b. grantee.   d. devisee.

6. Title to property transfers at the moment a deed is:
   a. signed.
   b. acknowledged.
   c. delivered and accepted.
   d. recorded.

7. Consideration in a deed refers to:
   a. gentle handling of the document.
   b. something of value given by each party.
   c. the habendum clause.
   d. the payment of transfer tax stamps.

8. A declaration before a notary or other official providing evidence that a signature is genuine is an:
   a. affidavit.   c. affirmation.
   b. acknowledgment.   d. estoppel.

9. In order to be recorded a document must be:
   a. witnessed.   c. acknowledged.
   b. sealed.   d. considered.

10. Alvin Rosewell executes a deed to Sylvia Plat as grantee, has it acknowledged, and receives payment from the buyer. Rosewell holds the deed, however, and arranges to meet Plat the next morning at the courthouse to deliver the deed to her. In this situation at this time:
    a. Plat owns the property because she has paid for it.
    b. title to the property will not officially pass until Plat has been given the deed the next morning.
    c. title to the property will not pass until Plat has received the deed and recorded it the next morning.
    d. Plat will own the property when she has signed the deed the next morning.

11. The grantee receives greatest protection with what type of deed?
    a. Quitclaim
    b. Warranty
    c. Bargain and sale with covenant
    d. Executor's

12. A bargain and sale deed with covenant against grantor's acts is commonly used:
    a. by executors.
    b. Downstate.
    c. in divorce settlements.
    d. to clear cloud from a title.

13. Which of the following types of deeds most usually recites the full, actual consideration paid for the property?
    a. Full covenant and warranty deed
    b. Quitclaim deed
    c. Bargain and sale deed
    d. Referee's deed

14. The bond accompanying a mortgage is signed by the:
    a. mortgagor.   c. grantor.
    b. mortgagee.   d. lessee.

15. The borrower proves a mortgage has been paid off by recording a:
    a. reduction certificate.
    b. certificate of estoppel.
    c. certificate of satisfaction.
    d. notice of default.

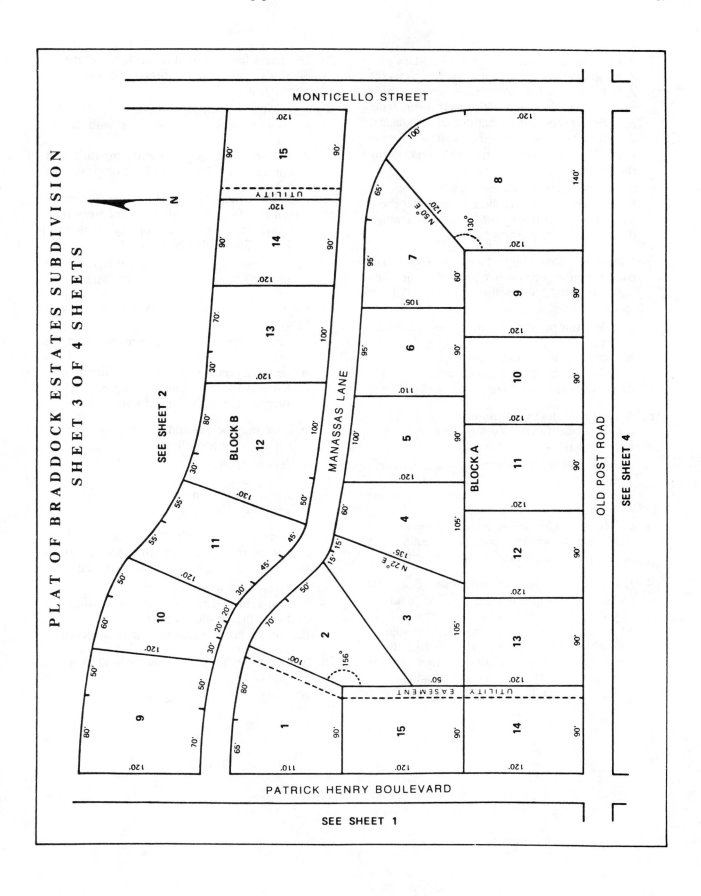

16. All on the same parcel: Charlie Feckless gives
    A a mortgage in return for a loan of $15,000.
    A fails to record the mortgage. Charlie then
    borrows an additional $40,000 from *B*, who
    records the mortgage. Charlie then persuades
    C to lend him $50,000 and *C* records his mort-
    gage. Which is now the first mortgage against
    the property?
    a. *A*'s because it was the loan first made
    b. *B*'s because it was the one first recorded
    c. *C*'s because it was for the largest amount
    d. *A*'s and *B*'s, sharing priority

17. Gloria Glamour allows Ron Rocker to take
    over the mortgage on her property when he
    buys the house. She will receive the most pro-
    tection if Ron:
    a. takes the property subject to the existing
       loan.
    b. assumes the existing loan.
    c. acknowledges the present loan.
    d. subordinates the loan.

18. A mortgage document requires the mortga-
    gor to perform certain duties. Which of the
    following is *not* one of these?
    a. Maintain the property in good condition
       at all times
    b. Obtain the mortgagee's permission before
       renting a room to a boarder
    c. Maintain adequate insurance on the property
    d. Obtain the lender's permission before mak-
       ing major alterations to the property

19. A savings and loan association lent Bob Blue-
    collar $60,000 to buy a house. The local fac-
    tory closed down and real estate values fell.
    At a foreclosure auction the property sold
    for only $50,000. To make up its loss the
    lender may seek a deficiency judgment against:
    a. Bob.   c. the appraiser.
    b. the new owner.   d. no one.

20. Jim has a lease until June on his apartment at
    $400 a month. The building is sold in Feb-
    ruary. Jim:
    a. must vacate by March 30.
    b. should negotiate a new lease with the new
       owner.
    c. can stay if he pays an extra month's rent.
    d. can abide by the terms of the original lease.

21. Ms. Black manufactures knitwear in a small
    rented building. In addition to monthly rent
    she pays heat, light and property taxes on the
    building. She probably has a:
    a. net lease.   c. percentage lease.
    b. periodic lease.   d. security lease.

22. In New York, a tenant may usually sublet an
    apartment if the:
    a. new tenant is paying a premium over the
       rent.
    b. building contains four or more living units.
    c. lease is for three years or more.
    d. original tenant has a written lease.

23. A lease may be entered in the public records
    if it is for a period of:
    a. less than one year.
    b. two years.
    c. three years or more.
    d. any length of time.

24. Tom says to Jim: "I'll let you rent my attic
    apartment for $200 a month until the first of
    the year." Jim agrees. The agreement:
    a. constitutes a binding lease.
    b. is invalid because it is not in writing.
    c. binds the landlord only.
    d. will be enforceable only if it is recorded.

25. The tenant who rents property is known as a:
    a. lessor.   c. lessee.
    b. grantor.   d. grantee.

Appendix: Excerpts from New York State's Study Booklet for Brokers

DEEDS

Ordinarily, a "deed" is understood to be an instrument in writing duly executed and delivered, that conveys title to real property. A deed is "duly executed" when it is signed and acknowledged by the maker thereof, who is usually termed the "grantor."

Essentials of a valid deed. They are as follows:

1. It must be in writing;
2. The grantor thereto must be competent (sane adult);
3. It must contain an adequate expression of intent to convey real property;
4. There must be a definite description of the real property conveyed;
5. It must include an "habendum" clause ("to have and to hold the above granted premises unto the party of the second part, ..., his heirs and assigns forever");
6. It must be signed by the grantor;
7. There must be an acknowledgment of its execution by grantor (see Acknowledgments);
8. It must be delivered to the grantee (purchaser).

Kinds of deeds. The forms of deeds in general use in the State of New York are: (a) deed with full covenants; (b) bargain and sale deed, without covenant against grantor; (c) bargain and sale deed with covenant against grantor; (d) quitclaim deed; (e) executor's deed; and (f) referee's deed. Short forms of all the foregoing conveyances are prescribed by the Real Property Law.

Deed with full covenants. This form of conveyance is usually styled a "full covenant and warranty deed" and is most advantageous to the purchaser of real property."

The following are the five covenants found in the full covenant and warranty deed:

First. That said..............is seized of said premises in fee simple, and has good right to convey the same;

Second. That the party of the second part shall quietly enjoy the said premises;

Third. That the said premises are free from encumbrances;

Fourth. That the party of the first part will execute or procure any further necessary assurance of the title to said premises;

Fifth. That said.............will forever warrant the title to said premises.

Bargain and sale deed without covenant against grantor. This is the simplest form of a deed. It is generally used when the purpose is to convey all the right, title and interest of the owner of record in the real property described in the document, and the grantor is not under contract to deliver a deed containing specified covenants.

Bargain and sale deed with covenant against the grantor. This form of deed contains the following covenant by the grantor: "And the party of the first part covenants that he has not done or suffered anything, whereby the said premises have been encumbered in any way whatever."

Quitclaim deed. The usual purpose of this form of deed is to remove a cloud from the title to real property. Its statutory short form is practically identical with the short form of a bargain and sale deed, without covenant against the grantor as prescribed by the statute and hereinbefore quoted, the only difference being the use of the word "quitclaim" in the conveying clause of the deed so named.

Executor's deed. This form of deed is used to convey title to a decedent's real property. It will be noted that the statutory short form of such a deed, contains only the covenant against encumbrances that is included in the form of bargain and sale deed with covenant against grantor, prescribed by the statute.

Referee's deed. This form of deed is used for the conveyance of real property sold pursuant to a judicial order, in an action for the foreclosure of a mortgage or for partition. This deed does not contain any covenants.

MORTGAGES

The term "mortgage" means an instrument in writing, duly executed and delivered, that creates a lien, upon the real property described therein, as security for the payment of a specified debt, which may be in the form of a bond or note. Essentials of a valid mortgage:

1. It must be in writing;
2. The parties thereto must be competent (sane adults);
3. Its purpose must be stated (to secure payment of a specified bond or obligation);
4. There must be an appropriate mortgaging clause (the mortgagor hereby mortgages to the mortgagee");
5. The description of the property mortgaged must be stated definitely;
6. It must be signed by the mortgagor;
7. It must be acknowledged by the mortgagor;
8. It must be delivered to the mortgagee.

The statutory short form of mortgage contains the following covenants:

1. That the mortgagor will pay the indebtedness as hereinbefore provided.
2. That the mortgagor will keep buildings on the premises insured against loss by fire for the benefit of the mortgagee.
3. That no building on the premises shall be removed or demolished without the consent of the mortgagee.
4. That the whole of said principal sum shall become due after default in the payment of any installment of principal or of interest for.......... days, or after default in the payment of any tax, water rate or assessment for..........days after notice and demand.
5. That the holder of this mortgage in any action to foreclose it, shall be entitled to the appointment of a receiver.
6. That the mortgagor will pay all taxes, assessments or water rates, and in default thereof, the mortgagee may pay the same.
7. That the mortgagor within..........days upon request in person or within.............days upon request by mail will furnish a statement of the amount due on this mortgage.
8. That notice and demand or request may be in writing and may be served in person or by mail.
9. That the mortgagor warrants the title to the premises.

Bond. A bond is evidence of the debt which creates the obligation for repayment of a loan, while a mortgage is the security for the debt with specific property as a pledge.

Acknowledgments and proofs within the state. The acknowledgment or proof, within this state, of a conveyance of real property situate in this state may be made:

1. At any place within the state, before (a) a justice of the supreme court; (b) an official examiner of title; (c) an official referee; or (d) a notary public.
2. Within the district wherein such officer is authorized to perform official duties, before (a) a judge or clerk of any court or record; (b) a commissioner of deeds outside of the city of New York, or a commissioner of deeds of the city of New York within the five counties comprising the city of New York; (c) the mayor or recorder of a city; (d) a surrogate, special surrogate, or special county judge; or (e) the county clerk or other recording officer of a county.
3. Before a justice of the peace, town councilman, village police justice or a judge of any court of inferior local jurisdiction, anywhere within the county containing the town, village or city in which he is authorized to perform official duties.

A certificate of authentication of an acknowledgment made anywhere in the State as to the execution of a conveyance, is required to entitle a conveyance to be recorded when acknowledged or proved before a commissioner of deeds, justice of the peace, town councilman or village police justice.

The usual form of acknowledgment by an individual is as follows:

STATE OF NEW YORK,

ss.:
County of ....

On this .... day of ...., before me came ...., to me known to be the individual described in, and who executed the foregoing instrument, and acknowledged that he executed the same.

....
Notary Public,
..........................County, No......

5

Law of Contracts

Overview

"Get it in writing" is a phrase commonly used to warn one party to an agreement to protect his or her interests by entering into a written *contract* with the other party, outlining the rights and obligations of both. The real estate business makes use of many different types of contracts, including listing agreements, leases and sales contracts. Brokers and salespeople must understand the content and uses of such agreements and must be able to explain them to buyers and sellers. This chapter first will deal with the legal principles governing contracts in general and then will examine the types of contracts used in the real estate business in particular.

Contract Law

Brokers and salespeople use many types of contracts and agreements in the course of their business in order to carry out their responsibilities to sellers, buyers and the general public. Among these are listing agreements, sales contracts, option agreements, land contracts and leases.

The general body of law that governs the operations of such agreements is known as *contract law.*

A **contract** may be defined as a *voluntary agreement between legally competent parties to perform or refrain from performing some legal act, supported by legal consideration.*

Depending on the situation and the nature or language of the agreement, a contract may be: (1) expressed or implied, (2) unilateral or bilateral, (3) executory or executed, and (4) valid, unenforceable, voidable or void.

Express and Implied Contracts

Depending on how a contract is created, it may be express or implied. In an **express contract** the parties state the terms and show their intentions in words. An express contract may be either oral or written. In an **implied contract** the agreement of the parties is demonstrated by their acts and conduct. The patron who orders a meal in a restaurant has implied a promise to pay for the food.

In the usual agency relationship a listing agreement is an *express* contract between the seller and the broker that names the broker as the fiduciary representative of the seller.

Bilateral and Unilateral Contracts

According to the nature of the agreement made, contracts also may be classified as either bilateral or unilateral. In a **bilateral contract** both parties promise to do something; one promise is given in exchange for another. A real estate sales contract is a bilateral contract because the seller promises to sell a parcel of real estate and deliver title to the property to the buyer, who promises to pay a certain sum of money for the property. "I will do this *and* you will do that." "Okay."

A **unilateral contract,** on the other hand, is a one-sided agreement whereby one party makes a promise in order to induce a second party to do something. The second party is not legally obligated to act; however, if the second party does comply, the first party is obligated to keep the promise. An offer of a reward would be an example of a unilateral contract; under this agreement a law enforcement agency offers a monetary payment (reward) to anyone who can aid in the capture of a criminal. "I will do this *if* you will do that." Only if someone *does* aid in the capture is the reward to be paid.

Executed and Executory Contracts

A contract may be classified as either executed or executory, depending on whether the agreement is completely performed. A fully **executed contract** is one in which both parties have fulfilled their promises and thus performed the contract. An

executory contract exists when something remains to be done by one or both parties. A real estate sales contract is executory before final settlement; after the closing it is an executed contract.

Validity of Contracts

A contract can be described as either valid, void, voidable or unenforceable (*see* Table 5.1), depending on the circumstances.

Table 5.1
Legal Effects of Contracts

Type of Contract	Legal Effect	Example
Valid	Binding and Enforceable on Both Parties	Agreement Complying with Essentials of a Valid Contract
Void	No Legal Effect	Contract for an Illegal Purpose
Voidable	Valid, but May Be Disaffirmed by One Party	Contract with a Minor
Unenforceable	Valid Between the Parties, but Neither May Force Performance	Certain Oral Agreements

A **valid contract** complies with all the essential elements (which will be discussed later in this chapter) and is binding and enforceable on both parties.

A **void contract** is one that has no legal force or effect because it does not meet the essential elements of a contract. One of the essential conditions for a contract to be valid is that it be for a legal purpose; thus a contract to commit a crime would be void.

A **voidable contract** is one that seems on the surface to be valid but may be rescinded, or disaffirmed, by one of the parties. For example, a contract entered into with a minor usually is voidable; a minor generally is permitted to disaffirm a real estate contract within a reasonable time after reaching legal age. A voidable contract is considered by the courts to be a valid contract if the party who has the option to disaffirm the agreement does not do so within a prescribed period of time.

An **unenforceable contract** also seems on the surface to be valid; however, neither party can sue the other to force performance. Unenforceable contracts are said to be "valid as between the parties" because if both desire to go through with it, they can do so.

Elements Essential to a Valid Contract

The essentials of a valid contract vary somewhat from state to state. Those elements that are uniformly required are:

1. **Competent parties:** To enter into a binding contract in New York a person must be at least 18 years old and of sound mind. A married person under 18 is considered adult. Persons under 18 may enter into a valid contract but the contract is voidable by the minor until a reasonable time after he or she reaches

the age of 18. A contract performed by a person judicially declared insane may be held void. Contracts for the sale of real property entered into on Sunday are enforceable in New York.

2. **Offer and acceptance:** This requirement, also called *mutual assent,* means that there must be a meeting of the minds. The wording of the contract must express all the agreed-upon terms and must be clearly understood by the parties.

3. **Consideration:** The agreement must be based upon good or valuable consideration. Consideration is what the parties promise in the agreement to give to or receive from each other. Consideration may consist of legal tender, exchange of value, or love and affection. The price or amount must be definitely stated and payable in exchange for the deed or right received.

4. **Legality of object:** To be valid and enforceable a contract must not involve a purpose that is illegal or against public policy.

5. **Agreement in writing and signed:** New York's **statute of frauds** requires certain types of contracts to be in writing. These include all contracts for the sale of real estate and for leasing or listing for one year or more.

In addition to these elements, a real estate sales contract must contain an adequate description of the property being conveyed. The **parol evidence** rule states that the written contract takes precedence over oral agreements or promises.

Undue influence and duress. Contracts signed by a person under duress or undue influence are voidable (may be canceled) by such person or by a court. Extreme care should be taken when one or more of the parties to a contract is elderly, sick, in great distress or under the influence of drugs or alcohol. To be valid every contract must be signed as the free and voluntary act of each party.

Performance of Contract

Occasionally a contract may call for a specific time at or by which the agreed-on acts must be completely performed. In addition many contracts provide that **"time is of the essence."** This means that the contract must be performed within the time limit specified and any party who has not performed on time is guilty of a breach of contract. This powerful phrase is a two-edged sword and brokers should leave its use to attorneys.

When a contract does not specify a date for performance, the acts it requires should be performed within a reasonable time. The interpretation of what constitutes a reasonable time will depend on the situation.

In the most common situation a real estate sale contract stipulates a target date and place for closing. If that date comes and goes without settlement the contract is still valid. Either party may later make time of the essence; again, that action should be taken only with a lawyer's advice.

Assignment and Novation

Often, after a contract has been signed one party may want to withdraw without actually terminating the agreement. This may be accomplished through either assignment or novation.

Assignment refers to a transfer of rights and/or duties under a contract. Generally, rights may be assigned to a third party unless the agreement forbids such an assignment. Obligations also may be assigned but the original obligor remains secondarily liable for them (after the new obligor) unless he or she is specifically released from this responsibility. Most contracts include a clause that either permits or forbids assignment.

A contract also may be performed by **novation,** or the substitution of a new contract for an existing agreement. The new agreement may be between the same parties or a new party may be substituted for either (this is *novation of the parties*).

Discharge of Contract

A contract may be completely performed, with all terms carried out, or it may be breached (broken) if one of the parties defaults. In addition there are various other methods by which a contract may be discharged (canceled). These include:

1. *Partial performance* of the terms along with a written acceptance by the person for whom acts have not been done or to whom money has not been paid.
2. *Substantial performance,* in which one party has substantially performed the contract but does not complete all the details exactly as the contract requires. Such performance may be sufficient to force payment with certain adjustments for any damages suffered by the other party.
3. *Impossibility of performance,* in which an act required by the contract cannot be legally accomplished.
4. *Mutual agreement* of the parties to cancel.
5. *Operation of law,* as in the voiding of a contract by a minor, as a result of fraud, the expiration of the statute of limitations, or as a result of a contract being altered without the written consent of all parties involved.

Default—Breach of Contract

A **breach** of contract is a violation of any of the terms or conditions of a contract without legal excuse, as when a seller breaches a sales contract by not delivering title to the buyer under the conditions stated in the agreement.

If the seller defaults, the buyer has three alternatives:

1. The buyer may *rescind, or cancel, the contract* and recover the earnest money.
2. The buyer may file a court suit, known as an action for **specific performance,** to force the seller to perform the contract (*i.e.,* convey the property).
3. The buyer may *sue the seller for compensatory damages*.

A suit for damages seldom is used in this instance, however, because in most cases the buyer would have difficulty proving the extent of damages.

If the *buyer defaults,* the seller may pursue one of the following courses:

1. The seller may *declare the contract forfeited*. The right to forfeit usually is provided in the terms of the contract and the seller usually is entitled to retain the earnest money and all payments received from the buyer.
2. The seller may *rescind the contract;* that is, he or she may cancel, or terminate, the contract as if it had never been made. This requires the seller to return all payments the buyer has made.
3. The seller may *sue for specific performance*. This may require the seller to offer, or tender, a valid deed to the buyer to show the seller's compliance with the contract terms.
4. The seller may *sue for compensatory damages*.

Statute of Limitations. New York allows a specific time limit of *six years* during which parties to a contract may bring legal suit to enforce their rights. Any party who does not take steps to enforce his or her rights within this **statute of limitations** may lose those rights. The six-year period applies to contracts, foreclosures, mortgages and cases of fraud. Lawsuits to recover real property have a ten-year statute of limitations in New York.

Contracts Used in the Real Estate Business

The written agreements most commonly used by brokers and salespeople are listing agreements, real estate sales contracts, option agreements, contracts for deed and leases.

Broker's Authority to Prepare Documents

The manual for real estate brokers issued by the New York Department of State expressly states that the real estate broker's license does not confer the right to draw legal documents or give legal advice. A recent decision by the New York Appellate Court stated that a broker has a right to draw a simple contract. No court decisions have yet been made as to what constitutes a "simple" contract. The preparation of legal documents by a broker may result in the loss of commissions, revocation of the license or other penalties or damages. In Upstate areas, many brokers fill in the blanks on forms or simple sales contracts; in the New York City area, the seller's attorney often prepares the contract.

Contract forms. *Printed forms* are used for all kinds of contracts because most transactions basically are similar in nature. The use of printed forms raises three problems: (1) what to *fill in the blanks,* (2) what printed matter is not applicable to a particular sale and can be *ruled out* by drawing lines through the unwanted words and (3) what additional clauses or agreements (called *riders*) are to be *added.* All changes and additions usually are initialed by both parties.

Listing Agreements

Listing agreements are contracts that establish the rights of the broker as agent and of the buyer or seller as principal. Explanations of the types of listing agreements will be presented in Chapter 9.

Sales Contracts

A **real estate sales contract** sets forth all details of the agreement between a buyer and a seller for the purchase and sale of a parcel of real estate. Depending on the locality this agreement may be known as an *offer to purchase, contract of purchase and sale, earnest money agreement, binder and deposit receipt* or other variations of these titles. New York does not mandate any specific form of listing or sales contract. An example of a real estate contract form used by some members of the Real Estate Board of Rochester appears as Figure 5.1.

In a few localities, notably in and around New York City, some brokers prepare a nonbinding **memorandum of sale.** This sheet of information states the essential terms of the agreement and negotiations of terms. The parties agree to have a formal and complete contract of sale drawn up by an attorney. Throughout the state a preliminary memorandum might be used in any situation where the details of the transaction are too complex for the standard sales contract form.

The contract of sale is the most important document in the sale of real estate because it sets out in detail the agreement between the buyer and the seller and establishes their legal rights and obligations. *The contract, in effect, dictates the contents of the deed.*

Offer and acceptance. One of the essential elements of a valid contract of sale is a meeting of the minds whereby the buyer and seller agree on the terms

Figure 5.1
Real Estate Sales
Contract

PURCHASE AND SALE CONTRACT
FOR RESIDENTIAL PROPERTY

Plain English Form Published by the Real Estate Board of Rochester, N.Y., Inc. and the Monroe County Bar Association.

COMMISSIONS OR FEES FOR REAL ESTATE SERVICES TO BE PROVIDED ARE NEGOTIABLE BETWEEN REALTOR AND SELLER.

When Signed, This Document Becomes A Binding Contract. Buyer And Seller May Wish To Consult Their Own Attorney.

TO: ___Mary and John Public___ (Seller) FROM: ___Debra and Arthur Byer___ (Buyer)

OFFER TO PURCHASE

Buyer offers to purchase the property described below from Seller on the following terms:

1. PROPERTY DESCRIPTION.
Property known as No. ___240 Hemingway Drive___ in the (Town) (City) (Village) of ___Brighton (Rochester 14620)___ State of New York, also
known as Tax No. ___080-557___ , including all buildings and any other improvements and all rights which the Seller has in or with the property.
Approximate Lot Size: ___85' x 185'___
Check if Applicable: [ ] As described in more detail in the attached description.

Description of Buildings on Property:

___8-room frame one-story house and attached one-car garage___

2. OTHER ITEMS INCLUDED IN PURCHASE. The following items, if any, now in or on the property are included in this purchase and sale: All heating, plumbing, lighting fixtures, flowers, shrubs, trees, windows shades, venetian blinds, curtain and traverse rods, storm windows, storm doors, screens, awnings, TV antennae, water softeners, sump pumps, window boxes, mail box, tool shed, fences, wall-to-wall carpeting and runners, exhaust fans, hoods, garbage disposal, electric garage door opener and remote control devices, intercom equipment, humidifier, security systems, smoke detectors, all fireplace screens and enclosures, swimming pool and all related equipment and accessories, and all built-in cabinets, mirrors, stoves, ovens, dishwashers, trash compactors, shelving, and air conditioning (except window) units. Buyer agrees to accept these items in their present condition. Other items to be included in the purchase and sale are:

___all drapes, washer, and dryer.___

Seller represents ___all of the above except built-in dishwasher___ to be in good working order.
Items not included are: ___dining-room chandelier.___

Seller represents that he has good title to all of the above items to be transferred to Buyer, and will deliver a Bill of Sale for the same at closing.

3. PRICE: AMOUNT AND HOW IT WILL BE PAID. The purchase price is ___Ninety-eight Thousand___ Dollars
$ ___$98,000.00___ Buyer shall receive credit at closing for any deposit made hereunder. The balance of the purchase price shall be paid as follows: (Check and complete applicable provisions.)

[ ] (a) Seller agrees to pay a loan fee of up to _____% of the mortgage amount as stated in paragraph 4 (a).

x⨯x(b) All in cash, or certified check at closing.

[ ] (c) By Buyer assuming and agreeing to pay according to its terms, the principal balance of the mortgage in the approximate amount of $ _____
held by _____ , provided that the mortgage is assumable without the holder's approval. Buyer
understands that the mortgage bears interest at the rate of _____% per year and the monthly payments are $_____ which includes principal,
interest, taxes and insurance (strike out any item not included in payment), with the last payment due on approximately _____, 19_____. Buyer agrees to pay the
balance of the purchase price over the amount of the assumed mortgage in cash or certified check at closing. Buyer understands that principal balance may be lower at time of closing because
of monthly payments made after this contract is signed. If the mortgage to be assumed provides for graduated or balloon payments, then a copy of the original bond and mortgage shall be
furnished to Buyer's attorney for approval within ten days after acceptance of this offer.

[ ] (d) By Buyer delivering a purchase money bond and mortgage to Seller at closing. This purchase money bond and mortgage shall be in the amount of $_____
shall be for a term of _____ years, shall bear interest at the rate of _____% per year, and shall be paid in monthly installments of
$_____ , including principal and interest. The entire principal balance shall be all due and payable _____ years from date of closing.

The mortgage shall contain the statutory clauses as to payment, insurance, acceleration on default of thirty days, taxes, assessments, and water rates and also shall provide for late charges of
2% of any monthly payment which is not paid within 15 days after it is due and for recovery of reasonable attorney's fees if the mortgage is foreclosed.

The mortgage shall allow Buyer to prepay all or part of the mortgage without penalty at any time but shall also provide that the mortgage be paid in full if Buyer sells the property, unless Seller
consents in writing to assumption of the mortgage debt. The balance of the purchase price will be paid at closing in cash, or certified check.

4. CONTINGENCIES. Buyer makes this offer subject to the following contingencies. If any of these contingencies is not satisfied by the dates specified, then either Buyer or Seller may cancel
this contract by written notice to the other.

[ ] (a) **Mortgage Contingency.** This offer is subject to Buyer obtaining a _____ mortgage loan in the amount of $_____ for a term of
_____ years. Buyer shall immediately apply for this loan and shall have until _____, to obtain a written mortgage commitment. The conditions of any such
mortgage commitment shall not be deemed contingencies of this contract but shall be the sole responsibility of Buyer. If the loan commitment requires repairs, replacements, or improvements
to be made, or painting to be done, before closing, then Seller shall do the work and install the materials and improvements needed or have the same done, at his expense, not to exceed,
however, $_____ . If the cost of doing so is more than that amount, Buyer will be allowed either to receive credit at closing for such amount and incur the
necessary expenses to comply with the loan commitment requirements, or to cancel this contract by written notice to Seller and receive back his deposit.

Figure 5.1
(continued)

[ ] (b) **Mortgage Assumption Contingency.** This offer is subject to Buyer obtaining permission to assume the existing mortgage loan balance referred to above (3c) by _____ 19____.
If the mortgage holder requires that the interest rate be increased for such approval to be given, Buyer agrees to assume the mortgage at such rate as long as it does not exceed _____%
at the time of commitment.

xxx (c) **Sale Contingency.** This offer is contingent upon Buyer securing a firm contract for the sale of his property located at _91 Salem Drive, Islip, NY_
no later than _May 1,19--_. If Buyer is unable to obtain a firm contract for the sale of his property by such date, then either he or Seller may cancel this contract by written notice to the
other. If Seller receives another acceptable purchase offer, Seller may notify Buyer in writing that Seller wants to accept the other offer and Buyer will then have _5 banking_ days to
remove this sale contingency by written notice to the Seller. If Buyer does not remove this contingency after receiving notice from Seller, Buyer's rights under this contract shall end, and Seller
shall be free to accept the other purchase offer and Buyer's deposit shall be returned. Buyer may not remove this contingency by such notice to Seller if Buyer's mortgage loan commitment
requires the sale and transfer of his property as a condition of the mortgage lender disbursing the mortgage loan proceeds, unless Buyer has a contract for the sale of his property which is not
then subject to any unsatisfied contingencies.

xxx (d) **Attorney Approval.** This offer is subject to approval by Buyer's and Seller's Attorney within ___3___ banking days after acceptance.

[ ] (e) **Waiver of Attorney Approval.** This offer is not subject to the Buyer's Attorney approval.

[ ] (f) **Other Contingencies.** _____

5. Closing Date and Place. The transfer of title shall take place at the _Monroe_ County Clerk's Office on or before the _1_ day of _July_, 19--.

6. Buyer's Possession of Property. Buyer shall have possession of the property on the day of closing.

7. Title Documents. Seller shall provide the following documents in connection with the sale:

A. Deed. Seller will deliver to Buyer at closing a properly signed and notarized Warranty Deed with lien covenant (or Executor's Deed, Administrator's Deed or Trustee's Deed, if Seller holds title as such).

B. Abstract, Bankruptcy and Tax Searches, and Instrument Survey Map. Seller will furnish and pay for and deliver to Buyer or Buyer's attorney at least 10 days prior to the date of closing, fully guaranteed tax, title and
United States Court Searches dated or redated after the date of this contract with a local tax certificate for Village, or City taxes, if any, and an instrument survey map dated or redated after the date of this contract. Seller
will pay for the map or redated map and for continuing such searches to and including the day of closing. Any survey map shall be prepared or redated and certified to meet the standards and requirements of Buyer's
mortgage lender and of the Monroe County Bar Association.

8. Marketability of Title. The deed and other documents delivered by Seller shall be sufficient to convey good marketable title in fee simple, to the property free and clear of all liens and encumbrances.
However, Buyer agrees to accept title to the property subject to restrictive covenants of record common to the tract or subdivision of which the property is a part, provided these restrictions have not been violated, or if
they have been violated, that the time for anyone to complain of the violations has expired. Buyer also agrees to accept title to the property subject to public utility easements along lot lines as long as those easements do
not interfere with any buildings now on the property or with any improvements Buyer may construct in compliance with all present restrictive covenants of record and zoning and building codes applicable to the
property.

9. Objections to Title. If Buyer raises a valid written objection to Seller's title which means that the title to the property is unmarketable, Seller may cancel this contract by giving prompt written notice of
cancellation to Buyer. Buyer's deposit shall be returned immediately, and if Buyer makes a written request for it, Seller shall reimburse Buyer for the reasonable cost of having the title examined. However, if Seller gives
written notice within five (5) days that Seller will cure the problem prior to the closing date, then this contract shall continue in force until the closing date subject to Seller performing as promised. If Seller fails to cure the
problem within such time, Buyer will not be obligated to purchase the property and his deposit shall be returned together with reimbursement for the reasonable cost of having the title examined.

10. Recording Costs, Mortgage Tax, Transfer Tax and Closing Adjustments. Seller will pay the real property transfer tax and special additional mortgage recording tax, if applicable.
Buyer will pay mortgage assumption charges, if any, and will pay for recording the deed and the mortgage, and for mortgage tax. Rent payments, if any, fuel oil on the premises, if any, water charges, pure water charges,
sewer charges, mortgage interest, prepaid or deferred F.H.A. insurance premium, current common charges or assessments, if any, and current taxes computed on a fiscal year basis, excluding any delinquent items,
interest and penalties, will be prorated and adjusted between Seller and Buyer as of the date of closing.

11. Zoning. Seller certifies that the property is in full compliance with all zoning or building ordinances for use as a _single-family dwelling._
If applicable laws require it, Seller will furnish at or before closing, a Certificate of Occupancy for the property dated within ninety (90) days of the closing, provided Seller need not spend more than
$ _N/A_ to make the property comply. If the cost of doing so is more than that amount, Buyer will be allowed either to receive credit at closing for such amount and incur the
expense himself, instead of receiving a Certificate of Occupancy, or to cancel this contract by written notice to Seller. If Buyer cancels, his deposit shall be returned.

12. Risk of Loss. Risk of loss or damage to the property by fire or other casualty until transfer of title shall be assumed by the Seller. If damage to the property by fire or such other casualty occurs
prior to transfer, Buyer may cancel this contract without any further liability to Seller and Buyer's deposit is to be returned. If Buyer does not cancel but elects to close, then Seller shall transfer to Buyer
any insurance proceeds, or Seller's claim to insurance proceeds payable for such damage.

13. Condition of Property. Buyer(s) agree to purchase the property "as is" except as provided in paragraph 2, subject to reasonable use, wear, tear, and natural deterioration between now and
the time of closing. However, this paragraph shall not relieve Seller from furnishing a Certificate of Occupancy as called for in paragraph 11, if applicable. Buyer shall have the right, after reasonable
notice to seller, to inspect the property within 48 hours before the time of closing.

14. Deposit. Buyer (has deposited) ~~(will deposit upon acceptance)~~ $ _1,000.00_ in the form of a _good check_ with _Sun City Realty_
which deposit is to become part of the purchase price or returned if not accepted or if this contract thereafter fails to close for any reason not the fault of Buyer. If buyer fails to complete his part of this
contract, seller is allowed to keep the deposit and may also pursue other legal rights he has against the buyer, including a law suit for any real estate brokerage commission paid by the seller.

15. Real Estate Broker.
xxx The parties agree that _Sun City Realty_ brought about this purchase and sale.

[ ] It is understood and agreed by both Buyer and Seller that no broker secured this contract.

16. Life of Offer. Buyer agrees not to withdraw this offer before _February 29_, 19--, at _10 p._m.

17. Responsibility of Persons Under This Contract; Assignability. If more than one person signs this contract as Buyer, each person and any party who takes over that person's
legal position will be responsible for keeping the promises made by Buyer in this contract. If more than one person signs this contract as Seller, each person or any party who takes over that person's
legal position, will be fully responsible for keeping the promises made by Seller. However, this contract is personal to the parties and may not be assigned by either without the other's consent.

18. Entire Contract. This contract when signed by both Buyer and Seller will be the record of the complete agreement between the Buyer and Seller concerning the purchase and sale of the
property. No verbal agreements or promises will be binding.

OK for buyers
2/29
L.H.

Dated: _February 26, 19--_   BUYER _Debra Byer_

Witness: _Susy Salesperson_   BUYER _Arthur Byer_

Figure 5.1
(continued)

ACCEPTANCE OF OFFER BY SELLER

Sellers certify that they own the property and have the power to sell the property. Sellers accept the offer and agree to sell on the terms and conditions set forth above and agree that the deposit may be held by _Sun City Realty._

[ ] Waiver of Seller's Attorney Approval. This offer is not subject to Seller's Attorney approval.

Dated: _February 27, 19—_   SELLER _Mary Public_

Witness: _Susy Salesperson_   SELLER _John Q. Public_

Approved for sellers as to form.
_J. M. 3/1/19—_

OPTION CLAUSE: VETERANS ADMINISTRATION AND FEDERAL HOUSING ADMINISTRATION LOANS ONLY

It is expressly agreed that, notwithstanding any other provisions of this contract, the purchaser shall not be obligated to complete the purchase of the property described herein or to incur any penalty by forfeiture of earnest money deposits or otherwise, in those cases involving a GI loan, if the contract purchase price or cost exceeds the reasonable value of the property established by the Veterans Administration or in those cases to be insured by the Federal Housing Administration unless the seller has delivered to the purchaser a written statement issued by the Federal Housing Commissioner setting forth the appraised value of the property (excluding closing costs) of not less than $_____ which statement the seller hereby agrees to deliver to the purchaser promptly after such appraised value statement is made available to the seller. The purchaser shall, however, have the privilege and option of proceeding with the consummation of this contract without regard to the amount of the appraised valuation if made by the Federal Housing Commissioner or reasonable value established by the Veterans Administration. In those cases involving FHA, **the appraised valuation is arrived at to determine the maximum mortgage the Department of Housing and Urban Development will insure. HUD does not warrant the value or the condition of the property. The purchaser should satisfy himself/herself that the price and the condition of the property are acceptable.**

BUYERS: _____ and _____

SELLERS: _____ and _____

CONTRACT OF SALE

Property Address: _240 Hemingway Drive, Rochester 14620_ Date _2/26/_ 19 _--_ To Be Closed _July 1,_ 19 _--_

Buyer: _Debra and Arthur Byer_		Seller: _John Q. and Mary Public_	
Address: _93 Salem Drive, Islip NY_		Address: _240 Hemingway Drive_	
_11751_		_Rochester, NY 14620_	
Zip: _(516)_ Phone: (H) _123-4567_ (B) _123-4000_		Zip: _(716)_ Phone: (H) _473-4973_ (B) _271-6230_	
Attorney: _Learned Hand, Esq._		Attorney: _John Marshall, Esq._	
Address: _480 Powers Building, Rochester_		Address: _Suite 1900, Executive Office Bld_	
Zip: _14614_ Phone: (B) _987-6543_ (H) _---_		Zip: _14614_ Phone: (B) _555-1212_ (H) _911-8000_	
Selling Broker _Sun City_		Listing Broker _Sun City Realty_	
Address: _____		Address: _400 Rainbow Plaza_	
Zip: ____ Phone: ____ Broker Code: _SUNC_		Zip: _14601_ Phone: _716-586-5028_ Broker Code: _SUNC_	
Selling Agent: _Susan Salesperson_ Phone: (H) _473-1755_		Listing Agent: _J. R. Ewing_ Phone: (H) _271-6265_	

of the sale. This usually is accomplished through the process of **offer and acceptance.**

A broker lists an owner's real estate for sale at the price and conditions set by the owner. A prospective buyer is found who wants to purchase the property at those terms or some other terms. Upstate, an offer to purchase is drawn up, signed by the prospective buye, and presented by the broker to the seller. This is an *offer.* If the seller agrees to the offer *exactly as it was made* and signs the contract, the offer has been *accepted* and the contract is *valid.* The broker then must advise the buyer of the seller's acceptance, obtain lawyers' approval if the contract calls for it and deliver a duplicate original of the contract to each party.

In some Downstate areas the broker prepares a precontract agreement, known as a binder, which may or may not be legally enforceable but which usually contains many of the essential terms that will later be included in a contract. In the New York City area purchase offers often are handled by attorneys.

Any attempt by the seller to change the terms proposed by the buyer creates a **counteroffer.** The buyer is relieved of his or her original offer because the seller has, in effect, rejected it. The buyer can accept the seller's counteroffer or can reject it and, if he or she wishes, make another counteroffer. Any change in the last offer made results in a counteroffer until one party finally agrees to the other party's last offer and both parties sign the final contract (*see* Figure 5.2).

An offer is not considered accepted until the person making the offer has been *notified of the other party's acceptance.* When the parties are communicating through an agent or at a distance, questions may arise regarding whether an acceptance, rejection or counteroffer has effectively taken place. The real estate broker or salesperson must transmit all offers, acceptances or other responses as soon as possible in order to avoid such problems.

Equitable title. When a buyer signs a contract to purchase real estate he or she does not receive title to the land; only a deed can actually convey title. However, after both buyer and seller have executed a sales contract the buyer acquires an interest in the land known as **equitable title.** In New York a buyer under a

Figure 5.2
Offer and Acceptance

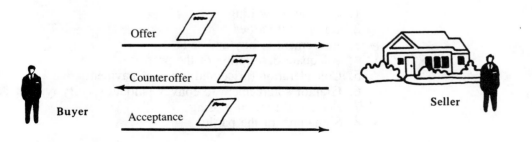

Offer

Counteroffer

Acceptance

Buyer

Seller

land contract also acquires equitable title. If the parties decide not to go through with the purchase and sale, they usually enter into a written **release,** freeing each other from any obligation under the contract.

Destruction of premises. New York State has adopted the *Uniform Vendor and Purchaser Risk Act,* which specifically provides that the seller (vendor) bears any material loss, most commonly a fire, that occurs before the title passes or the buyer (vendee) takes possession.

Earnest money deposits. It is customary, but not essential, for a purchaser to provide a cash deposit when making an offer to purchase real estate. This cash deposit, commonly referred to as **earnest money,** *gives evidence of the buyer's intention to carry out terms of the contract.* This deposit is given to the broker and the sales contract typically provides that the broker will hold the deposit for the parties. In some areas of New York it is common practice for deposits to be held in escrow by the seller's attorney. If the offer is not accepted, the earnest money deposit is returned to the would-be buyer immediately.

The amount of the deposit is a matter to be agreed upon by the parties. Under the terms of most listing agreements a real estate broker is required to accept a reasonable amount as earnest money. Generally the deposit should be sufficient to discourage the buyer from defaulting, compensate the seller for taking the property off the market and cover any expenses the seller might incur if the buyer defaulted. A purchase offer with no earnest money, however, is valid. Most contracts provide that the deposit becomes the seller's property if the buyer defaults. The seller might also claim further damages.

Earnest money must be held by a broker in a special *trust,* or *escrow, bank account.* This money cannot be *commingled,* or mixed, with a broker's personal funds. A broker may not use such funds for personal use; this illegal act is known as *conversion.* A broker need not open a special escrow account for each earnest money deposit received. One account into which all such funds are deposited is sufficient. A broker should maintain full, complete and accurate records of all earnest money deposits. Under no circumstances does the money belong to the broker, who must maintain it in his or her trust account. This uncertain nature of earnest money deposits makes it absolutely necessary that such funds be properly protected pending a final decision on their disbursement.

Parts of a sales contract. In New York the essentials of a valid contract for the sale of real property are:

1. Contract in writing
2. Competent parties
3. Agreement to buy and sell
4. Adequate description of the property
5. Consideration (price and terms of payment)
6. Grantor's agreement to convey (should specify type of deed)
7. Place and time of closing
8. Signatures of the parties

Usually included, but not essential for a valid contract, are provisions covering the following:

 9. Encumbrances to which the deed will be made subject
10. Earnest money deposit

11. Mortgage financing the buyer plans to obtain and other contingencies
12. Possession by the buyer
13. Title evidence
14. Prorations and adjustments
15. Destruction of the premises before closing
16. Default by either party
17. Miscellaneous provisions

The signature of a witness is not essential for a valid contract.

Miscellaneous Provisions

When the purchaser intends to secure an FHA or VA loan, special clauses must be included in the sales contract providing that the contract may be voided if the property appraises below the sales price. Provisions may be added stipulating that the seller will furnish satisfactory reports on such matters as termite or insect infestation, quality of a private water supply or condition of plumbing or heating equipment. In some transfers a certificate of occupancy must be obtained from a municipality; the contract should make it clear whose responsibility this will be. The purchaser may add a stipulation that allows inspection of the property shortly before settlement.

Among common provisions in the "subject to" section of the contract are: the purchaser's need to secure a specific loan; the purchaser's right to a satisfactory engineer's report on the property within a specified few days; approval of the contract by a family member or the purchaser's attorney, again within a short period of time; or the purchaser's need to sell a present home before buying the next residence. The last provision is known in some areas as a **contingency.** Where the purchaser has another home that must be sold first, the seller may insist on an **escape clause,** or kickout. Such a provision allows the seller to look for a more favorable offer, with the original purchaser retaining the right, if challenged, either to firm up the first sales contract (dropping the contingency) or to void the contract.

Liquidated damages are an amount of money, agreed to in advance by buyer and seller, which would serve as compensation if one party did not live up to the contract. If a sales contract specified that the earnest money deposit would serve as liquidated damages in case of default by the buyer, the seller would be entitled to keep the deposit if the buyer refused to perform for no good reason. The seller who does choose to keep the deposit as liquidated damages may not sue for any further damages.

The Duncan and Hill decision, described in Chapter 2, recommended that New York State brokers and salespersons who prepare purchase and sales contracts protect themselves against charges of unauthorized practice of law by making the contracts *subject to* (effective only after) approval by attorneys for buyer and seller. An attorney may then ask for changes to protect his or her client's interests; any such change constitutes a counteroffer and must be accepted by the other party.

In some cases the buyer who is having second thoughts may simply instruct the attorney to disapprove the contract. The appellate division, highest New York State court, has ruled that a buyer who did so was acting in bad faith and forfeited the right to attorney's approval—that the contract was valid.

Plain-Language Requirement (Sullivan Law)

New York law requires that certain written agreements for the sale or lease of residential property be written in a clear and coherent manner with words that are common in everyday usage. The copy also must be appropriately divided and captioned in its various sections. The plain-language requirement does not apply to agreements involving amounts over $50,000. Figure 5.1 is an example of a plain-English contract.

Option Agreements

An **option** is a *contract by which an* optioner *(generally an owner) gives an* optionee *(a prospective purchaser or lessee) the right to buy or lease the owner's property at a fixed price within a stated period of time.* The optionee pays a fee (the agreed-upon consideration) for this option right and assumes no other obligation until deciding, within the specified time, either to: (1) exercise his or her option right (to buy or lease the property) or (2) allow the option right to expire. The owner may be bound to sell; the optionee is not bound to buy. A common application of an option is a lease that includes an option for the tenant to purchase the property. Options must contain all the terms and provisions required for a valid contract of sale.

Land Contracts

A real estate sale can be made under a **land contract,** sometimes called *a contract for deed* or *installment contract.* Under a typical land contract, the seller, also known as the *vendor,* retains fee ownership while the buyer, known as the *vendee,* secures possession and an equitable interest in the property. The buyer agrees to give the seller a down payment and pay regular monthly installments of principal and interest over a number of years. The buyer also agrees to pay real estate taxes, insurance premiums, repairs and upkeep on the property. Although the buyer obtains possession when the contract is signed by both parties, *the seller is not obligated to execute and deliver a deed to the buyer until the terms of the contract have been satisfied.* This frequently occurs when the buyer has made a sufficient number of payments to obtain a mortgage loan and pay off the balance due on the contract.

Real estate is occasionally sold with the new buyer assuming an existing land contract from the original buyer/vendee. Generally, the seller/vendor must approve the new purchaser.

Land contracts require extensive legal input from lawyers experienced in real estate matters. The broker who negotiates a land contract should consult attorneys for both parties at every step of the way and refrain from specifying any detailed terms in the agreement.

Local Forms

To gain familiarity with the forms used in a local area the student should go to brokers or real estate companies and ask for copies of the sales contract, listing agreement and other forms they use. Usually such forms also can be obtained at a title or abstract company and some banks and savings and loan associations, or they may be purchased at local office supply and stationery stores.

Rescission

With contracts for the purchase of some types of personal property, the buyer has three days in which to reconsider and *rescind* (cancel) the contract. No such right of rescission applies to contracts for the purchase of real estate.

Borrowers who change their minds about a mortgage loan have three days in which to cancel the transaction if the mortgage was for *refinance* of presently owned property. No right of rescission, however, applies to mortgage loans used for the *purchase* of real estate.

Summary

A *contract* is defined as an agreement made by competent parties, with adequate consideration, to take or to refrain from some proper, or legal, action.

Contracts may be classified according to whether the parties' intentions are *expressed* or are *implied* by their actions. They also may be classified as *bilateral,* when both parties have obligated themselves to act, or *unilateral,* when one party is obligated to perform only if the other party acts. In addition, contracts may be classified according to their legal enforceability as either *valid, void, voidable* or *unenforceable.*

Many contracts specify a time for performance. In any case all contracts must be performed within a reasonable time. An *executed* contract is one that has been fully performed. An *executory* contract is one in which some act remains to be performed.

The *essentials of a valid contract* are: (1) competent parties, (2) offer and acceptance, (3) consideration, (4) legality of object and (5) agreement in writing and signed by the parties. A valid *real estate contract* also must include a description of the property.

In many types of contracts either of the parties may transfer his or her rights and obligations under the agreement by *assignment* of the contract or *novation* (substitution of a new contract).

Contracts usually provide that the seller has the right to declare a sale canceled if the buyer defaults. If either party has suffered a loss because of the other's default, he or she may sue for damages to cover the loss. If one party insists on completing the transaction, he or she may sue the defaulter for *specific performance* of the terms of the contract; a court can order the other party to comply with the agreement.

Contracts frequently used in the real estate business include listing agreements, sales contracts, options, land contracts (installment contracts) and leases.

A *real estate sales contract* binds a buyer and a seller to a definite transaction as described in detail in the contract. The buyer is bound to purchase the property for the amount stated in the agreement. The seller is bound to deliver title, free from liens and encumbrances (except those allowed by the "subject to" clause of the contract).

Under an *option* agreement, the optionee purchases from the optionor, for a limited time period, the exclusive right to purchase or lease the optionor's property. For a potential purchaser or lessee an option is a means of buying time to consider or complete arrangements for a transaction. A *land contract,* or *installment contract,* is a sales/financing agreement under which a buyer purchases a seller's real estate on time. The buyer takes possession of and responsibility for the property but does not receive the deed immediately.

Questions

1. A legally enforceable agreement under which two parties agree to do something for each other is known as a(n):

   a. escrow agreement. c. valid contract.
   b. legal promise.   d. option agreement.

2. Donna Bates drives into a filling station and tops off her gas tank. She is obligated to pay for the fuel through what kind of contract?

   a. Express   c. Oral
   b. Implied   d. Voidable

3. A contract is said to be *bilateral* if:

   a. one of the parties is a minor.
   b. the contract has yet to be fully performed.
   c. only one party to the agreement is bound to act.
   d. all parties to the contract are bound to act.

4. A seller gave an open listing to several brokers, specifically promising that if one of the brokers found a buyer for the seller's real estate, the seller then would be obligated to pay a commission to that broker. This offer by the seller is a(n):

   a. executed agreement.
   b. discharged agreement.
   c. implied agreement.
   d. unilateral agreement.

5. During the period of time after a real estate sales contract is signed but before title actually passes, the status of the contract is:

   a. voidable.   c. executed.
   b. executory. d. implied.

6. Dan Smith, who is 17 years old, signs a contract to buy a home for himself and his wife. The contract is:

   a. voidable.   c. executed.
   b. valid.   d. unilateral.

7. Broker Sam Manella has found a buyer for Joe Taylor's home. The buyer has indicated in writing his willingness to buy the property for $1,000 less than the asking price and has deposited $5,000 earnest money with broker Manella. Taylor is out of town for the weekend and Manella has been unable to inform him of the signed document. At this point the buyer has signed a(n):

   a. voidable contract.
   b. offer.
   c. executory agreement.
   d. implied contract.

8. Consideration offered in exchange for a deed might take the form of:

   a. love and affection.
   b. a purchase-money mortgage.
   c. cash.
   d. any of the above.

9. The statute of frauds requires that a contract must be in writing for:

   a. all real estate sales.
   b. all real estate contracts of any sort.
   c. all contracts.
   d. bilateral contracts only.

10. The seller told the buyer she'd leave the washing machine but instead took it with her. The written contract made no mention of the washing machine. The buyer has no right to complain because of the rule of:

    a. partial performance.
    b. novation.
    c. undue influence.
    d. parol evidence.

11. In New York State who fills out purchase contracts?

    a. Seller's attorney
    b. Buyer's attorney
    c. Real estate broker
    d. Either, according to local custom

12. If a real estate sales contract does not state that time is of the essence and the stipulated date of transfer comes and goes without a closing, the contract is then:
    a. binding for only 30 more days.
    b. novated.
    c. still valid.
    d. automatically void.

13. Tom has a contract to buy Blackacre but would rather let his friend Mary buy it instead. If the contract allows, Mary can take over Tom's obligation by the process known as:
    a. assignment.
    b. substantial performance.
    c. subordination.
    d. mutual consent.

14. A suit for specific performance of a real estate contract asks for:
    a. money damages.
    b. a new contract.
    c. a deficiency judgment.
    d. a forced sale or purchase.

15. In filling out a sales contract someone crossed out several words and inserted others. In order to eliminate future controversy as to whether the changes were made before or after the contract was signed, the usual procedure is to:
    a. write a letter to each party listing the changes.
    b. have each party write a letter to the other approving the changes.
    c. redraw the entire contract.
    d. have both parties initial or sign in the margin near each change.

16. In New York State the statute of limitations for enforcement of a contract is:
    a. three years.
    b. six years.
    c. ten years.
    d. 20 years.

17. The Foxes offer in writing to purchase a house for $120,000, drapes included, with the offer to expire Saturday at noon. The Wolfs reply in writing on Thursday, accepting $120,000 but excluding the drapes. On Friday while the Foxes are considering this counteroffer, the Wolfs decide to accept the original offer, drapes included, and state that in writing. At this point the Foxes:
    a. must buy and have a right to insist on the drapes.
    b. are not bound to buy and can forget the whole thing.
    c. must buy but are not entitled to the drapes.
    d. must buy and can deduct the value of the drapes from the $120,000.

18. In New York State a valid contract for the sale of real estate must include:
    a. an earnest money deposit.
    b. an adequate description of the property.
    c. the signatures of witnesses.
    d. all of the above.

19. The sales contract says Tom Jones will purchase only if his wife flies up and approves the sale by the following Saturday. Mrs. Jones's approval is a:
    a. contingency.   c. warranty.
    b. reservation.   d. consideration.

20. When the buyer promises to purchase only if he can sell his own present home, the seller gains some protection from an:
    a. escrow.   c. equitable title.
    b. option.   d. escape clause.

21. Real estate licensees who write contracts can protect themselves by making the contracts subject to:
    a. operation of law.
    b. novation.
    c. attorney's approval
    d. specific performance.

22. An option to purchase binds:
    a. the buyer only.
    b. the seller only.
    c. neither buyer nor seller.
    d. both buyer and seller.

23. Which of the following best describes a land contract, or installment contract?

    a. A contract to buy land only
    b. A mortgage on land
    c. A means of conveying title immediately while the purchaser pays for the property in installments
    d. A method of selling real estate whereby the purchaser pays in regular installments while the seller retains title

24. The purchaser of real estate under an installment contract:

    a. generally pays no interest charge.
    b. receives title immediately.
    c. is not required to pay property taxes for the duration of the contract.
    d. is called a vendee.

25. The consumer has the right to change his or her mind and rescind the transaction within three days after a:

    a. real estate purchase.
    b. firm purchase contract.
    c. refinance mortgage.
    d. lease option.

Appendix: Excerpts from New York State's Study Booklet for Brokers

CONTRACTS FOR THE SALE OR LEASE OF REAL PROPERTY

Essentials. 1. A contract for the leasing for a longer period than one year, or for the sale, of any real property, or an interest therein, is void, unless the contract, or some note or memorandum thereof, expressing the considerations, is in writing, subscribed by the party to be charged, or by the party's lawful agent thereunto authorized by writing. The other essentials of a valid contract for the sale of real property are:

2. Competent parties (sane adults);

3. An expression of their agreement to sell and buy;

4. An understandable and adequate description of the premises that are the subject of the transaction;

5. The consideration for the contemplated conveyance (price and terms of payment);

6. Agreement of grantor to convey title (although it is not essential, the contract should usually specify the form of the deed to be delivered to grantee);

7. Place and date of closing. (Again, this item may not be required to make the contract enforceable, but it is usually prudent to include this item.)

The contract speaks for itself. Care should be taken that the written contract includes all special terms and convenants that were verbally agreed upon by the parties.

For instance, if such a contract does not specifically provide that the grantor shall deliver a full covenant and warranty deed, the grantor may require the grantee to accept a bargain and sale deed. Under a contract providing that the seller shall deliver "a good and sufficient deed," the seller cannot be required to turn over a deed containing full covenants, for even a bargain and sale deed, without covenant against the grantor, is "a good and sufficient deed." A marketable title is one that a court will compel a buyer to accept in any action for specific performance of a contract.

Encumbrances. Where there are encumbrances,
or other flaws in the title to the property that is the subject of the contract, it is imperative that the contract shall express the agreement of the parties respecting them. Encumbrance is a right or interest in property held by a third party, which often limits the use and diminishes the value of the property, but usally does not prevent the transferring of title. The more common forms of encumbrances are:

1. Taxes, water rents and assessments for local improvements that have become liens upon the property to which a contract or conveyance relates;

2. Mortgages, upon such property;

3. Lease of property or any part thereof;

4. Judgments against the grantor, duly recorded in the country in which the property is located;

5. Mechanics' liens for work or labor done or material furnished for use upon such property;

6. *Lis pendens* (a legal document, filed in the office of the county clerk giving notice that an action or proceeding is pending in the courts affecting the title to the property);

7. Encroachments of a building, or other structure on the property, upon a street or other public place, or upon land of an adjoining owner*;

8. Easements (rights that may be exercised by the public or individuals on, over or through the lands of others; such as rights-of-way, rights to erect poles and string wires or cables overhead, or rights to construct and maintain conduits, pipes or mains underground);

9. Restrictive covenants (limitations upon the use of property, contained in these or other written instruments in the chain of title thereto, providing that the property shall not be used for specified purposes, or that buildings thereon must be set back from the property line for a given distance, or shall not be constructed of certain materials, etc.; zoning regulations, however, are not restrictions that, in a legal sense, are encumbrances);

10. Strictly speaking, violations are not considered encumbrances, although they may diminish the value of property. Violations (written notices

* In this sense, a party wall is an encumbrance, because it is a wall built along the line separating two properties, partly on each.

from state or municipal officers, addressed to the owners, lessees or occupants of specified real property, requiring compliance with definitely stated provisions of laws or ordinances relating to such property, which it is the duty of such officers to enforce).

"Time is of the essence of this contract." This clause is frequently found in real property contracts. It is useful where a quick "turn-over" is contemplated by the purchaser, or the seller has a special reason for closing title upon the date specified in the contract. Its legal effect is to require the seller to be able to deliver the required deed and the purchaser to be prepared to make payment of the agreed purchase price, upon the exact closing date fixed in the contract. If, then, either party is unprepared, the contract is breached and the delinquent is at a serious disadvantage and may suffer substantial financial loss. Obviously, neither party to a real property contract should bind himself/herself by such a provision, unless reasonably certain that the party can make good his/her part of the agreement precisely on the closing date specified therein.

Mortgage clauses. Contracts for the sale of real property frequently contain provisions relating to existing or contemplated mortgages upon the properties to which such contracts relate. It is particularly important for the purchaser to know whether he/she is to take the property "subject to" an existing mortgage, or is assuming payment of the mortgage indebtedness; for, in the latter case, in the event of the foreclosure of the mortgage, the purchaser will be liable for the deficiency, if the property sells for less than the mortgage debt.

Again, in the purchase of land intended for subdivision into building lots, it is usually to the interest of the purchaser to have the sale contract provide that a "release clause" shall be included in the mortgage to be given by the purchaser as security for the payment of a part of the purchase price. The purpose of such a provision is to enable the purchaser to give clear title to lots in the subdivision, which is possible only upon their release from the lien of the "blanket" mortgage.

Sometimes, what is known as a "mortgage subordination clause" is included in a contract for the sale of realty. The ordinary purpose of such a provision is to subordinate the mortgage to be taken by the seller, as a part of the purchase price, to a contemplated mortgage to secure a loan required to defray the cost of erecting a new building or altering an existing building upon the property. A sale contract should be carefully scrutinized and, if a mortgage subordination clause is included therein, the property owner should defer signing the contract until the property owner has had the advice thereon of a competent lawyer of his/her own selection.

Action for specific performance. This is a court action to compel defaulting principal to comply with provisions of contract.

Recording land contracts. Contracts for the sale of purchase or real property are usually not recorded, for, as a rule, they are not acknowledged by the parties thereto. They are recordable, if duly acknowledged.

Recording executory contracts and powers of attorney. 1. An executory contract for the sale, purchase or exchange of real property or an instrument canceling such a contract, or an instrument containing a power to convey real property, as the agent or attorney for the owner of the property, acknowledged or proved, and certified, in the manner to entitle a conveyance to be recorded, may be recorded.

General Obligations Law

Requirements for use of plain language in consumer transactions. a. Every written agreement, for the lease of space to be occupied for residential purposes, or to which a consumer is a party and the money, property or service which is the subject of the transaction is primarily for personal, family or household purposes must be:

1. Written in a clear and coherent manner using words with common and everyday meanings;

2. Appropriately divided and captioned by its various sections. . . . This subdivision shall not apply to agreements involving amounts in excess of fifty thousand dollars nor prohibit the use of words or phrases or forms of agreement required by state or federal law, rule or regulation or by a governmental instrumentality.

b. A violation of the provisions of subdivision a. of this section shall not render any such agreement void or voidable nor shall it constitute:

1. A defense to any action or proceeding to enforce such agreement; or

2. A defense to any action or proceeding for breach of such agreement.

c. In addition to the above, whenever the attorney general finds that there has been a violation of this section, he may proceed as provided in the executive law.

6

Land-Use Regulations

Overview

The ownership rights a person possesses in a parcel of real estate are subject to public and private land-use controls such as zoning ordinances, building codes and deed restrictions. The purpose of these controls is to ensure that our limited supply of land is being put to its highest and best use for the benefit of the general public as well as private owners. This chapter will discuss government powers, three types of land-use controls, and how they help shape and preserve the physical surface of our nation.

Government Powers

Although an individual in the United States has maximum rights in the land he or she owns, these ownership rights are subject to certain powers, or rights, held by federal, state and local governments. Because they are for the general welfare of the community, these limitations on the ownership of real estate supersede the rights of the individual. Government rights include the following:

1. **Taxation:** Taxation is a charge on real estate to raise funds to meet the public needs of a government.
2. **Police power:** This is the power vested in a state to establish legislation to preserve order, protect the public health and safety and promote the general welfare. A state's police power is passed on to municipalities and counties through legislation called *enabling acts*. The use and enjoyment of property is subject to restrictions authorized by such legislation, including both environmental protection laws and zoning and building ordinances regulating the use, occupancy, size, location, construction and rental of real estate.
3. **Eminent domain:** Through a condemnation suit a government may exercise this right to acquire privately owned real estate for public use. Three conditions must be met: (a) the proposed use must be declared by the court to be a public use; (b) just compensation must be paid to the owner; and (c) the rights of the property owner must be protected by due process of law.

   Decision-making under the right of eminent domain is granted by state laws to quasipublic bodies such as land-clearance commissions and public housing or redevelopment authorities, as well as to railroads and public utility companies.

   Condemnation proceedings are instituted only when the owner's consent cannot be obtained. Otherwise, public agencies acquire real property through direct negotiation and purchase from the owner.
4. **Escheat:** While escheat is not actually a limitation on ownership, state laws provide for ownership of real estate to revert, or escheat, to the state when an owner dies and leaves no heirs and no will disposing of his or her real estate.

Taxation

Ad valorem taxes are charged against each parcel according to the **assessed value** placed on land and improvements by a public official known as an *assessor*. Tax rates are set to raise whatever sum is needed for the public budget. A rate might be quoted as, for example, $26 per $1,000 of assessed valuation. The same rate, in a different community, might be expressed as $2.60 per $100, or 26 mills (a mill being 1/10th of a cent) per $1 of assessed value. At that rate, a house assessed at $100,000 would have a property tax bill of $2,600.

Special assessments are additional taxes that run for a few years to enable certain neighborhoods to pay for particular improvements. Property on one street might be subject to special assessment property taxes, for example, in order to install sidewalks or streetlights on that particular street.

Protesting assessments. Taxpayers who feel their assessment is unfair can research tax records to see how their valuation compares with that of their neighbors. Obtaining solid data on comparative parcels is of prime importance in protesting an assessment. Most assessors will visit the property and discuss the matter. If no agreement results, the next step is to present a grievance to the local assessment board of review. The taxpayer who wants to take matters beyond that point may go to court or take advantage of a simple small claims procedure intended for review of grievances on residential property.

Exemption from some property taxes may be available to qualified veterans, religious organizations and homeowners aged 65 or older who have limited income.

Property taxes have first priority as liens. Foreclosure of a tax lien is often *in rem,* against the property and not against the delinquent taxpayer personally. Property taxes are discussed at greater length in Chapter 25.

Land-Use Controls

The control and regulation of land use is accomplished through: (1) public land-use controls, (2) private land-use controls through deed restrictions, and (3) public ownership of land—including parks, schools and expressways—by the federal, state and local governments.

Public Land-Use Controls

Our largely urban population and the increasing demands placed on our limited natural resources have made it necessary for cities, towns and villages to increase their limitations on the private use of real estate. We now have controls over noise, air and water pollution, as well as population density. Regulations on privately owned real estate include planning; zoning; subdivision regulations; codes that regulate building construction, safety and public health; and environmental protection legislation.

The Master Plan

The primary method by which local governments recognize development goals is through the formulation of a comprehensive **master plan,** also commonly referred to as a *general plan.* Cities and counties develop master plans to ensure that social and economic needs are balanced against environmental and aesthetic concerns.

Economic and physical surveys both are essential in preparing a master plan. Countywide plans must also include the coordination of numerous civic plans and developments to ensure orderly city growth with stabilized property values. City plans are put into effect by enactment and enforcement of zoning ordinances.

Zoning

Zoning ordinances are laws of local government authorities (such as municipalities and counties) that regulate and control the use of land and structures within designated districts or zones. Zoning regulates and affects such things as use of the land, lot sizes, types of structures permitted, building heights, setbacks (the minimum distance away from streets or sidewalks that structures may be built) and density (the ratio of land area to structure area or population). Often the purpose of zoning is to implement a local master plan.

In New York State, zoning powers are given to municipal governments: There are no statewide zoning ordinances.

Zoning ordinances generally divide land use into three classifications: (1) residential, (2) commercial and (3) industrial. Now included by many communities are *cluster zoning* and *multiple-use zoning,* which permit planned unit developments. Zoning classifications found in a typical New York State community might include:

1. *R-1,* one-family residential;
2. *R-2,* multifamily residential;
3. *C-1,* commercial-retail;
4. *C-2,* heavy commercial; and
5. *I-1,* industrial.

To ensure adequate control, land-use areas are further divided into subclasses. For example, residential areas may be subdivided to provide for detached single-family dwellings, semidetached structures containing not more than four dwelling units, walk-up apartments, high-rise apartments and so forth. Variations exist between municipalities, and some may have as many as 15 classifications.

Adoption of zoning ordinances. Today approximately 98 percent of all cities with populations in excess of 10,000 have enacted comprehensive zoning ordinances governing the utilization of land located *within corporate limits*. New York City adopted one of the first in the country, shortly after World War I. In some cases the use of land located *within one to three miles* of an incorporated area must receive the approval and consent of the incorporated area even if the property is not contiguous to the village, town or city.

Zoning ordinances must not violate the rights of individuals and property holders or the various provisions of the state constitution. If the means used to regulate the use of property are destructive, unreasonable, arbitrary or confiscatory, the legislation is usually considered void. *Tests* commonly applied in determining the validity of ordinances require that the:

1. power must be exercised in a reasonable manner.
2. provisions must be clear and specific.
3. ordinance must be free from discrimination.
4. ordinance must promote public health, safety and general welfare under the police power concept.
5. ordinance must apply to all property in a similar manner.

When *downzoning* occurs in an area—for instance, when land zoned for single-family residences is rezoned to apartment use—the state usually is not responsible for compensating property owners for any resulting loss of value.

Zoning laws are enforced through local requirements that building permits be obtained before property owners build on their land. A permit will not be issued unless a proposed structure conforms to the permitted zoning, among other requirements.

Nonconforming use. A frequent problem is a building that does not conform to the zoning use because it was erected before the enactment of the zoning law. Such a **nonconforming use** is allowed to continue. If the building is destroyed or torn down, any new structure must comply with the current zoning ordinance. Local laws may say that the right to a nonconforming use is lost if it is discontinued for a certain period, usually one year.

Zoning boards of appeal. A **zoning appeals board** has been established in most communities to hear complaints about the effects of zoning ordinances on specific parcels of property. Petitions may be presented to the appeal board for exceptions to the zoning law. Determinations can be challenged in state courts.

Spot zoning affects only a small area. If it is not in harmony with the neighborhood (a chemical plant in a residential area, for example), it is illegal in New York.

Zoning variations. Each time a plan is created or a zoning ordinance enacted, some owners are inconvenienced and want to change the use of a property. Generally such owners may appeal for either a special-use permit or a variance to allow a use that does not meet zoning requirements.

A **special-use permit** is granted to allow a property owner a special use of property that is in the public interest. For example, a restaurant may be built in an industrially zoned area if it is deemed necessary to provide meal services for area workers, or a church in a residential area.

A **variance** may be sought by a property owner who has suffered hardship as a result of a zoning ordinance. For example, if an owner's lot is level next to a road but slopes steeply 30 feet back from the road, the zoning board may be willing to allow a variance so the owner can build closer to the road than normally would be allowed.

Subdivision Regulations

Most communities have adopted **subdivision regulations,** often as a part of a master plan. These will be covered in detail in Chapter 18. Subdivision regulations usually provide for the following:

1. Location, grading, alignment, surfacing and widths of streets, highways and other rights-of-way;
2. Installation of sewers and water mains;
3. Minimum dimensions of lots;
4. Building and setback lines;
5. Areas to be reserved or dedicated for public use, such as parks or schools; and
6. Easements for public utilities.

Subdivision regulations, like all other forms of zoning or building regulations, cannot be static. They must remain flexible to meet the ever-changing needs of society.

Building Codes

Most cities and towns have enacted ordinances to *specify construction standards* that must be met when repairing or erecting buildings. These are called **building codes** and they set the requirements for kinds of materials, sanitary equipment, electrical wiring, fire prevention standards and the like. New York has a statewide building code that is in force where no local code exists or where local codes are less restrictive.

Most communities require the issuance of a **building permit** by the *building department* or other authority before a person can build a structure or alter or repair an existing building on property within the municipality. Through the permit requirement officials can verify compliance with building codes and zoning ordinances by examining the plans and inspecting the work. After the new structure has been inspected and found satisfactory, the inspector issues a **certificate of occupancy** or, for an altered building, a certificate of compliance. The certificate of occupancy *(C of O)* is also required for some transfers of existing buildings.

If the construction violates a deed restriction (discussed later in this chapter), the issuance of a building permit will *not* cure this violation. A building permit is merely evidence of the applicant's compliance with *municipal* regulations.

The subject of city planning, zoning and restricting the use of real estate is extremely technical and the interpretation of the law is not altogether clear. Questions concerning any of these subjects should be referred to legal counsel.

Environmental Protection Legislation

Federal and state legislators have passed a number of environmental protection laws in an attempt to respond to the growing public concern over the improvement and preservation of America's natural resources.

The various states have responded to the environmental issue by passing a variety of localized environmental protection laws regarding all types of pollution—air, water, noise and solid waste disposal. For example, many states have enacted laws that prevent builders or private individuals from constructing septic tanks or other effluent-disposal systems in certain areas, particularly where public bodies of water—streams, lakes and rivers—are concerned.

Of particular importance are the New York Environmental Conservation Law and the federal Comprehensive and Environmental Response Cleanup and Liability Act of 1980 (CERCLA), discussed at greater length in Chapter 18.

In 1976 the New York legislature passed a law to protect designated wetlands. Improvements may be constructed only with a state permit; most agricultural uses are exempt from the law.

In addition to the states and the federal government, cities and counties also frequently pass environmental legislation of their own.

Landmark Preservation

In New York State, local governments may enact regulations intended to preserve individual buildings and areas of historical or architectural significance. Regulations setting up local historic areas or landmark preservation districts may restrict an owner's right to alter certain old buildings on the exterior. Interior remodeling is typically free from regulation. Individual buildings located outside a historic area also may be designated as landmarks.

Private Land-Use Controls

A real estate owner can create a **deed restriction** by including a provision for it in the deed when the property is conveyed. An individual seller or donor can set deed restrictions, giving property to a grandchild, for example, with the restriction that no intoxicating liquors ever be served on the premises. The restriction would be binding on future owners as well. The restriction is set by including a *restrictive covenant* in the deed.

In the past, deed restrictions might have forbidden any future sale of the property to a member of a particular religious or ethnic group. Such restrictions, in violation of modern human rights law, are not enforceable. Neither are restrictions that forbid the next owners selling in the future.

A subdivider may establish restrictions on the right to *use* land through a *covenant* in a deed or by a separate recorded declaration. These use restrictions are usually considered valid if they are reasonable restraints and are for the benefit of all property owners in the subdivision.

Plats of new subdivisions will frequently set forth on the face of the plat, or on a declaration attached thereto, restrictive covenants concerning the use of the land. When a lot in that subdivision is conveyed by an owner's deed, the deed refers to the plat or declaration of restrictions and incorporates these restrictions as limitations on the title conveyed by the deed. In this manner the restrictive covenants are included in the deed by reference and become binding on all grantees. Such covenants or restrictions usually relate to: (1) type of building, (2) use to which the land may be put, (3) type of construction, height, setbacks and square footage and (4) cost.

Some restrictions have a *time limitation*—for example, "effective for a period of 25 years from this date." Frequently the effective term of the restrictions may be extended with the consent of a majority (or sometimes two-thirds) of the owners in a subdivision.

Where a deed restriction and a zoning provision cover the same subject the more limiting restriction will prevail. If deed restrictions say lots in a subdivision must measure at least two acres but the town allows half-acre lots, the two-acre restriction is enforceable by neighbors.

Enforcement of deed restrictions. Subdividers place restrictions on the use of all lots of a subdivision as a *general plan* for the benefit of all lot owners. Each lot owner has the right to apply to the court for an *injunction* to prevent a neighboring lot owner from violating the recorded restrictions. If granted, the court injunction will direct the violator to stop the violation upon penalty of being in contempt of court. The court retains the power to punish the violator for failure to obey the court order.

If adjoining lot owners stand idly by while a violation is being committed, they can *lose the right* to the court's injunction by their inaction; the court might claim their right was lost through **laches,** that is, loss of a right through undue delay or failure to assert it. In New York, neighboring owners have a two-year statute of limitations on objections to violations of the general plan (type of building, height, setbacks) and ten years in which to object to violations of conditions mentioned in the deed.

Direct Public Ownership

Over the years the government's general policy has been to encourage private ownership of land. A certain amount of land is owned by the government for such use as municipal buildings, state legislature houses, schools and military stations. **Direct public ownership** is a means of land control.

Publicly owned streets and highways serve a necessary function for the entire population. In addition, public land is often used for such recreational purposes as parks. National and state parks and forest preserves create areas for public use and recreation and at the same time help to conserve our natural resources. At present the federal government owns approximately 775 million acres of land. Much of that is in Alaska. At times the federal government has held title to as much as 80 percent of the nation's total land area.

Summary

Government powers limiting private rights in land include *taxation, eminent domain, police power* and *escheat*.

The control of land use is exercised through public controls, through private (or nongovernment) controls and through public ownership.

Public controls are ordinances based on the states' *police power* to protect the public health, safety and welfare. Through power conferred by state enabling acts, cities and municipalities enact master plans and zoning ordinances.

Zoning ordinances segregate residential areas from business and industrial zones and control not only land use, but height and bulk of buildings and density of population. Zoning enforcement problems involve boards of appeal, special-use permits, variances and nonconforming uses. *Subdivision regulations* maintain control of the development of expanding community areas so that growth will be harmonious with community standards.

Building codes control construction of buildings by specifying standards for construction, plumbing, sewers, electrical wiring and equipment. A building inspector may issue a *certificate of occupancy* when a completed building meets standards.

In addition to land-use control on the local level, the state and federal governments occasionally have intervened to preserve natural resources through *environmental legislation*.

Private controls are exercised by owners, generally subdividers, who control use of subdivision lots by *deed restrictions* that are made to apply to all lot owners. The usual recorded restrictions may be enforced by adjoining lot owners obtaining a court *injunction* to stop a violator.

Public ownership provides land for such public purposes as parks, highways, schools and municipal buildings.

Questions

1. Real estate is evaluated for property tax purposes by a(n):
   a. appraiser.
   b. building inspector.
   c. assessor.
   d. zoning board.

2. A house valued at $120,000 is assessed for 80% of its value. The tax rate is $26.34 per $1,000. How much is the property tax bill?
   a. $252.86
   b. $316.08
   c. $2,528.64
   d. $3,160.80

3. A tax on the houses in one small neighborhood, to pay for new streetlamps in that area, would take the form of:
   a. ad valorem tax.
   b. eminent domain.
   c. special assessment.
   d. conditional-use tax.

4. An *in rem* tax foreclosure:
   a. shows up on the owner's record as a judgment.
   b. takes the property but ignores the owner's personal liability.
   c. gives first priority to any mortgages on the property.
   d. cannot take place unless taxes go unpaid for at least five years.

5. A homeowner who is dissatisfied with assessed valuation can take a complaint to:
   a. the assessor personally.
   b. a board of review.
   c. a small claims hearing.
   d. any of the above.

6. The government's police power allows it to regulate:
   a. law enforcement.
   b. fire codes.
   c. zoning.
   d. all of the above.

7. The state needs to run a new expressway through Martin's farm. Martin does not agree to sell the necessary land. The state then may try to exert its right of eminent domain through a court proceeding known as:
   a. escheat.
   b. variance.
   c. condemnation.
   d. downzoning.

8. The right of escheat allows New York State to acquire land:
   a. through an act of condemnation.
   b. when someone dies without leaving a will or heirs.
   c. through a gift from a donor.
   d. when property taxes are not paid as due.

9. Zoning ordinances control the use of privately owned land by establishing land-use districts. Which one of the following is not a usual zoning district?
   a. Residential
   b. Commercial
   c. Industrial
   d. Rental

10. A nonconforming use is allowed:
    a. only after a condemnation suit.
    b. if it is for a public purpose.
    c. with the approval of two-thirds of the neighbors.
    d. if it existed before the area was zoned.

11. Doctor Livingston goes before his local zoning board asking for permission to open an office in his residential neighborhood because the area has no medical facilities. He is asking for a:
    a. variance.
    b. nonconforming use.
    c. special-use permit.
    d. restriction.

12. Dan Hill asks the zoning board to allow him to build a fence to keep his children out of traffic on a busy corner, though he does not have room for the required ten-foot setback. He is asking for a:
    a. variance.
    b. nonconforming use.
    c. special-use permit.
    d. restriction.

13. Public land-use controls include all but which of the following?
    a. Subdivision regulations
    b. Deed restrictions
    c. Environmental protection laws
    d. Master plan specifications

14. Zoning boards of appeal are established to handle complaints about:
    a. restrictive covenants.
    b. building codes.
    c. zoning regulations.
    d. all of the above.

15. The building inspector who is satisfied that construction is satisfactory may issue a:
    a. certificate of occupancy.
    b. subdivision regulation.
    c. restrictive covenant.
    d. conditional-use permit.

16. The purpose of a building permit is to:
    a. override a deed restriction.
    b. maintain municipal control over the volume of building.
    c. provide evidence of compliance with municipal regulations.
    d. regulate area and bulk of buildings.

17. Miss Muffet's Greek Revival home is located in a historic preservation district. She probably may not change:
    a. the number of living units in the building.
    b. the exterior of the building.
    c. the interior of the building.
    d. either exterior or interior.

18. Every parcel in the subdivision has a deed restriction forbidding basketball backboards on front-facing garages. Wilt puts one up anyhow. Wilt's neighbors may force him to remove it by:
    a. calling the police.
    b. notifying the original developer of the subdivision.
    c. sending a petition to the town or city hall.
    d. going to court.

19. The grantor of real estate may place effective deed restrictions forbidding:
    a. any future sale of the property.
    b. rental of the property to a member of a particular ethnic group.
    c. division of the parcel into small building lots.
    d. any of the above.

20. The developer of Fancy Heights Subdivision placed a restriction in the deeds requiring 250 feet of road frontage for each building lot. The town building code requires only 100 feet, and Joe Doakes obtains permits to construct two houses on his 250-foot lot. His neighbors can:
    a. ask the court to order one house torn down.
    b. act only before he has obtained certificates of occupancy.
    c. do nothing because he complied with all town regulations.
    d. enforce their rights by calling the police.

7

Real Estate Financing

Key Terms

Adjustable rate mortgage (ARM)
Amortized loan
Annual percentage rate (APR)
Balloon payment
Biweekly mortgage
Buydown
Cap
Ceiling
Conventional loan
Fannie Mae (FNMA)
FHA loan
Freddie Mac (FHLMC)
Ginnie Mae (GNMA)
Graduated payment loan
Home equity loan
Imputed interest
Index
Interest

Jumbo loan
Loan-to-value ratio (l-v-r)
Margin
Mortgage insurance premium (MIP)
Negative amortization
PITI
Points
Prepayment penalty
Primary mortgage market
Private mortgage insurance (PMI)
Regulation Z
Secondary market
Shared equity mortgage
Sonny Mae (SONYMA)
Straight (term) loan
Underwriting
Usury
VA loan

Overview

Rarely is a parcel of real estate purchased for cash; almost every transaction involves some type of financing. An understanding of real estate financing is of prime importance to the real estate licensee. Most buyers report that they obtained their mortgage information from a broker or salesperson. This chapter will discuss the basic mortgage loan as well as alternative types of financing and payment plans. In addition the chapter will examine various sources of mortgage money and the role of the federal government in real estate financing.

Mortgage Financing

Liberalization of mortgage terms and payment plans over the past six decades has made the dream of home ownership a reality for more than 65 percent of the population. For example, the amount of a mortgage loan in relation to the value of a home, the **loan-to-value ratio**, has increased from 40 percent in 1920 to as much as 95 or 100 percent today. Payment periods have also extended, from five years in the 1920s to 30 years or more in the 1980s.

Interest rates charged by lending institutions on home mortgage loans vary as changes occur in the money market. As interest rates move up, an established fixed-rate mortgage with a lower interest rate may be a plus in selling a home if the new owner is able to assume the existing mortgage. On the other hand, if mortgage interest rates fall, the homeowner may seek to pay off the loan and refinance at a lower rate.

To buffer the effects of an unstable money market, lenders have been offering many alternative forms of mortgages in recent years, such as adjustable interest rate and graduated payment mortgages. Seller financing also gains popularity in times of tight mortgage money.

For years potential homeowners have been able to receive assistance in obtaining low–down-payment mortgage loans through the federal programs of the Federal Housing Administration (FHA) and the Veterans Administration (VA). In addition, private mortgage insurance companies offer programs to assist loan applicants in receiving higher loan-to-value ratios from private lenders than they could otherwise obtain.

Payment Plans

Many mortgage loans are **amortized loans.** Regular payments are applied first to the interest owed and the balance to the principal amount, over a term of perhaps 15 to 30 years. At the end of the term the full amount of the principal will have been paid off. Such loans are also called *self-liquidating loans*.

Most amortized mortgage loans are paid in monthly installments. These payments may be computed based on a number of payment plans, which tend to alternately gain and lose favor as the cost and availability of mortgage money fluctuate. These payment plans include the following; all are fixed-rate loans:

1. The most frequently used plan requires the mortgagor to pay a *constant amount*, usually each month. The mortgagee credits each payment first to the interest due and then applies the balance to reduce the principal of the loan. While each payment is the same, the portion applied toward repayment of the principal grows and the interest due declines as the unpaid balance of the loan is reduced. This is known as a *fully amortized loan*.
2. A mortgagor may choose a *straight payment plan* that calls for periodic payments of interest, with the principal to be *paid in full at the end of the loan term*. This is known as a **straight,** or **term, loan.** Such plans are generally used for home improvement loans and second mortgages rather than for residential first mortgage loans.

3. The mortgagor may elect to take advantage of a *graduated payment plan*, used to enable younger buyers and buyers in times of high interest rates to purchase real estate. Under this plan a mortgagor makes lower monthly payments for the first few years of the loan (typically the first five years) and larger payments for the remainder of the term, when the mortgagor's income is expected to have increased.
4. When a mortgage loan requires periodic payments that will not fully amortize the amount of the loan by the time the final payment is due, the final payment is a larger amount than the others. This is called a **balloon payment** and this type of loan is a *partially amortized loan*.

Adjustable rate mortgages (ARMs) shift the risk—or reward—of changing interest rates from the lender to the borrower, with corresponding changes in monthly payment or (occasionally) in the amount borrowed or the *term* (number of payments remaining). Adjustable rate mortgages will be discussed in detail in this chapter.

Biweekly mortgages involve payments every two weeks instead of monthly. This schedule, which may fit certain wage earners' budgets, produces the equivalent of 13 monthly payments a year. Because of the compounding effect of more frequent principal reduction, a 30-year loan can be paid off in 19 or 20 years. Prompt payment is essential to the plan, so most biweekly loans involve automatic payment from the borrower's checking or savings account.

Graduated payment loans are well suited to young professionals and other borrowers who can demonstrate to the satisfaction of lenders that they have reasonable expectations of rising income in the years ahead. With payments kept artificially low during the first few years of the loan, the borrowers can purchase property they might otherwise not qualify for. The shortfall in monthly payments may result in **negative amortization** (an increase in the principal owed) or be accounted for in some other way.

Interest

A charge for the use of money is called **interest.** A lender charges a borrower a certain percentage of the principal as interest for each year the debt is outstanding. The amount of interest due on any one installment payment date is calculated by computing the total yearly interest, based on the unpaid balance, and dividing that figure by the number of payments made each year.

On an amortized loan of $50,000 for 30 years at an annual interest rate of 13 percent, the amount due after the first month's payment has been made can be calculated as follows:

1. $50,000 × 13% = $6,500 annual interest
2. $6,500 ÷ 12 = $541.67 first month's interest
3. $553.10 monthly payment
   −$541.67 interest due
   $11.43 first month's principal reduction
4. $50,000   principal due at start of month
   −11.43 principal repayment
   $49,988.57 principal due at end of month

The following month, because less is now being borrowed, not quite so much interest will be due, and the principal can be reduced by a slightly larger amount.

Table 7.1 shows an *amortization schedule* for the first eight months of this 360-payment loan.

Interest is usually due at the *end* of each payment period (payment *in arrears,* as opposed to payment *in advance*). A table showing the amount of monthly payment needed to amortize a given loan is included as an appendix to this chapter. Most real estate salespersons and brokers carry small books of amortization tables or special hand calculators with built-in tables.

Table 7.1 Amortization Table for the First Few Months of a 30-Year Loan of $50,000 at 13 Percent with Monthly Payment of $553.10	Payment	Principal	Interest	Balance
	1	11.43	541.67	49,988.57
	2	11.56	541.54	49,977.01
	3	11.68	541.42	49,965.33
	4	11.81	541.29	49,953.52
	5	11.94	541.16	49,941.58
	6	12.07	541.03	49,929.51
	7	12.20	540.90	49,917.31
	8	12.33	540.77	49,904.98

Tax-Deductible Interest Payments

Taxpayers may take as a deduction on their federal income tax returns interest paid on mortgage loans up to a total of one million dollars for money used to acquire and/or improve both a first and a second (vacation) residence. Additional borrowing (second mortgages, home equity loans) of up to $100,000 also qualifies for income tax deduction, no matter what the money is used for. Homeowners may also deduct all property taxes, prepaid interest points (with a limit on refinance points as noted later) and any mortgage prepayment penalties. Different income tax regulations apply to mortgage loans on investment property.

Usury. The maximum rate of interest that may be charged on mortgage loans is set by state law. Charging interest in excess of this rate is called **usury** and lenders are penalized for making usurious loans. In New York a usurious lender may lose the entire amount of the loan in addition to the interest. Loans made to corporations are generally exempt from usury laws except for New York's criminal usury limit of 25 percent on loans up to $2,500,000.

Usury laws were enacted to protect borrowers from unscrupulous lenders who would charge unreasonably high interest rates. New York has a *floating interest rate.* The maximum rate that may be charged is adjusted up or down at specific intervals by the state banking board.

Money available for borrowing is a commodity subject to the economic laws of supply and demand, and lenders are in business to make money by lending money and charging interest. When there is plenty of money available, interest rates become fairly low. When money is scarce, interest rates go up. Table 7.2 tracks changing rates on FHA and/or VA loans for a 50-year period.

Sellers taking back purchase-money mortgages always have been exempt from usury limits. While lending institutions are also exempt up to the criminal usury limit (25 percent), *individuals making third-party mortgage loans are still bound by New York's usury limit.*

Points. When a new mortgage is placed, the lending institution may compensate for an interest rate that is below the current true cost of money by asking for extra prepaid interest in the form of up-front **points.** Each point is one percent of the new loan. On an $80,000 loan each point would be $800; a charge of two points would total $1,600. Payment of points is a one-time affair usually at time of closing but occasionally at mortgage application or issuance of a mortgage commitment by the lender.

Except with VA loans, points may be paid by either buyer or seller, depending on the terms of the sales contract. The buyer's points are interest payments, income–tax deductible in the year they are paid. The seller's points, because they are not paid on his or her own loan, are not deductible but merely one of the costs of selling. Points paid by investors or by refinancing homeowners must be *capitalized* or *amortized* (deducted gradually over the period of the loan).

Annual percentage rate. If a mortgage loan is made at 12 percent but also requires three points in prepaid interest or other service fees, the loan really costs the borrower more than 12 percent. The exact rate depends on the length of the proposed mortgage and requires some complicated calculations. The rate, which would total slightly over 12 percent, is known as the **annual percentage rate (APR).** Federal regulations require that the borrower be advised of the APR in advertisements and when a loan is placed.

Buydowns. With some mortgage plans, lending institutions are willing to lower the interest rate in return for extra payment of points. The arrangement is known as a **buydown.** Permanent buydowns keep the interest rate low for the entire life of the loan. Others may only lower the rate for a period of time, for example, by three percent the first year of the loan, two percent the second year, and one percent the third year (''3-2-1-buydown'').

Prepayment

Some mortgage notes require the borrower to pay a **prepayment premium,** or **penalty,** if the loan is paid off before its full term. For a one- to six-family dwelling, the maximum prepayment premium a lender can charge in New York is 90 days' interest on the unpaid balance of the mortgage when it is paid in full within one year of the date the mortgage is granted. Thereafter the borrower can prepay in whole or in part at any time without a premium. Federally chartered banks are under different regulations.

Tax and Insurance Reserves

Many lenders require borrowers to provide a reserve, or escrow, fund to meet future real estate taxes and insurance premiums. When the mortgage loan is made, the borrower starts the reserve by depositing funds to cover partial payment of the following year's tax bill. If a new insurance policy has been purchased, the insurance premium reserve will be started with the deposit of one-twelfth of the annual tax and insurance premium liability. Thereafter the monthly loan payments required of the borrower will include principal, interest, and tax and insurance reserves (**PITI**).

To be certain that these important bills are being met, the lender accumulates the borrower's money in the escrow account. Property tax bills and insurance premium bills are sent directly to the lending institution, which pays them and renders an accounting to the borrower. In most cases, the borrower is entitled to 2 percent interest on the money thus held. When the mortgage loan is

Table 7.2
*FHA/VA Mortgage
Rate Changes
1939–1988

Effective Date	Percent	Effective Date	Percent
August 1, 1939	4½	November 24, 1980	13½
April 24, 1950	4¼	March 9, 1981	14
May 2, 1953	4½	April 13, 1981	14½
December 3, 1956	5	May 8, 1981	15½
August 5, 1957	5¼	August 17, 1981	16½
September 23, 1959	5¾	September 14, 1981	17½
February 2, 1961	5½	October 12, 1981	16½
May 29, 1961	5¼	November 16, 1981	15½
February 7, 1966	5½	January 25, 1982	16½
April 11, 1966	5¾	March 2, 1982	15½
October 3, 1966	6	August 9, 1982	15
May 7, 1968	6¾	August 24, 1982	14
January 24, 1969	7½	September 24, 1982	13½
January 5, 1970	8½	October 13, 1982	12½
December 2, 1970	8	November 15, 1982	12
January 13, 1971	7½	May 9, 1983	11½
February 18, 1971	7	June 8, 1983	12
August 10, 1973	7¾	July 11, 1983	12½
August 25, 1973	8½	August 1, 1983	13½
January 22, 1974	8¼	August 23, 1983	13
April 15, 1974	8½	November 1, 1983	12½
May 13, 1974	8¾	March 21, 1984	13
July 5, 1974	9	May 8, 1984	13½
August 14, 1974	9½	May 29, 1984	14
November 24, 1974	9	August 13, 1984	13½
January 21, 1975	8½	October 22, 1984	13
March 3, 1975	8	November 21, 1984	12½
April 28, 1975	8½	March 25, 1985	13
September 3, 1975	9	April 19, 1985	12½
January 5, 1976	8¾	May 21, 1985	12
March 30, 1976	8½	June 5, 1985	11½
October 18, 1976	8	November 20, 1985	11
May 31, 1977	8½	December 13, 1985	10½
February 28, 1978	8¾	March 3, 1986	9½
May 23, 1978	9	November 24, 1986	9
June 29, 1978	9½	January 19, 1987	8½
April 23, 1979	10	April 13, 1987	9½
September 26, 1979	10½	May 11, 1987	10
October 26, 1979	11½	September 8, 1987	10½
February 11, 1980	12	October 5, 1987	11
February 28, 1980	13	November 10, 1987	10½
April 3, 1980	14	February 1, 1988	9½
April 28, 1980	13	April 3, 1988	10
May 15, 1980	11½	May 23, 1988	10½
August 20, 1980	12	November 1, 1988	10
September 22, 1980	13	December 19, 1988	10½

*FHA rates have ''floated free'' since November 30, 1983. VA rates are still set by the government.

eventually paid off, any money remaining in the escrow account is returned to the borrower.

RESPA, the federal Real Estate Settlement and Procedures Act (discussed in Chapter 11), limits the amount of tax and insurance reserves that a lender may require.

Conventional, Insured and Guaranteed Loans

Mortgage loans fall into several classifications:

1. *Conventional loans* are those arranged entirely between borrower and lending institution.
2. *Government-backed loans* include those *insured* by the Federal Housing Administration (FHA) or *guaranteed* by the Veterans Administration (VA). With both types the actual loan comes from a local lending institution.
3. *Loans directly from the government* include State of New York Mortgage Agency (SONYMA) mortgages and Farmer's Home Administration (FmHA) loans.

Conventional Loans

In making conventional loans, lending institutions set their own standards within the scope of banking regulations. As a result, a variety of mortgage plans is often offered and some flexibility is occasionally available. Conventional mortgages may be fixed rate, adjustable rate, graduated payment, or a combination of plans.

The time between loan application and loan commitment can sometimes be expedited with conventional loans. Most conventional mortgages are not assumable by a subsequent buyer of the property or are assumable only with the lender's approval.

Private mortgage insurance. In general, conventional loans call for higher down payments (lower loan-to-value ratio) than do government-backed mortgages. Banking theory holds that it risks depositors' money to lend more than 80 percent of the value of real estate. With any down payment below 20 percent, therefore, a conventional loan in New York State must be accompanied by **private mortgage insurance (PMI)**. The borrower pays a yearly premium for insurance that protects the lender in case of loss at a foreclosure.

Adjustable rate mortgages. Until the early 1980s almost all mortgages were fixed rate. As interest rates began to skyrocket, lenders found themselves locked in to unprofitable long-term commitments with money lent out at rates like 5, 6, and 7 percent—far below the then-current cost of money. This led to serious problems for lending institutions and many were reluctant to make any further fixed-interest loans, even at high rates.

Out of a chaotic variety of new mortgage instruments, the *adjustable rate mortgage (ARM)* emerged and became a national standard. As interest rates rose, borrowers across the country increasingly chose ARMs. The ARM shifts the risk of changing interest rates to the borrower, who also stands to benefit if rates drop during the period of the loan.

The vocabulary of ARMs includes the following:

Adjustment period: The anniversary on which interest rate adjustments may be made. Most borrowers elect one-year adjustments although they might be made more frequently or after three or five years.

Index: The interest rate on the loan may go up or down, following the trend for interest rates across the country. The lender must key changes to some national indicator of current rates. The most commonly chosen **index** is the rate paid on one-year U.S. Treasury bills. Next in popularity is a less-volatile, slower-changing index, the 11th District Federal Home Loan Bank Average Cost of Funds.

Margin: If Treasury bills are the chosen index and they are selling at 10 percent interest at the time the loan is adjusted, the borrower pays a specific percentage above that index. That percentage is known as the **margin.** With a 2 percent margin over Treasury bills the borrower would be charged 12 percent.

Cap: The loan agreement may set a **cap** of, for example, 2 percent on any upward adjustment. If interest rates (as reflected by the index) went up 3 percent by the time of adjustment, the interest rate could be raised only 2 percent. Depending on the particular mortgage, the extra 1 percent might be treated one of three ways:

1. It could be saved by the lender to be used at the next adjustment period, even though rates had fallen in the meantime.
2. It could be absorbed by the lender with no future consequences to the borrower.
3. The shortfall (the unpaid 1 percent) could be added to the amount borrowed so that the principal would increase instead of decreasing (negative amortization).

Ceiling: A **ceiling** (sometimes called a *lifetime cap*) is a maximum allowable interest rate. Typically, a mortgage may offer a five-point ceiling. If the interest rate started at 11 percent, it could never go beyond 16 percent no matter what happened to national rates. A ceiling allows the borrower to calculate the *worst case*.

Worst case: If a 30-year adjustable loan for $85,000 costs $809 a month for principal and interest at 11 percent, and if the ceiling is 5 percent, the worst that could happen is that the rate would go to 16 percent. The borrower can calculate in advance what that could cost—$1,143 a month.

Negative amortization: Negative amortization could result from an artificially low initial interest rate. It also could follow a hike in rates larger than a cap allows the lender to impose. Not all mortgage plans include the possibility of negative amortization. Sometimes the lender agrees to absorb any shortfalls. The possibility must always be explored, however, when an ARM is being evaluated.

Convertability: This feature offers the best of both worlds. The borrower may choose to change the mortgage to a fixed-rate mortgage at then-current interest levels. With some plans any favorable moment may be chosen. More commonly the option is available on the third, fourth or fifth anniversary of the loan. Cash outlay for the conversion is low compared with the costs of placing a completely new mortgage; one point, or 1 percent of the loan, is typical. The borrower may be charged a slightly higher interest rate in return for this option.

Initial interest rate: With many loan plans the rate during the first year, or the first adjustment period, is set artificially low to induce the borrower to enter into the agreement ("teaser" rate). This enables some buyers, whose income might not otherwise qualify, to place new mortgage loans. Buyers who plan to be in a house for only a few years may be delighted with such arrangements, especially if no interest adjustment is planned for several years. Other borrowers, however, may end up with negative amortization and payment shock at the first adjustment.

Assumability: Many ARMs are assumable by the next owner of the property, usually with the lender's approval and the payment of one point or more in service fees.

To help consumers compare different ARMs, lenders must give anyone considering a specific adjustable rate mortgage a uniform disclosure statement that lists and explains indexes, history of past interest rate changes and other information. A method for calculating the worst case is included. The disclosures must be furnished before the loan applicant has paid any nonrefundable application fee.

FHA-Insured Loans

The Federal Housing Administration (FHA) was created in 1934 under the National Housing Act to encourage improvement in housing conditions and exert a stabilizing influence on the mortgage market. The FHA was the government's response to the lack of housing, excessive foreclosures and collapsed building industry that occurred during the Great Depression in the 1930s.

The FHA, which operates under the Department of Housing and Urban Development (HUD), neither builds homes nor lends money itself. Rather, *it insures loans on real property made by approved lending institutions*. It does not insure the property but it does insure the lender against loss. The common term **FHA loan**, then, refers to a loan that is *not made* by the agency, but *insured* by it.

Most FHA loans are processed through *direct endorsement* with lenders handling the paperwork within their own organizations. Borderline cases are forwarded to the FHA for final decision; this can add several weeks to the loan process.

FHA 203(b). The most widely used FHA mortgage is known as 203(b) and may be placed on one- to four-family residences. Among the requirements set up by the FHA before it will insure a loan:

1. In addition to paying interest, the borrower is charged a lump sum of between 2.9 and 3.8 percent of the loan as a **mortgage insurance premium (MIP).** This amount is payable at the closing or (more commonly) it may be financed for the term of the loan. If the loan is subsequently paid off within the first ten years, some refund of unused premium is due the borrower from HUD. (With FHA loans made before September 1, 1983, the borrower pays ½ percent annually as an insurance premium instead of the lump-sum MIP.)
2. The real estate must be evaluated by an FHA-approved appraiser. The required down payment will be based on the appraised value; if the purchase price is higher, the buyer must pay the difference in a higher cash down payment. On Section 203(b) loans minimum down payment requirements are:

    a. for property appraised under $50,000, 3 percent. A house appraised at $40,000 would require $1,200 down with a $38,800 mortgage possible. A 3 percent down payment means a 97 percent loan-to-value ratio.

    b. for property over $50,000, the requirement is 3 percent down on the first $25,000 and 5 percent down on the rest. A house appraised at $75,000 would require a down payment of 3 percent on the first $25,000 ($750) plus 5 percent of the remaining $50,000 ($2,500) for a total down payment of $3,250.

c. for property to be purchased by an investor rather than an owner-occupant, the down payment requirement is a minimum of 25 percent. Some lenders charge additional points for such loans.

3. The FHA sets top limits on its loans, depending on price levels in different areas. Its loan maximums vary from one county to another within the state. In the least expensive areas the limits are:

single-family dwellings	$67,500
two-family dwellings	76,000
three-family dwellings	92,000
four-family dwellings	107,000

In Bronx, Nassau, Orange and Warren counties, the maximum may be as high as:

single-family dwellings	$101,250
two-family dwellings	114,000
three-family dwellings	138,000
four-family dwellings	160,000

In other areas the limits fall between these figures. The FHA raises these limits from time to time to meet changing conditions.

4. The FHA may stipulate repair requirements to be completed before it will issue mortgage insurance on a specific property.

Certain energy-saving improvements may be financed along with an FHA mortgage. No prepayment penalties are charged if an FHA loan is paid off before the end of the term. When the final payment is made on a long-standing FHA loan, some refund of unused premiums left in the mortgage insurance pool may be due the borrower.

Assumability: Older FHA loans may be assumed (taken over along with the house) by the next owner of the property, with no change in interest rate, no credit check on the buyer and only a small charge for paperwork. The original borrower is not released from liability, however, unless the new borrower is willing to go through a *formal assumption*, which involves the lender's approval of credit and income.

For FHA loans made after December 1, 1986, a check of creditworthiness is required of the new borrower if the loan is assumed within the first year (or within the first two years, if the original borrower was a nonoccupant investor). No change takes place, however, in the interest rate or terms of the mortgage, and charges for the assumption are limited to $500. Even without a formal assumption, the original borrower on these newer FHA loans will be released of liability if the mortgage is still current (paid up to date) five years after an assumption.

Other FHA programs. Among other FHA programs, which may or may not be handled by local lenders at any given time, are adjustable rate mortgages and special plans intended for veterans, for rehabilitation of housing being purchased, and for no–down-payment purchase of modest homes.

Other FHA programs are sometimes available to finance mobile homes, manufactured housing, condominiums and rehabilitation construction of housing. In 1989, the FHA initiated a Price Level Adjusted Mortgage (PLAM), which indexed payments and the remaining principal according to inflation. The rationale was that the borrower's income would keep pace with the inflation rate, so that higher payments and a larger debt would still represent the same proportion of family income in years to come.

VA-Guaranteed (GI) Loans

Under the Servicemen's Readjustment Act of 1944 and later legislation, the Veterans Administration (VA) can guarantee lending institutions against loss on mortgage loans to eligible veterans. Because the VA guarantees the top 40 percent of the loan, no down payment is required (though individual lenders may sometimes ask for a small down payment). Although no top limit is set for the loan, the guarantee is for up to $36,000, which in practice dictates a loan of up to $144,000.

VA mortgages are intended only for owner-occupied property, owned by veteran or veteran and spouse, and may be placed on one- to four-family residences. While the guarantee comes from the federal government, the loan itself is made by a local lending institution. The VA sets a standard nationwide interest rate and does not allow lenders to charge the veteran more than 1 percent as an origination fee; any other points must be paid by the seller. The veteran pays an additional 1 percent at closing, directly to the VA as a funding fee. As with FHA mortgages, no prepayment penalties may be charged.

Eligibility. The right to a VA guarantee does not expire. To qualify, a veteran must have a discharge that is "other than dishonorable," and the required length of service:

- For those who enlisted before September 7, 1980, 180 days' active service since September 16, 1940 (or 90 days' service during a war).
- For those who first enlisted after September 7, 1980, the requirement is for two years' active duty.

No amount of time in the reserves counts toward eligibility. Inservice VA loans are available to those still on active duty.

The veteran who applies for a VA loan must furnish a *certificate of eligibility*, which can be obtained by writing to:

VA Regional Office   VA Regional Office
Federal Building   252 7th Avenue
111 West Huron Street   or   New York, NY 10001
Buffalo, NY 14202   1-800-442-5882
1-800-462-1130

Even though the veteran has used some or all eligibility to guarantee one loan, it is sometimes possible to place another VA mortgage. Eligibility may still be available if:

- the first loan used only part of the $36,000 guarantee and the home has been sold (even with an assumption), or
- the original VA loan has been paid off, or
- the original VA loan was formally assumed by another veteran.

The widow or widower of a veteran who died of a service-connected disability and who has not remarried may use the veteran's eligibility.

Assumability. Any VA mortgage loan made before March 1, 1988, may be assumed by the next owner of the property, who need not be a veteran and need not prove qualification to the lender or the VA. For loans made after March 1, 1988, the assumer (who need not be a veteran) must prove creditworthiness, and a fee of up to $500 may be charged for the paperwork involved.

Additional Financing Techniques

A borrower and a lender can tailor financing instruments to suit the type of transaction and the financial needs of both parties by altering the terms of the basic mortgage and note. Especially in times of tight or expensive mortgage money, such *creative financing* gains prominence. In addition real estate may be financed using instruments other than mortgages, such as personal loans or barter.

Strictly speaking, a **purchase-money mortgage** is any mortgage placed when property is bought. This is in contrast to *refinancing*, further borrowing after the realty is already owned. In many areas, however, the term *purchase-money mortgage* is reserved for a mortgage taken by the seller to enable the buyer to purchase ("seller take-back financing"). A purchase-money mortgage is usually given to cover a portion of the purchase price; it may be given to finance the entire purchase price (especially in times of tight money). This may be a first or second mortgage. In the event of the foreclosure of a purchase-money mortgage, the lien takes priority over judgment liens against the borrower and homestead exemptions of the borrower and spouse. A purchase-money mortgage held by the seller is generally considered exempt from usury limitations on interest. If seller-financing is at an artificially low interest rate, however, the Internal Revenue Service will "impute" a higher rate and tax the recipient accordingly.

Imputed interest. If the amount of seller financing in a transaction is $2.8 million or less, the seller must charge no less than 9 percent interest or a rate equal to the applicable federal rate (AFR), whichever is lower. The AFR is set monthly by the federal government. If the seller charged a rate lower than required, he or she would be taxed as if income had been received at the required rate. An exception is made for certain transfers of vacant land within a family.

A **reverse annuity loan** is one in which regular monthly payments are made *to the borrower* based on the equity the homeowner has in the property given as security for the loan. A reverse mortgage allows senior citizens on fixed incomes to tap the equity buildup in their homes without having to sell. The loan accumulates interest and is eventually paid from the sale of the property or from the mortgagor's estate upon his or her death. New York allows such mortgages where the homeowner is at least 60 years old.

The American Association of Retired Persons has taken an active role in pioneering these loans, and the federal government experimented, in 1989, with a reverse mortgage it called a home equity conversion mortgage (HECM), intended for those 62 or older. The FHA-HUD program offered several options: homeowners could receive regular payments as long as they lived in the home, a set period of time could be arranged for payments or a letter of credit could establish a certain amount of money the homeowner could draw against at will.

The amount of monthly payments were based on factors like the age of the borrower(s) and the home's appraised value. If the borrower remained in the home, no repayment was due during the homeowner's lifetime.

Home equity loans, a form of second mortgage, have grown in popularity in recent years, following the limit of income–tax deductibility for consumer loans. Similar to older home-improvement loans, they may be used for any purpose. Homeowners whose property has appreciated in value may borrow up to new loan-to-value ratios or, in one popular version, establish a line of credit, borrowing against it as they choose.

The homeowner who is selling one residence and buying another may find it necessary to purchase the new home before the closing date on the present one. In that situation a temporary loan, variously called a *bridge loan, swing loan* or **interim financing** may be arranged. Such loans usually provide for interest-only payments and are intended for no more than six months.

Under a **shared equity mortgage** the purchaser receives some financial help in the form of a contribution toward the down payment, a concessionary interest rate or assistance with monthly payments. The "partner" may be a lending institution, the seller, the government or a relative. Typically the partner receives a share of profit when the property is sold.

A **package loan** not only includes the real estate but also *all fixtures and appliances on the premises*. In recent years this kind of loan has been used extensively in financing furnished condominium units. Such loans usually include the kitchen range, refrigerator, dishwasher and other appliances, as well as furniture, drapes and carpets in the sale price of the home.

A **blanket mortgage** covers *more than one parcel or lot* and is used to finance subdivision developments. These mortgages often include a provision, known as a *partial release clause,* that the borrower may obtain the release of any one lot or parcel from the lien by repaying a definite amount of the loan.

A **wraparound mortgage** is frequently used as a method of refinancing real property or financing the purchase of real property when an existing mortgage is to be retained. It is also used to finance the sale of real estate when the buyer wishes to put up a minimum of initial cash for the sale. The buyer gives a wraparound mortgage to the seller, who will collect payments on the new loan usually at a higher interest rate and continue to make payments on the old loan. The buyer should require a protective clause in the document granting him or her the right to make payments directly to the original lender in the event of a default by the seller. Wraparound mortgages, like all unusual arrangements, require careful study by the buyer's and seller's attorneys. The broker who negotiates one should exercise special care not to give legal advice.

An **open-end mortgage** is frequently used by borrowers to obtain additional funds to improve their property. The borrower "opens" the mortgage to increase the debt after the debt has been reduced by payments over a period of time. The lender is not obligated to advance the additional funds.

A **construction loan,** or *building loan agreement,* is made to *finance the construction of improvements* on real estate (homes, apartments, office buildings, and so forth). Under a construction loan the lender disburses the loan proceeds while the building is being constructed. A building loan can be difficult to secure if an individual is not working through a recognized builder or contractor.

Payments are made from time to time to the *general contractor* or owner for that part of the construction work that has been completed since the previous payment. Prior to each payment the lender usually inspects the work; the owner or general contractor must provide the lender with adequate waivers of lien releasing all mechanics' lien rights (*see* Chapter 24) for the work covered by the payment. This kind of mortgage loan generally bears a higher interest rate because of the risks assumed by the lender. This type of financing is short term. The borrower is expected to arrange for a permanent loan (also known as an *end,* or *take-out loan*) that will repay the construction lender when the work is completed.

Sale-and-leaseback arrangements are sometimes used as a means of financing large commercial or industrial plants. The land and building used by the seller for business purposes are sold to an investor such as an insurance company. The real estate is then leased back by the buyer (the investor) to the seller, who continues to conduct business on the property as a tenant. The buyer becomes the lessor and the original owner becomes the lessee. This enables a business firm that has money invested in a plant to free that money for working capital. The buyer benefits from an assured long-term tenant.

Sale-and-leaseback arrangements are complex. They involve complicated legal procedures and their success is usually related to the effects the transaction has on the firm's income tax liability. A real estate broker should consult with legal and tax experts when involved in this type of transaction.

As discussed in Chapter 5, real estate can be purchased under a **land contract,** also known as a contract for deed, installment contract, agreement of sale or articles of agreement for warranty deed. Real estate is often sold on contract in one of two situations: (1) when mortgage financing is not available or is too expensive or (2) when the purchaser does not have a sufficient down payment to cover the difference between a mortgage loan and the selling price of the real estate.

Sources of Real Estate Financing— The Primary Mortgage Market

The funds used to finance the purchase of real estate come from a variety of sources that comprise the **primary mortgage market**—lenders who supply funds to borrowers as an investment. Lenders may originate loans for the purpose of selling them to other investors as part of what is termed the *secondary mortgage market.* The secondary mortgage market is discussed later in this chapter.

Almost half the loans made to finance real estate purchases are obtained from financial institutions designed to hold individuals' savings ("thrifts"). These institutions lend out and invest these deposits to earn interest, some of which is directed back to the savers, some of which is retained as income. Mortgage loans are generally made by institutional lenders such as savings and loan associations, commercial banks, mutual savings banks, life insurance companies, mortgage banking companies, mortgage brokers, credit unions, pension and trust funds and finance companies. Individuals (sellers, investors, employers, brokers and relatives) occasionally are sources for financing.

Savings and loan associations are the most active participants in the home-loan mortgage market, specializing in long-term residential loans. A savings and loan earns money by paying less for the funds it receives than it charges for the loans it makes. Loan income includes loan origination fees, loan assumption fees and points.

Traditionally, savings and loan associations are the most flexible of all the lending institutions with regard to their mortgage lending procedures, and they are generally local in nature. In addition, they participate in FHA-insured and VA-guaranteed loans, though only to a limited extent.

All savings and loan associations must be chartered, either by the federal government or by the states in which they are located. *All* savings and loans are regulated by the Federal Home Loan Bank system (FHLB). The FHLB sets up mandatory guidelines for member associations and provides depositors with savings insurance through the Federal Savings and Loan Insurance Corporation (FSLIC).

Commercial banks are an important source of real estate financing. Primarily, bank loan departments handle such short-term loans as construction, home-improvement and mobile-home loans. In some areas, however, commercial banks originate one-quarter of home mortgages. Commercial banks usually issue a larger proportion of VA and FHA loans than do savings and loan associations. Like the savings and loan associations, banks must be chartered by the state or federal government. Bank deposits are insured by the Federal Deposit Insurance Corporation (FDIC).

These institutions, which operate like savings and loan associations, are located mainly in New York and New England. They issue no stock and are mutually owned by their investors. They are primarily savings institutions and are highly active in the mortgage market.

Insurance companies amass large sums of money from the premiums paid by their policyholders. A certain portion of this money is held in reserve to satisfy claims and cover operating expenses, but much of it is invested in profit-earning enterprises, such as long-term real estate loans.

Most insurance companies like to invest their money in large, long-term loans that finance commercial and industrial properties. They also invest in residential mortgage loans by purchasing large blocks of government-backed loans (FHA-insured and VA-guaranteed loans) from the Federal National Mortgage Association and other agencies that warehouse such loans for resale in the secondary mortgage market.

In addition, many life insurance companies seek to further ensure the safety of their investments by insisting on equity positions (known as *equity kickers*) in many projects they finance. This means that the company requires a partnership arrangement with, for example, a project developer or subdivider as a condition of making a loan. This is called *participation financing*.

Mortgage banking companies use money borrowed from other institutions and funds of their own to make real estate loans that may later be sold to investors (with the mortgage company receiving a fee for servicing the loans). Mortgage bankers are involved in all types of real estate loan activities and often serve as middlemen between investors and borrowers, but they are not mortgage *brokers*.

Mortgage banking companies are subject to considerably fewer lending restrictions than are commercial banks or savings and loans. Mortgage bankers originate about one-quarter of all home loans.

Mortgage brokers are individuals who are licensed to act as intermediaries in bringing borrowers and lenders together. Mortgage brokers charge a fee, often of the borrower, for their services. They usually handle large commercial transactions.

Credit unions are cooperative organizations in which members place money in savings accounts usually at higher interest rates than other savings institutions offer. In the past most credit unions made only short-term consumer and home-improvement loans but in recent years they have been branching out into originating longer-term first and second mortgage loans.

The **State of New York Mortgage Agency (Sonny Mae** or **SONYMA)** raises funds through the sale of bonds. The money is channeled into mortgages targeted for specific purposes in specific locations. Loans are made through local lending institutions, typically at below-market interest rates.

The **Farmer's Home Administration (FmHA)** is a federal agency of the Department of Agriculture that channels credit to rural residents as well as to certain small communities. FmHA loan programs fall into two categories: (1) guaranteed loans made and serviced by a private lender and guaranteed for a specific percentage by the FmHA and (2) insured loans that are originated, made and serviced by the agency. For low-income first-time homebuyers, mortgage interest may be subsidized as low as 1 percent. Only modest residences are eligible.

Application for Credit

All mortgage lenders require prospective borrowers to file an application for credit that provides the lender with basic information needed to evaluate the proposed loan. The application includes information regarding the purpose of the loan, the amount, rate of interest and the proposed terms of repayment.

A prospective borrower must submit personal information to the lender including age, family status, employment, earnings, assets and financial obligations. Details of the real estate that will be the security for the loan must be provided, including legal description, improvements, title, survey and taxes. For loans on income property or those made to corporations, additional information is required, such as financial and operating statements, schedules of leases and tenants and balance sheets. Those self-employed will be asked to show two years' income tax returns.

Through the process known as **underwriting** the lender carefully investigates the application information, studying credit reports and an appraisal of the property before deciding whether to grant the loan. The lender's acceptance of the application is written in the form of a *loan commitment*, which creates a contract to make a loan and sets forth the details.

Qualifying ratios. With each mortgage plan offered a lender will specify certain *qualifying ratios* that will be applied to each borrower. A typical ratio might be 25/33; the borrower will be allowed to spend up to 25 percent of gross monthly income for housing expense (PITI) or up to 33 percent of income after other payments on long-term debts have been subtracted. The lender calculates the maximum monthly payment each way and allows only the lower figure.

**Government
Influence in
Mortgage Lending**

Aside from FHA-insured and VA-guaranteed loan programs the federal government influences mortgage lending through the Federal Reserve System as well as through various federal agencies such as the Farmers' Home Administration. It also deals in the secondary mortgage market through the Federal National Mortgage Association, the Government National Mortgage Association and the Federal Home Loan Mortgage Corporation.

**Federal Reserve
System**

Established in 1913 under President Woodrow Wilson, the Federal Reserve System ("the Fed") operates to maintain sound credit conditions, help counteract inflationary and deflationary trends and create a favorable economic climate. The Fed regulates the flow of money and interest rates in the marketplace indirectly through its member banks by controlling their *reserve requirements* and *discount rates*.

Reserve controls. The Federal Reserve requires each member bank to keep a certain amount of its assets on hand as reserve funds unavailable for loans or any other use. By increasing its reserve requirements the Federal Reserve in effect limits the amount of money that member banks can use to make loans, causing interest rates to increase.

In this manner the government can slow down an overactive economy by limiting the number of loans that would have been directed toward major purchases of goods and services. The opposite is also true: By decreasing the reserve requirements the Federal Reserve can allow more loans to be made, thus increasing the amount of money circulated in the marketplace and causing interest rates to decline.

Discount rates. Federal Reserve member banks are permitted to borrow money from the district reserve banks. The interest rate that the district banks charge for the use of this money is called the *discount rate*. This rate is the basis on which the banks determine the percentage rate of interest that they in turn charge their loan customers. Theoretically when the Federal Reserve discount rate is high, bank interest rates are high; therefore fewer loans will be made and less money will circulate in the marketplace. Conversely a lower discount rate results in lower interest rates, more bank loans and more money in circulation.

**Government
Influence in the
Secondary Market**

Mortgage lending takes place in both the primary and secondary mortgage markets. The *primary market,* which this chapter has dealt with thus far, includes: (1) lenders who supply funds to borrowers as an investment and keep the loans in their own *portfolio* and (2) lenders who also originate loans for the purpose of selling them to investors. Loans are bought and sold in the **secondary market** after they have been originated. A lender may wish to sell a number of loans in order to raise immediate funds when it needs more money to meet the mortgage demands in its area.

A major source of secondary mortgage market activity is a *warehousing agency,* which purchases a number of mortgage loans and assembles them into one or more packages of loans for resale to investors. The major warehousing agencies are the Federal National Mortgage Association (FNMA), the Government National Mortgage Association (GNMA) and the Federal Home Loan Mortgage Corporation (FHLMC).

Federal National Mortgage Association. The Federal National Mortgage Association, often referred to as **Fannie Mae,** is a privately owned corporation that provides a secondary market for mortgage loans. The corporation raises funds to purchase loans by selling government-guaranteed FNMA bonds at market interest rates.

Mortgage bankers are actively involved with FNMA, originating loans and selling them to FNMA while retaining the servicing functions. FNMA is the nation's largest purchaser of mortgages.

When Fannie Mae talks, lenders listen. Because FNMA eventually purchases one mortgage out of every ten, it has great influence on lending policies. When Fannie Mae announces that it will buy a certain type of loan, local lending institutions often change their own regulations to meet the stated criteria. When lenders are experimenting with new types of loans, a Fannie Mae announcement can result in standardization of the innovative mortgage plans and bring order out of chaos.

Government National Mortgage Association. The common name for the Government National Mortgage Association is **Ginnie Mae.** The *Ginnie Mae pass-through certificate* lets small investors buy a share in a pool of mortgages that provides for a monthly "pass-through" of principal and interest payments directly to the certificate holder. The certificates are guaranteed by Ginnie Mae.

Federal Home Loan Mortgage Corporation. The Federal Home Loan Mortgage Corporation, or **Freddie Mac,** provides a secondary market for mortgage loans, primarily conventional loans. Freddie Mac has the authority to purchase mortgages, pool them and sell bonds in the open market with the mortgages as security.

Many lenders use the standardized forms and follow the guidelines issued by Freddie Mac because use of FHLMC forms is mandatory for lenders who wish to sell mortgages in the agency's secondary mortgage market. The standardized documents include loan applications, credit reports and appraisal forms.

Nonconforming Loans

Because each participant in the secondary market sets its own standards for the packages of mortgages it will buy, loans offered by local institutions tend toward uniformity. When Fannie Mae and Freddie Mac announce that they will buy loans of up to $187,600, for example, many local lenders will set that as their limit.

Loans higher than the secondary market's limit are known as **jumbo loans,** and the borrower who wants to place one would search for a local lending institution that is making portfolio loans—lending its own money and taking mortgages it intends to hold in its own portfolio without selling them to secondary investors. Portfolio loans, known as *nonconforming* mortgages because they do not have to meet uniform underwriting standards, can be flexible in their guidelines. The borrower with an unusual credit situation or the unique house may need a portfolio loan. A lending institution may want such loans at one time but not at other times. Following the rapidly changing mortgage market is often the largest part of a real estate broker's work.

Financing Legislation

The federal government regulates the lending practices of mortgage lenders through the Truth-in-Lending Act, Equal Credit Opportunity Act and the Real Estate Settlement Procedures Act.

Regulation Z

Commonly referred to as the *Truth-in-Lending Act,* **Regulation Z** requires credit institutions to inform borrowers of the true cost of obtaining credit so that the borrower can compare the costs of various lenders and avoid the uninformed use of credit. *All real estate transactions made for personal or agricultural purposes are covered.* The regulation does not apply to business or commercial loans.

Regulation Z requires that the customer be fully informed of all finance charges, as well as the true annual interest rate, before a transaction is consummated. In the case of a mortgage loan made to finance the purchase of a dwelling the lender must compute and disclose the annual percentage rate (APR).

Creditor. A *creditor,* for purposes of Regulation Z, is a person who extends consumer credit more than 25 times a year or more than five times a year if the transaction involves a dwelling as security. The credit must be subject to a finance charge or payable in more than four installments by written agreement.

Three-day right of rescission. In the case of most consumer credit transactions covered by Regulation Z, the borrower has three days in which to rescind the transaction merely by notifying the lender. This right of rescission does not apply to residential purchase-money first mortgage loans. In an emergency, the right to rescind may be waived in writing to prevent a delay in funding.

Advertising. Regulation Z provides strict regulation of real estate advertisements that include mortgage financing terms. General phrases like "liberal terms available" may be used, but if specifics are given they must comply with this act. By the provisions of the act, the APR—which includes all charges—rather than the interest rate alone *must be stated.* The total finance charge must be specified as well.

Specific credit terms, such as the down payment, monthly payment, dollar amount of the finance charge or term of the loan, may not be advertised unless the following information is set forth as well: cash price; required down payment; number, amounts and due dates of all payments; and annual percentage rate. The total of all payments to be made over the term of the mortgage must also be specified unless the advertised credit refers to a first mortgage to finance acquisition of a dwelling.

Penalties. Regulation Z provides penalties for noncompliance. The penalty for violation of an administrative order enforcing Regulation Z is $10,000 for each day the violation continues. A fine of up to $10,000 may be imposed for engaging in an unfair or deceptive practice. In addition, a creditor may be liable to a consumer for twice the amount of the finance charge, for a minimum of $100 and a maximum of $1,000, plus court costs. attorney's fees and any actual damages. Willful violation is a misdemeanor punishable by a fine of up to $5,000 or one year's imprisonment, or both.

Federal Equal Credit Opportunity Act

The Federal Equal Credit Opportunity Act (ECOA) prohibits lenders and others who grant or arrange credit to consumers from discriminating against credit applicants on the basis of race, color, religion, national origin, sex, marital status, age (provided the applicant is of legal age) or dependence on public assistance. Lenders must inform all rejected credit applicants in writing of the principal reasons why credit was denied or terminated.

Real Estate Settlement Procedures Act

The federal Real Estate Settlement Procedures Act (RESPA) was created to ensure that the buyer and seller in a residential real estate transaction involving a new first mortgage loan have knowledge of all settlement costs. This important federal law will be discussed in detail in Chapter 11.

Summary

The note for most common forms of mortgage loans provide for *amortization,* the gradual repayment of principal borrowed along with interest. The note also sets the rate of *interest* at which the loan is made that the mortgagor must pay as a charge for borrowing the money. Charging more than the maximum interest rate allowed by state statute is called *usury* and is illegal. Sellers taking back mortgages are exempt from usury limits.

Newly popular in recent years are *adjustable rate mortgages,* under which the interest rate is changed each *adjustment period* to a stipulated *margin* above a national *index* of current mortgage rates. A *cap* may limit the size of possible adjustments and a *ceiling* may limit the maximum adjustment over the life of the loan. In instances where monthly payments do not cover the interest due, *negative amortization* is possible, with the total debt increasing instead of decreasing as it does with normal *amortization.*

Mortgage loans include conventional loans, those *insured by the FHA or an independent mortgage insurance company,* and those *guaranteed by the VA.* FHA and VA loans must meet certain requirements in order for the borrower to obtain the benefits of the government backing that induces the lender to lend its funds. Fixed interest rates must be charged for VA loans. Lenders may charge *discount points;* each point is 1 percent of the new mortgage. FHA and VA mortgages are generally assumable, with some exceptions and regulations.

Other types of real estate financing include purchase-money mortgages, buydowns, graduated payment loans, shared equity loans, reverse mortgages, blanket mortgages, package mortgages, open-end mortgages, wraparound mortgages, construction loans, sale-and-leaseback agreements, land contracts and investment group financing.

The federal government affects real estate financing money and interest rates through the Federal Reserve Board's *discount rate* and *reserve requirements;* it also participates in the *secondary mortgage market.* The secondary market is composed of investors who ultimately purchase and hold the loans as investments. These include insurance companies, investment funds and pension plans. *Fannie Mae* (Federal National Mortgage Association), *Ginnie Mae* (Government National Mortgage Association) and *Freddie Mac* (Federal Home Loan Mortgage Corporation) take an active role in creating a secondary market by regularly purchasing mortgage loans from originators and retaining, or *warehousing,* them until investment purchasers are available.

Regulation Z, the federal Truth-in-Lending Act, requires institutional lenders to inform prospective borrowers who use their homes as security for credit of *all finance charges* involved in the loan. Severe penalties are imposed for noncompliance. The *Federal Equal Credit Opportunity Act* prohibits creditors from discriminat ing against credit applicants on the basis of race, color, religion, national origin, sex, marital status, age or dependence on public assistance. The *Real Estate Settlement Procedures Act* requires lenders to inform both buyers and sellers in advance of all fees and charges for the settlement or closing of a residential real estate transaction.

Questions

1. A savings and loan institution offers a mortgage plan with an 80 percent loan-to-value ratio. On the purchase of a $120,000 property, how much down payment will be required?
   a. $20,000   c. $40,000
   b. $24,000   d. $80,000

2. A borrower obtains a $76,000 mortgage loan at 11½ percent interest. If the monthly payments of $785 are credited first on interest and then on principal, what will the balance of the principal be after the borrower makes the first payment?
   a. $75,215.00   c. $75,543.66
   b. $75,943.33   d. $75,305.28

3. When Tiny Tim buys his house, Old Scrooge allows monthly mortgage payments to be figured on a 30-year basis so that Tim can handle them. At the end of the fifth year, however, Scrooge wants the whole remaining debt paid off in a:
   a. graduated payment.
   b. shared-equity payment.
   c. balloon payment.
   d. blanket payment.

4. With some exceptions, a homeowner may take as an income tax deduction:
   a. mortgage insurance premium.
   b. mortgage interest paid.
   c. property insurance premium.
   d. all of the above.

5. New York's usury limits still apply to interest on mortgage loans by:
   a. sellers.
   b. individuals other than sellers.
   c. regular lending institutions.
   d. the FHA.

6. Norman Emanuel sells his home for $150,000 and agrees to pay three points to his buyer's lending institution. The buyer is putting 20 percent down on the property. How much will the points cost Norman?
   a. $900   c. $4,500
   b. $3,600   d. $60,000

7. A lending institution may require the buyer to send in an extra monthly payment to cover future bills for:
   a. property taxes and insurance premiums.
   b. major repairs.
   c. possible default in monthly payments.
   d. all of the above.

8. Which of the following is an example of a conventional loan?
   a. A mortgage loan insured by the Federal Housing Administration
   b. A second loan for home improvements secured through a credit union
   c. A mortgage obtained through a private lender with a VA guarantee
   d. All of the above

9. Private mortgage insurance (PMI) is required whenever the:
   a. loan is to be placed with the FHA.
   b. property covers more than 2.5 acres.
   c. loan exceeds $67,500.
   d. buyer is putting less than 20 percent down on a conventional loan.

10. The Department of Housing and Urban Development insures mortgage loans made through:
    a. the FHA.   c. Fannie Mae.
    b. the VA.   d. Freddie Mac.

11. No down payment is required for loans made through:
    a. the FHA.   c. Fannie Mae.
    b. the VA.   d. Freddie Mac.

12. Money for FHA and VA mortgages comes from:
    a. different departments of the federal government.
    b. qualified local lending institutions.
    c. the Federal Reserve Bank.
    d. the secondary mortgage market.

13. The government lends money directly in which kind of loan?
    a. FHA   c. Farmer's Home
    b. VA   d. All of the above

14. The terms *index, margin* and *cap* are used in evaluating what type of mortgage?

    a. Package   c. Conventional
    b. Blanket   d. Adjustable rate

15. The Carters purchased a residence for $75,000. They made a down payment of $15,000 and agreed to assume the seller's existing mortgage, which had a current balance of $23,000. The Carters financed the remaining $37,000 of the purchase price by giving a mortgage and note to the seller. This type of loan, by which the seller becomes the mortgagee, is called a:

    a. wraparound mortgage.
    b. package mortgage.
    c. balloon note.
    d. purchase-money mortgage.

16. The bank that will make a lower-rate loan in return for the payment of extra points is offering a:

    a. reduced loan-to-value ratio.
    b. graduated payment loan.
    c. buydown.
    d. second mortgage.

17. Negative amortization refers to a situation in which:

    a. debt is gradually reduced through monthly payments.
    b. debt grows larger instead of smaller each month.
    c. regular adjustments reduce the interest rate.
    d. the interest rate may rise or fall according to an index.

18. The McBains are purchasing a lakefront summer home in a new resort development. The house is completely equipped and furnished and the McBains have obtained a loan that covers the purchase price of the residence including the furnishings and equipment. This kind of financing is called a(n):

    a. wraparound mortgage.
    b. package mortgage.
    c. blanket mortgage.
    d. unconventional loan.

19. A developer obtains one mortgage for a whole subdivision. As he sells each lot, he obtains a release of one parcel from the:

    a. package mortgage.
    b. reverse mortgage.
    c. balloon mortgage.
    d. blanket mortgage.

20. Tom Terrific buys a local factory from a company that intends to remain and rent it from him. Tom has put together an:

    a. equity-sharing transaction.
    b. sale and leaseback.
    c. secondary market.
    d. reserve for escrow.

21. Which of the following best defines the *secondary market?*

    a. Lenders who exclusively deal in second mortgages
    b. Lenders who buy and sell mortgages after they have been originated
    c. The major lender of residential mortgages
    d. The major lender of FHA and VA loans

22. Fannie Mae is:

    a. the leading purchaser of mortgages on the secondary market.
    b. a lender for homes in rural areas.
    c. a government agency that regulates interest rates.
    d. an old crone who lives in a cave.

23. The public can invest in mortgage pools by buying certificates issued by the:

    a. Federal Reserve Bank.
    b. Farmer's Home Administration.
    c. Government National Mortgage Association.
    d. Guaranteed Mortgage Fund.

24. Freddie Mac:

    a. mortgages are guaranteed by the full faith and credit of the federal government.
    b. buys and pools blocks of conventional mortgages, selling bonds with such mortgages as security.
    c. affects the mortgage market through adjustment of the discount rate.
    d. forbids the charging of more than one point to the buyer.

25. Regulation Z protects the consumer from:

    a. misleading advertising.
    b. fraudulent mortgage plans.
    c. discrimination in lending.
    d. substandard housing.

Appendix: Amortization Schedule

**Monthly Payment
Needed to Amortize a
Loan of $1,000**

			Numbers of Years		
Annual Interest Rate	1	5	15	25	30
8 %	86.99	20.27	9.56	7.72	7.34
8¼	87.10	20.40	9.70	7.88	7.51
8½	87.22	20.52	9.85	8.05	7.69
8¾	87.34	20.64	9.99	8.22	7.87
9	87.45	20.76	10.14	8.39	8.05
9¼	87.57	20.88	10.29	8.56	8.23
9½	87.68	21.00	10.44	8.74	8.41
9¾	87.80	21.12	10.59	8.91	8.59
10	87.92	21.25	10.75	9.09	8.78
10¼	88.04	21.38	10.90	9.27	8.97
10½	88.15	21.50	11.05	9.45	9.15
10¾	88.27	21.62	11.20	9.63	9.34
11	88.39	21.75	11.37	9.81	9.53
11¼	88.50	21.87	11.52	9.99	9.72
11½	88.62	22.00	11.69	10.17	9.91
11¾	88.73	22.12	11.84	10.35	10.10
12	88.85	22.25	12.00	10.54	10.29
12¼	88.97	22.38	12.16	10.72	10.48
12½	89.09	22.50	12.33	10.91	10.68
12¾	89.20	22.63	12.49	11.10	10.87
13	89.32	22.76	12.65	11.28	11.07
13¼	89.43	22.88	12.82	11.47	11.26
13½	89.56	23.01	12.98	11.66	11.45
13¾	89.68	23.14	13.15	11.85	11.65
14	89.79	23.27	13.32	12.04	11.85
14¼	89.91	23.40	13.49	12.23	12.05
14½	90.02	23.53	13.66	12.42	12.25
14¾	90.15	23.66	13.83	12.61	12.44
15	90.26	23.79	14.00	12.81	12.65
16	90.73	24.32	14.69	13.59	13.45
17	91.21	24.85	15.39	14.38	14.26

8

License Law and Ethics

Key Terms

Apartment information vendor
Article 12A
Associate broker
Blockbusting
Branch office
Broker
Code of Ethics
Commingle
Continuing education
Denial, suspension or revocation of license

Department of State (DOS)
Designation
GRI
Net listing
Principal broker
Qualifying course
Real estate license law
REALTOR®
Rules and regulations
Salesperson

Overview

Broker and salesperson license applicants are required to pass state examinations designed to test their knowledge of real estate principles and laws. Foremost among these is New York's real estate license law, which sets forth strict operating standards for licensees and penalties for noncompliance. This chapter will introduce the most basic provisions of New York's law as well as the rules and regulations of the Department of State, which administers real estate licensing services. An appendix reprints portions of the law as set forth in the state's study booklet for prospective licensees.

Real Estate License Laws in All States	All states, the District of Columbia, Puerto Rico and Canadian provinces have enacted **real estate license laws** that license and regulate the activities of real estate brokers and salespeople. Details of the law vary from state to state but the main provisions of state laws are similar. The purposes of the laws are: (1) to protect the public from dishonest or incompetent brokers or salespeople, (2) to prescribe qualifications for licensing brokers and salespeople and (3) to maintain high standards in the real estate business.
Basic Provisions of License Law	The New York Department of State, Division of Licensing Services has the power to issue licenses and enforce the real estate license law. The law is enforced through fines, reprimands and the **denial, suspension or revocation of licenses.**

The **Department of State (DOS)** has adopted a series of **rules and regulations** that further define the basic law, provide for its administration and set forth additional operating guidelines for brokers and salespeople. These administrative rules and regulations have the *same force and effect as the law* itself. Throughout this chapter all discussions of the license law also include the rules and regulations.

Violation of the license law is a misdemeanor punishable by up to a year in jail and a fine of up to $1,000.

The New York Real Property Law, **Article 12A,** which went into effect in 1922, is the main source of law for real estate licenses in New York. Copies of the law and regulations or a license application may be obtained by writing to:

New York Department of State
Division of Licensing Services
162 Washington Avenue
Albany, NY 12231

or to a local office listed in Table 8.1. The Licensing Division maintains a consumer assistance phone line in Albany at 518-474-4664.

Who Must Be Licensed?	Any person who for another and for a fee or the expectation thereof performs any of the activities described in the license law must hold a valid real estate license

Table 8.1 **Offices of the Department of State, Division of Licensing Services**		
	Albany	162 Washington Ave., Albany, NY 12231 518-474-4664
	Binghamton	State Office Bldg., Binghamton, NY 13901 607-773-7722
	Buffalo	65 Court St., Buffalo, NY 14202 716-847-7110
	Hauppauge	NYS Office Bldg., Veterans Hwy., Hauppauge, NY 11787 516-360-6579
	Mineola	114 Old Country Rd., Mineola, NY 11501 516-747-0700
	New York City	270 Broadway, New York, NY 10007 212-587-5747
	Rochester	189 N. Water St., Rochester, NY 14604 716-454-3094
	Syracuse	Hughes State Office Bldg., Syracuse, NY 13202 315-428-4258
	Utica	State Office Bldg., Utica, NY 13501 315-793-2533

Table 8.2	COUNTY	BROKERS	SALES-PERSONS	COUNTY	BROKERS	SALES-PERSONS
Real Estate Licensees by County in November 1988	ALBANY	704	1697	ONEIDA	302	803
	ALLEGANY	36	71	ONONDAGA	750	2489
	BRONX	817	1908	ONTARIO	161	505
	BROOME	360	1087	ORANGE	729	2337
	CATTARAUGUS	78	183	ORLEANS	41	152
	CAYUGA	88	199	OSWEGO	92	322
	CHAUTAUQUA	192	628	OTSEGO	103	369
	CHEMUNG	89	254	PUTNAM	279	881
	CHENANGO	74	226	QUEENS	3696	12848
	CLINTON	64	164	RENSSELAER	210	542
	COLUMBIA	177	438	RICHMOND	783	3087
	CORTLAND	48	126	ROCKLAND	802	2522
	DELAWARE	169	406	ST LAWRENCE	88	267
	DUTCHESS	700	2427	SARATOGA	355	2049
	ERIE	1067	4780	SCHENECTADY	283	932
	ESSEX	87	265	SCHOHARIE	52	207
	FRANKLIN	43	112	SCHUYLER	12	22
	FULTON	64	173	SENECA	39	91
	GENESEE	69	185	STEUBEN	84	255
	GREENE	169	418	SUFFOLK	4018	11595
	HAMILTON	21	52	SULLIVAN	216	553
	HERKIMER	72	267	TIOGA	47	123
	JEFFERSON	111	418	TOMPKINS	174	349
	KINGS	2793	7463	ULSTER	436	1059
	LEWIS	13	38	WARREN	222	701
	LIVINGSTON	61	186	WASHINGTON	61	228
	MADISON	67	235	WAYNE	93	274
	MONROE	1337	4481	WESTCHESTER	3364	7445
	MONTGOMERY	80	184	WYOMING	41	135
	NASSAU	4920	13708	YATES	30	116
	NEW YORK	8133	12849	OUTSIDE NYS	1632	969
	NIAGARA	203	725			
				STATE TOTAL	42101	110580

SOURCE: New York State, Department of State, Division of Licensing, "Report for the Month of November 1988."

unless specifically exempted. In 1989 New York State had more than 42,000 licensed brokers and 100,000 salespersons. Table 8.2 shows a breakdown of licenses by county.

Broker. A real estate broker is defined in the license law as any person, firm, partnership or corporation who for another and for a fee or the expectation of a fee performs any of the following services:

1. Negotiates any form of real estate transaction;
2. Lists or attempts to list real property for sale;
3. Negotiates a loan secured by a mortgage;
4. Negotiates or makes a lease;
5. Collects rents;
6. Sells a lot or parcel of land by auction;
7. Exchanges real property;
8. Relocates tenants;
9. Engages in resale of condominiums; or
10. Sells a business that includes real estate.

Soliciting, processing, placing and negotiating mortgage loans on one- to four-family dwellings for a fee also requires registration with the state banking department as a mortgage broker.

Salesperson. A real estate salesperson is one who assists in any of the services a broker performs and is associated with a broker.

A broker is authorized to operate his or her own real estate business; a salesperson can work only in the name of and under the supervision of a licensed broker. The salesperson may never accept any payment or commission from anyone except his or her supervising **(principal) broker.**

Exceptions. The provisions of the license law do not apply to:

1. public officers while they are performing their official duties.
2. persons acting under order of a court (executors, guardians, referees, administrators).
3. attorneys at law duly admitted to practice in the courts of New York. If an attorney employs real estate salespeople, however, he or she must obtain a real estate broker's license. Attorneys are not required to take the licensing examination.
4. a resident manager employed by one owner to manage rental property when the leasing of units or the collection of rents is part of the manager's regular duties.

Licensing Procedure

All applicants for a real estate license must submit a written application to the DOS on forms provided by the department, accompanied by the appropriate fees. To receive a license, applicants must pass an examination administered by the DOS. Persons who have been convicted of a felony may not obtain a New York real estate license unless they have received executive pardon or a certificate of good conduct from a parole board. The Department of State will also consider a *certificate of relief from disabilities* issued by a probation officer or a judge. A real estate licensee must be either a citizen of the United States or a permanent U.S. resident.

Broker's license. An applicant for the broker's license must be *19 years of age* or older. The license application must include:

1. the name and address of the applicant and the name under which he or she intends to conduct business. If the applicant is a partnership or corporation, the application must state the names and addresses of each partner or officer.
2. the place or places where business will be conducted.
3. the business or occupation held by the applicant for the two years preceding the date of application.
4. proof that the applicant successfully has completed *90 hours of real estate education* from an institution approved by the Department of State.
5. an affidavit stating that the applicant has actively participated in the real estate business as a licensed real estate salesperson under a broker's supervision for at least one year, or has at least two years' equivalent experience in the real estate business. The statement of experience, if used, must describe:
   - any transactions entered into during the two years (or more, if applicable).
   - the date and nature of each transaction, the names of the principals to each, the addresses of the subject properties and the nature and extent of the applicant's participation in each.
6. a passport-size photograph.

The broker who intends to do business under an assumed, partnership or corporate name must clear the name with the Division of Licensing Services, Department of State, before filing the application for a broker's license. A corporate name also must be cleared before filing with the Division of Corporations and State Records, and a trade name must be cleared with the county clerk.

Associate broker. A license as **associate broker** is available for the broker who wishes to work as a salesperson under the name and supervision of another broker. The associate broker must meet all the qualifications for a broker's license and pass the same examination, but transact business in the name of the sponsoring broker, exactly as a salesperson would. A separate application form is used and is signed not only by the applicant but also by the principal broker with whose firm the new broker will be associated.

Salesperson's license. An applicant for a salesperson's license must be *18 years of age* or older. The application must include:

1. proof that the applicant has successfully completed a 45-hour license qualifying course.
2. a statement by the sponsoring broker.
3. notice that the applicant has passed the license examination.
4. a $50 license fee.
5. the license application form, shown in Figure 8.1. (The application form is furnished by the school where the applicant completed the 45-hour course.)

Apartment information vendors. An apartment information vendor's license is available to anyone over the age of 18 who is trustworthy and able to maintain a $5,000 interest-bearing escrow account. The license is renewable annually for a $400 fee. Apartment information vendors must provide prospective tenants with a contract or receipt with specific information regarding the services they offer. They also must display a sign in all offices bearing the same information, post their license in all offices and notify the Department of State of any changes in name or address.

Fees. The Department of State charges the following application fees:

Broker, original license and renewal:	$150
Associate broker, original license and renewal:	150
Salesperson, original license and renewal:	50
Branch office, original and renewal:	150
Apartment information vendor's license:	400
License examination:	15

License Examinations

In approximately one-half the states, but not in New York, a uniform test is used. Furnished by Educational Testing Service (ETS) of Princeton, New Jersey, it contains nationwide material and a special state section for matters that differ from one area to another. Another uniform test, ACT, is used in some states. New York, however, has its own examinations.

Walk-in examinations are open to any interested person, either before or after completion of the 45-hour qualifying course. Applicants should arrive a half-hour before the scheduled examination times, 9:30 A.M., 11:00 A.M., and 1:30 P.M.

Figure 8.1
License Application

NYS DEPARTMENT OF STATE   162 WASHINGTON AVENUE
DIVISION OF LICENSING SERVICES   ALBANY, NY 12231-0001

Real Estate Salesperson Application

INSTRUCTIONS (READ CAREFULLY)

STATE

1. PRINT ALL RESPONSES IN INK, ONE CHARACTER FOR EACH SPACE PROVIDED. FOR EXAMPLE: N Y

2. A NONREFUNDABLE **$50** fee and your ORIGINAL EXAMINATION ADMISSION SLIP marked "PASSED" MUST ACCOM-
   PANY this application. The fee should be in the form of a check or money order made payable to the Department of
   State. DO NOT SEND CASH. Mail to the above address.

ELIGIBILITY

- You are not eligible to file this application if you are either a member of the partnership, or are an officer or own voting
  stock in the corporation that is the sponsoring broker.
- If you intend to be associated with any Real Estate Broker(s) other than the one named in this application, you must file
  separate applications and fees for each such association.

SOCIAL SECURITY NUMBER/EMPLOYER IDENTIFICATION NUMBER PRIVACY NOTIFICATION

The Department of State's Division of Licensing Services is required to collect the federal Social Security and Employer Identification
numbers of all licensees. The authority to request and maintain such personal information is found in section 5 of the Tax Law.
Disclosure by you is mandatory. The information is collected to enable the Department of Taxation and Finance to identify individuals,
businesses and others who have been delinquent in filing tax returns or may have understated their tax liabilities and to generally identify persons affected by the taxes administered by the Commissioner of Taxation and Finance. It will be used for tax administration
purposes and any other purpose authorized by the Tax Law, but will not be available to the public. A written explanation is required
where no numbers are provided. This information will be maintained in the Licensing Information System by the Director of Administration at the above address.

EXPLANATION OF NUMBER(S) NOT PROVIDED:

. . . .

_____
(Name of School)

CERTIFICATION OF SATISFACTORY COMPLETION

REAL ESTATE SALESPERSON COURSE (CODE) # S-_____

This certifies that _____ has satisfactorily completed a 45-hour
                                    (Name of Student)

salesperson qualifying education course in real estate approved by the Secretary of State in accordance with the provisions of Chapter 868 of the
Laws of 1977; that attendance of the student was in compliance with the law and that a passing grade was achieved on the final examination. The
course was completed on _____.

Authorized   X
Signature   _____

(SCHOOL
 SEAL)

Figure 8.1
(continued)

FOR OFFICE USE ONLY   CLASS   KEY   REG. NO.   CASH NO.   FEE
$50

E   W   S _ _ _   _ _ / _ _   B _ _ _   _ _ / _ _

READ ALL INSTRUCTIONS AND ELIGIBILITY REQUIREMENTS ON REVERSE BEFORE COMPLETING THIS APPLICATION.
REMEMBER: PRINT ALL RESPONSES IN INK: ONE CHARACTER FOR EACH SPACE PROVIDED.

1. APPLICANT'S NAME (LAST, FIRST, MI)

2. HOME ADDRESS (NUMBER AND STREET)

CITY   STATE   ZIP CODE

COUNTY   3. SOCIAL SECURITY NUMBER AND/OR FEDERAL EMPLOYER ID NUMBER (SEE OVER)

4. SPONSORING BROKER OR FIRM NAME (EXACTLY AS IT APPEARS ON THE BROKER'S LICENSE)

5. OFFICE ADDRESS AT WHICH APPLICANT WILL BE PERMANENTLY STATIONED (NUMBER AND STREET)

CITY   STATE   ZIP CODE

COUNTY

6. Are you 18 years of age or older? . . . . □ Yes □ No

7. Have you ever been convicted of a crime or offense (not a minor traffic violation) or has any license, commission
or registration ever been denied, suspended or revoked in this state or elsewhere?. . . . . □ Yes* □ No

   * If Yes, attach a statement of details.

8. Have you ever applied for or been issued a real estate broker's or salesperson's license in this state?. . . . . □ Yes* □ No

   * If Yes, in what year: _____   Under what name: _____

APPLICANT AFFIRMATION — I subscribe and affirm, under the penalties of perjury, that these statements are true and correct.

Applicant's Signature X_____ Date _____

REMEMBER: THE STATEMENT OF ASSOCIATION BELOW MUST BE COMPLETED; AND YOU MUST ENCLOSE YOUR $50
NONREFUNDABLE APPLICATION FEE AND ORIGINAL EXAMINATION APPLICATION SLIP MARKED "PASSED."

STATEMENT OF ASSOCIATION (MUST BE COMPLETED BY SPONSORING BROKER)

I am sponsoring the named applicant in accordance with the Real Property Law, section 441, 1(D).

BROKER NAME
(exactly as it appears
on Broker's License)
(Last, First, MI)

Signature X_____ Date _____

411201-554 (Rev. 6 88)

Examinations are held every *Monday* except legal holidays in Albany, Buffalo, Hauppauge, Mineola, New York City, Rochester and Syracuse.

Albany
Knights of Columbus Hall
375 Ontario Street

(Park in rear of building and enter through back door)

Buffalo
State Office Bldg.
65 Court Street
Hearing Rm. Part 5
Main Floor

Hauppauge
State Office Bldg.
Veterans Highway
2nd Floor
Room 2B-43

Mineola
Lever Building
114 Old Country Road
Dept. of State Office
3rd Floor

New York City
State Office Bldg.
270 Broadway
Sixth Floor

Rochester
State Office Bldg. Annex
189 North Water Street
1st Floor

(Off Andrews Street between St. Paul and State)

Syracuse
State Office Bldg.
333 Washington Street
Hearing Room
Main Floor

Walk-in examinations are held twice a month on Mondays in Binghamton, Newburgh, Utica and Yonkers. Examination times are 9:30 A.M., 11:00 A.M. and 1:30 P.M. (except Yonkers).

Binghamton
New York State Annex
164 Hawley Street
Room 303   3rd Floor

Newburgh
New York State Armory
355 South William Street

Utica
State Office Bldg.
207 Genesee Street
Dept. of State Office
7th Floor

Yonkers (at 4:00 P.M. and 5:30 P.M.)
Lincoln High School Cafeteria
375 Kneeland Ave.

(Thruway Exit 2 (Yonkers Raceway) West on Yonkers Ave. to St. Johns, South on St. Johns to Midland Terrace, one block to school)

Salespersons' examinations are held every other month in Plattsburgh and Watertown at 1:30 P.M.

Plattsburgh
Clinton County Community College
Lake Shore Drive
Route 9 South

Watertown
State Office Building
317 Washington Street
Dept. of State Office

The salesperson's examination covers material from both the state study booklet and the 45-hour license qualifying course. One hour is allowed for the test.

Examinees should bring to the examination two #2 pencils and a check or money order for $15 (no cash is accepted). An identifying thumbprint will be taken. Scrap paper is furnished and must be turned in before leaving the room. Calculators are allowed but must be noiseless and hand-held with no tape printout. Questions on each test are multiple-choice and true and false, and the passing grade is 70.

Notice of success or failure is mailed to the applicant's home address promptly. If the slip is marked "Passed," it is good for only 90 days toward a license application, which must also include proof of completion of the 45-hour qualifying course and a statement by the sponsoring broker. If 90 days elapse without a license application the state examination must be repeated. Unlimited retakes are allowed, each with a $15 fee.

In a typical recent year the Department of State administered 35,061 salespersons' examinations, with 28,285 passing and 6,776 failing, for a pass rate of better than 80%. Broker's examinations were taken by 4,164, of whom 3,328 passed and 836 failed, at about the same rate.

The *brokers' examination* contains 100 questions and runs for 2¾ hours. In recent years it has contained considerable material based on human rights and fair housing in addition to the subjects listed in the broker's study manual: Walk-in brokers' examinations are held two Tuesdays each month in most Department of State offices, less frequently in a few locations.

Issuing the License

Each license is issued for a two-year term. Each licensee receives a license and pocket card from the Department of State. A salesperson's principal broker must retain the salesperson's license. The pocket card must be carried by the salesperson. If a licensee does not renew the license within *two years* of its expiration, he or she must retake the licensing examination.

Summary of requirements. Table 8.3 shows the basic requirements for licensure as a real estate broker or salesperson in New York State.

The Department of State certifies certain educational institutions to offer two types of required courses, *qualifying* and *continuing education* courses.

One **qualifying course** covers the necessary 45 hours' instruction preliminary to a salesperson's license; the second 45-hour qualifying course completes the 90-hour prelicensing requirement for licensure as a broker. The courses must be taken in order. Topics to be covered and the time devoted to each are set by law. Successful completion requires 90% attendance and the passing of a final examination.

Continuing education courses fulfill requirements for *renewal* of licenses. In order to renew a broker's or salesperson's license, a licensee must fulfill a continuing education requirement consisting of study at an institution approved by the Department of State, during every four-year continuing education period. The requirement may be satisfied by successful completion during the four-year period of one of the following:

1. A 45-hour course that is *not* the original license-qualifying course, with at least 90% attendance, *or*
2. A 30-hour course with perfect attendance and a final examination, *or*
3. Three 15-hour modules, each with perfect attendance.

**Table 8.3
Requirements for
Licensing in New
York**

Salesperson:	Broker:
At least 18	At least 19
No felony*	No felony*
Permanent resident U.S.	Permanent resident U.S.
Sponsoring broker	Full year's experience*
45-hour course	90 hours' study
Pass state exam ($15)	Pass state exam ($15)
$50 (two years) license fee	$150 (two years)
*Some exceptions possible	

Unlike qualifying courses, continuing education courses may take several forms and may cover any material acceptable to the Department of State. Those exempted from the continuing education requirement include:

1. anyone who is a licensed broker at the time of license renewal and who has been continuously licensed as a full-time salesperson and/or broker for the preceding 15 years.
2. any licensee who took, during the preceding four-year period, a 45-hour license *qualifying course* for either a salesperson's or a broker's license.
3. New York State attorneys.

Licensing Corporations, Partnerships and Other Legal Entities

New York corporations, partnerships and other legal entities may obtain a real estate license from the Department of State. A license issued to a corporation entitles the president or other designated officers to act as a broker. A license must be secured by each officer who wishes to act as a broker; the appropriate fee must be paid for each license. Each partner in a partnership or each member of any other legal entity who desires to act as a broker in the firm's name also must pay a fee and obtain a license.

An associate broker could be a partner or part owner of a brokerage firm; a salesperson may not.

Licensing Nonresidents

Nonresidents of New York may be licensed as New York real estate brokers or salespersons by conforming to all the provisions of the license law except that they are not required to maintain a place of business within the state. The department will recognize the license issued to a real estate broker or salesperson by another state if the laws of his or her home state permit licenses to be issued to New York licensees without requiring them to take that state's licensing examination.

A list of the states that have such reciprocity agreements with New York is found in Table 8.4. If a particular state's laws do not include these provisions, the Department of State will require that the nonresident applicant meet the examination requirement.

Every nonresident applicant must file an irrevocable consent form, which would allow the nonresident to be sued in New York State.

Table 8.4 **States Offering** **Reciprocity with** **New York Licenses**	**Arkansas**	Broker only—two years licensure and current. (Business and Residence must be in Arkansas.)
	Connecticut	Broker and Sales—current licensure only. (Business and Residence must be in Connecticut.)
	Delaware	Broker and Sales—two years licensure and current. (Business and Residence must be in Delaware.)
	Massachusetts	Broker only—two years licensure and current. (Business and Residence must be in Massachusetts.)
	Nebraska	Broker and Sales—two years licensure and current. (Business and Residence must be in Nebraska.)
	New Jersey	Broker and Sales. Broker—two years licensure and current. Sales—current licensure only. (Must be licensed in same status as in New Jersey. Business and Residence must be in New Jersey.)
	Oklahoma	Broker only—two years licensure and current. (Business and Residence must be in Oklahoma.)
	Ohio	Broker and Sales. Two years licensure and current. (Business address must be in New York State. Residence address must be in Ohio.)
	West Virginia	Broker and Sales. Current licensure. (Business and Residence must be in West Virginia.)

All need *current* certification (dated within six [6] months, from the real estate commission where license was obtained), completed application, irrevocable consent form (except Ohio) and the appropriate fee.

Applicants from the state of New Jersey must also submit a completed licensure agreement form.

Applicants seeking a reciprocal real estate salesperson's license must be sponsored by a broker holding a current New York State broker's license.

General Operation of a Real Estate Business

Place of business. Every New York real estate broker must maintain a principal place of business within the state (with the rare exception of some nonresident brokers).

Business name and sign. Any business name used by a New York real estate broker must be approved by the Department of State. A sign readable from the sidewalk must be posted conspicuously on the outside of the building. If the office is located in an apartment building, office building or hotel, the broker's name and the words "Licensed Real Estate Broker" must be posted in the space that lists the names of the building's occupants.

Branch offices. A broker may maintain a branch office or offices; a supplemental license must be maintained for each branch. The principal broker must pay expenses for the branch office and supervise it closely.

Change of business address. Licensees must notify the department in writing of any change in their business address. A filing fee of $10 must accompany all such notifications. Failure to notify the department of a change is grounds for suspension of a license.

Display of licenses. The broker's license must be prominently displayed at his or her place of business. Salespersons' licenses need not be displayed.

Salesperson's transfer of employment. When a salesperson's employment is changed or terminated the supervising broker must notify the Department of State. The new supervising broker must notify the department that he or she will be holding the salesperson's license and must submit a $10 fee.

Blockbusting prohibited. Regulations prohibit licensees from inducing or attempting to induce an owner to sell, lease or list any property by using scare tactics regarding the entry into the neighborhood of a person or persons of a particular race, color, religion or national origin.

Net listings prohibited. Prohibited is the use of net listing agreements wherein the broker is promised as commission all of the sales price that exceeds an amount specified by the seller.

Offer to purchase. All offers to purchase property must be promptly presented to the owner of the property.

Maintaining documents. Every real estate broker must maintain a file of all listings, offers, closing statements and other documents for a period of three years. These records must contain the names and addresses of the sellers, buyers and mortgagees; the sales prices; the amount of deposit paid on contract; the commissions charged; and the expenses of procuring a mortgage loan or, if the broker has purchased for resale, the net profit and expenses that relate to the transaction. The broker must also keep copies of a statement showing all payments made by the broker. These records must be made available to the Department of State upon request. (Most brokers keep all records indefinitely as a matter of good business practice.)

Delivery of documents. A real estate broker must immediately deliver duplicate originals of any document relating to a real estate transaction prepared by the broker or one of his or her salespeople, to all parties signing the document.

Care and handling of funds. A real estate broker must not **commingle** money or other properties belonging to a principal with his or her own funds. The broker must maintain a separate *bank* account to be used exclusively for the deposit of these monies and must deposit them as promptly as possible. Within a reasonable time period the broker must render an account of the funds to the client and remit any funds collected. Interest earned, if any, does not belong to the broker. In the event of a dispute, the buyer's earnest money deposit may not be seized as a commission.

Commissions. No individual may legally accept a commission or other compensation for performing any of the activities regulated by the license law, unless he or she held a valid New York real estate license at the time the activity was performed. A salesperson may not accept a commission from anyone other than his or her supervising broker. Brokers and salespeople may not obtain compensation from more than one party to a transaction without the knowledge and consent of all parties involved. A broker may share a commission only with his or her own salespersons, or with another licensed broker.

Advertising. All real estate advertisements must contain the name of the broker's firm and must clearly indicate that the party who placed the ad is a real estate broker. Blind ads that contain only a telephone number are prohibited.

For Sale signs. A broker must obtain an owner's consent to place a For Sale sign on the owner's property.

Publishers. Article 12B of the Real Property Law requires real estate and business opportunity publishers or those who print, write or otherwise issue for the purpose of promoting for others the sale, lease or exchange of real estate or businesses to file a statement with the Department of State for its approval.

Disclosure of interest. Brokers may not buy or acquire an interest in property listed with them for their own account without first making their true position known to the owners involved. Similarly, a broker may not sell property in which he or she has an interest without revealing the interest to all parties to the transaction.

Substitution. The license law expressly prohibits the broker from interfering with or trying to frustrate other parties' existing contracts.

Obligations to other brokers. Brokers are prohibited from negotiating the sale, lease or exchange of any property belonging to an owner who has an existing written contract that grants exclusive authority to another broker.

No broker may compensate or accept the services of any other broker's associates without that broker's knowledge.

Suspension and Revocation of Licenses

The New York Department of State, Division of Licensing Services, may hear complaints and/or initiate investigations into any alleged violations of the license law or its rules and regulations. Anyone found guilty of any of the following violations may have his or her license suspended or revoked or may be fined or reprimanded:

1. Making any substantial misrepresentation;
2. Making any false promise likely to influence, persuade or induce;
3. Making a false statement or misrepresentation through agents, salespersons, advertising or otherwise;

4. Accepting a commission or valuable consideration (salesperson) for the performance of any service from any person except the licensed broker with whom the salesperson is associated;
5. Acting for more than one party in a transaction without the knowledge of all parties involved;
6. Failing within a reasonable amount of time to account for or remit any monies belonging to others that come into his or her possession;
7. Being unworthy or incompetent to act as a real estate licensee;
8. Paying a commission or valuable consideration (broker) to any person for services performed in violation of the law;
9. Obtaining a license falsely or fraudulently or making a material misstatement in the license application;
10. Engaging in any other conduct, whether of the same or of a different character from that just specified, that constitutes improper, fraudulent or dishonest dealing; and
11. Committing any violation of license law.

Investigation of complaint and hearing. If the department feels that a complaint against a licensee warrants further investigation, it will send an investigator to interview the alleged violator about the charge. In some cases the investigation is preceded by a formal letter of complaint from the department. If the investigation results in sufficient evidence, the department will conduct a hearing. Individuals accused of violation of the law may defend themselves or be represented by an attorney.

Penalties. If an offender has received any sum of money as commission, compensation or profit in connection with a license law violation, he or she may be held liable for up to *four times* that amount in damages in addition to having the license suspended or revoked. The Department of State may also impose a fine of *up to $1,000* on an offender. If an offense constitutes a misdemeanor, a licensee may be tried in court in addition to the hearing. Criminal actions will be prosecuted by the Attorney General of the State of New York.

Appeal. The action of the Department of State is subject to review. Any determination in granting or renewing a license, revoking or suspending a license, imposing a fine or reprimand, or the refusal to institute any of these penalties may be appealed.

Revocation of employer's license. Revocation of a broker's license automatically suspends the licenses of all salespeople in the broker's employ, pending a change of employer and the reissuing of their licenses accordingly.

When a salesperson is accused of violating license law the supervising broker is also held accountable if the broker knew or should have known of the violation or if, having found out about the problem, the broker retained any fees or commission arising from the transaction.

Professional Organizations

Years ago real estate brokers realized the need for an organization to assist them in improving their business abilities and to educate the public to the value of qualified real estate brokers. The National Association of REALTORS® (NAR) was organized in 1908 (as the National Association of Real Estate Boards) to meet this need. This association is the parent organization of most local real estate boards that operate throughout the United States, and the professional activities of all REALTORS®—active members of local boards that are affiliated with the national association—are governed by the association's Code of Ethics. The term REALTOR® is a registered trademark. In 1989, NAR had more than 800,000 members as REALTOR® and REALTOR®-ASSOCIATES.

The National Association of Real Estate Brokers (Realtists) was founded in 1947, and is particularly active in the South. Its membership includes individual members, as well as brokers who belong to state and local real estate boards affiliated with the organization. Members subscribe to a code of ethics that sets professional standards for all Realtists.

These are trade associations. Licensed brokers and salespersons are not required to join. In New York one licensee in four belongs to NAR. The NAR adopted its **Code of Ethics** in 1913. The REALTORS® Code of Ethics is reproduced in Figure 8.2.

New York State Association of REALTORS®

The New York State Association of REALTORS® is a member board of the National Association of REALTORS® that represents more than 45,000 REALTORS® and REALTOR-ASSOCIATES® in New York State. The objectives of the state association are carried out by volunteer officers, directors and committee members. The staff consists of an executive director, administrator, director of educational activities as well as groups responsible for legislative activities, communications and other membership services. The Commercial-Investment Division, the New York State Appraisal Society, and the Realtors Land Institute are divisions of the state association that serve specialized needs of the membership. Figure 8.3 lists the membership of 53 New York State Boards of REALTORS® in 1989.

Educational Services. The New York REALTORS® Institute administers a structured educational program. The prescribed course of study leads to the designation Graduate, REALTORS® Institute (GRI). To earn the **GRI** designation the candidate must successfully complete three courses. They are approved by the state for continuing education credit. GRI courses are offered during the year at various locations around the state and in summer at a week-long session at Ithaca College.

GRI course I covers residential property: valuation, listing, marketing and closings, business planning, and construction. Topics in GRI II include appraisal, financing, taxation, ethics and legal topics, and an overview of real estate management. GRI III covers commercial property: estimating cash flow, pricing, financing and appraising commercial property, federal taxation, exchanges and syndication.

Designations

Designations analogous to college degrees are awarded by various real estate organizations after study, examinations and experience. Various real estate bodies award these designations. Some are associated with the National Association of REALTORS® and some are independent organizations. Among the more well-known designations are:

American Institute of Real Estate Appraisers: MAI, Member Appraisal Institute; and RM, Residential Member;

American Society of Real Estate Counselors: CRE, Counselor of Real Estate;

Figure 8.2
Code of Ethics,
Standards of
Practice

Code of Ethics and Standards of Practice

of the
NATIONAL ASSOCIATION OF REALTORS®

Where the word REALTOR® is used in this Code and Preamble, it shall be deemed to include REALTOR-ASSOCIATE®. Pronouns shall be considered to include REALTORS® and REALTOR-ASSOCIATE®s of both genders.

Preamble...

Under all is the land. Upon its wise utilization and widely allocated ownership depend the survival and growth of free institutions and of our civilization. The REALTOR® should recognize that the interests of the nation and its citizens require the highest and best use of the land and the widest distribution of land ownership. They require the creation of adequate housing, the building of functioning cities, the development of productive industries and farms, and the preservation of a healthful environment.

Such interests impose obligations beyond those of ordinary commerce. They impose grave social responsibility and a patriotic duty to which the REALTOR® should dedicate himself, and for which he should be diligent in preparing himself. The REALTOR®, therefore, is zealous to maintain and improve the standards of his calling and shares with his fellow REALTORS® a common responsibility for its integrity and honor. The term REALTOR® has come to connote competency, fairness, and high integrity resulting from adherence to a lofty ideal of moral conduct in business relations. No inducement of profit and no instruction from clients ever can justify departure from this ideal.

In the interpretation of this obligation, a REALTOR® can take no safer guide than that which has been handed down through the centuries, embodied in the Golden Rule, "Whatsoever ye would that men should do to you, do ye even so to them."

Accepting this standard as his own, every REALTOR® pledges himself to observe its spirit in all of his activities and to conduct his business in accordance with the tenets set forth below.

Articles 1 through 5 are aspirational and establish ideals the REALTOR® should strive to attain.

ARTICLE 1

The REALTOR® should keep himself informed on matters affecting real estate in his community, the state, and nation so that he may be able to contribute responsibly to public thinking on such matters.

ARTICLE 2

In justice to those who place their interests in his care, the REALTOR® should endeavor always to be informed regarding laws, proposed legislation, governmental regulations, public policies, and current market conditions in order to be in a position to advise his clients properly.

ARTICLE 3

The REALTOR® should endeavor to eliminate in his community any practices which could be damaging to the public or bring discredit to the real estate profession. The REALTOR® should assist the governmental agency charged with regulating the practices of brokers and salesmen in his state. (Amended 11/87)

ARTICLE 4

To prevent dissension and misunderstanding and to assure better service to the owner, the REALTOR® should urge the exclusive listing of property unless contrary to the best interest of the owner. (Amended 11/87)

ARTICLE 5

In the best interests of society, of his associates, and his own business, the REALTOR® should willingly share with other REALTORS® the lessons of his experience and study for the benefit of the public, and should be loyal to the Board of REALTORS® of his community and active in its work.

Articles 6 through 23 establish specific obligations. Failure to observe these requirements subjects the REALTOR® to disciplinary action.

ARTICLE 6

The REALTOR® shall seek no unfair advantage over other REALTORS® and shall conduct his business so as to avoid controversies with other REALTORS®. (Amended 11/87)

• Standard of Practice 6-1

"The REALTOR® shall not misrepresent the availability of access to show or inspect a listed property. (Cross-reference Article 22.)" (Amended 11/87)

ARTICLE 7

In accepting employment as an agent, the REALTOR® pledges himself to protect and promote the interests of the client. This obligation of absolute fidelity to the client's interests is primary, but it does not relieve the REALTOR® of the obligation to treat fairly all parties to the transaction.

• Standard of Practice 7-1

"Unless precluded by law, government rule or regulation, or agreed otherwise in writing, the REALTOR® shall submit to the seller all offers until closing. Unless the REALTOR® and the seller agree otherwise, the REALTOR® shall not be obligated to continue to market the property after an offer has been accepted. Unless the subsequent offer is contingent upon the termination of an existing contract, the REALTOR® shall recommend that the seller obtain the advice of legal counsel prior to acceptance. (Cross-reference Article 17.)" (Amended 5/87)

• Standard of Practice 7-2

"The REALTOR®, acting as listing broker, shall submit all offers to the seller as quickly as possible."

• Standard of Practice 7-3

"The REALTOR®, in attempting to secure a listing, shall not deliberately mislead the owner as to market value."

**Figure 8.2
(continued)**

- **Standard of Practice 7-4**

  (Refer to Standard of Practice 22-1, which also relates to Article 7, Code of Ethics.)

- **Standard of Practice 7-5**

  (Refer to Standard of Practice 22-2, which also relates to Article 7, Code of Ethics.)

- **Standard of Practice 7-6**

  "The REALTOR®, when acting as a principal in a real estate transaction, cannot avoid his responsibilities under the Code of Ethics."

ARTICLE 8

The REALTOR® shall not accept compensation from more than one party, even if permitted by law, without the full knowledge of all parties to the transaction.

ARTICLE 9

The REALTOR® shall avoid exaggeration, misrepresentation, or concealment of pertinent facts relating to the property or the transaction. The REALTOR® shall not, however, be obligated to discover latent defects in the property or to advise on matters outside the scope of his real estate license. (Amended 11/86)

- **Standard of Practice 9-1**

  "The REALTOR® shall not be a party to the naming of a false consideration in any document, unless it be the naming of an obviously nominal consideration."

- **Standard of Practice 9-2**

  (Refer to Standard of Practice 21-3, which also relates to Article 9, Code of Ethics.)

- **Standard of Practice 9-3**

  (Refer to Standard of Practice 7-3, which also relates to Article 9, Code of Ethics.)

- **Standard of Practice 9-4**

  "The REALTOR® shall not offer a service described as 'free of charge' when the rendering of a service is contingent on the obtaining of a benefit such as a listing or commission."

- **Standard of Practice 9-5**

  "The REALTOR® shall, with respect to the subagency of another REALTOR®, timely communicate any change of compensation for subagency services to the other REALTOR® prior to the time such REALTOR® produces a prospective buyer who has signed an offer to purchase the property for which the subagency has been offered through MLS or otherwise by the listing agency."

- **Standard of Practice 9-6**

  "REALTORS® shall disclose their REALTOR® status when seeking information from another REALTOR® concerning real property for which the other REALTOR® is an agent or subagent."

- **Standard of Practice 9-7**

  "The offering of premiums, prizes, merchandise discounts or other inducements to list or sell is not, in itself, unethical even if receipt of the benefit is contingent on listing or purchasing through the REALTOR® making the offer. However, the REALTOR® must exercise care and candor in any such advertising or other public or private representations so that any party interested in receiving or otherwise benefiting from the REALTOR®'s offer will have clear, thorough, advance understanding of all the terms and conditions of the offer. The offering of any inducements to do business is subject to the limitations and restrictions of state law and the ethical obligations established by Article 9, as interpreted by any applicable Standard of Practice." (Adopted 11/84)

- **Standard of Practice 9-8**

  "The REALTOR® shall be obligated to discover and disclose adverse factors reasonably apparent to someone with expertise in only those areas required by their real estate licensing authority. Article 9 does not impose upon the REALTOR® the obligation of expertise in other professional or technical disciplines. (Cross-reference Article 11.)" (Amended 11/86)

ARTICLE 10

The REALTOR® shall not deny equal professional services to any person for reasons of race, creed, sex, or country of national origin. The REALTOR® shall not be party to any plan or agreement to discriminate against a person or persons on the basis of race, creed, sex, or country of national origin.

ARTICLE 11

A REALTOR® is expected to provide a level of competent service in keeping with the standards of practice in those fields in which the REALTOR® customarily engages.

The REALTOR® shall not undertake to provide specialized professional services concerning a type of property or service that is outside his field of competence unless he engages the assistance of one who is competent on such types of property or service, or unless the facts are fully disclosed to the client. Any person engaged to provide such assistance shall be so identified to the client and his contribution to the assignment should be set forth.

The REALTOR® shall refer to the Standards of Practice of the National Association as to the degree of competence that a client has a right to expect the REALTOR® to possess, taking into consideration the complexity of the problem, the availability of expert assistance, and the opportunities for experience available to the REALTOR®.

- **Standard of Practice 11-1**

  "Whenever a REALTOR® submits an oral or written opinion of the value of real property for a fee, his opinion shall be supported by a memorandum in his file or an appraisal report, either of which shall include as a minimum the following:

  1. Limiting conditions
  2. Any existing or contemplated interest
  3. Defined value
  4. Date applicable
  5. The estate appraised
  6. A description of the property
  7. The basis of the reasoning including applicable market data and/or capitalization computation

  "This report or memorandum shall be available to the Professional Standards Committee for a period of at least two years (beginning subsequent to final determination of the court if the appraisal is involved in litigation) to ensure compliance with Article 11 of the Code of Ethics of the NATIONAL ASSOCIATION OF REALTORS®."

- **Standard of Practice 11-2**

  "The REALTOR® shall not undertake to make an appraisal when his employment or fee is contingent upon the amount of appraisal."

Figure 8.2
(continued)

- **Standard of Practice 11-3**

"REALTORS® engaged in real estate securities and syndications transactions are engaged in an activity subject to regulations beyond those governing real estate transactions generally, and therefore have the affirmative obligation to be informed of applicable federal and state laws, and rules and regulations regarding these types of transactions."

ARTICLE 12

The REALTOR® shall not undertake to provide professional services concerning a property or its value where he has a present or contemplated interest unless such interest is specifically disclosed to all affected parties.

- **Standard of Practice 12-1**

(Refer to Standards of Practice 9-4 and 16-1, which also relate to Article 12, Code of Ethics.) (Amended 5/84)

ARTICLE 13

The REALTOR® shall not acquire an interest in or buy for himself, any member of his immediate family, his firm or any member thereof, or any entity in which he has a substantial ownership interest, property listed with him, without making the true position known to the listing owner. In selling property owned by himself, or in which he has any interest, the REALTOR® shall reveal the facts of his ownership or interest to the purchaser.

- **Standard of Practice 13-1**

"For the protection of all parties, the disclosures required by Article 13 shall be in writing and provided by the REALTOR® prior to the signing of any contract." (Adopted 2/86)

ARTICLE 14

In the event of a controversy between REALTORS® associated with different firms, arising out of their relationship as REALTORS®, the REALTORS® shall submit the dispute to arbitration in accordance with the regulations of their Board or Boards rather than litigate the matter.

- **Standard of Practice 14-1**

"The filing of litigation and refusal to withdraw from it by a REALTOR® in an arbitrable matter constitutes a refusal to arbitrate." (Adopted 2/86)

- **Standard of Practice 14-2**

"The obligation to arbitrate mandated by Article 14 includes arbitration requests initiated by the REALTOR®'s client." (Adopted 5/87)

- **Standard of Practice 14-3**

"Article 14 does not require a REALTOR® to arbitrate in those circumstances when all parties to the dispute advise the Board in writing that they choose not to arbitrate before the Board." (Adopted 5/88)

ARTICLE 15

If a REALTOR® is charged with unethical practice or is asked to present evidence in any disciplinary proceeding or investigation, he shall place all pertinent facts before the proper tribunal of the Member Board or affiliated institute, society, or council of which he is a member.

- **Standard of Practice 15-1**

"The REALTOR® shall not be subject to disciplinary proceedings in more than one Board of REALTORS® with respect to alleged violations of the Code of Ethics relating to the same transaction."

- **Standard of Practice 15-2**

"The REALTOR® shall not make any unauthorized disclosure or dissemination of the allegations, findings, or decision developed in connection with an ethics hearing or appeal." (Adopted 5/84)

- **Standard of Practice 15-3**

"The REALTOR® shall not obstruct the Board's investigative or disciplinary proceedings by instituting or threatening to institute actions for libel, slander or defamation against any party to a professional standards proceeding or their witnesses." (Adopted 11/87).

- **Standard of Practice 15-4**

"The REALTOR® shall not intentionally impede the Board's investigative or disciplinary proceedings by filing multiple ethics complaints based on the same event or transaction." (Adopted 11/88)

ARTICLE 16

When acting as agent, the REALTOR® shall not accept any commission, rebate, or profit on expenditures made for his principal-owner, without the principal's knowledge and consent.

- **Standard of Practice 16-1**

"The REALTOR® shall not recommend or suggest to a client or a customer the use of services of another organization or business entity in which he has a direct interest without disclosing such interest at the time of the recommendation or suggestion." (Amended 5/88)

- **Standard of Practice 16-2**

"When acting as an agent or subagent, the REALTOR® shall disclose to a client or customer if there is any financial benefit or fee the REALTOR® or the REALTOR®'s firm may receive as a direct result of having recommended real estate products or services (e.g., homeowner's insurance, warranty programs, mortgage financing, title insurance, etc.) other than real estate referral fees." (Adopted 5/88)

ARTICLE 17

The REALTOR® shall not engage in activities that constitute the unauthorized practice of law and shall recommend that legal counsel be obtained when the interest of any party to the transaction requires it.

ARTICLE 18

The REALTOR® shall keep in a special account in an appropriate financial institution, separated from his own funds, monies coming into his possession in trust for other persons, such as escrows, trust funds, clients' monies, and other like items.

ARTICLE 19

The REALTOR® shall be careful at all times to present a true picture in his advertising and representations to the public. The REALTOR® shall also ensure that his status as a broker or a REALTOR® is clearly identifiable in any such advertising. (Amended 11/86)

**Figure 8.2
(continued)**

- **Standard of Practice 19-1**

  "The REALTOR® shall not submit or advertise property without authority, and in any offering, the price quoted shall not be other than that agreed upon with the owners."

- **Standard of Practice 19-2**

  (Refer to Standard of Practice 9-4, which also relates to Article 19, Code of Ethics.)

- **Standard of Practice 19-3**

  "The REALTOR®, when advertising unlisted real property for sale in which he has an ownership interest, shall disclose his status as both an owner and as a REALTOR® or real estate licensee." (Adopted 5/85)

- **Standard of Practice 19-4**

  "The REALTOR® shall not advertise nor permit any person employed by or affiliated with him to advertise listed property without disclosing the name of the firm." (Adopted 11/86)

- **Standard of Practice 19-5**

  "The REALTOR®, when acting as listing broker, has the exclusive right to control the advertising of listed property prior to the closing. The listing broker may delegate the right to post 'For Sale' and 'Sold' signs and to make related advertising representations to a cooperating broker.

  After the transaction has been closed, the listing broker may not prohibit the cooperating broker from advertising his 'participation' or 'assistance' in the transaction." (Cross-reference Article 21.)" (Amended 2/89)

ARTICLE 20

The REALTOR®, for the protection of all parties, shall see that financial obligations and commitments regarding real estate transactions are in writing, expressing the exact agreement of the parties. A copy of each agreement shall be furnished to each party upon his signing such agreement.

- **Standard of Practice 20-1**

  "At the time of signing or initialing, the REALTOR® shall furnish to the party a copy of any document signed or initialed." (Adopted 5/86)

- **Standard of Practice 20-2**

  "For the protection of all parties, the REALTOR® shall use reasonable care to ensure that documents pertaining to the purchase and sale of real estate are kept current through the use of written extensions or amendments." (Adopted 5/86)

ARTICLE 21

The REALTOR® shall not engage in any practice or take any action inconsistent with the agency of another REALTOR®.

- **Standard of Practice 21-1**

  "Signs giving notice of property for sale, rent, lease, or exchange shall not be placed on property without the consent of the owner."

- **Standard of Practice 21-2**

  "The REALTOR® obtaining information from a listing broker about a specific property shall not convey this information to, nor invite the cooperation of a third party broker without the consent of the listing broker."

- **Standard of Practice 21-3**

  "The REALTOR® shall not solicit a listing which is currently listed exclusively with another broker. However, if the listing broker, when asked by the REALTOR®, refuses to disclose the expiration date and nature of such listing; i.e., an exclusive right to sell, an exclusive agency, open listing, or other form of contractual agreement between the listing broker and his client, the REALTOR®, unless precluded by law, may contact the owner to secure such information and may discuss the terms upon which he might take a future listing or, alternatively, may take a listing to become effective upon expiration of any existing exclusive listing." (Amended 11/86)

- **Standard of Practice 21-4**

  "The REALTOR® shall not use information obtained by him from the listing broker, through offers to cooperate received through Multiple Listing Services or other sources authorized by the listing broker, for the purpose of creating a referral prospect to a third broker, or for creating a buyer prospect unless such use is authorized by the listing broker."

- **Standard of Practice 21-5**

  "The fact that a property has been listed exclusively with a REALTOR® shall not preclude or inhibit any other REALTOR® from soliciting such listing after its expiration."

- **Standard of Practice 21-6**

  "The fact that a property owner has retained a REALTOR® as his exclusive agent in respect of one or more past transactions creates no interest or agency which precludes or inhibits other REALTORS® from seeking such owner's future business."

- **Standard of Practice 21-7**

  "The REALTOR® shall be free to list property which is 'open listed' at any time, but shall not knowingly obligate the seller to pay more than one commission except with the seller's knowledgeable consent. (Cross-reference Article 7.)" (Amended 5/88)

- **Standard of Practice 21-8**

  "When a REALTOR® is contacted by an owner regarding the sale of property that is exclusively listed with another broker, and the REALTOR® has not directly or indirectly initiated the discussion, unless precluded by law, the REALTOR® may discuss the terms upon which he might take a future listing or, alternatively, may take a listing to become effective upon expiration of any existing exclusive listing." (Amended 11/86)

- **Standard of Practice 21-9**

  "In cooperative transactions a REALTOR® shall compensate the cooperating REALTOR® (principal broker) and shall not compensate nor offer to compensate, directly or indirectly, any of the sales licensees employed by or affiliated with another REALTOR® without the prior express knowledge and consent of the cooperating broker."

- **Standard of Practice 21-10**

  "Article 21 does not preclude REALTORS® from making general announcements to property owners describing their services and the terms of their availability even though some recipients may have exclusively listed their property for sale or lease with another REALTOR®. A general telephone canvass, general mailing or distribution addressed to all property owners in a given geographical area or in a given profession, business, club, or organization, or other classification or group is deemed 'general' for purposes of this standard.

**Figure 8.2
(continued)**

Article 21 is intended to recognize as unethical two basic types of solicitation:

First, telephone or personal solicitations of property owners who have been identified by a real estate sign, multiple listing compilation, or other information service as having exclusively listed their property with another REALTOR®; and

Second, mail or other forms of written solicitations of property owners whose properties are exclusively listed with another REALTOR® when such solicitations are not part of a general mailing but are directed specifically to property owners identified through compilations of current listings, 'for sale' signs, or other sources of information required by Article 22 and Multiple Listing Service rules to be made available to other REALTORS® under offers of subagency or cooperation." (Adopted 11/83)

• Standard of Practice 21-11

"The REALTOR®, prior to accepting a listing, has an affirmative obligation to make reasonable efforts to determine whether the property is subject to a current, valid exclusive listing agreement." (Adopted 11/83)

• Standard of Practice 21-12

"The REALTOR®, acting as the agent of the buyer, shall disclose that relationship to the seller's agent at first contact. (Cross-reference Article 7.)" (Adopted 5/88)

• Standard of Practice 21-13

"On unlisted property, the REALTOR®, acting as the agent of a buyer, shall disclose that relationship to the seller at first contact. (Cross-reference Article 7.)" (Adopted 5/88)

• Standard of Practice 21-14

"The REALTOR®, acting as agent of the seller or as subagent of the listing broker, shall disclose that relationship to buyers as soon as practicable." (Adopted 5/88)

• Standard of Practice 21-15

"Article 21 does not preclude a REALTOR® from contacting the client of another broker for the purpose of offering to provide, or entering into a contract to provide, a different type of real estate service unrelated to the type of service currently being provided (e.g., property management as opposed to brokerage). However, information received through a Multiple Listing Service or any other offer of cooperation may not be used to target the property owners to whom such offers to provide services are made." (Adopted 2/89)

• Standard of Practice 21-16

"The REALTOR®, acting as subagent or buyer's agent, shall not use the terms of an offer to purchase to attempt to modify the listing broker's offer of compensation to subagents or buyer's agents nor make the submission of an executed offer to purchase contingent on the listing broker's agreement to modify the offer of compensation." (Adopted 2/89)

ARTICLE 22

In the sale of property which is exclusively listed with a REALTOR®, the REALTOR® shall utilize the services of other brokers upon mutually agreed upon terms when it is in the best interests of the client.

Negotiations concerning property which is listed exclusively shall be carried on with the listing broker, not with the owner, except with the consent of the listing broker.

• Standard of Practice 22-1

"It is the obligation of the selling broker as subagent of the listing broker to disclose immediately all pertinent facts to the listing broker prior to as well as after the contract is executed."

• Standard of Practice 22-2

"The REALTOR®, when submitting offers to the seller, shall present each in an objective and unbiased manner."

• Standard of Practice 22-3

"The REALTOR® shall disclose the existence of an accepted offer to any broker seeking cooperation." (Adopted 5/86)

• Standard of Practice 22-4

"The REALTOR®, acting as exclusive agent of the seller, establishes the terms and conditions of offers to cooperate. Unless expressly indicated in offers to cooperate made through MLS or otherwise, a cooperating broker may not assume that the offer of cooperation includes an offer of compensation. Entitlement to compensation in a cooperative transaction must be agreed upon between a listing and cooperating broker prior to the time an offer to purchase the property is produced." (Adopted 11/88)

ARTICLE 23

The REALTOR® shall not publicly disparage the business practice of a competitor nor volunteer an opinion of a competitor's transaction. If his opinion is sought and if the REALTOR® deems it appropriate to respond, such opinion shall be rendered with strict professional integrity and courtesy.

The Code of Ethics was adopted in 1913. Amended at the Annual Convention in 1924, 1928, 1950, 1951, 1952, 1955, 1956, 1961, 1962, 1974, 1982, 1986, and 1987.

EXPLANATORY NOTES (Revised 11/88)

The reader should be aware of the following policies which have been approved by the Board of Directors of the National Association:

"In filing a charge of an alleged violation of the Code of Ethics by a REALTOR®, the charge shall read as an alleged violation of one or more Articles of the Code. A Standard of Practice may only be cited in support of the charge."

The Standards of Practice are not an integral part of the Code but rather serve to clarify the ethical obligations imposed by the various Articles. The Standards of Practice supplement, and do not substitute for, the Case Interpretations in *Interpretations of the Code of Ethics.*

Modifications to existing Standards of Practice and additional new Standards of Practice are approved from time to time. The reader is cautioned to ensure that the most recent publications are utilized.

Articles 1 through 5 are aspirational and establish ideals that a REALTOR® should strive to attain. Recognizing their subjective nature, these Articles shall not be used as the bases for charges of alleged unethical conduct or as the bases for disciplinary action.

REALTOR®

EQUAL HOUSING OPPORTUNITY

©1989, NATIONAL ASSOCIATION OF REALTORS®
All Rights Reserved

Form No. 166-288-1 (2/89)

Figure 8.3 Members, New York State Association of REALTORS®, Early 1989	Board Name	Number of REALTORS®	Number of ASSOCIATES
X	Albany County Board of REALTORS®	210	1,495
X	Bronx Board of REALTORS®	144	154
X	Brooklyn Board of REALTORS®	218	31
X	Broome County Board of REALTORS®	258	735
X	Buffalo, Greater Board of REALTORS®	440	3,752
X	Cayuga County Board of REALTORS®	27	90
	Chenango County Board of REALTORS®	16	119
X	Clinton County Board of REALTORS®	44	107
X	Columbia County Board of REALTORS®	72	247
X	Cortland County Board of REALTORS®	111	0
	Dutchess County Board of REALTORS®	183	465
	Eastern Suffolk Board of REALTORS®	268	347
X	Elmira-Corning Rgl. Board of REALTORS®	226	0
	Essex County Board of REALTORS®	18	31
X	Finger Lakes Board of REALTORS®, Inc.	111	322
	Franklin County Board of REALTORS®	32	99
X	Fulton County Board of REALTORS®	34	105
	Genesee County Board of REALTORS®	42	107
X	Genesee Valley Real Estate Board	57	319
	Greene County Board of REALTORS®	37	159
	Greater Glens Falls & Warren County Board of REALTORS®	113	612
	Individual Membership Roster	25	155
X	Ithaca Board of REALTORS®	85	246
X	Jamestown, Greater Board of REALTORS®	60	295
X	Jefferson-Lewis Board of REALTORS®	60	209
X	Lockport Board of REALTORS®, Inc.	42	188
X	Long Island Board of REALTORS®[1]	1,612	8,739
X	Montgomery Cty Brd of REALTORS®, Inc.	19	103
	New York, Real Estate Board of	845	379
X	Niagara Falls Area Brd of REALTORS®	41	207
	Northern Chautauqua Board of REALTORS®	16	61
	Olean Board of REALTORS®	31	111
X	Orange County Board of REALTORS®	311	1,099
X	Oswego Board of REALTORS®	44	225
X	Otsego-Delaware Board of REALTORS®	430	1
	Putnam County Board of REALTORS®	67	244
X	Rochester, Greater Association of REALTORS®, Inc.	682	3,343
X	Rensselaer County Board of REALTORS®	50	389
	Rockland County Board of REALTORS®	145	667
X	Rome Board of REALTORS®	20	73
X	Saratoga County Board of REALTORS®	87	749
X	Schenectady Board of REALTORS®, Inc.	113	582
X	St. Lawrence County Board of REALTORS®	30	61
X	Staten Island Board of REALTORS®	289	730
	Steuben Allegany Board of REALTORS®	16	25
	Sullivan County Board of REALTORS®	55	146
X	Syracuse, Greater Board of REALTORS®	259	1,908
X	Ulster County Board of REALTORS®	152	568
X	Utica, Greater Board of REALTORS®	100	345
	Washington County Board of REALTORS®	19	38
	Wayne County Board of REALTORS®	52	178
X	Westchester Cty Brd of REALTORS®	1,016	2,642
	TOTAL	9,434	34,002

X—Administer multiple listing systems.
Putnam, Dutchess and Rockland counties have non–Board MLS.

[1]The Long Island Board also had 1,438 non–member salespersons.

Realtors National Marketing Institute: CCIM, Certified Commercial-Investment Member; CRB, Certified Real Estate Brokerage Manager; and CRS, Certified Residential Specialist;

Realtors Land Institute: ALC, Accredited Land Consultant;

Real Estate Securities and Syndication Institute: SRS, Specialist in Real Estate Securities;

International Real Estate Federation (FIABCI): CIPS, Certified International Property Specialist;

Institute of Real Estate Management: CPM, Certified Property Manager; ARM, Accredited Residential Manager; AMO, Accredited Management Organization;

Society of Industrial and Office Realtors: SIOR; PRE, Professional Real Estate;

Society of Real Estate Appraisers: SRA, Senior Residential Appraiser; SREA, Senior Real Estate Appraiser; SRPA, Senior Real Property Analyst;

American Society of Appraisers: ASA;

Real Estate Educators Association: DREI, Designated Real Estate Instructor; and

Women's Council of Realtors: LTG, Leadership Training Graduate.

Summary

The real estate license law was enacted by New York State to protect the public from dishonest brokers and salespeople, prescribe certain licensing standards, maintain high standards in the real estate profession and protect licensed brokers from unfair or improper competition.

In New York, licensees must be permanent residents of the United States, never convicted of a felony and must pass state examinations before licensure. A salesperson must have completed a prescribed 45-hour qualifying course, be at least 18 years old and sponsored by a licensed broker. A broker must be at least 19 years old, with an additional 45 hours of approved study and one full year's experience as a licensed salesperson. Some exceptions to these requirements are available.

The real estate license, which covers a two-year period, costs $50 for a salesperson and $150 for a broker. An associate broker license designates a fully qualified broker who chooses to remain in a salesperson's capacity under a supervising broker. Those exempt from licensing requirements include New York State attorneys, public officials while performing their public duties, persons acting under court order and resident managers employed by one owner to collect rents and manage property.

Every broker must have a principal place of business within the state, post a sign readable from the sidewalk or in the lobby of an office building, obtain a separate license for each branch office and display the broker's license prominently. Brokers are required to maintain a separate escrow account for deposit of other people's money and are prohibited from *commingling* their own funds with such funds. The broker must immediately deliver duplicate originals of all documents to the persons signing them and must keep a file of all documents relating to real estate transactions for at least three years.

Commissions may be collected only by the supervising broker and may be shared only with other brokers and the broker's own salespersons. Advertisements must contain the name of the broker's firm.

Laws, rules and regulations governing licensees are administered by the New York Department of State, which may, after hearings, suspend or revoke licenses.

Many licensees subscribe to a code of ethics as members of professional real estate organizations. The *Code of Ethics* of the National Association of REALTORS® is reprinted in this chapter.

Designations are awarded after study, examinations and experience by various organizations. The New York State Association of REALTORS® awards the GRI designation to graduates of the REALTORS® Institute.

Questions

1. Real estate license laws were instituted to:
   a. raise revenue through license fees.
   b. limit the number of brokers and salespersons.
   c. match the federal government's requirements.
   d. protect the public and maintain high standards.

2. In New York, real estate licenses are under the supervision of the:
   a. Real Estate Commission.
   b. Board of REALTORS®.
   c. Department of State.
   d. Department of Education.

3. New York's real estate license law is known as:
   a. the Statute of Frauds.
   b. Article 12A.
   c. the Law of Agency.
   d. Newton's Law.

4. A New York resident does *not* need a real estate license to perform which of the following actions?
   a. Selling a neighbor's house for a fee
   b. Offering tenants in a building that is to be rehabilitated a list of new rental spaces for a fee
   c. Entering into a lease with a prospective tenant for rental property he or she owns
   d. Buying lots in a particular area on behalf of a developer for a fee

5. Which of the following does *not* require a license in New York?
   a. Resale of condominiums
   b. Selling mobile homes
   c. Selling land at auction
   d. Selling shopping plazas

6. A duly licensed salesperson may accept a bonus from:
   a. a grateful seller.
   b. a grateful buyer.
   c. another salesperson.
   d. none of the above.

7. A fully qualified broker who chooses to remain as a salesperson under another broker's sponsorship is licensed as a(n):
   a. adjunct salesperson. c. associate broker.
   b. sales associate.   d. principal broker.

8. To obtain a broker's license one must reach the age of:
   a. 18.   c. 20.
   b. 19.   d. 21.

9. A broker must have completed how many hours of prescribed study?
   a. 15   c. 45
   b. 30   d. 90

10. A salesperson's license application must be accompanied by a fee of:
    a. $20.   c. $100.
    b. $50.   d. $250.

11. Subjects covered by the broker's license examination include:
    a. human rights and fair housing.
    b. deeds and mortgages.
    c. the English language.
    d. all of the above.

12. Every real estate license is good for a period of:
    a. one year.   c. three years.
    b. two years.   d. four years.

13. A continuing education course may consist of:
    a. a 45-hour course.
    b. a 30-hour course with examination.
    c. three 15-hour modules.
    d. any of the above.

14. A nonresident broker requesting a New York license must:
    a. post a bond of $5,000.
    b. be a citizen of the United States.
    c. find a New York sponsor.
    d. allow himself or herself to be sued in New York State.

15. A broker must post a sign at the place of business:

    a. inside the broker's office.
    b. on the outside door of the office.
    c. above each salesperson's desk.
    d. visible from the sidewalk or in a lobby.

16. A broker must display in the office:

    a. the broker's license.
    b. all salespersons' licenses.
    c. no licenses.
    d. all of the above.

17. A real estate broker must keep all documents pertaining to a real estate transaction on file for how long?

    a. Two years   c. Seven years
    b. Three years   d. Indefinitely

18. The term "commingling" pertains to:

    a. mixing the broker's funds with escrow deposits.
    b. soliciting the services of another broker's salespersons.
    c. failure to deliver duplicate originals of contracts.
    d. promoting business at social gatherings.

19. Every advertisement must contain the:

    a. sales associate's full name.
    b. address of the brokerage firm.
    c. name of the brokerage firm.
    d. full listing price of the property.

20. An infraction of the license law is legally classified as a(n):

    a. violation.   c. misdemeanor.
    b. offense.   d. felony.

21. The Department of State may impose a fine on an offending licensee of up to:

    a. $250.   c. $1,000.
    b. $500.   d. None of the above

22. If a principal broker loses her license, her associated salespersons must immediately:

    a. appoint one of their number to serve as supervisor.
    b. stop listing and selling.
    c. obtain brokers' licenses.
    d. move the office to another location.

23. A broker need *not* be:

    a. licensed by the state.
    b. over 19 years of age.
    c. a REALTOR®.
    d. already experienced in real estate.

24. The Code of Ethics is promulgated by the:

    a. National Association of REALTORS®.
    b. Department of State.
    c. Article 12A, Real Property Law.
    d. None of the above

25. The designation "GRI" stands for:

    a. general realty insurance.
    b. government regulatory institution.
    c. Graduate, REALTORS® Institute.
    d. guaranteed regular interest.

Appendix: Excerpts from New York State's Study Booklet for Brokers

SUMMARY OF ARTICLE 12-A OF THE REAL PROPERTY LAW

Purpose and effect. This statute was enacted, primarily, for the protection of the public against the dishonest practices of unscrupulous, and the costly blunderings of incompetent, real estate agents.

Real estate agents must be licensed. This statute forbids anyone who is not a duly licensed real estate broker or salesperson to negotiate any form of real estate transaction, for another and for compensation of any kind, in the State of New York. The provision covers the negotiation of (certain) mortgages and the collection of rents, as well as the making of leases of and sale by auction or otherwise of real property. In addition arranging the relocation of commercial or residential tenants for a fee is an activity restricted to real estate brokers. The negotiation of, or attempt to negotiate the sale of a lot or parcel for another, requires a real estate broker's license. A licensed broker may not employ an unlicensed person to assist in the negotiation of a real estate transaction. If the broker does, the broker forfeits rights to a commission on the transaction, is guilty of a misdemeanor and may have the license revoked.

Nonresident brokers. A nonresident of the State of New York may be licensed as a real estate broker in this State, upon the same terms as resident brokers, except that a nonresident broker must file a duly executed "irrevocable consent. . . ." A nonresident who is licensed in another state must demonstrate competency in the prescribed written examination, and must maintain an office in this State, unless in his/her state a New York broker may be licensed without passing the qualifying examination that is there required of resident applicants for real estate brokers' licenses, and is not required to maintain an office in that state.

Persons exempt from application of law. The provisions of the statute do not apply to public officers while performing their official duties, to persons acting in any capacity under the judgment or order of a court, or to attorneys-at-law duly admitted to practice in the courts of New York. Where an attorney employs a salesperson or salespersons, the attorney must obtain a license as real estate broker.

Eligibility for license. Applicants for salespersons' licenses are examined only to establish their character and general intelligence. Anyone age 18 or over may be licensed as a real estate salesperson. First time real estate salesperson applicants are required to take and pass an approved 45-hour qualifying course of study as a prerequisite to licensing.

Licenses to act as real estate brokers are granted to citizens of the United States or to persons who are legal resident aliens; persons under the age of 19 years are ineligible. No one may be licensed as a real estate broker without having actively participated in the general real estate brokerage business as a licensed real estate salesperson under the supervision of a licensed real estate broker for a period of at least one year, or has had the equivalent experience in general real estate business for a period of at least two years, and has attended for at least 90 hours and has successfully completed a real estate course or courses approved by the Secretary of State . . . and has demonstrated competency to act as a broker by passing the required written examination.

Each officer of a corporation or member of a copartnership who engages in any form of real estate brokerage, in behalf of a corporation or firm, must be licensed, as its representative, as a real estate broker. Salespersons' licenses are not issued to officers of corporations nor to members of copartnerships.

No person shall be entitled to a license as a real estate broker or real estate salesperson under this article who has been convicted in this State or elsewhere of a felony, and who has not subsequent to such conviction received executive pardon therefor or a certificate of good conduct from the parole board.

License fees. The nonrefundable fee for the issuance or renewal of a license authorizing a person, copartnership or corporation to act as a real estate broker is $150 and the fee for issuance or renewal of a salesperson's license is $50.

License terms. The license term for real estate brokers and salespersons is 2 years.

Renewal of license. A person who does not apply for renewal of either a broker's or salesperson's license within two years from expiration of a previously issued license must qualify by passing a written examination. No renewal license will be issued unless the licensee meets the continuing education requirement. Licensees must submit proof satisfactory to the Department of State that they have attended at least 45 hours of classroom instruction, and successfully completed a real estate course or courses approved by the Secretary of State, within the preceding 4 years. Licensed brokers with more than 15 years full-time experience and attorneys admitted to the bar in New York State are exempted from this requirement.

Compensation of salespersons. Real estate salespersons may not demand or receive compensation from any person other than a duly licensed real estate broker with whom the salesperson is associated. Payment of a commission to a licensed salesperson by the client does not cancel the claim of the broker for the services rendered by the salesperson.

Splitting commissions. No real estate broker may pay any part of a fee, commission or other compensation received, to any person for any service, help or aid rendered to such broker in the negotiation of any real estate transaction, unless such person is a duly licensed real estate salesperson associated with the broker, or is a licensed real estate broker of this State, or is engaged in the real estate brokerage business in another state or is exempt from the application of the license law. Further, a real estate broker may not pay or agree to pay any part of a fee, commission, or other compensation received or due, or to become due to the broker to any person who is or is to be a party to the transaction. (*"Kickback"*—*colloquial*)

Violations and penalties. A violation by any unlicensed person of any provision of Article 12-A of the Real Property Law is a class A mis-demeanor, which is punishable by a fine of not more than $1,000 or by imprisonment for not exceeding one year, or by both such fine and imprisonment. The commission of a single act prohibited by this article constitutes a violation thereof. In case the offender shall have received any sum of money, as compensation or profit by, or in consequence of offending, the offender is also liable to a civil penalty up to the sum of four times the amount of money so received by the offender, which may be sued for and recovered by the person aggrieved by the offender's misconduct. An unlicensed real estate agent cannot collect compensations for services by resort to the courts, for the agent must allege and prove that the agent is a duly licensed real estate broker or salesperson in order to be entitled to a judgment.

Disciplinary provisions. The license of any real estate broker or salesperson may be suspended pending hearing or may be suspended or revoked by the licensing authorities, after hearing and upon conviction of a violation of any provision of the license law, or for a material misstatement in the application for the broker's license, or for fraud, fraudulent practice, the use of dishonest or misleading advertising, or demonstrated untrustworthiness to act as a real estate broker or salesperson, as the case may be. The revocation of a broker's license operates to suspend the licenses of all real estate salespersons associated with the broker, pending a change of association and the reissuing of their licenses accordingly. All brokers' and salespersons' licenses and pocket cards shall be returned to the Department of State within five days after the receipt of notice of such revocation or suspension. Whenever the license of a broker or salesperson is revoked by the Department of State, such real estate broker or salesperson shall be ineligible to be relicensed either as a real estate broker or salesperson until after the expiration of a period of one year from the date of such revocation.

Drawing of legal documents. While the license as real estate broker gives the right to negotiate real estate transactions, it does not give the right to draw legal documents or give legal advice. The preparation of a legal document may result in the loss of commissions and the revocation of the license. It is essential that real estate brokers and their salespersons refrain from drawing legal instruments of any character.

Department of State
RULES AND REGULATIONS

Regulations Affecting Brokers and Salespersons

Commingling money of principal. A real estate broker shall not commingle the money or other property of his principal with his own and shall at all times maintain a separate, special bank account to be used exclusively for the deposit of said monies and which deposit shall be made as promptly as practicable. Said monies shall not be placed in any depository, fund or investment other than a federally insured bank account. Accrued interest, if any, shall not be retained by, or for the benefit of, the broker except to the extent that it is applied to, and deducted from, earned commission, with the consent of all parties.

Managing property for client. When acting as an agent in the management of property, a real estate broker shall not accept any commission, rebate or profit on expenditures made for his client without his full knowledge and consent.

Broker's purchase of property listed with him. A real estate broker shall not directly or indirectly buy for himself property listed with him, nor shall he acquire any interest therein without first making his true position clearly known to the listing owner.

Disclosure of interest to client. Before a real estate broker buys property for a client in the ownership of which the broker has an interest, he shall disclose his interest to all parties to the transaction.

Broker's sale of property in which he owns an interest. Before a real estate broker sells property in which he owns an interest, he shall make such interest known to the purchaser.

Compensation. A real estate broker shall make it clear for which party he is acting and he shall not receive compensation from more than one party except with the full knowledge and consent of all parties.

Negotiating with party to exclusive listing contract. No real estate broker shall negotiate the sale, exchange or lease of any property directly with an owner or lessor if he knows that such owner, or lessor, has an existing written contract granting exclusive authority in connection with such property with another broker.

Inducing breach of contract of sale or lease. No real estate broker shall induce any party to a contract of sale or lease to break such contract for the purpose of substituting in lieu thereof a new contract with another principal.

Broker's offering property for sale must be authorized. A real estate broker shall never offer a property for sale or lease without the authorization of the owner.

Sign on property. No sign shall ever be placed on any property by a real estate broker without the consent of the owner.

Delivering duplicate original of instrument. A real estate broker shall immediately deliver a duplicate original of any instrument to any party or parties executing the same, where such instrument has been prepared by such broker or under his supervision and where such instrument relates to the employment of the broker or to any matters pertaining to the consummation of a lease, or the purchase, sale or exchange of real property or any other type of real estate transaction in which he may participate as a broker.

Accepting services of another broker's salesman or employee. A real estate broker shall not accept the services of any salesman or employee in the organization of another real estate broker without the knowledge of the broker and no real estate broker should give or permit to be given or directly offer to give anything of value for the purpose of influencing or rewarding the actions of any salesman or employee of another real estate broker in relation to the business of such broker or the client of such broker without the knowledge of such broker.

Termination of salesman's association with broker. A real estate salesman shall, upon termination of his association with a real estate broker, forthwith turn over to such broker any and all listing information obtained during his association whether such information was originally given to him by the broker or copied from the records of such broker or acquired by the salesman during his association.

Automatic continuation of exclusive listing contract. No real estate broker shall be a party to an exclusive listing contract which shall contain an automatic continuation of the period of such listing beyond the fixed termination date set forth therein.

Prohibitions in relation to solicitation. No broker or salesperson shall induce or attempt to induce an owner to sell or lease any residential property or to list same for sale or lease by making any representations regarding the entry or prospective entry into the neighborhood of a person or persons of a particular race, color, religion or national origin.

Use of trade or corporate name. No licensed real estate broker or applicant applying for a real estate broker's license, may use a trade or corporate name which, in the opinion of the Department of State, is so similar to the trade name or corporate name of any licensed real estate broker that confusion to the public will result therefrom.

Net listing agreements. (a) The term *net listing* as used herein shall mean an agency or other agreement whereby a prospective seller of real property or an interest therein, lists such property or interest for sale with a licensed real estate broker authorizing the sale thereof at a specified net amount to be paid to the seller and authorizing the broker to retain as commission, compensation, or otherwise, the difference between the price at which the property or interest is sold and the specified net amount to be received by the seller.

(b) No real estate broker shall make or enter into a "net listing" contract for the sale of real property or any interest therein.

Branch offices. (a) Every branch office shall be owned, maintained and operated only by the licensed broker to whom the license for such office is issued. A branch office shall not be conducted, maintained and operated under an arrangement whereby a licensed salesman or employee of the broker shall pay, or be responsible for, any expense or obligation created or incurred in its conduct, maintenance or operation, or under any other arrangement, the purpose, intent or effect of which shall permit a licensed salesman or employee to carry on the business of real estate broker for his own benefit, directly, or indirectly, in whole or in part.

(b) Every branch office shall be under the direct supervision of the broker to whom the

license is issued, or a representative broker of a corporation or partnership holding such license. A salesman licensed as such for a period of not less than two years and who has successfully completed a course of study in real estate approved by the Secretary of State, may be permitted to operate such a branch office only under the direct supervision of the broker provided the names of such salesman and supervising broker shall have been filed and recorded in the division of licenses of the Department of State.

(c) Supervision of such a licensed salesman shall include guidance, oversight, management, orientation, instruction and supervision in the management and operation of the branch office and the business of real estate broker conducted therein.

(d) No broker shall relocate his principal office or any branch office without prior approval of the department.

Supervision of salesman by broker. (a) The supervision of a real estate salesman by a licensed real estate broker shall consist of regular, frequent and consistent personal guidance, instruction, oversight and superintendence by the real estate broker with respect to the general real estate brokerage business conducted by the broker, and all matters relating thereto.

(b) The broker and salesman shall keep written records of all real estate listings obtained by the salesman, and of all sales and other transactions effected by, and with the aid and assistance of, the salesman, during the period of his association, which records shall be sufficient to clearly identify the transactions and shall indicate the dates thereof. Such records must be submitted by the salesman to the Department of State with his application for a broker's license.

Ownership of voting stock by salesmen prohibited. No licensed real estate salesman may own, either singly or jointly, directly or indirectly, any voting shares of stock in any licensed real estate brokerage corporation with which he is associated.

Records of transactions to be maintained. (a) Each licensed broker shall keep and maintain for a period of three years records of each transaction effected through his office concerning the sale or mortgage of one to four family dwellings. Such records shall contain the names and addresses of the seller, the buyer, mortgagee, if any, the purchase price and resale price, if any, amount of deposit paid on contract, amount of commission paid to broker, or gross profit realized by the broker if purchased by him for resale, expenses of procuring the mortgage loan, if any, the net commission or net profit realized by the broker showing the disposition of all payments made by the broker. In lieu thereof each broker shall keep and maintain, in connection with each such transaction a copy of (1) contract of sale, (2) commission agreement, (3) closing statement, (4) statement showing disposition of proceeds of mortgage loan.

(b) Each licensed broker engaged in the business of soliciting and granting mortgage loans to purchasers of one to four family dwellings shall keep and maintain for a period of three years, a record of the name of the applicant, the amount of the mortgage proceeds, a copy of the verification of employment and financial status of the applicant, a copy of the inspection and compliance report with the Baker Law requirements of FHA with the name of the inspector. Such records shall be available to the Department of State at all times upon request.

Advertising. (a) All advertisements placed by a broker must indicate that the advertiser is a broker or give the name of the broker and his telephone number.

(b) All advertisements placed by a broker which state that property is in the vicinity of a geographical area or territorial subdivision must include as part of such advertisement the name of the geographical area or territorial subdivision in which such property is actually located.

Disclaimer. Nothing in this Part is intended to be, or should be construed as, an indication that a salesperson is either an independent contractor or employee of a broker.

Subjects for study—real estate salesperson. The following are the required subjects to be included in the course of study in real estate for licensure as a real estate salesperson, and the required minimum number of hours to be devoted to each such subject:

Subject	Hours
Real estate instruments	6
Law of agency	5
Real estate financing	5
Valuation and listing procedures	5
Law of contracts	5
License law and ethics	5
Human rights—fair housing	4
Closing and closing costs	4
Land use regulations	3
Real estate mathematics	3

Subjects for study—real estate broker. The following are the required subjects to be included in a course of study in real estate for licensure as a real estate broker and the required minimum number of hours to be devoted to each such subject:

Subject	Hours
Operation of a real estate broker's office	10
General business law	5
Construction	3
Subdivision and development	3
Leases and agreements	3
Liens and easements	3
Taxes and assessments	3
Investment property	3
Voluntary and involuntary alienation	3
Property management	2
Condominiums and cooperatives	2
Appraisal	2
Advertising	2
Rent regulations	1

9

Valuation and Listing Procedures

Key Terms

Arm's-length transaction
Comparative market analysis (CMA)
Cost approach
Demand
Depreciation
Direct sales comparison approach
DOM
Economic obsolescence
Exclusive-agency listing
Exclusive-right-to-sell listing
External obsolescence
Functional obsolescence
Income approach
Listing agreement

Locational obsolescence
Market
Market value
Multiple-listing service (MLS)
Net listing
Nonhomogeneity
Open listing
Physical deterioration
Present value of money
Situs
Subject property
Supply
Value

Overview

This chapter will discuss the nature and characteristics of land and the concept of value, particularly as it is tested by the influences of supply and demand in the real estate market. The listing agreement, which comprises the broker's stock in trade, can take many forms, each with its own rights and responsibilities for principal and agent. This chapter will examine these forms of listing agreements. The real estate broker needs at least a rudimentary knowledge of basic appraisal. A fuller treatment is found in Chapter 16, which some students may wish to read also at this point.

Characteristics of Real Estate

Unlike many commodities sold on the open market, real estate possesses unique characteristics that affect its use both directly and indirectly. These fall into two broad categories: economic characteristics and physical characteristics.

Economic Characteristics

The basic economic characteristics of land are: (1) relative scarcity, (2) improvements, (3) permanence of investment and (4) area preferences.

Relative scarcity. The total supply of land is fixed. While there is still a considerable amount of land not in use, land in a given location or of a particular quality is scarce in some areas.

Improvements. The building of an improvement on one parcel of land has an effect on the value and utilization of neighboring tracts. Not only does an improvement affect adjoining tracts, it often has a direct bearing on whole communities. For example, the improvement of a parcel of real estate by the construction of an assembly plant or the selection of a site for the building of a nuclear power facility can directly influence a large area favorably or unfavorably.

Permanence of investment. After land has been improved, the capital and labor needed to build the improvement represent a fixed investment. Although older buildings can be razed, improvements such as drainage, electricity, water and sewerage remain. The income return on such investments is long term and relatively stable and usually extends over what is referred to as the economic life of the improvement.

Area preference. This economic characteristic, often called **situs,** refers to people's choices and preferences for a given area. It is the unique quality of people's preferences that makes a house in a given location sell for twice as much as a similar one on the other side of town.

Physical Characteristics

The basic physical characteristics of land are: (1) immobility, (2) indestructibility and (3) nonhomogeneity.

Immobility. Land, which is the earth's surface, is immobile. It is true that some of the substances of land are removable and that topography can be changed but still that part of the earth's surface always remains. The geographic location of any given parcel of land can never be changed. It is rigid; it is fixed. Because land is immobile, *real estate laws and markets tend to be local in character*.

Indestructibility. Just as land is immobile, it is *durable* and *indestructible*. This permanence, not only of land but also of the improvements (including the buildings) that are placed on it, has tended to stabilize investments in land. The fact that land is indestructible does not, of course, change the fact that the improvements on land do depreciate and can become obsolete, thereby reducing—or possibly destroying—values.

Nonhomogeneity. The characteristic of **nonhomogeneity** stems from the fact that no two parcels of land are ever exactly the same. Although there may be substantial similarity, *all parcels differ geographically* as each parcel has its own location.

Characteristics Define Land Use

The various characteristics of a parcel of real estate affect its desirability for a specific use. Physical and economic factors that would affect land use include: (1) contour and elevation of the parcel, (2) prevailing winds, (3) transportation, (4) public improvements and (5) availability of natural resources, such as water. Hilly, heavily wooded land would need considerable work before it could be used for industrial purposes but would be ideally suited for residential use. Flat land located along a major highway network would be undesirable for residential use but well located for industry.

Real Estate—The Business of Value

The real estate industry deals with real estate and its value. Value is not the same as price; nor is it the same as cost. Specifically **value** can be defined as *the amount of goods or services that will be offered in the marketplace in exchange for any given product.* It also has been described as the *present worth of future benefits.*

The value of real property does not remain the same. Changes in the cost of construction material can increase the objective value of property and differing standards and needs can alter a personal estimate of value. A housing shortage may increase the market value of even older, less desirable houses, while building a better road may cause the value of property along an older road to decrease. Availability of financing also may affect the property's value.

In real estate the concept of *cost* generally relates to the past, *price* to the present and *value* to the future. Value does not rise in exact proportion to inflation or to the cost of living, as is illustrated in Table 9.1.

Vital to the appraisal of investment or income property is the concept of the **present value of money.** It considers the question: "Would you rather have $1 today

Table 9.1	1983	1984	1985	1986	1987	1988
Changing Values in						
Selected Cities: Median						
Sales Price of Existing Albany/Schenectady/Troy	$49,400	$52,900	$60,300	$72,700	$86,400	$93,300
Single-Family Homes for Buffalo/Niagara Falls	*	44,800	46,600	52,400	56,500	66,600
Metropolitan Areas New York/Northern New						
Jersey/Long Island	88,900	105,300	133,600	160,600	178,500	192,600
Rochester	54,800	59,600	64,200	68,300	72,200	78,300
Syracuse	*	50,700	58,800	64,300	68,900	75,400
Boston	82,600	100,000	134,200	159,200	176,800	184,100
Chicago	76,500	79,500	81,100	86,100	90,800	100,800
Cleveland	*	62,700	63,300	66,900	68,400	69,800
Los Angeles Area	112,700	115,300	116,900	128,800	147,700	190,900
Philadelphia	59,600	60,300	68,300	82,400	97,000	101,200
Washington, D.C.	89,400	93,000	97,100	101,200	108,500	135,800
United States	70,300	72,400	75,200	80,300	85,600	90,200

SOURCE: National Association of REALTORS®.
*Not available.

or $1 a year from now?'' Obviously, today's dollar is more valuable. The next question is: ''Would you rather have 95 cents today, or $1 a year from now?'' Depending on current interest rates and investment opportunities, one might even prefer 90 cents today. That figure would be the *present value* of next year's dollar. Much more complex calculations are used to determine the present value of, for example, rental income or a stream of mortgage payments over a period of many years.

The Real Estate Market

A **market** is a place where goods can be bought and sold, where a price can be established and where it becomes advantageous for buyers and sellers to trade. The function of the market is to facilitate this exchange by providing a setting in which the *supply and demand forces* of the economy can establish price levels.

Supply and Demand

The economic forces of supply and demand continually interact in the market to establish and maintain price levels. Essentially *when supply goes up, prices will drop; when demand increases, prices will rise* (*see* Figure 9.1).

Supply can be defined as *the amount of goods offered for sale within the market at a given price during a given time period.*

Demand can be defined as *the number of people willing and able to accept the available goods at any given price during a given time period.*

Supply and demand in the real estate market. Because of its characteristics of nonstandardization and immobility, the real estate market is relatively slow to adjust to changes in supply and demand. The product cannot be removed from the market or transferred to another market, so an oversupply usually results in a lowering of price levels. But because development and construction of real estate take a considerable period of time from conception to completion, increases in demand may not be met immediately. Building and housing construction may occur in uneven spurts of activity.

**Figure 9.1
Supply and Demand**

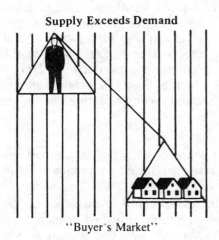

Supply Exceeds Demand

''Buyer's Market''

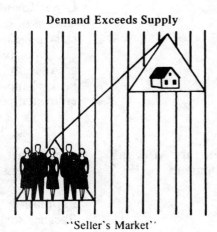

Demand Exceeds Supply

''Seller's Market''

Factors Affecting Supply

Factors that tend to affect supply in the real estate market include the labor supply, construction costs and government controls and financial policies (*see* Figure 9.2).

Labor supply and construction costs. A shortage of labor in the skilled building trades, an increase in the cost of building materials or a scarcity of materials will tend to lower the amount of housing that will be built. High interest rates also severely curtail construction. The impact depends on the extent to which higher costs can be passed on to the buyer or renter in the form of higher purchase prices or rentals.

Figure 9.2
Factors Affecting Supply and Demand

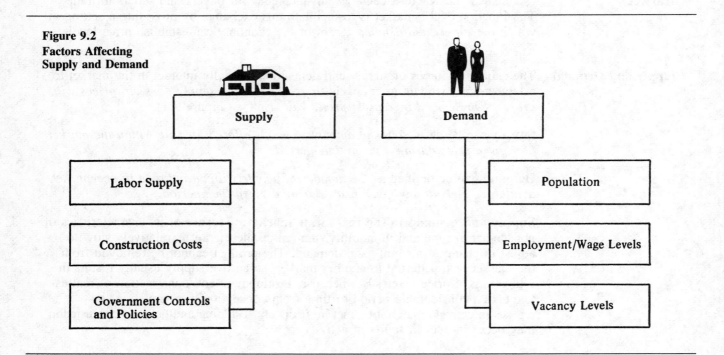

Government controls and financial policies. The government can influence the amount of money available for real estate investment through its fiscal and/or monetary policies. At the local level, policies on taxation of real estate can have either positive or negative effects. Health, fire, zoning and building ordinances are used by communities to control and stimulate the highest potential use of land. Community amenities such as churches, schools and parks and efficient governmental policies are influential factors affecting the real estate market.

Factors Affecting Demand

Factors that tend to affect demand in the real estate market include population, employment and wage levels, and vacancy levels (*see* Figure 9.2).

Population. Population trends have a basic influence on the sale of real estate. Because shelter (whether in the form of owned or rented property) is a basic human and family need, the general need for housing will grow as the population grows. Although the total population of the country is increasing, this trend is not uniform in all localities.

In a consideration of the impact of population on the real estate market, the makeup of the population, or *demographics,* also must be taken into account. In recent years an increasing number of residential units are being purchased by singles or one-parent families.

Employment and wage levels. Employment opportunities and wage levels in a small community can be drastically affected in a short period of time by decisions made by major employers in the area.

Vacancy levels. Vacancy levels in a community provide a good indication of the demand for housing. A growing shortage of housing (fewer vacancies) will result in increasing rents. Conversely because real estate is a fixed commodity and cannot be removed from the market, an increase in vacancies will force rents down.

Appraisal

Real estate usually is appraised using one of three different approaches: *cost approach, income approach* or *direct sales comparison approach*. Each is appropriate for a different type of real estate. Some elaborate appraisals study the **subject property** (the parcel being evaluated) through all three methods, reconciling the results for a final estimate of value.

Approaches to Appraisal

The **cost approach** estimates the amount needed to reproduce or replace the property being studied. This approach is most appropriate for non–income-producing buildings that cannot easily be compared with others: hospitals, schools, churches, fire stations. It also is used for insurance purposes. The cost approach considers not only the cost of reconstructing buildings but also the amount of **depreciation** that has already subtracted value from the property. Depreciation falls into three categories: **physical deterioration, functional obsolescence** (undesirable or outmoded features) and **external (economic or locational) obsolescence** (undesirable factors located beyond the property lines).

The **income approach** to appraisal estimates value by analyzing the income generated by the property being considered. It is appropriate for valuation of commercial, industrial and rental property.

The **direct sales comparison (market data) approach** evaluates property by careful study of similar parcels recently sold. The process is based on research and study of data. It is most appropriate for single residences. Chapter 16 contains a detailed discussion of appraisal.

Market Value

Market value is an important concept defined as the *probable price a property will bring in a competitive and open market, offered by an informed seller and allowing a reasonable time to find a purchaser who buys the property with knowledge of all the uses to which it is adapted, neither buyer nor seller being under duress.*

In other words, market value is the likely price obtainable in a free, open and informed market. The concept of market value also supposes an **arm's-length transaction,** defined as one between relative strangers, each trying to do the best for himself or herself. A sale between mother and son, for example, is not likely to be an arm's-length transaction and may not yield full market value for the property.

Market value is not to be confused with cost or even with selling price. In an ideal market each parcel would sell for its exact value but outside factors may cause a sale to be made below market value and sometimes above market value.

Listing Property

To acquire their inventories brokers and salespeople must obtain listings. **Listing agreements** generally are written contracts of employment although in New York oral agreements may be used if the term of the listing is for less than one year. Only a broker can act as agent to list, sell or rent another person's real estate. These acts must be done in the name and under the supervision of the broker, never in the name of the salesperson.

Listing Agreements

The forms of listing agreements, or employment contracts, used in New York are: (1) open listing, (2) exclusive-agency listing and (3) exclusive-right-to-sell listing. Their similarities and differences are examined in Table 9.2.

Table 9.2 Listing Agreements

Type of Listing	Listing Agent Entitled to Commission if Sold by:		
	Seller	Agent	Other Broker
Open Listing		x	
Exclusive-Agency Listing		x	x
Exclusive-Right-to-Sell Listing	x	x	x

Open listing. In an **open listing** the seller retains the right to employ any number of brokers to act as agents. The seller is obligated to pay a commission only to that broker who successfully produces a ready, willing and able buyer. If the seller personally sells the property *without the aid of any of the brokers,* he or she is not obligated to pay any of them a commission. A listing contract generally creates an open listing unless wording that specifically provides otherwise is included.

Exclusive-agency listing. In an **exclusive-agency listing** *only one broker* is specifically authorized to act as the exclusive agent of the principal. The *seller* under this form of agreement *retains the right to sell the property himself or herself* without obligation to the broker.

Exclusive-right-to-sell listing. In an **exclusive-right-to-sell listing** one broker is appointed as sole agent of the seller and is given the exclusive *authorization* to represent the property in question. The seller must pay the broker a commission *regardless of who sells the property* if it is sold while the listing is in effect. If the seller gives a broker an exclusive-right-to-sell listing but finds a buyer without the broker's assistance, the seller must still pay the broker a commission. (An example of this form of agreement is reproduced in Figure 9.4.)

Net listing. A **net listing** is based on the amount of money the seller will receive if the property is sold. The broker is free to offer the property for sale at any price. If the property is sold, the broker pays the seller only the net amount previously agreed on and keeps the rest. *This type of listing is illegal in New York*. It lends itself to fraud and is seldom in the seller's best interest.

Multiple Listing

A **multiple-listing service (MLS)** is usually organized within a geographic area by a group of brokers who agree to pool their listings.

The multiple-listing agreement, while not actually a separate form of listing, is in effect an *exclusive-right-to-sell* or *exclusive-agency agreement* with an additional authority to *distribute the listing to other brokers who belong to the multiple-listing service*. The contractual obligations among the member brokers of a multiple-listing organization vary widely. Most provide that upon sale of the property *the commission is divided between the listing broker and the selling broker*. Terms for division of the commission vary by individual arrangement between brokers.

Under most multiple-listing contracts the broker who secures the listing is not only authorized but *obligated* to turn the listing over to his or her multiple-listing service within a definite period of time so that it can be distributed to other member brokers.

The broker who chooses to show property listed by another MLS firm has taken on the duties of seller's subagent. Unless specifically retained as a buyer's broker, the selling broker is working *for* the seller, just as the listing agent is.

A multiple-listing service offers advantages to broker, buyer and seller. Brokers develop a sizable inventory of properties to be sold and are assured of a portion of the commission if they list the property or participate in its sale. Sellers gain because all members of the multiple-listing organization work to sell their property. Buyers have efficient access to a large selection of listings.

Termination of Listings

As discussed in Chapter 2, a listing agreement—or any agency relationship—may be terminated for any of the following reasons: (1) performance by the broker, (2) expiration of the time period stated in the agreement, (3) abandonment by the broker if he or she spends no time on the listing, (4) revocation by the owner (although the owner may be liable for the broker's expenses), (5) cancellation by the broker or by mutual consent, (6) bankruptcy, death or insanity of either party, (7) destruction of the property or (8) a change in property use by outside forces (such as a change in zoning).

Expiration of listing period. All listings should specify a definite period of time during which the broker is to be employed. The use of automatic extensions of time in exclusive listings is illegal in New York.

Obtaining Listings

All legal owners of the listing property or their authorized agents as well as the listing salesperson and/or broker should sign the listing agreement. The listing salesperson can sign the contract in the broker's name if authorized by the broker.

Information needed for listing agreements. When taking a listing it is important to obtain as much information as possible concerning a parcel of real estate. This ensures that all possible contingencies can be anticipated, particularly when the listing will be shared with other brokers and salespeople in a multiple-listing arrangement. This information includes the following (where appropriate):

1. Names and addresses of owners;
2. Adequate description of the property;
3. Size of lot (frontage and depth);
4. Number and size of rooms and total square footage;
5. Construction and age of the building;
6. Information relative to the neighborhood (schools, churches, transportation);
7. Current taxes;
8. Amount of existing financing (including interest, payments and other costs);
9. Utilities and average payments;
10. Appliances to be included in the transaction;
11. Date of occupancy or possession;
12. Possibility of seller financing;
13. Zoning classification (especially important for vacant land); and
14. A detailed list of exactly what will and what will not be included in the sales price.

A real estate broker, as an agent of the seller, is responsible for the disclosure of any material information regarding the property. Getting as much initial information from the seller as possible—even if it becomes necessary to ask penetrating and possibly embarrassing questions—will pay off in the long run by saving both principal and agent from potential legal difficulties. The agent also should assume the responsibility of searching the public records for such pertinent information as zoning, lot size and yearly taxes.

The *true tax* figure should be used, disregarding any present veteran's, aged or religious exemption, or any addition for unpaid water bills.

In the sale of multiple dwellings the seller should be ready to present a statement of rents and expenses, preferably prepared by an accountant. Prospective buyers will want statements on leases and security deposits. The listing agent should verify zoning and the legality of existing use. The seller should be informed of any necessity for a certificate of occupancy at transfer. Arranging with tenants to show the property at reasonable times is also of vital importance.

Truth-in-Heating Law. New York's Truth-in-Heating Law requires the seller to furnish upon written request two past years' heating and cooling bills to any prospective buyer of a one- or two-family home. Sellers also must furnish a statement on the extent and type of insulation they have installed together with any information the seller may have on insulation installed by previous owners.

If the federal Department of Housing and Urban Development has determined that the property is in a flood-prone area, a buyer may need to obtain flood insurance before placing certain kinds of mortgages. The listing agent can anticipate this by consulting a flood area map at the time of listing. Maps may be ordered from the federal Emergency Management Agency, Flood Map Distribution Center, 6930 (A-F) San Tomas Road, Baltimore, Maryland 21227-6227, or by calling toll-free 1-800-333-1363.

Some municipalities may have restrictive ordinances like aquifer protection zones, wetlands protection or steep slope ordinances. Listing agents should keep current with all potential restrictions to use of land.

Pricing the Property   The pricing of the real estate is of primary importance. Even though it is the responsibility of the broker or salesperson to advise, counsel and assist, it is ultimately the *seller* who must determine a listing price for his or her property. However, because the average seller usually does not have the background to make an informed decision about a fair market price, the real estate agent must be prepared to offer knowledge, information and expertise in this area.

A broker or salesperson can help the seller determine a listing price for the property through a **comparative market analysis (CMA).** This is a comparison of the prices of recently sold homes that are similar in location, style and amenities to that of the listing seller.

Although it has some resemblance to a direct sales comparison approach appraisal, a CMA differs from an appraisal in several important ways. It is usually offered as a free service by a salesperson or broker, contrasting with the paid appraisal rendered by a fee appraiser. Both studies analyze recent sales of similar properties, but the CMA does so in a more superficial manner. The CMA includes material not usually considered in regular appraisals: information on nearby properties that *failed* to sell, for example, and a list of competing property currently on the market. It also includes significant **DOM** (days on market) information. Broker ethics dictate that a CMA must never be called a free appraisal. A comparative market analysis form is illustrated in Figure 9.4, page 169.

The broker should convey to the seller the fact that the eventual selling price is set by the buying public through the operation of supply and demand in the open market. Among factors that should not determine listing price are the original cost, assessed value, replacement cost and the amount the seller needs to realize from the property.

New York State Requirements

The New York Real Property Law requires that the broker must have attached to or printed on the reverse side of an exclusive agreement a statement to the following effect:

> An exclusive-right-to-sell listing means that if you, the property owner, find a buyer for your house or if another broker finds a buyer, you must pay the agreed-upon commission to the present broker.

> An exclusive-agency listing means that if you, the property owner, find a buyer, you will not have to pay a commission to the broker. However, if another broker finds a buyer you will owe a commission to both the selling broker and your present broker.

If an exclusive listing of residential property is obtained by a broker who is a member of a multiple-listing service: (1) the broker must give the homeowner a list of the names and addresses of all member brokers and (2) the listing agreement must allow the seller to choose whether all negotiated offers to purchase will be submitted through the listing broker or through the selling broker.

Sample Listing Agreement

The individual specifics of a listing may vary from area to area. Following is a section-by-section analysis of the sample agreement; numerical references are to the specific provisions of the contract (See Figure 9.3) used by the Westchester Multiple Listing Service.

1. *Exclusive right to sell*. The title specifies that this document is an "exclusive right to sell" real property.
2. *Date*. The date of the listing contract is the date it is executed; this may not necessarily be the date the contract becomes effective.
3. *Names*. The names of all persons having an interest in the property should be specified and should enter into the agreement. If the property is owned under one of the forms of co-ownership discussed in Chapter 3, that fact should be clearly established.
4. *Broker or firm*. The name of the broker or firm entering into the listing must be clearly stated in the agreement.
5. *Contract*. This section establishes the document as a *bilateral contract* and states the promises by both parties that create and bind the agreement.
6. *Termination of agreement*. Both the exact time and date serve to remove any ambiguity in regard to termination of the contract.
7. *Listing price*. The listing price is a gross sales price and the owner should understand that any obligations such as taxes, mortgages and assessments remain his or her responsibility and must be paid out of the proceeds of the sale.
8. *Commission rate*. This paragraph establishes the broker's rate of commission. Each brokerage firm is free to set its own fee schedule and to negotiate commission rates if it wishes to.
9. *Extension clause*. This section, permitted in New York, will protect the broker if the owner or another person sells the property after the listing expires to a person with whom the original broker negotiated. In other words the broker is guaranteed a commission for a set period of time after the agreement expires (generally three to six months) if he or she was the procuring cause of the sale even if the broker did not actually consummate the transaction. This extension clause does not apply, however, if the owner signs a new listing agreement with another broker after the original agreement expires.
10. *Negotiation*. The owner agrees to refer all inquiries to the agent and chooses to have any offers submitted either by the listing agent or the selling agent, who may belong to a different firm.
11. *Multiple-listing service*. The agent will circulate information on the listing to all members of the multiple-listing service—immediately. In some other areas the listing office may have one, two or three days of "office exclusive" before the listing is submitted to the MLS.
12. *For Sale sign*. The agent may not place a sign on the property without authorization.
13. *Additional points*. Anything not illegal may be agreed on by seller and agent. For example, an understanding that "no commission will be due if seller's brother purchases within 30 days" would go here.
14. *Signatures*. The contract should be signed by all owners. The sales associate signs on behalf of the broker or firm; the contract is *not* made with the individual salesperson.
15. *Definitions*. The seller must receive an explanation of types of listings and a list of all MLS participants, as required by the New York Department of State.
16. *Civil rights legislation*. This clause serves to alert the owner that both federal and state legislation protects against discrimination.
17. *Owner's acknowledgment*. The seller acknowledges notification of listing definitions and of civil rights legislation.

Figure 9.3
Listing Agreement

8/88

(1) **EXCLUSIVE RIGHT TO SELL AGREEMENT**

THIS AGREEMENT is effective (2) _____ 19___, and confirms that (3) _____
_____ has (have) appointed (4) _____ to act as Agent for the
sale of property known as _____, New York.

(5) In return for the Agent's agreement to use Agent's best efforts to sell the above property, the Owner(s) agree(s) to grant the Agent the exclusive right to sell this property under the following terms and conditions:

PERIOD OF AGREEMENT

1. This agreement shall be effective from the above date and shall expire at midnight on (6) _____, 19___

PRICE AT WHICH PROPERTY WILL BE OFFERED

2. The property will be offered for sale at a list price of $ (7) _____ and shall be sold, subject to negotiation, at such price and upon such terms to which Owner(s) may agree.

(8) **COMMISSION TO BE PAID TO AGENT**

3. The Agent shall be entitled to one commission of _____% of the selling price. Both the Owner(s) and the Agent acknowledge that the above commission rate was not suggested nor influenced by anyone other than the parties to this Agreement. Any commission due for a sale brought about by a Sub-agent (another broker who is authorized by the Agent to assist in the sale of your property) shall be paid by the Agent from the commission received by the Agent.

(9) **OWNER(S) OBLIGATIONS AFTER THE EXPIRATION OF THIS AGREEMENT**

4. Owner(s) understands and agrees to pay the commission referred to in paragraph 3, if this property is sold or transferred or is the subject of a contract of sale within____ months after the expiration date of this agreement involving a person with whom the Agent or Sub-agent or the Owner(s) negotiated or to whom the property is offered, quoted or shown during the period of this listing agreement. Owner(s) will not, however, be obligated to pay such commission if Owner(s) enters into a valid Exclusive Listing Agreement with another New York State licensed real estate broker after the expiration of this agreement.

(10) **WHO MAY NEGOTIATE FOR OWNER(S)**

5. Owner(s) agree(s) to direct all inquiries to the Agent. Owner(s) elect(s) to have all negotiations submitted through Agent ❑ or Sub-agent ❑.

(11) **SUBMISSION OF LISTING TO MULTIPLE LISTING SERVICE**

6. Both Owner(s) and Agent agree that the Agent immediately is to submit this listing agreement to the Westchester Multiple Listing Service, Inc., for dissemination to its Participants. No provision of this agreement is intended to nor shall be understood to establish or imply any contractual relationship between the Owner(s) and the Westchester Multiple Listing Service, Inc., nor has the Westchester Multiple Listing Service, Inc., in any way participated in any of the terms of this agreement, including the rate of commission. Owner(s) acknowledge(s) that the Agent's ability to submit this listing to the Westchester Multiple Listing Service, Inc., or to maintain such listing amongst those included in any compilation of listing information published by Westchester Multiple Listing Service, Inc., is subject to Agent's continued status as a member in good standing of the Westchester County Board of REALTORS, Inc., and Agent's status as a Participant in good standing of the Westchester Multiple Listing Service, Inc.

(12) **AUTHORIZATION FOR "FOR SALE" SIGN**

7. Agent ❑ is (❑ is not) authorized to place a "For Sale" sign on the property.

REQUIREMENTS FOR PUBLICATION IN WMLS COMPILATION

8. This listing agreement is not acceptable for publication by the Westchester Multiple Listing Service, Inc. unless and until the owner(s) has duly signed both the face of this agreement and the reverse side or an attachment to the listing agreement reflecting receipt of the definitions of "Exclusive Right to Sell" and "Exclusive Agency" required by New York State Department of Law - Division of Licensing Services.

9. Additional Points of Agreement, if any: (13) _____

ALL MODIFICATIONS TO BE MADE IN WRITING

10. Owner(s) and Agent agree that no change, amendment, modification or termination of this Agreement shall be binding on any party unless the same shall be in writing and signed by the parties.

_____ _____ (14)   _____ _____
(OWNER)   (DATE)   (AGENT)

_____ _____   By: _____
(OWNER)   (DATE)   (Authorized Representative)   (DATE)

Owner's Mailing Address: _____   Agent's Address: _____

_____   _____

Owner's Telephone: _____   Agent's Telephone: _____

Figure 9.3
(continued)

DEFINITIONS ⑮

In accordance with the requirements of the New York State Department of State the undersigned owner(s) does (do) hereby acknowledge receipt of the following:
1. Explanation of "Exclusive Right to Sell" listing;
2. Explanation of "Exclusive Agency" listing;
3. A list of Participants of Westchester Multiple Listing Service, Inc.

EXPLANATION OF EXCLUSIVE RIGHT TO SELL: (As worded verbatim by the Department of State)
"An Exclusive Right to Sell listing means that if you, the owner of the property, find a buyer for your house, or if another broker finds a buyer, you must pay the agreed commission to the present broker."

EXPLANATION OF EXCLUSIVE AGENCY: (As worded verbatim by the Department of State)
"An Exclusive Agency listing means that if you, the owner of the property, find a buyer, you will not have to pay commission to the broker. However, if another broker finds a buyer, you will owe a commission to both the selling broker and your present broker".

⑯ "THE FAIR HOUSING ACT"

The Civil Rights Act of 1968 known as the Federal Fair Housing Law makes illegal any discrimination based on race, color, religion, sex or national origin in connection with the sale or rental of housing."

Article X of the REALTOR Code of Ethics states:

"The REALTOR shall not deny any equal professional services to any person for reasons of race, creed, sex, or country of national origin. The REALTOR shall not be a part to any plan or agreement to discriminate against a person or persons on the basis of race, creed, sex or country of national origin."

⑰

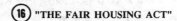

_____
                                                              Owner

Courtesy of the Westchester Multiple   _____
Listing Service, Inc.   Owner

Income Tax Benefits for Home Sellers

Although sellers should be referred to their accountants or attorneys for specific information, many ask the real estate broker about the regulations on profit from the sale of real estate. Where a primary residence is being sold, two special tax treatments apply.

In New York State, federal tax benefits for homeowners will also apply to state income tax. Special tax breaks are available if the homeowner is over 55 at the time of sale or if the residence is replaced with another.

Deferment of tax. If a main residence is replaced with another within 24 months before or after the sale of the first home, profit on the first property is not immediately taxable but is rolled over (buried) in the cost basis of the new residence. It will not be taxed until some time in the future, when the next home is sold. If the replacement residence costs less than the first one sold for, a portion of the profit may be immediately taxable; the rest qualifies for postponement.

Over-55 exclusion. A homeowner who sells or exchanges his or her principal residence and (1) was 55 or older by the date of sale or exchange and (2) owned and used the property sold or exchanged as a principal residence for a period totaling at least three years within the five-year period ending on the date of the

Figure 9.4
Comparative Market Analysis

Comparative Market Analysis for _____

Date _____

Sugg. list price
$ _____

Address	Style	Const	Age	No. of Rms	No. of Bdrms	No. of Baths	Gar	Fplc	Pool	C/A	Size Prop	Assess Value	Taxes	Comments & Extras	Fair Market Value

1. SIMILAR HOMES RECENTLY SOLD: These tell us what people are willing to pay . . . for this kind of home . . . in this area . . . at this time

Closed Date Adjustd
Price   Price

2. SIMILAR HOMES FOR SALE NOW: These tell us what we are competing against. Buyers will compare your home against these homes.

Askg   Days On
Price Mkt.

3. EXPIRED LISTINGS — SIMILAR HOMES UNSOLD FOR 90 DAYS OR MORE: These illustrate the problems of over pricing.

PROBLEMS OF OVERPRICING:

A.   HARD to get salespeople excited.
B.   HARD to get people to make an offer.
C.   HARD to get good buyers to look.
D.   HARD to get financing.

SOURCE: John E. Cyr and Joan m. Sobeck, *Real Estate Brokerage: A Success Guide*, 2nd Ed. (Chicago: Real Estate Education Company, 1988), p. 175.

sale, may exclude from income part or all of the capital gain on that sale or exchange. Taxpayers who meet these requirements can exclude the first *$125,000* of gain. A homeowner may exclude gains under the over-55 provision *only once in a lifetime* even if the total gain excluded is less than the $125,000 limit. Because a spouse must join in the election to use the over-55 exclusion it may not be taken by anyone whose spouse has already used the exclusion, even in a previous marriage, or on a home owned solely by a former spouse. New York State imposes a 10 percent capital gains tax on real estate transfers for property that is not the seller's main residence where the sales price is more than $1,000,000. Installment sale treatment, which taxes profit year by year as it is received, is available for nonrental property (one's own home, vacant land) and for investment property with some exceptions for recapture of excellerated depreciation.

Summary

The unique nature of land is apparent in both its economic and physical characteristics. The economic characteristics consist of *scarcity, improvements, permanence of investment* and *area preferences*. The physical characteristics are *immobility, nonhomogeneity* and *indestructibility*.

Real estate is the business of *value*. A property's value is the present worth of its future benefits. Value is not the same as *price;* price is determined in the marketplace.

A *market* is a place where goods and services can be bought and sold and relatively stable price levels established. Because of its unique characteristics, real estate is relatively slow to adjust to the forces of supply and demand.

Supply can be defined as the amount of goods available in the market for a given price. *Demand* is defined as the number of people willing to accept those available goods at a given price.

The supply of and demand for real estate are affected by many factors including *population changes, wage and employment levels, percentage of unoccupied space, construction costs and availability of labor,* and *governmental monetary policy and controls*.

Real estate is appraised through the use of three different methods. The *cost approach* estimates the money needed to reconstruct the building and subtracts any loss in value due to *depreciation*. Depreciation may be *physical* (wear and tear), *functional* (outmoded features) or *external* (*locational*—due to features beyond the property boundaries).

The *income approach* calculates value based on income generated by the *subject property*.

The *direct sales comparison approach* evaluates property by analysis of similar nearby properties recently sold.

Market value is defined as the probable price a property will bring in a competitive and open market, offered by an informed seller and allowing a reasonable time to find a purchaser who buys the property with knowledge of all the uses to which it is adaptable, neither buyer nor seller being under duress.

An *open listing* is one in which the broker's commission depends on his or her finding a buyer before the property is sold by the seller or another broker. Under an *exclusive-agency listing* the broker is given the exclusive right to represent the seller but the seller can avoid paying the broker a commission if he or she sells the property without the broker's help. With an *exclusive-right-to-sell listing* the seller appoints one broker to represent him or her and must pay that broker a commission regardless of whether it is the broker or the seller who finds a buyer for it, if the buyer is found within the listing period. *Net listings* are illegal in New York.

A *multiple listing* is an exclusive listing with the additional authority and obligation on the part of the listing broker to distribute the listing to other brokers in his or her multiple-listing organization.

A listing agreement may be terminated for the same reasons as any other agency relationship.

The *comparative market analysis* is a rudimentary form of direct sales comparison appraisal.

When a homeowner sells a principal residence, income tax on any gain is deferred if the homeowner purchases another residence within 24 months before or after the sale. Homeowners over the age of 55 are given additional benefits.

Questions

1. Any two parcels of real estate:
   a. can never be the same.
   b. can be the same only with identical tract houses.
   c. are considered the same if they have identical sales prices.
   d. are identical because of situs.

2. The benefits anticipated from property in the future are a measure of its:
   a. value.   c. obsolescence.
   b. depreciation.   d. nonhomogeneity.

3. In real estate the concept of cost is related to the:
   a. past.   c. future.
   b. present.   d. sales price.

4. If six houses are offered for sale on the same street, sales prices will probably:
   a. be identical.
   b. be disappointingly low.
   c. set new highs for that neighborhood.
   d. None of the above

5. Real estate markets tend to be:
   a. similar across the country.
   b. statewide in their characteristics.
   c. stable despite economic changes.
   d. local in character.

6. The three approaches to appraisal do *not* include the:
   a. cost method.
   b. income approach.
   c. comparative market analysis.
   d. direct sales comparison method.

7. Tom Wills is asked to estimate the market value of a church. He will give most emphasis to which appraisal approach?
   a. Cost   c. Competitive analysis
   b. Income   d. Direct sales comparison

8. The income approach to appraisal is most appropriate for a:
   a. tract ranch house.   c. apartment house.
   b. library.   d. vacant lot.

9. The market data approach to appraisal utilizes:
   a. asking prices for property on the market.
   b. building costs in the area.
   c. analysis of functional obsolescence.
   d. recent sale prices of similar parcels.

10. If the roof of a building is near the end of its useful life, an appraiser will subtract value because of:
    a. physical deterioration.
    b. functional obsolescence.
    c. external obsolescence.
    d. situs.

11. An office building that cannot be centrally air-conditioned suffers from:
    a. physical deterioration.
    b. functional obsolescence.
    c. external obsolescence.
    d. situs.

12. An example of external obsolescence might be a:
    a. faulty heating system.
    b. poor floor plan.
    c. tenant who will not pay rent.
    d. used car lot next door.

13. The highest price that would be paid by an informed buyer when property is widely exposed on the market is known as:
    a. cost.   c. sales price.
    b. listing price. d. market value.

14. In the final analysis selling price for real estate is set by:
    a. the seller.
    b. the broker.
    c. comparative market analysis.
    d. the buying public.

15. Ned Neighbor tells Betty Broker over the phone that if she sells his house before Christmas, he will pay her a 5 percent commission. Betty produces a buyer and negotiates a written sales agreement. Betty:

    a. cannot claim a commission because the listing was oral.
    b. cannot claim it because it is not an arm's-length transaction.
    c. can claim a commission only if Ned is still willing to pay.
    d. has a legal claim for commission as agreed over the phone.

16. Susy promised a commission to Broker *A* if he sold the property, then turned around and made the same arrangement with Broker *B*. Susy must be entering into a(n):

    a. open listing.
    b. exclusive-agency listing.
    c. exclusive-right-to-sell listing.
    d. multiple listing.

17. Leon Ericsson arranged to let Don Hotshot be his only broker, but when Leon sold the property himself, he owed Don nothing. Their agreement must have been a(n):

    a. multiple listing.
    b. exclusive-agency listing.
    c. exclusive-right-to-sell listing.
    d. net listing.

18. In the question above, Don could have claimed a commission if their agreement had been a(n):

    a. open listing.
    b. exclusive-agency listing.
    c. exclusive-right-to-sell listing.
    d. net listing.

19. In New York State every listing contract must include:

    a. an automatic extension clause.
    b. a net listing provision.
    c. the broker's license number.
    d. an explanation of types of listings.

20. Under a multiple-listing system if Broker *A* lists the property and Broker *B* with another firm sells it:

    a. no commission need be paid.
    b. Broker *A* is entitled to the full commission.
    c. Broker *B* receives the full commission.
    d. the commission is shared between the two offices.

21. The Truth-in-Heating Law requires a seller to disclose to prospective buyers:

    a. any flaws in the heating system.
    b. a detailed list of which tenants pay their own utilities.
    c. two years' past heating bills.
    d. receipts for installation of furnace and air-conditioner.

22. A property was listed with a broker who belonged to a multiple-listing service. It was sold for $93,500 by another broker member. The total commission was 6 percent of the sales price; of this commission the selling broker received 60 percent and the listing broker received the balance. How much was the listing broker's commission?

    a. $3,366   c. $5,610
    b. $2,019.60   d. $2,244

23. The Internal Revenue Service offers special income tax treatment for profit from the sale of one's primary residence. New York State:

    a. taxes such profit as ordinary income.
    b. goes along with the federal tax treatment.
    c. imposes its own capital gains tax.
    d. allows the first $10,000 of profit tax free.

24. Tax on profit from the sale of one's home is postponed if another home of equal or greater value is bought within:

    a. six months.
    b. one year.
    c. two years.
    d. three out of five years.

25. Mr. Spock is 56 when he sells his long-time home for a profit of $110,000. If he chooses to, Mr. Spock may have income tax on his profit:

    a. depreciated.   c. amortized.
    b. capitalized.   d. excluded.

10

Human Rights and Fair Housing

Key Terms

Affirmative marketing agreement (NAR)
Blockbusting
Civil Rights Act of 1866
Code for Equal Opportunity
Department of Housing and Urban
  Development
Executive Law
Federal Fair Housing Act of 1968

New York Human Rights Law
Protected classes
Real Property Law
Redlining
Reverse discrimination
State Division of Human Rights
Steering
Testers

Overview

To ensure equal opportunity in housing for everyone, federal and state governments have enacted laws that require ethical practices from real estate licensees dealing with the public. In addition brokers and salespeople have an obligation to educate their clients about fair housing laws affecting sellers and landlords. This chapter will deal with such fair housing laws and will examine the codes of ethical practices in this matter followed by most licensees.

Equal Opportunity in Housing

Brokers and salespeople who offer residential property for sale or rent must be aware of the federal, state and local laws pertaining to human rights and non-discrimination. These laws, under such titles as open housing, fair housing or equal opportunity housing prohibit undesirable and discriminatory activities. Their provisions affect every phase of the real estate sales process from listing to closing and *all brokers and salespersons must comply with them.*

The goal of legislators who have enacted fair housing laws and regulations is to create a single, unbiased housing market—one in which every homeseeker has the opportunity to buy any home in the area he or she chooses provided that the home is within the homebuyer's financial means. As a potential licensee the student of real estate must be aware of undesirable and illegal housing practices in order to avoid them. Failure to comply with fair housing practices is not only grounds for license revocation but also a criminal act.

Federal Fair Housing Laws

The efforts of the federal government to guarantee equal housing opportunities to all U.S. citizens began more than 100 years ago with the passage of the **Civil Rights Act of 1866.** This law, an outgrowth of the Fourteenth Amendment, prohibits any type of discrimination based on **race.** "All citizens of the United States shall have the same right in every state and territory as is enjoyed by white citizens thereof to inherit, purchase, lease, sell, hold, and convey real and personal property." A summary of fair housing laws appears in Table 10.1.

Federal Fair Housing Act of 1968. In 1968 two major events greatly encouraged the progress of fair housing. The first was the passage of the **Federal Fair Housing Act of 1968,** which is contained in *Title VIII of the Civil Rights Act of*

Table 10.1 Summary of Fair Housing Laws	Law	Protected Classes
	Civil Rights Act of 1866	Prohibits discrimination in housing based on race without exception
	Title VIII of the Civil Rights Act of 1968 (Federal Fair Housing Act)	Prohibits discrimination in housing based on race, color, religion or national origin with certain exceptions
	Housing and Community Development Act of 1974	Extends prohibitions to discrimination in housing based on sex (gender)
	Fair Housing Amendments Act of 1988	Extends protection to cover persons with handicaps and families with children (with exceptions)
	New York Executive Law	Covers race, creed, color, national origin, sex, disability, age and marital status (some exceptions)
	New York Real Property Law	Prohibits discrimination based on presence of children in a family or pregnancy

1968. This law provides that it is unlawful to discriminate on the basis of **race, color, religion, or national origin** when selling or leasing residential property.

In 1974, an amendment added **sex** (gender) as a **protected class,** and in 1988 two new classes were added: those with mental or physical **handicaps** and **familial status** (presence of children in the family). Drug abusers are not protected as handicapped, nor are those who pose a threat to the health or safety of others. Housing intended for older persons is exempt if it is solely occupied by persons 62 and older, or if 80 percent of its units are occupied by at least one person 55 or older and special facilities for the elderly are provided.

The Federal Fair Housing Act covers dwellings and apartments as well as vacant land acquired for the construction of residential buildings and prohibits the following discriminatory acts:

1. Refusing to sell, rent or negotiate with any person, or otherwise making a dwelling unavailable to any person;
2. Changing terms, conditions or services for different individuals as a means of discrimination;
3. Practicing discrimination through any statement or advertisement that restricts the sale or rental of residential property;
4. Representing to any person, as a means of discrimination, that a dwelling is not available for sale or rental;
5. Making a profit by inducing owners of housing to sell or rent because of the prospective entry into the neighborhood of persons of a particular race, color, religion, national origin, handicap or familial status;
6. Altering the terms or conditions for a home loan to any person who wishes to purchase or repair a dwelling, or otherwise denying such a loan as a means of discrimination; and
7. Denying people membership or limiting their participation in any multiple-listing service, real estate brokers' organization or other facility related to the sale or rental of dwellings, as a means of discrimination.

The following exemptions to the Federal Fair Housing Act are provided:

1. The sale or rental of a single-family home is exempted when the home is owned by an individual who does not own more than three such homes at one time and when the following conditions exist: (a) **a broker, salesperson, or agent is not used** and (b) discriminatory advertising is not used. If the owner is not living in the dwelling at the time of the transaction or was not the most recent occupant, only one such sale by an individual is exempt from the law within any 24-month period.
2. The rental of rooms or units is exempted in an owner-occupied one- to four-family dwelling.
3. Dwelling units owned by religious organizations may be restricted to people of the same religion if membership in the organization is not restricted on the basis of race, color, national origin, handicap or familial status.
4. A private club that is not in fact open to the public may restrict the rental or occupancy of lodgings that it owns to its members as long as the lodgings are not operated commercially.

Jones vs. Mayer. The second significant fair housing development of 1968 was the Supreme Court decision in the case of *Jones vs. Alfred H. Mayer Company,* 392, U.S. 409(1968). In its ruling the Court upheld the Civil Rights Act of 1866, which "prohibits all racial discrimination, private or public, in the sale and rental of property."

The importance of this decision rests in the fact that while the 1968 federal law exempts individual homeowners and certain groups, the 1866 law *prohibits all racial discrimination without exception*. So despite any exemptions in the 1968 law, an aggrieved person may seek a remedy for racial discrimination under the 1866 law against *any* homeowner regardless of whether the owner employed a real estate broker and/or advertised the property. *Where race is involved, no exceptions apply.*

In 1987, U.S. Supreme Court decisions implied that the 1866 no-exceptions law extended to ethnic and/or religious groups.

Equal Housing Poster. An amendment to the Federal Fair Housing Act of 1968 instituted the use of an equal housing opportunity poster. This poster, which can be obtained from HUD (illustrated in Figure 10.1), features the equal housing opportunity slogan, an equal housing statement pledging adherence to the Fair Housing Act and support of affirmative marketing and advertising programs, and the equal housing opportunity logo.

When HUD investigates a broker for discriminatory practices it considers failure to display the poster evidence of discrimination.

Blockbusting and Steering

Blockbusting and steering are undesirable housing practices frequently discussed in connection with fair housing. While they are not mentioned by name in the Federal Fair Housing Act of 1968, both are prohibited by that law and by New York State law.

Blockbusting means *inducing homeowners to sell by making representations regarding the entry or prospective entry of minority persons into the neighborhood.* The blockbuster frightens homeowners into selling and makes a profit by buying the homes cheaply and selling them at considerably higher prices to minority persons. The Federal Fair Housing Act prohibits this practice.

Steering is the channeling of homeseekers to particular areas on the basis of race, religion, country of origin or other protected class. On these grounds it is prohibited by the provisions of the Federal Fair Housing Act. Steering is often difficult to detect, however, because the steering tactics can be so subtle that the homeseeker is unaware that his or her choices have been limited. Steering may be done unintentionally by agents who are not aware of their own unconscious assumptions.

Redlining

Refusing to make mortgage loans or issue insurance policies in specific areas without regard to the economic qualifications of the applicant is known as **redlining.** This practice, which often contributes to the deterioration of older, transitional neighborhoods, is frequently based on racial grounds rather than on any real objections to the applicant.

In an effort to counteract redlining the federal government passed the *Home Mortgage Disclosure Act* in 1975. This act requires all institutional mortgage lenders with assets in excess of $10 million and one or more offices in a given geo-

Figure 10.1
Equal Housing
Opportunity Poster*

U.S.. Department of Housing and Urban Development

**EQUAL HOUSING
OPPORTUNITY**

We Do Business in Accordance With the Federal Fair Housing Law
(The Fair Housing Amendments Act of 1988)

It is Illegal to Discriminate Against Any Person Because of Race, Color, Religion, Sex, Handicap, Familial Status, or National Origin

- In the sale or rental of housing or residential lots
- In advertising the sale or rental of housing
- In the financing of housing

- In the provision of real estate brokerage services
- In the appraisal of housing
- Blockbusting is also illegal

Anyone who feels he or she has been discriminated against may file a complaint of housing discrimination with the:

**U.S. Department of Housing and
Urban Development
Assistant Secretary for Fair Housing and
Equal Opportunity
Washington, D.C. 20410**

Previous editions are obsolete   form HUD-928.1 (3-89) graphic area to make annual reports by census tracts of all mortgage loans the institution makes or purchases. This law enables the government to detect lending or insuring patterns that might constitute redlining. A lending institution that refuses a loan solely on sound economic grounds cannot be accused of redlining.

Enforcement. A person who believes illegal discrimination has occurred has up to one year after the alleged act to file a charge with the **Department of Housing and Urban Development (HUD),** or may bring a federal suit within two years. HUD will investigate, and if the department believes a discriminatory act has occurred or is about to occur, it may issue a charge. Any party involved (or HUD) may choose to have the charge heard in a federal district court. If no one requests the court procedure the charge will be heard by an administrative law judge within HUD itself.

The administrative judge has the authority to issue an *injunction*. This would order the offender to do something—rent to the complaining party, for example—or to refrain from doing something. In addition, penalties can be imposed, ranging from $10,000 for a first violation, to $25,000 for a second violation within five years, and $50,000 for further violations within seven years. If the case is heard in federal court an injunction, actual and punitive damages are possible, with no dollar limit. In addition to offended parties, the Department of Justice may itself sue anyone who seems to show a pattern of illegal discrimination. Dollar limits on penalties in such cases are set at $50,000, with a $100,000 penalty for repeat violations.

In all such cases mentioned, the guilty party may be required to pay the other side's legal fees and court costs, which can add up to substantial amounts.

Complaints brought under the Civil Rights Act of 1866 must be taken directly to a federal court. The only time limit for action would be three years, New York's statute of limitation for *torts,* injuries done by one individual to another. There would be no dollar limit on damages.

Threats or Acts of Violence

The Federal Fair Housing Act of 1968 contains criminal provisions protecting the rights of those who seek the benefits of the open housing law as well as owners, brokers or salespeople who aid or encourage the enjoyment of open housing rights. Unlawful actions involving threats, coercion and intimidation are punishable by appropriate civil action. In such cases the victim should report the incident immediately to the local police and to the nearest office of the Federal Bureau of Investigation.

New York Human Rights Law

Blockbusting, forbidden under federal statutes, is specifically mentioned in the **New York Human Rights Law** (Article 15, Executive Law) and is also prohibited by a Department of State regulation. A person discriminated against is able to initiate a private lawsuit (with no dollar limit mentioned under state law) and also to lodge a complaint with the Department of State if the offender is a licensed broker or salesperson. A complaint may be filed with the **New York State Division of Human Rights** also within a one-year period.

Under sections of the **Executive Law,** New York statutes broaden the nondiscrimination rules to cover commercial real estate. In addition several other categories are added in which discrimination is prohibited. These include *age* and *marital status*. Further provisions forbidding discrimination on the basis of age apply to transactions involving commercial space and public housing but not to housing in general. The age provisions apply only to those 18 and over. Local governments may add other groups to the list of protected categories. New York City has prohibited housing discrimination based on sexual orientation or lawful occupation.

The **Real Property Law** forbids a landlord to deny rental housing because of children and also prohibits an eviction because of a tenant's pregnancy or new child. The rules extend to mobile homes.

Various exceptions are made to the New York State rules but these exceptions will not apply where the discrimination is racially based because the Federal Civil Rights Law of 1866, which covers *race, permits no exceptions*. With that in mind, the New York State exceptions are:

1. Public housing that may be aimed at one specific age group;
2. Rental of a duplex in which the owner or his or her family occupies the other unit;
3. Restriction of all rooms rented to members of the same sex;
4. Rental of a room in one's own home; and
5. Restriction of rentals to persons 55 years of age or older.

While an owner sometimes may discriminate under these exemptions, a *licensee may not participate in the transaction*. In general the New York statutes, which are reprinted at the end of this chapter, cover all fields: renting, selling, leasing and advertising. Public accommodations are also included. The law further forbids any real estate board to discriminate in its membership because of any of the listed categories, which in this case include age. New York regulations are generally more restrictive than federal laws. Table 10.2 summarizes the categories covered by the various federal and New York State laws.

Table 10.2 Protected Classes		Civil Rights Act of 1866	Fair Housing Act of 1968	New York Law
	Race	Yes	Yes	Yes
	Color	Yes	Yes	Yes
	Religion		Yes	Yes ("creed")
	National origin		Yes	Yes
	Sex		Yes (1974)	Yes
	Age			Yes (over 18)
	Handicapped		Yes (1988)	Yes (Disability)
	Marital status			Yes
	Children in family (Familial Status)		Yes (1988)	Yes (Children in family)
	Exceptions	No	Yes	Yes

Code for Equal Opportunity

The National Association of REALTORS® has adopted a **Code for Equal Opportunity.** The Code sets forth suggested standards of conduct for REALTORS® so that they may comply with both the letter as well as the spirit of the fair housing laws.

Affirmative Marketing Agreement

The National Association of REALTORS® also has entered into an agreement with HUD for a program of voluntary affirmative action to eliminate fair housing violations. After a local board of REALTORS® has voluntarily accepted the **affirmative marketing agreement,** individual member brokers are asked to voluntarily join. The broker's salespersons are referred to as associated with the agreement. In New York, 95 percent of NYSAR's (New York State Association of Realtors) members have signed the agreement.

Information about the affirmative marketing agreement is available from the National Association of REALTORS® and also from the following HUD offices:

Albany: Equal Opportunity Officer, HUD
O'Brien Federal Bldg.
N. Pearl & Clinton
Albany, NY 12207

Buffalo: Equal Opportunity Officer, HUD
107 Delaware Ave.
Buffalo, NY 14203

New York: Equal Opportunity Officer, HUD
26 Federal Plaza
New York, NY 10278

In order to be eligible for certain FHA, HUD and VA transactions, brokers who do not belong to an affirmative marketing agreement will be asked to take equivalent steps individually.

Implications for Brokers and Salespersons

To a large extent the laws place the burden of responsibility for effecting and maintaining fair housing on real estate licensees—brokers and salespeople. The laws are clear and widely known. *The complainant does not have to prove guilty knowledge or specific intent—only the fact that discrimination occurred.*

How does a broker go about complying with the laws and making that policy known? HUD regulations suggest that a public statement in the form of an approved fair housing poster be displayed by a broker in any place of business where housing is offered for sale or rent (including model homes). HUD also offers guidelines for nondiscriminatory language and illustrations for use in real estate advertising.

In addition the National Association of REALTORS® suggests that a broker's position can be emphasized and problems can be avoided by the prominent display of a sign stating that it is against company policy as well as state and federal laws to offer any information on the racial, ethnic or religious composition of a neighborhood or to place restrictions on listing, showing or providing information on the availability of homes for any of these reasons.

If a prospect still expresses a locational preference for housing based on race, the association's guidelines suggest the following response: "I cannot give you that kind of advice. I will show you several homes that meet your specifications. You will have to decide which one you want.''

Discrimination involves a sensitive area, human emotions—specifically fear and self-preservation based on considerable prejudice and misconception. The broker or salesperson who keeps his or her own actions in check by complying with the law still has to deal in many cases with a general public whose attitudes cannot be altered by legislation alone. Therefore a licensee who wishes to comply with the fair housing laws and also succeed in the real estate business must work to educate the public.

In recent years brokers sometimes have been caught in the middle when local governments enacted well-meaning **reverse discrimination** regulations. Intended to preserve racial balance in given areas, local laws sometimes run counter to federal and state rules, posing a real problem for the conscientious licensee.

From time to time real estate offices may be visited by **testers** or *checkers,* undercover volunteers who want to see whether all customers and clients are being treated with the same cordiality and are being offered the same free choice within a given price range. The courts have held that such practice is permissible as the only way to test compliance with the fair housing laws that are of such importance to American society.

When a real estate broker is charged with discrimination, it is *no defense* that the offense was unintentional. Citing past service to members of the same minority group is of little value as a defense. The agent's best course is to study fair housing law, develop sensitivity on the subject and follow routine practices designed to reduce the danger of unintentionally hurting any member of the public. These practices include careful record-keeping for each customer: financial analysis, properties suggested, houses shown, check-back phone calls. Using a standard form for all qualifying interviews is helpful. Special care should be taken to be on time for appointments and to follow through on returning all phone calls. Besides helping to avoid human rights violations, these practices are simply good business and should result in increased business.

Summary

Federal regulations regarding equal opportunity in housing are principally contained in two laws. The *Civil Rights Act of 1866* prohibits all racial discrimination and the *Federal Fair Housing Act* (Title VIII of the Civil Rights Act of 1968) prohibits discrimination on the basis of race, color, religion, sex, national origin, handicap or the presence of children in a family, in the sale or rental of residential property. Discriminatory actions include refusing to deal with an individual or a specific group, changing any terms of a real estate or loan transaction, changing the services offered for any individual or group, making statements or advertisements that indicate discriminatory restrictions or otherwise attempting to make a dwelling unavailable to any person or group because of membership in a protected class. Some exceptions apply to owners but *none to brokers,* and *none when the discriminatory act is based on race.*

Complaints under the Federal Fair Housing Act may be reported to and investigated by the *Department of Housing and Urban Development* and may be taken to a U.S. district court. Complaints under the Civil Rights Act of 1866 must be taken to a federal court.

New York's *Executive Law (Human Rights Law)* adds age and marital status to the grounds on which discrimination is forbidden.

The National Association of REALTORS® Code for Equal Opportunity suggests a set of standards for all licensees to follow.

Questions

1. After John Wilson lists a summer home with salesperson Sharon Sikes, he informs her of his general dislike of members of a particular ethnic minority group. Sikes later shows the home to two prospective buyers, one of whom is a member of this group, and both make an offer. When Wilson contacts her again she does not present him with the lower offer, which was made by the member of the minority. Sikes has violated:
   a. regulations of the New York Real Estate License Law.
   b. the law of agency.
   c. both a and b.
   d. no law.

2. Which of the following acts is permitted under the Federal Fair Housing Act?
   a. Advertising property for sale only to a special group
   b. Altering the terms of a loan for a member of a minority group
   c. Refusing to sell a home to an individual because he or she has a poor credit history
   d. Telling an individual that an apartment has been rented when in fact it has not

3. The Civil Rights Act of 1866 is unique because it:
   a. covers only the area of race.
   b. provides no exceptions.
   c. requires a federal court suit by the complainant.
   d. does all of the above.

4. "I hear they're moving in; there goes the neighborhood. Better sell to me today!" is an example of:
   a. steering.   c. redlining.
   b. blockbusting.   d. testing.

5. The act of channeling homeseekers to a particular area either to maintain or to change the character of a neighborhood is:
   a. blockbusting.
   b. redlining.
   c. steering.
   d. permitted under the Fair Housing Act of 1968.

6. Which would *not* be permitted under the Federal Fair Housing Act?
   a. The Harvard Club in New York will rent rooms only to graduates of Harvard who belong to the club.
   b. The owner of a 20-unit apartment building rents to women only.
   c. A convent refuses to furnish housing for a Jewish man.
   d. All of the above

7. Under federal law, families with children may be refused rental or purchase in buildings where occupancy is reserved exclusively for those aged at least:
   a. 55.   c. 62.
   b. 60.   d. 65.

8. Guiding prospective buyers to a particular area because the agent feels they belong there may lead to:
   a. blockbusting.   c. steering.
   b. redlining.   d. bird-dogging.

9. Refusal to rent to someone because they receive public assistance violates:
   a. no law.
   b. the New York Executive Law.
   c. the Fair Housing Act of 1968.
   d. the Civil Rights Act of 1866.

10. A policy of never renting to college students violates:
    a. no law.
    b. the New York Executive Law.
    c. the Fair Housing Act of 1968.
    d. the Civil Rights Act of 1866.

11. Refusing an apartment to a couple because they are unmarried violates:
    a. no law.
    b. the New York Executive Law.
    c. the Fair Housing Act of 1968.
    d. the Civil Rights Act of 1866.

12. The EZ-Go Mortgage Co. makes it a practice not to lend money to potential homeowners attempting to purchase property located in predominantly black neighborhoods. This practice is known as:

    a. redlining.
    c. steering.
    b. blockbusting.
    d. qualifying.

13. A court found Landlord Sneed guilty of illegal discrimination and ordered him to rent his next available apartment to the person who was unfairly hurt. The court order is an example of:

    a. punitive damages.
    b. actual damages.
    c. an injunction.
    d. a monetary penalty.

14. The seller who requests prohibited discrimination in the showing of a home should be told:

    a. "As your agent I have a duty to warn you that such discrimination could land you in real trouble."
    b. "I am not allowed to obey such instructions."
    c. "If you persist, I'll have to refuse to list your property."
    d. All of the above

15. A good precaution against even unconscious discrimination is:

    a. detailed recordkeeping on each customer.
    b. use of a standard financial interview form.
    c. routine follow-up phone calls.
    d. all of the above.

16. The Federal Fair Housing Amendments of 1988 added which of the following as new protected classes?

    a. Occupation and source of income
    b. Handicap and familial status
    c. Political affiliation and country of origin
    d. Prison record and marital status

17. The fine for a first violation of the Federal Fair Housing Act could be as much as:

    a. $500.
    c. $5,000.
    b. $1,000.
    d. $10,000.

18. The only defense against an accusation of illegal discrimination is proof that it:

    a. was unintentional.
    b. didn't cause financial loss to anyone.
    c. arose because the agent was ignorant of the law.
    d. didn't occur.

19. Undercover investigation to see whether fair housing practices are being followed is sometimes made by:

    a. testers.
    c. operatives.
    b. evaluators.
    d. conciliators.

20. Participation in the REALTORS® Affirmative Marketing Agreement is:

    a. required by law.
    b. automatic when regular dues are paid.
    c. voluntary.
    d. open to brokers only.

Appendix: Excerpts from New York State's Study Booklet for Brokers

DISCRIMINATORY PRACTICES

The Executive Law prohibits discrimination because of race, creed, color, national origin or sex by brokers, salespersons, employees or agents thereof in selling or renting housing or commercial space covered by the law, and in advertising the sale or rental of any housing or commercial space.

Moreover, under a rule promulgated by the Secretary of State, licensed real estate brokers and salespersons are prohibited from engaging in the practice of "blockbusting"—the solicitation of the sale or lease of property due to a change in the ethnic structure of a neighborhood.

In addition, no broker or salesperson may, either directly or by implication, encourage or discourage the purchase of property by referring to the race, color, religion or national origin of persons living in or near or moving into or near to any particular neighborhood.

Except with regards to senior citizens housing subsidized, insured, or guaranteed by the federal government, it is illegal to discriminate in the rental of housing on the basis that the prospective tenant has or may have a child or children, and no broker or salesperson may participate in such discrimination.

Extracts from the Executive Law

It shall be an unlawful discriminatory practice for any real estate broker, real estate salesman or employee or agent thereof:

To refuse to sell, rent or lease any housing accommodation, land or commercial space to any person or group of persons or to refuse to negotiate because of the race, creed, color, national origin, sex, or disability or marital status of such person or persons, or in relation to commercial space because of the age of such person or persons, or to represent that any housing accommodation, land or commercial space is not available for inspection, sale, rental or lease when in fact it is so available, or otherwise to deny or withhold any housing accommodation, land or commercial space or any facilities of any housing accommodation, land or commercial space from any person or group of persons because of the race, creed, color, national origin, sex, or disability or marital status of such person or persons or in relation to commercial space because of the age of such person or persons.

The provisions of this paragraph shall not apply (1) to the rental of a housing accommodation in a building which contains housing accommodations for not more than two families living independently of each other, if the owner or members of his family reside in one of such housing accommodations, (2) to the restriction of the rental of all rooms in a housing accommodation to individuals of the same sex or (3) to the rental of a room or rooms in a housing accommodation, if such rental is by the occupant of the housing accommodation or by the owner of the housing accommodation and he or members of his family reside in such housing accommodation.

It shall be an unlawful discriminatory practice for the owner, lessee, sublessee, or managing agent of, or other person, to print or circulate or cause to be printed or circulated any statement, advertisement or publication, or to use any form of application for the purchase, rental or lease of any housing accommodation, land or commercial space or to make any record or inquiry which expresses, directly or indirectly, any limitation, specification, or discrimination as to race, creed, color, national origin, sex, or disability or marital status, or in relation to commercial space as to age; or any intent to make any such limitation, specification or discrimination.

It shall be an unlawful discriminatory practice for any real estate board, because of the race, creed, color, national origin, age, sex, or disability or marital status of any individual who is otherwise qualified for membership, to exclude or expel such individual from membership, or to discriminate against such individual in the terms, conditions and privileges of membership in such board.

The provisions of this subdivision, as they relate to age, shall not apply to persons under the age of eighteen years.

11

Closing and Closing Costs

Key Terms

Abstract of title
Accrued item
Actual notice
Adjustments
Affidavit
Attorney's opinion of title
Caveat emptor
Chain of title
Closing statement
Coinsurance clause
Constructive notice
Credit
Debit
Escrow
Evidence of title

Homeowner's policy
Liability coverage
Marketable title
Mortgage reduction certificate
Prepaid item
Priority
Proration
Public records
Real Estate Settlement Procedures Act (RESPA)
Replacement cost
Suit to quiet title
Title insurance policy
Torrens system
Uniform Settlement Statement

Overview

The final step in the real estate transaction is the closing, a procedure that includes both title and financial considerations. For the protection of real estate owners, taxing bodies, creditors and the general public, public records are maintained in every county and borough. Such records help to establish ownership, give notice of encumbrances and establish priority of liens. The placing of documents in the public records is known as *recording*. This chapter will discuss title records and then go on to the real estate closing, focusing on the licensee's role in this concluding phase of a real estate transaction. Emphasis will be placed on the computations necessary to settle all relevant expenses between buyer and seller and between seller and broker.

Public Records and Recording

Before an individual purchases a parcel of real estate, he or she wants to be sure that the seller can convey good title to the property. The present owner of the real estate undoubtedly purchased from a previous owner, so the same question of *kind and condition* of title has been inquired into many times in the past.

Recording Acts

The state legislature has passed laws that allow owners or parties interested in real estate to record, or file, in the **public records** all documents affecting their interest in real estate in order to give *legal, public and constructive notice* to the world of their interest.

Public records are maintained by the recorder of deeds, county clerk, county treasurer, city clerk and collector, and clerks of various courts of record. Records involving taxes, special assessments, ordinances, and zoning and building records also fall into this category. All these records are open for public inspection.

Necessity for Recording

New York's laws provide that a *deed or mortgage may not be effective as far as later purchasers* are concerned unless such documents have been *recorded.* Thus the public records should reveal the condition of the title and a purchaser should be able to rely on a search of such public records. From a practical point of view the recording acts give **priority** to those interests that are recorded first.

In New York in order to give subsequent purchasers constructive notice of a person's interest, all deeds, mortgages or other written instruments affecting an interest in real estate must be recorded in the county clerk's office of the county where the real estate is located. All documents must be properly acknowledged and show proof of payment of the real estate transfer tax on deeds or the mortgage tax on mortgages before the documents will be accepted for recording.

A deed will not be accepted for recording unless it is accompanied by a *real property transfer report,* which will be used by the New York State Board of Equalization and Assessment. A *real estate transfer gains* **affidavit** (sworn statement) also must be filed. In New York City a deed may not be recorded unless it is accompanied by a *multiple dwelling registration statement,* or an affidavit that no statement is due.

The recording office in the county clerk's office maintains general indexes of instruments recorded in that office. Documents are also recorded in the Office of the New York City Register in borough offices in Manhattan (New York County), Brooklyn (Kings County), Bronx, and Jamaica (Queens).

Notice

Through the legal maxim of **caveat emptor** (''let the buyer beware'') the courts charge a prospective real estate buyer or mortgagee (lender) with the responsibility of inspecting the property and searching the public records to ascertain the interests of other parties. **Constructive notice** assumes that the information is available, therefore the buyer or lender is responsible for learning it.

Constructive notice, or what a buyer could find out, is distinguished from **actual notice,** or what the person actually knows (*see* Figure 11.1). After an individual has searched the public records and inspected the property, he or she has actual notice, or knowledge, of the information learned. An individual is said to have actual notice of any information of which he or she has *direct knowledge*.

In New York it is the *duty of the purchaser* to investigate the title of property to be conveyed. The purchaser will be held to constructive notice of any outstanding rights on the title that could be discovered by a diligent search, including possible rights of persons in physical possession of the property.

**Figure 11.1
Notice**

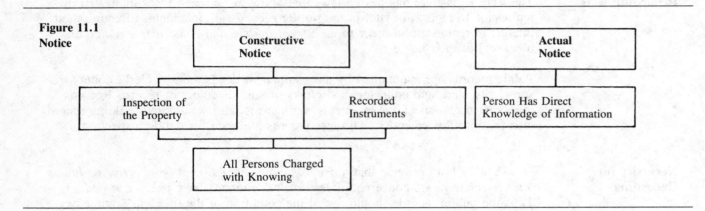

Real estate taxes and special assessments are automatically direct liens on specific parcels of real estate and need not be recorded. Other liens such as inheritance taxes and franchise taxes are placed by statutory authority against all real estate owned either by a decedent at the time of death or by a corporation at the time the franchise tax became a lien; these liens also are not recorded.

Recording sales contracts. It can occasionally be desirable to enter a contract for the sale of real property in the public records. Any document to be filed must be acknowledged. If neither the buyer nor seller can be reached for an acknowledgment, it will be sufficient if a witness to their signatures appears before a notary.

Chain of Title

The **chain of title** shows the record of ownership of the property over a period of time. An **abstract of title** is a condensed history of all the instruments affecting a particular parcel of land. In New York, chains of title frequently date back to a grant from the king of England, or a grant to a Dutch patroon.

Through the chain of title, the ownership of the property can be traced from its origin to its present owner. If this cannot be done it is said that there is a *gap* in the chain. In such cases it is usually necessary to establish ownership by a court action called a **suit to quiet title,** or an Article 15 proceeding.

Evidence of Title

When dealing with an owner of real estate, a purchaser or lender requires satisfactory proof that the seller is the owner and has good title to the property. This documentary proof is called **evidence of title.**

There are four generally used forms of title evidence: (1) abstract of title and lawyer's opinion, (2) title insurance policy, (3) Torrens certificate and (4) certificate of title.

A deed is not proof of title; it proves the grantor sold the property but does not prove the grantor had good title in the first place. The only effective proof must be one of the evidences of title, based on an adequate search of the public records.

Abstract of Title and Lawyer's Opinion

An abstract of title is a brief history of the instruments appearing in the county record that affect title to the parcel in question. The legal description of the property is in the abstract's caption. Abstracts usually consist of several sections, or continuations. It is necessary for each section of the abstract to begin with a search of the public record from a date immediately following the date of the previous section. If this were not done, there would be a gap in the abstract.

When an abstract is first prepared or is continued, the abstractor lists and summarizes each instrument in chronological order along with information relative to taxes, judgments, special assessments and the like. The abstractor concludes with a certificate indicating which records were examined and when, and then he or she signs the abstract. Abstractors must exercise due care because they can be liable for negligence for any failure to include or accurately record all pertinent data. An *abstractor does not, however, pass judgment on or guarantee the condition of the title*.

The abstract illustrated in Figure 11.2 shows that on June 3, 1947 Ida Hughey mortgaged her property at 47 Rowley Street to Rochester Savings Bank for $5,000. The rubber stamp on the record shows that the mortgage was paid off in 1958. The mortgage document evidently carried two legal descriptions: one by plat of subdivision, the other by metes and bounds.

In 1952 Hughey granted a five-year lease on the property to Michael and Mildred Franco, who recorded the document. The next year the Francos bought the property. This particular abstract later goes on to report a driveway easement the Francos negotiated with their neighbors to the north and then traces the property through several later owners with mortgages placed and paid off along the way.

In a sale of land the seller's attorney usually orders the abstract continued to cover the current date. It is then submitted to the buyer's attorney, who must *examine the entire abstract*. Following his or her detailed examination the attorney must evaluate all the facts and material in order to prepare a written report for the purchaser on the condition of the ownership; this report is called an **attorney's opinion of title.**

As transfers of title have accumulated through the years, each abstract of title to individual property has become more and more voluminous and the time needed by an attorney to examine an abstract has therefore increased. In many ways the title evidence system of abstract examination and opinion and the certification of title by attorneys (discussed later in this chapter) are imperfect and open to objection. It is difficult to detect forged deeds or false statements including incorrect marital information and transfers involving incompetent parties or minors. An honest mistake could be made against which the owner of real estate had no recourse. To provide purchasers with protection against this type of error title insurance is used increasingly in New York. It is usually required by the lending institution when a new mortgage is to be placed.

Figure 11.2
Portion of an Abstract

A B S T R A C T   O F   T I T L E

- T O -

#47 West side Rowley Street, being
Part of Lots #27 and 28 of the
Brooks Tract (N. Part) in the
City of Rochester

Maps: Liber 2 of Maps, page 120 and 138
Liber 3 of Maps, page 45
1935 Hopkins Atlas, Vol. 1, Plate 4

1 Ida May Hughey — Mortgage to secure $5000.00

-To- Dated June 3, 1947
Ack. same day
Rec. same day at 12:30 P. M.

Rochester Savings Bank
47 Main Street West
Rochester, New York — Liber 1800 of Mortgages, page 344

CORRECTLY DISCHARGED OF RECORD
BY MORTGAGEE 12/19/58
BY ASSIGNEE
BY ASSIGNMENT OF RECORD
ABSTRACT & TITLE INSURANCE CORPORATION
PER

Conveys land in the City of Rochester, being on the west side of Rowley Street in said City and being part of lots Nos. 27 and 28 in the Brooks Tract as shown on a map of said Tract made by M. D. Rowley, surveyor, May 15, 1869, and filed in Monroe County Clerk's Office and counded and described as follows:

Beginning at a point in the west line of Rowely Street 15 feet northerly from the southeast corner of said lot #27; thence northerly on the west line of Rowley Street, forth (40) feet; thence westerly on a line parallel with the south line of said lot #27, 121 feet; thence southerly on a line parallel with the west line of Rowley Street, 40 feet; thence easterly 121 feet to the place of beginning.

Figure 11.2
(continued)

Being the same premises conveyed to the mortgagor
by Liber 2258 of Deeds, page 178.

Subject to any restrictions and public utility
easements of record.

- -

2 Ida May Hughey, Landlord   Lease

      -To-   Dated May 23, 1952
                                Ack.   same day
Michael Franco   Rec.   August 4, 1952
Mildred Franco,his wife,
Tenants, 17 Glendale Park,   Liber 2769 of Deeds, page 290
Rochester, N.Y.,(Second
parties not certified)

First party leases to second parties premises described as #47 Rowley Street, Rochester, New York, being a
12 room house for a term of 5 years commencing July 16, 1952
and ending July 15, 1957 on certain terms and conditions set
forth herein.

Second parties shall have the right of renewal on
the same terms and conditions as herein for an additional
period of 5 years provided that written notice of intention to
renew is served upon Landlord or her assigns at least 30 days
prior to end of initial term hereof.

- -

3 Ida May Hughey,   Warranty Deed

      -To-   Dated Oct. 30, 1953
                                Ack. Same day
Michele Franco, Mildred   Rec. Same day at 10:50 A.M.
Franco, his wife, as
tenants by the entirety,   Liber 2861 of Deeds, page 411
#47 Rowley St., Rochester,
N.Y. (Second parties not
certified).

Conveys same as #1.

Subject to all covenants, easements and restrictions

Title Insurance

A buyer or seller seeking to obtain a **title insurance policy** as evidence of ownership makes an application to the title insurance company. The company examines the title records and agrees to insure against certain undiscovered defects. Exactly which defects the company will insure against depends on the type of policy it issues; the New York State Insurance Department sets standards. A policy will usually insure against defects that may be found in the public records and such items as forged documents, documents of incompetent grantors, incorrect marital statements and improperly delivered deeds. The company does not agree to insure against any defects in or liens against the title that are specifically listed in the policy as exceptions.

Upon completion of the examination the title company usually issues a report of title, or a commitment to issue a title policy. This describes the policy that will be issued. An *owner's policy will usually exclude coverage* against the following exceptions: unrecorded documents, unrecorded defects of which the policyholder has knowledge, rights of parties in possession and facts discoverable by survey. The title insurance company agrees to defend the title at its own expense and to reimburse the policyholder up to the amount of the policy for damages sustained by reason of any defect not excepted. Title companies in New York must offer a homeowner the right to purchase insurance covering future market value.

Title companies issue various forms of title insurance policies, the most common of which are the *owner's* title insurance policy (a *fee policy*), the *mortgage* title insurance policy and the *leasehold* title insurance policy. As the names indicate, each of these policies is issued to insure specific interests. A mortgage title insurance policy ensures a lender that it has a valid first lien against the property. The owner's policy (usually available at an additional charge when a mortgage policy is purchased) insures the property owner's interests.

The Torrens System

In New York the **Torrens system** of land registration is a valid method of recording title. The method, however, is used only occasionally in this state.

Under the Torrens system a written application to register a title to real estate is made with the clerk of the court of the county in which the real estate is located. If the applicant proves that he or she is the owner, the court enters an order to register the real estate and the *registrar of titles* is further directed to issue a certificate of title. At any time, the Torrens original certificate of title in the registrar's office reveals the owner of the land and all mortgages, judgments and similar liens. It does not reveal federal or New York State taxes and some other items.

Certificate of Title

In some rural localities a *certificate of title prepared by an attorney* is used and no abstract is prepared. The attorney examines the public records and issues a certificate of title that expresses his or her opinion of the title's status. It is not, however, a title insurance policy and does not carry the full protection of such a policy.

A lawyer's opinion of title is often oral, or implied, representation; the person who sustains damages by relying upon it may look to the lawyer for satisfaction.

Marketable Title

Under the terms of the usual real estate sales contract the seller is required to deliver marketable or insurable title to the buyer at the closing. Generally, a **marketable title** is one that is so free from significant defects (other than those specified in the sales contract) that the purchaser can be assured against having to defend the title. Proper evidence of title is proof that the title is in fact marketable.

A buyer cannot be forced to accept a conveyance that is materially different from the one bargained for in the sales contract; he or she cannot be forced to buy a lawsuit. Questions of marketable title must be raised by a purchaser (or his or her broker or attorney) prior to acceptance of the deed. If a buyer accepts a deed with unmarketable title, the only available legal recourse is to sue the seller under the covenants of warranty (if any) contained in the deed.

Closing the Transaction

Although salespeople usually are not burdened with the technicalities of closing, they must clearly understand what takes place. A real estate specialist should be able to assist in preclosing arrangements and advise the parties in estimating their expenses and the approximate amounts the buyer will need and the seller will receive at the closing.

Generally the closing of a real estate transaction involves a gathering of interested parties at which the promises made in the *real estate sales contract* are kept, or *executed;* that is, a deed is delivered in exchange for the purchase price. In many sales transactions two closings actually take place at this time: (1) the closing of the buyer's loan—the disbursal of mortgage funds in exchange for the note and mortgage—and (2) the closing of the sale.

As discussed in Chapter 5, a sales contract is the blueprint for the completion of a real estate transaction. The buyer will want to be sure that the seller is delivering good title and that the property is in the promised condition. This involves inspecting the title evidence, the deed the seller will give, any documents representing the removal of undesired liens and encumbrances, any survey, termite report, or leases if there are tenants on the premises. The seller will want to be sure that the buyer has obtained the stipulated financing and has sufficient funds to complete the sale. Both parties will wish to inspect the closing statement to make sure that all monies involved in the transaction have been properly accounted for. In doing this the parties most likely will be represented by attorneys.

When the parties are satisfied that everything is in order, the exchange is made and all pertinent documents are then recorded. The documents must be recorded in the correct order to avoid creating a defect in the title. For example, if the seller is paying off an existing loan and the buyer is obtaining a new loan, the seller's satisfaction of mortgage must be recorded before the seller's deed to the buyer. The buyer's new mortgage must be recorded after the deed because the lender cannot have a security interest in the buyer's property until it belongs to the buyer.

Where Closings Are Held and Who Attends

Closings may be held at a number of locations including the offices of the title company, the lending institution, the office of one of the parties' attorneys, the broker's office, the office of the county clerk (or other local recording official) or an escrow company. Those attending a closing may include any of the following interested parties: buyer; seller; real estate agent(s); attorney(s) for the seller and/or buyer; representatives for lending institutions involved; and representative of the title insurance company.

Broker's Role at Closing

Depending on the locality, the broker's role at a closing can vary from simply collecting his or her commission to conducting the proceedings. Because a real estate broker is not authorized to give legal advice or otherwise engage in the practice of law, a broker's job is essentially over when there has been a meeting of the minds. At that point, the attorneys take over. Even so a broker's service generally continues after the contract is signed as he or she advises the parties in practical matters, aids the buyer with a mortgage application and makes sure all details are taken care of so that the closing can proceed smoothly.

In this capacity the broker might make arrangements for such items as appraisals, termite inspections and repairs, or might suggest sources of these services to the parties.

Lender's Interest in Closing

When a buyer is obtaining a new loan, the lender wants to protect its security interest in the property—to make sure that the buyer is getting good, marketable title and that tax and insurance payments are maintained so that there will be no liens with greater priority than the mortgage lien, and the insurance will be paid up if the property is damaged or destroyed. For this reason the lender frequently will require the following items: (1) a title insurance policy or abstract of title; (2) a fire and hazard insurance policy with receipt for the premium; (3) additional information such as a survey, a termite or other inspection report or a certificate of occupancy (for newly constructed buildings, multiple dwellings and in a few areas in and around New York City, all buildings); (4) establishment of a reserve, or escrow, account for tax and insurance payments; and (5) representation by its own attorney at the closing.

Homeowner's Insurance

Where mortgaging is involved the buyer must bring to the closing proof of insurance on the property and, occasionally, proof of flood insurance. The insurance policy or binder usually names the lender as lienholder and copayee in case of loss under the policy.

Although it is possible for a homeowner to obtain individual policies for each type of risk (*see* Chapter 21 for a discussion of various kinds of available coverage), most residential property owners take out insurance in the form of a packaged **homeowner's policy.** These standardized policies insure holders against the destruction of their property by fire or windstorm, injury to others that occurs on the property and theft of any personal property on the premises that is owned by the insured or members of his or her family.

The package homeowner's policy also includes **liability coverage** for: (1) personal injuries to others resulting from the insured's acts or negligence, (2) voluntary medical payments and funeral expenses for accidents sustained by guests or resident employees on the property of the owner and (3) physical damage to the property of others caused by the insured.

Characteristics of Homeowners' Packages

There are four major forms of homeowners' policies. The *basic* form, known as *HO-1,* provides property coverage against the following perils: fire or lightning; glass breakage; windstorm or hail; explosion; riot or civil commotion; damage by aircraft; damage from vehicles; damage from smoke; vandalism and malicious mischief; theft; and loss of property removed from the premises when endangered by fire or other perils.

Increased coverage is provided under a *broad* form, known as *HO-2,* that covers the following additional perils: falling objects; weight of ice, snow or sleet; collapse of the building or any part of it; bursting, cracking, burning or bulging of a steam or hot water heating system, or of appliances used to heat water; accidental discharge, leakage or overflow of water or steam from within a plumbing, heating or air-conditioning system; freezing of plumbing, heating and air-conditioning systems and domestic appliances; and injury to electrical appliances, devices, fixtures and wiring from short circuits or other accidentally generated currents.

Further coverage is provided by *comprehensive* forms *HO-3,* the most popular form, and *HO-5;* these policies cover all possible perils except flood, earthquake, war and nuclear attack. Other policies include *HO-4,* a form designed specifically for apartment renters, and *HO-6,* a broad-form policy for condominium owners. Apartment and condominium policies generally provide fire and windstorm, theft and public liability coverage for injuries or losses sustained within the unit but do not usually extend to cover losses or damages to the structure. The structure is insured by either the landlord or the condominium owners' association.

Claims. Most homeowners' insurance policies contain a **coinsurance clause.** This provision requires the insured to maintain fire insurance on his or her property in an amount equal to at least 80 percent of the **replacement cost** of the dwelling (not including the price of the land). If the owner carries such a policy a claim may be made for the cost of the repair or replacement of the damaged property without deduction.

In any event *the total settlement cannot exceed the face value of the policy.* Because of coinsurance clauses it is important for homeowners to periodically review all policies to be certain that the coverage is equal to at least 80 percent of the current replacement cost of their homes. Some policies carry automatic increases in coverage to adjust for inflation.

Federal Flood Insurance Program

A subsidized program authorized by Congress requires property owners in certain areas to obtain flood damage insurance on properties financed by mortgages or other loans, grants or guarantees obtained from federal agencies and federally insured or regulated lending institutions. The program seeks to improve future management for floodplain areas through land-use and control measures. The Department of Housing and Urban Development (HUD), which administers the flood program, has prepared maps and identified specific flood-prone areas throughout the country.

RESPA Requirements

The federal **Real Estate Settlement Procedures Act (RESPA),** enacted in 1974 and revised in 1975, was created to ensure that the buyer and seller in a *residential real estate transaction* have knowledge of all settlement costs. *RESPA requirements apply when the purchase is financed by a federally related mortgage loan.* Federally related loans include those (1) made by banks, savings and loan associations or other lenders whose deposits are insured by federal agencies (FDIC or FSLIC); (2) insured by the FHA or guaranteed by the VA; (3) administered by the U.S. Department of Housing and Urban Development; or (4) intended to be sold by the lender to Fannie Mae, Ginnie Mae or Freddie Mac.

RESPA regulations apply only to transactions involving new first mortgage loans. A transaction financed solely by a purchase-money mortgage taken back by the seller, land contract, or the buyer's assumption of the seller's existing loan would not be covered by RESPA unless the terms of the assumed loan are modified or the lender charges more than $50 for the assumption. When a transaction is covered by RESPA, the following requirements must be met:

1. *Special information booklet:* Lenders must give a copy of the HUD booklet *Settlement Costs and You* to every person from whom they receive or for whom they prepare a loan application.
2. *Good faith estimate of settlement costs:* At the time of the loan application or within three business days the lender must provide the borrower with a good faith estimate of the settlement costs the borrower is likely to incur. In addition if the lender requires use of a particular attorney or title company to conduct the closing, the lender must state whether it has any business relationship with that firm and must estimate the charges for this service.
3. *Uniform Settlement Statement (HUD Form 1):* Loan closing information must be prepared on a special HUD form, the **Uniform Settlement Statement,** designed to detail all financial particulars of a transaction. The completed statement must itemize all charges imposed by the lender. Items paid for prior to the closing must be clearly marked as such on the statement and are omitted from the totals. Upon the borrower's request, *the closing agent must permit the borrower to inspect the settlement statement, to the extent that the figures are available, one business day before the closing.* Lenders must retain these statements for two years after the date of closing unless the loan (and its servicing) is sold or otherwise disposed of.
4. *Prohibition against kickbacks:* RESPA explicitly prohibits the payment of kickbacks, or unearned fees, such as when an insurance agency pays a kickback to a lender for referring one of the lender's recent customers to the agency. This prohibition does *not* include fee splitting between cooperating brokers or members of multiple-listing services, brokerage referral arrangements or the division of a commission between a broker and his or her salespeople.

RESPA is administered by HUD.

The Title Procedure

On the date when the sale is actually completed, that is, the date of delivery of the deed, the buyer has a title commitment or an abstract that was issued several days or weeks before the closing. For this reason the title or abstract company is usually required to make a second search of the public records. A supplemental telephone search by the abstracting company is often made at the moment of closing.

The seller is usually required to execute an *affidavit of title*. This is a sworn statement in which the seller assures the title company (and the buyer) that since the date of the title examination there have been no judgments, bankruptcies, or divorces involving the seller; no repairs or improvements that have not been paid for; and that he or she is in possession of the premises. Through this affidavit the title company obtains the right to sue the seller if his or her statements in the affidavit prove incorrect.

Checking the Premises

It is important for the buyer to inspect the property to determine the interests of any parties in possession or other interests that cannot be determined from inspecting the public record. A *survey* is frequently required so that the purchaser will know the location, size and legal description of the property. The contract should specify whether the seller is to pay for this. It is usual for the survey to spot the location of buildings, driveways, fences and other improvements on the premises being purchased as well as any improvements on adjoining property that may encroach upon the premises. The survey also sets out in full any existing easements and encroachments. So that the survey will clearly identify the location of the property the house number, if any, should be stated.

The buyer should also make a last-minute inspection before closing to check that the house remains in the condition originally presented and that the seller is leaving behind any appliances or other personal property stipulated in the written sales contract.

Releasing Existing Liens

When the purchaser is paying cash or is obtaining a new mortgage in order to purchase the property, the seller's existing mortgage usually is paid in full and released in the public record. In order to know the exact amount required to pay the existing mortgage the seller secures a current *payoff statement* from the mortgagee. This payoff statement sets forth the unpaid amount of principal, interest due through the date of payment, any fee for issuing the release, credits, if any, for tax and insurance reserves, and any penalties that may be due because the loan is being prepaid before its maturity. The same procedure would be followed for any other liens that must be released before the buyer takes title.

When the buyer is assuming the seller's existing mortgage loan, the buyer will want to know the exact balance of the loan as of the closing date. In some areas it is customary for the buyer to obtain a **mortgage reduction certificate** (sometimes inaccurately referred to as an estoppel certificate) from the lender, stating the exact balance due and the last interest payment made.

Closing in Escrow

In the western section of the country the majority of transactions are closed in escrow but the system is almost never used in New York State.

In an **escrow** closing a disinterested third party authorized to act as escrow agent coordinates the closing activities. The escrow agent may be an attorney, a title company, a trust company, an escrow company or the escrow department of a lending institution. Buyer and seller choose an escrow agent and execute an escrow agreement after the sales contract is signed. This agreement sets forth the details of the transaction and the instructions to the escrow agent. Buyer and seller deposit all pertinent documents and other items with the escrow agent before the specified date of closing.

When all other conditions of the escrow agreement have been met, the agent is authorized to disburse the purchase price to the seller and to record the deed and mortgage (if a new mortgage has been executed by the purchaser).

Preparation of Closing Statements

A typical real estate sales transaction involves numerous expenses for both parties in addition to the purchase price. There are a number of property expenses that the seller will have paid in advance for a set period of time or that the buyer will pay in the future. The financial responsibility for these items must be **prorated,** (adjusted or divided) between the buyer and the seller. In closing a transaction it is customary to account for all these items by preparing a written statement to determine how much money the buyer needs and how much the seller will net after the broker's commission and expenses. There are many different formats of closing statements, or settlement statements, but all are designed to achieve the same results.

Closing statements in New York are prepared by the buyer's and seller's attorneys or bank representatives. The broker should, however, possess the necessary knowledge to prepare statements in order to give the seller an accurate estimate of sale costs. In addition the buyer must be prepared with the proper amount of money to complete the purchase and, again, the broker should be able to assist by making a reasonably accurate estimate.

How the Closing Statement Works

The completion of a **closing statement** involves an accounting of the parties' debits and credits. A **debit** is a charge, an amount that the party being debited owes and must pay at the closing. A **credit** is an amount entered in a person's favor—either an amount that the party already has paid, an amount that he or she must be reimbursed for or an amount the buyer promises to pay in the form of a loan.

To determine the amount the buyer needs at the closing, the buyer's debits are totaled. Any expenses and prorated amounts for items prepaid by the seller are added to the purchase price. Then the buyer's credits are totaled. These would include the earnest money (already paid), the balance of the loan the buyer is obtaining or assuming and the seller's share of any prorated items that the buyer will pay in the future. Finally the total of the buyer's credits is subtracted from the total amount the buyer owes (debits) to arrive at the actual amount of cash the buyer must bring to the closing. Usually the buyer brings a bank cashier's check or a certified personal check.

A similar procedure is followed to determine how much money the seller actually will receive. The seller's debits and credits are each totaled. The credits would include the purchase price plus the buyer's share of any prorated items that the seller has prepaid.

The seller's debits would include expenses, the seller's share of prorated items to be paid later by the buyer and the balance of any mortgage loan or other lien that the seller is paying off. Finally the total of the seller's charges is subtracted from the total credits to arrive at the amount the seller will receive.

Expenses

In addition to the payment of the sale price and the proration of taxes, interest and the like, a number of other expenses and charges may be involved in a real estate transaction. These may include the following items.

Broker's commission. The broker's commission is usually paid by the seller because the broker is usually the seller's agent. When the buyer has employed the broker, the buyer may pay the commission.

Attorney's fees. If either of the parties' attorneys will be paid from the closing proceeds, that party will be charged with the expense in the closing statement.

Recording expenses. Charges for recording documents vary from one county to another. A county may typically charge $5.50 for recording a document plus $3 per page. Thus a single-page deed would cost $8.50 to record while the charge for a four-page mortgage would be $17.50. These charges are established by law and are based on the number of pages in the document. The licensee should verify local recording charges.

The *seller* usually pays for recording charges (filing fees) that are necessary in order to clear all defects and furnish the purchaser with a clear title in accordance with the terms of the contract. Items usually charged to the seller would include the recording of satisfaction of mortgages, quitclaim deeds, affidavits and satisfaction of mechanic's lien claims. The *purchaser* pays for recording charges incident to the actual transfer of title. Items usually charged to the purchaser include recording the deed that conveys title to the purchaser and a mortgage executed by the purchaser.

Transfer tax stamps. Any New York State conveyance is taxed at a rate of $2 per $500 or fraction thereof of the property's value minus any mortgage being assumed. Before 1983, the rate was $0.55. The transfer tax must be paid, usually by the seller, when the deed is recorded through the purchase of *stamps* from the county recorder of the county in which the deed is recorded. Local taxes also may be due. Shares in a cooperative are taxed at $.05 per share.

New York City levies a transfer tax of 1 percent on sales of less than $500,000 and on one- to three-family dwellings. Other transfers require payment of a 2 percent city tax. The tax is paid by the grantor.

Personal property transferred with the real estate (drapes, for example) is covered by a bill of sale and is subject not to transfer tax but to state sales tax.

In 1985 the U.S. Supreme Court let stand a New York State capital gains tax of 10 percent, due on any transfer where consideration totals more than $1,000,000. Any sale between $500,000 and $1,000,000 does not require this capital gains tax but must be accompanied by an affidavit detailing the transaction. The affidavit must be filed or the tax paid before the deed may be recorded.

State mortgage tax. New York State imposes a tax of $0.75 for each $100 or fraction thereof for every mortgage recorded within the state and in many counties there is an additional $0.25 for each $100 or fraction thereof. The first $10,000 of a mortgage for any one- or two-family residence is taxed at a rate of $0.50 for each $100. If the mortgage covers property improved by a structure with six or fewer cooking units, the mortgagee must pay a portion of the mortgage tax—$0.25 for each $100 or fraction thereof. Private lenders do not pay the $0.25 portion; lending institutions do. When a land contract is recorded, mortgage tax is due on the amount "borrowed." New York City imposes an additional tax of $0.50 for each $100 or fraction thereof for every mortgage recorded on property located in the city. In counties that levy additional tax, none is due on the first $10,000 of the loan for a one- or two-family residence.

Title expenses. The responsibility for title expenses will vary according to the contract, which usually follows local custom. If the buyer's attorney will inspect the evidence or if the buyer purchases title insurance policies, the buyer will be charged for these expenses. In some situations the title or abstract company is required to make two searches of the public records: the first showing the status of the seller's title on the date of the sales contract and the second continuing after the closing and through the date the purchaser's deed is recorded. In some areas the seller pays for the initial search and the purchaser pays for the "re-date" charge. Elsewhere, buyer pays for the full search.

Loan fees. When the purchaser is securing a mortgage to finance the purchase, the lender (mortgage company) will usually charge a service charge or origination fee. The fee is a flat charge and is usually paid by the purchaser at the time the transaction is closed. In addition the buyer may be charged an assumption fee if he or she assumes the seller's existing financing and in some cases may pay discount points. The seller also may be charged discount points as discussed in Chapter 7.

Tax reserves and insurance reserves (escrows). A *reserve* is a sum of money set aside to be used later for a particular purpose. The mortgage lender usually requires the borrower to establish and maintain a reserve so that the borrower will have sufficient funds to pay general taxes and renew insurance when these items become due. To set up the reserve the borrower is required to make a lump-sum payment to the lender when the mortgage money is paid out (usually at the time of closing). Thereafter the borrower is required to pay into the reserve an amount equal to one month's portion of the *estimated* general tax and insurance premium as part of the monthly payment made to the mortgage company.

Additional fees. An FHA borrower owes a lump sum for prepayment of the mortgage insurance premium (MIP) if it is not being financed as part of the loan. A VA mortgagor pays a 1 percent fee directly to the VA at closing. If a conventional loan carries private mortgage insurance the buyer prepays one year's insurance premium at closing.

Appraisal fees. Either the seller or the purchaser pays appraisal fees. When the buyer obtains a mortgage, it is customary for the lender to require an appraisal, which the buyer pays for.

Survey fees. If the purchaser obtains new mortgage financing, he or she customarily pays the survey fees. In some cases the sales contract may require the seller to furnish a survey.

Prorations

Most closings involve the dividing of financial responsibility between the buyer and seller for such items as loan interest, taxes, rents, fuel and utility bills. These allowances are called **prorations** or **adjustments.** Prorations are necessary to ensure that expenses are fairly divided between the seller and the buyer. For example, where taxes have been paid in advance, the seller would be entitled to reimbursement at the closing. If the buyer assumes the seller's existing mortgage, the seller usually owes the buyer an allowance for accrued interest through the date of closing.

As interest is usually paid in arrears, each payment covers interest for the preceding month. At a mid-month closing, the seller who has not made the current month's payment might owe six weeks' back interest on a mortgage.

Accrued items are items to be prorated (such as water bills and interest on an assumed mortgage) that are owed by the seller but eventually will be paid by the buyer. The seller therefore gives the buyer credit for these items at closing.

Prepaid items are items to be prorated (such as taxes or fuel oil left in the tank) that have been prepaid by the seller but not fully earned (not fully used up). They are therefore credits to the seller.

General rules for prorating. The rules or customs governing the computation of prorations for the closing of a real estate sale vary:

1. In New York it is generally provided that the buyer owns the property on the closing date. In practice, however, either buyer or seller may be charged with that day's expenses.
2. Mortgage interest, general real estate taxes, water taxes, and similar expenses are computed in some areas by using *360 days in a year and 30 days in a month*. However, the rules in other areas provide for computing prorations on the basis of the actual number of days in the calendar month of closing.
3. *Special assessments* for such municipal improvements as sewers, water mains or streets are usually paid in annual installments over several years. Sellers are sometimes required to pay off special assessments entirely. In other cases, buyers may agree to assume future installments.
4. *Rents* are usually adjusted on the basis of the *actual* number of days in the month of closing. It is customary for the seller to receive the rents for the day of closing and to pay all expenses for that day. If any rents for the current month are uncollected when the sale is closed, the buyer often will agree in the contract or by a separate letter to collect the rents if possible and remit a share to the seller.
5. *Security deposits* are generally transferred by the seller to the buyer; the tenant must be notified of the transfer of deposit.
6. Unpaid *wages of building employees* are prorated if the sale is closed between wage payment dates.

Accounting for Credits and Charges

The items that must be accounted for in the closing statement fall into two general categories: (1) prorations or other amounts due to either the buyer or seller (credit to) and paid for by the other party (debit to) and (2) expenses or items paid by the seller or buyer (debit only).

<table>
<tr><th>Items Credited to Buyer (debited to seller)</th><th>Items Credited to Seller (debited to buyer)</th></tr>
<tr><td>

1. buyer's earnest money*
2. unpaid principal balance of outstanding mortgage being assumed by buyer*
3. interest on existing assumed mortgage not yet paid (accrued)
4. unearned portion of current rent collected in advance
5. earned janitor's salary (and sometimes vacation allowance)
6. tenants' security deposits*
7. purchase-money mortgage (*see* Chapter 7)
8. unpaid water bills

</td><td>

1. sales price*
2. fuel oil on hand, usually figured at current market price (prepaid)
3. insurance and tax reserve (if any) when outstanding mortgage is being assumed by buyer (prepaid)
4. refund to seller of prepaid water charge and similar expenses
5. portion of general real estate tax paid in advance

</td></tr>
</table>

Items marked by an asterisk (*) are not prorated; they are entered in full as listed. The *buyer's earnest money*, while credited to the buyer, *is not usually debited* *to the seller.* The buyer receives a credit because he or she has already paid that amount toward the purchase price. Under the usual sales contract the money is held by the broker or attorney until the settlement, when it will be included as part of the total amount due the seller. If the seller is paying off an existing loan and the buyer is obtaining a new one, these two items are accounted for with a debit only to the seller for the amount of the payoff and a credit only to the buyer for the amount of the new loan.

Accounting for expenses. Expenses paid out of the closing proceeds are usually debited only to the party making the payment.

The Arithmetic of Proration

There are three basic methods of calculating prorations:

1. The yearly charge is divided by a *360-day year,* or 12 months of 30 days each.
2. The monthly charge is divided by the *actual number of days in the month of closing* to determine the amount.
3. The *yearly charge is divided by 365* to determine the daily charge. Then the actual number of days in the proration period is determined and this number is multiplied by the daily charge.

In some cases when a sale is closed on the fifteenth of the month the one-half month's charge is computed by simply dividing the monthly charge in two.

The final proration figure will vary slightly depending on which computation method is used.

Sample Closing Statements

Figure 11.3 on page 206 details a buyer's closing statement and Figure 11.4 on page 207 a seller's closing statement for the same transaction. The property is being purchased for $89,500, with $49,500 down and the seller taking back a mortgage for $40,000. Closing takes place on August 12.

Prorations. The buyer is taking over a house on which taxes have been paid, in one case until the end of the year. The buyer will therefore reimburse the seller for the time in which the buyer will be living in a tax-paid house. Specifically, the seller paid city and school taxes of $1,176.35 for the tax year that started July 1 and will receive a large portion of that back as a credit from the buyer. County taxes of $309.06 were paid January 1 for the year ahead so the buyer will also credit the seller for the four months and 18 days remaining in the year, an adjustment of $118.52.

The buyer owes the seller ("total seller's credits") the purchase price plus unearned taxes, for a total of $90,657.68. Toward this sum the buyer receives credit for an earnest money deposit of $500 in a broker's escrow account. (The seller's attorney and the broker will later take this sum into consideration when commission is paid.) The buyer also receives credit for the $40,000 bond and mortgage given to the seller at closing. The buyer therefore gives the seller cash (or a certified check) for the remaining sum, $50,157.68.

The upper half of the closing statement accounts for the transaction between buyer and seller; the lower part details each one's individual expenses. The buyer pays to record the deed and mortgage and pays the mortgage tax. The buyer also pays his or her attorney.

The seller's expenses involve last-minute payment of the school tax (plus a small late-payment penalty) for which the seller is largely reimbursed, the required lender's share of the mortgage tax (seller/lender is a corporation), the remaining real estate commission, legal costs of proving title, transfer tax, and incidental out-of-pocket expenses incurred by seller's attorney, who also deducts his or her own fee and turns over to the seller the net proceeds.

A more complex closing statement is found in Figure 11.5. The purchaser has placed a new mortgage and carries private mortgage insurance. The down payment is small. The buyer's costs include funds to establish an escrow account with the lender.

Other Documents at Closing

The state requires that the seller of a one- or two-family building furnish the buyer, at closing, with an affidavit stating that the residence complies with the New York fire code requirement for a working smoke alarm on the premises.

The Tax Reform Act of 1986 requires every real estate sale to be reported to the Internal Revenue Service by one of the following: the person conducting the closing, the seller's attorney, the buyer's attorney, the title company or the real estate broker involved. The report is made on IRS Form 1099-S and includes the seller's name, address and tax identification number and the full sale price. The seller furnishes to the individual making the report a certificate showing his or her correct social security number or other tax identification number.

Summary

The purpose of the recording acts is to give legal, public and *constructive notice* to the world of parties' interests in real estate. *Possession* of real estate is generally interpreted as notice of the rights of the person in possession. *Actual notice* is knowledge acquired directly and personally.

Four forms of *title evidence* are commonly in use throughout the United States: (1) abstract of title and lawyer's opinion, (2) owner's title insurance policy, (3) Torrens certificate and (4) certificate of title. A deed is evidence that a grantor has conveyed his or her interest but it does not *prove* that the grantor had any interest at all. Each of the forms of title evidence bears a date and is evidence up to and including that date. All forms of title evidence show the previous actions that affect the title. Each must be *re-dated* or continued or reissued to cover a more recent date. Title evidence shows whether a seller is conveying *marketable title*. Marketable title is generally one that is so free from significant defects that the purchaser can be assured against having to defend the title.

Closing a sale involves both title procedures and financial matters. The broker, as agent of the seller, is often present at the closing to see that the sale is actually concluded and to account for the earnest money deposit.

At closing a buyer may be required to prove hazard insurance coverage to a lender. A standard *homeowner's insurance policy* covers fire, theft and liability and can be extended to cover many types of less common risks. Another type of

**Figure 11.3
Buyer's
Closing
Statement,
Closing on
August 12, 1989**

SELLER'S CREDITS

Sale Price _____ $ 89,500.00

ADJUSTMENT OF TAXES

School Tax 7/1/89 to 6/30/90   Amount $ 1176.35   Adj. 10 mos. 18 days $ 1,039.16

City, School Tax 7/1/   to 6/30/   Amount $_____   Adj. ____ mos. ____ days $_____

County Tax 19 89   Amount $ 309.06   Adj. 4 mos. 18 days $ 118.52

Village Tax 6/1/   to 5/31/   Amount $_____   Adj. ____ mos. ____ days $_____

City Tax Embellishments   Amount $_____   Adj. ____ mos. ____ days S_____

_____

_____

_____

Total Seller's Credits $ 90,657.68

PURCHASER'S CREDITS

Deposit with ___Nothnagle_____ $ 500.00

(~~Assumed~~) (New) Mortgage with Seller $480.07 p/m $ 40,000.00

beg. 9-12-89, 12% int., 15 yrs. $_____

_____ $_____

_____ $_____

_____ $_____

_____ $_____

_____ $_____

Total Purchaser's Credits $ 40,500.00

Cash (~~Rec'd~~) (Paid) at Closing $ 50,157.68

EXPENSES OF PURCHASER

Mortgage Tax	$ 275.00
Recording Mortgage...............	$ 11.00
Recording Deed...................	$ 12.00

ESCROWS:

____ mos. insurance	$ _____	
____ mos. school tax	$ _____	
____ mos. county tax	$ _____	
____ mos. village tax	$ _____	
PMI FHA Insurance	$ _____	
	Total: $ _____	

Bank Attorney Fee.................	$ _____
Points..........................	$ _____
Title Insurance..................	$ _____
Interest.........................	$ _____
....	$ _____
....	$ _____
....	$ _____
Legal Fee........................	$ 500.00
Total...........................	$ 798.00

Cash paid to Seller:	$ 50,157.68
Plus Purchaser's Expenses:	$ 798.00
Total Disbursed:	$ 50,955.68

EXPENSES OF SELLER

Title Search Fee	$_____
Transfer Tax on Deed	$_____
Filing of Gains Tax Affidavit ..	$_____
Discharge Recording Fee	$_____
Mortgage Tax	$_____
Surveyor's Fees	$_____
Points	$_____
Mortgage Payoff	$_____
Real Estate Commission	$_____
Water Escrow	$_____
....	$_____
....	$_____
....	$_____
....	$_____
Legal Fee...................	$_____
Total......................	$_____

Cash Received:	$
Less Seller's Expenses:	$
Net Proceeds:	$

**Figure 11.4
Seller's
Closing
Statement,
Closing on
August 12, 1989**

SELLER'S CREDITS

Sale Price _____ $ 89,500.00

ADJUSTMENT OF TAXES

School Tax 7/1/89 to 6/30/90   Amount $ 1176.35   Adj. 10 mos. 18 days $ 1,039.16

City/School Tax 7/1/ to 6/30/   Amount $_____ Adj. _____ mos. _____ days $_____

County Tax 19 89   Amount $ 309.06   Adj. 4 mos. 18 days $ 118.52

Village Tax 6/1/ to 5/31/   Amount $_____ Adj. _____ mos. _____ days $_____

City Tax Embellishments   Amount $_____ Adj. _____ mos. _____ days $_____

Total Seller's Credits $ 90,657.68

PURCHASER'S CREDITS

Deposit with ___ Nothnagle _____ $ 500.00

~~(Assumed)~~ (New) Mortgage with seller $ 40,000.00

12% interest, 15 years, payments $_____

$ 480.07, beginning 9/12/89 _____ $_____

_____ $_____

_____ $_____

_____ $_____

_____ $_____

_____ $_____

Total Purchaser's Credits $ 40,500.00

Cash (Rec'd) ~~(Paid)~~ at Closing $ 50,157.68

EXPENSES OF PURCHASER		**EXPENSES OF SELLER**	
Mortgage Tax .... $_____		Title Search Fee .... $ 220.00	
Recording Mortgage.............. $_____		Transfer Tax on Deed .... $ 358.00	
Recording Deed.................. $_____		Filing of Gains Tax Affidavit .. $ 1.00	
ESCROWS:		Discharge Recording Fee ...... $_____	
___ mos. insurance $_____		Mortgage Tax .... $ 100.00	
___ mos. school tax $_____		Surveyor's Fees .... $_____	
___ mos. county tax $_____		Points .... $_____	
___ mos. village tax $_____		Mortgage Payoff .... $_____	
PMI/FHA Insurance $_____		Real Estate Commission ...... $ 4870.00	
Total: $_____		Water Escrow .... $_____	
Bank Attorney Fee................ $_____		1989-1990 school tax $ 1,182.14	
Points........................... $_____		Federal express $ 14.00	
Title Insurance................... $_____		.... $_____	
Interest......................... $_____		.... $_____	
.... $_____		Legal Fee................ $ 550.00	
.... $_____		Total................. $ 7,295.14	
.... $_____			
Legal Fee........................ $_____		Cash Received: $ 50,157.68	
Total............................ $_____		Less Seller's Expenses: $ 7,295.14	
Cash paid to Seller: $		Net Proceeds: $ 42,862.54	
Plus Purchaser's Expenses: $_____			
Total Disbursed: $			

**Figure 11.5
Buyer's
Closing
Statement
(New Mortgage)**

STATEMENT OF CLOSING

In the matter of the _____ of premises situate _____

_____

Seller: _____ Purchaser: _____

Closed __September 12__ 19_89_

Adjustments as of __October 28__ 19_89_

SELLER'S CREDITS

Sale Price _____ $__62,000.00__

ADJUSTMENT OF TAXES

School Tax 7/1/ to 6/30/	Amount $_____	Adj. _____mos._____	days $_____
City/School Tax 7/1/ to 6/30/	Amount $_____	Adj. _____mos._____	days $_____
County Tax 19_89_	Amount $__631.16__	Adj. _4_ mos. _2_	days $__213.90__
Village Tax 6/1/89 to 5/31/90	Amount $__382.80__	Adj. _9_ mos. _2_	days $__289.22__
City Tax Embellishments	Amount $_____	Adj. _____mos._____	days $_____

Rent 8/28 - 9/12 - 15 days @ $ 14.12/day   211.80

Total Seller's Credits $__62,714.92__

PURCHASER'S CREDITS

Deposit with _Nothnagle Gallery of Homes_ $__1000.00__

(Assumed) (New) Mortgage with _Nothnagle Home Securities_ $__58,900.00__

(assigned to Citibank) $_____

Adjustable Rate Mortgage (see reverse for term) $_____

1st due 11/1/89 $_____

Monthly payments (see below) $_____

1989-90 school tax $738.24, adj. 1 mo. 28 days $__118.92__

_____ $_____

Total Purchaser's Credits $__60,018.92__

Cash (Rec'd) (Paid) at Closing $__2,696.00__

EXPENSES OF PURCHASER		EXPENSES OF SELLER	
Mortgage Tax .... $__416.75__		Title Search Fee .... $_____	
Recording Mortgage.............. $__35.00__		Transfer Tax on Deed .... $_____	
Recording Deed.................. $__12.00__		Filing of Gains Tax Affidavit .. $_____	
		Discharge Recording Fee ...... $_____	
ESCROWS:		Mortgage Tax .... $_____	
_2_ mos. insurance $__43.50__		Surveyor's Fees .... $_____	
_2_ mos. school tax $__123.04__		Points .... $_____	
_9_ mos. county tax $__473.37__		Mortgage Payoff .... $_____	
_4_ mos. village tax $__127.60__		Real Estate Commission ...... $_____	
PMI FHA Insurance $__23.56__		Water Escrow .... $_____	
Total: $__791.07__		.... $_____	
Bank Attorney Fee................. $__549.25__		.... $_____	
Points............................ $_____		.... $_____	
Title Insurance.................... $_____		.... $_____	
Interest 9/12 - 9/30............ $__268.28__		Legal Fee................... $_____	
1989-90 school tax .... $__738.24__		Total...................... $_____	
PMI - 1 year premium.......... $__471.20__			
TAX SERVICE FEE-charged by bank $__39.00__		Cash Received: $_____	
Legal Fee...................... $__410.00__		Less Seller's Expenses: $_____	
Total........................ $__3730.79__		Net Proceeds: $_____	

Cash paid to Seller: $ 2696.00

Plus Purchaser's Expenses: $ 3730.79

Total Disbursed: $ 6426.79

Monthly Payments

Principal and Interest	463.37
Taxes	146.01
Home Owners Policy	21.75
Private Mortgage Insurance	11.78
Total Monthly Payments	642.91

insurance, which covers personal property only, is available to those in apartments and condominiums. In addition to homeowner's insurance, the federal government makes flood insurance mandatory for people living in flood-prone areas who wish to obtain federally regulated or federally insured mortgage loans. Many homeowners' policies contain a *coinsurance clause* that requires the policyholder to maintain fire insurance in an amount equal to 80 percent of the replacement cost of the home. If this percentage is not met the policyholder may not be reimbursed for the full repair costs in case of loss.

The federal *Real Estate Settlement Procedures Act (RESPA)* requires disclosure of all settlement costs when a residential real estate purchase is financed by a federally related mortgage loan. RESPA requires lenders to use a *Uniform Settlement Statement* to detail the financial particulars of a transaction.

Usually the buyer's attorney examines the title evidence to ensure that the seller's title is acceptable. The sale may be closed in *escrow* by a neutral third party or escrow agent.

The actual amount to be paid by the buyer at the closing is computed by preparation of a *closing,* or *settlement, statement.* This lists the sales price, earnest money deposit and all adjustments and prorations due between buyer and seller. The purpose of this statement is to determine the net amount due the seller at closing. The buyer reimburses the seller for *prepaid* items like unused taxes or fuel oil. The seller credits the buyer for bills the seller owes that will be paid by the buyer (*accrued* items), such as unpaid water bills.

Questions

1. Public records may be inspected by:
   a. anyone.
   b. New York attorneys and abstractors only.
   c. attorneys, abstractors and real estate licensees only.
   d. anyone who obtains a court order under the Freedom of Information Act.

2. The date and time a document was recorded establish which of the following?
   a. Priority   c. Subrogation
   b. Chain of title   d. Marketable title

3. An instrument affecting title to a parcel of real estate gives constructive notice to the world when it is filed with the:
   a. city clerk.
   b. county clerk.
   c. secretary of state.
   d. title insurance company.

4. In New York no deed may be recorded unless:
   a. it has been acknowledged.
   b. the transfer tax has been paid.
   c. there is a Real Property Transfer Report.
   d. All of the above

5. The principle of *caveat emptor* states that if the buyer buys into a title problem the fault lies with the:
   a. buyer.   c. broker.
   b. seller.   d. lender.

6. Which of the following is *not* acceptable proof of ownership?
   a. A Torrens certificate
   b. A title insurance policy
   c. An abstract and lawyer's opinion
   d. A deed signed by the last seller

7. In locations where the abstract system is used, an abstract is usually examined by the:
   a. broker.
   b. abstract company.
   c. seller.
   d. attorney for the purchaser.

8. Proof of the kind of estate and all liens against an interest in a parcel of real estate can usually be found through:
   a. a recorded deed.
   b. a court suit for specific performance.
   c. one of the four evidences of title.
   d. a foreclosure suit.

9. A fee title insurance policy generally will defend the property owner against problems arising from:
   a. unrecorded documents.
   b. facts discoverable by survey.
   c. forged documents.
   d. all of the above.

10. If a property has encumbrances, it:
    a. cannot be sold.
    b. can be sold only if title insurance is provided.
    c. cannot have a deed recorded without a survey.
    d. can be sold if a buyer agrees to take it subject to the encumbrances.

11. Mortgage title policies protect which parties against loss?
    a. Buyers   c. Lenders
    b. Sellers   d. Buyers and lenders

12. Sally Seller is frantic because she cannot find her deed and now wants to sell the property. Sally:
    a. may need a suit to quiet title.
    b. will have to buy title insurance.
    c. does not need the deed to sell if it had been recorded.
    d. should execute a replacement deed to herself.

13. At closing the seller of a single home must give the buyer an affidavit that the house has:
    a. flood insurance.
    b. title insurance.
    c. a working smoke alarm.
    d. insulation.

14. R. Crusoe is selling a two-family dwelling. The buyer's lending institution is likely to request:

    a. proof of hazard insurance.
    b. a certificate of occupancy.
    c. title insurance.
    d. all of the above.

15. The terms *basic*, *broad* and *comprehensive* describe types of:

    a. title insurance.
    b. attorney's services.
    c. mortgage documents.
    d. homeowner's insurance.

16. A coinsurance clause can penalize the homeowner who does not carry insurance coverage for at least what percent of replacement cost?

    a. 50 percent   c. 100 percent
    b. 80 percent   d. 125 percent

17. Flood insurance is required for mortgaging property if it is:

    a. a multiple dwelling.
    b. on a flood-prone area on a special map.
    c. owned by HUD.
    d. going to have title insurance.

18. The RESPA Uniform Settlement Statement must be used to illustrate all settlement charges for:

    a. every real estate transaction.
    b. transactions financed by VA and FHA loans only.
    c. residential transactions financed by federally related mortgage loans.
    d. all transactions involving commercial property.

19. A mortgage reduction certificate is executed by a(n):

    a. abstract company.
    b. attorney.
    c. lending institution.
    d. grantor.

20. The earnest money left on deposit with the broker is a:

    a. credit to the seller.
    b. credit to the buyer.
    c. debit to the seller.
    d. debit to the buyer.

21. The buyers are assuming a mortgage loan that had a principal balance of $27,496 as of June 1. Interest is at 12 percent per annum. Interest is payable in arrears. The June payment has not been made and closing is on June 15. Which of the following is true?

    a. Credit buyer $274.95; debit seller $274.95.
    b. Credit buyer $412.44; debit seller $412.44.
    c. Credit seller $137.48; debit buyer $137.48.
    d. No adjustment is necessary.

22. The year's town, county and state taxes amount to $1,800 and have been paid ahead for the calendar year. If closing is set for June 15, which of the following is true?

    a. Credit seller $825; debit buyer $975.
    b. Credit seller $1,800; debit buyer $825.
    c. Credit buyer $975; debit seller $975.
    d. Credit seller $975; debit buyer $975.

23. Which one of the following items is *not* usually prorated between buyer and seller at the closing?

    a. Recording charges
    b. Property taxes
    c. Rents
    d. Interest on assumed mortgage

24. The seller collected rent of $400, payable in advance, from the attic tenant on June 1. At the closing on June 15:

    a. seller owes buyer $400.
    b. buyer owes seller $600.
    c. seller owes buyer $200.
    d. buyer owes seller $200.

25. Security deposits should be listed on a closing statement as a credit to the:

    a. buyer.   c. lender.
    b. seller.   d. broker.

Real Estate Mathematics

Overview

This review is designed to familiarize the student with some basic mathematical formulas that are most frequently used in the computations required on state licensing examinations. These same computations are also important in day-to-day real estate transactions. If you feel you need additional help in working these problems, you may want to consult *Mastering Real Estate Mathematics,* Fourth Edition, by Ventolo, Allaway and Irby. The order form at the back of this book includes this self-instructional text.

Percentages

Many real estate computations are based on the calculation of percentages. A percentage expresses a portion of a whole. For example, 50 percent means 50 parts of the possible 100 parts that comprise the whole. Percentages greater than 100 percent contain more than one whole unit. Thus 163 percent is one whole and 63 parts of another whole. A whole is always expressed as 100 percent.

Unless a calculator with a percent key is being used, *the percentage must be converted either to a decimal or to a fraction.* To convert a percentage to a decimal, move the decimal two places to the left and drop the percent sign. Thus:

$$60\% = .6 \qquad 7\% = .07 \qquad 175\% = 1.75$$

To change a percentage to a fraction, place the percentage over 100. For example:

$$50\% = \frac{50}{100} \qquad 115\% = \frac{115}{100}$$

These fractions may then be *reduced* to make it easier to work the problem. To reduce a fraction, determine the largest number by which both numerator and denominator can be evenly divided. For example:

$$25/100 = 1/4 \text{ (both numbers divided by 25)}$$

$$49/63 = 7/9 \text{ (both numbers divided by 7)}$$

Percentage problems contain three elements: *percentage, total* and *part.* To determine a specific percentage of a whole, multiply the percentage by the whole:

$$\textbf{percent} \times \textbf{whole} = \textbf{part}$$

$$5\% \times 200 = 10$$

For example: A broker is to receive a 7 percent commission on the sale of a $100,000 house. What will the broker's commission be?

$$.07 \times \$100,000 = \$7,000 \text{ broker's commission}$$

This formula is used in calculating mortgage loan interests, brokers' commissions, loan origination fees, discount points, amount of earnest money deposits and income on capital investments.

A variation, or inversion, of the percentage formula is used to find the total amount when the part and percentage are known:

$$\text{total} = \frac{\text{part}}{\text{percent}}$$

For example: The Masterson Realty Company received a $4,500 commission for the sale of a house. The broker's commission was 6 percent of the total sales price. What was the total sales price of this house?

$$\frac{\$4,500}{.06} = \$75,000 \text{ total sales price}$$

This formula is used in computing the total mortgage loan principal still due if the monthly payment and interest rate are known. It is also used to calculate the total sales price when the amount and percentage of commission are known and the market value of property if the assessed value and the ratio (percentage) of assessed value to market value are known.

The formula may be used by a real estate salesperson thus: Bertha Buyer has $19,500 available for a down payment and she must make a 25 percent down payment. How expensive a home can she purchase? The question is: $19,500 is 25 percent of what figure?

$$\frac{\$19,500}{.25} = \$78,000$$

Such a problem also may be solved by the use of ratios. Thus: $19,500 is to what number as 25 percent is to 100 percent?

$$\frac{\$19,500}{?} = \frac{25}{100}$$

One type of percentage problem, which may take several forms, is often found on the New York State licensing examinations. For example: Joe Brown sold property for $90,000. This represents a 20 percent loss from his original cost. What was his cost?

In this problem the student must resist the impulse to multiply everything in sight. Taking 20 percent of $90,000 yields nothing significant. The $90,000 figure represents 80 percent of the original cost and the question resolves itself into: $90,000 is 80 percent of what figure?

$$\frac{\$90,000}{.80} = \$112,500$$

Again: Hester Prynne clears $88,200 from the sale of her property after paying a 10 percent commission. How much did the property sell for? Taking 10 percent of $88,200 is an incorrect approach to the problem because the commission was based not on the seller's net but on the full, unknown sales figure; $88,200 represents 90 percent of the sales price.

$$\frac{\$88,200}{.90} = \$98,000$$

To determine the percentage when the amounts of the part and the total are known:

$$\text{percent} = \frac{\text{part}}{\text{total}}$$

This formula may be used to find the tax rate when taxes and assessed value are known or the commission rate if sales price and commission amount are known.

Rates

Property taxes, transfer taxes and insurance premiums are usually expressed as rates. A rate is the cost expressed as the amount of cost per unit. For example, tax might be computed at the rate of $5 per $100 assessed value in a certain county. The formula for computing rates is:

$$\frac{\text{value}}{\text{unit}} \times \text{rate per unit} = \text{total}$$

For example: A house has been assessed at $90,000 and is taxed at an annual rate of $2.50 per $100 assessed valuation. What is the yearly tax?

$$\frac{\$90,000}{\$100} \times \$2.50 = \text{total annual tax}$$

$$\$90,000 \div \$100 = \$900 \text{ (increments of \$100)}$$

$$\$900 \times \$2.50 = \$2,250 \text{ total annual tax}$$

Basic to investment problems is the IRV formula, which should be memorized.

Income = Rate × Value

Areas and Volumes

To compute the area of a square or rectangular parcel, use the formula:

width × depth = area

The area of a rectangular lot that measures 100 feet wide by 200 feet deep would be:

$$100' \times 200' = 20,000 \text{ square feet}$$

The first figure given always represents *front feet;* a lot described as "80′ × 150′" is 80 feet across and 150 feet deep. *Area is always expressed in square units.*

To compute the amount of surface in a triangular-shaped area, use the formula:

area = ½ (base × height)

The base of a triangle is the bottom, upon which the triangle rests. The height is an imaginary straight line extending from the point of the uppermost angle straight down to the base:

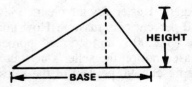

Example: A triangle's base is 50 feet, and it's height is 30 feet. What is its area?

$$\text{½ } (50' \times 30') = \text{area in square feet}$$

$$\text{½ } (1500) = 750 \text{ square feet}$$

To compute the area of an irregular room or parcel of land, divide the shape into regular rectangles, squares or triangles. Next, compute the area of each regular figure and add the areas together to obtain the total area.

Example: Compute the area of the hallway shown below:

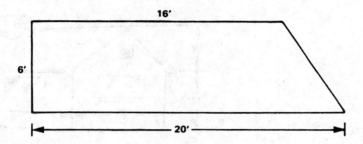

Make a rectangle and a triangle by drawing a single line through the figure:

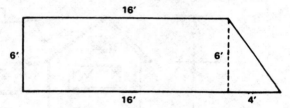

Compute the area of the rectangle:

area = length × width   16′ × 6′ = 96 square feet

Compute the area of the triangle:

area = ½ (base × height)   ½(4′ × 6′) = ½ (24) = 12 square feet

Total the two areas:

96 + 12 = 108 square feet in total area

The cubic capacity of an enclosed space is expressed as volume, which is used to describe the amount of space in any three-dimensional area, for example, in measuring the interior airspace of a room to determine what capacity heating unit is required. The formula for computing cubic or rectangular volume is:

volume = length × width × height

Volume is always expressed in cubic units.

For example: The bedroom of a house is 12 feet long, 8 feet wide, and has a ceiling height of 8 feet. How many cubic feet does the room enclose?

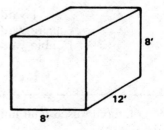

8′ × 12′ × 8′ = 768 cubic feet

To compute the volume of a triangular space, such as the airspace in an *A*-frame house, use the formula:

volume = ½ (base × height × width)

For example: What is the volume of airspace in the house shown below?

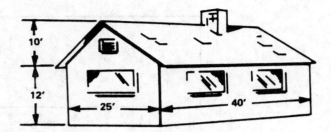

First, divide the house into two shapes, rectangular and triangular, as shown:

Find the volume of *T*:

volume = ½ (base × height × width)

½ (25′ × 10′ × 40′) = ½ (10,000) = 5,000 cubic feet

Find the volume of *R*:

25′ × 40′ × 12′ = 12,000 cubic feet

Total volumes *T* and *R*:

5,000 + 12,000 = 17,000 cubic feet of airspace in the house

Cubic measurements of volume are used to compute the construction costs per cubic foot of a building, the amount of airspace being sold in a condominium unit or the heating and cooling requirements for a building. When either area or volume is computed, *all dimensions used must be given in the same unit of measure*. For example, one may not multiply two feet by six inches to get the area; two feet must be multiplied by ½ foot. Thus it is important to remember that:

1 yard = 3 feet,
1 square yard = 3 × 3 = 9 square feet, and
1 cubic yard = 3 × 3 × 3 = 27 cubic feet.

Land Units and Measurements

Some commonly used land units and measurements follow:

1. A *rod* is 16½ feet.
2. A *chain* is 66 feet, or 100 links.

3. A *mile* is 5,280 feet.
4. An *acre* contains 43,560 square feet. **Memorize this one.**
5. A *section* of land is one square mile and contains 640 acres; a *quarter section* contains 160 acres; a *quarter of a quarter section* contains 40 acres.
6. A *circle* contains 360 degrees; a *quarter segment* of a circle contains 90 degrees; a *half segment* of a circle contains 180 degrees. One *degree* (1°) can be subdivided into 60 minutes (60'), each of which contains 60 seconds (60"). One-and-a-half degrees would be written 1°30'0".

Questions

1. A rectangular lot measures 60 feet wide and has an area of 1,200 square yards. What is the depth of the lot?

   a. 20 feet   c. 20 yards
   b. 180 feet   d. 90 yards

2. A buyer is applying for an FHA mortgage on a house priced at $68,000. The minimum down payment required is 3 percent of the first $25,000 of the purchase price and 5 percent of the remaining purchase price. What is the minimum down payment?

   a. $2,040   c. $1,790
   b. $3,400   d. $2,900

3. Ebenezer Scrooge intends to put up a fence between his lot and his neighbor's. The fencing comes in six-foot sections. For a fence 120 feet long, how many fence posts will be required?

   a. 19   c. 21
   b. 20   d. 22

4. A house is valued at $98,000. It is to be insured for 80 percent of its cost. Insurance will cost $0.60 per $100. What is the annual insurance premium?

   a. $470.40   c. $588.00
   b. $47.04   d. $58.80

5. John Walton received a net amount of $74,000 from the sale of his house after paying $1,200 in legal and other fees and 6 percent sales commission. What was the selling price of the house?

   a. $80,000   c. $79,640
   b. $78,440   d. $79,000

6. A lending institution will allow its borrowers to spend 25 percent of their income for housing expense. What will be the maximum monthly payment allowed for a family with annual income of $37,000 and no other debts?

   a. $9,250   c. $925
   b. $770.83   d. None of the above

7. Sally Sellright works on a 50/50 commission split with her broker. If she lists a house at $56,000 for 6 percent commission and sells it for $54,000, how much will Sally receive?

   a. $3,360   c. $3,240
   b. $1,680   d. $1,620

8. Dudley Doright's monthly mortgage payment for principal and interest is $628.12. His property taxes are $1,800 a year and his annual insurance premium is $365. What is his total monthly payment for PITI (principal, interest, taxes and insurance)?

   a. $808.54   c. $778.12
   b. $1,921.24   d. None of the above

9. A lot measuring 120' × 200' is selling for $300 a front foot. What is its price?

   a. $720,000   c. $36,000
   b. $60,000   d. $800,000

10. A five-acre lot has front footage of 300 feet. How deep is it?

    a. 145.2 feet   c. 88 feet
    b. 726 feet   d. 160 feet

11. Broker Sally Smith of Happy Valley Realty recently sold Jack and Jill Hawkins's home for $79,500. Smith charged the Hawkinses a 6½ percent commission and will pay 30 percent of that amount to the listing salesperson and 25 percent to the selling salesperson. What amount of commission will the listing salesperson receive from the Hawkins sale?

    a. $5,167.50   c. $3,617.25
    b. $1,550.25   d. $1,291.87

12. Susan Silber signed an agreement to purchase a condominium apartment from Perry and Marie Morris. The contract stipulated that the Morrises replace the damaged bedroom carpet. The carpet Silber has chosen costs $16.95 per square yard plus $2.50 per square yard for installation. If the bedroom dimensions are as illustrated, how much will the Morrises have to pay for the job?

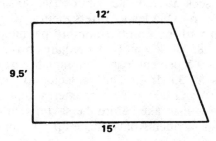

a. $241.54   c. $277.16
b. $189.20   d. $2,494.46

13. Hal, Olive, Ron and Marvin pooled their savings and purchased a vacation home for $125,000. If Hal invested $30,000 and Olive and Ron each contributed $35,000, what percentage of ownership was left for Marvin?

a. 20 percent   c. 28 percent
b. 24 percent   d. 30 percent

14. Harold Barlow is curious to know how much money his son and daughter-in-law still owe on their mortgage loan. Barlow knows that the interest portion of their last monthly payment was $391.42. If the Barlows are paying interest at the rate of 11½ percent, what was the outstanding balance of their loan before that last payment was made?

a. $43,713.00   c. $36,427.50
b. $40,843.83   d. $34,284.70

15. Nick and Olga Stravinski bought their home on Sabre Lane a year ago for $98,500. Property in their neighborhood is said to be increasing in value at a rate of 5 percent annually. If this is true, what is the current market value of the Stravinskis' real estate?

a. $103,425
b. $93,575
c. $104,410
d. None of the above is within $50.

16. The DeHavilands' home on Dove Street is valued at $95,000. Property in their area is assessed at 60 percent of its value and the local tax rate is $2.85 per hundred. What is the amount of the DeHavilands' monthly taxes?

a. $1,111.50   c. $111.15
b. $926.30   d. $135.38

17. The Fitzpatricks are planning to construct a patio in their backyard. An illustration of the surface area to be paved appears here. If the cement is to be poured as a six-inch slab, how many cubic feet of cement will be poured into this patio?

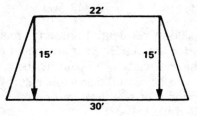

a. 660 cubic feet   c. 330 cubic feet
b. 450 cubic feet   d. 195 cubic feet

18. Happy Morgan receives a monthly salary of $500 plus 3 percent commission on all of his listings that sell and 2.5 percent on all his sales. None of the listings that Morgan took sold last month but he received $3,675 in salary and commission. What was the value of the property Morgan sold?

a. $147,000   c. $122,500
b. $127,000   d. $105,833

19. The Salvatinis' residence has proven difficult to sell. Salesperson Martha Kelley suggests it might sell faster if they enclose a portion of the backyard with a privacy fence. If the area to be enclosed is as illustrated, how much would the fence cost at $6.95 per linear foot?

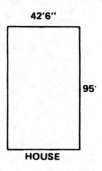

a. $1,911.25   c. $1,615.88
b. $1,654.10   d. $955.63

20. Andrew McTavish leases the 12 apartments in the Overton Arms for a total monthly rental of $4,500. If this figure represents an 8 percent annual return on McTavish's investment, what was the original cost of the property?
    a. $675,000   c. $54,000
    b. $450,000   d. $56,250

21. A 100-acre farm is divided into house lots. The streets require one-eighth of the whole farm and there are 140 lots. How many square feet are there in each lot?
    a. 35,004   c. 27,225
    b. 31,114   d. 43,560

22. In a sale of residential property, real estate taxes for the current year amounted to $975 and have already been paid by the seller. The sale is to be closed on October 26; what is the amount of real estate proration to be credited the seller?
    a. $173.33   c. $798.96
    b. $162.50   d. $83.96

23. The buyer is assuming the seller's mortgage. The unpaid balance after the most recent payment (the first of the month) was $61,550. Interest is paid in arrears each month at 13 percent per annum. The sale is to be closed on September 22; what is the amount of mortgage interest proration to be credited to the buyer at the closing?
    a. $666.97   c. $177.82
    b. $488.97   d. $689.01

24. Riley's commission on a sale was $14,100, which was 6 percent of the sales price. What was the sales price?
    a. $235,000   c. $846,000
    b. $154,255.31   d. $234,500

25. A 30-year fixed-rate amortized mortgage for $100,000 at 11 percent interest requires monthly payments of $952.34 for principal and interest. What is the total amount of interest paid on this loan during the life of the mortgage?
    a. $114,280.00   c. $314,272.60
    b. $242,842.40   d. $330,000.00

26. The Duffys are buying a house for $120,000 and seek a fixed-rate loan of $90,000 for 25 years. One lender offers them a 10 percent loan with no points, monthly payments of $817.85. A second lender requires two points for a 9.5 percent loan, with monthly payments of $786.35. If the Duffys decide to pay the points and take the lower-interest loan, how long will it take before the savings on their lower payments have made up for that extra cost at closing?
    a. Two years, eight months
    b. Three years, two months
    c. Four years, nine months
    d. Seven years, four months

27. The Sterns receive two offers for their property at the same time. The Avilas offer $95,000 all cash. The Browns offer $100,000 subject to obtaining a conventional mortgage loan with 20 percent down payment, and ask the Sterns to pay three points to their lending institution. The Sterns decide to accept the all-cash offer. If they had accepted the Browns' offer instead they would have received:
    a. $2,600 more at closing.
    b. $2,000 more at closing.
    c. $2,400 less at closing.
    d. $3,000 less at closing.

Salesperson's Review Examination

The following questions cover topics found on the salesperson's examination given by the state of New York. Allow yourself one hour to complete the review. Each correct answer is worth two points on this exam. A grade of 70% is passing.

Those who desire additional exam preparation may obtain a copy of *New York Real Estate Exam Guide*, by Judith Deickler, which is available from Real Estate Education Company, Chicago.

1. A deed is valid when it is:
   a. delivered.   c. signed.
   b. recorded.   d. notarized.

2. Which type of deed is used to convey title to a parcel of land through a foreclosure proceeding?
   a. Bargain and sale   c. Referee's
   b. Quitclaim   d. Warranty

3. In which clause in a deed would you find metes and bounds and monuments?
   a. Demising   c. Description
   b. Defeasance   d. Habendum

4. If Mr. Jones owns his home free and clear of encumbrances and can will it to his daughter, this type of ownership is a(n):
   a. life estate.   c. estate at will.
   b. fee simple.   d. freehold.

5. An instrument in writing that is the security for a debt with specific property as a pledge is a:
   a. bond.   c. deed.
   b. mortgage.   d. lease.

6. A legally enforceable agreement between competent parties in which each party acquires a right is called a:
   a. certiorari.   c. contract.
   b. consideration.   d. clause.

7. The usual listing agreement between a seller and a real estate agent is a(n):
   a. implied contract.
   b. express contract.
   c. breach of contract.
   d. discharge of contract.

8. When a buyer defaults on a contract, an optional choice for the seller would *not* be to:
   a. sue for partition
   b. sue for damages.
   c. sue for specific performance.
   d. rescind the contract.

9. Land contracts are:
   a. reportable.   c. recorded.
   b. recordable.   d. revocable.

10. A contract with a minor is:
    a. void.   c. not recordable.
    b. voidable.   d. unilateral.

11. Something given to induce a party to enter into a contract, such as money or services, is known as:
    a. condemnation.   c. conversion.
    b. caveat emptor.   d. consideration.

12. All brokers are REALTORS®.
    a. True   b. False

13. A broker's fiduciary duty is always to the seller.
    a. True   b. False

14. Only the grantor can establish deed restrictions.
    a. True   b. False

15. To be valid, a purchase contract must be accompanied by an earnest money deposit.
    a. True   b. False

16. If the closing date stipulated in a purchase contract passes without settlement, the contract is still valid.
    a. True   b. False

17. A lot zoned for business use was 95 feet wide and 125 feet deep. It sold for $155,000. What was the sale price per front foot?
   a. $2,110.41   c. $1,631.58
   b. $1,240.00   d. $1,334.21

18. A house sold for $385,000. The broker received $27,912.50. What rate of commission did this broker charge?
   a. 6%   c. 7%
   b. 7¼%   d. 10%

19. What is the amount of New York State transfer tax to be paid on the sale of a property for $405,575?
   a. $405.00   c. $1,208.00
   b. $811.15   d. $1,624.00

20. A salesperson sells another firm's listing for $462,500. The 7% commission is to be shared 50/50 by the two companies. The salesperson receives 60% of her offices share. What will her broker receive?
   a. $6,475.00   c. $8,421.50
   b. $7,216.75   d. $9,712.50

21. What should the asking price be if an owner wishes to clear (net) $247,000 and the broker charges a real estate fee of 6%?
   a. $233,180   c. $261,820
   b. $262,765   d. $262,800

22. A broker may legitimately pay all or part of a real estate commmission to:
   a. the seller.   c. his or her salesperson.
   b. the buyer.   d. the house inspector.

23. When an owner lists property for sale with a number of brokers, this form of listing is known as a(n):
   a. exclusive agency.
   b. open listing.
   c. exclusive right to sell.
   d. net listing.

24. Minimum age for a New York real estate broker's license is:
   a. 18.   c. 20.
   b. 19.   d. 21.

25. In the usual transaction, the listing agent owes fiduciary duties to the seller, and the selling agent owes those duties to the:
   a. buyer.   c. Department of State.
   b. seller.   d. listing broker.

26. Which of the following happenings would *not* cause the termination of an open listing agreement?
   a. Death or insanity of either party
   b. Bankruptcy of either party
   c. A kitchen fire
   d. Sale by another broker

27. Which of the following acts would require a real estate license in New York?
   a. Sale of one's own property
   b. Sale by owner's lawyer
   c. Sale of land by auctioneer
   d. Foreclosure sale by court order

28. An associate broker may:
   a. sponsor a person for a salesperson's license.
   b. work as a salesperson for a principal broker.
   c. collect his or her own real estate fees.
   d. act as a principal broker for another broker.

29. When applying for a New York State real estate broker's license, which of the following is *not* necessary?
   a. Completion of 90 hours of approved instruction
   b. U.S. residence
   c. Posting a bond
   d. One year's experience as a salesperson

30. When a real estate license is revoked, how long must the licensee wait before applying to have the license reinstated?
   a. one year   c. six months
   b. one and a half years   d. two years

31. The officer of a corporation who actively practices real estate for the corporation must:
   a. have a salesperson's license.
   b. own 75% of the corporation's stock.
   c. have a broker's license.
   d. be a director of the corporation.

32. Civil rights legislation forbids discrimination on the basis of:
    a. political affiliation.
    b. source of income.
    c. country of origin.
    d. prison record.

33. The Civil Rights Act of 1866:
    a. prohibits any type of discrimination based on race.
    b. prohibits discrimination in federally funded housing.
    c. allows an exception to racial discrimination for an owner-occupied two-family house.
    d. does not apply to nonlicensed persons.

34. Redlining is defined as:
    a. steering homeseekers to a particular neighborhood.
    b. drawing red lines on a local map indicating what areas to look for listings.
    c. denying or restricting loans in a certain area by a lending institution.
    d. a zoning procedure.

35. New York State goes beyond federal human rights law when it forbids discrimination based on:
    a. race.
    b. marital status.
    c. religion.
    d. children in a family.

36. A summary of data affecting title to property, arranged in the order of recording is called:
    a. marketable title.
    b. evidence of title.
    c. abstract of title.
    d. color of title.

37. Which of the following instruments does not always have to be in writing in New York State?
    a. Listing agreement
    b. Deed
    c. Mortgage
    d. Option to purchase

38. An item credited to the buyer at a closing would be:
    a. sale price.
    b. unpaid water bills.
    c. prepaid insurance.
    d. fuel oil on hand.

39. A Veteran's Administration loan is:
    a. insured.
    b. guaranteed.
    c. conventional.
    d. prepaid.

40. A written document that creates a lien on real estate as security for the payment of a debt is a:
    a. bond.
    b. deed.
    c. encroachment.
    d. mortgage.

41. A mortgage with a final payment larger than the preceeding ones is known as a(n):
    a. blanket mortgage.
    b. balloon mortgage.
    c. open mortgage.
    d. variable rate mortgage.

42. Discount charges imposed by a lender to raise the yield on a loan are called:
    a. negative amortization.
    b. points.
    c. laches.
    d. lis pendens.

43. Which of the following is *not* essential to a valid mortgage?
    a. To be in writing
    b. To have competent parties
    c. To be paid in full
    d. A description of the property

44. Value of real property is best defined as:
    a. cost.
    b. present worth of future benefits.
    c. price.
    d. attractiveness and location.

45. Which type of listing agreement is illegal in New York State?
    a. Net listing
    b. Exclusive agency
    c. Exclusive right to sell
    d. Open listing

46. Which of the following items need not be included in the listing information on a property?
    a. Lot size
    b. Legal description
    c. Current taxes
    d. Number and size of rooms

47. When a comparative market analysis is done, which approach to real estate appraisal is being used?
    a. Income approach
    b. Cost approach
    c. Direct sales comparison approach
    d. Guesstimate

48. When a property owner dies leaving no will or heirs ownership reverts to the state through:

    a. redemption.   c. escheat.
    b. revulsion.   d. accretion.

49. Which of the following is *not* a basic zoning classification?

    a. Commercial   c. Industrial
    b. Residential   d. Municipal

50. The tenant who pays property taxes and heating bills for the store he or she rents probably has what type of lease?

    a. Net   c. Percentage
    b. Participation   d. Gross

Part Two

Real Estate Broker

13

Opening a Broker's Office

Key Terms

Call forwarding
Closing room
Conference capability
Corporation
DBA
Errors and omissions insurance
FAX machine
Franchise
Fringe benefits

General partnership
Limited partnership
Market share
NYSAR
Sales manager
S corporation
Sole proprietorship
Startup expenses
Umbrella policy

Overview

An ambition to open one's own office is common among successful real estate salespersons. Any licensee contemplating such a move needs to plan well in advance, reach some basic decisions about the form the new firm will take and carefully estimate projected expenses. This chapter will discuss matters a broker has to consider before going into business and will offer advice on planning the office itself.

Real Estate in New York

As of 1989, New York State counted licenses for 43,000 real estate brokers and 111,000 salespeople. Approximately one-half were licensed in and around New York City and the other half Upstate. Many of the 154,000 licensees are inactive. The New York State Association of REALTORS (**NYSAR**) estimates that its members handle between 80 and 90 percent of all brokered sales although they constituted only 44,000, less than one-third of those licensed.

Making the Break

A successful salesperson often aspires to open an office operating either as a sole practitioner, earning the same money more easily by keeping the entire commission, or by taking on associates and moving into sales management.

The success of these plans may depend on the individual's ability to run a business. The qualities that mark a star salesperson may or may not be the same as those contributing to successful management. After breaking away from an established office the new broker lacks the accustomed support system. Even with the relatively few transactions generated by one person, paperwork accumulates. Many successful salespeople are by nature uninterested in detail work, but someone must maintain accurate records, handle mail, make copies, write checks and keep careful books. The lone broker soon discovers that even a bare-bones operation requires an extra telephone, a typewriter, new furniture, a filing cabinet, signs, stationery, promotional material, advertising and possibly a computer terminal or copier. These expenses must be paid from that 100 percent commission that looks so inviting. The broker who plans to move into sales management must understand that experience as a successful salesperson is not sufficient preparation for the different skills needed in hiring, training, motivating and supervising others.

License Application

The broker's license application is shown in Figure 13.1 The applicant must include original school certificates (not copies) as proof of completion of the required 90 hours of qualifying courses. If the certificate for the first 45-hour course was already sent to Albany with a previous application for a salesperson's license, that fact can be noted on the application.

A fee of $150 (good for a two-year license) must accompany the application in the form of a check or money order, not cash. In addition, the applicant will complete a supplemental form detailing at least one full year's experience as a licensed real estate salesperson; such experience is defined by the state as at least 50 35-hour weeks of work. The required experience can be gained part-time over a period of years. For those in fields other than brokerage, it is possible to substitute at least two years' equivalent experience in some other field of real estate. The Department of State will examine the record of experience and rule on whether it is sufficient to qualify toward a broker's license.

The applicant must indicate an intention either to operate as an independent *principal broker*, or else become an *associate broker*, retaining the status of a salesperson in association with another broker, using that broker's business name and

**Figure 13.1
Broker's License
Application**

FOR OFFICE USE ONLY

CLASS	KEY	REG. NO.							CASH NO.	FEE
3										**$150**

E   W   S ___ ___ ___   ___ ___ / ___ ___   B ___ ___ ___ ___   ___ ___ / ___ ___

Application as (check one):   ☐ Broker   ☐ Associate Broker

1. APPLICANT'S NAME (LAST, FIRST, MI)

2. HOME ADDRESS (NUMBER AND STREET)

CITY   STATE   ZIP

COUNTY   3. SOCIAL SECURITY NUMBER AND/OR FEDERAL EMPLOYER ID NUMBER (SEE OVER)

4. BUSINESS NAME

5. BUSINESS ADDRESS AT WHICH APPLICANT WILL OPERATE

CITY   STATE   ZIP

COUNTY

6. Are you 19 years of age or older?...... ☐ Yes ☐ No   7. Have you been admitted to the NYS Bar ?..... ☐ Yes ☐ No

8. A Real Estate license was last issued to   FROM   TO
   me by the State of New York.................. 19 ☐ 19 ☐   Registration No. _____

9. Have you ever been convicted of a crime or offense (not a minor traffic violation) or has any license, commission
   or registration ever been denied, suspended or revoked in this state or elsewhere? .... ☐ Yes ☐ No
   • If Yes, attach a statement of details.

10. I own this business and the trade name certificate has been filed in the office of the County Clerk where our
    business is located .... ☐ Yes ☐ No

11. I am a member of this partnership and the partnership certificate has been filed in the office of the County
    Clerk where our business is located .... ☐ Yes ☐ No

12. I am an officer of this corporation and the New York State Charter of Incorporation providing the power to
    engage in the business of real estate brokerage has been filed in the Division of Corporations .... ☐ Yes ☐ No

13. ALL NEW APPLICANTS (except attorneys admitted to the Bar in New York State) MUST PASS a written examination and provide
    proof of work experience as indicated in the instructions. Please circle the city in which you wish to take your examination. You
    will be notified by mail of the date, time and location.

ALBANY   BINGHAMTON   BUFFALO   HAUPPAUGE   MINEOLA   NEWBURGH   NEW YORK CITY
PLATTSBURGH   ROCHESTER   SYRACUSE   UTICA   WATERTOWN

APPLICANT AFFIRMATION

I subscribe and affirm, under the penalties of perjury, that these statements are true and correct.

Applicant's
Signature X _____ Date _____

FOR ASSOCIATE BROKER APPLICANTS ONLY:

ASSOCIATION STATEMENT — I am sponsoring this applicant in accordance with the Real Property Law, section 441.1(d).

Sponsoring Broker's Signature X _____ Date _____

office facilities. Associate brokers are fully qualified for principal broker and may simply request a change of license status if they later decide to go into business for themselves. The associate broker's application is signed by the sponsoring principal broker.

Advance Preparations

The broker's first step should be to review the law of agency and New York's license law (Chapters 2 and 8). In addition the new broker can learn a great deal quickly by attending a national convention of the National Association of REALTORS®. These week-long gatherings, held every November, include hundreds of educational sessions (many of them geared to office management) and offer exhibits by manufacturers of necessary office equipment and service companies like franchisors, referral networks and insurance firms. The New York State Association of REALTORS® holds a similar convention every September. Management seminars are also available at different times and locations across the state.

Basic Decisions

Before opening an office the new broker must decide on specialty, groups to affiliate with, size, location, form of organization, office layout and budgeting, among other items. Seven out of ten firms in this country list single-family sales as their major source of income, but the broker who has acquired expertise in commercial and industrial property, multiple dwellings or farm and land sales will be drawn to those fields.

Organizations and Franchises

The broker's first decision is whether to become a REALTOR® and whether to join an available multiple-listing arrangement. In 1986 the National Association of REALTORS® found 80 percent of surveyed firms associated with multiple-listing systems and 15 percent with franchises. Asked to list the aspects of franchising that most appealed to them, member firms mentioned the national identity that made their names readily recognized and expressed satisfaction with the training programs offered by franchises. Items singled out for criticism were high franchise fees, not enough assistance with local advertising and too few intercity referrals.

Size of Office

Despite a trend toward larger offices and multioffice firms, nine out of ten real estate companies in a National Association of REALTORS® survey had only one office and fewer than ten salespersons. Five or fewer salespersons were found in more than one-half the offices, as shown in Figure 13.2. Three percent of the firms had 50 or more associates.

The survey showed the majority of small firms as having no management except that provided by the owner. Large companies usually employed part-time or full-time managers most often called **sales managers** or administrative managers. Some firms achieve a sales force of 50 or more within two or three years. After five years in business no relationship was found between length of time in business and size of firm. By then the majority of brokers evidently reached the form of business they preferred and stayed there.

The *one-person office* involves less responsibility to and for others, more flexibility and lower initial investment. Its disadvantages include uneven flows of income,

Figure 13.2
Size of Firms, 1979–1986
(Percentage Distributions)

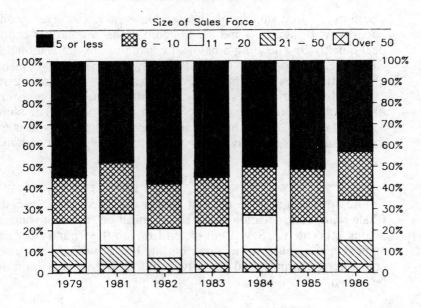

TRENDS IN THE PERCENT OF FIRMS
IN VARIOUS SIZE CATEGORIES: 1979 – 1986
(Percentage Distributions)

SOURCE: National Association of REALTORS®: Economics and Research Division.

no backup in emergencies and less prestige and ego satisfaction than a larger firm would provide. Profits are limited to one person's efforts.

Also classified as small companies are one-manager offices with a sales force of between two and ten persons. Such a firm usually employs one secretary, possibly only part-time. As the number of associates approaches ten the managing broker usually stops selling. Salespersons resent the broker who remains in competition with them, appropriates leads and is unavailable for the management support they require. On the other hand the manager who sells remains in close contact with the market and with current financing and is in a position to spot weak points. Many managers compromise by handling only personal requests from their own past customers and clients. Advantages of an office this size include a more even flow, more freedom to take vacations or attend conventions and seminars, availability of backup in emergencies and tight control of business decisions. Income is less limited but sometimes may not exceed that attainable in the one-person office. Drawbacks include considerably more overhead, more responsibility to others and the need for management skills. A hired manager is still not cost-effective with this size of operation.

Site Selection

Site selection should follow careful analysis of goals. The broker should study *demographics* (the population characteristics in the area) and identify a target clientele. Research into sales activity in the area can aid in setting a goal for **market share** in terms of gross sales or number of transactions.

A *downtown* location is close to accountants, lawyers, courthouse records and the business community. Parking costs and expensive office rentals, particularly for ground floor locations, often make it inappropriate for residential firms. Offices specializing in commercial property are more likely to choose this type of location.

Suburban locations follow customers and clients of those brokers specializing in residential property sales. Before selecting an area the broker will consider growth patterns and present competition. A location on a well-traveled road offers high visibility and may produce some stop-ins. In addition it is easy to direct callers to a main road address. From such a location salespersons find it possible to cover more territory. The specific site should provide easy access and ample free parking.

Shopping centers attract walk-in traffic. Mall locations can be expensive and a strip location offers better sign visibility. Parking density and sign regulations should be investigated before choosing shopping center space, as well as the questions: Will the mall be open after store hours? May the sign be lighted at night?

Status of Associates   The NAR survey found nine out of ten of the real estate firms listing their sales associates as independent contractors. Brokers traditionally have maintained this relationship to avoid the bookkeeping problems of withholding taxes, social security payments, unemployment insurance and other such items that become complex when based not on a regular salary but on unpredictable commissions. The broker who chooses independent contractor status for associates should keep on file agreements signed by the associates with the wording provided by the broker's attorney. Recent "safe-harbor" guidelines provide that the Internal Revenue Service will not challenge independent contractor status where the associate (1) is licensed as a real estate broker or salesperson, (2) has income based on sales output and subject to fluctuation and (3) performs services pursuant to a written contract specifying independent contractor status.

In 1986, New York state adopted similar guidelines on independent contractor status for real estate licensees, whose situation had been unclear with regard to state programs like unemployment insurance and workers' compensation insurance.

The New York Department of Labor, in evaluating associates' status, also stresses the importance of a current, written contract between broker and salesperson (*see* end-of-chapter Appendix). A sample contract, suggested by the New York State Association of REALTORS®, is shown in Figure 13.3.

Employee status for salespersons has some advantages for the broker: closer control over salesperson activities and the ability to mandate sales meetings, floor duty, dress codes and sales quotas. It also may retain skilled salespersons.

Fringe benefits like health insurance, pension plans, sick leave and paid vacations are variously estimated to add 25 to 50 percent to base salary. The broker who chooses to regard salespersons as employees must take such costs into consideration when working out commission schedules.

Part-timers. Almost 60 percent of the firms surveyed, many of them the smaller firms, had part-time sales associates; 40 percent, probably larger firms, did not.

Figure 13.3
Sample Independent
Contractor Agreement

AGREEMENT

THIS AGREEMENT, (hereinafter "Agreement") made and entered into this _____ day of _____ 198_____, by and between _____ (hereinafter "Sales Associate") and _____ (hereinafter "Broker").

WHEREAS, the Sales Associate and the Broker are both duly licensed pursuant to Article 12-A of the Real Property Law of the State of New York; and

WHEREAS, the Sales Associate and the Broker wish to enter into this Agreement in order to define their respective rights, duties and obligations.

NOW THEREFORE, in consideration of the terms, covenants, conditions and mutual promises contained herein, and other good and valuable consideration, it is hereby stipulated and agreed as follows:

1. The Sales Associate is engaged as an independent contractor associated with the Broker pursuant to Article 12-A of the Real Property Law and shall be treated as such for all purposes, including but not limited to Federal and State taxation, withholding, unemployment insurance and workers' compensation; and

2. The Sales Associate (a) shall be paid a commission on his or her gross sales, if any, without deducation for taxes, which commission shall be directly related to sales or other output; (b) shall not receive any remuneration related to the number of hours worked; and (c) shall not be treated as an employee with respect to such services for Federal and State tax purposes; and

3. The Sales Associate shall be permitted to work out of his or her own home or the office of the Broker; and

5. The Sales Associate shall be free to engage in outside employment; and

6. The Broker may provide office facilities and supplies for the use of the Sales Associate, but the Sales Associate shall otherwise bear his or her own expenses, including but not limited to automobile, travel and entertainment expenses; and

7. The Broker and Sales Associate shall comply with the requirements of Article 12-A of the Real Property Law and the regulations pertaining thereto, but such compliance shall not affect the Sales Associate's status as an independent contractor nor would it be construed as an indication that the Sales Associate is an employee of the Broker for any purpose whatsoever; and

8. This contract and the association created hereby may be terminated by either party hereto at any time upon notice given to the other; and

9. This Agreement is deemed to have been entered into in, and will be construed and interpreted in accordance with the laws of the State of New York; and

10. BY SIGNING BELOW THE UNDERSIGNED STIPULATE AND AGREE THAT THEY HAVE COMPLETELY READ THIS AGREEMENT, THAT THE TERMS HEREOF ARE FULLY UNDERSTOOD AND VOLUNTARILY ACCEPTED BY THEM AND THAT THIS AGREEMENT IS NOT SIGNED UNDER DURESS.

IN WITNESS WHEREOF, the parties hereto have executed this Agreement as of the day and year first above written.

_____
SALES ASSOCIATE

_____
BROKER

PREPARED BY THE NEW YORK STATE ASSOCIATION OF REALTORS, INC.

Name of Firm

The choice of a business name has an important connection with the public image planned for the firm. If a broker's name is well known in the community, that name is the logical choice. Sometimes the name suggests a logo or motto for the firm. The proposed business name must be cleared in advance by the Department of State, which will veto any name too closely resembling another in the community or any deemed misleading to the public. The word "REALTOR®" is a trademark and may not be used in the firm name. Any **DBA** (doing business as) name must be registered with the county clerk, who will issue a certificate, without which the broker will have trouble opening a business bank account.

The new business will need a checking account and an escrow account. Department of State regulations stipulate that escrow deposits shall be held in a separate, special *bank* account, which may or may not be an interest-bearing one. The DOS states clearly that any interest earned does not belong to the broker. The account should be clearly identified as an escrow account to avoid any confusion with the broker's own funds in the event of a lawsuit, bankruptcy or death.

Form of Organization

A real estate business may be run as a **sole proprietorship** with the broker as single owner. The broker may draw a regular salary or take profits as income. This type of business has the virtue of simplicity and probably offers the best tax advantage for a small office. One major drawback is the owner's unlimited financial liability if problems of damages, judgments or bankruptcy arise.

A **corporation** offers limited personal liability. Its profits are taxed twice, once to the corporation and again to stockholders as individual income. Because salaries are not taxed twice, however, and generous arrangements can be made for pension funds, some flexibility is possible. The corporate form of ownership is appropriate for larger companies. The **S corporation** is often ideal for a brokerage or rental business. It avoids the tax disadvantages of a regular corporation but still offers some limited liability, continuity of life and retirement fund advantages. It may not have more than 35 stockholders and is appropriate for proprietorships and partnerships.

General partnership in New York State requires that all partners be licensed brokers. Tax treatment of a partnership is simple: Losses, gains and income are shared directly by each partner. A well-drafted partnership agreement is necessary; otherwise problems can arise if one partner dies, files bankruptcy or wishes to sell his or her share. **Limited partnerships** are usually employed for acquiring investments, not for usual brokerage operations. Overall, partnership organization is used for eight percent of real estate firms (*see* Figure 13.4).

Outside Help

Ideally, an *attorney* for a real estate firm should be available by telephone in the evenings and on weekends to provide counsel if unusual situations arise in the course of business. Sometimes a yearly retainer is appropriate compensation. Among the attorney's contributions to the organization before operations begin will be advising which form of ownership to choose, drawing up partnership or corporation documents, reviewing a lease or a franchise contract and assisting with independent contractor agreements and other forms to be used in the business.

Although the firm's bookkeeping can be handled by the broker, *secretary* or *bookkeeper* (often part-time), the books should be set up by an *accountant,* who should also look over the initial budget for any flaws. The accountant will offer advice, provide periodic reports of the firm's financial condition and prepare income tax returns. Because tax considerations often arise in real estate brokerage, it is helpful if the accountant is also available by telephone after normal business hours. Many computer software programs specifically designed for real estate office management are available.

An *insurance broker* should be consulted before the office opens. An **umbrella** liability **policy** protects the broker beyond any automobile insurance protection that associates carry and can be written to cover accidents occurring in the showing of property. More costly is **errors and omissions insurance,** increasingly

Figure 13.4
Organization of Real Estate Firms, 1986 Percentage Distributions

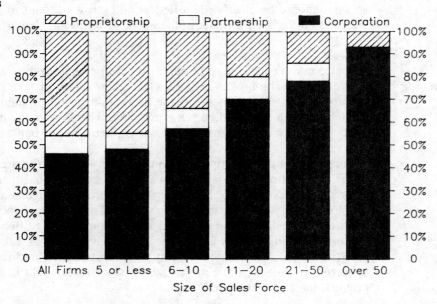

LEGAL ORGANIZATION OF REAL ESTATE IN 1986
(Percentage Distributions)

SOURCE: NATIONAL ASSOCIATION OF REALTORS®, Economics and Research Division.

necessary as society becomes more litigious. Analogous to legal or medical malpractice insurance, it is carried by about one-half of today's real estate firms.

Office Layout

Bare necessities for any one-person office include a *desk, restroom* for the public, *files* and *storage space* for signs and supplies. Whether in one room or an entire building, the real estate office must provide areas for different activities: a *reception area,* with *coat storage* and a place for customers to wait in comfort, and *desk space,* preferably for each salesperson. A popular arrangement provides a number of desks in one large room. Such an arrangement saves space and facilitates easy communication. Also needed is a private *conference area* or **closing room** for confidential interviews and the serious business of signing contracts. If residential sales are to be the company's specialty, a separate children's *play corner* is useful. A kitchen area or small refrigerator is welcome. Space is needed for the *manager's desk,* often in a separate office, and for the secretary, receptionist or bookkeeper. A computer terminal can be coupled with files, bookcases or copier to provide a *research area.* The large office will also provide for a *training center* or *meeting room.*

Equipment

Modern office equipment and telephone gadgets can be seductive, but every piece of equipment must be analyzed carefully to determine its cost-effectiveness. Will it contribute to the company's image, pay for itself in time saved or produce higher sales volume?

Telephone service is the lifeblood of a real estate office. An unlisted line is useful for outgoing calls so that the main line is free for incoming ones. Telephone coverage must be provided around the clock either with an answering service or an *answering machine*. Some offices make use of **call forwarding** to shunt calls to the home of the broker or associate responsible for overnight coverage. Also useful is **conference capability** that allows two or more lines to be linked.

Initially a *copier* may be rented rather than purchased. Copiers were found in almost all surveyed offices. The machine must take legal-size paper, and a basic model is usually sufficient. An electric *typewriter* with a carbon cartridge provides a crisp, professional image and is a handy supplement to any word-processing equipment. **FAX (facsimile) machines** are expected to become a commonplace in real estate offices in the 1990s.

When a *filing cabinet* is purchased a standard one can be matched later as another is required. If the startup budget is limited, files can be purchased secondhand or at office supply sales. *Desks, chairs* and *tables* should be chosen for utility as well as decor. However, round conference tables with comfortable armchairs create a more reassuring and friendly atmosphere than an authoritative desk-and-straight-chair arrangement.

In the 1986 survey 74 percent of real estate firms had *computer* capability. This figure had more than doubled since 1981. Although the most common use was for access to a multiple-listing system, firms specializing in nonbrokerage activities were more likely to use in-house systems and word processors.

Smaller items to be purchased include lamps, bookcases, coffee or side tables and a fireproof safe for records. The office's *outside sign* should be lighted at night. New York license law also requires that each broker be listed on a sign visible from the sidewalk or in the lobby of an office building with the words "licensed real estate broker."

Budgeting

Before the office is opened a careful budget is made to estimate **startup expenses** and costs for the first six months of operation. A sample budget for one-time and annual expenses, shown as Figure 13.5, is reprinted from *Real Estate Brokerage: A Success Guide,* by John E. Cyr and Joan m. Sobeck (Chicago: Real Estate Education Company, second edition, 1988), which also provided much of the information in this and the next chapter. Ideally the broker should have the necessary cash in hand, as indicated on the bottom line, before starting. A broker confident of success can sometimes borrow the money to open, however. In that case periodic repayments of the loan must be added to operating expenses.

Opening the Office

A good way to introduce the new brokerage is to hold an opening celebration complete with refreshments. Invitations can be sent to former customers (*not* to clients presently listed with one's former brokerage), neighboring business establishments, lawyers and bankers with whom the broker has ties, and nearby real estate offices that are curious to see the new competition. The hours between business day and dinnertime are probably best. The firm's brand new Open House signs can be positioned near the door and in the office.

High visibility in the community may be accomplished in several ways. Newspapers should be sent a brief, businesslike news release announcing the new firm. While the interior is being readied, a large window sign outside can announce that the

Figure 13.5
Sample Budget

One-Time Expenses

Legal fees (to establish corporation or partnership) $ _____
Accounting fees (advice, start-up, books)   _____
Telephone installation   _____
Initiation fees, board of REALTORS®, MLS   _____
License fees—state, city   _____
Office space costs—deposit, remodeling   _____
Office equipment—typewriters, files, desks   _____
Office supplies—stationery, cards, forms   _____
Automobile purchase or lease   _____
Artist work for logo, signs, stationery   _____
Advertising agency cost (if applicable)   _____
Stock of lawn signs   _____
Office sign—purchase or lease   _____

TOTAL ONE-TIME EXPENSES $ _____ $ _____

Monthly Expenses

Office rent $ _____
Office salaries   _____
Legal and accounting fees   _____
Insurance premiums   _____
Automobile cost   _____
Utilities (if applicable)   _____
Office supplies   _____
Janitorial wages (if applicable)   _____
Telephone expense   _____
Newspaper advertising   _____
Your salary   _____
Miscellaneous dues and subscriptions   _____
Sign repair and replacement   _____
Entertainment   _____
Reserve for contingencies   _____

TOTAL MONTHLY EXPENSES $ _____ x 6 mo. $ _____
GROSS AMOUNT NEEDED $ _____
LESS PROJECTED INCOME FOR SIX MONTHS $ _____
MINIMUM CASH NEEDED TO START $ _____

brokerage is "Coming Soon. . . ." Announcements can be mailed to old customers and clients. With the first listings the office acquires, extra money should be budgeted for newspaper classified advertising, so that the firm logo is prominently displayed for a few months.

Summary

Operating a broker's office requires skills beyond those needed for successful listing and selling of property. Expenses are incurred in even bare-bones operation. The new broker may prepare by reviewing law of agency and license law and by attending management seminars and REALTORS® conventions.

Among early decisions a broker needs to make are what specialty to pursue, groups to affiliate with, size, location, form of ownership, office layout and budgeting. Franchise affiliation should be considered. Even with a trend toward larger offices most real estate firms in this country are still small businesses with no sales management beyond the owner's services. Site selection must take into account ease of access, parking facilities and the firm's desired public image.

The majority of brokers elect *independent contractor status* for associates. The name of the new firm must be cleared with the Department of State and should be registered with the county clerk. A separate bank account is required for escrow deposits. The firm may be organized as a *sole proprietorship, corporation, S corporation* or *general partnership*. A salesperson may not be a partner with a broker. Corporate ownership may lead to double taxation but has the advantage of limited personal financial liability.

Outside assistance may include the services of an *attorney, accountant, bookkeeper, insurance broker, artist* or *advertising agency, answering service* and *notary public*. Office layout must provide a *reception area, desk space, research area* and a *private conference* or *closing room*. Equipment should be carefully chosen for cost-effectiveness.

The opening of the office can be celebrated with an open house to which clients, customers, neighbors and business associates are invited. Newspaper releases and extra exposure of the new office's logo will increase community awareness of the firm.

Questions

1. The number of real estate licensees in New York State is approximately:
   a. 154,000.   c. 650,000.
   b. 15,500.   d. 31,000.

2. Approximately what portion of real estate licensees in New York State belong to the State Association of REALTORS®?
   a. 10 percent   c. 50 percent
   b. 30 percent   d. All

3. Among the requirements for successful sales management are:
   a. motivational skills.
   b. attention to detail.
   c. careful budgeting.
   d. all of the above.

4. The majority of the real estate firms in this country specialize in:
   a. full-service brokerage.
   b. farm and land sales.
   c. commercial property.
   d. residential sales.

5. Approximately what proportion of REALTORS® offices are affiliated with a franchise organization?
   a. 10 percent   c. 50 percent
   b. 15 percent   d. 90 percent

6. Most REALTORS® offices in this country have how many salespersons?
   a. 1–10   c. 21–50
   b. 11–20   d. More than 50

7. The IRS allows independent contractor tax status for an associate who:
   a. holds a real estate license.
   b. is paid irregularly, by commission.
   c. works under a written contract that specifies independent contractor status.
   d. does all of the above.

8. The initials "DBA" are used for:
   a. Department of State.
   b. Department of Business Administration.
   c. Doing business as.
   d. Downtown Broker's Association.

9. The business name of a prospective real estate company must be cleared with the:
   a. NAR.   c. DOS.
   b. NYSAR.   d. IRS.

10. The broker's escrow account:
    a. may be a brokerage money market account.
    b. must be non–interest-bearing.
    c. may also contain earned commissions.
    d. should be clearly identified as a trust account.

11. Which of the following forms of organization does *not* involve personal liability for the firm's financial debts?
    a. Sole proprietorship
    b. Corporation
    c. Monolithic office
    d. Partnership

12. Just as a physician carries malpractice insurance many real estate brokers carry:
    a. health and accident insurance.
    b. incompetence insurance.
    c. errors and omissions insurance.
    d. partnership insurance.

13. Computers are most often used by real estate firms for:
    a. word processing.
    b. playing games.
    c. in-house management systems.
    d. accessing multiple-listing information.

14. New York license law requires:
    a. an accountant's yearly report to the Department of State.
    b. a sign visible from the sidewalk with the words "licensed real estate broker."
    c. membership in the New York State Association of REALTORS®.
    d. all of the above.

15. The advertising budget for a newly opened real estate office should:
    a. be held to a cautious minimum.
    b. be more lavish than usual.
    c. be discussed with the firm's attorney.
    d. include provisions for skywriting.

Appendix: Independent Contractor Guidelines

NEW YORK STATE,
DEPARTMENT OF LABOR,
UNEMPLOYMENT INSURANCE
DIVISION
NOTICE TO EMPLOYERS

Persons Engaged in Real Estate Sales

Effective October 1, 1986, services performed by a licensed real estate broker or sales associate are excluded from coverage if it can be proven that all of the following conditions are met:

(A) substantially all of the remuneration (whether or not paid in cash) for the services performed by such broker or sales associate is directly related to sales or other output (including the performance of services) rather than to the number of hours worked;

and

(B) the services performed by the broker or sales associate are performed pursuant to a written contract executed between such broker or sales associate and the person for whom the services are performed within the past twelve to fifteen months;

and

(C) such contract was not executed under duress and contains the following provisions:

1. that the broker or sales associate is engaged as an independent contractor associated with the person for whom services are performed pursuant to Article 12-A of the Real Property Law and shall be treated as such for all purposes;

2. that they (a) shall be paid a commission directly related to their gross sales or other output without deduction for taxes; (b) shall not receive any remuneration related to the number of hours worked; and (c) shall not be treated as employees with respect to such services for federal and state tax purposes;

3. that they shall be permitted to work any hours they choose;

4. that they shall be permitted to work out of their own homes or the office of the person for whom services are performed;

5. that they shall be free to engage in outside employment;

6. that the person for whom the services are performed may provide office facilities and supplies for the use of the broker or sales associate, but that they shall otherwise bear their own expenses, including but not limited to automobile, travel, and entertainment expenses;

7. that the person for whom the services are performed and the broker or sales associate shall comply with the requirements of Article 12-A of the Real Property Law and the regulations pertaining thereto, but such compliance shall not affect their status as independent contractors nor should it be construed as an indication that they are employees of such person for any purpose whatsoever;

8. that the contract and the association may be terminated by either party at any time upon notice to the other.

14

Operation of a Broker's Office

Overview   Careful planning, close regular supervision and constant monitoring are essential if a real estate brokerage is to prosper in a competitive market. This chapter examines standard techniques for achieving these ends, from budgeting through selecting and training sales associates and evaluating the firm's performance. It also considers the broker's liability for breaches of fiduciary duty, conflict of interest, misrepresentation and required standard of care.

Budgeting

The difference between firms that fail and those that stay in business during difficult times is often careful financial planning, budgeting and control of expenses. Unique to real estate brokerage is the concept of the **company dollar**—Funds left from gross income after commissions have been shared with salespersons, other brokers and franchise networks. The company dollar represents the money available for the firm's expenses and for profit.

Budgets for real estate companies vary widely. A recent national survey found that the average firm paid 43 percent of commissions received to its associates, forwarded another 6 percent in cobrokerage commissions to other offices, credited 6 percent as the owner's own commissions on transactions personally negotiated and spent approximately 1 percent for franchise fees, board or MLS costs. Of gross income, 44 percent was company dollar for the average firm.

Breakdown of Company Dollar

Advertising averaged 16 percent of the company dollar spent. Most went for newspaper advertising, but also included were radio and television, signs and yellow pages advertising (often incorrectly included with communications expense). *Sales promotion* expense, including entertainment, education, travel, sales awards, business gifts and charitable contributions, averaged 5 percent. *Sales management expense* varied widely with small firms reporting no outlay in this category and large ones about 9 percent. The average was 3 percent. *Salary* figures included managers other than sales managers, secretarial and clerical help, payroll taxes and employee benefits. This category totaled 13 percent. *Owner's nonselling services* were computed by estimating the hours the owner spent and their value if the same services were being performed on an hourly basis by someone else. This cost averaged 11 percent of company dollars. *Communications expense,* including telephone, telegrams, long-distance networks and answering service, averaged 7 percent. *Occupancy* included rent, janitorial services and utilities. If the premises were owned the cost of occupancy was calculated from fair market rental for the space. The category accounted for about 12 percent of company dollar. *Operating expenses* (20 percent of the budget) covered licenses, dues, legal and accounting fees, office supplies, equipment rental, repairs and depreciation, insurance, postage, business loan interest, auto expenses and computer costs. *Profit* was reported by a few firms to be as high as 40 percent of company dollar while others operated at a net loss. Average net income, pretax, was reported at around 11 percent of the company dollar, or less than 5 percent of gross income. This analysis had, of course, already compensated the owner for time spent in management and for commissions on his or her own sales.

Other Methods of Financial Analysis

Other methods of expense analysis are available. Total expenses divided by the number of associates gives a figure called **desk cost** per salesperson. In a 1984–85 survey, desk cost per associate averaged $12,618. Small firms reported higher desk costs but showed higher production per employee. The associate who does not bring in enough company dollars to pay his or her desk cost is a drain on the firm. Besides representing a net loss, such a person costs the firm something in lost opportunities; valuable leads that might have been followed up successfully by someone else may be wasted. The inept salesperson also saps office morale and tarnishes the company's public image.

The company's revenue also may be measured by calculating the company dollar per average transaction (dividing total company dollars by number of transactions in a given period). Company figures can be calculated for items like advertising expense per salesperson or per listing, amount of money spent to produce each telephone inquiry, ratio of listings to sales, cost to service the average listing and monthly **nut** (amount in company dollars that must be generated to cover expenses). Careful analysis of the figures is valuable in budgeting, goal setting, and long-term planning.

Policy and Procedures Guide

A written **policy and procedures guide** contributes to the smooth running of the company, heads off misunderstandings, serves as a reference for settling disputes and can be an excellent tool in recruiting and training associates. A loose-leaf format makes revisions simple. Care must be taken not to violate the salesperson's independent contractor status through inappropriate wording. "Suggested Procedures Guide" is a suitable title. Except where legal and ethical considerations are under discussion, the word "must" is inappropriate. "Sales meetings are held each Monday morning at 9:30" is better than "Associates are required to attend each Monday . . ."; "Associates may sign up for floor duty" is preferable to "Each associate must spend four hours a week on floor duty." The guide should be as concise as possible. It should say nothing, for example, about how to secure a listing. Instead it can detail procedures to follow after the listing is obtained.

Company Policy. A typical guide starts with a sketch of the company's *history* and *goals*. *Background information* on the owner and manager is appropriate, with *names* and *responsibilities* of *personnel*. A *job description* for the associates follows. *Independent contractor* status is briefly reviewed with a list of items provided by the company and another list of those to be paid by the associate. A concise treatment of *ethical* and *legal* considerations is appropriate: *civil rights* guidelines to be followed both within the office and in listing and selling (*see* Chapter 10), a review of the *fiduciary duty* to clients, the theory of *hidden defects, nonsolicitation* orders that may be in effect in the area and local *sign restrictions* or regulations. Company policy regarding the *termination* of a salesperson is also discussed.

The associate needs to know the procedures followed in relationships with *attorneys*, a *franchise* or *multiple-listing system* to which the office belongs and *cooperating offices*. The guide may suggest (but not dictate) appropriate *goals* for an associate in terms of number of listings and sales, hours of floor duty and attendance at sales meetings and it may discuss the desk cost per associate.

Paperwork and Housekeeping. *Paperwork* should be described in detail: what *forms* are available; what *reports* are to be turned in with listings, contracts or deposits, and to whom. A *sample* of each form and sales aid used in the office should be included. *Supplies, signs, lockboxes, business cards* and use of equipment like the *copier, FAX machine* or *computer terminal* are discussed. Housekeeping information includes rules on *desk use,* lights, heat, ashtrays, coffee or kitchen equipment, *parking* and *office hours*.

Office Procedures. *Sales meetings, caravan tours, open houses* and *floor duty* (opportunity time, office time) should all be covered in the guide. The responsibilities and opportunities of the associate on floor duty are spelled out in detail to prevent misunderstandings. *Advertising* policy includes a discussion of frequency and size of ads, paperwork procedures, deadlines, individual budgets and follow-up reports to be turned in. A section on *telephones* describes the answering service used, specifies policy on long-distance calls and entries in a long-distance log, briefly discusses standard telephone-answering techniques and sets standards for customer rotation and the channeling of calls.

Compensation. Office morale benefits from the inclusion of a set *commission schedule*. Future disputes can be anticipated and avoided if the guide spells out commission divisions in unusual situations: when the associate buys or sells his or her own house, when the office furnishes interim financing to a buyer or seller, when unusual expenses or legal fees are incurred in the course of a transaction or when one associate makes a sale while holding an open house at another's listing.

Antitrust. Individual real estate brokers, boards of REALTORS®, and multiple-listing systems have come under close scrutiny by agencies intent on ensuring free and active competition. The Sherman Antitrust Act sets penalties as high as $1 million for corporations and $100,000 and three years in prison for individuals who operate in restraint of trade. Even seemingly casual and well-meant conversations have had devastating results for some companies. Brokers should refrain from *any* discussion with anyone from a competing firm anywhere, about *commission rates,* except as necessary for a specific cooperative transaction between two firms. Also suspect is any conversation with competitors about *geographical* or sociological *division* of business and *refusal to deal* with a competitor. The guide should tell associates to avoid conversation with members of another firm by leaving the premises if the talk turns to commission rates or geographical division of the market.

Recruiting

Before taking on associates the owner must consider the company's overall goals, public image and available space. A decision should be made beforehand on whether the firm wants part-time salespersons or only full-timers. Recruiting must be coordinated with training. The small office that offers informal one-on-one training may recruit on a continuing basis. The large firm may prefer a single recruitment campaign followed by a number of classroom training sessions.

Advertising, career nights and *trial training sessions* are often used for recruitment. Classified or small display ads in newspapers are common. A single sentence of invitation to discuss a real estate career may be appended to the company's other advertising. Care must be taken that advertising is not discriminatory. The phrase "experienced only," for example, has been held discriminatory in an area where experienced salespersons are almost all white, or male. "Experience desirable or we will train you" is more acceptable.

The broker who takes on anyone who walks in the door risks a loss in office morale, the financial drain of an unproductive associate and legal problems arising from unethical associates. Common methods of selection include *application forms, aptitude tests* and *personal interviews.*

An application form reveals, if nothing else, whether the would-be salesperson can write legibly and fill in forms, useful attributes for a real estate agent. Any application form should be reviewed by the firm's attorney before it is first used, however. Charges of discrimination in this matter can be serious. Questions about address, education and former employment are considered relevant. Among those forbidden are queries about race, religion, age (except as necessary to meet licensure requirements) and spouse's employment. There is also a growing belief that many aptitude tests may be discriminatory; in any event the value of tests in predicting success in real estate is questionable.

Among topics explored during an interview may be the applicant's attitude toward number of hours worked, weekend and evening work and the amount of income anticipated from commissions. Other jobs presently held should be discussed. The prospective associate's attitudes toward ethics and civil rights should be explored. The manager often cautions the applicant that no income may be forthcoming for three to six months, and explains that a regular **draw** against future commissions is inconsistent with independent contractor status. In explaining the nature of real estate brokerage the manager can stress the necessity for a salesperson to handle stress, face disappointments and accept occasional rejection. The decision to take on a particular salesperson should consider not only the profit potential but also whether the individual fits the company image and will contribute to office harmony.

Training

A good company training program aids in recruitment and builds reputation. The well-trained associate requires less time-consuming attention during early transactions and is eager to try out the techniques taught. The educated salesperson is more likely to succeed and to remain with the company.

An old jingle sums up the attitude in a few old-fashioned offices: "Here's the desk, there's the phone. Lots of luck, you're on your own." The small office, however, can offer excellent one-on-one, *on-the-job* training with the newcomer led step-by-step through the first few transactions. The *sales meeting* technique is often utilized in medium-size offices. Periodic training sessions are integrated into sales meetings. Full coverage of the material requires a number of months with this method. *Organized classrooms* are most often run by multiple-office companies or franchise operations. They offer efficient instruction and are one of the main inducements for franchise affiliation. Occasionally several small independent firms combine to operate an organized classroom.

The instructor should set down beforehand the objectives for each session. Visual aids (blackboard, videotapes, overhead projector) greatly enhance learning. Instruction may be varied with guest speakers, perhaps a mortgage counselor or the firm's attorney. Student involvement is encouraged through discussions, questions, role playing and small–group work on case studies. Students may be taken on field trips to an abstract company, settlement session or the office of the multiple-listing system or real estate board. The instructor need not be the broker; good teaching skills might be found in some other member of the staff.

Course Content

The following outline of topics is adapted from Cyr and Sobeck's *Real Estate Brokerage: A Success Guide,* second edition, 1988. The individual office will probably cover only some of these topics:

1. The philosophy of the firm regarding ethics, Board of REALTORS® membership, MLS participation, cooperation with other firms and the real estate sales process. Human rights and fair-housing laws.
2. The jobs and duties of the broker and sales manager and what the new associate should expect of them; the jobs, duties and responsibilities of other employees of the firm; what trainees may ask of associates and tasks they cannot expect others to perform for them; and the office layout and organizational chart.
3. The job description of a professional salesperson; what is expected of the trainee in the way of objectives, goals, working habits, demeanor, dress and attitude toward fellow associates.
4. The contract between the broker and the sales associate, what it contains and why; independent contractor versus employer-employee relationship, with an explanation of the different responsibilities of each party; why the company has chosen this specific form of contract and what it entails.
5. Reviewing the policy and procedures manual (if employer-employee relationship) or the suggested procedures guide (if independent contractor status).
6. How the associate can plan and manage time wisely.
7. Explanation of the company referral system; how referrals from other firms, former customers and clients are handled.
8. The importance of communicating properly: handling letters, telephone calls, brochures and other communication devices.
9. The law of agency and the exclusive listing; various kinds of listings and the company's attitude toward each type.
10. The multiple-listing system to which the firm belongs, its rules and regulations, how it works and how best to use it correctly.
11. Prospecting for listings, sources and methods.
12. The farm method of obtaining listings—setting up a market and research program.
13. Handling objections from For-Sale-by-Owners (FSBOs); using role playing.
14. Planning the listing presentation—use of the listing kit.
15. The first listing interview—role playing between trainees.
16. Pricing the listing; the dangers of overpricing; and how to use the comparative market analysis form.
17. The appraisal process for residential properties.
18. The listing agreement: gathering the data, measuring the house, computing the square footage and filling out the form properly.
19. Processing the listing by compiling the in-house records needed to service it adequately; installing the sign; lockboxes; counseling the seller about showings.
20. Servicing the listing: advertising, touring the property, holding open house for inspection—callback reports, obtaining new loan commitments.
21. How to write compelling and attention-getting classified and display ads about the listing.
22. When and how to advertise the listing by using brochures.
23. Renewing expiring exclusives.
24. Touring the listings and competing properties (improving product knowledge).
25. Prospecting for Buyers, Part One: advertising policy and techniques.
26. Prospecting for Buyers, Part Two: how to answer ad calls, getting the name and pertinent information, making the appointment, the use of "switch" sheets.
27. Prospecting for Buyers, Part Three: the use of open houses, how to conduct an open house properly, separating the buyers from the lookers.
28. Arranging for and conducting the showings correctly: cooperating with other firms, making the appointments, picking up and returning the keys, office policy regarding lockboxes.

29. Learning how to qualify buyers by using role playing for the trainees.
30. Techniques for obtaining the offer: countering prospects' objections, when and how to close.
31. Handling offers and counteroffers, closing techniques, contingency clauses, the art of negotiating.
32. The memorandum or purchase agreement: how to fill it out correctly and pitfalls to avoid.
33. Follow-through on the transaction: obtaining required inspections, permits and appraisals.
34. Estimating buyer and seller closing costs: how to prepare for the settlement, prorating customary charges in the locality.
35. The importance of after-sale servicing. (This is a good subject to "brainstorm.")
36. Financing, Part One: investigating and verifying the existing loan(s), obtaining the correct principal balance and interest rate; finding out if it is assumable and at what rate of interest; explaining the due-on-sale clause and use of amortization tables or financial hand calculator.
37. Financing, Part Two: finding out if the owner will carry back part of the purchase price, the use of the land contract, first and second mortgages, wrap-around or all-inclusive mortgages, fixed-rate mortgages versus ARMs.
38. Financing, Part Three: explaining government-supported financing; FHA, VA, Farmer's Home Administration loans, SONYMA loans.
39. Financing, Part Four: creative financing; the various sources coupled with the right tools.
40. Clauses to watch for on loans, such as subordination clause, "lock-in" loans, due-on-sale (alienation), notice of default, request for notice of default, acceleration clauses of various types and release clause. Caution against unauthorized practice of law.
41. Income tax implications in the sale of single-family residence, the avoidance or postponement of capital gains tax, the one-time after-55 credit and new laws affecting same.
42. The use of the installment sale method in order to spread out the tax on the sale of a home or farm.
43. Explanation of terms regarding the sale and exchange of real property; meaning of terms such as *basis, depreciation, "like-kind" property, tax shelter and leverage.*
44. IRS rules and regulations affecting the exchange of property and the mechanics of effecting a tax-deferred exchange.
45. Exchanges: two-party, three-party and multiparty.
46. Listing and selling small-income properties.
47. Analyzing a Real Estate Investment, Part One: arriving at the NOI (net operating income).
48. Analyzing a Real Estate Investment, Part Two: basic knowledge.
49. Analyzing a Real Estate Investment, Part Three: advanced knowledge.
50. Discussion about and commitment to a personal success plan for each trainee.

Sales Management

Where the sales force numbers more than 12, the owner often adds a sales manager and moves on to administrative and public relations activities. The manager handles recruiting, training, setting goals, motivation and evaluations and is available as a resource for difficult transactions, backup support for associates, and counsel for personal and professional problems. A good manager can also spot particular talents (working with transferees, obtaining listings, handling income property) and thus guide associates toward suitable specialties.

Compensation. The majority of nonowner sales managers are employees rather than independent contractors. As an incentive to increased production an override is sometimes offered in addition to salary. The manager whose primary income comes from commissions personally earned is in the difficult position of competing with the associates he or she is supposed to be helping.

Motivation. Even though sales associates often state they are in real estate to make money, other important factors are also at work. Among them are the desire to belong, to be liked, to create, to achieve and to receive recognition for achievement. These needs may be particularly strong in those individuals drawn to sales work. Significant findings emerged from a study conducted at the University of Alberta that investigated the efficacy of various forms of motivation for real estate salespersons. Financial incentives (higher commission splits, prizes, bonuses) were found to be less effective in raising production than close supervision, goal setting, sales meetings and individual attention. Other studies have shown that almost any new system, if accompanied by careful individual supervision, results in increased production.

Sales Meetings

Properly planned sales meetings contribute to production and to office morale. Selling can be lonely work and associates look forward to good meetings as enjoyable social occasions. Meetings impart technical knowledge, provide data on current market conditions and disseminate information on the associates' listings, transactions and issues of general interest.

The sales manager might start by calling upon each associate for a brief report on new sales and listings. Activity at weekend open houses is then canvassed. Financial information is updated with associates sharing any news or rumors they have encountered about interest rate changes, points and SONYMA money. Upcoming seminars and board meetings are publicized and goals and sales contests updated. A short presentation on a single training topic serves as a refresher and may stimulate discussion. Outside speakers may appear; bankers, appraisers, home inspection engineers and Department of State examiners are often willing to address groups, even small ones. The sales meeting also can serve as a forum for ventilating office problems.

Evaluating Performance

A broker cannot require independent contractors to file regular reports, but such records are valuable for analyzing each salesperson's working habits and production. Figure 14.1 is an activity report that might be used as the basis for an individual counseling session with the manager. Figure 14.2 aids in monitoring the goals set by the associate in consultation with the manager.

Broker's Liability

It is possible to incur liability even though acting in all honesty and with goodwill. Situations that may lead to professional liability fall under four main headings: breach of fiduciary duties; failure to observe standard of care; conflict of interest; and misrepresentation. Possible results include loss of client and list-

Figure 14.1
Monthly Activity Sheet

Name _____ Month _____

Sales . . . .
1.
2.
3.
4.
5.
_____

Listings Sold . . . .
1.
2.
3.
4.
5.
_____

New Listings . . . .
1.
2.
3.
4.
5.
_____

Total Activities . . . .
_____

Current Listing Inventory
1.
2.
3.
4.
5.
6.
7.
Total Current Listing Inventory . . . .
_____

ing, loss of customer and sale, loss of commission, civil lawsuit for damages, criminal prosecution, and suspension or loss of license. In many of the following situations full disclosure in advance will prevent liability. If on the other hand the problem is not immediately obvious, disclosure as soon as it is discovered may limit liability.

Breach of Fiduciary Duty

In essence fiduciary duty requires the agent to put the principal's interest above everyone else's, including the agent's own. Besides setting forth specific rules and regulations in this matter, New York's license law mandates "trustworthy" service. As noted in Chapter 2, the agent owes the principal:

- notice (calling to attention any material facts).
- obedience (not to deviate from instructions);

Figure 14.2
Self-Imposed Goals and
Actual Evaluation

	GOALS					ACTUAL				
INVENTORY LISTINGS		Sales	Listings	Total Activities	Earnings	Sales	Actual Listings	Total Activities	Earnings	
Goal	Actual									
198___										
JANUARY										
FEBRUARY										
MARCH										
1st QUARTER TOTALS										
APRIL										
MAY										
JUNE										
2nd QUARTER TOTALS										
JULY										
AUGUST										
SEPTEMBER										
3rd QUARTER TOTALS										
OCTOBER										
NOVEMBER										
DECEMBER										
4th QUARTER TOTALS										
YEAR-END TOTAL										

SIGNED _____

- care (acting in a competent manner);
- accounting (of all monies involved in a transaction); and
- loyalty (acting in client's best interest, above others').

Notice. The law considers that any notice given the agent has been given to the principal. The agent therefore has a duty to pass on any material information; all offers must be presented immediately. The broker must volunteer any facts that might be of value to the seller. Details of the buyer's financial condition should be disclosed as well as information that the buyers have indicated they might pay a higher price. The duty of notice also places on the broker an obligation to explain to the seller matters that might otherwise escape notice or be misunderstood, details of proposed financing, or drawbacks in a purchase offer.

Obedience. The agent must obey all the client's lawful instructions. Any order to conceal a hidden defect or to practice discrimination in the sale or rental of property should not be obeyed and the agent has a duty to explain to property owners their own legal liability in such cases. An agent may not advertise property below the price stipulated by the seller; thus "try the $90s" or "make offer" may be in violation of the duty of obedience. It is also a violation to suggest that the buyer offer anything below the asking price unless the seller has authorized the broker to do whatever negotiating is necessary to effect a sale. Instructions like "24 hours' notice for showing" or "all offers through listing broker" must be scrupulously obeyed by any subagents in a multiple-listing system.

Care. This duty requires the broker to further the client's goals by all reasonable and lawful means. If property has been listed the agent owes a sincere attempt to market it, as evinced by advertising the property, showing it to buyers, and advising the seller on ways to effect the sale.

Accounting. Handling of earnest money deposits is set forth in New York's license law, rules and regulations. A common source of trouble arises when the prospective buyer who does not keep large sums in a checking account, gives an agent a check to be held for a few days. If the seller accepts the purchase offer based on the representation that the earnest money is in the broker's possession, trouble may ensue. The broker clearly owes the seller an accounting of the exact status of the deposit.

Loyalty. Because the agent may not advance his or her interest at the expense of the principal's, any attempt to profit from a transaction except through the agreed-upon commission signals a situation in which loyalty might be breached. Profiting from a client's misfortune is forbidden. The agent who subtly discourages efforts by cobrokers in a multiple-listing system in hopes of securing a sale within the listing office, is not acting in the seller's best interest.

Buyer's Broker

When the agent is acting as buyer's broker, fiduciary duty to the buyer/principal may entail opposite obligations: conveying to the buyer any information about the seller's willingness to accept a lower price, about other offers or about the value of the property. No confidentiality would apply to the seller's disclosures. Trustworthy and straightforward treatment of all parties, however, dictates that all understand the agent's status from the outset.

Disclosure Notice

Figure 14.3 shows a disclosure notice recommended for use by members of the National Association of REALTORS®, when—as in the most common situation—they are acting as agents for the seller.

Figure 14.3
Suggested Disclosure
Notice

NOTICE TO PROSPECTIVE REAL ESTATE PURCHASERS

As a prospective purchaser you should know that:

• Generally, the listing and cooperating ("selling") brokers are the agents of the seller.

• Their fiduciary duties of loyalty and faithfulness are owed to their client (the seller).

• While neither broker is your agent, they are able to provide you with a variety of valuable market information and assistance in your decision-making process.

For example, a real estate broker representing the seller can:

• Provide you with information about available properties and sources of financing.

• Show you available properties and describe their attributes and amenities.

• Assist you in submitting an offer to purchase.

Both the listing broker and the cooperating broker are obligated by law to treat you honestly and fairly. They must:

• Present all offers to the seller promptly.

• Respond honestly and accurately to questions concerning the property.

• Disclose material facts the broker knows or reasonably should know about the property.

• Offer the property without regard to race, creed, sex, religion or national origin.

You can, if you feel it necessary, obtain agency representation of a lawyer or a real estate broker, or both.

If you choose to have a real estate broker represent you as your agent, you should:

• Enter into a written contract that clearly establishes the obligations of both parties.

• Specify how your agent will be compensated.

If you have any questions regarding the roles and responsibilities of real estate brokers, please do not hesitate to ask.

I have received, read and understand the information in this "Notice to Prospective Real Estate Purchasers."

Name of Prospective Purchaser:

Signature:

Address:

Telephone:

Date:

I certify that I have provided the Prospective Purchaser named above with a copy of this "Notice to Prospective Purchasers."

Name of Broker or Sales Agent:

Signature:

Date:

Failure to Observe Standard of Care

Standard of care requires the agent to deliver the quality of service expected of a reasonably prudent broker. New York license law expects the broker to be "competent." Actions breaching this obligation might be failing to present an offer before it expires, neglecting to mention in the purchase contract any fixtures or personal property desired by one of the parties, neglecting the property being managed for another, improperly handling escrow deposits or failing to obtain all necessary signatures on a contract. The cost of drapes might be sought by the buyer who was assured they would be mentioned in the contract. The seller who did not receive an offer in time to consider it might subsequently look to the broker for a sum known as **loss-of-bargain.** If the lost offer was for $125,000 and the property later sold for $115,000, the seller may look to the broker for the lost $10,000.

The courts and the New York Department of State set differing standards of care for brokers and salespersons. The broker is held to higher expectations than the salesperson. Special training, designations, education and experience may all increase the standard required of an agent. Brokers are unwise to represent themselves as qualified appraisers or experienced syndicators if they are unable to deliver service of acceptable quality. The neophyte residential agent confronted with an opportunity to list a shopping plaza should probably approach an experienced commercial broker with a request that they work together to list and sell the property. Otherwise the duty of observing an appropriate standard of care may be breached by the inexperienced agent.

Conflict of Interest

In the mid-1980s a federal survey disclosed that approximately 75 percent of the buying public thought they were being represented by the selling broker. Even worse, some brokers had the same impression. Long discussions took place on the question of **dual agency,** sometimes designated as the *subagency* question, because of the position of a cooperating broker in a multiple-listing system. In one state after another, legislatures wrestled with the problem of informing the public and controlling the agent's fiduciary position.

New York's license law forbids the agent from representing both parties unless each knows of the arrangement and consents to it. Where the agent is being paid by both, the situation is clear. More difficult, however, is the common situation in which the agent, being paid by the seller, comes to identify with the buyer and furnishes encouragement, advice and assistance to the buyer. Under a multiple-listing system, the selling agent may never even have met the seller. Many agents—and some lawyers—have difficulty remembering that the seller is usually the principal and owed first loyalty.

Advising the buyer on how to negotiate with the seller may even put the broker in the position of serving two masters. Without such advice, of course, most transactions would not take place at all. The broker has been retained to produce a ready, willing and able buyer; to accomplish this, negotiation and compromise are usually necessary. Nevertheless an unintended result may follow, with the agent now representing both parties. If the transaction falls through, either buyer or seller might claim damages based on the broker's conflict of interest. That the actions are performed with good intentions does not change the situation. The problem is a difficult one, faced daily by brokers and with no simple solution. One remedy might be to obtain the seller's authorization to perform whatever negotiation and service to the buyer might be necessary to secure an offer.

Conflict of interest may occur when the agent is called to a listing interview and finds a seller ready to let the property go at a ridiculously low price. The courts have held that even though the property is not yet listed the seller is relying on the broker's expertise. The broker who wants to buy the property immediately without notifying the seller of its true value is operating under a conflict between his or her own interest and that of the seller.

Indirect interest is a more subtle situation occurring where no financial advantage accrues to the agent. The agent should disclose, for example, if he is a member of a Boy Scout committee looking for a campsite or if he is trying to locate a home for his mother to purchase.

Misrepresentation	Misrepresentation covers more than a deliberate lie intended to mislead someone, which is called **intentional (fraudulent) misrepresentation.** There are two other classifications. **Negligent (unintentional) misrepresentation** covers false statements made by someone who *should* have known better. **Innocent (honest) misrepresentation** is a false statement by someone who believes the information to be true but is not expected to have expertise in the subject.

In order for the agent to be liable there must be:

- a false or misleading statement (or concealment of a material fact), by
- a person who knows (or should have known) that the information is false, with
- intent to deceive or defraud (or, where there is no such intent, the effect is still to deceive or defraud), and
- damages suffered by the party who relied on the information.

It is relatively easy for an agent to avoid intentional misrepresentation simply by sticking to the truth. But omissions and half-truths may misrepresent as readily as actual misstatements and the offense may be committed inadvertently. The buyer looking at rural property may be told "the septic system works well" when in fact it does not. If the agent knew the true state of affairs, *intentional misrepresentation* has occurred. If the agent did not know the condition of the system, the potential buyer is still being misled by *negligent misrepresentation*. The half-truth that might mislead would be a statement like "most people out here have septic systems." True in itself, this skirts the issue in a manner that may be misleading to an ignorant buyer. No mention at all of the septic system might also be misleading, particularly to an urban buyer who assumed sewers were available everywhere.

It will be little defense that the broker knew nothing of the condition of that system if brokers in that community *should* know about such matters. Even if the intention is not to defraud, the buyer who purchases the property and discovers the septic system inoperative has suffered damages and may seek to recover them from the broker.

In recent years buyers and sellers have become increasingly aware of the possible danger posed by urea-formaldehyde foam insulation (UFFI), radon, asbestos building materials and other environmental hazards. Some brokers insist on written statements from each party about the presence or absence of such problems so that they can prove the subject was discussed. Other brokers feel that they should not assume any responsibility for matters they prefer to keep outside their field of expertise.

In some parts of the state there is growing use of a *seller's disclosure form,* a check-off list signed by the seller at the time of listing, which may offer some protection to the listing agent from liability for undisclosed problems.

Among areas where problems frequently arise are statements about the value of property ("Sure to go up 10 percent a year in this area"); title ("The judgments have all been cleared up"); utilities ("No problem hooking in to the sewers"); boundaries; zoning; and size. In a recent case in another state the buyer of a house that turned out to contain 100 square feet fewer than promised in the listing data was awarded the current construction cost of 100 square feet in that area. The buyer may prefer to sue the broker, who still has an office in town and a vulnerable reputation, rather than the seller, who may have already moved out of town.

To Avoid Misrepresentation

Never present opinions as facts. Not "We can certainly get you $200,000 for this house" but "I don't see why we might not . . ." or "It should probably bring as much as these recent sales did." Absolute statements should be avoided. Not "all copper plumbing" but "It looks from here as if. . . ." The phrases "I believe" or "I was told by the seller" are more accurate than "The roof is five years old," where the agent has no direct knowledge of its age.

Many requests for information should be met by referring the questioner directly to an expert source: city zoning bureau, mortgage counselor, building inspection engineer or lawyer. The agent thus shifts responsibility and cuts down the chances of giving faulty information in specialized areas.

Department of State Determinations

Analyzing a group of offenses for which licensees were disciplined, the Department of State found the most common complaint from the public was a licensee's retaining an unearned commission. Among other offenses frequently listed were: broker's failure to supervise salesperson; salesperson acting as a broker; misuse of escrow funds; and broker using services of an unlicensed person.

Offenses that brought license suspension, fines or revocation of license during the period surveyed included:

- racial steering;
- discrimination;
- violation of nonsolicitation orders;
- failure to disclose licensee's interest in a transaction;
- failure to disclose dual compensation;
- unauthorized practice of law;
- failure to deliver copies of documents;
- net listing;
- inducing breach of another's contract;
- material misstatement on a license application;
- deceptive and improper advertising;
- improper information on stationery and business cards; and
- personal offenses not necessarily related to real estate (fraud, failure to pay a judgment, conviction of a felony).

Brokers and salespersons were cited for breach of fiduciary duties (failure to explain the nature of exclusive-right-to-sell listing, failure to follow principal's directions).

Defense Against Claims of Liability

Staying alert to situations that might pose problems is a first defense. Disclaimers that "the information furnished is believed correct but not warranted" are of little value. They cannot cover spoken repetition of the material and they cannot acquit the broker of liability. The fact that the misleading material may have been furnished by the seller is also of little value in defense.

The best protection against possible damage to others and possible claims for those damages is disclosure. "This is my mother; I'm helping her look for a house" treats the seller fairly by putting him or her on notice of a possible conflict of interest. "The listing sheet says 1,600 square feet but I think it's closer to 1,500." "The contract says the buyer is putting down $2,000 earnest money; we haven't deposited the check yet." If made in time such disclosure prevents the client from making decisions based upon faulty data. Actions taken after disclosure are the client's own responsibility. The broker will not have caused damages.

Even if the problem has been discovered after the buyer or seller has acted, timely disclosure may limit the damages incurred. Consider the buyer who asks the broker to hold a deposit check for a few days "until I can get the money into my account." Subsequently the buyer tells the broker "Don't cash the check at all; I'll make it good on the day of closing." Feeling that the damage already has been done, the broker hesitates to notify the seller of a potential problem. The seller meanwhile moves out of the house in anticipation of closing. If the buyer then refuses to perform, the seller may claim **loss-of-the-bargain,** loss of the escrow deposit that was to serve as damages, moving expenses, and rent or the cost of holding a vacant house. Damages could have been limited if the problem had been disclosed when it became apparent the transaction might be shaky. The seller's actions after that disclosure—the moving expenses and rent, for example—would not be the broker's fault and liability could have been somewhat mitigated.

Every disclosure should be made in writing, without admission of wrongdoing, in a businesslike manner. Although the letter should come from the broker, an attorney's advice and assistance with wording should be sought.

Errors and omissions insurance is to real estate practitioners what malpractice insurance is to physicians. It covers legal fees to defend against claims for liability and payment of any damages, less a deductible amount. Such insurance, however, does not cover dishonest or deliberately fraudulent acts.

Summary

Budgeting is essential to survival in today's real estate business. Unique to real estate is the concept of the *company dollar,* defined as those funds remaining after commissions have been shared with salespersons and other brokers. Nationwide, real estate firms spend the greatest share of the company dollar for advertising and operating expenses. Dividing total expenses by the number of salespersons yields a figure known as *desk cost.*

A written *policy and procedures guide* contributes to the smooth running of a real estate office. Procedures are suggested for independent contractors, who cannot be bound by specific requirements. To avoid any suspicion that they are acting in restraint of trade, brokers should avoid any discussion with competitors of *commission rates* or *geographical division* of business.

Recruiting is often done through advertising, career nights and trial training sessions. Advertisements must be carefully worded to avoid discrimination. Application forms and aptitude tests also should be cleared with an attorney before use. The most common method of *selecting* associates is through interviews. *Training* may be informal in the small company, take place within a series of sales meetings or follow standard classroom procedures.

A nonowner sales manager is usually found in firms with more than 12 sales associates. Most sales managers are employees, often receiving an override based on profits. Studies have shown that *sales meetings, goal setting* and *close supervision* motivate higher production from associates than do financial incentives.

The successful *sales meeting* is prompt, brisk and short. An agenda planned in advance may include reports on associates' activities, news of the financial market, a training topic and outside speakers.

Liability claims against brokers for damages caused to buyers or sellers may arise from *breach of fiduciary duty, failure to observe standard of care, conflict of interest,* or *misrepresentation*. Misrepresentation need not be *intentional*; unintentional or *negligent misrepresentation* and *innocent misrepresentation* are also possible. The best defense against claims arising from such situations is *disclosure*, either before the client has acted or as soon as the problem is discovered.

Questions

1. The term "company dollar" refers to:

    a. gross commissions received.
    b. firm's share of commissions.
    c. percentage forwarded to a franchise.
    d. net profit.

2. Yellow pages costs are budgeted under:

    a. communications.
    b. advertising.
    c. operating expense.
    d. telephone.

3. The largest single expense for most real estate firms is:

    a. advertising.
    b. rent and occupancy.
    c. telephone and telegraph.
    d. sales promotion.

4. The term "desk cost" refers to:

    a. expenses for sales management.
    b. equipment rental.
    c. share of expenses for each associate.
    d. cost of training one salesperson.

5. A policy and procedures guide is best described as:

    a. a multiple-listing system's contract with brokers.
    b. board of REALTORS® rules and regulations.
    c. independent contractor agreements with associates.
    d. a statement of a company's basic philosophy and guidelines.

6. Brokers can be held guilty of restraint of trade if they are suspected of:

    a. regulating commission rates.
    b. dividing up the market geographically.
    c. refusing to deal with competitors.
    d. any of the above.

7. Violation of the Sherman Antitrust Act is punishable by:

    a. a fine of up to $1 million for a corporation.
    b. up to three years in prison.
    c. a fine of up to $100,000 for an individual.
    d. all of the above.

8. Advertisements for associates, application forms and aptitude tests must be carefully monitored for:

    a. cost-effectiveness.
    b. conformity to community practice.
    c. evidence that discrimination is not practiced.
    d. goal setting.

9. Which of the following is a legitimate question for an application form?

    a. Age
    b. Spouse's employment
    c. Religion
    d. Former employment

10. One of the main reasons cited for affiliation with a franchise is:

    a. aptitude testing.
    b. training program.
    c. assistance with budgeting.
    d. sales contests.

11. The Alberta study found that associates earned more in firms that offered:

    a. a sliding scale of commissions.
    b. sales contests.
    c. no sales quotas.
    d. frequent sales meetings.

12. Sales meetings should be:

    a. scheduled frequently and regularly.
    b. started promptly even if not all associates have arrived.
    c. planned to allow group discussion.
    d. All of the above

13. The setting of sales quotas by a broker:

    a. results in lower production.
    b. violates the independent contractor relationship.
    c. brings up the dual agency question.
    d. involves indirect interest.

14. Misrepresentation may occur when:
    a. the speaker knows the statement is false.
    b. the speaker should know the statement is false.
    c. the speaker is not expected to have knowledge in the matter under discussion.
    d. All of the above

15. The broker charged with professional liability may suffer:
    a. civil damages.
    b. loss of commission.
    c. loss of license.
    d. all of the above.

16. The duty of loyalty forbids the broker from:
    a. mentioning the condition of the house in ads.
    b. placing a sign on the property.
    c. suggesting an offer under the listed price.
    d. giving information over the telephone.

17. When the buyer gives a broker information about possible financial problems in completing the purchase, the broker should:
    a. respect the confidence and let it go no further.
    b. inform the seller immediately.
    c. offer to lend the buyer extra funds needed.
    d. ask for a written confirmation of the situation.

18. If the agent in the previous question is acting as a buyer's broker, the most correct response for the broker is to:
    a. say nothing to the seller because of the duty of confidentiality to the principal.
    b. explain to the buyer that not revealing the problem to the seller will constitute concealment of a material defect.
    c. tell the seller, at the same time asking the seller not to reveal to the buyer that confidentiality was breached.
    d. try to find another buyer for the property.

19. Negligent misrepresentation occurs when:
    a. the speaker knows the statement is false.
    b. the speaker should know the statement is false.
    c. the speaker is not expected to have knowledge in the matter under discussion.
    d. no harm is done by the falsehood.

20. The best defense against a breach of fiduciary duty is:
    a. concealment of defects.
    b. indirect interest.
    c. timely disclosure.
    d. loss-of-bargain.

15

Advertising

Key Terms

Annual percentage rate
Blind ads
Display advertising

Regulation Z
Truth-in-Lending Act

Overview

Advertising, the largest single item in most brokerage budgets, is designed to "make the phone ring." Motivating prospective buyers and sellers to call requires skill that can be acquired. State and federal regulations call for honesty and fairness. This chapter will discuss advertising media open to the broker, techniques for creating effective advertising and regulations to be observed.

Function of Advertising

Advertising real estate must accomplish a dual function. It attracts prospective purchasers to the real estate broker's office to inspect specific properties and it attracts prospective sellers to the office. Only by obtaining listings of property does the broker have anything to sell. Advertising therefore is both an integral part of the process of securing listings and a useful selling tool.

A broker usually pays the expenses of advertising property. On occasion, however, a broker may persuade a homeowner to pay for some or all of the advertising, especially if the seller needs a quick sale. Sometimes a broker has an agreement with associates whereby each salesperson may choose to place or pay for advertising on houses listed. In any case the cost of advertising reduces the profit made on a sale. The need to make advertising effective and productive is obvious.

Advertising Media

Aside from costs, a broker must take two important factors into consideration when selecting an advertising medium: (1) the *geographic area* covered by the medium and (2) the *demographic makeup* of the people that the advertising will reach. For example, it would probably be foolish to advertise a plush mansion in the local newspaper of a lower–middle-income suburb. The broker must *aim advertising at those most likely to respond favorably and take action and place it where such people are likely to see it*. Care must be taken, however, that such targeted advertising does not lay the broker open to charges of steering when the assumption that a certain group of people will be interested in a specific property is based on ethnic, religious or other prohibited considerations.

Stationery and business cards. A letter on business stationery along with a business card are often the first items a potential prospect receives from a broker and both must create a good impression. A distinctive, easy-to-recognize company logo should be designed and incorporated into both letterheads and business cards. A printer or commercial artist usually can design company stationery and cards relatively inexpensively. Every salesperson on a broker's staff should have personalized business cards. Such cards tend to present the salesperson as a competent, expert representative of the firm. Business cards are also an excellent way for real estate people to introduce themselves to potential clients and give contacts something to remember them by. Any item of information or memorandum should be jotted down and handed out on the back of the agent's card. Business cards are probably the least expensive form of advertising.

The New York Department of State requires that the broker's or company's name be featured more prominently on business cards than that of the salesperson. Regulations that prohibited the use of residence telephone numbers on business cards are no longer in effect.

Signs. Both For Sale and Sold signs can draw people to the real estate office that posted them. People may interpret such signs as indications of an active and effective business and therefore one that may be able to satisfy their needs. In addition many people drive through neighborhoods in which they are thinking of living. When they notice a house they like with a lawn sign they will contact the real estate company involved. The lawn sign (the "free billboard") is regarded by many as the most effective form of advertising.

Display boards. Display boards are used to attract walk-by traffic. They are usually large boards or space in the brokerage firm's front widow that display photographs of property for sale and pertinent data about the homes. The descriptions could be the same ones used in other kinds of ads. A display board may also attract the interest of walk-in buyers while they wait for someone in the office to help them.

Open houses. An open house is based on a public announcement that a particular piece of real estate is for sale and that anyone interested may visit the property at a specific time. The announcement is usually made by placing signs on major roads near the property and advertising in the newspaper. An open house may attract potential *sellers* as well as potential buyers, for people often examine the market before offering their own homes for sale. To build traffic, a sign in front of the house during the week might say "Open Sunday 2–4."

Classified ads. Classified advertising, generally concerning one or only a few parcels of real estate, is designed to be read line by line. It is assumed that in reading the ad, prospects will look for those words, phrases and features that interest them or capture and stimulate their imaginations. A buyer seldom purchases the house whose ad originally attracted him or her to the real estate office. Thus ads bring in potential buyers to be qualified and then shown houses to fit their needs.

New York's license laws prohibit a broker from running **blind ads**—ads that do not identify the advertiser as a real estate broker. In addition the state license laws prohibit a salesperson from running real estate ads in his or her own name. If an ad mentions a salesperson it must also clearly show the relationship between the salesperson and the broker. Advertisements claiming that property is in a "vicinity" or geographic area must name the territorial subdivision or geographic area where the property is actually located. It should also be noted that any advertisement of a price lower than the listed price violates the broker's fiduciary duty to the seller.

Display ads. Real estate firms most often use newspaper **display advertising** for public relations purposes to build prestige and remind people that the firm is in business. When such an ad is intended to attract buyers, several For Sale offerings usually are combined in one attractive display. Its purpose is to describe a variety of the firm's best homes that are currently most in demand in order to create the impression that the broker can satisfy the needs of a variety of buyers. This type of ad often includes photographs of the houses along with their descriptions. An advantage of display ads is that they can be used as reprints for direct mail and other forms of promotion.

Direct mail. The usual direct mail ad is a "choose your neighbor" letter sent to families in an area where the broker has one or more listings. The letter notifies families in the area that a particular property is for sale and asks them to consider the possibility of having a friend or relative look at the available home. Those interested are invited to contact the broker. Expensive property is often marketed through direct mail distribution of lavish color brochures.

Press releases. Press releases are an institutional form of publicity or advertising. Their purpose is to call attention to a real estate firm involved in a newsworthy event. For example, news releases should be sent to the real estate editors of local newspapers when a large and/or prestigious property has been either listed or sold by a firm. Although a press release does not specifically advertise the property for sale, it does notify people in the area that a well-known property is available and calls their attention to the firm that is selling it.

Billboards. Billboard advertising is an expensive yet highly successful method of advertising. It cannot be used to sell a specific property but it is a good way to convey *institutional advertising,* such as a company name and service, to passersby. Some large brokerage firms use this form of advertising successfully to establish their names and reputations in a given area.

Radio and television. Some brokerages use short radio and television ads in their institutional advertising programs. Franchised brokerage firms may run a standard commercial for the chain in which the local broker's name and address will be mentioned if he or she agrees to pay a small percentage of the ad's cost. In recent years, TV programs that consist entirely of homes on the market may offer 10-, 20- or 30-second exposure.

Developing Good Advertising

The best advertisements stimulate the imagination and attract interest. The most successful real estate firms use their ads to impress the public. Every broker can build a strong public image through consistent use of a symbol or trademark on all letterheads, advertising copy and signs, combined with a distinctive advertising style.

An advertisement can be monitored in several useful ways. A simple check to see that the ad actually ran should be routine. Publications make mistakes, particularly with last-minute classified ads. If the same classified ad is to run next week, the broker may want to check it for *widows,* lines having only a word or part of a word. A slight change may result in more cost-effectiveness.

Written reports on the response to individual advertisements can pinpoint surefire phrases and information of special appeal to the public. A broker can also monitor responses to estimate the amount of advertising money that has been spent to produce each phone inquiry; associates often treat phone calls with more care when they realize how expensive each one is.

The broker may distribute copies of each ad to all salespeople so they will be able to discuss the specific parcel of property when inquiries are received. Each salesperson should review the ads before they are published. This gives them the opportunity to participate in the preparation of the ad and to relate it directly to the property.

Time factors should be considered in preparing classified ads. For example, if immediate possession of the property is possible, such information could be included. During the month of August it is appropriate to relate the ad to the beginning of the school year and refer to the opening dates of both public and parochial schools. With seller's permission, it can be effective to advertise that the seller has been transferred and that therefore the property has been priced to sell quickly. Relate the ad to the natural assets of the specific property: proximity to lakes, availability of swim club membership and the like.

Ad writing. Rules for effective ads: Be careful in choosing the words used to describe a house or property offered for sale. *Words communicate images.* Some synonyms that may technically share the same meaning may communicate *widely varying images*. For example, the words *big, substantial, massive, huge, immense, enormous, mammoth, colossal, jumbo, whoppingly big,* and *king-size* all mean the same but each conveys a strikingly different thought. Another example of this phenomenon is found in the words *charming, polished, refreshing, mellow, refined, gracious, cordial, cheerful, delightful, lived-in, dignified,* and *inviting*.

Studies have shown that ad readers look first for information about location, number of rooms, number of bedrooms and energy-related improvements. Many of those surveyed claimed they would not read ads that did not indicate price. Here are some sample ads and phrases that use price as a selling point: "$150,000 and your garden and landscaping are complete!" (excellent where the property described is in a new subdivision and competing with new homes that are not landscaped for the initial owner); "Ready to move into for $95,000"; "More than you'd expect—for only $125,000"; "No need to buy appliances—all included at $92,000." Keep a "choose a better word chart" handy. Such a chart lists the words frequently used to describe homes and property.

There are many ways to make display and classified advertising more effective. It pays to *use a provocative lead*. Such phrases as "first ad today" and "unusual opportunity" are attention-getters. *Be sure the style and wording of ads are up to date*. Read professionally written classified ads and clip examples of good advertising from newspapers and magazines. Become aware of the words and phrases professional ad writers use. *Whet the reader's curiosity—don't tell everything*. Surprise the reader into wanting to know more so that he or she will call. *Play on the reader's imagination*. Use words that stimulate the imagination and encourage the reader to complete the picture. *Use emotion*. Purchasers frequently buy homes solely for emotional reasons. The pride of ownership is often cited as the primary reason. Many people also buy homes because of a strong sense of parental responsibility. They may feel a strong need to provide their children with a better way of life than they themselves had as children. *Be sincere*. Advertising is telling the truth attractively.

The New York Department of State has prepared a pamphlet to help brokers avoid some of the more common violations of law or department policy in advertising. This pamphlet is reproduced at the end of the chapter.

Regulation Z

The federal **Truth-in-Lending Act,** known as **Regulation Z,** provides for the strict regulation of real estate advertisements that include mortgage financing terms. General phrases such as "liberal terms available" may be used, but if details are given they must comply with this act. By the provisions of the act the **annual percentage rate,** *which includes all charges rather than the interest rate alone, must be stated*.

Regulation Z applies to all credit advertising. If any of the following *triggering terms* is used, three further items of information also must be included. The triggering terms are:

- amount or percentage of down payment (unless none is required);
- number of payments or period of repayment;

- amount of any payment; and
- amount of any finance charge.

If any of the items listed is mentioned, the advertisement also must include:

- amount or percentage of down payment;
- number of payments or term of loan; and
- the words "Annual percentage rate," so identified, and whether that rate is to be increased after consummation.

Full disclosure would be necessary if any of the following terms were used:

- 30-year loan available;
- Payment $853.26 including principal and interest;
- Only 5 percent down; or
- Assume mortgage with five years left to go.

These terms would *not* trigger the required disclosures:

- Financing available;
- Terms negotiable;
- Owner may finance;
- No down payment;
- Assume 13 percent annual percentage rate loan;
- Attractive financing; and
- $90,000 mortgage available.

In the summer of 1983 the New York Bureau of Consumer Frauds surveyed real estate advertisements in six major newspapers from Buffalo to Long Island and found more than one-half the real estate advertisements contained triggering terms. Of those ads requiring full disclosure, only 4 percent were in compliance with the Truth-in-Lending Act. The most common violations were failure to disclose that an interest rate was variable and failure to mention annual percentage rate.

Summary

Advertising must perform a dual function in the real estate business—attract prospective sellers as well as prospective buyers. Forms of brokerage advertising include stationery, business cards, signs, display boards, open houses, classified ads, display ads, direct mail, press releases, billboards, radio and television. A broker usually pays the cost of advertising a home. All real estate advertising should be aimed at those people most likely to respond favorably and take action because of it.

New York Department of State regulations forbid blind ads, misleading geographic terms and advertising by a salesperson that does not also identify the supervising broker. *Regulation Z* sets standards to prevent misleading statements about financing. If certain *triggering terms* are mentioned, the advertisement must disclose full loan information.

Questions

1. Institutional advertising:
   a. gives information about unique property like a school or library.
   b. keeps the firm's name before the public.
   c. meets the requirements of antidiscrimination laws.
   d. must be approved by the Department of State.

2. The least expensive form of advertising is probably a:
   a. business card.   c. billboard.
   b. For Sale lawn sign.   d. classified ad.

3. The most effective form of advertising is probably a:
   a. business card.   c. display ad.
   b. Sold lawn sign.   d. blind ad.

4. The classified ad usually:
   a. triggers a response from someone who will buy that exact house.
   b. brings in potential buyers for other property.
   c. is intended for institutional advertising.
   d. sounds as if it is run by the owner.

5. The Department of State looks with disfavor on:
   a. blind ads.
   b. vague and misleading geographic terms.
   c. ads in the salesperson's own name.
   d. all of the above.

6. Buyers report they are most interested in an ad that tells about:
   a. location, number of rooms, insulation.
   b. landscaping, trees, pools or patio.
   c. appliances, drapes, carpeting.
   d. the makeup of the neighborhood.

7. Many buyers say they will not answer ads that have no information about:
   a. school system.   c. price level.
   b. number of baths.   d. garages.

8. Regulation Z provides that:
   a. buyers must be provided with information on heating costs.
   b. brokers must clear all ads with the Department of State.
   c. if certain financing terms are mentioned, others also must be included.
   d. vague, misleading geographic terms must not be used.

9. Which of the following is a triggering term that mandates inclusion of full details in an advertisement?
   a. Assume 12 percent FHA loan
   b. Less than 10 percent down
   c. Owner may finance
   d. No down payment

10. If a triggering term is included, an ad must go on to explain:
   a. amount or percentage of down payment.
   b. number of payments.
   c. annual percentage rate.
   d. all of the above.

Appendix: Department of State Guidelines on Advertising for Brokers

DISCRIMINATORY PRACTICES. The Executive Law, Federal Fair Housing Laws and rules governing discriminatory practices prohibit a broker from using advertisements where there is any expression of limitation because of race, creed, color, national origin, sex or disability or marital status in any of the activities defined as those of a real estate broker.

PROPERTY DESCRIPTION AND BROKER IDENTIFICATION. The General Business Law and License Law rules and regulations contain provisions which regulate both blind ads and advertising according to geographic location. A "blind ad" is one where there is no indication given in the ad that the advertiser is a broker. Property ads which give only a telephone number or a street address would be considered as blind ads. The owner of a parcel of real property might use a blind ad but brokers may not; even if they own the property advertised. Brokers may indicate their status by giving their licensed name or use the word "broker" and list an office telephone number.

Brokers are required to post a sign or directory notice at their principal and branch offices which must give their full licensed name and indicate their business to be "Licensed Real Estate Broker."

It is an important consideration for the potential home buyer to know the location of property listed in an advertisement. At the same time, when a broker is employed by a seller, there is an agency duty to present the property to be sold in the most favorable light. Whenever a broker places an ad describing the location of a property as being in the vicinity of an area or location, the actual name of the area or location of the property must also be included.

SALESPERSONS. While a real estate advertisement may include a salesperson's name as a part of the ad, such use may occur only when the name is subordinate to that of the name of the broker with whom the salesperson is associated. Additionally, ads must clearly indicate that the status is that of a "Salesman."* Substitute words such as "Salesperson," "Saleswoman," "Sales Associate," "Sales Agent" or "Sales Representative" may be used. While this does not prevent

the use of additional descriptive terms such as "Relocation Manager," such should always be subordinate to the required term.

Additionally, the use of a salesperson's principal residence telephone number in advertisements is permitted as is the use of the home phone number of a broker, provided that the ad includes a notation that such is a residence number and, further, that such use is not extended to any activity that would constitute branch office operation. A separate branch office license is required for use beyond the listing of a home telephone number.

Business cards and stationery should be prepared using the same guidelines that exist for advertising. The broker's name must be predominate in size of print and location, and the "salesman" identifying term should follow the salesperson's name.

BROKER ASSOCIATE. For specific application filings, a person, licensed as a real estate broker, may retain that status but perform salesperson activity in association with another broker (primary broker) and using that broker's business name and office facilities. Those so licensed would follow the same guidelines applicable to salespersons except that, as an identifying term, the words "Broker Associate" would be used.

GENERAL. Any advertisement, irrespective of the medium used, should give an honest and accurate description of the property to be sold or leased; and the broker using such advertisement should include an honest and accurate representation of agency, status and associate standings. The ability and status of even unnamed competitors should not be derogated nor should there be unfair or incomplete representations of the real property involved or of others' real property by comparison.

If a broker chooses to make reference to any financing terms in an advertisement, he is required by the "Truth in Lending Law" to disclose *all* financing terms.

---

*The word "salesman" is taken from the text of Section 440 of the Real Property Law as a legal definition of one engaged in the specific activities listed and may denote either male or female gender.

16

Appraisal

Overview

Real estate is the business of value. Members of the general public informally estimate this value when they buy, sell or invest in real estate. A formal estimate of value generally is conducted by a real estate appraiser and serves as a basis for the pricing, financing, insuring or leasing of real property. This chapter will examine value—what determines it, adds to it and detracts from it. It also will discuss in detail the various methods professional appraiser use to estimate the value of residential as well as commercial and industrial real estate.

Appraising

An **appraisal** is an estimate or opinion of value. In the real estate business the highest level of appraisal activity is conducted by professional real estate appraisers who are recognized for their knowledge, training, skill and integrity in this field. Formal appraisal reports are relied on in important decisions made by mortgage lenders, investors, public utilities, governmental agencies, businesses and individuals.

Not all estimates or real estate value are made by professional appraisers; often the real estate licensee must help a seller arrive at a market value for his or her property without the aid of a formal appraisal report. It is necessary for everyone engaged in the real estate business, even those who are not experts in appraisal, to possess at least a fundamental knowledge of real estate valuation. Appraisals may be required in a number of situations. Among them:

- *Estate purposes,* to establish taxable value or facilitate fair division among heirs;
- *Divorce proceedings*, where real estate forms part of property to be shared;
- *Financing*, when the amount to be lent depends on the value of the property;
- *Taxation*, to furnish documentation for a taxpayer's protest of assessment figures;
- *Relocation*, establishing the amount to be guaranteed to a transferred employee;
- *Condemnation*, arriving at fair compensation for property taken by government;
- *Insurance*, estimating possible replacement expense in cases of loss;
- *Damage loss*, used to support income tax deductions; and
- *Feasibility*, to study possible consequences of a particular use for property.

A **fee appraiser** works as an independent contractor offering services to a number of different clients. A **staff appraiser** is an in-house employee of an organization like the FHA, a lending institution or a large corporation.

Value

Value in an abstract word with many acceptable definitions. In terms of real estate appraisal, **value** may be described as the *present worth of future benefits arising from the ownership of real property*. For a property to have a value in the real estate market it must have four characteristics:

1. *Utility:* the capacity to satisfy human needs and desires;
2. *Scarcity:* a limited supply;
3. *Demand:* the need or desire for possession or ownership backed up by the financial means to satisfy that need;
4. *Transferability:* the ability to transfer ownership rights from one person to another with relative ease.

Market Value

While a given parcel of real estate may have many different kinds of value at the same time (as illustrated in Figure 16.1), generally the goal of an appraiser is an estimate of *market value*. The market value of real estate is the most probable price that a property will bring in a competitive and open market, allowing a

**Figure 16.1
Kinds of Value**

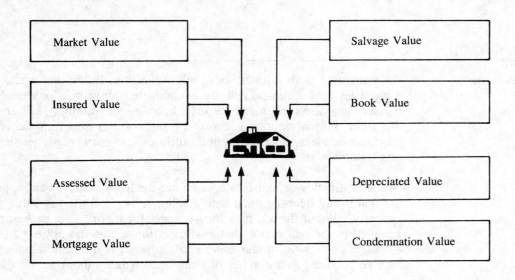

reasonable time to find a purchaser who buys the property with knowledge of all the uses to which it is adapted and for which it is capable of being used, neither buyer nor seller under duress. Included in this definition are the following key points:

1. Market value is the *most probable* price a property will bring.
2. Payment must be made in *cash* or its equivalent.
3. Both buyer and seller must act without *undue pressure*.
4. A *reasonable length of time* must be allowed for the property to be exposed in the *open market*.
5. Both buyer and seller must be *well informed* of the property's assets, defects and potential.

Market value presupposes an *arm's-length* transaction, one between relative strangers, each of whom is trying to do the best for himself or herself.

Market value versus market price. Market value is an estimate based on an analysis of comparable sales and other pertinent market data. *Market price*, on the other hand, is what a property *actually* sells for—its selling price. Theoretically the ideal market price would be the same as the market value. There are circumstances under which a property may be sold below market value, however, as when a seller is forced to sell quickly or when a sale is arranged between relatives. Thus the market price can be taken as accurate evidence of current market value only after considering the relationship of the buyer and the seller, the terms and conditions of the market and the effect of the passage of time since the sale was made.

Market value versus cost. It is important also to distinguish between market value and *cost*. One of the most common errors made in valuing property is the assumption that cost represents market value. Cost and market value *may* be equal and often are when the improvements on a property are new and represent the highest and best use of the land.

More often, cost does not equal market value. Two homes may be similar in every respect except that one is located on a street with heavy traffic and the other on a quiet, residential street. The value of the former may be less than that of the latter although the cost to construct each was exactly the same.

Basic Principles of Value

A number of economic principles affect the value of real estate. The most important of these principles are defined in the following paragraphs.

Highest and best use. The most profitable use to which the property is adapted and needed or the use that is likely to be in demand in the reasonably near future is the **highest and best use.** For example, a highest-and-best-use study may show that a parking lot in a busy downtown area should, in fact, be replaced by an office building. To place a value on the property based on its present use would be erroneous because a parking lot is not the highest and best use of the land. **Amenities** or owner satisfaction—an unusual view of the mountains, for instance—may be a key factor.

Substitution. The principle of **substitution** states that the maximum value of a property tends to be set by the cost of purchasing an equally desirable and valuable substitute property, assuming that no costly delay is encountered in making the substitution. For example, if two similar houses are for sale in an area, the one with the lower asking price normally would be purchased first.

Supply and demand. This principle states that the value of a property will increase if the supply decreases and the demand either increases or remains constant—and vice versa. For example, the last lot to be sold in a desirable residential area would probably be worth more than the first lot sold in that area.

Conformity. Maximum value is realized if the use of land conforms to existing neighborhood standards. There should also be a reasonable degree of conformity along social and economic lines. In residential areas of single-family houses, for example, buildings should be similar in design, construction, size and age to other buildings in the neighborhood and they usually will house families of similar social and economic status. Subdivision restrictions rely on the principle of conformity to protect maximum future value.

Anticipation. This principle holds that value can increase or decrease in anticipation of the same future benefit or detriment affecting the property. For example, the value of a house may be affected by rumors that an adjacent parcel may be converted to commercial use in the near future.

Increasing and diminishing returns. Improvements to land and structures will eventually reach a point at which they will no longer have an effect on property values. As long as money spent on improvements produces an increase in income or value, the *law of increasing returns* is applicable. But at the point where additional improvements will not produce a proportionate increase in income or value, the *law of diminishing returns* applies.

Regression and progression. The principle that, between dissimilar properties the worth of the better property is adversely affected by the presence of the lesser-quality property is known as **regression.** Thus, in a neighborhood of modest homes, a structure that is larger, better maintained and/or more luxurious, would tend to be valued in the same range as the others. Conversely, the principle of **progression** states that the worth of a lesser property tends to increase if it is located among better properties.

Plottage. The principle of **plottage** holds that the merging or consolidation of adjacent lots held by separate land owners into one larger lot may produce a higher total land value than the sum of the two sites valued separately. For example, if two adjacent lots are valued at $35,000 each, their total value if consolidated into one larger lot under a single use might be $90,000. The process of merging the two lots under one owner is known as **assemblage.**

Contribution. The value of any component of a property is what its addition contributes to the value of the whole or what its absence detracts from that value. For example, the cost of installing an air-conditioning system and remodeling an older office building may be greater than is justified by the increase in market value (a function of expected rent increases) that may result from the improvement to the property.

Competition. This principle states that excess profits tend to attract competition. For example, the success of a retail store may attract investors to open similar stores in the area. This tends to mean less profit for all stores concerned unless the purchasing power in the area increases substantially.

Change. No physical or economic condition remains constant. Real estate is subject to natural phenomena such as tornadoes fires and routine wear and tear of the elements. The real estate business is also subject to the demands of its market, just as in any business. It is an appraiser's job to be knowledgeable about the past and, therefore perhaps predictable, effects of natural phenomena and the behavior of the marketplace.

The Three Approaches to Value

In order to arrive at an accurate estimate of value three basic approaches, or techniques, are traditionally used by appraisers: the direct sales comparison approach, the cost approach and the income approach. Each method serves as a check against the others and narrows the range within which the final estimate of value will fall. Each method is generally considered most reliable for certain types of property.

The Direct Sales Comparison Approach

In the **direct sales comparison approach,** an estimate of value is obtained by comparing the **subject property** (the property under appraisal) with recently sold comparable properties (**comparables** or **comps**) (properties similar to the subject). This approach is most often used by brokers and salespeople when helping a seller to set a price for residential real estate in an active market. Because no two parcels of real estate are exactly alike, each comparable property must be compared to the subject property, and the sales prices must be adjusted for any dissimilar features. The principal factors for which adjustments must be made fall into four basic categories:

1. *Date of sale:* An adjustment must be made if economic changes occur between the date of sale of the comparable property and the date of the appraisal.
2. *Location:* An adjustment may be necessary to compensate for locational differences. For example, similar properties might differ in price from neighborhood to neighborhood, or even in more desirable locations within the same neighborhood.
3. *Physical features:* Physical features that may require adjustments include age of building, size of lot, landscaping, construction, number of rooms, square

feet of living space, interior and exterior condition, presence or absence of a garage, fireplace, or air-conditioner and so forth.

4. *Terms and conditions of sale:* This consideration becomes important if a sale is not financed by a standard mortgage procedure.

After a careful analysis of the differences between comparable properties and the subject property, the appraiser assigns a dollar value to each of these differences. On the basis of their knowledge and experience, appraisers estimate dollar adjustments that reflect actual values assigned in the marketplace. The value of a feature present in the subject property but not in the comparable property is *added* to the sales price actually recieved for the comparable. This presumes that, all other features being equal, a property having a feature (such as a fireplace or wet bar) not present in the comparable property would tend to have a higher market value because of this feature. (The feature need not be a physical amenity; it could be a locational or aesthetic feature.) Likewise, the value of a feature present in the comparable but not the subject property is *subtracted.*

The terms **CPA** and **CBS** are useful guides—''Comparable Poorer: Add'' and ''Comparable Better: Subtract.'' The adjusted sales price represents the probable value range of the subject property. From this range a single market value estimate can be calculated using a weighted average to emphasize those properties most closely comparable.

The direct sales comparison approach is essential in almost every appraisal of real estate. It is considered the most reliable of the three approaches in appraising residential property, where the amenities (intangible benefits) are so difficult to measure. An example is shown in Table 16.1.

The Cost Approach

The **cost approach** to value is based on the principle of substitution, which states that the maximum value of a property tends to be set by the cost of acquiring an equally desirable and valuable substitute property. The cost approach is sometimes called appraisal by summation. The cost approach consists of five steps:

1. Estimate the value of the land as if it were vacant and available to be put to its highest and best use.
2. Estimate the current cost of constructing the building(s) and site improvements.
3. Estimate the amount of accrued depreciation resulting from physical deterioration, functional obsolescence and/or external (locational) obsolescence.
4. Deduct accrued depreciation from the estimated construction cost of new building(s) and site improvements.
5. Add the estimated land value to the depreciated cost of the building(s) and site improvements to arrive at the total property value.

Land value (step 1) is estimated by using the market comparison approach; that is, the location and improvements of the subject site are compared to those of similar nearby sites, and adjustments are made for significant differences.

There are two ways to look at the construction cost of a building for appraisal purposes (step 2): reproduction cost and replacement cost. **Reproduction cost** is the dollar amount required to construct an *exact duplicate* of the subject building at current prices. **Replacement cost** of the subject property would be the construction cost at current prices of a property that is not necessarily an exact duplicate, but serves the same purpose or function as the original. Replacement

Table 16.1
Direct Sales Comparison
Approach to Value

	Subject Property	Comparables				
		A	B	C	D	E
Sales Price		$118,000	$112,000	$121,000	$116,500	$110,000
Location	good	same	poorer +4,500	same	same	same
Age	6 years	same	same	same	same	same
Size of Lot	60' × 135'	same	same	larger −5,000	same	larger −5,000
Landscaping	good	same	same	same	same	same
Construction	brick	same	same	same	same	same
Style	ranch	same	same	same	same	same
No. of Rooms	6	same	same	same	same	same
No. of Bedrooms	3	same	same	same	same	same
No. of Baths	1½	same	same	same	same	same
Sq. Ft. of Living Space	1,500	same	same	same	same	same
Other space (basement)	full basement	same	same	same	same	same
Condition— Exterior	average	better −1,500	poorer +1000	better −1,500	same	poorer +2,000
Condition— Interior	good	same	same	better −500	same	same
Garage	2-car attached	same	same	same	same	same +5,000
Other Improvements						
Financing Date of Sale		current	1 yr. ago +3,500	current	current	current
Net Adjustments		−1,500	+9,000	−7,000	-0-	+2,000
Adjusted Value		$116,500	$121,000	$114,000	$116,500	$112,000

Note: Because the value range of the properties in the comparison chart (excluding comparable B) is close, and comparable D required no adjustment, an appraiser would conclude that the indicated market value of the subject is $116,500.

cost is more often used in appraising, because it eliminates obsolete features and takes advantage of current construction materials and techniques.

An example of the cost approach to value is shown in Table 16.2

Table 16.2
Cost Approach to Value

Land Valuation: Size 60' × 135' @ $450 per front foot		= $27,000
Plus site improvements: driveway, walks, landscaping, etc.		= 8,000
Total Land Valuation		$35,000

Building Valuation: Replacement Cost
1,500 sq. foot @ $65 per sq. ft. = $97,500

Less Depreciation:

Physical depreciation, curable (items of deferred maintenance)		
exterior painting	$4,000	
incurable (structural deterioration)	9,750	
Functional obsolescence	2,000	
External obsolescence	-0-	
Total Depreciation		−15,750

Depreciated Value of Building — $ 81,750
Indicated Value by Cost Approach — $116,750

Determining reproduction or replacement cost. An appraiser using the cost approach computes the reproduction or replacement cost of a building using one of the following methods:

1. **Square-foot method:** The cost per square foot of a recently built comparable structure is multiplied by the number of square feet in the subject building; this is the most common method of cost estimation. The example in Table 16.3 uses the square-foot method.

   For some property, the cost per *cubic* foot of a recently built comparable structure is multiplied by the number of cubic feet in the subject structure.

2. **Unit-in-place method:** The replacement cost of a structure is estimated based on the construction cost per unit of measure of individual building components, including material, labor, overhead and builder's profit. Most components are measured in square feet, although items like plumbing fixtures are estimated by unit cost.

3. **Quantity-survey method:** An estimate is made of the quantities of raw materials needed to replace the subject structure (lumber, plaster, brick and so on), as well as of the current price of such materials and their installation costs. These factors are added to indirect costs (building permit, survey, payroll taxes, builder's profit) to arrive at the total replacement cost of the structure.

4. **Index method:** A factor representing the percentage increase to the present time of construction costs is applied to the original cost of the subject property.

Depreciation. In a real estate appraisal, **depreciation** refers to any condition that adversely affects the value of an *improvement* to real property. Land usually does not depreciate, except in such rare cases as misused farmland, downzoned urban parcels or improperly developed land. For appraisal purposes (as opposed to depreciation of tax purposes, which will be discussed in Chapter 17), depreciation is divided into three classes according to its cause:

1. **Physical deterioration**—*curable:* Repairs that are economically feasible and would result in an increase in appraised value equal to or exceeding their cost. Routine maintenance, such as painting, falls in this category.

Physical deterioration—incurable: Repairs to the separate structural components of a building, which deteriorate at different rates. Roof, electrical system and plumbing fall in this category.

2. **Functional obsolescence**—*curable:* Physical or design features that are no longer considered desirable by property buyers, but could be replaced or redesigned at low cost. Outmoded fixtures, such as plumbing, are usually easily replaced. Room function might be redefined at no cost if the basic room layout allows for it. A bedroom adjacent to a kitchen, for instance, may be converted to a family room.

   Functional obsolescence—incurable: Currently undesirable physical or design features that could not be easily remedied. Many older multistory industrial buildings are considered less suitable than one-story buildings. An office building that cannot be air-conditioned suffers from functional obsolescence.

3. **External (locational) obsolescence**—*incurable only:* Caused by factors not on the subject property, so that this type of obsolescence cannot usually be considered curable. Proximity to a nuisance, such as a polluting factory, would be an unchangeable factor that could not be expected to be cured by the owner of the subject property.

The cost approach is most helpful in the appraisal of special-purpose buildings such as schools, churches and public buildings. Such properties are difficult to appraise using other methods because there are seldom many local sales to use as comparables, and the properties do not ordinarily generate income.

The Income Approach

The **income approach** to value is based on the present worth of the future rights to income. It assumes that the income derived from a property will control the value of that property. The income approach is used for valuation of income-producing properties—apartment buildings, office buildings, shopping centers and the like. In using the income approach to estimate value, an appraiser must go through the following steps:

1. Estimate annual potential *gross rental income*.
2. Based on market experience, deduct an appropriate allowance for vacancy and rent collection losses, and add income from other sources, such as concessions and vending machines, in order to arrive at the *effective gross income*.
3. Based on appropriate operating standards, deduct the annual *operating expenses* of the real estate from the effective gross income in order to arrive at the annual *net operating income*. Management costs are always included as operating expenses even if the current owner also manages the property. Mortgage payments, however (including principal and interest), are debt service and *not* considered operating expenses.
4. Estimate the price a typical investor would pay for the income produced by this particular type and class of property. This is done by estimating the rate of return (or yield) that an investor will demand for the investment of capital in this type of building. This rate of return is called the **capitalization** (or "cap") **rate** and is determined by comparing the relationship of net operating income to the sales price of similar properties that have sold in the current market. For example, a comparable property that is producing an annual net income of $15,000 is sold for $187,500. The capitalization rate is $15,000 ÷ $187,500 or 8 percent. If other comparable properties sold at prices that yield substantially the same rate, it may be assumed that 8 percent is the rate that the appraiser should apply to the subject property.

5. Finally, the capitalization rate is applied to the property's annual net income, resulting in the appraiser's estimate of the property value.

With the appropriate capitalization rate and the projected annual operating net income, the appraiser can obtain an indication of value by the income approach in the following manner:

$$\text{Net Operating Income} \div \text{Capitalization Rate} = \text{Value}$$

Example: $15,000 income ÷ 8% cap rate = $187,500 value

This formula and its variations are important in dealing with income property.

$$\frac{\text{Income}}{\text{Rate}} = \text{Value} \qquad \frac{\text{Income}}{\text{Value}} = \text{Rate} \qquad \text{Value} \times \text{Rate} = \text{Income}$$

A simplified version of the computations used in applying the income approach is illustrated in Table 16.3.

The most difficult step in the income approach to value is determining the appropriate capitalization rate for the property. This rate must be selected to recapture the original investment over the building's economic life, give the owner an acceptable rate of return on investment and provide for the repayment of borrowed capital. An income property that carries with it a great deal of risk as an investment generally requires a higher rate of return than would a property considered a safe investment.

Gross rent or income multipliers. Certain properties such as single-family homes or two-flat buildings, are not purchased primarily for income. As a substitute for a more elaborate income analysis, the **gross rent multiplier** (GRM) method is often used in appraising such properties. The GRM relates the sales price of

**Table 16.3
Income Approach to
Value**

Gross Annual Rental Income Estimate		$60,000
Less vacancy and collection losses (estimated) @ 6%		– 3,600
		$56,400
Income from other sources		+ 600
Effective Gross Income		$57,000
Expenses:		
Real estate taxes	$9,000	
Insurance	1,000	
Heat	2,800	
Maintenance	6,400	
Utilities, electricity, water, gas	800	
Repairs	1,200	
Decorating	1,400	
Replacements of equipment	800	
Legal and accounting	600	
Management	3,000	
Total Expenses		$27,000
Annual Net Operating Income		$30,000

Capitalization Rate = 10%

Capitalization of annual net income: $\frac{\$30,000}{.10}$

Indicated Value by Income Approach = $300,000

a property to its rental income. (Gross *monthly* income is used for residential property; gross *annual* income is used for commercial and industrial property.) The formula is as follows:

$$\frac{\text{Sales Price}}{\text{Rental Income}} = \text{Gross Rent Multiplier}$$

For example, if a home recently sold for $82,000 and its monthly rental income was $650, the GRM for the property would be computed thus:

$$\frac{\$82,000}{\$650} = 126.2 \text{ GRM}$$

To establish an accurate GRM, an appraiser should have recent sales and rental data from at least four properties similar to the subject property. The most appropriate GRM can then be applied to the estimated fair market rental of the subject property in order to arrive at its market value. The formula would then be:

$$\text{Rental Income} \times \text{GRM} = \text{Estimated Market Value}$$

Table 16.4 shows some examples of GRM comparisons.

Table 16.4 Gross Rent Multiplier	Comparable No.	Sales Price	Monthly Rent	GRM
	1	$93,600	$650	144
	2	78,500	450	174
	3	95,500	675	141
	4	82,000	565	145
	Subject	?	625	?

Note: Based on an analysis of these comparisons, a GRM of 145 seems reasonable for homes in this area. In the opinion of an appraiser, then, the estimated value of the subject property would be $625 × 145, or $90,625.

If a property's income also comes from nonrental sources (such as sales concessions), a **gross income multiplier** (GIM) is similarly used.

Much skill is required to use multipliers accurately, because there is no fixed multiplier for all areas or all types of properties. Therefore many appraisers view the technique simply as a quick, informal way to check the validity of a property value obtained by one of the other appraisal methods.

Reconciliation

If more than one of the three approaches to value are applied to the same property, they will normally produce as many separate indications of value. **Reconciliation** is the art of analyzing and effectively weighing the findings from the different approaches used.

Although each approach may serve as an independent guide to value, whenever possible all three approaches should be used as a check on the final estimate of value. The process of reconciliation is more complicated than simply taking the average of the derived value estimates. An average implies that the data and logic applied in each of the approaches are equally valid and reliable, and should therefore be given equal weight. In fact, however, certain approaches are more valid and reliable with some kinds of properties than with others.

For example, in appraising a home the income approach is rarely used, and the cost approach is of limited value unless the home is relatively new; therefore, the market data approach is usually given greatest weight in valuing single-family residences. In the appraisal of income or investment property, the income approach would normally be given the greatest weight. In the appraisal of churches, libraries, museums, schools and other special-use properties where there is little or no income or sales revenue, the cost approach would usually be assigned the greatest weight. From this analysis, or reconciliation, a single estimate of market value is produced.

| **The Appraisal Process** | The key to an accurate appraisal lies in the methodical collection of data. The appraisal process is an orderly set of procedures used to collect and analyze data in order to arrive at an ultimate value conclusion. The data are divided into two basic classes: |

1. *Specific data,* covering details of the subject property as well as comparative data relating to costs, and income and expenses of properties similar to and competitive with the subject property.
2. *General data,* covering the nation, region, city and neighborhood. Of particular importance is the neighborhood, where an appraiser finds the physical, economic, social and political influences that directly affect the value and potential of the subject property.

Figure 16.2 outlines the steps an appraiser takes in carrying out an appraisal assignment.

1. *State the problem:* The kind of value to be estimated must be specified, and the valuation approach(es) most valid and reliable for the kind of property under appraisal must be selected.
2. *List the data needed and their sources:* Based on the approach(es) the appraiser will be using, the types of data needed and the sources to be consulted are listed.
3. *Gather, record and verify the general data:* Detailed information must be obtained concerning the economic, political and social conditions of the nation, region, city and neighborhood, and comments on the effects of these data on the subject property also must be obtained.
4. *Gather, record and verify the specific data on the subject property:* Specific data include information about the subject site and improvements.
5. *Gather, record and verify the data for the valuation approach used:* Depending on the approach(es) used, comparative information relating to sales, income and expenses and construction costs of comparable properties must be collected. In the case of sales data, one source should be a person directly involved in the transaction.
6. *Analyze and interpret the data:* All information collected must be reviewed to ensure that all relevant facts have been considered and handled properly and that no errors have been made in calculations.
7. *Reconcile data for final value estimate:* The appraiser makes a definite statement of conclusions reached. This is usually in the form of a value estimate of the property.

Figure 16.2
The Appraisal Process

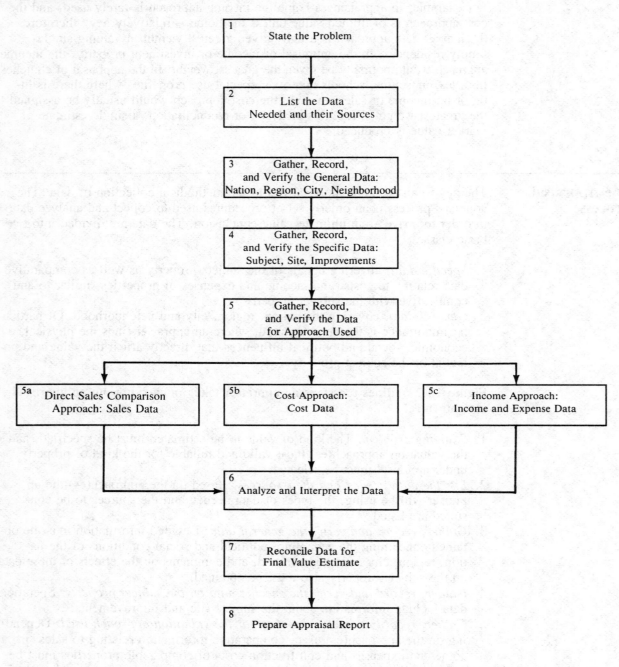

1   State the Problem

2   List the Data
Needed and their Sources

3   Gather, Record,
and Verify the General Data:
Nation, Region, City, Neighborhood

4   Gather, Record,
and Verify the Specific Data:
Subject, Site, Improvements

5   Gather, Record,
and Verify the Data
for Approach Used

5a   Direct Sales Comparison
Approach: Sales Data

5b   Cost Approach:
Cost Data

5c   Income Approach:
Income and Expense Data

6   Analyze and Interpret the Data

7   Reconcile Data for
Final Value Estimate

8   Prepare Appraisal Report

8. *Prepare appraisal report:* After the three approaches have been reconciled and an opinion of value reached, the appraiser prepares a formal written report for the client. The statement may be a completed *form,* a *letter* or a lengthy written *narrative.* The most complete appraisal report would contain the following information:

    a. The estimate of value and the date to which it applies;
    b. The purpose for which the appraisal was made;
    c. A description of the neighborhood and the subject property;
    d. Factual data covering costs, sales, and income and expenses of similar, recently sold properties;
    e. An analysis and interpretation of the data collected;
    f. A presentation of one or more of the three approaches to value in enough detail to support the appraiser's final value conclusion;
    g. Any qualifying conditions;
    h. Supportive material, such as charts, maps, photographs, floor plans, leases and contracts; and
    i. The certification and signature of the appraiser.

Some institutions in the secondary mortgage market require floor plans of the subject property and photographs of both subject property and comparables. Figure 16.3 shows the uniform residential appraisal form widely used for mortgage financing.

The Profession of Appraising

Although appraising has existed since the origin of the concept of property, the huge number of foreclosures during the depression of the 1930s resulted in the beginning of appraising as an organized profession. Courses have been established in universities and colleges; books, journals and other publications devoted to various aspects of appraising have come into existence. Appraising has now become the most specialized branch of real estate.

In 1987 Nebraska became the first state to license appraisers, and California set standards for certified appraisals. Louisiana and Florida instituted certification for appraisers in 1988. Legislation for certification is federally mandated for every state. The leading appraisal societies have founded an overall Appraisal Foundation, with one of its primary objectives being the establishment of recommended guidelines for state and federal legislation regulating appraisers.

Professional designation of qualified appraisers is traditionally made through membership in appraisal societies. Different designations require varying levels of education, specific courses in appraisal, examinations, demonstration appraisals, experience, and continuing education. The two largest societies are the American Institute of Real Estate Appraisers (associated with the National Association of REALTORS®) and the Society of Real Estate Appraisers. **AIREA** offers the designation RM (Residential Member) and MAI (Member, Appraisal Institute). The difficulty of attaining the coveted and relatively rare MAI level is indicated by the fact that among other qualifications, a college degree and 16 hours of examinations are required. **SRA** offers the designations SRA (Senior Residential Appraiser), SRPA (Senior Real Property Appraiser), and SREA (Senior Real Estate Analyst).

The National Association of Review Appraisers awards the CRA (Certified Review Appraiser); the National Association of Independent Fee Appraisers offers

Figure 16.3
Residential Appraisal Report

Property Description & Analysis **UNIFORM RESIDENTIAL APPRAISAL REPORT** File No.

SUBJECT

Property Address	Census Tract	LENDER DISCRETIONARY USE
City / County / State / Zip Code	Sale Price $
Legal Description	Date
Owner/Occupant	Map Reference	Mortgage Amount $
Sale Price $ / Date of Sale	PROPERTY RIGHTS APPRAISED	Mortgage Type
Loan charges/concessions to be paid by seller $	☐ Fee Simple	Discount Points and Other Concessions
R.E. Taxes $ / Tax Year / HOA $/Mo.	☐ Leasehold	Paid by Seller $
Lender/Client	☐ Condominium (HUD/VA)	
	☐ De Minimis PUD	Source

NEIGHBORHOOD

	Urban	Suburban	Rural	NEIGHBORHOOD ANALYSIS	Good	Avg	Fair	Poor
LOCATION	☐ Urban	☐ Suburban	☐ Rural	Employment Stability				
BUILT UP	☐ Over 75%	☐ 25-75%	☐ Under 25%	Convenience to Employment				
GROWTH RATE	☐ Rapid	☐ Stable	☐ Slow	Convenience to Shopping				
PROPERTY VALUES	☐ Increasing	☐ Stable	☐ Declining	Convenience to Schools				
DEMAND/SUPPLY	☐ Shortage	☐ In Balance	☐ Over Supply	Adequacy of Public Transportation				
MARKETING TIME	☐ Under 3 Mos	☐ 3-6 Mos.	☐ Over 6 Mos.	Recreation Facilities				

PRESENT LAND USE %	LAND USE CHANGE	PREDOMINANT OCCUPANCY	SINGLE FAMILY HOUSING		
Single Family	Not Likely	☐ Owner	PRICE $(000) / AGE (yrs)	Adequacy of Utilities
2-4 Family	Likely	☐ Tenant		Property Compatibility
Multi-family	In process	☐ Vacant (0-5%)	Low	Protection from Detrimental Cond
Commercial	To:	☐ Vacant (over 5%)	High	Police & Fire Protection
Industrial			Predominant	General Appearance of Properties
Vacant				Appeal to Market

Note: Race or the racial composition of the neighborhood are not considered reliable appraisal factors.
COMMENTS:

SITE

Dimensions ___
Site Area ___ Corner Lot ___ Topography ___
Zoning Classification ___ Zoning Compliance ___ Size ___ Shape ___
HIGHEST & BEST USE: Present Use ___ Other Use ___ Drainage ___

UTILITIES	Public	Other	SITE IMPROVEMENTS	Type	Public	Private		
Electricity			Street				View	
Gas			Curb/Gutter				Landscaping	
Water			Sidewalk				Driveway	
Sanitary Sewer			Street Lights				Apparent Easements	
Storm Sewer			Alley				FEMA Flood Hazard Yes* / No	
							FEMA* Map/Zone	

COMMENTS (Apparent adverse easements, encroachments, special assessments, slide areas, etc.):

IMPROVEMENTS

GENERAL DESCRIPTION	EXTERIOR DESCRIPTION	FOUNDATION	BASEMENT	INSULATION
Units	Foundation	Slab	Area Sq. Ft.	Roof
Stories	Exterior Walls	Crawl Space	% Finished	Ceiling
Type (Det./Att.)	Roof Surface	Basement	Ceiling	Walls
Design (Style)	Gutters & Dwnspts.	Sump Pump	Walls	Floor
Existing	Window Type	Dampness	Floor	None
Proposed	Storm Sash	Settlement	Outside Entry	Adequacy
Under Construction	Screens	Infestation		Energy Efficient Items:
Age (Yrs.)	Manufactured House			
Effective Age (Yrs.)				

ROOM LIST

ROOMS	Foyer	Living	Dining	Kitchen	Den	Family Rm.	Rec. Rm.	Bedrooms	# Baths	Laundry	Other	Area Sq. Ft.
Basement												
Level 1												
Level 2												

Finished area **above** grade contains: ___ Rooms; ___ Bedroom(s); ___ Bath(s); ___ Square Feet of Gross Living Area

INTERIOR

SURFACES	Materials/Condition	HEATING	KITCHEN EQUIP.	ATTIC	IMPROVEMENT ANALYSIS	Good	Avg	Fair	Poor
Floors		Type	Refrigerator	None	Quality of Construction				
Walls		Fuel	Range/Oven	Stairs	Condition of Improvements				
Trim/Finish		Condition	Disposal	Drop Stair	Room Sizes/Layout				
Bath Floor		Adequacy	Dishwasher	Scuttle	Closets and Storage				
Bath Wainscot		COOLING	Fan/Hood	Floor	Energy Efficiency				
Doors		Central	Compactor	Heated	Plumbing-Adequacy & Condition				
		Other	Washer/Dryer	Finished	Electrical-Adequacy & Condition				
		Condition	Microwave		Kitchen Cabinets-Adequacy & Cond				
Fireplace(s) #		Adequacy	Intercom		Compatibility to Neighborhood				

CAR STORAGE			ATTIC entries	IMPROVEMENT				
No. Cars	Garage / Carport	Attached / Detached	Adequate / Inadequate	House Entry / Outside Entry	Appeal & Marketability				
Condition	None	Built-In	Electric Door	Basement Entry	Estimated Remaining Economic Life ___ Yrs
					Estimated Remaining Physical Life ___ Yrs

Additional features: ___

COMMENTS

Depreciation (Physical, functional and external inadequacies, repairs needed, modernization, etc.) ___

General market conditions and prevalence and impact in subject/market area regarding loan discounts, interest buydowns and concessions ___

Freddie Mac Form 70 10 86   Fannie Mae Form 1004 10 86

**Figure 16.3
(continued)**

Valuation Section

UNIFORM RESIDENTIAL APPRAISAL REPORT   File No.

Purpose of Appraisal is to estimate Market Value as defined in the Certification & Statement of Limiting Conditions.

COST APPROACH

BUILDING SKETCH (SHOW GROSS LIVING AREA ABOVE GRADE)
If for Freddie Mac or Fannie Mae show only square foot calculations and cost approach comments in this space

ESTIMATED REPRODUCTION COST – NEW – OF IMPROVEMENTS

Dwelling _____ Sq. Ft. @ $ _____	= $ _____	
_____ Sq. Ft. @ $ _____	= _____	
Extras _____	= _____	
_____	= _____	
Special Energy Efficient Items _____	= _____	
Porches, Patios, etc. _____	= _____	
Garage/Carport _____ Sq. Ft. @ $ _____	= _____	
Total Estimated Cost New	= $ _____	

	Physical	Functional	External
Less Depreciation			

Depreciation _____	= $ _____
Depreciated Value of Improvements	= $ _____
Site Imp. "as is" (driveway, landscaping, etc.)	= $ _____
ESTIMATED SITE VALUE	= $ _____
(If leasehold, show only leasehold value.)	
INDICATED VALUE BY COST APPROACH	= $ _____

(Not Required by Freddie Mac and Fannie Mae)

Does property conform to applicable HUD/VA property standards? ☐ Yes ☐ No

If No, explain: _____

Construction Warranty ☐ Yes ☐ No

Name of Warranty Program _____

Warranty Coverage Expires _____

The undersigned has recited three recent sales of properties most similar and proximate to subject and has considered these in the market analysis. The description includes a dollar adjustment, reflecting market reaction to those items of significant variation between the subject and comparable properties. If a significant item in the comparable property is superior to, or more favorable than, the subject property, a minus (−) adjustment is made, thus reducing the indicated value of subject; if a significant item in the comparable is inferior to, or less favorable than, the subject property, a plus (+) adjustment is made, thus increasing the indicated value of the subject.

SALES COMPARISON ANALYSIS

ITEM	SUBJECT	COMPARABLE NO. 1		COMPARABLE NO. 2		COMPARABLE NO. 3	
Address							
Proximity to Subject							
Sales Price	$		$		$		$
Price/Gross Liv. Area	$	$		$		$	
Data Source							
VALUE ADJUSTMENTS	DESCRIPTION	DESCRIPTION	+ (−) $ Adjustment	DESCRIPTION	+ (−) $ Adjustment	DESCRIPTION	+ (−) $ Adjustment
Sales or Financing Concessions							
Date of Sale/Time							
Location							
Site/View							
Design and Appeal							
Quality of Construction							
Age							
Condition							
Above Grade Room Count	Total Bdrms Baths	Total Bdrms Baths		Total Bdrms Baths		Total Bdrms Baths	
Gross Living Area	Sq. Ft.	Sq. Ft.		Sq. Ft.		Sq. Ft.	
Basement & Finished Rooms Below Grade							
Functional Utility							
Heating/Cooling							
Garage/Carport							
Porches, Patio, Pools, etc.							
Special Energy Efficient Items							
Fireplace(s)							
Other (e.g. kitchen equip., remodeling)							
Net Adj. (total)		☐ + ☐ − $		☐ + ☐ − $		☐ + ☐ − $	
Indicated Value of Subject		$		$		$	

Comments on Sales Comparison: _____

INDICATED VALUE BY SALES COMPARISON APPROACH ... $ _____

INDICATED VALUE BY INCOME APPROACH (If Applicable) Estimated Market Rent $ _____ /Mo. x Gross Rent Multiplier _____ = $ _____

This appraisal is made ☐ "as is" ☐ subject to the repairs, alterations, inspections or conditions listed below ☐ completion per plans and specifications

Comments and Conditions of Appraisal: _____

RECONCILIATION

Final Reconciliation: _____

This appraisal is based upon the above requirements, the certification, contingent and limiting conditions, and Market Value definition that are stated in

☐ FmHA, HUD &/or VA instructions.

☐ Freddie Mac Form 439 (Rev 7/86)/Fannie Mae Form 1004B (Rev 7/86) filed with client _____ 19 _____ ☐ attached.

I (WE) ESTIMATE THE MARKET VALUE, AS DEFINED, OF THE SUBJECT PROPERTY AS OF _____ 19 _____ to be $ _____

I (We) certify: that to the best of my (our) knowledge and belief the facts and data used herein are true and correct; that I (we) personally inspected the subject property, both inside and out, and have made an exterior inspection of all comparable sales cited in this report; and that I (we) have no undisclosed interest, present or prospective therein

Appraiser(s) SIGNATURE _____   Review Appraiser SIGNATURE _____   ☐ Did ☐ Did Not

NAME _____   (if applicable)   NAME _____   Inspect Property

Freddie Mac Form 70 10/86   Fannie Mae Form 1004 10/86 the designations FA (Member) and FAS (Senior Member). Some professional appraisers belong to more than one society. Those along the Niagara Frontier, for example, may join an international society, FIABCI.

Where expert testimony is provided for court proceedings or before a public body such as zoning board, specific credentials (MAI, SRA or the like) may be required.

Summary

To *appraise* real estate is to *estimate its value*. Although there are many types of value, the most common objective of an appraisal is to estimate *market value*—the most probable sales price of a property.

While appraisals are concerned with values, prices and costs, it is vital to understand the distinctions among the terms. *Value* is an estimate of future benefits, *cost* represents a measure of past expenditures and *price* reflects the actual amount of money paid for a property.

Basic to appraising are certain underlying economic principles such as highest and best use, substitution, supply and demand, conformity, anticipation, increasing and diminishing returns, regression, plottage, contribution, competition and change.

A professional appraiser analyzes a property through three approaches to value. In the *direct sales comparison approach* the value of the subject property is compared with the values of others like it that have sold recently. Because no two properties are exactly alike, adjustments must be made to account for any differences. With the *cost approach,* an appraiser calculates the cost of building a similar structure on a similar site. Then he or she subtracts depreciation (losses in value), which reflects the differences between new properties of this type and the present condition of the subject property. The *income approach* is an analysis based on the relationship between the rate of return that an investor requires and the net income that a property produces.

A special version of the income approach called the *gross rent multiplier* (GRM), is computed by dividing the sale price of a property by its gross monthly rent.

The application of the three approaches normally will result in three different estimates of value. In the process of *reconciliation* the validity and reliability of each approach are weighed objectively to arrive at the single best and most supportable conclusion of value.

Questions

1. Jim Jordan is a fully qualified appraiser. As such he:

   a. discovers value.   c. estimates value.
   b. insures value.   d. sets value.

2. In order to do his work, Jim is legally required to:

   a. have a real estate license.
   b. have a separate appraiser's license.
   c. register with the state attorney general.
   d. do nothing specific.

3. The appraiser who works for a number of different clients is known as a(n):

   a. fee appraiser.
   b. freelance appraiser.
   c. staff appraiser.
   d. in-house appraiser.

4. Value is the:

   a. relationship between desired object and potential buyer.
   b. power of a good to command other goods in exchange.
   c. present value of future benefits.
   d. All of the above

5. A house should bring $100,000 but is sold for $90,000 by a hard-pressed seller in a hurry, is then mortgaged for $80,000 and insured for $95,000. Its market value is:

   a. $80,000   c. $95,000
   b. $90,000   d. $100,000

6. An example of an arm's-length transaction is one between:

   a. father and daughter.
   b. employer and employee.
   c. broker and salesperson.
   d. two strangers.

7. The seller's concessionary financing is taken into account when a comparable is adjusted for:

   a. plottage.   c. obsolescence.
   b. cash equivalent. d. regression.

8. Market value and cost are often equal when property:

   a. remains in the family a long time.
   b. was recently constructed.
   c. is sold in an arm's-length transaction.
   d. receives a weighted appraisal.

9. Highest and best use of real estate is defined as the use that produces the most:

   a. benefit to the community.
   b. conformity.
   c. progression.
   d. money.

10. "Why should I pay more when I can buy almost the same house new for less?" is an example of the principle of:

    a. substitution.   c. anticipation.
    b. conformity.   d. change.

11. Houses are likely to reach their maximum value when:

    a. a wide range of price levels is represented.
    b. neighbors hold a mix of executive, blue-collar and white-collar jobs.
    c. each house is unique.
    d. jobs, houses and price levels are similar.

12. The principle of value that states the two adjacent parcels of land combined into one larger parcel may have a greater value than the two parcels value separately is called:

    a. substitution.   c. highest and best use.
    b. plottage.   d. contribution.

13. You are appraising the house at 23 Oak. The house recently sold at 54 Oak is similar but has a fireplace. What use do you make of the value of the fireplace?

    a. Subtract it.   c. Ignore it.
    b. Add it.   d. Reconcile it.

14. The cost approach is most useful for:

    a. a library.
    b. insurance purposes.
    c. new construction.
    d. all of the above.

15. From the reproduction or replacement cost of the building an appraiser deducts depreciation, which represents:

    a. the remaining useful economic life of the building.
    b. remodeling costs to increase rentals.
    c. loss of value due to any cause.
    d. costs to modernize the building.

16. The difference between reproduction cost and replacement cost involves:

    a. functional obsolescence.
    b. estimated land value.
    c. modern versus obsolete methods and materials.
    d. effective gross income.

17. The appraised value of a residence with five bedrooms and one bathroom would probably be reduced because of:

    a. locational obsolescence.
    b. functional obsolescence.
    c. physical deterioration—curable.
    d. physical deterioration—incurable.

18. The term *external obsolescence* refers to:

    a. poor landscaping.
    b. faulty floor plan.
    c. wear and tear.
    d. problems beyond the property line.

19. If a property's annual net income is $37,500 and it is valued at $300,000 what is its capitalization rate?

    a. 12.5 percent   c. 15 percent
    b. 10.5 percent   d. 18 percent

20. Certain data must be determined by an appraiser before value can be computed by the income approach. Which of the following is *not* required for this process?

    a. Annual net income
    b. Proper capitalization rate
    c. Accrued depreciation
    d. Annual gross income

21. Capitalization is the process by which the estimated future annual net income is used as the basis to:

    a. determine cost.
    b. estimate value.
    c. establish depreciation.
    d. determine potential tax value.

22. Which of the following factors would *not* be important in comparing properties under the Direct sales comparison approach to value?

    a. Difference in dates of sale
    b. Difference in real estate taxes
    c. Difference in appearance and condition
    d. Difference in original cost

23. *Reconciliation* refers to which of the following?

    a. Loss of value due to any cause
    b. Separating the value of the land from the total value of the property in order to compute depreciation
    c. Analyzing the results obtained by the three approaches to value to determine a final estimate of value
    d. The process by which an appraiser determines the highest and best use for a parcel of land

24. A fully qualified appraiser will probably hold a:

    a. fellowship.   c. designation.
    b. license.   d. degree.

25. Some of the country's foremost appraisers have earned the designation:

    a. MAI.   c. SRE.
    b. REA.   d. ARE.

17

Real Estate Investment

Key Terms

Adjusted basis	Inflation
Appreciation	Installment sale
Basis	Leverage
Boot	Limited partnership
Capital gain	Pyramiding
Cash flow	Real estate investment syndicate
Cost recovery	Real estate investment trust
Depreciation	Real estate mortgage investment conduit
Exchanges	Return
General partnership	Tax credits

Overview

The market for real estate investment is one of the most active in the country. Real estate can be used to generate income, build up equity and, to a limited extent, provide tax deductions that can be used to offset income from other sources. This chapter will present a basic introduction to real estate investment. Major emphasis is placed on investment opportunities open to small or beginning investors. Note that the examples and computations given in this chapter are symbolic and used for *illustrative purposes only*. Such examples are included in the discussion in order to explain a particular feature or concept of investment, *not to teach the reader how, when or what amount of money to invest*.

Investing in Real Estate

Often, customers expect a real estate broker or salesperson to act as an investment counselor. The broker or salesperson should always *refer a potential real estate investor to a competent tax accountant, attorney or investment specialist* who can give expert advice regarding the investor's specific interest.

Advantages of Real Estate Investment

Traditionally, real estate investments have shown an overall *high rate of return,* generally higher than the prevailing interest rate charged by mortgage lenders. Theoretically, this means that an investor can use the *leverage* of borrowed money to finance a real estate purchase and feel relatively sure that, if held long enough, the asset will yield more money than it costs to finance the purchase.

Real estate values usually keep pace with the rate of inflation. Such an *inflation hedge* provides the real estate investor with relative assurance that if the purchasing power of the dollar decreases, the value of the investor's assets will increase to offset the inflationary effects. Inflation will be discussed in detail later in this chapter. In addition, real estate entrepreneurs may enjoy various tax advantages that will also be discussed later in this chapter.

Disadvantages of Real Estate Investment

Unlike stocks and bonds, *real estate is not highly liquid* over a short period of time. This means that an investor cannot usually sell real estate quickly without taking some sort of loss. An investor in listed stocks need only call a stockbroker in order to liquidate a certain portion of such assets quickly when funds are needed. In contrast, even though a real estate investor may be able to raise a limited amount of cash by refinancing the property, that property is usually listed with a real estate broker and the investor may have to sell at a substantially lower price than full market value in order to facilitate a quick sale.

In addition, *it is difficult to invest in real estate without some degree of expert advice.* Investment decisions must be made based on a careful study of all the facts in a given situation, reinforced by a broad and thorough knowledge of real estate and the manner in which it affects and is affected by the marketplace— the human element. As mentioned earlier, *all investors should seek legal and tax counsel before making any real estate investments.*

Rarely can a real estate investor sit idly by and watch his or her money grow. *Management decisions must be made.* For example, can the investor effectively manage the property personally, or would it be preferable to hire a professional property manager? How much rent should be charged? How should repairs and tenant grievances be handled? "Sweat equity" (physical improvements accomplished by the investor personally) may be required to make the asset profitable.

Finally, a *high degree of risk* is often involved in real estate investment. There is always the possibility that an investor's property will decrease in value during the period it is held or that it will not generate an income sufficient to make it profitable.

The Investment   Property held for **appreciation** is generally expected to increase in value and to show a profit when sold at some future date. Income property is just that— property held for current income as well as a profit upon its sale.

Appreciation   Real estate is an avenue of investment open to those interested in holding property *primarily* for appreciation.

Two main factors affect appreciation: inflation and intrinsic value. **Inflation** is defined as the *increase in the amount of money in circulation, which results in a decline in its value coupled with a rise in wholesale and retail prices.* The *intrinsic value* of real estate is the result of a person's individual choices and preferences for a given geographical area, based on the features and amenities that the area has to offer. For example, property located in a well-kept suburb near business and shopping areas would have a greater intrinsic value to most people than similar property in a more isolated location. As a rule, the greater the intrinsic value, the more money a property can command upon its sale.

Quite often an investor speculates in purchases of either agricultural (farm) land or undeveloped (raw) land, located in what is expected to be a major path of growth. This type of investment carries with it many inherent risks. The investor must consider such questions as: How fast will the area develop? Will it grow sufficiently for the investor to make a good profit? Will the expected growth even occur? More important, will the profits eventually realized from the property be granted enough to offset the costs (such as property taxes) of holding the land?

Despite these risks, land has historically been a good inflation hedge if held for a long term. It can also be a source of income to offset some of the holding costs. For example, agricultural land can be leased out for crops or timber production, or grazing. On the downside, the Internal Revenue Service does not allow the depreciation (cost recovery) of land. Also, such land may not be liquid (salable) at certain times under certain circumstances, because few people are willing to purchase raw or agricultural land on short notice.

Income   The wisest initial investment for a person who wishes to buy and personally manage real estate may be the purchase of rental income property.

Cash flow. The object of income property is to generate spendable income, usually called cash flow. The **cash flow** is the total amount of money remaining after all expenditures have been paid, including taxes, operating costs and mortgage payments. The cash flow produced by any given parcel of real estate is determined by at least three factors: amount of rent received, operating expenses and method of debt repayment.

Generally, the amount of *rent* (income) that a property may command depends on a number of factors, including location, physical appearance and amenities. If the cash flow from rents is not enough to cover all expenses, a *negative cash flow* will result.

To keep cash flow high, an investor should *keep operating expenses low*. Such operating expenses include general maintenance of the building, repairs, utilities, taxes and tenant services (switchboard facilities, security systems and so forth). Poor or overly expensive management can result in negative cash flow.

An investor often stands to make more money by investing borrowed money, usually obtained through a mortgage loan. *Low mortgage payments* spread over a long period of time result in a higher cash flow because they allow the investor to retain more income each month; conversely, higher mortgage payments would contribute to a lower cash flow.

Return is the sum of appreciation and amortization, plus or minus cash flow and tax benefits.

Investment opportunities. Traditional income-producing property investments include apartment and office buildings, hotels, motels, shopping centers and industrial properties. Investors have historically found well-located, one- to four-family dwellings to be favorable investments.

Leverage

Leverage is the use of *borrowed money to finance the bulk of an investment*. As a rule, an investor can receive a maximum return from the initial investment (the down payment and closing and other costs) by: 1. making a small down payment; 2. paying a low interest rate; and 3. spreading mortgage payments over as long a period as possible.

As an example, the use of leveraging allows a person of modest income to buy a home valued at several times that amount, as the following figure illustrates.

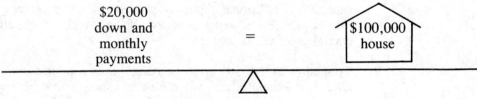

The effect of leveraging on an investor is to provide, on a sale of the asset, a return that is a reflection of the effect of market forces on the entire amount of the original purchase price, but is measured against only the actual cash invested. For example, if an investor spends $100,000 for rental property and makes a $20,000 down payment, then sells that property five years later for $125,000, the return over five years is $25,000. Disregarding ownership expenses, the return is not 25 percent ($25,000 compared to $100,000), but 125 percent of the original amount invested ($25,000 compared to $20,000).

Risks are generally proportionate to leverage. A high degree of leverage gives the investor and lender a high degree of risk; lower leverage results in a lower risk.

Equity buildup. Equity buildup is that portion of the payment directed toward the principal rather than the interest, *plus* any gain in property value due to appreciation. In a sense, equity buildup is like money in the bank to the investor. Although this accumulated equity is not realized as cash unless the property is sold or refinanced, the equity interest may be sold, exchanged or mortgaged (refinanced) to be used as leverage for other investments.

Pyramiding through refinancing. By holding and refinancing using equity and appreciation buildup, rather than selling or exchanging already-owned properties, an investor's holdings can be increased without investment of any additional capital. This practice is known as **pyramiding.** By reinvesting and doubling his or her holdings periodically, it is conceivable that an investor who started out with a small initial cash down payment could own (heavily mortgaged) properties worth hundreds of thousands or millions of dollars. With sufficient cash flow to cover all costs, if market values hold steady, the income derived from such assets could pay off the various mortgage debts and show a handsome profit.

Tax Benefits

One of the main reasons real estate investments were popular—and profitable—in the past was that federal law allowed investors to use losses generated by the investments to shelter income from other sources. The Tax Reform Act of 1986 (TRA) has eliminated some tax advantages of owning investment real estate, but with professional tax advice the investor can still make a wise real estate purchase.

Internal Revenue Service regulations are subject to frequent change. Too much tax shelter, however, can backfire by making the investor subject to *alternative minimum tax*.

Exchanges

Real estate investors can defer taxation of capital gains by a property exchange. Even if property has appreciated greatly since its initial purchase, it may be exchanged for other property and the property owner will incur tax liability on the sale only if additional capital or property is also received. Note, however, that *the tax is deferred, not eliminated*. If the investor ever sells the property, the capital gain will be taxed.

To qualify as a tax-deferred exchange, the properties involved must be of *like kind*—for example, real estate for real estate. Any additional capital or personal property included with the transaction to even out the exchange is considered **boot,** and the party receiving it is taxed at the time of the exchange. The value of the boot is added to the basis of the property with which it is given.

For example, investor Brown owns an apartment building with an adjusted basis of $225,000 and a market value of $375,000. Brown exchanges the building plus $75,000 cash for another apartment building having a market value of $450,000. That building, owned by investor Grey, has an adjusted basis of $175,000. Brown's basis in the new building will be $300,000 (the $225,000 basis of the building exchanged plus the $75,000 cash boot paid) and Brown has no tax liability on the exchange. Grey must pay tax on the $75,000 boot received and has a basis of $175,000 (the same as the previous building) in the building now owned.

Capital Gains

The tax law no longer favors long-term investments by reducing taxable gain (profit) on their sale or exchange. *Capital gain* is still defined as the difference between the adjusted basis of property and its net selling price. At various times, tax law has excluded a portion of capital gains from income tax, in percentages ranging from 0 to 50 percent.

Basis. A property's cost basis will determine the amount of gain to be taxed. The **basis** of property is the investor's initial cost for the real estate. The investor adds to the basis the cost of any physical improvements subsequently made to the property, and subtracts from the basis the amount of any depreciation claimed as a tax deduction (explained later), to derive the property's **adjusted basis.** When the property is sold by the investor, the amount by which the sale price exceeds the property's adjusted basis is the capital gain taxable as income.

For example, an investor purchased a one-family dwelling for us as a rental property. The purchase price was $45,000. The investor is now selling the property for $100,000. Shortly before the sale date, the investor made $3,000 worth of capital improvements to the home. Depreciation of $10,000 on the property improvements has been taken during the term of the investor's ownership. The investor will pay a broker's commission of 7 percent of the sale price and will also pay closing costs of $600. The investor's capital gain is computed as follows:

Selling price:		$100,000
Less:		
7% commission	$7,000	
closing costs	+ 600	
	$7,600	−7,600
Net sales price:		$ 92,400
Basis:		
original cost	$45,000	
improvements	+ 3,000	
	$48,000	
Less:		
depreciation	−10,000	
Adjusted basis:	$38,000	−38,000
Total capital gain:		$ 54,400

Depreciation (Cost Recovery)

Depreciation, or **cost recovery,** is an accounting concept. Depreciation allows an investor to recover the cost of an income-producing asset by way of tax deductions over the period of the asset's useful life.

While investors rarely purchase property without the expectation that it will appreciate over time, the view of the Internal Revenue Service is that all physical structures will deteriorate and hence lose value over time. Cost recovery deductions may be taken only on personal property and improvements to land, and only if they are used in a trade or business or for the production of income. Thus a cost recovery deduction cannot be claimed on an individual's personal residence. *Land cannot be depreciated*—technically it never wears out or becomes obsolete.

If depreciation is taken in equal amounts over an asset's useful life, the method used is called *straight-line depreciation*. For certain property purchased before 1987, it is also possible to use an *accelerated cost recovery system (ACRS)* to claim greater deductions in the early years of ownership, gradually reducing the amount deducted in each year of the useful life.

For property placed in service as of January 1, 1987, the Tax Reform Act increased the recovery period or residential rental property to 27.5 years and nonresidential property to 31.5 years. Just as important, only straight-line depreciation is allowed.

Deductions and TRA '86

The Tax Reform Act of 1986 (TRA '86) limits the deductibility of losses from rental property. The first $25,000 of loss can be used to offset income from any source provided that the investor *actively participates* in the management and operation of the property and has taxable income of no more than $100,000 before the deduction is made. The deduction is reduced by $.50 for every dollar of income over $100,000, and is thus eliminated completely when income reaches $150,000. Two examples will help to illustrate the impact of this law.

1. Harvey has adjusted gross income of $130,000 and losses of $20,000 from three apartment buildings that he owns and personally manages. Harvey is entitled to a deduction of only $10,000 (because the $25,000 maximum is reduced by $.50 for every dollar of the $30,000 Harvey earned over $100,000), reducing his taxable income to $120,000.
2. Helen has adjusted gross income of $100,000 and losses of $20,000 from rental property that she actively manages. Helen is entitled to a deduction of the full $20,000 (her income doesn't exceed $100,000), reducing her taxable income to $80,000.

The deduction applies only when the taxpayer actively participates in managing the rental property. The involvement may be as great as personally managing the day-to-day operation of the rental property with no outside assistance, or as minimal as simply making management decisions, such as the approval of new tenants and lease terms, while hiring others to provide services.

The Tax Reform Act prevents an investor from using a loss from a passive activity (one in which the taxpayer is not an active participant) to shelter "active income" (such as wages) or "portfolio income" (such as stock dividends, bank interest and capital gains). An example of passive investor is a limited partner, someone who contributes investment monies but has no voice in the operation of the investment.

Generally, a passive investor can offset investment losses only against investment income. If the passive investor has no other current investment income, the loss may be carried over to offset investment income in future years. If the investment is sold before the loss is used, it may offset what would otherwise be taxable gain on the sale.

To ease the effect of the new law, investors could write off 20 percent of passive losses against noninvestment income in 1989, and 10 percent in 1990.

Tax credits. A **tax credit** is a direct reduction in tax due, rather than a deduction from income before tax is computed. A tax credit is therefore of far greater value.

Investors in older building renovations and low-income housing projects may use the designated tax credits (described below) to offset tax on up to $25,000 of other income. This is a major exception to the rule requiring active participation in the project. Even passive investors can take advantage of the tax credits. The maximum income level at which the credits can be taken is also higher. Investors with adjusted gross income of up to $200,000 are entitled to the full $25,000 offset, which is reduced by $.50 for every additional dollar of income, and eliminated entirely for incomes above $250,000.

Since 1976, tax credits have been provided for taxpayers who renovate historic property. Historic property is property so designated by the Department of the Interior and listed in the *National Register of Historic Landmarks,* or property of historic significance that is located in an area certified by a state as a historic district. The Tax Reform Act reduced the allowable credit from 25 percent of the money spent on renovation of historic property to 20 percent of money so spent. The property can be depreciated, but the full amount of the tax credit must be subtracted from the basis derived by adding purchase cost and renovation expenses.

The work must be accomplished in accordance with federal historic property guidelines and certified by the Department of the Interior. After renovation, the property must be used as a place of business or rented—it cannot be used as the personal residence of the person taking the tax credit.

There is a credit of 10% of rehabilitation costs for nonhistoric buildings placed in service before 1936. Nonhistoric buildings must be nonresidential property. Special transition rules may make a rehabilitated property eligible for 19-year recovery period.

The law also provided tax credits ranging from 4 percent to 9 percent each year over a 10-year period for expenditures on new construction or renovation of certain low-income housing.

Installment Sales

A taxpayer who sells real property and receives payment on an installment basis, may report any profit on the transaction year by year as it is collected. Any accelerated depreciation previously taken, however, must be recaptured immediately. There are many complex provisions regarding installment sales.

Income tax calculations are usually figured at the investors *marginal tax rate,* that rate at which his or her top dollar of income is taxed.

Real Estate Investment Syndicates

A **real estate investment syndicate** is a form of business venture in which a group of people pool their resources to own and/or develop a particular piece of property. In this manner, people with only modest capital can invest in large-scale, high-profit operations, such as high-rise apartment buildings and shopping centers. A certain amount of profit is realized from rents collected on the investment, but the main return usually comes when the syndicate sells the property after sufficient appreciation.

Syndicate participation can take many different legal forms, from tenancy in common and joint tenancy to various kinds of partnerships, corporations and trusts. *Private syndication,* which generally involves a small group of closely associated and/or widely experienced investors, is distinguished from *public syndication,* which generally involves a much larger group of investors who may or may not be knowledgeable about real estate as an investment. Any pooling of individuals' funds raises questions of registration of securities under federal securities laws and state securities laws, commonly referred to as *blue-sky laws.*

Securities laws include provisions to control and regulate the offering and sale of securities. This is to protect members of the public who are not sophisticated investors but may be solicited to participate. Real estate securities must be registered with state officials and/or with the federal Securities and Exchange Commission (SEC) when they meet the defined conditions of a public offering. The number of prospects solicited, the total number of investors or participants, the financial background and sophistication of the investors and the value or price per unit of investment are pertinent facts. *Salespeople of such real estate securities may be required to obtain special licenses and registration with the state's attorney general.*

Forms of Syndicates   A **general partnership** is organized so that *all members of the group share equally in the managerial decisions, profits and losses involved with the investment.* A certain member (or members) of the syndicate is designated to act as trustee for the group and holds title to the property and maintains it in the syndicate's name.

Under a **limited partnership** agreement, *one party* (or parties), usually a property developer or real estate broker, *organizes, operates and is responsible for the entire syndicate.* This person is called the *general partner.* The other members of the partnership are merely investors; they have no voice in the organization and direction of the operation. These *passive investors are called limited partners.*

The limited partners share in the profits and compensate the general partner out of such profits. The limited partners stand to lose only as much as they invest—nothing more. The general partner(s) is (are) totally responsible for any excess losses incurred by the investment. The sale of a limited partnership interest involves the sale of an *investment security*, as defined by the SEC. Therefore, such sales are subject to state and federal laws concerning the sale of securities. Unless exempt, the securities must be registered with the federal Securities and Exchange Commission and the appropriate state authorities.

Real Estate Investment Trusts   By directing their funds into **real estate investment trusts (REITs),** real estate investors can take advantage of the same tax benefits as mutual fund investors. A real estate investment trust does not have to pay corporate income tax as long as 95 percent of its income is distributed to its shareholders and certain other conditions are met. There are three types of investment trusts: equity trusts, mortgage trusts and combination trusts. To qualify as a REIT, at least 75 percent of the trust's income must come from real estate.

Equity trusts. Much like mutual fund operations, equity REITs pool an assortment of large-scale income properties and sell shares to investors. This is in contrast to a real estate syndicate, through which several investors pool their funds in order to purchase *one* particular property. An equity trust also differs from a syndicate in that the trust realizes and directs its main profits through the *income* derived from the various properties it owns rather than from the sale of those properties.

Mortgage trusts. Mortgage trusts operate similarly to equity trusts, except that the mortgage trusts buy and sell real estate mortgages (usually short-term, junior instruments) rather than real property. A mortgage trust's major sources of income are mortgage interest and origination fees. Mortgage trusts may also make construction loans and finance land acquisitions.

Combination trusts. Combination trusts invest shareholders' funds in both real estate assets and mortgage loans. It has been predicted that these types of trusts will be best able to withstand economic slumps because they can balance their investments and liabilities more efficiently than can the other types of trusts.

Real Estate Mortgage Investment Conduits

The Tax Reform Act created a new tax entity that may issue multiple classes of investor interests (securities) backed by a pool of mortgages.

The **real estate mortgage investment conduit (REMIC)** has complex qualification, transfer and liquidation rules. Qualifications include the "asset test" (substantially all assets after a startup period must consist of qualified mortgages and permitted investments) and the requirement that investors' interests consists of one or more classes of regular interests and a single class of residual interests. Holders of regular interests receive interest or similar payments based on either a fixed rate or variable rate, is allowed. Holders of residual interests receive distributions (if any) on a pro rata basis.

Summary

Traditionally, real estate investment has offered a *high rate of return* while at the same time acting as an effective *inflation hedge* and allowing an investor to make use of other people's money to make investments through *leverage*. There may also be tax advantages to owning real estate. On the other hand, real estate is *not a highly liquid investment* and often carries with it a *high degree of risk*. Also, it is difficult to invest in real estate without *expert advice,* and a certain amount of involvement is usually required to establish and maintain the investment.

Investment property held for *appreciation* purposes is generally expected to increase in value to a point where its selling price is enough to cover holding costs and show a profit as well. The two main factors affecting appreciation are *inflation* and the property's present and future *intrinsic value*. Real estate held for *income* purposes is generally expected to generate a steady flow of income, called *cash flow,* and to show a profit upon its sale.

An investor hoping to use maximum *leverage* in financing an investment should make a small down payment, pay low interest rates and spread mortgage payments over as long a period as possible. By holding and refinancing properties, known as *pyramiding,* an investor may substantially increase investment holdings without contributing additional capital.

By *exchanging* one property for another with an equal or greater selling value, an investor can *defer* paying tax on the gain realized until a sale is made. A total tax deferment is possible only if the investor receives no cash or other incentive to even out the exchange. If received, such cash or property is called *boot* and is taxed.

Depreciation (cost recovery) is a concept that allows an investor to recover in tax deductions the basis of an asset over the period of its useful life. Only costs of improvements to land may be recovered, not costs for the land itself. The Tax Reform Act of 1986 greatly limited the potential for investment losses to shelter other income, but *tax credits* are still allowed for projects involving low-income housing and older buildings.

An investor may defer federal income taxes on gain realized from the sale of an investment property through an *installment sale* of property.

Individuals may also invest in real estate through an *investment syndicate;* these generally include *general and limited partnerships*. Other forms of real estate investment are the *real estate investment trust* (REIT) and the *real estate mortgage investment conduit* (REMIC).

The real estate broker and salesperson should be familiar with the rudimentary tax implications of real property ownership, but should refer clients to competent tax advisers for answers to questions on specific matters.

Questions

1. Among the advantages of real estate investment is:
   a. illiquidity.
   b. need for expert advise.
   c. hedge against inflation.
   d. degree of risk.

2. Among the disadvantages of real estate investment is:
   a. leverage.
   b. need for physical and mental effort.
   c. tax shelter.
   d. equity buildup.

3. Vacant land can be a good investment because:
   a. it must appreciate enough to cover expenses.
   b. it can have intrinsic value.
   c. bank financing is easily arranged.
   d. it may not be depreciated.

4. The increase of money in circulation coupled with a sharp rise in prices, resulting in an equally sharp decline in the value of money, is called:
   a. appreciation.   c. negative cash flow.
   b. inflation.   d. recapture.

5. A small multifamily property generates $50,000 in rental income with expenses of $45,000 annually, including $35,000 in debt service. The property appreciates about $25,000 a year. The owner realizes another $5,000 through income tax savings. On this property, the cash flow is:
   a. $5,000.   c. $25,000.
   b. $15,000.   d. $35,000.

6. In the example above, the owner's return is:
   a. $5,000.   c. $25,000.
   b. $15,000.   d. $35,000.

7. Leverage involves the extensive use of:
   a. cost recovery.
   b. borrowed money.
   c. government subsidies.
   d. alternative taxes.

8. A property's equity represents its current value less which of the following?
   a. Depreciation
   b. Mortgage indebtedness
   c. Physical improvements
   d. Selling costs and depreciation

9. An investor's marginal tax rate is the:
   a. total tax bill divided by net taxable income.
   b. extra tax if he has too many tax shelters.
   c. top applicable income tax bracket.
   d. percentage taxable on an installment sale.

10. The primary source of tax shelter in real estate investments comes from the accounting concept known as:
    a. recapture.   c. depreciation.
    b. boot.   d. net operating income.

11. For tax purposes the initial cost of an investment property plus the cost of any subsequent improvements to the property, less depreciation, represents the investment's:
    a. adjusted basis.   c. basis.
    b. capital gains.   d. salvage value.

12. The money left in an investor's pocket after expenses, including debt service, have been paid is known as:
    a. net operating income.
    b. gross income.
    c. cash flow.
    d. internal rate of return.

13. The investor who secures what the IRS regards as excessive tax shelter may be subject to:
    a. recovery.
    b. recapture.
    c. alternative minimum tax.
    d. pyramiding.

14. Julia Kinder is exchanging her apartment building for an apartment building of greater market value and must include a $10,000 boot to even out the exchange. Which of the following may she use as a boot?

    a. $10,000 cash
    b. Common stock with a current market value of $10,000
    c. A parcel of raw land with a current market value of $10,000
    d. Any of the above if acceptable to the exchangers

15. In the question above, which is true?

    a. Julia may owe income tax on $10,000.
    b. Each may owe tax on $10,000.
    c. The other investor may owe tax on $10,000.
    d. No one owes any tax at this time.

16. An investment syndicate in which all members share equally in the managerial decisions, profits and losses involved in the venture would be an example of which of the following?

    a. Real estate investment trust
    b. Limited partnership
    c. Real estate mortgage trust
    d. General partnership

17. Shareholders in a real estate trust generally:

    a. receive most of the trust's income each year.
    b. take an active part in management.
    c. find it difficult to sell their shares.
    d. realize their main profit through sales of property.

18. In an installment sale of one's own home, taxable gain is received and must be reported as income by the seller:

    a. in the year the sale is initiated.
    b. in the year the final installment payment is made.
    c. in each year that installment payments are received.
    d. at any one time during the period installment payments are received.

19. Depreciation allows the investor to charge as an expense on each year's tax return part of the:

    a. purchase price.
    b. down payment.
    c. mortgage indebtedness.
    d. equity.

20. A separate license and/or registration is required for the sale of:

    a. all investment property.
    b. real estate securities.
    c. installment property.
    d. boots.

21. In 1989, the Smiths received capital gains of $22,000, which was:

    a. deductible only from passive income.
    b. taxed at their regular rate on 40 percent of value.
    c. included in their ordinary income.
    d. subject to the purchase price rule.

22. Harvey, a limited partner in a partnership that is renovating a historic waterfront property, is entitled to offset up to $25,000 in tax credits against:

    a. no more than the amount he has at risk.
    b. income up to $100,000.
    c. income up to $200,000.
    d. income up to $250,000.

23. Helen has purchased a dilapidated town house that is 40 years old and of no particular historic value. Helen intends to renovate the town house and live in it. On her renovation expenditures, Helen will be entitled to tax credits of:

    a. $25,000.   c. $12,500.
    b. $0.   d. 25 percent.

24. Jim traded his office building purchased for $475,000 and valued at $650,000 for an office building valued at $750,000. Jim also paid $100,000 cash to the owner of the other building. Jim:

    a. received $100,000 "boot."
    b. must report $100,000 as income.
    c. must reduce his adjusted basis by $100,000.
    d. now has a property basis of $575,000.

25. A new tax entity that issues securities backed by a pool of mortgage is a:

    a. REIT.   c. TRA.
    b. REMIC.   d. general partnership.

18

Subdivision and Development

Key Terms

Clustering
Curvilinear system
Dedicated
Density zoning
Department of Environmental
   Conservation (DEC)
Developer
Environmental impact studies
Gridiron pattern
Impact fees

Interstate Land Sales Full Disclosure
   Act
Moratorium
Planned Unit Development (PUD)
Planning board
Plat of subdivision
Property report
Subdivider
Subdivision

Overview

Subdividers and property developers convert raw land, or property that is no longer serving its highest and best use, into subdivisions for residential and other uses. These subdividers and developers, working with local officials, are largely responsible for the orderly growth of such communities. This chapter will deal with the process of developing and subdividing property and also will discuss some of the legal aspects of selling subdivided land.

Developing and Subdividing Land

Land in large tracts must receive special attention before it can be converted into sites for homes, stores or other uses. A **subdivider** buys undeveloped acreage and divides it into smaller lots for sale to individuals or developers or for the subdivider's own use. A **developer** (who may also be a subdivider) builds homes or other buildings on the lots and sells them. Developing is generally a much more extensive activity than is subdividing. A developer may have a sales staff or may use the services of local real estate brokerage firms.

Regulation of Land Development

As discussed in Chapter 6, *no uniform city planning and land development legislation effects the entire country*. Laws governing subdividing and land planning are controlled by the state and local governmental bodies. New York State sets standards for villages, cities and towns. Local governments may adopt more restrictive policies. **Article IX-A** of New York's Real Property Law governs subdivision.

Land Planning

The recording of a plat of subdivision of land prior to public sale for residential or commercial use is usually required, but land planning precedes the actual subdividing process. The development plan must comply with any overall local *master land plan* adopted by the county, city, village or town. In doing so, the developer must consider zoning laws and land-use restrictions adopted for health and safety purposes. Basic city plan and zoning requirements are not inflexible, but long, expensive and frequently complicated hearings are usually required before alterations can be authorized.

Most villages, cities and other areas that are incorporated under state laws have **planning boards** or *planning commissioners*. Communities establish strict criteria before approving new subdivisions. The following are frequently included: (1) *dedication* of land for streets, schools, parks; (2) assurance by *bonding* that sewer and street costs will be paid; and (3) *compliance with zoning ordinances* governing use and lot size along with fire and safety ordinances.

Local authorities usually require land planners to submit information on how they intend to satisfy sewage-disposal and water-supply requirements. Development and/or septic tank installation may first require a *percolation test* of the soil's absorption and drainage capacities. Frequently a planner will also have to submit an *environmental impact report*.

Environmental Hazards

The Environmental Protection Agency has identified 403 chemicals as highly toxic, and innocent future purchasers of land can be held liable. Previous use of land being considered for development should be carefully investigated at the outset. Chemical companies, dry cleaners, old farms with trash dumps or underground gas tanks, airports, warehouses, gas stations and factories of all sorts may have produced potentially dangerous chemical wastes.

Problems faced by unaware future owners could include liability for cleanup, liability for health problems, unfavorable publicity and restrictions on future use of the land. More and more, developers are turning to specialists trained in environmental compliance and documentation.

Subdividing

The process of **subdivision** involves three distinct stages of development: (1) initial planning, (2) final planning and (3) disposition or start-up.

During the *initial planning stage* the subdivider seeks out raw land in a suitable area that he or she can profitably subdivide. After the land is located the property is analyzed for it highest and best use, and preliminary subdivision plans are drawn up accordingly. As previously discussed, close contact is initiated between the subdivider and local planning and zoning officials: If the project requires zoning variances, negotiations begins along these lines. The subdivider also locates financial backers and initiates marketing strategies.

Next, during the *final planning stage,* plans are prepared, approval is sought from local officials, permanent financing is obtained, the land is purchased, final budgets are prepared and marketing programs are designed.

The *disposition, or start-up*, carries the subdividing process to a conclusion. Subdivision plans are recorded with local officials, and streets, sewers and utilities are installed. Buildings, open parks and recreational areas are constructed and landscaped if they are part of the subdivision plan. Marketing programs are then initiated and title to the individual parcels of subdivided land is transferred as the lots are sold.

Subdivision Plans

In plotting out a subdivision according to local planning and zoning controls, a subdivider determines the size as well as the location of the individual lots. The size of the lots, front footage, depth and square footage are generally regulated by local ordinances. Frequently ordinances regulate both the minimum and maximum lot size.

The land itself must be studied, usually in cooperation with a surveyor, so that the subdivision can be laid out with consideration of natural drainage and land contours. A site planner and an engineer are also employed.

In laying out a subdivision a subdivider should provide for *utility easements* as well as easements for water and sewer mains. Usually the water and sewer mains will be laid in the street with connecting junction boxes available for each building site. When the city, town or village installs the water or sewer mains connecting a new building with the junction box in the street, a tie-in or connection fee is frequently charged to help the authority defray the cost of such installation.

A large development may also be charged controversial **impact fees,** intended to help a community cope with increased demand for schools and other services.

Most subdivisions are laid out by use of *lots and blocks*. An area of land is designated as a block, and the area making up this block is divided into lots. Both lots and blocks are numbered consecutively. If a developer does not intend to subdivide an entire tract of land at one time, however, some variation from consecutive numbering may be granted.

Although subdividers may designate areas reserved for schools, parks and future church sites, this practice can have some drawbacks. If in the future any such purpose is not appropriate, it will become difficult for the developer to abandon the original plan and use that property for residential purposes. To get around this situation, many developers designate such areas as *out-lot A, out-lot B* and so forth. Then, for example, if one of these areas is to be used for church purposes, it can be so conveyed and so used. If on the other hand the out-lot is not to be used for such a purpose, it can be resubdivided into residential properties without the burden of securing the consent of the lot owners in the area.

Plat of subdivision. The subdivider's completed **plat of subdivision,** a map of development indicating the location and boundaries of individual properties, must contain all necessary approvals of public officials and must be recorded in the county where the land is located.

After the plat has been filed for record, all areas that have been set aside for street purpose are considered to be **dedicated.** This means that the land shown as streets now belongs to the city or town. If this is not the subdivider's intention, the plat should specify that the streets are private. Filing the map protects the developer in the event the local government should later declare a **moratorium,** a halt to further development in the area.

Because the plat will be the basis for future conveyances, the subdivided land should be carefully measured with all lot sizes and streets noted by the surveyor and accurately entered on the document. Survey monuments should be established and measurements made from these monuments, with the location of all lots carefully marked.

Covenants and restrictions. Deed restrictions, discussed in Chapters 3 and 6, are originated and recorded by the subdivider as a means of *controlling and maintaining the desirable quality and character of the subdivision*. These restrictions can be included in the subdivision plat or they may be set forth in a separate recorded instrument, commonly referred to as a *declaration of restrictions*.

FHA standards. FHA *minimum standards* have been established for residential area subdivisions that are to be submitted for approval for FHA loan insurance.

There are also FHA standards applicable to building construction. Since 1986, in recognition of the more stringent local codes in effect, FHA has allowed local building codes (where preapproved by HUD—the Department of Housing and Urban Development) to serve as the standards. Exceptions generally include site conditions, thermal (insulation) standards and certain other material standards.

Development costs. The subdivider, developer and builder frequently invest many hundreds of thousands of dollars (and in larger developments, several million dollars) before the subdivision is even announced to the public. An analysis of these development costs will substantiate the sale price for a typical building lot of four to six times the cost of the raw land.

In the subdivision of a typical parcel of raw land, a lot's sale price will reflect such expenses as cost of land; installation of sewers, water mains, storm drains, landscaping and streetlights; earthworks (mass dirt removal, site grading and similar operations); paving; engineering and surveying fees; brokers' commissions; inspections; bonding costs; filing and legal fees; sale costs; and overhead. In certain areas a subdivider also may be required to give financial assistance to school districts, park districts and the like, either in the form of donated school or parksites or in the form of a fixed subsidy per subdivision lot. Should such further costs be incurred they must, of course, be added proportionately to the sale price of each building site.

Subdivision Density   Zoning ordinances often include minimum lot sizes and population density requirements for subdivisions and land developments. For example, a typical zoning restriction may set the minimum lot area on which a subdivider can build a single-family housing unit at 10,000 square feet. This means that the subdivider will be able to build four houses per acre. Many zoning authorities now establish special density zoning standards for certain subdivisions. **Density zoning** ordinances restrict the *average maximum number of houses per acre* that may be built within a particular subdivision. If the area is density zoned at an average maximum of four houses per acre, for example, by *clustering* building lots, the developer is free to achieve an open effect. Regardless of lot size or the number of units, the subidivider will be consistent with the ordinance as long as the average number of units in the development remains at or below the maximum density. This average is called *gross density*.

Street patterns. By varying street patterns and clustering housing units, a subdivider can dramatically increase the amount of open and/or recreational space in a development. Some of these patterns are illustrated in Figure 18.1.

The **gridiron pattern** evolved out of the government rectangular survey system. Featuring large lots, wide streets and limited-use service alleys, the system works reasonably well up to a point. An overabundance of grid-patterned streets often results in monotonous neighborhoods, with all lots facing busy streets. In addition, sidewalks are usually located adjacent to the streets, and the system provides for little or no open, park or recreational space.

The **curvilinear system** integrates major arteries of travel with smaller secondary and cul-de-sac streets carrying minor traffic. In addition, small open parks are often provided at intersections.

Figure 18.1
Street Patterns

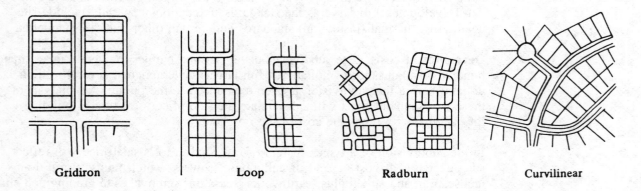

Gridiron   Loop   Radburn   Curvilinear

Clustering for open space. By slightly reducing lot sizes and **clustering** them around varying street patterns, a developer can house as many people in the same area as could be done using traditional subdividing plans, but with substantially increased tracts of open space.

For example, compare the two illustrations in Figure 18.2 The first is a plan for a conventionally designed subdivision containing 368 housing units. It uses 23,200 linear feet of street and leaves only 16 acres open for park areas. Contrast this with the second subdivision pictured. Both subdivisions are equal in size and terrain. But when lots are minimally reduced in size and clustered around limited-access, cul-de-sac streets, the number of housing units remains nearly the same (366), with less street area (17,700 linear feet) and drastically increased open space (23.5 acres). In addition, with modern building designs this clustered plan could be modified to accommodate 550 patio homes or 1,100 town houses.

Cluster housing may take the form of a **Planned Unit Development (PUD),** with some or all of an entire community's land use established by the developer's original plan.

Interstate Land Sales Full Disclosure Act

The **Interstate Land Sales Full Disclosure Act** requires those engaged in the interstate sale or leasing of 25 or more lots to file a *statement of record* and *register* the details of the land with HUD.

The seller is also required to furnish prospective buyers a **property report** containing all essential information about the property, such as distance over paved roads to nearby communities, number of homes currently occupied, soil condi-

Figure. 18.2 Clustered Subdivision Plan

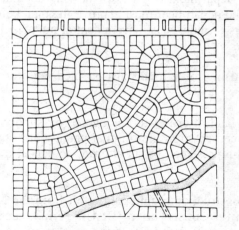 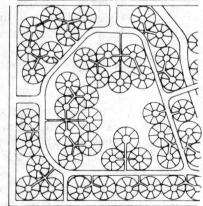

Conventional Plan
12,500-square-foot lots
368 housing units
1.6 acres of parkland
23,200 linear feet of street

Cluster Plan
7,500-square-foot lots
366 housing units
23.5 acres of parkland
17,700 linear feet of street

tions affecting foundations and septic systems, type of title a buyer will receive and existence of liens. The property report must be given to a prospective purchaser at least three business days before any sales contract is signed.

If a buyer does not receive a property report, the purchaser can cancel such a contract without further liability within two years. Any buyer of land covered by this act has the right to rescind a contract within seven days after signing. If the seller misrepresents the property in any sales promotion, a buyer induced by such a promotion is entitled to sue the seller for civil damages under federal law. Failure to comply with the law also may subject a seller to criminal penalties of up to five years' imprisonment and a $10,000 fine for each violation.

New York State Subdivided Land Sales Law

Land sold within New York State on the installment plan by a subdivider, and out-of-state land offered for sale in New York in any manner, may not be offered for sale until at least two documents have been filed with the Department of State. The first covers the identity and address of the offerer, the names of owners of the land, a statement on the subdivider's previous experience with vacant land, any criminal activity, a description of the land complete with maps, a title statement including any encumbrances of liens and the terms on which the land will be sold, with a copy of the contract to be used.

The second document is a copy of the offering statement to be furnished to each buyer with a full financial statement of the assets and liabilities of the subdivider, a description of the subdivision and each lot, information on existing liens and encumbrances, existing or proposed utilities, area, community and recreational facilities and even the weather conditions of the area as well as the terms of sale.

In addition, New York's Public Health Laws require any subdivider offering for sale or rent five or more residential building lots to file a map of the proposed subdivision with the Department of Health, showing adequate water supply and sewerage facilities. The department must approve the plan before it can be filed. A development of 50 lots or more must have a central municipal water supply rather than individual wells.

A copy of any advertising to be used must be filed with the Department of State.

New York considers land offerings to be covered by subdivision regulations as soon as a fifth lot is carved from the original parcel. The state allows any purchaser who is not represented by an attorney to cancel a contract within ten days.

In some instances, construction requires a permit from the New York **Department of Environmental Conservation (DEC).** Permits are necessary for work in a protected wetland or the 100-foot buffer zone around a wetland. Depending on the circumstances, permits may be needed for work that disturbs the banks of streams, for some water supplies, sewage discharges and sewer extensions. The sale of more than 1,000 tons of fill dirt or gravel per year requires a DEC mining permit. **Environmental impact studies** of varying complexity may be required when the parcel is ruled environmentally sensitive: large projects or those located in floodplains, wetlands, steep slopes, or other environmentally fragile areas.

Rehabilitation

Upgrading older buildings for modern use can take different forms. Among them:

- *Adaptive reuse:* finding a new use that varies from the building's original function—loft apartment developments in old warehouses, for example;
- *Preservation:* careful maintenance of a building in its present state;
- *Reconstruction:* recreation of the original building that may have been damaged or destroyed;
- *Recycling:* any process that makes possible further use of an old building;
- *Rehabilitation (reconditioning):* making a building sound and usable, with some consideration for original architectural features;
- *Renovation (restoration):* reconditioning with a greater use of new materials, keeping intact or recreating original architectural elements;
- *Remodeling:* changing the appearance of a building with the use of modern materials;
- *Restoration:* returning a structure to the appearance it had some point in the past, removing later additions and adding some that might have been removed.

Summary

A *subdivider* buys undeveloped acreage, divides it into smaller parcels and sells it. A *land developer* builds homes on the lots and sells them, either through an in-house sales organization or through local real estate brokerage firms. City planners and land developers, working together, plan whole communities that are later incorporated into cities, towns or villages.

Land development must generally comply with master land plans adopted by counties, cities, villages or towns. This may entail approval of land-use plans by local *planning boards* or *commissioners*.

The process of subdivision includes dividing the tract of land into *lots and blocks* and providing for *utility easements,* as well as laying out street patterns and widths. A subdivider must generally record a completed *plat of subdivision* with all necessary approvals of public officials in the county where the land is located. Subdividers usually place *restrictions* on the use of all lots in a subdivision as a general plan for the benefit of all lot owners.

By *varying street patterns and housing density* and *clustering housing units,* a subdivider can dramatically increase the amount of open and recreational space within a development.

Subdivided land sales are regulated on the federal level by the *Interstate Land Sales Full Disclosure Act.* This law requires developers engaged in interstate land sales or the leasing of 25 or more units to register the details of the land with HUD. Such developers also must provide prospective purchasers with a property report containing all essential information about the property at least three business days before any sales contract is signed.

Subdivided land sales are also regulated by New York laws. For the sale of subdivided land on an installment basis, and of any out-of-state land offered in New York, documents must be filed in advance with the Department of State, and an offering statement furnished to buyers. The sale of any subdivision of five or more lots requires approval of a water and sewage plan by the Department of Health, and 500 or more lots require a central municipal water system.

Questions

1. Lila Hurwitz buys farmland near the city and turns it into usable building lots. She is a:

   a. site planner.   c. surveyor.
   b. developer.   d. subdivider.

2. Overall subdivision guidelines are set by:

   a. the federal government.
   b. New York State.
   c. the Department of Health.
   d. the Department of Environmental Conservation.

3. Local governments often regulate subdivision through their:

   a. planning boards.
   b. conservationists.
   c. site planners.
   d. building inspectors.

4. A particular subdivision plan may require the services of a(n):

   a. surveyor.   c. engineer.
   b. site planner.   d. All of the above

5. A map illustrating the sizes and locations of streets and lots in a subdivision is called a:

   a. gridiron pattern.   c. plat of subdivision.
   b. survey.   d. property report.

6. Which of the following items are *not* usually designated on the plat for a new subdivision?

   a. Easements for sewer and water mains
   b. Land to be used for streets, schools and civic facilities
   c. Numbered lots and blocks
   d. Prices of residential and commercial lots

7. A subdivider turns over streets to public ownership through:

   a. development.   c. dedication.
   b. eminent domain.   d. condemnation.

8. Deed restrictions are usually placed on an entire subdivision by the:

   a. building inspector. c. planning board.
   b. state government.   d. subdivider.

9. Which of the following would *not* be a part of the development cost of land?

   a. Curbs and gutters
   b. Installation of telephone lines
   c. Raw land cost
   d. Developer's overhead.

10. *Gross density* refers to which of the following?

    a. The maximum number of residents that may by law, occupy a subdivision
    b. The average maximum number of houses per acre that may, by law, be built in a subdivision
    c. The maximum size lot that may, by law, be built in a subdivision
    d. The minimum number of houses that may, by law, be built in a subdivision

11. A street pattern based on the rectangular survey system is called a:

    a. block plan.
    b. gridiron system.
    c. loop streets plan.
    d. cul-de-sac system.

12. A street pattern featuring clusters of housing units grouped into large, cul-de-sac blocks is generally called a:

    a. block Plan.
    b. curvilinear system.
    c. loop street system.
    d. gridiron system.

13. Which of the following kinds of information need *not* be included in a property report given to a land buyer in compliance with the Interstate Land Sales Full Disclosure Act?

    a. Soil conditions affecting foundations
    b. Financial condition of the seller
    c. Number of homes currently occupied
    d. Existence of liens

14. The Marshes received a property report and consulted a lawyer a week before they signed a contract to buy a lot in a retirement community in Florida covered by the Interstate Land Sales Full Disclosure Act. They may change their minds and cancel the contract within:

    a. seven days.   c. two years.
    b. ten days.   d. They may not cancel.

15. Subdivision regulations apply in New York State as soon as one offers:

    a. the first lot.   c. the fifth lot.
    b. the third lot.   d. the seventh lot.

16. A subdivider can increase the amount of open and/or recreational space in a development by:

    a. establishing out-lots.
    b. meeting FHA standards.
    c. clustering housing units.
    d. dedicating roads.

17. Turning an old warehouse into a discount shopping mall is an example of:

    a. restoration.   c. adaptive reuse.
    b. preservation.   d. reconstruction.

Appendix: Excerpt from New York State's Study Booklet for Brokers

SUMMARY OF ARTICLE 9-A OF THE REAL PROPERTY LAW

Subdivided Lands

No real estate broker or real estate salesperson should be involved in any way, in the State of New York, with the sale or lease of subdivided lands located within or without the State, unless the subdivider offering the property for sale or lease has complied with the provisions of Article 9-A of the Real Property Law.

Article 9-A of the Real Property law is designed to protect the residents of New York State in the purchase or lease of subdivided lands located within the State of New York where sold on an installment plan, and located without the State of New York whether offered on the installment or any other plan, terms and conditions of sale or lease.

Safeguards are inserted into the law to prevent fraud or fraudulent practices which might be employed to include the purchase or lease of vacant subdivided lands. Among such safeguards is the requirement that the subdividers file with the Department of State a statement, with substantiating documentation, including a certified copy of a map of the subdivided lands, a search of the title to the land reciting in detail all the liens, encumbrances and clouds upon the title which may or may not render the title unmarketable.

A subdivider, in addition to the statement required under the law, must file with the Department of State an Offering Statement. The Offering Statement must contain among other facts, detailed information about the subdivision including a description of the land, existence of utilities, area, community and recreational facilities, restriction, weather conditions and financial statement of the subdivider. The Offering Statement must be revised yearly. It must clearly indicate that the Department of State has not passed on the merits of the offering.

No sale or lease or subdivided lands shall be made without prior delivery of an Offering Statement to the prospective customer. Any offer to sell or lease subdivided lands prior to filing of both the Offering Statement and the statement constitutes a felony.

Where the land is affected by mortgages or other encumbrances, it is unlawful for the subdivider to sell such vacant lands in the subdivision unless appropriate provisions in the mortgage or lien enable the subdivider to convey valid title to each parcel free of such mortgage or encumbrance. A mortgage on an entire subdivision will usually provide for a release of individual lots from that mortgage on payment of a specified amount of money. If the land is being sold on an installment plan, the law provides that where the amount paid to the subdivider by the purchaser reaches the point where the balance owing is the amount required to release that lot from the mortgage, all moneys thereafter received by the seller from the purchaser must be deemed trust funds, be kept in a separate account, and applied only toward clearance of title from the lien of the mortgage.

If, after investigation, the Secretary of State believes that the subdivider is guilty of fraud or that certain sales methods may constitute a fraud on the public, court proceedings to stop these practices may be instituted. The Secretary of State may also withdraw the acceptance previously granted and may order that all sales and advertising in New York State stop.

The law, as amended, also makes it mandatory that all advertising prior to publication be submitted to the Department for acceptance for filing. Misrepresentations in the sale or lease of subdivided lands constitute a misdemeanor.

The law now also provides that in every contract of sale or lease of subdivided lands, if the purchaser or lessee is not represented by an attorney, he or she has a 10-day cancellation privilege.

Sales may not be made based on the representation that the purchase of the property is a good investment, that the purchaser will or may make money on the transaction, or that the property can be readily resold. Nothing may be promised which is not contained in the written contract and Offering Statement.

19

Construction

Key Terms

Asphalt
British Thermal Unit (BTU)
Blueprints
Casement window
Ceiling joists
Circuit breaker box
Concrete slab foundation
Crawl space
Dormer window
Double-hung window
Drywall
Eaves
Floating slab foundation
Floor joists
Footing
Foundation
Framing
Gambrel roof

Heat pump
Hip roof
Insulation
Jalousie window
Mansard roof
110-volt wiring
Pier and beam foundation
Rafters
Sash window
Sheathing
Siding
Slider window
Solar collector
Solar heating
Studs
220-volt wiring
Urea-formaldehyde foam insulation
Veneer

Overview

A real estate licensee who has a general familiarity with basic construction details is better able to recognize and evaluate the quality of a finished house. Because most houses today are constructed with wood frames, this chapter will concentrate on the elements involved in the construction and design of wood-frame residences.

Wood-Frame Construction

Most houses are built with a basic underlying wood-frame construction covered with an exterior of brick, stone, wood or vinyl siding. Wood-frame houses are preferred in New York State because they are less expensive; they can be built rapidly; they are easy to insulate; and they allow greater flexibility of design.

Throughout this chapter, certain terms will be followed by a bold number in brackets. The number in the brackets refer to the numbered terms in the house diagram in Figure 19.1, which provides an overall picture of how housing components fit into the end product.

Regulation of Residential Construction

New York State has a minimum standards building code, but local municipalities may add to it or impose tighter restrictions. Examples of local codes in certain New York communities: requiring sprinkler systems in all new residential construction, banning the use of PVC for plumbing, licensing plumbers, electricians, carpenters or builders. New York's Board of Fire Underwriters must approve all electrical installations, independent of local approval.

Adaptable Housing for the Disabled

As of September, 1991, federal law requires new multifamily housing developments with four or more units to include easy access for the disabled and the elderly. The law calls for ground-level entrances and ramp or elevator access to basement laundry or recreation rooms. Older buildings need not be modified unless a tenant requests a ramp or widened doorway, is willing to pay for it and will return the premises to original, condition upon moving out.

New apartments and condos covered by the law must conform to certain standards: wide doorways and hallways, light switches and wall thermostats lower than usual and electric outlets higher to facilitate wheelchair access, and bathroom walls reinforced for possible future installation of grab bars. Kitchens and bathrooms must be arranged for wheelchair maneuverability.

New York City. In New York City, Local Law 58 requires handicap access for new and renovated apartments and offices. New York State has a similar law, which specifically excludes the city.

New Home Warranty

New York real estate law requires that the buyer of a new home receive the following warranties: one year's protection against faulty workmanship and defective materials; two years' protection against defective installation of plumbing, electrical, heating, cooling and ventilation systems; and six years of protection against major structural defects (a foundation that settles, a roof that sags, a wall that bows).

Some builders carry warranty insurance, at a cost of several hundred dollars per house.

Warranty law allows builders a reasonable time to make repairs and does not cover construction done by the buyer that is beyond the builder's control.

Figure 19.1
House Diagram

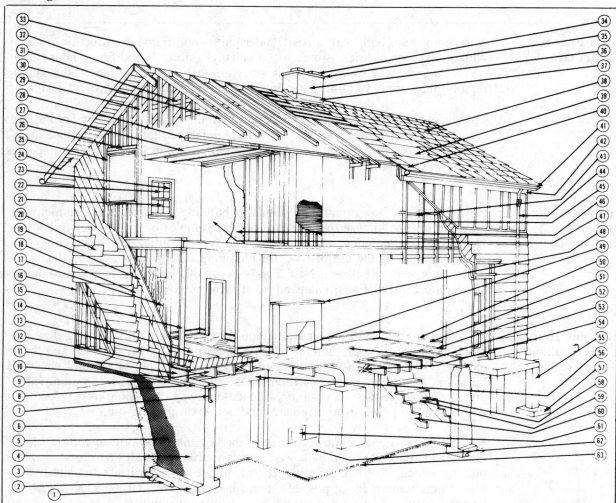

1. FOOTING	22. MUNTIN	43. FIRESTOP
2. FOUNDATION DRAIN TILE	23. WINDOW SASH	44. DOWNSPOUT
3. FELT JOINT COVER	24. EAVE (ROOF PROJECTION)	45. LATHS
4. FOUNDATION WALL	25. WINDOW JAMB TRIM	46. PLASTER BOARD
5. DAMPPROOFING OR	26. DOUBLE WINDOW HEADER	47. PLASTER FINISH
WEATHERPROOFING	27. CEILING JOIST	48. MANTEL
6. BACKFILL	28. DOUBLE PLATE	49. ASH DUMP
7. ANCHOR BOLT	29. STUD	50. BASE TOP MOULDING
8. SILL	30. RAFTERS	51. BASEBOARD
9. TERMITE SHIELD	31. COLLAR BEAM	52. SHOE MOULDING
10. FLOOR JOIST	32. GABLE END OF ROOF	53. FINISH MOULDING
11. BAND OR BOX SILL	33. RIDGE BOARD	54. BRIDGING
12. PLATE	34. CHIMNEY POTS	55. PIER
13. SUBFLOORING	35. CHIMNEY CAP	56. GIRDER
14. BUILDING PAPER	36. CHIMNEY	57. FOOTING
15. WALL STUD	37. CHIMNEY FLASHING	58. RISER
16. DOUBLE CORNER STUD	38. ROOFING SHINGLES	59. TREAD
17. INSULATION	39. ROOFING FELTS	60. STRINGER
18. BUILDING PAPER	40. ROOF SHEATHING	61. CLEANOUT DOOR
19. WALL SHEATHING	41. EVE TROUGH OR GUTTER	62. CONCRETE BASEMENT FLOOR
20. SIDING	42. FRIEZE BOARD	63. GRAVEL FILL
21. MULLION		

Notice of problems must be given the builder within 30 days after expiration of the warranty. Lawsuits must be filed within four years for the one-year and two-year warranties, and within seven years for the six-year warranty. If the home is sold within the warranty period, the new owner is covered as the original owner was.

Architectural Styles

Although details of construction are rigidly specified by building codes, the architectural styles of houses may vary greatly. Some popular styles include colonial, Georgian, ranch, Cape Cod, contemporary, split-level, Dutch colonial, French provincial and Spanish. Examples of several typical architectural styles are shown in Figures 19.2 and 19.3

Plans and Specifications

Working drawings called plans or **blueprints** show the construction details of the building, while specifications are written statements that establish the quality of the materials and workmanship required.

The following specialists may be involved in residential construction:

1. A mechanical engineer, who provides the heating, air-conditioning, septic and plumbing plans and specifications;
2. A structural engineer, who ensures that the foundation will support the structure and is responsible for specifying the amount of steel required to reinforce the foundation and the type and mix of concrete to be used; and
3. A soil engineer, who may assist in determining the stability of the land on which the foundation will be built and whose investigation, coupled with the structural engineer's knowledge, will determine details of the foundation.

An owner may engage an architect to design a house and prepare plans and specifications for its construction. Professional architects are recognized as members of the American Institute of Architects (AIA). The architect's services may include negotiating with the builder and inspecting the progress of the construction as well as preparing plans and specifications. In New York, plans must be signed by a licensed architect or engineer.

Foundations

The term **foundation** includes the footings, foundation walls, column, pilasters, slab and all other parts that provide support for the house and transmit the load of the superstructure to the underlying earth. Foundations are constructed of cut stone, stone and brick, concrete block, poured concrete and recently, specially treated wood. Poured concrete and concrete block are the most common foundation material because of their strength and resistance to moisture. The two major types of foundations are **concrete slab** and **pier and beam.**

Concrete slab. *A concrete slab foundation is composed of a concrete slab supported around the perimeter and in the center by concrete beams sunk into the earth.* It is made of poured concrete reinforced with steel rods. The foundation slab rests directly on the earth, with only a waterproofing membrane between the concrete and the ground. Foundations formed by a single pouring of concrete are called *monolithic*, while those in which the footings and the slab are poured separately are referred to as **floating.**

Pier and beam. In a pier and beam foundation, shown in Figure 19.4, the foundation slab rests on a series of isolated columns, called piers, that extend above

Figure 19.2
Architectural Styles

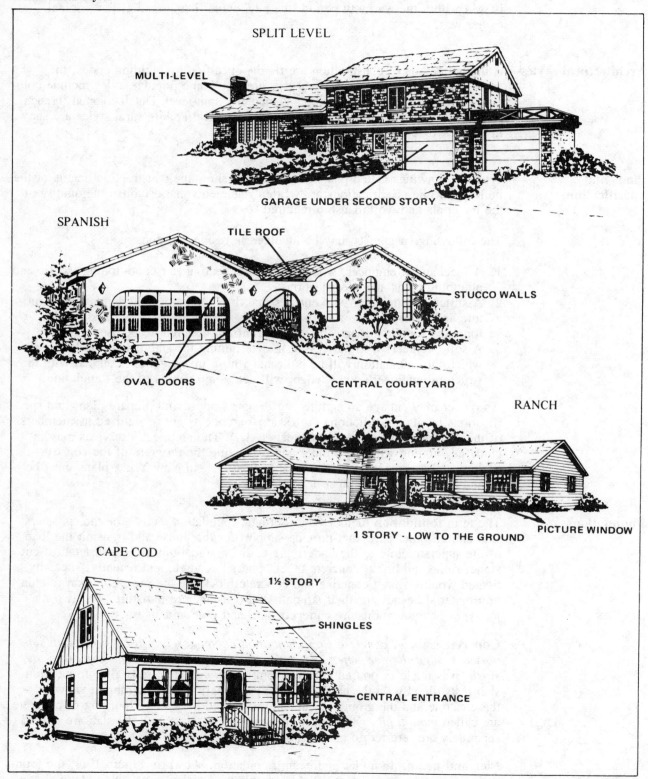

**Figure 19.3
Architectural Styles**

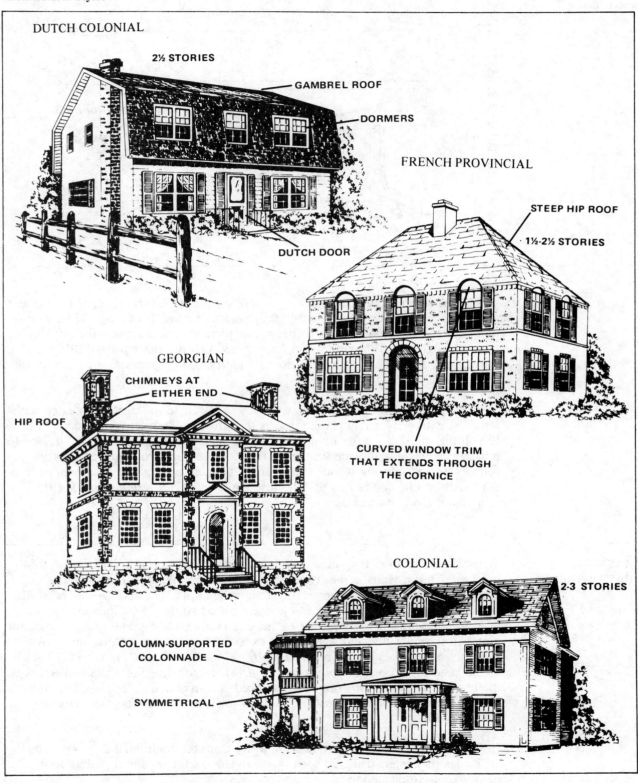

**Figure 19.4
Pier and Beam
Foundation**

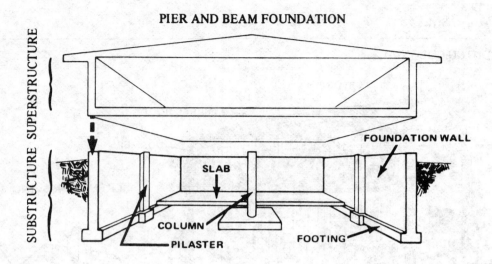

PIER AND BEAM FOUNDATION

ground level. The space between the ground and the foundations is called the **crawl space.** Each support of a pier and beam foundation consists of a *pier* **[55]**, or column, resting on a **footing [1]**, or base. The pier, in turn, supports the *sill* **[8]**, which is attached to the pier by an *anchor bolt* **[7]**. the **floor joists [10]** that provide the major support for the flooring are placed perpendicular to and on top of the sills.

Termite protection. In some areas of New York State the earth is infested with termites, extremely active antlike insects that are very destructive to wood. Prior to pouring the slab for the foundation, the ground should be chemically treated to poison termites and thus prevent them from coming up through or around the foundation and into the wooden structure. Chemical or pressure treatment of lumber used for sills and beams and the installation of *metal termite shields* **[9]** will also provide protection.

Exterior Construction

Walls and Framing

When the foundation is in place the exterior walls are erected. The first step in erecting exterior walls is the **framing.** The skeleton members of a building to which the interior and exterior walls are attached are called its *frame*. The walls of a frame are formed by vertical members called **studs [15].** Studs are spaced at even intervals and are attached to the sill. Many building codes require that for a one-story house the stud spacing not exceed 24 inches on centers. For a two-story house the spacing may not exceed 16 inches. Studs rest on *plates* **[12]**, which are secured to and rest on *foundation wall* **[4].** In constructing walls and floors the builder will install *firestops* **[43]** as needed or required. These are boards or blocks nailed horizontally between studs or joists to stop drafts and retard the spread of fire.

In framing, many builders are moving away from the traditional 2 × 4s placed 16 inches on center, using 2 × 6s instead. This facilitates the installation of more extensive insulation.

Figure 19.5
Frame Construction

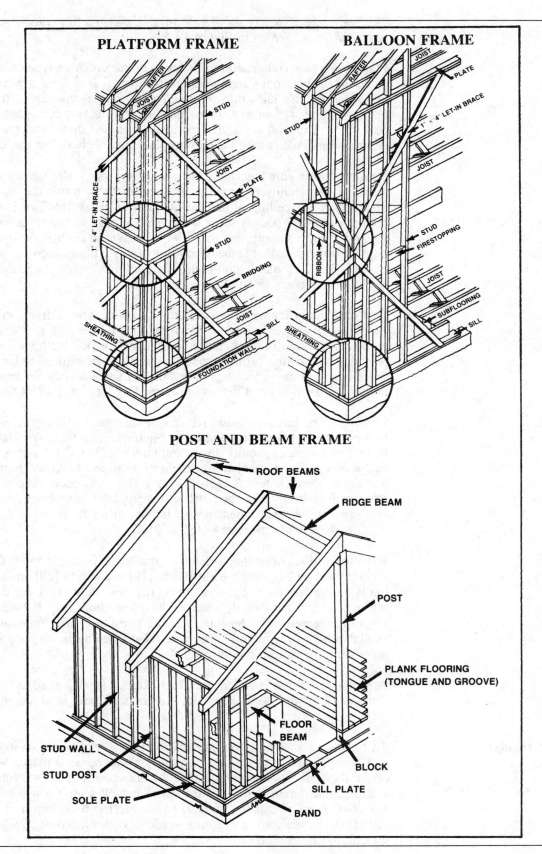

PLATFORM FRAME

BALLOON FRAME

POST AND BEAM FRAME

There are three basic types of wood-frame construction: *platform, balloon* and *post and beam*, shown in Figure 19.5.

Platform-frame construction. Today the most common type of wall-framing construction for both one- and two-story residential structures is *platform framing construction*, also known as *western frame construction*. In platform construction only one floor is built at a time, and each floor serves as a platform for the next story. The wall studs are first attached to the upper and lower plates and the entire assemblage is then raised into place and anchored to the sill.

Balloon-frame construction. The second type of wall framing is *balloon* construction, which differs from the platform method in that the studs extend continuously to the ceiling of the second floor. The second-floor joists rest on *ledger boards or ribbon boards* set into the interior edge of the studs. The balloon method gives a smooth, unbroken wall surface on each floor level, thus alleviating the unevenness that sometimes results from settling when the platform method is used. The balloon method is usually employed when the exterior finish will be brick, stone veneer or stucco.

Post and beam frame construction. The third type of frame construction is *post and beam frame construction*. With this method the ceiling planks are supported on beams that rest on posts placed on intervals inside the house. Because the posts provide some of the ceiling support, rooms can be built with larger spans of space between the supporting side walls. In some houses the beams are left exposed and the posts and beams are stained to serve as part of the decor.

Lumber. The lumber used in residential construction is graded according to moisture content and structural quality as established by the 1970 National Grade Rule. Grading rules require dimension lumber (2″ × 4″, 2″, 2″ × 6″) that is classified as *dry* to have a moisture content of 19 percent or less. Lumber that has a higher moisture content is classified as *green*. All species and grades are assigned stress ratings to indicate their strength when used in spanning distances between two supports. Actual dimensions of lumber differ from nominal measurements. A 2″ × 4″ actually measures 1½″ × 3½″.

Exterior walls. After the skeleton of the house is constructed, the exterior wall surface must be built and the **sheathing [19]** and **siding [20]** applied. The sheathing is nailed directly to the wall studs **[15]** to form the base for the siding. Sheathing is generally hardboard, insulated board or chipboard. If the house is to have a masonry veneer, the sheathing may be gypsum board. Fabricated sheathings are available both in strip and sheet material. Sheathing is wrapped in tar paper or more recently in a plastic material.

After the sheathing is added, the final exterior layer, called *siding*, is applied. This may be vinyl, asphalt, wood, aluminum, stone, brick or other material.

Insulation

To ensure adequate protection, **insulation [17]** should be placed in the exterior walls and upper floor ceilings. *Band insulation* of fiberglass is placed with a sill sealer above the foundation walls. The New York code requires varying amounts of insulation in different regions of the state, as well as storm windows and doors. For conversion of existing units to gas or electric heat, cap insulation (under the attic floor) is required, and storm windows or insulated glass where single-glazing has been used.

Commonly used insulation materials are rock wool, fiberglass and cellulose. Combinations of material such as fiberglass wrapped in aluminum foil or rock wool formed into batt sections that can be placed between the studs are available. Proper insulation will contribute to the efficiency of both heating and air-conditioning systems.

Urea-formaldehyde foam insulation (UFFI) has been blamed for respiratory problems, nausea and flulike illnesses. It was used in some new homes and pumped into the walls of older homes during the 1970s. Determining if it is in place can sometimes be difficult. Older homes may be insulated with undesirable *asbestos* which is wrapped around basement heat runs or water pipes.

Window and Door Units

After the foundation has been completed and the exterior walls constructed, the next step is the construction of exterior window and door units. Windows and doors come in many styles and materials. Windows may either be side-hinged or vertical hinges **(casement)** or slide up and down **(sash)**. Basic window styles include the following:

1. **Single-hung window:** A sash window of which only one sash, usually the bottom one, is movable;
2. **Double-hung window:** A sash window with two vertically sliding sashes; both single- and double-hung window sashes are held in place after movement by friction of the sash (frame) as controlled by springs or weights;
3. **Slider window:** A sash window that opens by moving horizontally;
4. **Casement window:** A window that has a sash hinged like a door and opens or closes by the action of a gear complex; and
5. **Jalousie window:** A window formed by horizontal slats of glass that open or close horizontally by the action of a gear complex.

The materials most commonly found in window frames are wood, steel and aluminum. The quality of a window depends on its construction, additional security and insulating factors. State code requires either double-glazing (two panes of sealed glass with insulating airspace between) or storm windows.

The thickness of an interior door is usually 1⅜ inches; an exterior door is usually 1¾ inches. The majority of doors are made of mahogany, birch, walnut or oak. Glass doors, screen doors with aluminum or steel frames, and insulated metal doors are primarily exterior doors used for patios, porches or garden areas. Energy considerations dictate triple-glazing for many windows in recent years.

Roof Framing and Coverings

The construction of the skeleton framing for the roofing material is the next step in building a house. Residential roofs are made in several styles including gabled, shed, salt box and flat. Roof construction includes the *rafters* [30], *sheathing* [39], and *exterior trimming* [42]. Skeleton framings are classified as either conventional or truss (*see* Figures 19.6 and 19.7).

Joist and rafter roof framing. A joist and rafter roof consists of *rafters* [30]), *collar beams* [31], *ceiling joists* [27] and *ridge board* [33]. **Rafters** are the sloping timbers that support the weight of the roof and establish the roof's pitch, or slant. The collar beams give rigidity to the rafters, and the ridge board aligns and receives the rafters.

Figure 19.6
Roof Construction

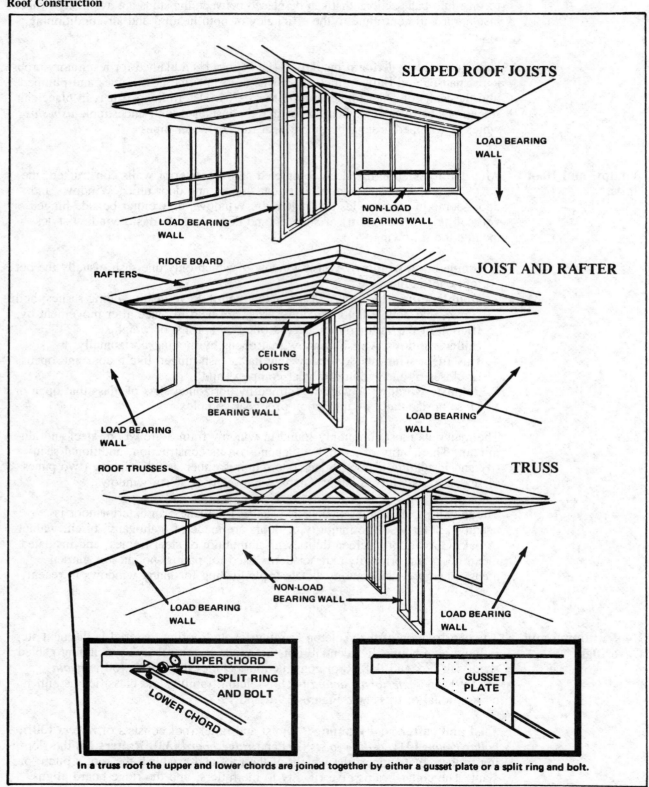

SLOPED ROOF JOISTS

LOAD BEARING WALL

NON-LOAD BEARING WALL

LOAD BEARING WALL

JOIST AND RAFTER

RIDGE BOARD

RAFTERS

CEILING JOISTS

CENTRAL LOAD BEARING WALL

LOAD BEARING WALL

LOAD BEARING WALL

TRUSS

ROOF TRUSSES

NON-LOAD BEARING WALL

LOAD BEARING WALL

LOAD BEARING WALL

UPPER CHORD

SPLIT RING AND BOLT

LOWER CHORD

GUSSET PLATE

In a truss roof the upper and lower chords are joined together by either a gusset plate or a split ring and bolt.

**Figure 19.7
Roof Styles**

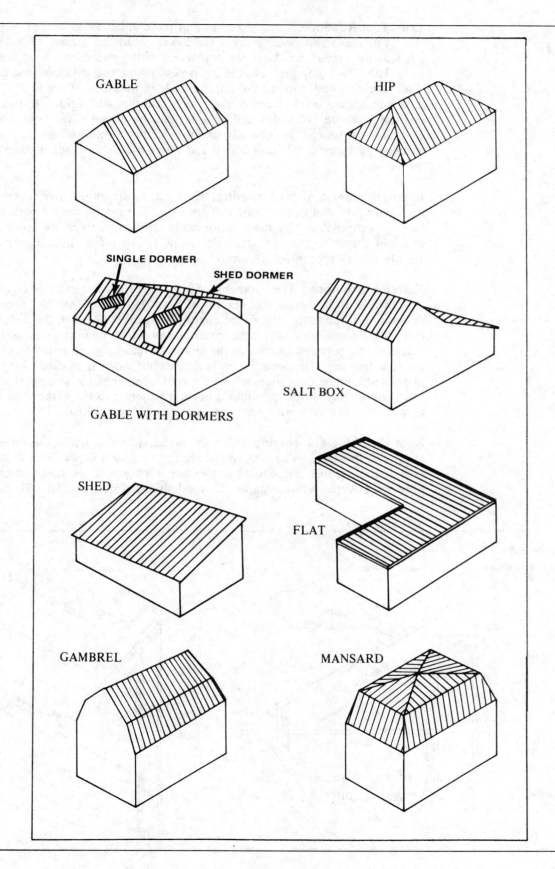

GABLE

HIP

SINGLE DORMER

SHED DORMER

GABLE WITH DORMERS

SALT BOX

SHED

FLAT

GAMBREL

MANSARD

Truss roof framing. A *truss* roof has four parts. It has *lower chords, upper chords,* "W" *diagonals* and *gusset plates.* The lower chords are similar to ceiling joists, whereas the upper chords are the equivalent of the rafters in a joist and rafter roof. The "W" diagonals are the equivalent of the collar beams and are called "W" because they support the rafter chords in the form of the letter "W". The gusset plates are solid pieces of metal or wood that add rigidity to the roof. All integral parts are assembled and held in place by gusset plates, bolt connections or nails. A truss roof is generally prefabricated at a mill and set in place in sections by a crane, whereas a joist and rafter roof is assembled piece by piece on the site.

Exposed rafter and roof framing. *Exposed,* or *sloping, rafter* roofs are often used with post and beam frame construction. The rafters are supported by central support posts and by the exterior walls. However, there are no ceiling joists or lower chords to provide additional support. The rafters in this type of roof are often left exposed for decorative purposes.

Exterior trimming. The overhang of a pitched roof that extends beyond the exterior walls of the house is called the **eaves [41],** or *cornice.* The cornice is composed of the soffit, the frieze board, the facia board, and the extended rafters. The *frieze board* **[42]** is the exterior wood trim board used to finish the exterior wall between the top of the siding or masonry and eave, or overhang, of the roof framing. The *facia board* is an exterior wood trim used along the line of the butt end of the rafters where the roof overhangs the structural walls. The overhang of the cornice provides a decorative touch to the exterior of a house as well as some protection from sun and rain (Figure 19.8).

Roof sheathing and roofing. With the skeleton roof in place, the rafters are covered with sheathing. The type of sheathing to be used depends on the choice of outside roofing material. Most shingles are composed of **asphalt** and are laid over plywood covered with tar paper. If wood shingles are used, spaced sheathing of

**Figure 19.8
Eave or Cornice**

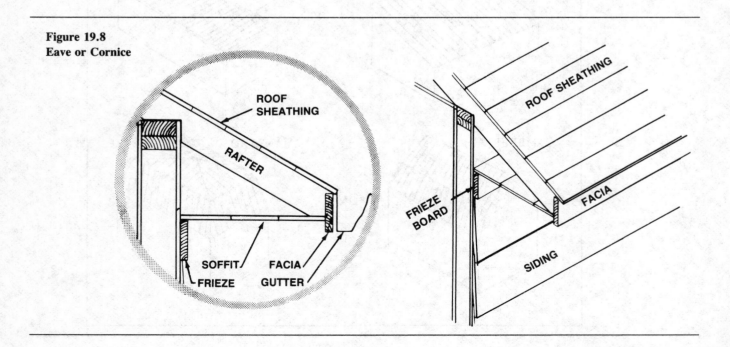

1″ × 4″ boards may be used to provide airspace to allow the shingles to dry after rain. Other materials, including fiberglass, may also be used for roofing.

Interior Construction

Walls and Finishing

Interior walls are the partitioning dividers for individual rooms and are usually covered with *plasterboard* [46], although *lath* [45] and *plaster* [47] may be used. The terms **drywall** and *wallboard* are synonymous with plasterboard. Plasterboard is finished by a process known as *taping and floating*. Taping covers the joints between the sheets of plasterboard. Floating is the smoothing out of the walls by the application of a plaster texture over the joints and rough edges where nails attach the plasterboard to the wall studs. Texturing may be used in some areas as a final coating applied with a roller onto the plasterboard prior to painting, wood paneling or wallpapering.

The final features added to a home include: (1) *floor covering*, (2) *trim*, (3) *cabinet work* and (4) *wall finishings* of paint, wallpaper or paneling. Floor coverings of vinyl, asphalt tile, wood (either in strips of blocks), carpet, brick, stone or terrazzo tile are applied over the wood or concrete subflooring. Trim masks the joints between the walls and ceiling and gives a finished decorator touch to the room. Cabinet work in the home may be either built in on the job or prefabricated in the mill.

Plumbing

Plumbing must be installed subject to strict inspections and in accordance with local building codes that dictate the materials to be used and the method of installation. Sewer pipes are of cast iron, concrete or plastic, while water pipes are of copper, plastic or galvanized iron. Recently, plastic has been used more frequently for waste lines because it eliminates piping joints in the foundation slab. Domestic hot water may be supplied directly from a coil in the heating system or by a separate hot-water heater. If a separate unit is used, the water is heated by electricity, gas or oil. Well water supplies may require water softeners.

Lead-tin solder, used widely for copper plumbing, has been under scrutiny by the Environmental Protection Agency, which limits lead content to 8 percent and recommends the use of tin-antimony solder instead.

Bathtubs, toilets and sinks are made of cast iron or pressed steel casted with enamel, plastic or artificial marble. Fiberglass is gaining in popularity.

Heating and Air-Conditioning

Warm-air heating systems and hot-water baseboards are the most common heating systems in use today. Steam heat is found in some older homes. In recent years some areas of northern New York have seen increasing dependence on wood as a fuel. A forced warm-air system consists of a furnace, warm-air distributing ducts and ducts for the return of cool air. Each furnace has a capacity rated in **British Thermal Units (BTUs).** The number of BTUs given represents the furnace's heat output from either gas, oil or electric firing. A heating and cooling engineer can determine the cubic area of the building, as well as its construction, insulation, and window and door sizes, and from this data compute the furnace capacity required to provide heat for the building in the coldest possible weather.

All gas pipes for heating and cooking are made of black iron. Gas pipes are installed in the walls or run overhead in the attic where adequate ventilation is possible. They are never placed in the slab.

Air-conditioning units are rated either in BTUs or in tons. Twelve thousand BTUs are the equivalent of a one-ton capacity. An engineer can determine the measurements and problems inherent in the construction and layout of the space, and from this information specify the cooling capacity required to adequately service the space or building.

Combination heating-cooling systems are common in new homes. The most common is the conventional warm-air heating system with a cooling unit attached.

Solar heating. The increased demand for fossil fuels in recent years has forced builders to look for new sources of energy. One of the most promising sources of heat for residential buildings is *solar energy.* Most **solar heating** units suitable for residential use operate by gathering the heat from the sun's rays with one or more **solar collectors.** Water or air is forced through a series of pipes in the solar collector to be heated by the sun's rays. The hot air or water is then stored in a heavily insulated storage tank until it is needed to heat the house.

More immediately practical in the New York State area is *passive solar* heating. Without any additional special equipment, a house may be built or remodeled to take advantage of the sun's rays. Large areas of glass on a southern exposure and few windows on the north side of a building are typical of passive solar arrangements. Substantial savings in fuel may be obtained.

Heat pumps, which utilize heat from outside air in a form of reverse air-conditioning, are often used in conjunction with backup heating units of more conventional design. Where electricity is expensive, use of a heat pump may bring down costs. The heat pump also serves in summer for air-conditioning. Geothermal systems utilize the constant temperature underground to aid in heating and cooling. At depths of 4-6 feet and greater, the earth maintains about the same temperature year-round—approximately 52°F in New York State—no matter what the climatic conditions are above the surface.

Electrical Services

Electrical services from the power company is brought into the home through the transformer and the meter into a **circuit-breaker box** or fuse box. The circuit-breaker box is the distribution panel for the many electrical circuits in the house. In case of a power overload the heat generated by the additional flow of electrical power will cause the circuit breaker to open at the breaker box, thus reducing the possibility of electrical fires. It is the responsibility of the architect or the builder to adhere to local building codes that regulate electrical wiring. All electrical installations are inspected by the New York Board of Fire Underwriters.

Residential wiring circuits are rated by the voltage they are designed to carry. In the past, most residences were wired only for **110-volt** capacity. Today because of the many built-in appliances in use, **220-volt** service is generally necessary. New York State standards require at least 100-ampere service and, for new home construction, a 110-volt smoke detector and a *ground fault interrupter* on each water hazard circuit (kitchen, baths, exterior outlets). The ground fault interrupter is a supersensitive form of circuit breaker.

A typical schedule for new home construction is shown in Table 19.1.

**Table 19.1
New Home Construction
Schedule**

Preliminary Work: Site engineering, evaluation, preliminary plan, environmental review, etc., county and local agency reviews, signatures and filing of plan. Obtain letter of credit. Site development.

Construction Schedule:

Building permit	Rough electrical
Surveyor stakes out lot and house.	Electrical inspection—rough wiring
Excavator digs basement.	Prewire telephone, cable TV and security system
Plumber installs sanitary sewer/water service.	Insulation
Building inspector inspects sewer.	Drywall: hanging and finishing
Excavator backfills sewer/water trench.	Mason pours concrete floors.
Mason forms the footings and pours shallow footing concrete.	Interior trim
	Interior painting
Mason lays up concrete block walls.	Ceramic tile walls/floors
Concrete block wall dampproofing	Kitchen cabinets/vanities
Backfill basement walls	Finish flooring—hardwood/vinyl
Excavator digs trench footings.	Finish plumbing
Mason pours trench footing concrete.	Finishing heating
Box out driveway and spread gravel.	Finish electrical
Framer sets steel beams and columns.	Electrical inspection—final
Framer frames house.	Mirror/shower doors
Mason builds fireplace.	Storms and screens
Mason lays up exterior brick or stone.	Blacktop
Roofing	Landscaping
Siding	Appliances
Exterior painting/staining	Cleanup
Gutters	Certificate of occupancy inspection
Garage door	Surveyor prepares instrument survey "as built."
Rough plumbing	Building department issues Certificate of Occupancy.
Rough heating	
Building inspector reviews framing, plumbing and heating.	Final inspection and closing

Recent Developments

Recent developments in foundation materials include superplasticizers and light-weight aggregates added to concrete mixtures. In colder areas where concrete is not available during winter, some builders use pressure-treated wood foundations, which may even have some value in radon abatement.

For framing, new cores of particleboard with plywood surfaces have some advantages over solid wood. Panelized walls are available with exterior and interior surface material filled with foam insulation. Various sheathing materials, construction adhesives and laminated veneer lumber, polybutylene piping and high-efficiency heating systems are all gaining wider acceptance.

Looking Over an Older Home

In general, houses built after World War II are more or less modern with copper plumbing, adequate electric service and compact furnaces. Houses built before the 1940s require more stringent inspection. The buyer of such a house, where no inspection by lender, FHA or VA will be involved, may want to retain a building inspection engineer or construction engineer for advice before a purchase contract becomes firm.

Exterior condition. Well-fitting older wood storms and screens can be even more efficient than modern self-storing ones. Asphalt roofs can be expected to last 15 or 20 years. Binoculars can sometimes be useful in examining a roof for missing shingles, patched spots or a dried-up, crinkled condition. Moss growing on a roof, particularly on the north side, may indicate a moisture problem within. In mid-winter a roof clear of snow often means that heat is being lost because of inadequate insulation. Downspouts should be firmly attached; gutters with holes will have to be replaced.

Electric service. Ideally each room should have an outlet on each wall and one every 12 feet. A tangle of extension cords signals potential problems. A circuit-breaker box in the basement indicates that the system has been modernized. An old fuse system, however, can be satisfactory if enough circuits were carefully installed.

Plumbing. Old galvanized pipes suffer from corrosion and deposits can eventually clog them enough to impede the flow of water. The classic test for water pressure is to open all taps in an upstairs bathroom and then flush the toilet to see if the flow from the faucets diminishes. Hot-water lines corrode most quickly; a quick check of the water heater should show whether copper pipes have been installed. Particularly vulnerable are patch jobs, where copper has been joined to galvanized pipe to solve a particular emergency. Where kitchen and bath have been modernized, it is likely that copper plumbing was used.

Basement. In much of New York State a completely dry basement is an unattainable goal. A *sump pump,* installed in a corner of the basement to pump accumulated water up into a sewer, does not necessarily signal trouble; sump pumps are routinely required by many local building codes. Inspecting an older home, one may gain some clue from the amount of material (newspapers, storage boxes) kept directly on the basement floor. Rust on the bottom of the furnace or the hot-water heater or a newly painted stripe across the bottom might indicate an earlier flood, which might have been a one-time occurrence.

Insulation. Many older homes show plugged holes in the attic stair risers, where insulation has been blown in. Often the owner of an older home does not know how much insulation has been installed. Inspection under the attic floor may involve prying up a floorboard; sidewalls can sometimes be accessed by removing a switchplate. Sellers are required by New York State law to make past heating bills available to prospective purchasers and to furnish statements on insulation.

Home-Improvement Law

New York State requires that the sale of home-improvement goods and services costing more than $500 to homeowners, co-op owners or tenants conform to certain regulations.

A copy of a written, plain-English contract must be given to the customer before any work is done. It must contain the contractor's name, address and telephone number; approximate start and completion dates; specifics of the work and materials (brands, model numbers, price); and a notice that the customer has an unconditional right to cancel the contract in writing within three days after it is signed.

Contractors are required to put into a trust (escrow) account in a New York State bank any contract payments by a customer, to be withdrawn only under a reasonable payment schedule agreed to by contractor and customer, or upon substantial completion of the job. If the customer violates the contract, funds may be withdrawn only to the amount of the contractor's reasonable costs. As an alternative to the escrow account the contractor may deliver to the customer, within 10 days of receiving funds, a bond guaranteeing that the customer's money will be properly used or returned.

The customer may sue for damages, legal fees and a $500 penalty in case of fraudulent written statements. The attorney general may also institute lawsuits. VIolation of the law is also subject to $100 in civil fines, or $250 where the violation is related to protection of the customer's payments.

Summary

State and local building codes set standards for health and safety in construction. Starting in September 1991, federal law requires access for the disabled in new multifamily buildings containing four or more units. New York City and New York State have similar adaptation requirements, for both apartments and offices.

Buyers of new homes in New York State receive a one-year warranty on materials and workmanship; a two-year warranty on installation of heating, cooling, ventilation, plumbing and electrical systems; and a six-year warranty on structural defects.

Working drawings and supplemental written specifications are prepared to establish the quality of materials and workmanship needed to produce the desired residence and conform to local building codes. An architect may be employed to design the building, prepare plans and specifications and supervise construction as it progresses.

Foundations include footings, foundation walls and slabs. The two major types of foundations are *concrete slab* and *pier and beam*.

Wood-frame construction is the type most frequently used in building single-family houses. The three basic types of exterior wall framing are *platform, balloon*, and *post and beam*. Multilevel balloon construction differs from the platform method in that the studs extend continuously to the ceiling of the second floor, while with the platform method only one floor is built at a time. Post and beam construction utilizes interior posts to support the roof.

Windows may be *sash windows,* which are single-hung, double-hung or of the slider type; *casement windows,* which are side-hinged or vertical hinges; or *jalousie windows,* which are formed of horizontal slats of glass. Door styles include *panel, slab,* and *hollow* or *solid core.*

Skeleton roof framing may be either *joist and rafter, exposed rafter or truss*. The parts of the joist and rafter roof are the joists, rafters, collar beams and ridge. The parts of the truss roof are the lower and upper chords, the "W" diagonals and the gusset plates. The skeleton roof rafters or upper chords are covered with sheathing, generally plywood.

Interior walls are generally covered with plasterboard and finished with paint or wallpaper. Final interior features include wall finishings, trim, floor covering and cabinet work. Plumbing, heating, air-conditioning and electrical wiring require careful installation to adhere to building codes.

Brokers must be alert to the possible presence of asbestos, radon or urea-formaldehyde foam insulation in residential property.

An older home in good condition should have a tight roof with no missing or patched shingles, a complete set of storm windows and screens, and firmly attached gutters and downspouts, without holes. Proper electric systems provide better than 100-amp service, an adequate number of circuits, 220 as well as 110-volt service and outlets on each wall or every 12 feet. Plumbing should be all copper. Basements should be relatively dry; adequate insulation should have been installed at least under the attic floor.

Home-improvement contractors must give customers a written contract before work starts where goods or services will exceed a cost of $500. They must keep customers' funds in a separate escrow account, to be drawn on only according to an agreed-on schedule.

Questions

1. Most building codes place emphasis on:
   a. safety.   c. structural strength.
   b. sanitation.   d. all of the above.

2. Which is described as a 1½-story house?
   a. Split-level   c. Colonial
   b. Ranch   d. Cape Cod

3. A gambrel roof is found on what type of house?
   a. Dutch Colonial   c. Georgian
   b. French Provincial   d. Spanish

4. In New York State, building plans must be signed by a:
   a. fire underwriter.
   b. licensed architect or engineer.
   c. site planner.
   d. primary contractor.

5. Which is a type of foundation?
   a. Balloon   c. Floating slab.
   b. Post and beam   d. Chord

6. The components of a pier and beam foundation include:
   a. the footings.   c. the anchor bolts.
   b. the sill or beam.   d. all of the above.

7. Which of the following are installed in a house in horizontal position?
   a. Joists   c. Rafters
   b. Studs   d. Posts

8. Blocks nailed between studs and joists are called:
   a. trusses.   c. bolts.
   b. firestops.   d. sills.

9. In building a frame or wooden skeleton, studs rest on:
   a. plates.   c. joists.
   b. balloons.   d. ridges.

10. Which of the following characteristics is considered when grading lumber?
    a. Age   c. Fragrance
    b. Color   d. Moisture content

11. Sheathing is found on the outside:
    a. walls.   c. foundation.
    b. windows.   d. doors.

12. Cap insulation, which has the greatest payback in lowered fuel bills, is found:
    a. under the attic floor.
    b. on the basement ceiling.
    c. in sidewalls.
    d. just under the roof.

13. Band insulation is placed:
    a. under the attic floor.
    b. above the foundation.
    c. on the basement ceiling.
    d. inside exterior walls.

14. Roof framing constructed on the site, with sloping rafters supported by ceiling joists, is called:
    a. truss.   c. exposed rafter.
    b. joist and rafter. d. platform.

15. A cornice provides some protection against:
    a. fire.   c. rain.
    b. lightning. d. cold.

16. Plasterboard is also known as:
    a. drywall.   c. sheathing.
    b. siding.   d. paneling.

17. Heat from outside air is utilized through a:
    a. reverse conditioner.
    b. passive solar system.
    c. heat pump.
    d. cold air return.

18. Buyers of an older home may want to consult a:
    a. building inspection engineer.
    b. soil engineer.
    c. framer.
    d. firestop specialist.

19. Which of the following signals trouble when found on a roof?
    a. Snow   c. Birds
    b. Moss   d. Asphalt

20. A contractor must give the customer a written contract in advance of any work when home-improvement goods and services will cost more than:
    a. $100.   c. $500.
    b. $250.   d. $750.

21. A new home buyer receives a warranty of six years' protection against:
    a. defective materials.
    b. structural defects.
    c. defective installation of heating systems.
    d. all of the above.

22. The Environmental Protection Agency considers solder materials dangerous when they contain more than 8 percent of:
    a. copper.   c. lead.
    b. tin.   d. antimony.

23. Handicap access is required in construction or renovation of apartments in buildings containing at least how many living units?
    a. Two   c. Six
    b. Four   d. Eight

24. Wheelchair adaptation includes changes in the usual placement of:
    a. door handles.   c. drapery pulls.
    b. light switches.   d. All of the above

25. Federal law as of September 1991, requires a landlord to modify an older building at the request of a handicapped tenant who:
    a. qualifies for a handicap parking certificate.
    b. produces a doctor's letter.
    c. agrees to a rent increase.
    d. is willing to pay for the modifications.

20

Condominiums and Cooperatives

Key Terms

Black book
Board of directors
Board of managers
Bylaws
Common elements
Covenants, conditions and restrictions (CC&Rs)
Conversions
Declaration
Disclosure statement
Eviction plan
Homeowners' association

Letter of intent
Noneviction plan
Proprietary lease
Prospectus
Public offering
Red herring
Reserves
Sponsor
Time-sharing
Town house

Overview

The advantages of home ownership and the amenities of apartment living may be combined through relatively new forms of ownership: condominiums and cooperatives. This chapter will examine these forms as well as planned unit developments, town houses and time-sharing.

Growth of Condominiums and Cooperatives

Condominium and *cooperative* ownership of housing has been on the rise in the second half of the twentieth century. Together with town houses and *planned unit developments (PUDs),* condos and co-ops offer the emotional, financial and tax advantages of home owning, combined with various forms of apartment living.

As inflation and interest rates escalate, the *economies* of such housing become more attractive. As opposed to traditional single-family homes, condos and co-ops offer more efficient use of ever-scarcer building land, *lower costs* for lot development, less outlay for construction per living unit and some *savings* in maintenance and heating bills.

Contributing to the growth of condos and co-ops are changes in population patterns with increasing numbers of single homeowners, one-parent families and senior citizens. To such groups, community living offers *security* and *sociability,* ease of *maintenance* and sometimes the opportunity for a share in expensive *recreational facilities* like swimming pools.

In addition, landlords plagued by rent control or by rising costs have turned to conversion of existing apartment buildings as a profitable method of disposing of property.

Looking at a shared housing complex will give no clue as to whether it is a condominium, cooperative or (in some cases) PUD. The buildings themselves may be high-rises, town houses, patio homes, garden apartments or even single detached houses. The differences arise from the legal forms of ownership.

Condominium Ownership

The buyer of a condominium receives a *deed* conveying *fee simple ownership* of two things: the living unit and an undivided interest in the **common elements** (*see* Figure 20.1). Chief among the common elements are the land and the exteriors of the buildings. Also common property are hallways, basements, elevators, stairwells, driveways, private roads, sidewalks, lawns, landscaping and recreational facilities.

In many respects a condominium owner may be regarded in the same light as the owner of a single detached house. Title may be held in severalty, by the entirety, as joint tenants or tenants in common. The unit receives an individual tax account number and tax bill and may be mortgaged as a house would be. The owners place a separate insurance policy on the living space. Income tax advantages are identical to those on single homes. The owners are free to sell the property, lease it, give it away or leave it to heirs. Each unit is a financial entity and if an adjoining unit is foreclosed, no obligation is incurred by the other owners.

Owners are, however, bound by the bylaws of a **homeowners' association** to which all belong. Monthly fees are levied for the maintenance, insurance and management of common elements. If unpaid, these *common charges* become a lien against the individual unit and may even be enforced by foreclosure. The bylaws also

**Figure 20.1
Condominium
Ownership**

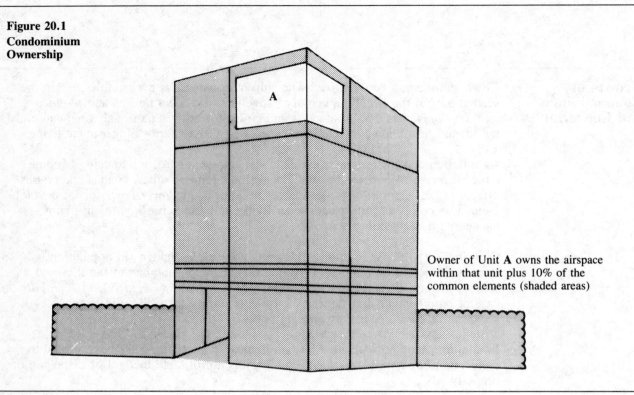

Owner of Unit **A** owns the airspace
within that unit plus 10% of the
common elements (shaded areas)

set up **covenants, conditions and restrictions (CC&Rs),** which, for example,
may prohibit the display of For Sale signs or the painting of a front door bright
red.

A condominium is usually managed by an elected **board of managers.** With
more than 25 units, a board often hires professional management.

Several national organizations offer support, education and publications to residents, board members and professional managers of condominiums and cooperatives. Seminars in maintenance, accounting, law, association operations and
management practices, for example, are offered by the Community Associations
Institute, 1423 Powhatan Street, Suite 7, Alexandria, VA 22314. The organization publishes a regular newsletter and offers a designation in professional management. It has local branches within New York that hold regular meetings.

**Selling
Condominiums**

While the selling of new condominiums requires the broker to register with the
attorney general's office, resale is among the activities covered by a broker's or
salesperson's license. The broker who deals in such properties must be concerned
with some items that do not apply to the marketing of single homes. The buyer
of a condominium must receive detailed statements about the property, should read
the CC&Rs and must be alerted to any unpaid common charges against the unit.
Analysis of the health of a project also should include an examination of the
reserves, those funds set aside to accumulate for large expenses like new roofs
or heating units. The sale of a condominium is arranged on a special form of
contract.

Although it is most widely used for residential property, condominium ownership is growing for professional buildings, office buildings and even shopping malls.

Cooperative Ownership

Cooperative ownership is common in the New York City metropolitan area. In the city, condominium organization is generally used only for the more expensive developments. Under the usual *cooperative* arrangement, title to land and building is held by a *corporation*. Each purchaser of an apartment in the building receives stock in the corporation. The purchaser then becomes a stockholder of the corporation and, *by virtue of that stock ownership receives a* **proprietary lease** to his or her apartment.

The cooperative building's real estate taxes are assessed against the corporation as owner. The mortgage is signed by the corporation, creating one lien on the entire parcel of real estate. Taxes, mortgage interest and principal, and operating and maintenance expenses on the property are shared by the tenant-shareholders in the form of monthly *maintenance charges*.

Thus even though the cooperative tenant-owners do not actually own an interest in real estate (they own stock, which is *personal property*), for all practical purposes they control the property through their stock ownership and their voice in the management of the corporation. For example, the bylaws of the corporation generally provide that each prospective purchaser of an apartment lease must be approved by a **board of directors.**

One disadvantage of cooperative ownership became particularly evident during the Great Depression and must still be considered. This is the possibility that if enough owner-occupants became financially unable to make prompt payment of their monthly assessments, the corporation might be forced to allow mortgage and tax payments to go unpaid. Through such defaults the entire property could be ordered sold by court order in a foreclosure suit. Such a sale might destroy the interests of all occupant-shareholders, even those who paid their assessments. Accumulation of a substantial reserve fund offers some protection to the cooperative as a whole.

The tenant-owner, who does not have fee simple ownership, may not place a regular mortgage against the unit. Financing is usually arranged at a slightly higher interest rate and with perhaps a shorter term than with regular mortgages. Boards of directors, sensitive to the financial dependence of one tenant on the others, sometimes set down payment requirements more stringent than those asked by lending institutions. In some cases they may even refuse prospective tenants unless the purchase is to be made for all cash. Some boards also have the right of first refusal, allowing the corporation a chance to buy back an apartment by meeting any bona fide offer from a prospective buyer.

As with a condominium, the owner of a cooperative has all the income tax advantages that accrue to the owner of a single home. That portion of maintenance charges attributable to property taxes and mortgage interest may be taken as deductions.

Outside the New York metropolitan area, cooperatives are most often found in parts of Chicago, San Francisco, Miami and Buffalo. They are being used for conversion of resort property (motels, for example) in parts of Long Island.

Cooperative living tends to develop somewhat differently than condominium occupancy. Long-term stability of tenants is common. The corporation's right to accept or reject any new owner is aimed at safeguarding present owners who would share financial responsibility for a defaulting neighbor but it is often used to maintain a particular level of occupancy. Thus, not long after Watergate, residents of a New York City cooperative rejected a proposed sale to Richard Nixon on the grounds that they simply did not want him as a neighbor.

Town Houses and PUDs

The term **town house,** as it refers to shared housing, describes a type of ownership rather than an architectural style. Although the organization, similar to a planned unit development, often does take the form of town houses (attached row houses), it also may refer to attached ranch homes or even to small single dwellings in close proximity.

A town-house owner has title to the land beneath the individual unit and owns a share in the common elements, most often in the form of shares in a corporation. Town-house arrangements differ: In some, the unit owner may also own outright a small front yard or back patio; in others the individual roof may be owned. The legal process of development for town houses can differ somewhat from that of condominiums and may sometimes be simpler from the developer's point of view.

Construction and Conversion

Until about 1977 the majority of cooperatives and condominiums were new construction. Since then, particularly in the New York City area, most are **conversions** from rental properties. The sale of any form of shared housing is considered a **public offering** and is under the jurisdiction of the New York attorney general's office. The **sponsor,** the organizer of the proposed project, files a **declaration** with the county clerk that contains a complete description of the proposed land, buildings and individual units. If the proposal is for a condominium, floor plans for each unit are included. Common elements are described and the percentage of ownership for each unit is stated.

Bylaws

Also included in the enabling declaration are the plans for the governing homeowners' association and its **bylaws.** By statute, the bylaws must contain numerous provisions concerning the election, term of office, compensation and powers of the board of managers and officers. Provisions for meetings, quorums, budget, collection of charges and assessments, use of common property, and architectural control are included, along with procedures for the collection of unpaid charges. The developer also submits a list of the covenants, conditions and regulations.

Whether for new construction or a conversion, the developer or sponsor must file a **disclosure statement** with the attorney general's office. The statement includes an architect's or engineer's report, statement of past or projected expenses, prices for each unit and expected amount of tax deductions, management arrangements, description of the corporation (if a cooperative) and master deed and sample unit deed (for a condominium). The declaration is also forwarded with the disclosure statement.

After it has been reviewed by the attorney general's office, the preliminary **prospectus (red herring)** is available for inspection by present tenants. At this point it is subject to modification. When the plan is accepted for filing by the attorney general's office, it is issued as a **black book** to potential buyers.

Conversion Restrictions

If the property is occupied, special regulations safeguarding the rights of tenants are in effect in New York City, Westchester, Nassau and Rockland counties. Under a **noneviction plan,** unless at least 15 percent of present tenants furnish the sponsor with **letters of intent** to purchase their units, the property may not be converted to condominium or cooperative ownership. If the sponsor intends to evict present tenants **(eviction plan)** at the expiration of their leases, the requirement is that at least 51 percent of the tenants must evince their intention to purchase. Depending on which regulations have been adopted by various communities, areas in Westchester, Rockland and Nassau counties may require either 51 percent or 35 percent tenant participation for an eviction plan. Other communities across the state are eligible to adopt the regulations if they choose. Exempt from eviction are disabled persons and those over 62 who have occupied the apartments for at least two years and have income under $50,000 a year. To encourage tenant participation, the sponsor may offer discounts averaging one-third off the list price.

Nonpurchasers may have three-year protection from eviction, and tenants in occupancy have a 90-day exclusive right to purchase and other benefits. In 1983 the state empowered town, city and village governments elsewhere in the state to pass noneviction prohibitions for the elderly and disabled.

If the sponsor elects the noneviction (15 percent) route, all those tenants who do not wish to purchase remain as tenants under whatever rent regulations may be in effect.

The sponsor's inside sales staff, working as employees, do not require any license. In contrast, the broker who sells new condominiums, town houses or cooperatives, as an agent and not as an employee of the sponsor, must file with the Department of Law for a modified form of securities license. Application includes the submission of a work history and a photograph; the license is good for a four-year period and costs $100 for a broker and $25 for associates.

Time-Sharing

A relatively new form of ownership known as **time-sharing** has become popular in resort and vacation areas in recent years, with annual sales topping $1 billion. The buyer of a time-share receives a fraction of a year's ownership of property that might be a condominium, town house, single-family detached home, campground or even a motel. In some cases only right-to-use is purchased rather than fee simple.

Although the concept is most popular in resort areas such as the Caribbean, Colorado, Vermont and Florida, it has been used in Long Island, the Catskills and a few other areas of New York State. The property owner is entitled to some income tax deductions and can exchange, sell or rent the time slot subject only to any restrictions in the prospectus of the organization administering the property. As many as 13, 26 or 52 different owners might share a unit at designated times of the year. Each owner receives a deed entitling use of the property for a specified period each year.

In New York, time-sharing is regulated under Article 23A of the General Business Law (*blue-sky securities statute*) administered by the Department of Law and the Department of State. Sellers must file a public offering statement and buyers have a 10-day rescission period in which to withdraw from a contract. Real estate licenses are required of those handling such sales.

Summary

Condominium and *cooperative* arrangements for homeowning are becoming more frequent due to scarcity of land, the need for economy of construction and operation, and changing lifestyles. Both terms refer to forms of ownership and not to the type of buildings involved.

Condominiums provide *fee simple* ownership of the living unit and an undivided interest in common elements. The owner may mortgage the unit, receives individual tax bills and arranges homeowners' insurance. Owners bear no direct financial liability for adjoining units. Management of common elements is administered by a homeowners' association, which levies monthly fees. Bylaws provide regulations binding upon all owners in the form of *covenants, conditions and restrictions*.

The owner of a *cooperative* apartment receives *shares in a corporation* that owns the entire building, and a *propietary lease* to his or her apartment. Financing is arranged through a single mortgage on the entire property; individual financing comes through personal loans. Each owner shares responsibility for the debts of the corporation. The corporation has the right to reject prospective buyers.

A *town-house development* involves fee simple ownership of the living unit and the land beneath it. All other land and common elements are owned by a homeowners' association in which owners are members.

Plans for construction or conversion or a condominium or cooperative must be filed with the *county recorder* and reviewed by the *attorney general*'s office. In the New York City area at least 15 percent of present tenants must agree to buy their apartments before conversion may take place. If *eviction* is planned, at least 51 percent must agree to buy. Differing regulations in parts of Westchester, Rockland and Nassau counties (and some Upstate communities) may require 51 percent or 35 percent tenant participation. Certain *disabled persons* and *senior citizens* are exempt from eviction in any case.

Time-sharing involves the purchase of a resort or vacation property for a portion of the year.

Questions

1. Condominium living provides:
   a. economy of construction and operation.
   b. increased square footage per occupant.
   c. accelerated cost recovery.
   d. inexpensive vacations.

2. A high-rise building is likely to be organized as:
   a. a condominium project.
   b. a cooperative development.
   c. rented apartments.
   d. any of the above.

3. A separate tax account number, insurance policy and mortgage are available to the owner of:
   a. a cooperative apartment.
   b. a condominium
   c. both.
   d. neither.

4. Common elements include:
   a. stairwells.   c. foyers.
   b. swimming pool.   d. all of the above.

5. The term *CC&R* refers to:
   a. clubhouse, courts and recreation.
   b. covenants, conditions and restrictions.
   c. Chesapeake, Charleston and Richmond.
   d. contracts, citations and releases.

6. The owner of a cooperative apartment receives:
   a. a deed.
   b. a property tax bill.
   c. a life estate.
   d. shares in a corporation.

7. Condominium units in New York may be held by:
   a. one person.   c. tenants in common.
   b. joint tenants.   d. any of the above.

8. The right to reject prospective new owners is held by the board of directors of a:
   a. town house.   c. cooperative.
   b. time-share.   d. condominium.

9. The land immediately under the unit is owned individually in a:
   a. condominium.   c. town house.
   b. cooperative.   d. time-share.

10. A declaration must be accepted by the:
    a. sponsor.
    b. attorney general.
    c. homeowners' association.
    d. Department of State.

11. The changing of a rental building into shared ownership is called:
    a. conversion.   c. disclosure.
    b. declaration.   d. offering.

12. Restrictions may be set on exterior architectural changes by the association of a:
    a. condominium.
    b. cooperative.
    c. planned unit development.
    d. All of the above

13. What percentage of New York City tenants must plan to buy before an existing development is changed to a condominium or cooperative under a noneviction plan?
    a. 10 percent   c. 35 percent
    b. 15 percent   d. 51 percent

14. In New York City what percentage of tenants must plan to buy before other tenants may be evicted at the expiration of leases?
    a. 10 percent   c. 35 percent
    b. 15 percent   d. 51 percent

15. Time-sharing is a technique most often used for the shared ownership of:
    a. high-rise buildings.
    b. resort property.
    c. town houses.
    d. office buildings.

21

Property Management—Rent Regulations

Key Terms

Business interruption insurance
Casualty insurance
Certified Property Manager (CPM)
Contents and personal property insurance
Division of Housing and Community
    Renewal (DHCR)
Fire and hazard insurance
Liability insurance

Management agreement
Multiperil policies
Property manager
Rent control
Rent stabilization
Replacement cost
Surety bond
Workers' compensation acts

Overview

A real estate owner who rents out the upstairs apartment in the building where he or she resides generally has no problem with property management—setting and collecting rents, maintenance and repairs are easy enough with only one tenant. But the owners of large, multiunit developments often lack the time and/or expertise to manage their properties successfully. Enter the *property manager,* hired to maintain the property and ensure profitability of the owner's investment. This chapter will examine the growing property management field and will include discussions of the types of property insurance available to further protect an owner's real estate investment. It also will discuss rent control and rent stabilization in effect in some parts of New York State.

Property Management	In recent years the increased size of buildings; the technical complexities of construction, maintenance and repair; and the trend toward absentee ownership by individual investors and investment groups have led to the expanded use of professional property managers for both residential and commercial properties.
	Property management has become so important that many brokerage firms maintain separate management departments staffed by carefully selected, well-trained people. Many corporate and institutional owners of real estate have also established property management departments. Many real estate investors will still manage their own property, however, and thus must acquire the knowledge and skills of a property manager. In some instances, property managers must be licensed real estate brokers.
Functions of the Property Manager	In the simplest terms, a **property manager** is someone who *preserves the value of an investment property while generating income as an agent for the owners.* A property manager is expected to merchandise the property and control operating expenses so as to maximize income. A property manager chooses the best possible means to carry out an agent's responsibilities, and has more authority and discretion than an employee. A manager should maintain and modernize the property to preserve and enhance the owner's capital investment. The manager carries out these objectives by: (1) securing suitable tenants, (2) collecting the rents, (3) caring for the premises, (4) budgeting and controlling expenses, (5) hiring and supervising employees and (6) keeping proper accounts and making periodic reports to the owner.
Securing Management Business	In today's market, property managers may look to corporate owners, apartment and condominium associations, homeowners' associations, investment syndicates, trusts and absentee owners as possible sources of management business. In securing business from any of these sources, word of mouth is often the best advertising. A manager who consistently demonstrates the ability to increase property income over previous levels should have no difficulty finding new business.
The Management Agreement	The first step in taking over the management of any property is to enter into a **management agreement** with the owner. This agreement creates an agency relationship between the owner and the property manager. A property manager is usually considered to be a *general agent*, whereas a real estate broker is usually considered to be a *special agent*. As agent, the property manager is charged with the same agency responsibilities as the listing broker—notice, obedience, care, accounting and loyalty (NO-CAL). (Agency responsibilities were discussed at length in Chapters 2 and 14.)
	The management agreement should be in writing and should cover the following points:

1. *Description* of the property.
2. *Time period* the agreement will be in force.

3. *Definition of management's responsibilities.* All of the manager's duties should be stated in the contract; exceptions should be noted.
4. *Extent of manager's authority as an agent.* This provision should state what authority the manager is to have in such matters as hiring, firing and supervising employees, fixing rental rates for space, making expenditures and authorizing repairs within the limits established previously with the owner. (Repairs that exceed a certain expense limit may require the owner's written approval.)
5. *Reporting.* Agreement should be reached on the frequency and detail of the manager's periodic reports on operations and financial position. These reports serve as a means for the owner to monitor the manager's work and as a basis for both the owner and the manager to assess trends that can be used in shaping future management policy.
6. *Management fee.* The fee can be based on a percentage of gross or net income, a commission on new rentals, a fixed fee or a combination of these.
7. *Allocation of costs.* The agreement should state which of the property management expenses, such as custodial and other help, advertising, supplies and repairs, are to be charged to the property's expenses and paid by the owner.

Management Considerations

A property manager must live up to both the letter and the spirit of the management agreement. The owner must be kept well informed on all matters of policy as well as on the financial condition of the property and its operation. A manager must keep in contact with others in the field, thus becoming increasingly knowledgeable on the subject and keeping informed on current policies pertaining to the profession.

Budgeting Expenses

Before attempting to rent any property, a property manager should develop an operating budget based on anticipated revenues and expenses and reflecting the long-term goals of the owner. In preparing a budget, a manager should begin by allocating money for such continuous fixed expenses as employees' salaries, real estate taxes, property taxes and insurance premiums.

Next, the manager should establish a cash reserve fund for such variable expenses as repairs, decorating and supplies. The amount allocated for the reserve fund can be computed from the previous yearly costs of variable expenses.

Capital expenditures. If an owner and a property manager decide that modernization or renovation of the property would enhance its value, the manager should budget money to cover the costs of remodeling. The property manager should be thoroughly familiar with the principle of *contribution* or seek expert advice when estimating any increase in value expected by an improvement. In the case of large-scale construction, the expenses charged against the property's income should be spread over several years. Although budgets should be as accurate an estimate of cost as possible, adjustments may sometimes be necessary, especially in the case of new properties.

Renting the Property

The role of the manager in managing a property should not be confused with that of a broker acting as a leasing agent and solely concerned with renting space. The property manager may use the services of a leasing agent, but that agent does not undertake the full responsibility of maintenance and management of the property.

Setting rental rates. In establishing rental rates for a property, a basic concern must be that, in the long term, the income from the rentable space cover the fixed charges and operating expenses and also provide a fair return on the investment. Consideration must also be given to the prevailing rates in comparable buildings and the current level of vacancy in the property to be rented—supply and demand. Following a detailed survey of the competitive space available in the neighborhood, prices should be noted and adjusted for differences between neighboring properties and the property being managed. Annual rent adjustments are usually warranted.

While apartment rental rates are stated in monthly amounts, office and commercial space rentals are usually stated according to either the annual or the monthly rate per square foot of space.

If a high level of vacancy exists, an immediate effort should be made to determine why. *A high level of vacancy does not necessarily indicate that rents are too high.* The trouble may be inept management or defects in the property. The manager should attempt to identify and correct the problems first, rather than immediately lower rents. Conversely, *while a high percentage of occupancy may appear to indicate an effective rental program, it could also mean that rental rates are too low.* With an apartment house or office building, any time the occupancy level exceeds 95 percent serious consideration should be given to raising the rents.

Tenant selection. Generally, the highest rents can be secured from satisfied tenants. While a broker may sell a property and then have no further dealings with the purchaser, a building manager's success is greatly dependent on retaining sound, long-term relationships. In selecting prospective commercial or industrial tenants, a manager should be sure that each person will "fit the space." The manager should be certain that: (1) the *size of the space* meets the tenant's requirements, (2) the tenant will have the *ability to pay* for the space for which he or she contracts, (3) the *tenant's business will be compatible* with the building and the other tenants and (4) if the tenant is likely to expand in the future, there will be *expansion space available.* After a prospect becomes a tenant, *the manager must be sure that the tenant remains satisfied in all respects commensurate with fair business dealing.*

In selecting tenants, the property manager must comply with all federal and local fair housing laws (*see* Chapter 10).

Collecting rents. The best way to minimize problems with rent collection is to make a *careful selection* of tenants in the first place. A desire to have a high level of occupancy should not override good judgment in accepting only tenants who meet their financial obligations. A property manager should investigate financial references given by the prospect, local credit bureaus and, when possible, the prospective tenant's former landlord.

The terms of rental payment should be spelled out in detail in the lease agreement. A *firm and consistent collection plan* with a sufficient system of notices and records should be established. In cases of delinquency, every attempt must be made to make collections without resorting to legal action. For those cases in which it is required, a property manager must be prepared to initiate and follow through with legal counsel.

Maintaining the Property

One of the most important functions of a property manager is the supervision of property maintenance. A manager must learn to balance the provided services with the costs they entail so as to satisfy the tenants' needs while minimizing operating expenses. *Maintenance* covers several types of activities. First, the manager must *protect the physical integrity of the property* to ensure that the condition of the building and its grounds is kept at present levels over the long term. Repainting the exterior or replacing the heating system will help to keep the building functional and decrease routine maintenance costs.

A property manager must also *supervise routine cleaning and repairs* of the building, including cleaning common areas, minor carpentry and plumbing, and regularly scheduled upkeep of heating, air-conditioning and landscaping.

In addition, especially when dealing with commercial or industrial space, a property manager will be called on to make tenant improvements—alterations to the interior of the building to meet the functional demands of the tenant. These alterations range from repainting to completely gutting the interior and redesigning the space. Tenant improvements are especially important when renting new buildings, since the interior is usually left incomplete so that it can be adapted to the needs of the individual tenants ("make-ready").

Supervision of modernization or renovation of buildings that have become functionally obsolete and thus unsuited to today's building needs is also important (see Chapter 16 for a definition of *functional obsolescence*). The renovation of a building often increases the building's marketability and thus its possible income.

Hiring employees versus contracting for services. One of the major decisions a property manager faces is whether to contract for maintenance services from an outside firm or hire on-site employees to perform such tasks. This decision should be based on a number of factors, including size of the building, complexity of tenants' requirements and availability of suitable labor.

Tenants' Rights

New York's Multiple Dwelling Law, in effect in New York City and Buffalo, sets the following requirements for buildings with three or more living units: automatic self-closing and self-locking doors, two-way voice buzzers (for buildings with eight or more units), mirrors in each self-service elevator, and peepholes and chain door-guards on the entrance door of each apartment. Tenants may install their own additional locks but must provide the landlord with a duplicate key upon request. Heat must be provided from October 1 to May 31. Additional regulations apply in various communities.

Postal regulations require landlords of buildings with three or more units to provide secure mailboxes. The majority of municipalities have smoke detector regulations. In New York City, tenants with children under 11 years of age must receive window-guards upon request. Protective guards also must be installed on all public hall windows.

Throughout the state the landlord of a building with three or more apartments must keep the apartments and public areas in good repair, maintaining electrical, plumbing, sanitary, heating and ventilation systems in good working order. Landlords also must maintain appliances that are furnished to tenants. Landlords have a legal duty to keep buildings free of vermin, dirt or garbage.

A landlord may enter the tenant's apartment only with reasonable prior notice, to provide repairs or service in accordance with the lease, or to show the apartment to prospective tenants or purchasers. The landlord may enter without prior permission only in an emergency.

Mobile-home park tenants. Mobile-home park tenants must be offered at least a one-year written lease. If they do not have leases they are entitled to 90 days' written notice before rent increases. Rules must not be changed without 30 days' written notice. Late rent payment charges are limited to 5 percent, after a ten-day grace period.

Owners may not discriminate against mobile-home tenants with children. Owners have the right to sell their homes within the park with the consent of the park owner, which consent may not be unreasonably withheld. Park owners cannot require any fee or commission in connection with the sale of a mobile home unless they act as sales agent pursuant to a written contract. Owners may not foster park monopolies.

Owners of mobile-home parks with more than two units must register with the New York Division of Housing and Community Renewal, which will enforce the rights of mobile-home tenants in the state.

Insurance

One of the most important responsibilities of a property manager is to protect the property owner against all major insurable risks. In some cases a property manager or a member of the firm may be a licensed insurance broker. In any case a competent, reliable insurance agent who is well versed in all areas of insurance pertaining to property should be selected to survey the property and make recommendations. If the manager is not completely satisfied with these recommendations, additional insurance surveys should be obtained. Final decisions, however, must be made by the property owner. *An insurance broker must have passed a state examination to secure a special license to sell insurance.*

Types of Coverage

Many kinds of insurance coverage are available to income-property owners and managers. Some of the more common types include the following:

- **Fire and hazard:** Fire insurance policies provide coverage against direct loss or damage to property from a fire on the premises. Standard fire coverage can be extended to cover hazards such as windstorm, hail, smoke damage or civil insurrection. Most popular today is the *all-risks* or *special form.*
- **Business interruption:** Most hazard policies insure against the actual loss of property but do not cover loss of revenues from income property. Interruption insurance covers the loss of income that occurs if the property cannot be used to produce income.
- **Contents and personal property:** *Inland marine insurance* covers building contents and personal property during periods when they are not actually located on the business premises.
- **Liability:** Public liability insurance covers the risks an owner assumes when the public enters the building. Medical expenses are paid for a person injured in the building as a result of landlord negligence. Another liability risk is that of medical or hospital payments for injuries sustained by building employees hurt in the course of their employment. These claims are covered

by state laws known as **workers' compensation acts.** These laws require a building owner who is an employer to obtain a workers' compensation policy from a private insurance company.

- **Casualty:** Casualty insurance policies include coverage against theft, burglary, vandalism, machinery damage and health and accident insurance. Casualty policies usually are written on specific risks such as theft, rather than being all-inclusive.
- **Surety bonds:** Surety bonds cover an owner against financial losses resulting from an employee's criminal acts or negligence while carrying out his or her duties. A *blanket crime policy* is most often chosen.
- **Boiler and machinery coverage:** This covers repair and replacement of heating plants, central air-conditioning units and major equipment.

Lower premiums may be offered property that qualifies as a *highly protected risk (HPR)* based on the quality of water supply, sprinklers, alarms, security personnel and loss-control programs. Many insurance companies offer **multiperil policies** for apartment and business buildings. These include standard types of commercial coverage: fire, hazard, public liability and casualty.

Claims

When a claim is made under a policy insuring a building or other physical object, either of two methods can determine the amount of the claim. One is the *depreciated*, or actual, cash value of the damaged property; the other is replacement cost. If a 30-year-old building is damaged, the timbers and materials are 30 years old and therefore do not have the same value as new material. Thus in determining the amount of the loss under what is called *actual cash value,* the cost of new material would be reduced by the estimated depreciation, based on the time the item had been in the building.

The alternate method is to cover **replacement cost.** This would represent the actual amount a builder would charge to replace the damaged property at the time of the loss, including materials. When purchasing insurance, a manager must assess whether the property should be insured at full replacement cost or at a depreciated cost. As with the homeowners' policies discussed in Chapter 11, commercial policies usually carry *coinsurance clauses* that require coverage up to 80 percent of the building's replacement value.

The Management Field

For those interested in pursuing a career in property management, most large cities have local associations of building and property owners and managers that are affiliates of regional and national associations. The Institute of Real Estate Management was founded in 1933 and is part of the National Association of REALTORS®. Members may earn the designation **Certified Property Manager (CPM).** The Building Owners and Managers Association International (BOMA International) is a federation of local associations of owners and managers, primarily of office buildings. Participation in groups like these allows property managers to gain valuable professional knowledge and to discuss their problems with other managers facing similar issues. Management designation also is offered by the National Association of Home Builders, the New York Association of Building Owners and the International Council of Shopping Centers.

A growing field is the management of cooperatives and condominiums. The manager hired by a homeowners' organization must develop different techniques because owners and tenants are one and the same. The Community Associations Institute (CAI) is a nonprofit organization founded in 1974 to research and distribute information on association living and offers training and designation for specialized management.

Rent Regulations

Rent regulation in New York State is administered by the Office of Rent Administration of the New York State **Division of Housing and Community Renewal (DHCR).** It includes two programs: **rent control** and **rent stabilization.**

Rent Control

Rent control dates back to the housing shortage that followed World War II and generally covers property containing three or more units constructed before February 1947 and located in one of the 64 municipalities where the system is in effect. These include New York City, Albany, Buffalo and parts of the following counties: Albany, Erie, Nassau, Rensselaer, Schenectady and Westchester. Table 21.1 lists participating municipalities. Also covered are tenants who have been in continuous residence since May 1, 1953, in one- or two-family dwellings in the participating communities.

For buildings with three or more units, the regulations apply to an apartment continuously occupied by the present tenant since July 1, 1971 (with some exceptions in Nassau County). When such an apartment is vacated, it moves to rent stabilization status or is removed from regulation, depending on the municipality.

Rents in controlled apartments initially were based on rentals in effect when rent control was first imposed in 1943. Outside New York City the DHCR determines maximum allowable rates of rent increases, which are available to landlords every two years. Within New York City a *Maximum Base Rent (MBR)* is established for each apartment and is adjusted every two years. Landlords may raise rents by 7.5 percent each year until they reach the maximum base rental figure. Tenants may challenge proposed increases if the building has been cited for violations or the owner's expenses do not warrant an increase.

Under rent control, rent may be increased (1) if the landlord increases services, (2) if landlord installs a major capital improvement, (3) in cases of hardship and (4) to cover high labor and fuel costs. Rents will be reduced if the landlord fails to correct violations or reduces essential services. The law prohibits harassment of rent-controlled tenants or retaliatory eviction of tenants who exercise their right to complain to a government agency about violations of health or safety laws.

In 1989, 155,000 units in New York City remained under rent control, with another 936,000 under the later arrangement known as rent stabilization.

Rent Stabilization

In New York City, **rent stabilization** applies to apartments in buildings of six or more units constructed between February 1, 1947, and January 1, 1974. For buildings older than that, tenants are covered if they moved in after June 30, 1971. Buildings with three or more units that were constructed or extensively renovated since 1974 with special tax benefits are also subject to rent stabilization while the tax benefits continue.

**Table 21.1
Municipalities Outside
New York City Covered
by Rent Control or That
Have Adopted the
Emergency Tenant
Protection Program Act
as of March 1986.**

County	Locality	Rent Control	Rent Stabilized	County	Locality	Rent Control	Rent Stabilized
Albany	Albany	X			Lynbrook		X
	Watervliet	X			Rockville Center		X
	Bethlehem	X			Russell Gardens		X
	(Town) Green Island	X			Thomaston		X
	New Scotland	X		Rensselaer	Rensselaer	X	
	(Village) Green Island	X			Hoosick	X	
	Voorheesville	X			North Greenbush	X	
Erie	Buffalo	X			Hoosick Falls	X	
	Cheektowaga	X		Rockland	Haverstraw		X
	Depew	X			Spring Valley		X
	Sloan	X		Schenectady	Niskayuna	X	
Nassau	Glen Cove	X	X		Princeton	X	
	Long Beach	X	X	Westchester	Mount Vernon	X	X
	(Town) Hempstead	X			New Rochelle	X	X
	North Hempstead	X	X		White Plains	X	X
	Oyster Bay	X			Yonkers	X	X
	Bellerose	X			Eastchester	X	X
	Cedarhurst	X	X		Greenburgh	X	X
	Floral Park	X	X		Harrison	X	X
	Freeport	X	X		(Town) Mamaroneck	X	X
	(Village) Hempstead	X	X		Ardsley	X	
	Mineola	X			Dobbs Ferry	X	X
	New Hyde Park	X			Hastings-on-Hudson	X	X
	Roslyn	X	X		Larchmont	X	X
	Sea Cliff	X			(Village) Mamaroneck	X	X
	Valley Stream	X			North Tarrytown	X	X
	Westbury	X			Tarrytown	X	X
	Williston Park	X			Tuckahoe	X	
	Baxter Estates		X		Irvington		X
	Flower Hill		X		Mt. Kisco		X
	Great Neck		X		Pleasantville		X
	Great Neck Estates		X		Port Chester		X
	Great Neck Plaza		X				

Outside New York City, rent stabilization applies in those communities that have adopted the Emergency Tenant Protection Act (EPTA). Each community sets a limit on the size of buildings to be covered; in no case is the program applied to property with fewer than six living units.

Where rent stabilization applies, maximum allowable rent increases are set annually by local rent stabilization boards. Tenants may choose one- or two-year renewal leases.

To be eligible for rent increases, owners must file an annual statement with DHCR, listing the rental for each unit under rent stabilization. Copies must be furnished to the tenants. Tenants may challenge the figures and receive a refund of any overcharges during the preceding four years plus treble damages for two years if the overcharge was willful. Administrative penalties for a landlord found guilty of harassment of tenants are set as $1,000 for a first offense and $2,500 thereafter.

Where units should have been registered with the DHCR and were not, any future purchaser could be liable to tenants for the refund of unauthorized rent increases. This provision is important to the real estate broker who may be handling the sale of a building that is not in compliance.

A *Senior Citizen Rent Increase Exemption (SCRIE)* is in effect for some rent-controlled and rent-stabilized apartments in New York City and in some other areas. Tenants 62 or older may qualify for full or partial exemption from rent increases if their income falls below levels set by the municipality, if they pay at least one-third of their income for rent and if they are not on welfare. Among municipalities that have adopted the SCRIE are North Hempstead, Great Neck, Great Neck Plaza, Thomaston, Mount Vernon, New Rochelle, White Plains, Yonkers, Greenburgh, Spring Valley, Seacliff, Mamaroneck, Tarrytown and Irvington.

The DHCR has set up a special unit to assist the owners of small buildings, those with fewer than 50 rental units, in filling out registration forms and with record-keeping and bookkeeping. The Department's main office is located in the World Trade Center. District offices administering rent regulations are listed in Table 21.2.

Summary

Property management is a specialized service to owners of income-producing properties in which the managerial function may be delegated to an individual or a firm with particular expertise in the field. The manager, as agent of the owner, becomes the administrator of the property.

A *management agreement* must be carefully prepared to define and authorize the manager's duties and responsibilities.

The first step a property manger should take when managing a building is to draw up a budget of estimated variable and fixed expenses. The budget also should allow for any proposed expenditures for major renovations or modernizations. These projected expenses, combined with the manager's analysis of the condition of the building and the rent patterns in the neighborhood, will form the basis on which rental rates for property are determined.

After a rent schedule is established, the property manager is responsible for soliciting tenants needs are suited to the available space and who are financially capable of meeting the proposed rents. The manager usually is obligated to collect rents, maintain the building, hire necessary employees, pay taxes for the building and deal with tenant problems.

One of the manager's primary responsibilities is supervising maintenance. Maintenance includes safeguarding the physical integrity of the property and performing routine cleaning and repairs as well as adapting the interior space and overall design of the property to suit the tenants' needs and meet the demands of the market.

In addition the manager is expected to secure adequate insurance coverage for the premises. The basic types of coverage applicable to commercial structures include

Table 21.2
Department of Housing and Community Renewal Offices, New York State

New York City Office
One Fordham Plaza
Bronx, NY 10458
(212) 519-5700
FAX: 212-519-5840
       212-519-5518

Buffalo Office
Ellicott Square Building
295 Main Street
Room 446
Buffalo, NY 14203
716-856-1382
FAX: 716-847-3087

Central Rent Office
and Queens Rent Office
92-31 Union Hall Street
Jamaica, NY 11433
718-739-6400
FAX: 718-262-4008

Upper Manhattan Rent Office
Adam Clayton Powell, Jr.
State Office Building
163 West 125th Street
5th Floor
New York, NY 10027
212-870-8930

Lower Manhattan Rent Office
Two Lafayette Street
12th Floor
New York, NY 10007
212-566-7970

Brooklyn Rent Office
91 Lawrence Street, 2nd Floor
Brooklyn, NY 11201
718-643-7570

Staten Island Rent Office
350 St. Mark's Place
Room 105
Staten Island, NY 10301
718-816-0277

Albany Office
Hampton Plaza
38–40 State Street
Albany, NY 12207
518-474-8580
FAX: 518-473-9462
       518-473-3260

Watertown Office
State Office Building
6th Floor
317 Washington Street
Watertown, NY 13601
315-785-2459
FAX: 315-785-2581

Nassau Rent Office
50 Clinton Street
6th Floor, Room 605
Hempstead, NY 11550
516-481-9494

District Rent Office
10 Columbus Circle
11th Floor
New York, NY 10019
FAX: 212-708-0782

Westchester Rent Office
55 Church Street
3rd Floor
White Plains, NY 10601
914-948-4434
FAX: 914-948-7783

Harassment Unit
17 John Street, 3rd Floor
New York, NY 10038
212-566-3945

Employee Assistance Program
One Fordham Plaza
Bronx, NY 10458
212-519-5443

Rent Hotline: 212-519-5700
Public Information: 212-307-5760

fire and hazard insurance on the property and fixtures; *business interruption insurance* to protect the owner against income losses; and *casualty insurance* to provide coverage against such losses as theft, vandalism and destruction of machinery. The manager also should secure *public liability insurance* to insure the owner against claims made by people injured on the premises and *workers' compensation policies* to cover the claims of employees injured on the job.

The Multiple Dwelling Law in New York City and Buffalo sets health and safety standards for apartment buildings. Local communities have additional regulations. The state also regulates mobile-home parks.

The Institute of Real Estate Management, a branch of the National Association of REALTORS®, awards the most widely recognized designation in the field, the *CPM, Certified Property Manager*.

Rent regulations in New York are administered by the *Department of Housing and Community Renewal (DHCR)*. *Rent control* is in effect in some localities around New York City, Albany and Buffalo. A less rigid *rent stabilization* program applies in New York City, and as the *Emergency Tenant Protection Act* in parts of Nassau, Rockland, and Westchester counties. The tenant who successfully challenges rent overcharges may collect a rebate for *four years* past and may not be harassed or evicted.

Questions

1. An owner-manager agreement should include:
   a. a statement of the owner's purpose for the building.
   b. a clear definition of the manager's authority.
   c. agreement on what portion of the property manager's personal operating expenses will be paid by the owner.
   d. all of the above.

2. An operating budget for income property usually is prepared on what basis?
   a. Daily   c. Monthly
   b. Weekly   d. Annual

3. In the absence of rent regulations the amount of rent charged is determined by the:
   a. management agreement.
   b. principle of supply and demand.
   c. operating budget.
   d. toss of a coin.

4. Office rentals usually are figured by the:
   a. front foot.
   b. amount of desk space.
   c. number of rooms.
   d. square foot.

5. From a management point of view, apartment building occupancy that reaches as high as 98 percent would tend to indicate that:
   a. the building is poorly managed.
   b. the building is run-down.
   c. the building is a desirable place to live.
   d. rents should be raised.

6. Which of the following should *not* be a consideration in selecting a tenant?
   a. The size of the space versus the tenant's requirements
   b. The tenant's ability to pay
   c. The racial and ethnic backgrounds of the tenant
   d. The compatibility of the tenant's business to other tenants' businesses

7. A property manager may be reimbursed with:
   a. a percentage of rentals.
   b. rebates from suppliers.
   c. key money.
   d. any of the above.

8. In some situations, municipal or state law may require a landlord to install:
   a. elevator mirrors.
   b. window guards.
   c. intercoms and buzzers.
   d. all of the above.

9. While her tenants are at work, Laura Landlady may enter their apartment:
   a. to leave them a note.
   b. to check on their housekeeping.
   c. in case of fire.
   d. all of the above.

10. Which insurance insures the property owner against the claims of employees injured on the job?
    a. Business interruption
    b. Workers' compensation
    c. Casualty
    d. Surety bond

11. A deliveryman slips on a defective stair in an apartment building and is hospitalized. A claim against the building owner for medical expenses will be made under which of the following policies held by the owner?
    a. Workers' compensation
    b. Casualty
    c. Liability
    d. Fire and hazard

12. Property manager Frieda Jacobs hires Albert Weston as the full-time janitor for one of the buildings she manages. While repairing a faucet in one of the apartments, Weston steals a television set. Jacobs could protect the owner against liability for this type of loss by purchasing:
    a. liability insurance.
    b. worker's compensation insurance.
    c. a surety bond.
    d. casualty insurance.

13. The initials CPM stand for:
    a. chargeback percentage mortgage.
    b. contract priority maintenance.
    c. Certified Property Manager.
    d. cardiopulmonary manipulation.

14. Rent regulations in this state are administered by:
    a. the New York City Housing Bureau.
    b. the Department of State.
    c. HUD.
    d. the New York Department of Housing and Community Renewal.

15. Rent control regulations are found mainly around the:
    a. Adirondacks.   c. Finger Lakes.
    b. Southern tier.   d. New York City area.

16. When the original tenant dies or moves out, a rent-controlled apartment may become eligible for:
    a. rent control.
    b. rent stabilization.
    c. comparative hardship.
    d. freeze.

17. The rent stabilization program is known outside New York City as:
    a. ETPA.   c. CPR.
    b. DHCR.   d. HPR.

18. A rent stabilization tenant may collect unauthorized overcharges going back how far?
    a. Six months   c. Four years
    b. Two years   d. Indefinitely

19. Jim Ordway should have registered his Manhattan apartment building for rent stabilization but failed to do so. He sells it to Sam Simple. Tenants may file to collect their past rent increases from:
    a. the City of New York.
    b. the Department of Housing and Community Renewal.
    c. Jim.
    d. Sam.

20. The DHCR considers small apartment buildings to be those with fewer than:
    a. three units.   c. 50 units.
    b. eight units.   d. 100 units.

22

Leases and Agreements

Key Terms

Actual eviction
Constructive eviction
Estate for years
Gross lease
Ground lease
Holdover tenancy
Implied warranty of habitability
Lease
Leasehold estate
Lessee

Lessor
Month-to-month tenancy
Net lease
Percentage lease
Periodic estate
Sublease
Suit for possession
Tenancy at sufferance
Tenancy at will

Overview

When an owner of real property does not wish to use the property personally but wants to derive some measure of income from it, he or she can allow it to be used by another person in exchange for consideration. Any type of real property may be leased. This chapter will examine the various leasehold estates a landlord and a tenant may enter into and the types and specific provisions of lease agreements commonly used in the real estate business.

Leasing Real Estate

A **lease** is a conveyance from an owner of real estate (known as the **lessor**) to a tenant (the **lessee**) that transfers the right to possession and use of the owner's property to the tenant for a specified period of time. This agreement sets forth the length of time the contract is to run, the amount to be paid by the lessee for the right to use the property and other rights and obligations of the parties.

The landlord grants the tenant the right to occupy the premises and use them for purposes stated in the lease. In return the landlord retains the right to receive payment for the use of the premises as well as a *reversionary right* to retake possession after the lease term has expired.

The statute of frauds requires that a *lease for a term of more than one year must be in writing* to be enforceable. It also should be signed by both lessor and lessee. A lease for one year or less is enforceable even if it is entered into orally.

Leasehold Estates

A tenant's right to occupy land is called a **leasehold estate.** Just as there are several types of freehold (ownership) estates, there are various leasehold estates. The four most important are: (1) estate for years; (2) periodic estate, or estate from period to period; (3) tenancy at will; and (4) tenancy at sufferance (*see* Table 22.1). All are recognized in New York State.

Table 22.1 Leasehold Estates

Type of Estate	Distinguishing Characteristics
Estate for Years	For Definite Period of Time
Periodic Estate	Automatically Renews
Tenancy at Will	For Indefinite Period of Time
Tenancy at Sufferance	Without Landlord's Consent

Estate for Years

A leasehold estate that continues for a *definite period of time* is an **estate for years.** When a definite term is specified in a written or oral lease and that period of time expires, the lessee is required to vacate the premises and surrender possession to the lessor. *No notice is required* to terminate such a lease at the end of the term. A lease for years may be terminated prior to the expiration date by the mutual consent of both parties but otherwise neither party may terminate without showing that the lease agreement has been breached.

An estate for years need not necessarily last for years or even for one year. Its distinguishing characteristic is that it begins and ends at a specific time.

Periodic Estates

Periodic estates, sometimes called *estates from period to period,* are created when the landlord and tenant enter into an agreement that continues for an *indefinite length of time without a specific expiration date;* rent, however, is payable at definite intervals. These tenancies generally run for a certain amount of time; for instance, month to month, week to week or year to year. The agreement is automatically renewed for similar succeeding periods until one of the parties gives notice to terminate.

A **month-to-month tenancy** is created when a tenant takes possession with no definite termination date and pays rent on a monthly basis.

A tenancy from year to year is created when a tenant for a term of years remains in possession, or holds over, after the expiration of the lease term. When no new lease agreement has been made, the landlord may either evict the tenant or acquiesce in the **holdover tenancy.**

A New York tenant who remains in possession of leased premises after giving notice of intention to quit the premises (holding over) may be held liable for double rent if he or she holds possession beyond the date stated in the notice. When the lease term is longer than one month, the landlord may commence proceedings to remove a tenant who has held over. The subsequent acceptance of rent by the landlord will create a tenancy from month to month. Some leases stipulate that in the absence of a renewal agreement, a tenant who holds over does so as a month-to-month tenant.

In order to *terminate* a periodic estate, either the landlord or the tenant must give *proper notice*. To end a month-to-month tenancy New York State requires one month's written notice: New York City requires 30 days' notice, from the day the rent is due (usually the first of the month).

Tenancy at Will

An estate that gives the tenant the right to possess with the *consent of the landlord* is a **tenancy at will.** It may be created by express agreement or by operation of law, and during its existence the tenant has all the rights and obligations of a lessor-lessee relationship including the payment of rent at regular intervals.

For example, at the end of a lease period a landlord informs a tenant that in a few months the city is going to demolish the apartment building to make way for an expressway. The landlord gives the tenant the option to occupy the premises until demolition begins. If the tenant agrees to stay, a tenancy at will is created. The term of an estate at will is indefinite but the estate may be terminated by giving proper notice. An estate at will is automatically terminated by the death of either the landlord or the tenant.

Tenancy at Sufferance

A **tenancy at sufferance** arises when a tenant who lawfully came into possession of real property continues, after his or her rights have expired, to hold possession of the premises *without the consent of the landlord*. Two examples of estates at sufferance are: (1) when a tenant for years *fails to surrender* possession at the expiration of the lease and (2) when a mortgagor, without consent of the purchaser, continues in possession after the foreclosure sale. In New York a tenant may be charged up to double rent for the period while he or she was in possession as a tenant at sufferance after notice to quit the premises had been given.

Standard Lease Provisions

The lease may be written, oral or implied, depending on the circumstances. New York State requires a *plain-English* format. The requirements for a valid lease are essentially the same as those for any other real estate contract. In New York the essentials of a valid lease include the following:

1. *Capacity to contract:* The parties must be sane adults.
2. A *demising clause:* The lessor to let and the lessee to take the premises.
3. *Description of the premises:* A description of the leased premises should be clearly stated. If the lease covers land, the legal description of the real estate should be used. If on the other hand the lease is for a part of the building, such as office space or an apartment, the space itself should be clearly and carefully described. If supplemental space is to be included, the lease should clearly identify it.
4. A clear statement of the *term* (duration) of the lease must be provided.
5. *Specification of the rent and how it is to be paid:* In New York, unless the lease states otherwise, rent is considered due in arrears rather than in advance.
6. The *lease must be in writing* if it is to be for more than one year.
7. *Signatures:* A lease should be signed by both parties.

Use of Premises

A lessor may restrict a lessee's use of premises through provisions included in the lease. This is most important in leases for stores or commercial space. For example, a lease may provide that the leased premises are to be used *only* for the purpose of a real estate office *and for no other*. In the absence of such limitations a lessee may use the premises for any lawful purpose.

Term of Lease

The term of a lease is the period for which the lease will run and it should be set out precisely. The date of the beginning of the term and the date of its ending should be stated together with a statement of the total period of the lease: for example, "for a term of thirty years beginning June 1, 1990 and ending May 31, 2020."

Security Deposits

Many leases require the tenant to provide some form of security. This security, which guarantees payment of rent and safeguards against a tenant's destruction of the premises, may be established by: (1) contracting for a lien on the tenant's property, (2) requiring the tenant to pay a portion of the rent in advance, (3) requiring the tenant to post security and/or (4) requiring the tenant to have a third person guarantee the payment of the rent. Where trade fixtures are to be installed, the landlord may want an extra deposit to ensure that the property will be restored to its original state when they are removed.

Under the New York General Obligations Law a landlord must hold all security deposits in trust and must not commingle them with his or her own funds because *such deposits continue to belong to the tenants who have advanced them* throughout the term of the lease. If the landlord owns six or more units, the landlord must notify tenants in writing where the security funds are being held in a New York interest-bearing bank account and must turn over to them all but 1 percent of any interest earned. Any provisions in a lease requiring a tenant to waive any provisions of this law are void. The rules also apply to mobile-home parks.

When a landlord conveys rental property he or she must turn over any security deposits to the new owner within five days of the deed's delivery. He or she must also notify tenants by registered or certified mail that their deposits have been turned over; such notification must include the new owner's name and address. With a rent-stabilized apartment only one month's rent may be charged for security deposit.

Legal Principles of Leases

New York provides that leases can be recorded in the county in which the property is located when a lease runs for a period of *three years* or longer. The recording of a *long-term lease* places the world on notice of the long-term rights of the tenant. The recordation of such a lease is usually required if the tenant intends to mortgage his or her leasehold interest.

Possession of Leased Premises

Leases carry the implied convenant that the landlord will give the tenant possession of the premises. Thus, if the premises are occupied by a holdover tenant at the beginning of the new lease period, it is the landlord's duty to bring whatever action is necessary to recover possession and to bear the expense of this action.

Improvements

The tenant may make improvements with the landlord's permission but any such alterations generally become the property of the landlord; that is, they become fixtures. However, a tenant may be given the right to install trade fixtures or chattel fixtures by the terms of the lease. It is customary to provide that such trade fixtures may be removed by the tenant before the lease expires, provided the tenant restores the premises to the same condition as when he or she took possession.

Maintenance of Premises

Every residential New York lease, oral or written, is considered to contain an **implied warranty of habitability.** The landlord guarantees that the leased property is fit for human habitation and that the tenant will not be subjected to any conditions that could endanger life, health or safety. The landlord is required to maintain dwelling units in a habitable condition and to make any necessary repairs to common elements such as hallways, stairs or elevators. The tenant does not have to make any repairs (unless otherwise provided in the lease) but must return the premises in the same condition they were received with allowances for wear and tear occasioned by ordinary use.

Constructive Eviction

Assignment and Subleasing

The tenant may assign the lease or may sublease if the lease terms do not prohibit it, or if the building contains four or more units (in New York State). A tenant who transfers the entire remaining term of his or her lease *assigns* the lease. One who transfers most of the term but retains a small part of it **subleases** (*see* Figure 22.1). In most cases the sublease or assignment of a lease does not relieve the original tenant of the obligation to make rental payments unless the landlord agrees to waive such liability. Most leases prohibit the tenant from assigning or subletting without the landlord's consent; this allows the landlord to retain control over the occupancy of the leased premises. The (original landlord's) interest in the real estate is known as a *sandwich lease*. In New York, where the lessor's consent is required for sublease or assignment, it may not be unreasonably withheld. If it is, the tenant is released from the lease with 30 days' notice.

New York's Real Property Law sets guidelines for a detailed written request from the tenant; the landlord's right to ask for additional information within ten days; and the landlord's written response, including the reasons for any

Figure 22.1
Assignment versus
Subletting

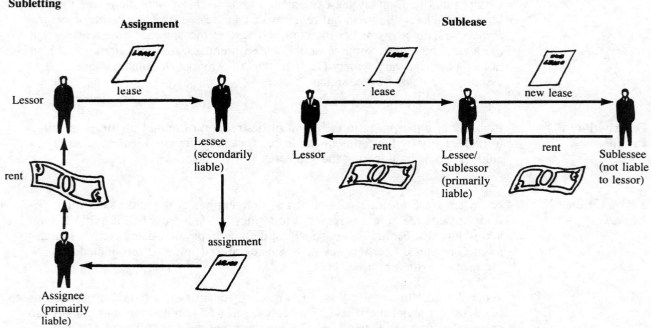

denial, within 30 days. The landlord's failure to respond is considered consent for the sublet.

Special regulations apply to the subletting of rent-stabilized apartments: For a furnished sublet, rent may exceed the original tenant's figure by 10 percent. The original tenant must establish that the apartment is his or her primary residence and will be reoccupied at the end of the sublet. A rent-stabilized apartment may not be sublet for more than one-half of any four-year period. The original tenant, not the subtenant, is entitled to the rights of a renewal lease and any right resulting from a co-op conversion.

Apartment-Sharing

In New York State a lease may not restrict occupancy of an apartment to the named tenant and that tenant's immediate family. The apartment may be shared with one additional occupant and that occupant's dependent children. If the lease names more than one tenant and one of them moves out, that tenant may be replaced with another occupant and that person's dependent children. At least one of the original tenants named in the lease, or that person's spouse, must continue to occupy the shared apartment as a primary residence.

Tenants must inform their landlords of the name of any occupant within 30 days after the occupant moves into an apartment. Landlords may, however, limit the total number of occupants to comply with health laws on overcrowding.

Renewals

Sometimes a lease contains a clause stating that it will be *automatically renewed unless* the tenant gives *notice* that he or she intends not to renew. No such clause is valid unless the landlord reminds the tenant about the automatic renewal provision 15 to 30 days before the tenant's notice would be due.

On the other hand many leases contain an *option* that grants the lessee the privilege of *renewing* the lease but requires that the lessee give *notice* on or before a specific date of his or her intention to exercise the option. Some leases grant to the lessee the option to purchase the leased premises; the provisions for the option to purchase vary widely (*see* Chapter 5). Any option must contain all the essential elements of a contract.

Destruction of Premises

Liability of either party in the event of destruction of leased premises is controlled largely by the terms of the lease. Carefully prepared leases generally include a provision covering the subject.

Termination of Lease

A written lease for a definite period of time expires at the end of that time period; no separate notice is required to terminate the lease when it expires. Oral and written leases that do not specify a definite expiration date (such as month-to-month or year-to-year tenancy or a tenancy at will) may be terminated by giving proper written notice.

When the conditions of a lease are breached, or broken, a landlord may terminate the lease and evict the tenant. This action must be handled through a court proceeding according to state law. The landlord who wishes to be rid of a tenant is not allowed to use threats of violence, change locks, discontinue essential services like water or heat or seize the tenant's possessions.

It is possible for the parties to a lease to agree to cancel the lease. The tenant may offer to surrender the lease and acceptance by the landlord will result in termination. A tenant who abandons leased property, however, remains liable for the terms of the lease—including the rent. The terms of the specific lease will usually dictate whether the landlord is obligated to try to rerent the space.

When the owner of leased property dies or the property is sold, *the lease does not terminate*. The heirs of a deceased landlord are bound by the terms of existing valid leases. In addition, if a landlord conveys leased real estate, the new landlord takes the property subject to the rights of the tenant. The lease *survives* the sale. If a tenant dies, the lease will remain in effect; the deceased lessee's heirs will be bound by the terms of the lease.

Breach of Lease

When a tenant breaches any lease provision, the landlord may sue the tenant to obtain a judgment to cover past-due rent, damages to the premises or other defaults. Likewise, when a landlord breaches any lease provision, the tenant is entitled to remedies. The landlord's nonperformance of some obligation under the lease, short of eviction, does not, however, affect the tenant's obligation to pay rent.

In this state, grounds for which the landlord can institute proceedings include nonpayment of rent, illegal use of the premises, tenant remaining in possession after expiration of the lease without permission and bankruptcy or insolvency of the tenant.

Suit for possession—actual eviction. When a tenant breaches a lease or improperly retains possession of leased premises the landlord may regain possession through a **suit for possession** or *summary proceeding to recover possession of real estate*. This process is known as **actual eviction.** Law requires the landlord to serve *notice* on the tenant before commencing the suit. In New York, only a three-day notice must be given before filing a suit for possession based on a default in payment of rent. When a court issues a judgment for possession to a landlord, the tenant must peaceably remove or the landlord can have the judgment enforced by a sheriff, constable or marshal, who will *forcibly remove* the tenant and his or her possessions.

Tenants' remedies—constructive eviction. If a landlord breaches any clause of a lease agreement, the tenant has the right to sue, claiming a judgment for damages against the landlord. If an action or omission of the landlord's part results in the leased premises becoming uninhabitable for the purpose intended in the lease, the tenant may have the right to abandon the premises. This action, called **constructive eviction**, terminates the lease agreement if the tenant can prove that the premises have become uninhabitable because of the landlord's neglect. In order to claim constructive eviction the tenant must actually move from the premises while the uninhabitable condition exists.

For example, a lease requires the landlord to furnish steam heat; because of the landlord's failure to repair a defective heating plant, the heat is not provided. If this results in the leased premises becoming uninhabitable, the tenant may abandon them. Some leases provide that if the failure to furnish heat is accidental and not the landlord's fault, it is not grounds for constructive eviction.

Pro-Tenant Legislation

In New York State a landlord may not legally retaliate because a tenant joins a tenants' organization. The landlord or his or her agent may not willfully violate any provision of a lease requiring the furnishing of heat, lights, water and like utilities. If the landlord fails to furnish heat as stipulated in the lease, tenants in New York may pay a utility company directly and deduct the sum from rent due. In New York City at least one-third of the tenants of a multiple-unit dwelling, having agreed to participate together, may start a special court proceeding to use their rent money to remedy conditions dangerous to life, health or safety. Retaliatory evictions are illegal.

The federal government also took steps to increase tenants' protection with the implementation of the Tenants' Eviction Procedures Act in 1976. This act establishes standardized eviction procedures for people living in *government-subsidized housing*. It requires that the landlord have a valid reason for evicting the tenant and that the landlord give the tenant proper notice of eviction. This act does not supersede state laws in this area; however, it does provide recourse for tenants in states that have no such laws. The act applies only to multiunit residential buildings that are owned or subsidized by the Department of Housing and Urban Development and to buildings that have government-insured mortgages.

Types of Leases

Three primary types of leases are outlined in Table 22.2.

Gross Lease

In a **gross lease** the tenants' obligation is to pay a *fixed rental* and the landlord pays all taxes, insurance, mortgage payments, repairs and the like connected with

Table 22.2 Types of Leases	Type of Lease	Tenant Pays	Landlord Pays

	Gross Lease
	  Residential (also small
	  commercial)
		Basic Rent	Property Charges (taxes,
			  repairs, insurance, etc.)

	Net Lease
	  Commercial/Industrial
		Basic Rent Plus Most or
		  All Property Charges
			Few or No Property Charges
			  Mortgage (if any)

	Percentage Lease
	  Commercial/Industrial
		Basic Rent Plus Percent of
		  Gross Sales (may pay some or
		  all property costs)
			Any Agreed Property Charges

the property (usually called *property charges*). This type of lease most often is used for residential rentals.

Net Lease

The **net lease** provides that in addition to the rent, the *tenant pays some or all of the property charges*. The monthly rental paid to the landlord is in addition to these charges and so is net income for the landlord. Leases for entire commercial or industrial buildings and the land on which they are located, ground leases and long-term leases are usually net leases. With a *triple-net* lease, the tenant pays taxes, insurance and all other expenses except debt service.

Percentage Lease

Either a gross lease or a net lease may be a **percentage lease.** A percentage lease provides that the rental is based on a *percentage of the gross or net income* received by the tenant doing business on the leased property. This type of lease is normally used in the rental of retail business locations.

The percentage lease provides for a minimum fixed rental fee plus a percentage of that portion of the tenant's business income that exceeds a stated minimum. For example, a lease might provide for a minimum monthly rental of $1,200 with the further agreement that the tenant pay an additional amount each month equivalent to 5 percent of all gross sales in excess of $30,000. The percentage charged in such leases varies widely with the nature of the business and is negotiable between landlord and tenant. A tenant's bargaining power is determined by the volume of business.

Other Lease Types

Variable leases. Several types of leases allow for increases in the fixed rental charge during the lease period. Two of the more common ones are the *graduated lease,* which provides for increases in rent at set future dates, and the *index lease,* which allows rent to be increased or decreased periodically based on changes in the government cost-of-living index.

Ground leases. When a landowner leases his or her land to a tenant who agrees to *erect a building* on it, the lease is referred to as a **ground lease.** Such a lease must be for a long enough term to make the transaction desirable to the tenant making the investment in the building. These leases are generally *net leases* that require the lessee to pay rent as well as real estate taxes, insurance, upkeep and repairs. Net ground leases often run for terms of 50 years or longer and a lease for 999 years is not impossible. Although these leases are considered to be personal property, law may give leaseholders some of the rights and obligations of real property owners.

Oil and gas leases. When oil companies lease land to explore for oil and gas, a special lease agreement must be negotiated. Usually the landowner receives a cash payment for executing the lease. If no well is drilled within the period stated in the lease, the lease expires; however, most oil and gas leases provide that the oil company may continue its rights by paying another flat rental fee. Such rentals may be paid annually until a well is produced. If oil and/or gas is found, the landowner usually receives a fraction of its value as a royalty. In this case the lease will continue for as long as oil or gas is obtained in significant quantities. Oil and gas leases are common across the Southern Tier and in the western part of New York State. An oil or gas lease constitutes a cloud on title, and a buyer may refuse to consummate a purchase unless he or she has specifically agreed to take title subject to such a lease.

Summary

A *lease* grants one person the right to use the property of another for a certain period in return for consideration. The lease agreement is a combination of a conveyance creating a leasehold interest in the property and a contract outlining the rights and obligations of landlord and tenant.

A leasehold estate that runs for a specific length of time creates an *estate for years*, while one that runs for an indefinite period creates a *periodic tenancy* (year to year, month to month) or a *tenancy at will*. A leasehold estate is generally classified as personal property.

The requirements of a valid lease include the capacity to contract, a demising clause, description of premises, statement of terms, rent and signatures. The state statute of frauds requires that any lease that will not be executed within one year be in writing. Most leases also include clauses relating to such rights and obligations of the landlord and tenant as the use of the premises, subletting, judgments, maintenance of the premises and termination of the lease period.

In New York an oral lease is valid if it is for a period of less than one year. A lease for three years or more, if properly acknowledged, may be entered in the public records. State regulations require the owner of six or more units to hold security deposits in an interest-bearing New York bank account with all interest less a 1-percent fee due the tenant. State law gives the tenant in any building with four or more units the right to sublet, subject to the landlord's consent, which may not be unreasonably withheld.

Leases may be terminated by the expiration of the lease period, the mutual agreement of the parties, or a breach of the lease by either landlord or tenant. Neither the death of the tenant nor the landlord's sale of the rental property terminates a lease.

Upon a tenant's default on any of the lease provisions, a landlord may sue for a money judgment or for *actual eviction* where a tenant has improperly retained possession of the premises. If the premises have become uninhabitable due to landlord's negligence, the tenant may exercise *constructive eviction*, the right to abandon the premises and refuse to pay rent until the premises are repaired.

Basic types of leases include *net leases, gross leases* and *percentage leases*, classified according to the method used in determining the rental rate of the property.

Questions

1. In order to be considered valid in New York a two-year lease must:
   a. be in writing.
   b. be signed by the parties involved.
   c. state the terms of the agreement.
   d. All of the above.

2. A lease for more than one year must be in writing because:
   a. the landlord or tenant may forget the terms.
   b. the tenant must sign the agreement to pay rent.
   c. the statute of frauds requires it.
   d. it is the customary procedure to protect the tenant.

3. A lease is considered to be:
   a. a freehold estate.
   b. personal property.
   c. a reversionary interest.
   d. real property.

4. Willie James agrees to rent Dana Gibson her upstairs apartment for the next six months. Dana has a(n):
   a. estate for years.
   b. periodic estate.
   c. tenancy at will.
   d. tenancy at sufferance.

5. Willie James agrees to rent Dana Gibson her upstairs apartment from month to month. To end the arrangement Willie must:
   a. file a court suit to recover possession.
   b. give at least 60 days' notice from the day the rent is due.
   c. give at least 30 days' notice from the day the rent is due.
   d. simply refuse to accept the next month's rent, on the day it is due.

6. A tenant's lease has expired, the tenant has neither vacated nor negotiated a renewal lease and the landlord has declared that she does not want the tenant to remain in the building. The tenancy is called:
   a. estate for years.
   b. periodic estate.
   c. tenancy at will.
   d. tenancy at sufferance.

7. Mary Withers sells her six-unit apartment building in Queens to George Brown. Now:
   a. George may give all the tenants 30 days' notice.
   b. tenants should collect their security deposits from Mary.
   c. George must renegotiate all leases with the tenants.
   d. Mary must turn over security deposits to George.

8. A lease, properly acknowledged, may be recorded if it is for a period of at least:
   a. one year.   c. three years.
   b. two years.   d. four years.

9. Steve Jackson rents a single-family house under a one-year lease. Two months into the rental period Jackson installs awnings over the front windows to keep the sun from some delicate hanging plants. The awnings:
   a. may be removed by Jackson any time before the year is over.
   b. are classified as trade fixtures.
   c. are now the landlord's property.
   d. are known as chattels.

10. If a tenant is unable to receive hot water because of a faulty hot-water heater, which of the following remedies may the tenant take if the landlord refuses to fix the equipment?
    a. The tenant may sue the landlord for damages.
    b. The tenant may abandon the premises.
    c. The tenant may terminate the lease agreement.
    d. The tenant may exercise all these options.

11. A tenant who transfers the entire remaining term of his or her lease to a third party is:

    a. a sublettor.
    b. assigning the lease.
    c. automatically relieved of any further obligation under it.
    d. giving the third party a sandwich lease.

12. Unless otherwise stated in the lease, in New York State:

    a. rent is payable in arrears.
    b. the tenant is not entitled to interest on the security deposit.
    c. the tenant may not sublet.
    d. the lease is automatically terminated when the property is sold.

13. An automatic renewal clause in a lease:

    a. is not allowed on rent-stabilized apartments.
    b. is granted every tenant in a building with four or more units.
    c. is illegal in New York State.
    d. requires notice from the landlord calling the tenants' attention to the clause.

14. Jane Miller's apartment lease agreement states that it will expire on April 30, 1992. When must her landlord give notice that her tenancy is to terminate?

    a. January 31, 1992.
    b. March 31, 1992.
    c. April 1, 1992.
    d. No notice is required.

15. If a tenant falls three months behind in rent payments, a landlord may:

    a. turn down the heat.
    b. move out the tenant's possessions, storing them carefully.
    c. start a court suit for possession.
    d. All of the above.

16. In the preceding question, the landlord who turns down the heat has terminated the lease through:

    a. the demising clause.
    b. constructive eviction.
    c. payment in arrears.
    d. assigning the lease.

17. A gross lease is most likely to be used for rental of:

    a. an apartment.
    b. a factory building.
    c. land under a post office.
    d. a farm.

18. With a triple-net lease, the tenant pays:

    a. rent only.
    b. rent plus a share of business profits.
    c. rent plus any increase in property taxes.
    d. everything but the mortgage.

19. A percentage lease provides for a:

    a. rental of a percentage of the value of a building.
    b. definite periodic rent not exceeding a stated percentage.
    c. definite monthly rent plus a percentage of the tenant's gross receipts in excess of a certain amount.
    d. graduated amount due monthly and not exceeding a stated percentage.

20. A ground lease is usually:

    a. terminable with 30 days' notice.
    b. based on percentages.
    c. long term.
    d. a gross lease.

Appendix: Excerpts from New York State's Study Booklet for Brokers

LEASES

A lease is a contract whereby, for a consideration, usually termed rent, one who is entitled to the possession of real property grants such right to another for life, for a term of years, or at will.

Essentials of a valid lease. These are:
1. Competent parties (sane adults):
2. A definite demising clause, whereby the lessor (landlord) leases and the lessee (tenant) takes the property leased;
3. A reasonably definite description of the property leased;
4. A clear statement of the term (duration) of the letting;
5. Specification of the rent payable and how it is to be paid;
6. If the term of the lease is for more than one year it must be in writing, signed by all parties thereto and duly delivered.

A net lease is one that provides that the tenant, in addition to paying the agreed rent, shall defray the expense of all repairs, taxes, water rents, insurance, premiums, and such other items of the carrying charges upon the leased property, as may be specified.

Section 5—905 of the General Obligations Law reads as follows: "No provision of a lease of any real property or premises which states that the term thereof shall be deemed renewed for a specified additional period of time unless the tenant gives notice to the lessor of his intention to quit the premises at the expiration of such term shall be operative unless the lessor, at least fifteen days and not more than thirty days previous to the time specified for the furnishing of such notice to him, shall give to the tenant written notice, served personally or by registered or certified mail, calling the attention to the tenant to the existence of such provision in the lease."

The results that may flow from the omission of a necessary or desirable covenant or condition are often annoying and, sometimes, may prove serious to the landlord or the tenant, as the case may be. *For instance, rent is not payable in advance unless the lease so provides.* So, too, a landlord has no right to send mechanics into leased premises, to make alterations or to install new equipment, unless the lease authorizes the landlord to do so. On the other hand, the tenant should carefully consider the negative convenants the lease contains. A negative covenant binds the tenant not to do specified acts, such as assigning the lease, subletting, or using the premises for other than a specified purpose, etc. The tenant should also bear in mind that, unless the lease provides that the landlord shall make all repairs, or such of them as the landlord has agreed to make, the tenant must bear the cost of even the most necessary repairs to the leased premises. Under section 226-b of the Real Property Law, a tenant of a residence of four or more units is given the right to sublet the premises or to assign his or her lease, such subletting or assignment being subject to the landlord's prior approval. If, however, the landlord unreasonably withholds consent, the landlord upon request must release the tenant from the lease. These provisions are applicable to all leases or renewals of leases now entered into. Every residential lease is also deemed to contain a covenant by the landlord that the premises are fit for human habitation and for the uses for which they were reasonably intended by the parties. The tenant's rights under this covenant cannot be waived.

Form. There is no statutory form of lease. The law does require, however, that a residential lease be written in a clear and coherent manner, using words with every day meaning—that is, in plain language.

Recording leases. A lease is not recordable unless it is for a term of three years, or more, and has been duly signed and acknowledged by the parties thereto.

Voluntary and Involuntary Alienation

Key Terms

Adverse possession
Descent
Escheat
Executor
Heir
Intestate
Involuntary alienation

Last will and testament
Probate
Testate
Testator
Title
Voluntary alienation

Overview

A parcel of real estate may be transferred from one owner to another in a number of different ways. It may be given *voluntarily* by sale or gift, or it may be taken *involuntarily* by operation of law. In addition it may be transferred by the living or it may be transferred by will or descent after a person has died. In every instance, however, a transfer of title to a parcel of real estate is a complex legal procedure involving a number of laws and documents. This chapter will discuss the four methods of title transfer.

Title

Title to real estate means the right to or ownership of the land; in addition it represents the *evidence* of ownership. The term *title* has two functions. It represents the "bundle of rights" the owner possesses in the real estate and it also denotes the facts that, if proven, would enable a person to recover or retain ownership or possession of a parcel of real estate.

The laws of each state govern real estate transactions for land located within its boundaries. Title to real estate may be transferred by: (1) voluntary alienation, (2) involuntary alienation, (3) will and (4) descent.

Voluntary Alienation

Voluntary alienation (transfer) of title may be made by either gift or sale. To transfer title by voluntary alienation during his or her lifetime, an owner must use some form of deed of conveyance.

In New York the following deeds are used to convey title to property: (1) deeds with full covenants (warranty deeds); (2) bargain and sale deeds, without covenant against grantor's acts; (3) bargain and sale deeds, with covenant against grantor's acts; (4) quitclaim deeds; (5) executor's deeds; and (6) referees' deeds.

The full covenants and warranty deed contains the following five covenants:

1. That the grantor is *seized* of (owns) the premises and has good right to convey the same (covenant of seizin);
2. That the grantor will have the right to a property free of interference from the acts or claims of third parties (covenant of quiet enjoyment);
3. That the premises are free from *encumbrances* (covenant against encumbrances);
4. That the grantor will execute or procure any *further* necessary *assurance* of the title to the premises (covenant of further assurances); and
5. That the grantor will *forever warrant* the title to the premises (covenant of warranty forever).

Title to land may be transferred voluntarily between an individual and the government through dedication or public grant. A developer passes ownership of subdivision lands earmarked for streets and roads to a city, town or village through the process of *dedication*. Lands owned by the government may be transferred to individuals through *public grant*, as when available public land is earned through the process of homesteading.

Involuntary Alienation

Title to property can be transferred by **involuntary alienation,** that is, without the owner's consent (*see* Figure 23.1). Such transfers are usually carried out by operations of law ranging from government condemnation of land for public use to the sale of property to satisfy delinquent tax or mortgage liens. When a person dies intestate and leaves no heirs, the title to his or her real estate passes to the state by operation of law based on the principle of **escheat.**

Figure 23.1
Involuntary Alienation

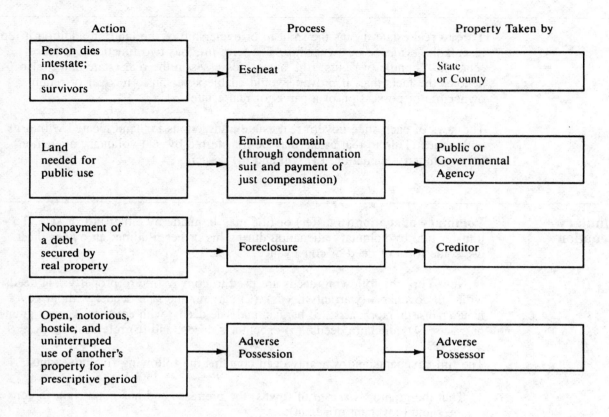

Action	Process	Property Taken by
Person dies intestate; no survivors	Escheat	State or County
Land needed for public use	Eminent domain (through condemnation suit and payment of just compensation)	Public or Governmental Agency
Nonpayment of a debt secured by real property	Foreclosure	Creditor
Open, notorious, hostile, and uninterrupted use of another's property for prescriptive period	Adverse Possession	Adverse Possessor

Federal, state and local governments, school boards, some government agencies and certain public and quasi-public corporations and utilities (railroads and gas and electric companies) have the power of *eminent domain*. Under this power, private property may be taken for public use through a *suit for condemnation*. The exercise of eminent domain is subject to a court's determination of two necessary conditions: (1) that the use is for the benefit of the public and (2) that an equitable compensation, as set by the court, will be paid to the owner. Whenever private property is taken in New York, the owner is given the opportunity to challenge in court the amount of money offered.

Land also may be transferred without an owner's consent in order to satisfy debts contracted by the owner. In such cases the debt is foreclosed, the property is sold and the proceeds of the sale are applied to pay off the debt. Debts that could be foreclosed include mortgage loans, real estate taxes, mechanics' liens or general judgments against the property owner (*see* Chapter 24).

In addition to the involuntary transfer of land by legal processes, land may be transferred by natural forces. Owners of land bordering on rivers, lakes and other bodies of water may acquire additional land through the process of *accretion,* the slow accumulation of soil, rock or other matter deposited by the movement of water on an owner's property. The opposite of accretion is *erosion*, the gradual wearing away of land by the action of water and wind. In addition property may be lost through *avulsion,* the sudden tearing away of land by natural means like earthquakes or tidal waves.

Involuntary alienation also may occur as a result of court action. In a *partition proceeding* one co-owner seeks to force another to divide or sell property. An *action to quiet title* requests that the court rule on a clouded or disputed title, quashing one claim in favor of another.

Adverse Possession

Adverse possession is another means of involuntary transfer. An owner who does not use his or her land or does not inspect it for a number of years may lose title to another person who has some claim to the land, takes possession and, most important, uses the land. In New York a person may acquire title by adverse possession to land owned by another by the continuous, open, notorious, hostile and exclusive occupation of the property for *ten years*. After that time the user may perfect the claim of title to land by adverse possession by bringing a court suit to quiet title.

Through a process known as *tacking,* continuous periods of adverse possession may be combined by successive users, thus enabling a person who had not been in possession for the entire ten years to establish a claim of adverse possession. The process is not automatic; legal action is necessary to *perfect* the claim. Adverse possession is not possible against publicly owned property.

Transfer of a Deceased Person's Property

Every state has a law known as the *statute of descent and distribution*. When a person dies **intestate** (without having left a will), the decedent's real estate and personal property pass to his or her heirs according to this statute. In effect the state makes a will for such decedents. In contrast a person who dies **testate** has prepared a will indicating the way his or her property will be disposed of after death.

Legally, when a person dies title to his or her real estate immediately passes either to the heirs by descent or to the persons named in the will. However, the will must be probated and all claims against the estate must be satisfied.

Probate Proceedings

Probate or administration is a legal process by which a court determines who will inherit the property of a deceased person and what the assets of the estate are. Surrogate's court proceedings must take place in the county where the deceased person lived. In the case of a person who has died testate, the court also rules on the validity of the will. If the will is upheld, the property is distributed according to its provisions. If a person has died without a will, the court determines who inherits by reviewing a *proof of heirship*. This statement, usually prepared by an attorney, gives personal information regarding the decedent's spouse, children and relatives. From this document the court decides which parties will receive what portion of the estate.

To initiate probate or administration proceedings, the custodian of the will, an heir or another interested party must petition the court. The court then holds a hearing to determine the validity of the will and/or the order of descent, should no valid will exist. If for any reason a will is declared invalid by the court, any property owned by the decedent will pass by the laws of descent. The court will appoint an **executor,** usually named in the will, or an *administrator* to oversee the administration and distribution of the estate.

Transfer of Title by Will

A **last will and testament** is an instrument made by an owner to voluntarily convey title to the owner's property after his or her death. A will takes effect only after the death of the decedent; until that time, any property covered by the will can be conveyed by the owner.

A party who makes a will is known as a **testator,** or *testatrix* (female); the gift of real property by will is known as a *devise*, and a person who receives real property by will is known as a *devisee*. A gift of personal property is a *legacy* or *bequest;* the person receiving the personal property is a *legatee*.

In New York, children can be disinherited but a surviving spouse is entitled to at least one-third of the estate. In a case where a will does not provide the minimum statutory inheritance, the surviving spouse has the option of informing the court that he or she will take the minimum statutory share rather than the lesser share provided in the will. This practice, called a right of election, is a right reserved only to a surviving spouse.

A will differs from a deed in that a deed conveys a present interest in real estate during the lifetime of the grantor, while a will conveys no interest in the property until after the death of the testator. To be valid a deed *must* be delivered during the lifetime of the grantor. The parties named in a will have no rights or interests as long as the party who has made the will is still alive; they acquire interest or title only after the owner's death. The will must be filed with the court and *probated* in order for title to pass to the devisees.

Legal requirements for making a will (*see* Figure 23.2). A person must be of *legal age* and of *sound mind* when he or she executes the will. There are no rigid tests to determine the capacity to make a will. Usually the courts hold that to make a valid will the testator must have sufficient mental capacity to understand the nature and effect of his or her acts and to dispose of the property according to some plan. The courts also hold that the drawing of a will must be a voluntary act, free of any undue influence by other people.

New York law provides that any person of sound mind who is 18 years of age or older can make a will devising his or her real property. All wills must be in

**Figure 23.2
Requirements for a
Valid Will**

WILL
1. Legal Age
2. Sound Mind
3. Proper Wording
4. No Undue Influence
5. Witnesses

writing and signed by the testator in the presence of at least two witnesses. A holographic will is one that is written entirely in the testator's own handwriting and is not property attested in the manner just described. Such a document will be enforced by New York courts only under limited circumstances.

Transfer of Title by Descent

Title to real estate and personal property of a person who dies intestate passes to heirs. Under the **descent** statutes the primary **heirs** of the deceased are his or her spouse and close blood relatives. When children have been legally adopted, most states consider them to be heirs of the adopting parents but not heirs of ancestors of the adopting parents. In most states illegitimate children inherit from the mother but do not inherit from the father unless he has admitted parentage in writing or parentage has been established legally. If he legally adopts such a child, that child will inherit as an adopted child.

Intestate property will be distributed according to the laws of the state in which the property is located. The New York law of descent and distribution provides that real property belonging to an individual who has died intestate is distributed in the order listed below. This law and the estate discussed apply only to what remains of the estate after payment of all debts. If a decedent is survived by:

- a spouse and children or grandchildren, the spouse receives money or personal property not to exceed $4,000 in value and one-third of what remains of the estate. The balance of the estate passes to the children or to grandchildren.
- a spouse and only one child, or a spouse and the children of only one child, the spouse receives money or personal property not to exceed $4,000 in value and one-half of what remains of the estate. The balance passes to the child or his or her children.
- a spouse and both parents only, $25,000 and one-half the estate passes to the spouse. The parents (or parent) receive the balance, or the whole estate if there is no surviving spouse.
- a spouse only, the spouse receives the entire estate.
- children only, the children receive the entire estate.
- siblings only, or their children, they receive the entire estate.

If there are no heirs, the decedent's property escheats to the state of New York.

Summary

Title to real estate is the right to, and evidence of, ownership of the land. It may be transferred in four ways: (1) voluntary alienation, (2) involuntary alienation, (3) will and (4) descent.

An owner's title may be transferred without his or her permission by a court action such as a *foreclosure* or judgment sale, a tax sale, *condemnation* under the power of eminent domain, *adverse possession* or *escheat*. Land also may be transferred by the natural forces of water and wind, which either increase property by *accretion* or decrease it through *erosion* or *avulsion*.

The real estate of an owner who makes a valid *will* (who dies testate) passes to the devisees through the probating of the will. Generally, an heir or a devisee does not receive a deed, because title passes by the law or the will. The title of an owner who dies without a will (intestate) passes according to the provisions of the *laws of descent* of the state in which the real estate is located.

Questions

1. Title to real estate may be transferred during a person's lifetime by:

   a. devise.
   c. involuntary alienation.
   b. descent.
   d. escheat.

2. Title to an owner's real estate can be transferred at the death of the owner by which of the following documents?

   a. Warranty deed
   b. Quitclaim deed
   c. Referee's deed
   d. Last will and testament

3. Matilda Fairbanks bought acreage in a distant county, never went to see the acreage and did not use the ground. Harold Sampson moved his mobile home onto the land, had a water well drilled and lived there for 12 years. Sampson may become the owner of the land if he has complied with the state law regarding:

   a. requirements for a valid conveyance.
   b. adverse possession.
   c. avulsion.
   d. voluntary alienation

4. Which of the following is *not* one of the manners in which title to real estate may be transferred by involuntary alienation?

   a. Eminent domain
   c. Erosion
   b. Escheat
   d. Seisin

5. A person who has died leaving a valid will is called a(n):

   a. devisee.
   c. legatee.
   b. testator.
   d. intestate.

6. Claude Johnson, a bachelor, died owning real estate that he devised by his will to his niece, Annette. In essence, at what point does title pass to his niece?

   a. Immediately upon Johnson's death
   b. After his will has been probated
   c. After Annette has paid all inheritance taxes
   d. When Annette executes a new deed to the property

7. An owner of real estate who was adjudged legally incompetent made a will during his stay at a nursing home. He later died and was survived by a wife and three children. His real estate will pass:

   a. to his wife.
   b. to the heirs mentioned in his will.
   c. according to the state laws of descent.
   d. to the state.

8. In New York, land may be acquired by adverse possession after a period of:

   a. three years.
   c. ten years.
   b. seven years.
   d. twenty years.

9. The acquisition of land through deposit of soil or sand washed up by water is called:

   a. accretion.
   c. erosion.
   b. avulsion.
   d. condemnation.

10. The person whose land is taken for public use in New York State:

    a. may or may not receive compensation.
    b. may refuse to give up the property.
    c. may still devise it by will.
    d. may challenge a money award in court.

24

Liens and Easements

Overview

The ownership interest a person has in real estate can be diminished by the interests of others. Taxing bodies, creditors and courts can lessen an ownership interest by making a financial claim—called a *lien*—against a person's property to secure payment of taxes, debts and other obligations. In addition, rights to use another's real estate can be acquired; these rights are called *easements*. This chapter will discuss the nature of liens and easements that affect both real and personal property.

Liens

A **lien** is defined as a charge against property that provides security for a debt or obligation. A lien allows a creditor (lienor) to force the sale of the property to satisfy the debt in case of default. A lien does not constitute ownership; it is a type of *encumbrance*—a charge or burden on a property that may diminish its value. While all liens are encumbrances, encumbrances are not necessarily liens. As discussed in Chapter 3, encumbrances that are not liens (easements and deed restrictions) give the parties in question certain rights, or interest, in the real estate. Generally liens are enforced by court order. A creditor must institute a legal action for the court to sell the real estate in question for full or partial satisfaction of the debt.

A lien may be voluntary or involuntary. A **voluntary lien** is created by the owner's action such as taking out a mortgage loan. An **involuntary lien** is created by law. Involuntary liens are either statutory or equitable. A **statutory lien** is created by statute. An **equitable lien** arises out of common law. A real estate tax lien, for example, is an involuntary, statutory lien; that is, it is created by statute without any action by the property owner. A court-ordered judgment requiring payment of the balance on a delinquent charge account would be an involuntary, equitable lien on the debtor's property.

Liens may be classified into two categories: general and specific. As illustrated in Figure 24.1, **general liens** usually affect all the property of a debtor, both real and personal, and include judgments, estate and inheritance taxes, debts of a deceased person, corporation franchise taxes and Internal Revenue Service taxes. **Specific liens** on the other hand are secured by a specific parcel of real estate and affect only that particular property. As illustrated in Figure 24.2, these in-

Figure 24.1
General Liens

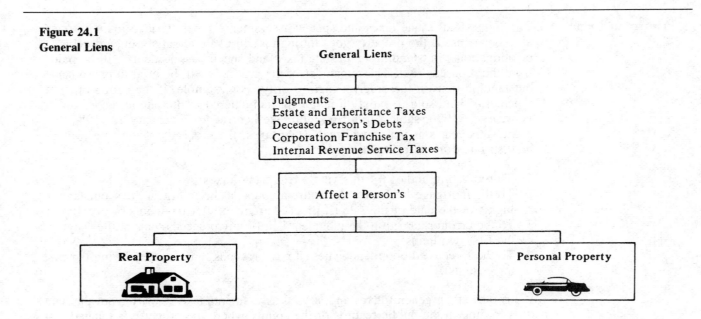

Figure 24.2
Specific Liens

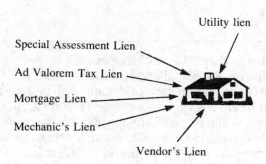

clude mechanics' liens, mortgages, taxes, special assessment, liens for certain public utilities, vendors' liens, vendees' liens and surety bail bond liens.

Effects of Liens on Title

Although the fee simple estate held by a typical real estate owner can be reduced
in value by the lien and encumbrance rights of others, the owner is still free to
convey title to a willing purchaser. This purchaser, however, will buy the property subject to any liens and encumbrances because liens *run with the land;* that
is, they will bind successive owners if steps are not taken to clear the liens.

Liens attach to property, not to the property owner. Although a purchaser who
buys real estate under a delinquent lien is not responsible for payment of the
debt secured by the lien, he or she faces a possible loss of the property if the
creditors take court action to enforce payment of their liens.

Priority of Liens

Tax liens. Real estate taxes and special assessments generally take **priority** over
all other liens. If the property goes through a court sale to satisfy unpaid debts
or obligations, outstanding real estate taxes and special assessments will be paid
from the proceeds *first*. The remainder of the proceeds will be used to pay other
outstanding liens in the order of their priority. For example, if the courts ordered
a parcel of land sold to satisfy a judgment lien entered in the public record on
February 7, 1990, subject to a first mortgage lien recorded January 22, 1984,
and to this year's as-yet unpaid real estate taxes, the proceeds of the sale would
be distributed in the following order:

1. To the taxing bodies for this year's real estate taxes;
2. To the mortgage lender for the entire amount of the mortgage loan outstanding as of the date of the sale (if proceeds remain after payments of taxes);
3. To the creditor named in the judgment lien (if any proceeds remain after paying
   the first two items);
4. To the foreclosed-upon landowner (if any proceeds remain after paying the first
   three items).

Liens other than general taxes and special assessments take priority from the date
of recording in the public records of the county where the property is located
(*see* Figure 24.3).

Figure 24.3
Priority of Liens

First Priority   Real Estate Taxes/Special Assessments

Next Priority
According to   Property   *1024 First St.*
Order of Filing   *Anytown, USA.*
in Public Record   *10-14-82 .. First Mortgage lien--*
                     U.S.A.--Federal Savings & Loan
                     2-17-83--Mechanic's lien filed
                     J.W. Adams Construction
                     3-1-84--Second Mortgage lien--
                     American Finance Co.

Subordination agreements are written agreements between lineholders to change the priority of mortgage, judgment and other liens under certain circumstances. Priority and recording of liens are discussed in detail in Chapter 11.

Liens Other Than Real Estate Taxes

Aside from real estate tax and special assessment liens, the following types of liens may be charged against real property either voluntarily or involuntary: mortgage liens, mechanics' liens, judgments, estate and inheritance tax liens, vendors' liens, vendee's liens, liens for municipal utilities, surety bail bond liens, corporation franchise tax liens and Internal Revenue Service tax liens.

Mortgage Liens

In general a **mortgage lien** is a voluntary lien on real estate given to a lender by a borrower as security for a mortgage loan. It becomes a lien on real property when the mortgage funds are disbursed and when the lender files or records the mortgage in the office of the county clerk or registrar of the county where the property is located. Mortgage lenders generally require a preferred lien, referred to as a *first mortgage lien;* this means that (aside from taxes) no other major liens against the property would take priority over the mortgage lien. This requirement does not apply to second mortgages or home equity loans. Mortgages and mortgage liens are discussed in detail in Chapter 7.

Mechanics' Liens

The purpose of the **mechanic's lien** is to *give security to those who perform labor or furnish material in the improvement of real property.* A mechanic's lien is a specific, involuntary lien.

In order for a person to be entitled to a mechanic's lien, the work that was done must have been by contract (expressed or implied consent) with the owner or owner's authorized representative. Such a lien is relied on to cover situations in which the owner has not fully paid for the work or when the general contractor has been paid but has not paid the subcontractors or suppliers of materials.

A notice of a mechanic's lien must be filed in the office of the clerk of the county in which the property is located. The lien must be filed within four months for work on a single residence and eight months on all other property, from the date the last item of labor was performed or material furnished. The mechanic's lien attaches immediately upon filing. New York's lien law requires the lienor to serve a copy of the lien upon the property owner within 30 days of filing, and an affidavit that service was made must be filed with the county clerk within 35 days.

If a landowner has paid a **general contractor** in full and the general contractor has failed to pay the **subcontractor** or materialmen, the general contractor may be in violation of the trust provisions of the New York State lien law. Proof of payment in full by the landowner will be a defense to the claim under the mechanic's lien law; the subcontractor must look to the contractor.

A mechanic's lien does not have priority over any prior recorded lien provided the prior liens are proper in all respects. A mechanic's lien for private improvements is valid for one year from the date of filing and can be renewed by a court order.

New York's lien law allows certain brokers' claims for commissions to be filed as mechanics' liens. On the theory that the negotiation of a long-term lease constitutes an improvement of commercial property, a broker may enter a mechanic's lien in the public records for unpaid commissions. Such a lien may be filed only if the property is to be used for other than residential purposes and if the lease is for three years or longer.

Similarly, real property law allows a broker to file an affidavit of entitlement to commission for negotiation of a contract for the purchase or lease of any real property. Such an affidavit, although entered in the public records, does not become a lien against the property.

Judgments

A **judgment** is a *decree issued by a court*. When the decree provides for the awarding of money and sets forth the amount of money owed by the debtor to the creditor, the judgment is referred to as a *money judgment*.

A judgment becomes a *general, involuntary lien on real property* owned by the debtor when it is docketed (filed) with the county clerk. A lien covers only property located within the county in which the judgment is issued. Transcripts of the lien must be filed in other counties when a creditor wishes to extend the lien coverage. A judgment differs from the mortgage in that a *specific* parcel of real estate was not given as security at the time that the debtor-creditor relationship was created.

A judgment becomes a lien against the debtor's real property in each county where the judgment is docketed—a judgment acquired in one county can be docketed in any county of New York. A judgment is a lien against the property for ten years and can be renewed for ten more. (A judgment remains a valid lien against *personal* property for 20 years.)

A judgment takes its priority as a lien on the debtor's property from the date the judgment was docketed in the county clerk's office. Judgments are enforced through the sale of the debtor's real or personal property by a sheriff. When the property is sold and the sale yields enough to satisfy the debt, the debtor may demand a legal document known as a *satisfaction of judgment,* or *satisfaction piece,* which should be filed with the clerk of the court and the county clerk where the judgment was filed or docketed so that the record will be cleared of the judgment. Normally the sheriff files a writ of execution showing that it has been returned satisfied; this is generally sufficient. A judgment can also be satisfied, of course, by the debtor's payment of the debt in full.

Lis pendens. A judgment or other decree affecting real estate is rendered at the conclusion of a lawsuit. Generally, considerable time elapses between the filing of a lawsuit and the rendering of a judgment. When any suit is filed that affects title to a specified parcel of real estate (such as a foreclosure suit), a notice known as a *lis pendens* is recorded. A lis pendens is not a lien but rather a *notice of a possible future lien*. Recording of the lis pendens gives notice to all interested parties such as prospective purchasers and lenders and establishes a priority for the later lien, which is dated back to the date the lis pendens was filed for record. The lis pendens creates a cloud on the title until the lawsuit is determined. In New York a lis pendens is also known as a **notice of pendency.**

Other Liens

Federal **estate taxes** and state **inheritance taxes** (as well as the debts of deceased persons) are *general, statutory, involuntary liens* that encumber a deceased person's real and personal property. These are normally paid or cleared in probate court proceedings. Probate and issues of inheritance are discussed in Chapter 23.

A **vendor's lien** is a *seller's claim* against the title of property he or she conveyed to a buyer; it occurs in cases where the seller did not receive the full, agreed-on purchase price. This is a *specific, equitable, involuntary lien* for the amount of the unpaid balance due the seller but is not enforceable without the decree of a court of competent jurisdiction.

A **vendee's lien** is a *buyer's claim* against a seller's property in cases where the seller failed to deliver title. This may occur when property is purchased under an installment contract (contract for deed, land contract) and the seller fails to deliver title after all other terms of the contract have been satisfied. A vendee's lien is a *specific, equitable, involuntary lien* for any money paid plus the value of any improvements made to the property by the buyer. The contract terms often define the lien and extend it to include the costs of a survey and title examination as well. This lien does not have to be filed in the clerk's office. If it is not filed, however, it will be subordinate to those liens that have been filed. The buyer may notify third parties of the claim by filing a lis pendens, the contract itself, or a memorandum of contract.

Municipalities that furnish water or services like refuse collection to property owners are given the right to a *specific, involuntary lien* on the property of an owner who refuses to pay bills for water or any other such municipal utility services.

A real estate owner charged with a crime for which he or she must face trial may choose to put up real estate instead of cash as surety for bail. The execution and recording of such a **surety bail bond** creates a *specific, voluntary lien* against the owner's real estate. This lien is enforceable by the state through a sheriff or other court officer if the accused person does not appear in court as required.

State governments levy a **corporation franchise tax** on corporations as a condition of allowing them to do business in the state. Such a tax is a *general, involuntary, statutory* lien on all property, real and personal, owned by the corporation and need not be specifically filed.

An **Internal Revenue Service (IRS) tax lien** results from a person's failure to pay any portion of his or her federal IRS taxes such as income and withholding taxes. A federal tax lien is a *general, statutory, involuntary lien* on all real and personal property held by the delinquent taxpayer.

Other possibilities include liens for New York State Tax Commission Warrants, special liens in the City of New York such as parking violations and emergency repairs, and certain Uniform Commercial Code (UCC) filings where real estate is specifically included in the lien.

Easements

A right acquired by one party to use the land of another party for a special purpose is an **easement.** Although this is the common definition of an easement, a party may also have an easement right in the air above a parcel of real estate or land. Since 1979 the New York Real Property Law provides for the recording of solar energy easements. Because *an easement is a right to use land* it is classified as an interest in real estate, but it is not an estate in land. The holder of an easement has only a right. He or she does not have an estate or ownership interest in the land over which the easement exists. An easement is sometimes referred to as an *incorporeal right* in land (a nonpossessory interest). An easement may be either appurtenant or in gross.

Easement Appurtenant

An easement that is *annexed to the ownership and used for the benefit of another's parcel of land* is an **easement appurtenant.** For example, if *A* and *B* both own adjacent properties in a resort community and only *A*'s property borders the lake, *A* may grant *B* a right-of-way across *A*'s property to the beach (*see* Figure 24.4).

For an easement appurtenant to exist there must be two adjacent tracts of land owned by different parties. The tract over which the easement runs is known as the *servient tenement;* the tract that is to benefit from the easement is known as the *dominant tenement.*

An easement appurtenant is considered part of the dominant tenement, and if the dominant tenement is conveyed to another party, the easement passes with the title. In legal terms it is said that *the easement runs with the land.* However, title to the land over which an easement actually runs is still retained by the servient tenement.

Easement in Gross

A mere personal interest in or right to use the land of another is an **easement in gross.** Such an easement is not appurtenant to any ownership estate in land. Examples of easements in gross are the easement rights a railroad has in its right-of-way or the right-of-way for a pipeline or high-tension power line. Commercial easements in gross may be assigned or conveyed and may be inherited. However, personal easements in gross usually are not assignable and terminate upon the death of the easement owner. Easements in gross are often confused with the similar personal right of license. A license may be withdrawn, an easement may not.

Easement by Necessity

An appurtenant easement that arises when an owner sells part of his or her land that has no access to a street or public way except over the seller's remaining land is an **easement by necessity.**

Figure 24.4
Easements

The owner of Lot A has an **easement appurtenant** across Lot B to gain access to his property from the paved road. The owner of Lot B has an **easement by necessity** across Lot A so that she may reach the road. The utility company has an **easement in gross** across both parcels of land for its electric power lines.

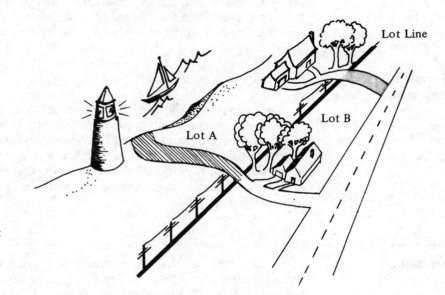

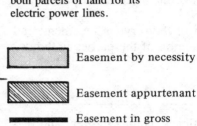

Easement by necessity

Easement appurtenant

Easement in gross

Easement by Prescription	When the claimant has made use of another's land for a certain period of time as defined by state law, an **easement by prescription** may be acquired. This *prescriptive period* is ten years in New York. The claimant's use must have been continuous, adverse to owner's title, exclusive and without the owner's approval. Additionally the use must be visible, open and notorious so that the owner could readily learn of it.
	Through the concept of **tacking,** a party not in possession of real property for the entire required statutory period may successfully establish a claim of an easement by prescription. Successive periods of continuous, uninterrupted occupation by different parties may be tacked on, or combined, to reach the prescriptive period. In order to tack on one person's possession to that of another, the parties must have been *successors in interest* such as an ancestor and his or her heir, landlord and tenant, or seller and buyer. Legal action must be taken to perfect the easement.
Party Walls	A party wall is a wall of a building that straddles the boundary lines between two owners' lots. Each lot owner owns half of the wall (on his or her own side) and each has an easement right in the other half of the wall for support of the building. A written party wall agreement should be used to create these easement rights. Each owner must pay half of expenses to maintain the wall.
Creating an Easement	Easements are commonly created by written agreement between the parties establishing the easement right. They also may be created in a number of other ways: (1) by express grant from the owner of the property over which the easement will run; (2) by the grantor in a deed of conveyance either *reserving* an ease-

ment over the sold land or *granting* the new owner an easement over the grantor's remaining land; (3) by longtime usage, as in an easement by prescription; (4) by necessity; and (5) by *implication*, that is, the situation of the parties' actions may imply that they intend to create an easement. Court action would be necessary to perfect the easement created by implication.

Terminating an Easement

Easements may be terminated:

1. when the purpose for which the easement was created no longer exists;
2. when the owner of either the dominant or the servient tenement becomes the owner of the other, provided there is an expressed intention of the parties to extinguish the easement (this is called a *merger*);
3. by release of the right of easement to the owner of the servient tenement; and
4. by abandonment of the easement (again, the intention of the parties is the determining factor).

Summary

Liens are claims, or charges, of creditors or tax officials against the real and personal property of a debtor. A lien is a type of encumbrance. All liens are encumbrances, but not all encumbrances are liens. Liens are either *general*, covering all real and personal property of a debtor-owner, or *specific*, covering only the specific parcel of real estate described in the mortgage, tax bill, building or repair contract or other document.

With the exception of real estate tax liens and mechanics' liens, the priority of liens is generally determined by the order in which they are placed in the public record of the county in which the debtor's property is located.

Mortgage liens are voluntary, specific liens given to lenders to secure payment for mortgage loans. *Mechanics' liens* protect general contractors, subcontractors and material suppliers whose work enhances the value of real estate.

A *judgment* is a court decree obtained by a creditor, usually for a monetary award from a debtor. The lien of a judgment can be enforced by issuance of a *writ of execution* and sale by the sheriff to pay the judgment amount and costs. *Lis pendens*, or *notice of pendency*, is a recorded notice that a lawsuit is awaiting trial in court and may result in a judgment that will affect title to a parcel of real estate.

Federal estate taxes and *state inheritance taxes* are general liens against a deceased owner's property.

Vendors' liens and *vendees' liens* are liens against a specific parcel of real estate. A vendor's lien is a seller's claim against a purchaser who has not paid the entire purchase price, and a vendee's lien is a purchaser's claim against a seller under an installment contract who has not conveyed title.

Liens for *water charges or other municipal utilities* and *surety bail bond liens* are specific liens, while *corporation franchise tax liens* are general liens against a corporation's assets.

Internal Revenue Service tax liens are general liens against the property of a person who is delinquent in payment of income tax.

An *easement* is the right acquired by one person to use another's real estate. Easements are classified as interests in real estate but are not estates in land. *Easements appurtenant* involve two separately owned tracts. The tract benefited is known as the *dominant tenement;* the tract that is subject to the easement is called the *servient tenement.* An *easement in gross* is a personal right such as that granted to utility companies to maintain poles, wires and pipelines.

Easements may be created by agreement, express grant, grant or reservation in a deed, implication, necessity, prescription, or party wall agreement. They can be terminated when the purpose of the easement no longer exists, by merger of both interests with an express intention to extinguish the easement, by release or by an intention to abandon the easement.

Questions

1. Which of the following is considered a lien on real estate?

    a. An easement running with the land
    b. An unpaid mortgage loan
    c. A public footpath
    d. A license to erect a billboard

2. General contractor Ralph Hammond was hired to build a room addition to Thom and Harriet Elkin's home. Hammond completed the work several weeks ago but still has not been paid. In this situation Hammond is entitled to a mechanic's lien; it will be:

    a. general lien.   c. statutory lien.
    b. specific lien.   d. voluntary lien.

3. When the Micawbers failed to pay for their bedroom furniture the store secured a judgment against them. The judgment becomes what kind of lien?

    a. Specific   c. Voluntary
    b. General   d. Statutory

4. Which of the following best refers to the type of lien that affects all real and personal property of a debtor?

    a. Specific lien   c. Involuntary lien
    b. Voluntary lien   d. General lien

5. Which of the following is a voluntary, specific lien?

    a. IRS tax lien   c. Mortgage lien
    b. Mechanic's lien   d. Vendor's lien

6. Which of the following liens usually would be given higher priority?

    a. A mortgage dated last year
    b. The current real estate tax
    c. A mechanic's lien for work started before the mortgage was made
    d. A judgment rendered yesterday

7. Jim Chard was not paid for roofing the Hills' ranch home. How long does he have to file a mechanic's lien?

    a. Four months   c. One year
    b. Eight months   d. Ten years

8. Jim's mechanic's lien will remain against the property for at least:

    a. four months.   c. one year.
    b. eight months.   d. ten years.

9. In New York a lis pendens:

    a. is known as a notice of pendency.
    b. gives notice of a lawsuit involving a particular party.
    c. is filed in the county clerk's office.
    d. All of the above.

10. General contractor Kim Kelly is suing homeowner Bob Baker for nonpayment of services; suit will be filed in the next few weeks. Recently Kelly learned that the homeowner has listed his property with a local real estate broker for sale. In this instance which of the following will probably be used by Kelly and her attorneys to protect her interest?

    a. Lis pendens
    b. Prescription
    c. Affidavit of entitlement
    d. Satisfaction piece

11. Suzy Soldsine secured an excellent buyer for the Tightes' split-level home but she suspects they will not pay her commission. Suzy may file a(n):

    a. mechanic's lien.
    b. lis pendens.
    c. affidavit of entitlement.
    d. statutory lien.

12. When the Cratchetts failed to pay for Tim's orthopedic surgery Dr. Kildare obtained a money judgment, which he can now file against the Cratchetts':

    a. car.   c. apartment house.
    b. home.   d. All of the above

13. Donny Prelate sold Erneste Tully a parcel of real estate; title has passed but to date Tully has not paid the purchase price in full as originally agreed. If Prelate does not receive payment, which of the following could he sue to enforce?

    a. Mortgage lien   c. Lis pendens
    b. Venedee's lien   d. Vendor's lien

14. Which of the following is classified as a general lien?

    a. Vendor's lien
    b. Surety bail bond lien
    c. Debts of a deceased person
    d. General real estate taxes

15. When the Cratchetts pay off their doctor's judgment they should:

    a. record a satisfaction certificate.
    b. put a lis pendens on the apartment house.
    c. notify their mortgagee.
    d. grant an easement appurtenant.

16. In New York City, property may receive a lien for the owner's:

    a. jaywalking.   c. shoplifting.
    b. traffic tickets.   d. public disturbance.

17. A telephone company runs its poles and wires with the rights granted by an easement:

    a. by necessity.   c. by prescription.
    b. appurtenant.   d. in gross.

18. A license differs from an easement in that it:

    a. runs with the land.
    b. requires a court order.
    c. may be withdrawn.
    d. allows use of someone else's land.

19. The farmer who allowed promoters to run the Woodstock rock festival on his land granted them a(n):

    a. easement by necessity.
    b. dominant tenement.
    c. equitable lien.
    d. license.

20. To establish an easement by prescription in New York a person must use another's property for an uninterrupted period of:

    a. five years.   c. fifteen years.
    b. ten years.   d. twenty years.

21. After Peter Desmond had purchased his house and moved in, he discovered that his neighbor regularly used Desmond's driveway to reach a garage located on the neighbor's property. Desmond's attorney explained that ownership of the neighbor's real estate includes an easement over the driveway. Desmond's property is properly called:

    a. the dominant tenement.
    b. a tenement.
    c. a leasehold.
    d. the servient tenement.

22. If the owner of real estate does not take action before the prescriptive period has passed, then someone could acquire:

    a. an easement by necessity.
    b. a license.
    c. an easement by implication of law.
    d. none of the above.

23. A shared driveway agreement will probably take the form of a(n):

    a. voluntary lien.
    b. easement appurtenant.
    c. affidavit of entitlement.
    d. certificate of satisfaction.

24. A party wall:

    a. straddles a boundary line.
    b. faces a main road.
    c. is located only on a servient tenement.
    d. is owned by one party.

25. Bob buys a vacation cottage whose owner has an easement appurtenant for access to the lake across a neighbor's land. If Bob wants to reach the lake, he must:

    a. renegotiate with the neighbor.
    b. apply to a court for an easement by necessity.
    c. pay a token rental to the neighbor.
    d. simply go ahead and use the crossing.

25

Taxes and Assessments

Key Terms

Ad valorem tax - *according to value*
Assessment roll
Equalization factor
Full-value assessment
In rem
Mill

Special assessment
Statutory redemption period
Tax foreclosure
Tax lien
Tax sale
True tax

Overview

Among the powers of government over ownership of real estate is the right to levy taxes. This chapter will discuss real estate tax liens, which affect every owner of real estate.

Tax Liens

As discussed in Chapter 6, the ownership of real estate is subject to certain government powers. One of these powers is the right of state and local governments to impose **tax liens** for the support of their governmental functions. Because the location of real estate is permanently fixed, the government can levy taxes with a rather high degree of certainty that the taxes will be collected. Because the annual taxes levied on real estate usually have priority over other previously recorded liens, they may be enforced by the court-ordered sale of the real estate.

Real estate taxes can be divided into two types: (1) *general real estate tax,* or **ad valorem tax,** and (2) **special assessment**, or *improvement tax*. Both taxes are levied against specific parcels of property and automatically become liens on those properties.

General Tax (Ad Valorem Tax)

The general real estate tax is made up of the taxes levied on real estate by various governmental agencies and municipalities. These include cities, towns, villages and counties. Other taxing bodies are school districts, park districts, lighting districts, drainage districts, water districts and sanitary districts. Municipal authorities operating recreational preserves such as forest preserves and parks also may be authorized by the legislature to levy real estate taxes.

General real estate taxes are levied for the *general support or operation* of the governmental agency authorized to impose the levy. These taxes are known as *ad valorem* taxes because the amount of the tax varies in accordance with the *value of the property being taxed*.

Exemptions from general taxes. Certain real estate is exempt from real estate taxation. Certain property owned by cities, various municipal organizations (schools, parks and playgrounds), the state and federal governments, religious corporations, hospitals or educational institutions is tax exempt. The property must be used for tax-exempt purposes by the exempted group or organization. If it is not so used, it will be subject to tax.

New York also allows special exemptions to reduce real estate tax bills for certain property owners or land uses. Homeowners 65 or older on limited incomes and veterans may be eligible for reductions in some property taxes. Real estate tax reductions are sometimes granted to attract industries. In specific agricultural districts New York may offer reductions for agricultural land to encourage the continuation of agricultural uses.

The real estate broker taking the listing of a parcel of real estate should be alert to the possibility of exemptions and exercise diligence in ascertaining the **true tax** figure.

Special Assessments (Improvement Taxes)

Special assessments are *special taxes levied on real estate that require property owners to pay for improvements that benefit the real estate they own*. These taxes are often levied to pay for such improvement as streets, alleys, street lighting, curbs and similar items and are enforced in the same manner as general real estate taxes.

The authority to recommend or initiate the *specific improvement* is vested in either the property owners, who may petition for an improvement, or in a proper legislative authority such as the city council or board of trustees, which may initiate the proposal for an improvement. Hearings are held and notices given to the owners of the property affected.

After preliminary legal steps have been taken, the legislative authority authorized by statute to act in such cases adopts an *ordinance* that sets out the nature of the improvement, its cost and a description of the area to be assessed.

The proper authority spreads the assessment (called the **assessment roll**) over the various parcels of real estate that will benefit. The amount of the assessment for each parcel is determined by the estimated benefit each tract will receive by reason of the assessment. The assessment usually will vary from parcel to parcel, as all will not benefit equally from the improvement.

The Taxation Process

Assessments in New York are made by municipal officials known as assessors. Assessments are made by towns, villages, cities and, in a few cases, by counties. The assessment roll contains an assessment for land and a total value for land and improvements, if any.

In 1788 New York law mandated **full-value assessment.** The requirement was largely ignored, with most municipalities assessing at less than full value. In 1975 the court of appeals ordered the state either to enforce the law or to change it. More than 400 communities then went to full-value assessment voluntarily or under court order. In 1982 the legislature repealed the 200-year-old requirement. Under the regulations that went into force at that time, Upstate communities were simply required to assess all property at a "*uniform* percentage of value" while New York City and Long Island were allowed to divide real property into four different classes for tax purposes. The question of full-value assessment remains controversial and hotly debated, with court challenges frequently occurring.

Property owners who claim that errors were made in determining the assessed value of their property may present their objections, usually to a local board of review. Protests or appeals regarding tax assessments ultimately may be taken to court.

Such cases generally involve a proceeding whereby the court reviews the certified assessment records of the tax assessment official. Since 1982, a simple, inexpensive "small claims" procedure is available in New York for owner-occupied one- to four-family dwellings if the property has an equalized value of less than $150,000 or if the reduction in assessment being sought is less than 25 percent.

Equalization. When it is necessary to correct general inequalities in statewide tax assessments, uniformity is achieved by use of an **equalization factor.** The New York State Board of Equalization and Assessment issues an equalization rate for each municipality. This factor is intended to equalize the assessments in every taxing jurisdiction across the state. No equalization factor applies where full-value assessment is used. Westchester County establishes its own equalization rate. The assessed value of each property is multiplied by the equalization factor and the tax rate is then applied to the equalized assessment. For example, the assessments in one district are determined to be 20 percent lower than the average assessments throughout the rest of the state. This underassessment can be corrected by decreeing the application of an equalization factor of 125 percent to each assessment in that district. Thus, a parcel of land assessed for tax purposes at $98,000 would be taxed on an equalized value of $122,500 ($98,000 × 1.25 = $122,500).

Tax rates. The process of arriving at a real estate tax rate begins with the *adoption of a budget* by each county, city, school board or other taxing district (*see* Figure 25.1). Each budget covers the financial requirements of the taxing body for the coming fiscal year, which may be the January-to-December calendar year or some other 12-month period. The budget must include an estimate of all expenditures for the year and indicate the amount of income expected from all fees, revenue-sharing and other sources. The net amount remaining to be raised from real estate taxes is then determined from these figures.

Figure 25.1
Ad Valorem Taxation

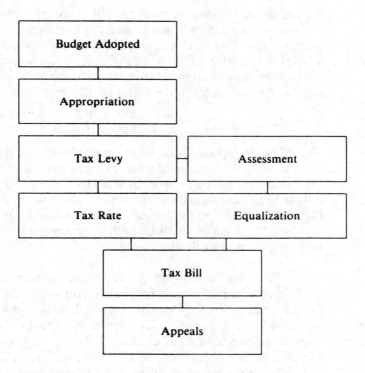

The next step is *appropriation*, the action taken by each taxing body that authorizes the expenditure of funds and provides for the sources of such monies. Appropriation involves the adoption of an ordinance or the passage of a law setting forth the specifics of the proposed taxation.

The amount to be raised from the general real estate tax is then imposed on property owners through a *tax levy*, the formal action taken to impose the tax, by a vote of the taxing district's governing body.

The *tax rate* for each individual taxing body is computed separately. To arrive at a tax rate, the total monies needed for the coming fiscal year are divided by the total assessments of all real estate located within the jurisdiction of the taxing body. For example, a taxing district's budget indicates that $300,000 must be raised from real estate tax revenues, and the assessment roll (assessor's record) of all taxable real estate within this district equals $10,000,000. The tax rate is computed thus:

$$\$300,000 \div \$10,000,000 = .03 \; or \; 3\%$$

The tax rate may be stated in a number of different ways. In many areas it is expressed in mills. A **mill** is *1/1,000 of a dollar, or $.001*. The tax rate may be expressed as a mill ratio, in dollars per hundred or in dollars per thousand. The tax rate computed in the foregoing example could be expressed as:

30 mills (per $1 of assessed value)
or
$3 per $100 of assessed value
or
$30 per $1,000 of assessed value

Tax bills. A property owners' tax bill is computed by applying the tax rate to the assessed valuation of the property. For example, on property assessed for tax purposes at $90,000, at a tax rate of 3 percent, or 30 mills, the tax will be $2,700 ($90,000 × .030 = $2,700). If an equalization factor is used, the computation on a property with an assessed value of $120,000 and a tax rate of 4 percent with an equalization factor of 120 percent would be as follows:

$$\$120,000 \times 1.20 = \$144,000$$
$$\$144,000 \times .040 = \$5,760 \; tax$$

Taxing bodies operate on different taxing years, so the homeowner may receive separate bills for various taxes at different times during the year. (Where a lending institution maintains an escrow account to meet a mortgagor's taxes, tax bills may be sent directly to the lender. After the taxes are paid the receipted bills are forwarded to the property owner.) Penalties in the form of monthly interest charges are added to all taxes that are not paid when due. The due date is also called the *penalty date*.

New York cities, towns, villages and school districts generally send out their own tax bills that in many municipalities often include the county tax levy. Improvement district charges are usually included in the town tax bill; benefit charges are often billed separately. State, town and county taxes run from January to December and are payable in advance. Villages may begin their tax year either in March or, more commonly, in June. School taxes are levied from July 1 through June 30, but the tax may not be payable until September or October in some areas, and may be payable in installments. School taxes, therefore, are paid in arrears for several months. City taxes frequently are payable in two or four installments during the year.

Enforcement of Tax Liens

To be enforceable, real estate taxes must be valid, which means they must be: (1) properly levied, (2) used for a legal purpose and (3) applied equitably to all affected property. Real estate taxes that have remained delinquent for the period of time specified by state law can be collected by the tax-collecting officer through either **tax foreclosure** (similar to mortgage foreclosure) or **tax sale.** Many cities and villages enforce their own tax liens through tax sales; in most cases towns do not.

Tax sales are held pursuant to a published notice and often are conducted by the tax collector as an annual public sale. The purchaser must pay at least the amount of delinquent tax and penalty owing. Some foreclosures are **in rem,** against the property on which taxes are delinquent, without proceeding against the individual owner.

The delinquent taxpayer can redeem the property at any time before the tax sale by paying the delinquent taxes plus interest and charges (any court costs or attorney's fees); this is known as an *equitable right of redemption.* State laws also grant a period of redemption *after the tax sale* during which the defaulted owner or lienholders (creditors of the defaulted owner) may redeem the property by paying the amount paid at the tax sale plus interest and charges. This is known as the *statutory right of redemption.* During the **statutory redemption period** the property owner and other parties who have an interest in the property, including a mortgagee, can redeem the property by payment of the back taxes together with penalties and interest. Counties, cities and villages have different statutory redemption periods.

County tax sales. The owner of the property encumbered by the delinquent tax lien is entitled to redeem the property from the tax lien (as sold) within one year following the date of the tax sale. If the property is actually occupied (not vacant land) or if the property is mortgaged, the period for redemption is extended for an additional two years (three years total, following the date of the tax sale). This period may be shortened by a procedure involving service of a notice to redeem upon the owner.

Village tax sales. The owner of the property encumbered by the delinquent tax lien is entitled to redeem the property from the tax lien (as sold) within two years following the date of the tax sale.

In most cases the purchasers of tax titles in New York secure title insurance or bring actions to quiet any outstanding claims against the property and do not rely only on the tax deed issued by the municipality.

Summary

Real estate taxes are levied by local authorities. Tax liens are generally given priority over other liens. Payments are required before stated dates, after which penalties accrue. An owner may lose title to his or her property for nonpayment of taxes because such tax-delinquent property can be sold at a tax sale. New York allows a time period during which a defaulted owner can redeem his or her real estate from a tax sale.

Special assessments are levied to spread the cost of improvements such as new sidewalks, curbs or paving to the real estate that benefits from them.

The appraisal process begins with assessment of the taxable value of each parcel. New York mandates either *equitable* or *full-value assessment* with variations from one jurisdiction to another adjusted through the use of equalization rates. The money budgeted to be raised through taxation is then divided by the total assessment roll to arrive at the *tax rate.* The tax bill for each parcel is determined by multiplying the tax rate by assessed valuation.

Various taxing authorities send tax bills at different times of the year. Unpaid taxes become a lien against property, usually taking precedence over other liens, and may be enforced through tax foreclosure or sale.

Questions

1. Some exemptions from real estate taxes may be granted to certain:

   a. veterans.
   b. senior citizens.
   c. religious organizations.
   d. Any of the above

2. Which of the following taxes is used to distribute the cost of civic services among real estate owners?

   a. Personal property tax
   b. Inheritance tax
   c. Ad valorem tax
   d. Sales tax

3. A lien on real estate made to secure payment for specific improvements made to a local community is a(n):

   a. mechanics' lien.
   b. special assessment.
   c. ad valorem tax.
   d. utility lien.

4. Which of the following steps is usually required before a special assessment becomes a lien against a specific parcel of real estate?

   a. The state of New York must verify the need.
   b. An ordinance is passed.
   c. The improvement is completed.
   d. A majority of affected property owners must approve.

5. New York statutes require that property be assessed for taxes at which percentage of its value?

   a. 33⅓   c. Any uniform percentage
   b. 50   d. 100

6. When real estate is assessed for tax purposes:

   a. the homeowner may appeal to a local board of review.
   b. a protest must take the form of a personal suit against the assessor.
   c. the appeal process must start in state court.
   d. no appeal is possible.

7. A specific parcel of real estate has a market value of $80,000 and is assessed for tax purposes at 25 percent of market value. The tax rate for the county in which the property is located is 30 mills. The tax will be:

   a. $500.   c. $600.
   b. $550.   d. $700.

8. What is the annual real estate tax on a property that is valued at $135,000 and assessed for tax purposes at $47,250 with an equalization factor of 125 percent, when the tax rate is 25 mills?

   a. $1,417.50   c. $4,050.00
   b. $1,476.56   d. None of the above

9. An *in rem* foreclosure proceeds against:

   a. the property.
   b. the owner of the property.
   c. the mortgagee on the property, if any.
   d. all of the above.

10. During the statutory period of redemption. New York property sold for delinquent taxes may:

    a. be redeemed by payment of back taxes, penalties and interest.
    b. be redeemed by payment of four times the delinquent taxes.
    c. be redeemed only through a court proceeding.
    d. not be redeemed.

26

General Business Law

Key Terms

Administrator
Appellate divisions
Bankruptcy
Board of directors
Certificate of incorporation
Chapter 7
Chapter 11
Chapter 13
Civil law
Commercial paper
Common law
Court of appeals
Criminal law
Endorsement
Executor
Financing statement

Holder in due course
Injunction
Involuntary bankruptcy
Marital deduction
Negotiable instrument
Personal representative
Precedent
Procedural law
Security agreement
Small claims court
Statute of limitations
Substantive law
Torts
Unified credit
Uniform Commercial Code (UCC)
Voluntary bankruptcy

Overview

Real estate brokers and salespersons must have a broad understanding of law and how various laws affect real estate. The broker is already familiar with several aspects of this topic, including law of agency, law of contracts and real property law. This chapter will discuss the sources of law, commercial paper, business organizations, the court system, torts, bankruptcy and the settlement of estates.

Sources of Law

There are *seven sources of law* in the United States, all of which affect the ownership and transfer of real estate. These are: *the Constitution of the United States; laws passed by Congress; federal regulations adopted by the various agencies and commissions created by Congress; state constitutions; laws passed by state legislatures; ordinances passed by cities, towns and other local governments;* and *court decisions.*

The primary purpose of the *U.S. Constitution and the individual state constitutions* is to establish the rights of citizens and delineate the limits of governmental authority.

Laws passed by Congress and by state and local legislative bodies may establish specific provisions on any issue or they may simply set broad standards of conduct and establish administrative and enforcement agencies.

Governmental agencies that enact rules and regulations range from the Federal Housing Administration through state real estate commissions to local zoning boards. These regulations are a means of implementing and enforcing legislative acts; they provide detailed information on legal and illegal actions and practices and they designate penalties and violations. These regulations have the effect of law.

Court decisions of federal, state and muncipal courts serve to clarify and interpret laws, regulations and constitutional provisions. By applying and interpreting the laws in relation to a specific event, a court decision expands the meaning of the law. For example, an attorney draws up what is considered to be a valid contract under the provisions of state law. If the court disallows the contract, it will render an opinion as to why the contract does not fulfill the legal requirements for such a document. Future contracts in the state then will be based on the **precedent** of the requirements established by prior court decisions as well as on the statutes governing contracts.

The courts are not always bound by the established precedent. Courts in one jurisdiction (area of authority) may not be bound by the decisions of courts in other jurisdictions. In addition, a court with superior authority in its jurisdiction may at its discretion reverse the ruling of a lower court.

Common law. In addition to the aforementioned sources of law, real estate ownership and transfer are indirectly affected by what is known as the **common law,** that body of rules and principles founded on custom, usage and the decisions and opinions of the courts. It is derived mainly from practices developed in England and, as it applies to the United States, dates back to the practices that were in effect at the time of the American Revolution. Today the common law includes not only custom but previous court decisions.

Commercial Paper

A written promise to pay money is known as **commercial paper.** *Promissory notes, checks, drafts* and *certificates of deposit*—all forms of commercial paper— are also known as **negotiable instruments.** Negotiability means that they can be freely transferred from one person to another. Commercial paper serves as a convenient substitute for actual money and also can be used to extend credit. The *Uniform Commercial Code (UCC)* divides commercial paper into four types: notes, drafts, checks and certificates of deposit.

Promissory Notes

The simplest form of commercial paper, the note, is a promise by one person (the *maker*) to pay money to another (the *payee*). A promissory note may be made payable to a specific payee or simply to anyone who presents it for payment (the *bearer*). If it can be collected at any time, it is a *demand* note. Often, however, notes are used as a device for extending credit and are not due until a specified time in the future. The bond or note accompanying a mortgage, for example, is a form of promissory note.

Drafts

A *draft* is a form of commercial paper involving three parties. Sometimes known as a *bill of exchange*, a draft is issued by the *drawer*, who orders another party (the *drawee*) to pay money to the payee. Like a note, a draft may be payable either to a specific payee or to a bearer and may be payable on demand or on a certain date. Drafts are often used in connection with goods being shipped from seller to buyer. A *trade acceptance* is a form of time draft.

Checks

A check is a special type of draft, ordering a bank to pay money to the payee upon demand. A check may name a specific payee or be payable to the bearer (often, in that case, made out to "cash"). A *cashier's check*, issued by the bank, is a type of draft in which two of the three parties (drawer and drawee) are the same party: the bank. The bank orders itself to make the payment.

Certificates of Deposit

A *certificate of deposit* is a bank's receipt for a sum of money with a promise to repay it. Certificates of deposit (CDs) are devices for investing large amounts of cash, often at relatively high rates of interest. They run for a specific length of time.

Negotiability

The Uniform Commercial Code sets standards for a negotiable instrument. It must be in writing, signed by the maker or drawer, contain an unconditional promise or order to pay a specific sum of money either on demand or at a definite time and payable either to order or to a bearer. If a third-party instrument, it must identify the drawee.

Writing. The instrument must be written on material relatively permanent and portable. It may be written in ink or pencil, typed or printed. Standard printed forms are used most often.

Signed. A simple *X* made by a person unable to write can constitute a legal signature. Initials or a thumbprint are also acceptable. A trade name or a rubber stamp, when used by someone authorized to do so, is also permitted.

Promise. The promise or order to pay must be unconditional. Because it may pass from one person to another and be used in place of money, the instrument cannot be dependent on other happenings. The promise or order to pay must be clear. A simple IOU acknowledging that "I owe you $1,000" is not a promise to pay and not a negotiable instrument. A promise to pay "to Mary Doe" implies no promise to pay to anyone else. In order for Mary to sell the instrument or otherwise turn it over to someone else, it should contain a promise to pay "*to the order of* Mary Doe." Mary could then order the sum paid to another party.

Specific sum. Negotiable paper must be payable only in money. It cannot promise payment in goods or services. If interest is involved, it must be stated so clearly that a computation of the sum promised is possible. Any recognized foreign currency may be stipulated in place of U.S. currency.

Demand or time. A negotiable instrument must be payable "on *demand*" or at a definite time. Most checks are payable immediately (*on sight*, or upon presentation). A note also may be payable *after sight*—for example, one month after it is presented for payment. It may state that it will be paid "on or before" a specific date. If it is payable in installments, it may contain an acceleration clause, allowing the full amount to fall due immediately if some event occurs, like default on payment.

Endorsement. Instruments payable to bearer may be transferred by *delivery*. Instruments payable to order must be transferred by **endorsement.** A note may be transferred from one party to another by one of four types of endorsements (*see* Figure 26.1):

**Figure 26.1
Endorsements**

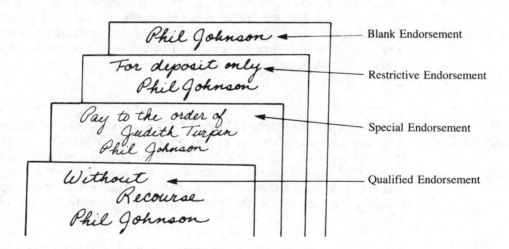

- Blank Endorsement
- Restrictive Endorsement
- Special Endorsement
- Qualified Endorsement

1. *Blank endorsement,* in which the payee signs the back of the note without further explanation. It is the riskiest form of endorsement because the note remains negotiable for any purpose, even if the holder acquired it illegally. It is almost equivalent to cash.
2. *Restrictive endorsement,* in which the negotiability of the instrument is restricted to a specific purpose, stated in the endorsement.
3. *Special endorsement,* in which the payee specifically names the next holder in due course.
4. *Qualified endorsement,* in which the phrase "without recourse" is written as part of the endorsement in order to relieve the person making the endorse-

ment from any liability if the check or note is not honored. A qualified endorsement specifies that the person who originated the check remains liable for the note.

If an instrument is payable to John *or* Mary Doe, one endorsement is sufficient to transfer it. If it is payable to John *and* Mary Doe, both must endorse it.

Holder in due course. The holder of an instrument is the person in possession of it, but only if the instrument is payable to bearer or properly endorsed to the person holding it. That person is entitled to receive payment. Special rights accrue to a **holder in due course,** who has more claim than an ordinary holder against potential conflicting claims to the payment. A holder in due course must meet specific requirements, taking the instrument for *value exchanged,* in *good faith*, and *without having notice* that it was *overdue, dishonored* (payment previously refused) or *having a claim against it*. A holder in due course has a stronger legal case for enforcing payment than an ordinary holder.

Defenses. Legal defense against paying on an instrument might include claims that the maker was under duress, that the instrument was intended for some illegal purpose (payment of a gambling debt or for the purchase of illegal drugs), that the instrument was obtained by fraud or that the instrument has been altered after it was signed.

Discharge

The most common method of discharging commercial paper is by *payment*. It also may be *canceled* by the holder either by marking it paid or by destroying it. The destruction must be deliberate, not accidental, for the instrument to be discharged. The instrument also may be *renounced* by the holder or, in the case of a check, the maker may issue a *stop-payment* order.

Uniform Commercial Code

The **Uniform Commercial Code (UCC)** is a codification of commercial law that has been adopted, wholly or in part, in all states. While this code generally does not apply directly to real estate, it has replaced state laws relating to chattel mortgages, conditional sales agreements, and liens on chattels, crops or items that are to become fixtures. Shares in an apartment cooperative are personal property, and security interests in them generally involve the use of UCC filings.

To create a security interest in a chattel, including chattels that will become fixtures, the code requires the use of a **security agreement,** which must contain a complete description of the items against which the lien applies. A short notice of this agreement, called a **financing statement** or UCC-1, which includes the identification of any real estate involved, must be filed for fixtures with the clerk of the county where the debtor resides and for other personal property with the secretary of state in Albany. The recording of the financing statement constitutes notice to subsequent purchasers and mortgagees of the security interest in chattels, and fixtures on the real estate. Many mortgagees require the signing and recording of a financing statement when the mortgaged premises include chattels or readily removable fixtures (washers, dryers and the like) as part of the security for the mortgage debt. If the financing statement has been properly recorded, upon the borrower's default the creditor could repossess the chattels and cause them to be sold and apply the proceeds to the debt payment.

Business Organizations

Partnerships

Partnership is defined by partnership law as an association of two or more persons to carry on a business for profit as co-owners. Each partner is considered an agent of the other as concerns the partnership and each shares the profits or losses. While the stockholders of a *corporation* are liable only to the extent of their investment in the firm, the members of a *general partnership* are personally liable for debts and losses and liable for each other's acts within the scope of the business.

A specific *partnership agreement* sets up the powers and duties of the partners. Unless the agreement specifies otherwise, some common arrangements are that new members must be approved by all the existing partners and every member is entitled to equal participation in the management and to a specific share of profits.

When the question arises as to whether two persons are in fact partners, the chief test is whether each receives a share of profits. Partners have a fiduciary duty to each other. Notice given to one is considered given to all.

Partnership property. Property contributed to the partnership when it is formed is considered to be partnership property. Property acquired with the firm's assets is also partnership property. No one partner can assign partnership property unless all consent. Creditors of the individual partners may not attach the assets of the partnership for a partner's personal debts but may attach the partner's interest in the partnership.

If one partner assigns his or her share of profits to a third person, that person may be entitled to profits but does not become a partner and has no right to share in management or examine the firm's books.

Dissolution. The partnership is dissolved at a specific time originally agreed on or if any one partner requests *dissolution*. It is also dissolved upon the death or bankruptcy of a partner. A court order can dissolve the partnership if it is shown that one partner is insane or incapacitated, that the business cannot be operated at a profit or that one partner is involved in impropriety affecting the partnership.

Upon dissolution the partnership may no longer transact new business but the partnership continues through the process of *winding-up*. Assets are distributed first to creditors who are not partners, next to partners who have lent money to the partnership, then in a refund of capital contributed by each partner. Anything remaining is distributed among the partners according to their respective interests.

Limited partnerships. Limited partnerships are generally formed for commercial investment. The general partner takes management responsibility and unlimited personal liability for the partnership's debts; the limited partners contribute cash but do not share in management and are liable only to the amount of their contributions.

Corporations

A corporation is an organization that is recognized by the law as a legal person. It may buy, sell, lease, mortgage, make contracts and perform most other acts allowed to persons. It is entitled to most of the same protection guaranteed other persons by the Bill of Rights.

Its authority to act is separate from the persons who own shares in it and, in most cases, they bear no individual liability for the corporation's actions or debts. Likewise, the corporation cannot be held liable for the shareholders' debts.

Creation of a corporation. A corporation is created by the filing of a **certificate of incorporation** with the secretary of state. The incorporator(s) must sign the certificate, giving their names and addresses, the name of the intended corporation and its purposes, intended duration (usually perpetual), address and number of shares of stock authorized to be issued. Upon payment of a fee and approval of the secretary of state, the corporation becomes a legal entity. Bylaws, the rules and regulations under which the corporation will operate, are usually adopted at the first organizational meeting after the certificate of incorporation has been secured.

Management. A corporation is managed by a **board of directors** elected by shareholders. Shareholders who cannot attend meetings, which are usually held annually, may vote by *proxy*. Once elected, the board of directors selects officers who administer the business of the corporation. Directors and officers have a fudiciary duty to the corporation and may not profit personally at its expense. Each shareholder has the right to examine the company's books.

A *closely held corporation* is one owned by a single individual or a small number of shareholders, perhaps members of the same family. The shareholders usually manage the business themselves.

Corporations, considered as persons, are subject to income tax on profits. One of the major disadvantages to corporate organization is double taxation, with profits taxed once to the firm and again when received (in the form of dividends) by shareholders. Corporations are also subject to the New York State franchise tax (another term for corporate income tax).

One of the major advantages of corporate organizations, however, is the ability to shelter some income through pension and profit-sharing plans and to consider as business expense fringe benefits like health or life insurance. In recent years, however, liberalized tax-deferment possibilities for individuals through various retirement plans have lessened the appeal of this aspect of incorporation.

S corporations. The S corporation, intended for a small group of shareholders, allows the firm to be taxed as a partnership would be—passing profit and loss directly to shareholders, so that profits are taxed only once. Losses also may be passed to shareholders, although only to the limit of their investments, and used to offset ordinary income. An S corporation may have no more than 35 shareholders.

Termination. *Dissolution* is the legal death of the corporation. *Liquidation* is the winding-up process. A corporation may be dissolved by an act of the legislature, expiration of the time originally planned for the business, approval of the shareholders and board of directors, unanimous action of all the shareholders, failure to pay franchise taxes or court order. A *certificate of dissolution* is filed with the secretary of state and assets are distributed first to creditors, next to holders of preferred stock and last to holders of common stock.

The Federal Court System

The federal court system includes specialized courts, district courts, courts of review (appellate courts) and the Supreme Court, as shown in Figure 26.2. Federal judges receive lifetime appointments, subject to confirmation by the Senate.

District courts cover specific geographical areas, with at least one in each state. New York has four *districts,* referred to as the northern, eastern, southern and western districts. District courts are the point of origin for civil cases arising from federal law and for federal crimes. They also serve as appellate courts for the U.S. bankruptcy court.

Specialized courts are established by Congress. Among them are tax court, court of claims and bankruptcy court. The *U.S. court of appeals* provides review for district courts and for decisions made by federal agencies such as HUD. The United States is divided into 11 judicial circuits. Appeals from district courts located in this state are heard by the second circuit court of appeals, which also covers part of Connecticut. Decisions of this court are generally final, with further appeal to the Supreme Court the only possibility.

The *Supreme Court of the United States* consists of nine justices. It serves mainly as a court of appeals for cases involving federal law or constitutionality, but it also has original, or trial, jursidiction in a few situations.

New York Court System

In New York State the supreme court is paradoxically one of the lowest courts in the system, so named because of its wide jurisdiction and because it originates most lawsuits. New York's court system is complicated by differing arrangements in the New York City area (first and second departments) and Upstate (third and fourth departments) as diagramed in Figure 26.3. The highest court in the state is the **court of appeals.** *Supreme court* is the lowest court of unlimited jurisdiction and unlimited dollar amount of claims. It has branches in every county. Supreme court justices are also assigned to criminal cases when the caseload requires it.

**Figure 26.2
Federal Court System**

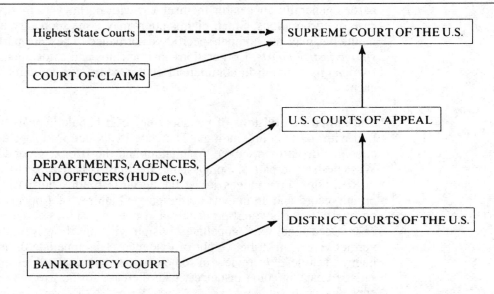

Figure 26.3
New York Court System

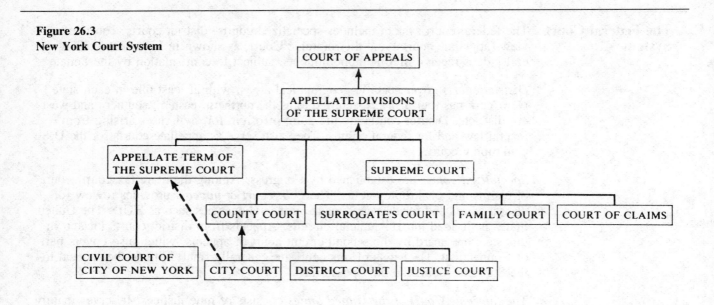

County court is a court of criminal jurisdiction, also handling some civil cases and appeals from lower courts. *Surrogate court* handles decedents' estates, will contests, probates, adoptions (with family court) and incompetency proceedings.

Family court combines the old domestic relations and children's courts for family complaints, delinquencies, child abuse and adoptions. Divorces, however, are heard in supreme court.

The *court of claims* has jurisdiction over claims against the state.

Small claims courts are set up for prompt and informal treatment of disputes and complaints involving less than $2,000. Fees and paperwork are nominal and the parties generally appear for themselves, with no lawyers involved except in the case of corporations. Small claims court may issue monetary awards and judgments but may not compel specific performance. They are part of *city, town* and *village justice courts*. Corporations, partnerships and associations may initiate up to five claims a month in commercial claims court, for amounts of up to $1,500 each.

The **appellate divisions** of the supreme court handle appeals by parties dissatisfied with lower court findings. The state is divided into four departments: first appellate department covers Manhattan and the Bronx; second covers Brooklyn, Westchester and part of Long Island; the third is based in Albany; and the fourth in Rochester. Five judges serve, taking no testimony but basing their decisions on the record and arguments by the parties' attorneys. Appeals are usually based on questions of law and procedure and not on disputes about the facts in the case. Occasionally the appellate division will rule, however, that the original verdict was against the weight of evidence. The appellate divisions serve as an intermediate level of review in some cases and as final arbiter in others. Those dissatisfied can, in some instances, take the case further, to the court of appeals.

The *court of appeals* is the highest court in the state. Seven judges sit. There is generally no further appeal from this court although U.S. constitutional questions can be taken to the Supreme Court of the United States.

Substantive and Procedural Law

The whole body of law falls into two categories: **substantive law,** which defines the rights of individuals, and **procedural law,** which establishes the methods of enforcing those rights. *Substantive law* includes some subjects with which the real estate broker is already familiar, among them Law of Agency and Real Property Law. Other major areas of substantive law include Administrative Law, Commercial Law, Constitutional Law, Law of Contracts, Corporation Law, Criminal Law, Personal Property Law (Uniform Commercial Code), Partnership, Trusts and Wills, Torts and Taxes.

Procedural law includes Law of Evidence, Civil Procedure, Criminal Procedure, Administrative Procedure and Appellate Procedure.

Torts

The state prosecutes criminals who commit acts that injure the state or society as a whole under the provisions of **criminal law. Civil law,** on the other hand, is concerned, among other matters, with **torts,** the injuries one person does another. While criminal law concentrates on punishing the culprit, the law of torts is intended to compensate the injured party. A single act may result in both civil and criminal court action as well as administrative procedure. The commission of a fraud, for example, may result in criminal prosecution, a civil suit by the defrauded person and administrative action such as the revocation of a real estate license.

For a tort to be committed, three factors must exist: The plaintiff must have suffered a loss or injury; the damage must have been caused by the defendant; and the defendant must usually have failed to exercise reasonable care. Torts are generally classified into three groups: intentional torts, negligence and strict liability. Wrongs against the person include *assault* (threatening behavior), *battery* (physical contact, even without actual injury), *false imprisonment* (sometimes charged, for example, in the detention of a suspected shoplifter) and the *infliction of mental distress* through harassment. *Defamation* covers *slander* (oral) and *libel* (written), actions that tend to falsely hold a person up to contempt, ridicule or hatred. Slander or libel arise when third parties can read or overhear the material. Among the grounds for libel that may concern real estate brokers are statements that another person has committed improprieties while engaging in a profession or trade. In a lawsuit the truth of the statement is almost always a complete defense. False statements about products, businesses or title to property also can result in tort liability if actual damages occur. Torts against the person also include *misrepresentation, fraud* and *invasion of the right to privacy.*

Wrongs against property include *trespass,* unauthorized intrusion upon another's land. No actual damage need be shown; the landowner's right to exclusive possession has been violated by the trespass. Damage to landscaping by workers who could have avoided it through reasonable care becomes a tort against the property. *Trespass to personalty* occurs when personal property is injured or the owner's right to enjoyment of it is interfered with. When property is stolen, the tort of *conversion* (to someone else's use) had occurred. Conversion also can occur if another's property is mistakenly taken or accidentally damaged.

Nuisances are acts that interfere with another's enjoyment or health. Barking dogs, searchlights that shine onto another's property and business activities that cause unpleasant odors are typical nuisances. In addition to seeking money damages, the plaintiff will usually ask the court for an **injunction,** an order forbidding the offending activity.

Negligence covers actions that tend to wrong another through carelessness without any intent to cause damage. Such torts are often committed in accidents and the court may apportion negligence between the parties. *Business torts* include infringement of copyrights, patents and trademarks, and unfair competition. A business venture that is entered into for the single purpose of harming another established business becomes the tort known as *malicious injury to business*. *Strict liability* (usually in product liability cases) covers damages caused by unusual and abnormally dangerous activities in the course of business such as improper manufacturing procedures that create dangerous products. Failure to warn the user of the dangers in using such an item is also covered by strict liability.

Statute of Limitations

Lawsuits must be commenced within a given period after damages have occurred. In some cases, it is necessary only to file notice within the period, that a suit may be instituted. The **statute of limitations** (time within which suit must be commenced) varies for different matters in New York State:

- To sue a governmental agency: notice of claim within 90 days;
- To recover real property: 10 years;
- Contracts, foreclosures, fraud: six years;
- Personal or property injury, malpractice (other than dental and medical): three years;
- Medical or dental malpractice: two years (six months or one year after discovery of a foreign object in the body); and
- Assault, battery, false arrest, right of privacy, libel and slander: one year.

Divorce in New York

Divorce in New York State is not granted on the grounds of incompatibility or irreconcilable differences. No-fault divorce is possible after one year of living apart under a separation agreement or a court-ordered separation decree. Four grounds for divorce in New York hold one party at fault: cruel and inhuman treatment, abandonment for one or more years, imprisonment for three years or more and adultery.

Grounds for divorce. Cruel and inhuman treatment involves either mental or physical cruelty that has a serious effect on the spouse's health. Alcoholism and mental illness are not considered under this category unless they result in maltreatment. The cruel and inhuman treatment must have occurred within five years before the divorce is sought.

Abandonment occurs when a spouse leaves voluntarily (or refuses to have sexual relations), or when a spouse with no career refuses to follow the other in a move. It must exist for at least one year before the divorce action is started.

If imprisonment of a spouse is the grounds cited, the spouse must have served three or more years before the divorce action is brought.

Adultery is difficult to prove and may be overturned as grounds for a divorce if the spouse encouraged the adultery, forgave it to the extent of resuming sexual relations after discovering the action, also committed adultery or failed to bring the action within five years.

Living apart. Living apart for at least one year, if cited as grounds for a divorce, requires either a detailed separation agreement prepared by attorneys or a decree granted by the Supreme Court. Grounds for the decree include abandonment for less than a year and nonsupport. At the end of a year apart, either spouse may sue for a no-fault divorce.

Annulment. At the court's discretion, a marriage may be voided if either spouse is incapable of sexual intercourse, was under the age of 18 at marriage, has become incurably insane for five or more years, was married under duress or force, or consented to the marriage because of fraud (but not if there was forgiveness in the form of sexual intercourse after the fraud was discovered).

Special proceeding. A marriage may be dissolved if a spouse has been absent for five years and efforts to discover whether he or she is still living have been to no avail.

Equitable distribution. In New York, the courts can order division of marital property (all property acquired during the marriage except inheritance, gifts from third parties and compensation for personal injuries.) Court-ordered division can take place no matter who holds title to the property, and need not be on a 50/50 basis. Maintenance may be ordered for one spouse on a limited or permanent basis.

Bankruptcy

Bankruptcy is a legal proceeding through which a debtor may seek relief from overwhelming financial problems and a chance at a fresh start. Creditors are assured a fair share of any assets that may be available. Bankruptcy is a federal proceeding brought in bankruptcy court, a special federal court. Three general types of bankruptcy are known by the chapter numbers in the Bankruptcy Reform Act of 1978. **Chapter 7** provides for the total liquidation of the debtor's assets (less certain exempt items available to individuals.) **Chapter 11** and **Chapter 13** provide for the debtor's retention of assets and a corresponding adjustment in the payment of the outstanding debts. The purposes of bankruptcy law are to allow a debtor whose debts have become unmanageable to be protected from the creditors, to give the debtor a chance to start over and to distribute the debtor's available assets fairly to the creditors.

Chapter 7, often known as straight bankruptcy, requires the debtor (either an individual or a corporation) to disclose all debts and to disclose and surrender all assets to a trustee. The process starts with the filing of a petition in bankruptcy court, either by the debtor (**voluntary bankruptcy**) or by creditors (**involuntary bankruptcy**). Filing of the petition automatically freezes actions against the debtor, providing temporary relief. *The filing of any bankruptcy case automatically halts any pending foreclosure suit.* Lawsuits in progress and other actions against the debtor are halted, and no new actions may be commenced. However, if a creditor is *secured* (where his debt is backed by a lien on debtor's real property or personal property), the secured creditor may request the court to permit the creditor to pursue foreclosure or repossession remedies. The bankruptcy judge may or may not grant this request or may require the debtor to make some payments to the secured creditor to forestall foreclosure.

At the time of the filing of the petition for bankruptcy, an interim trustee is appointed. A meeting of the creditors provides an opportunity for questioning of the debtor and confirmation of the amounts owed. The creditors also may vote for the election of a permanent trustee. The trustee takes over the debtor's assests and distributes the net proceeds proportionately to creditors. The balance of the debts are canceled or *discharged*. The law provides guidelines for the priority or payment of the claims. The debtor is allowed by law to retain up to $5,000 worth of household furnishings, equity in an automobile up to $2,400 and up to $10,000 equity in a homestead. If husband and wife file bankruptcy together, they may protect up to $20,000 in homestead equity. To exercise the homestead equity, it is required that the debtor reside in the real property.

The property of the debtor at the time the bankrupty petition is filed is known as the *property of the estate*. Any property the debtor acquires after the bankruptcy petition is filed is not included in the property of the estate and belongs to the debtor (with the exception of an inheritance within six months after the petition was filed).

A *corporation* filing for *Chapter 11* relief receives the same automatic stay or freeze on creditors' actions as provided by Chapter 7 proceedings. The goal of Chapter 11, however, is not immediate liquidation of the debtor's business or total distribution of assets. Instead, the debtor and a creditors' committee formulate a plan for paying a portion of the debts while the debtor continues in business under the scrutiny of the bankruptcy court and the creditors' committee. Chapter 11 plans may provide for a gradual, orderly winding-up of the business or may aim at total recovery.

Persons holding mortgages on real property may be delayed in foreclosing those mortgages by order of the bankruptcy judge until a plan is proposed by the bankrupt party and either accepted or rejected by the creditors and the court. Thus although a creditor holds a mortgage on real property of the debtor, the mortgagee may have to wait a considerable time, sometimes years, before the mortgage can be foreclosed.

After the Chapter 11 petition is filed, the debtor continues to operate the business, free of the claims and judgments that beset the debtor prior to such filing. *Debtor-in-possession* (DIP) is the term used to designate the situation. The court may allow the debtor to continue in the operation of the business or upon a showing of fraudulent practices or waste may appoint a trustee to do so. In either event a creditor's committee is appointed to oversee the management. After a plan is proposed (by the debtor or by the creditor's committee) a vote of the creditors is taken. If the creditors' vote favors the plan and the court approves it, it is put into effect. If no plan is presented or the creditors and/or the court turn down the plan, the proceeding is generally converted into a straight Chapter 7 bankruptcy.

Chapter 13 is available only to *individuals* with regular income (including those on welfare, social security and retirement income) or those who operate a small business. It offers a chance to work out financial problems over a period of up to five years. Creditors may be paid in part or in full as in Chapter 11 but under Chapter 13 the proposed plan is not voted on by creditors. The court, in its sole discretion, makes the decisions on the viability of the plan and the best interests of the creditors. Chapter 13 can be initiated only by a voluntary petition and tends to avoid the stigma of bankruptcy. The automatic stay halting all pending actions and prohibiting new actions exists just as under Chapter 7 and Chapter 11.

The trustee appointed in a bankruptcy replaces the debtor in exercising control over the debtor's property. His or her function is to take control of the debtor's (bankrupt's) assets, manage them until they are disposed of, and then distribute the net proceeds pro rata among the creditors in the order of the statutory priorities.

If the secured creditor is permitted by the bankruptcy court to foreclose the lien on the secured property (real or personal property or both) and the value of the foreclosed property is less than the amount of mortgagee's debt, the secured creditor becomes unsecured for the excess amount and to that extent shares pro rata with the other unsecured creditors in the property of the estate.

Certain claims cannot be discharged in bankruptcy:

- Income taxes accruing within three years of the bankruptcy filing;
- Sales taxes and withholding taxes collected from customers and employees but not paid over to the taxing authorities;
- Claims not listed on the bankruptcy schedule;
- Claims based on fraud (misrepresentation or false pretenses):
- Alimony and child support;
- Claims based on willful injury (except under Chapter 13);
- Some fines or penalties due to the government; and
- Some student loans (except where the court determines there is undue hardship or under Chapter 13).

Occasionally debtors do not receive their discharge. Discharges may be withheld where proof is offered that the debtor has concealed assets, obtained credit under false financial statements or failed to cooperate with the trustee.

Estates

A decedent's estate is administered and settled by a **personal representative** appointed by surrogate's court. A will may name an **executor** to serve as personal representative. If no will can be found or no executor is named, the court will appoint an **administrator,** who serves as a personal representative and performs the same duties as an executor. The executor first inventories the estate to determine its extent and value. The will, insurance policies, deeds, car registrations, birth and marriage certificates are located. Safe deposit boxes are inventoried and the executor takes possession of property such as bank accounts, real estate and personal property. Names, addresses and social security numbers of all heirs are obtained. The executor files claims for social security, pension and veterans benefits.

The personal representative then administers the estate as the decedent would have done, collecting debts, managing real estate, collecting insurance proceeds, continuing a family business and arranging for the support of a family pending final distribution of the estate. The executor also pays rightful claims against the estate, negotiates the most favorable treatment for taxes and sells selected assets to pay taxes in time to avoid any penalties.

Final winding-up of the estate involves arranging proper division of the assets, selling some to pay cash bequests and transferring title to real and personal property. Final estate costs are paid and an accounting is prepared.

Estate and Gift Taxes

Both the federal government and one or more state governments may levy taxes on the assets of the decedent's estate. The executor or other personal representative of the estate generally pays estate taxes from the assets of the estate. Any amount may be transferred between spouses during a lifetime or by will with no federal gift or estate tax due. Transfer to a spouse by will is known as the **marital deduction.** The remainder of an estate, beyond property passing through the marital deduction and certain other deductions, is subject to substantial federal estate tax if it exceeds $600,000.

Gifts made during a lifetime in excess of the *annual exclusion* ($10,000 to any individual each year, or $20,000 if the donor's spouse joins in the gift) are subject to federal gift tax. They may, however, be subtracted from the **unified credit.** A gift of $100,000 during the decedent's lifetime, for example, would be free of gift tax but at death only $500,000 would be covered by the remaining unified exclusion.

New York also allows annual gifts of $10,000 each to any number of individuals, free of any gift tax. Gifts of up to $100,000 may go to a spouse during one's lifetime, untaxed. A limited amount of unified credit is also available at the state level.

An unlimited amount may pass to a surviving the spouse free of New York estate tax. After this marital deduction and certain other deductions, approximately $108,000 of the estate's assets are free from New York estate tax.

If estate or gift tax is due and not paid, the federal government and New York State may impose a lien on property. With certain exceptions, after a tax lien attaches to property, it continues even though the property is transferred to another. Thus until taxes are paid, a cloud on the title may render the property subject to the lien unmarketable.

Summary

The *seven sources of law* in the United States are the U.S. Constitution, laws passed by Congress, federal regulations, state constitutions, laws passed by state legislatures, local ordinances and court decisions.

Common law in the United States evolved predominantly from custom and usage in early England. Gradually the basis of common law expanded to include the precedent or prior court decisions as well as custom. Much of real property law is founded in common law.

Commercial paper, or *negotiable instruments*, is comprised of written promises or orders to pay money that may be transferred from one person to another. The Uniform Commercial Code divides commercial paper into *notes, drafts, checks* and *certificates of deposit*. Commercial paper must be in writing, signed by the maker or drawer, payable either to bearer or a specific payee, for a specific sum of money at a definite time or on demand. It may be transferred by four types of *endorsement: blank, restrictive, special* or *qualified. A holder in due course* has a stronger claim to payment in case of dispute than an ordinary holder.

Under the Uniform Commercial Code, security interests in chattels must be recorded using a *security agreement* and *financing statement*. The recording of a financing statement gives notice to purchasers and mortgagees of the security interest in chattels and fixtures on the specific parcel of real estate.

A *partnership* is an association of two or more persons to carry on a business for profit as co-owners. Profit and loss are passed directly through to individual partners for taxation. Partners have unlimited individual liability for the partnership's debts. *Limited partnerships* have one general partner who takes on management and unlimited debt liability, and limited partners who are liable only to the extent of their investment.

A *corporation* is a legal person owned by any number of shareholders who have limited individual liability for the corporation's debts. It is formed through the approval of a *certificate of incorporation* by the secretary of state. A *board of directors,* elected by the shareholders, selects officers to manage the business. Profits are taxed twice, once to the corporation and once to the shareholder who receives dividends.

The federal court system includes *district courts, specialized courts, courts of review* and the *Supreme Court.* New York State has four federal judicial district courts, which originate federal cases. Appeals from this state are heard by the *second circuit court of appeals.*

In New York State different court systems originate cases in New York City area and Upstate. *Small claims court* is part of a court of local jurisdiction for the prompt and informal treatment of disputes. *Appeals* from lower courts are handled by the *appellate divisions of the supreme court.* The highest court in the state is the *court of appeals.*

The whole body of law falls into two categories, *substantive* law, which defines the rights of individuals, and *procedural* law, which establishes methods for enforcing those rights. *Criminal law* covers acts that injure society or the state; *civil law* is concerned with *torts,* the injuries one person does another. Torts may be against a person or against property. Civil lawsuits are intended to recompense the injured party.

Bankruptcy is a federal proceeding through which a debtor seeks relief from overwhelming financing problems. *Chapter 7* provides for immediate liquidation of debts, *Chapter 11* for reorganization or the orderly winding-down of *businesses* and *Chapter 13* for gradual payment over a period of time, either in part or in full, by *individual* debtors.

A decedent's estate is settled by a *personal representative,* either an *executor* named in a will or an *administrator* appointed by the court. The executor inventories the estate, administers it, collects debts and pays claims, divides the assets and distributes them to heirs. Federal and state governments levy *estate taxes.*

Questions

1. Among the seven sources of law are:
   a. court decisions.
   b. governmental agencies' regulations.
   c. state laws.
   d. all of the above.

2. A written promise to pay money made by one individual directly to another is most often a:
   a. promissory note:
   b. draft.
   c. check.
   d. certificate of deposit.

3. To be negotiable, an instrument must:
   a. mention a consideration.
   b. conform with Chapter 11 rules.
   c. mention a specific sum of money.
   d. qualify for dissolution.

4. In case of a dispute, the person with the best claim to payment is a(n):
   a. ordinary holder.
   b. holder in due course.
   c. drawer.
   d. maker.

5. The Uniform Commercial Code covers:
   a. bequests.   c. chattels.
   b. realty.   d. services.

6. Writing "for deposit only" on a check constitutes a:
   a. blank endorsement.
   b. special endorsement.
   c. qualified endorsement.
   d. restrictive endorsement.

7. Co-owners have no individual liability for the debt of a:
   a. corporation.   c. tort.
   b. partnership.   d. private offering.

8. The general partner has unlimited liability in a:
   a. corporation.
   b. real estate investment trust.
   c. limited partnership.
   d. closely held corporation.

9. Most federal lawsuits and prosecution for federal crimes originate in:
   a. supreme court.   c. district court.
   b. court of claims.   d. court of appeals.

10. New York State's highest court is the:
    a. supreme court.   c. district court.
    b. court of claims.   d. court of appeals.

11. Disputes of limited dollar value may be settled at nominal cost and without the use of lawyers in:
    a. small claims court.   c. civil court.
    b. court of claims.   d. justice court.

12. Law of agency and real property law fall under the category known as:
    a. substantive law.   c. criminal law.
    b. procedural law.   d. law of contracts.

13. Slander, libel, assault and battery are types of torts known as:
    a. negligence.
    b. wrongs against property.
    c. wrongs against the person.
    d. strict liability.

14. A court order forbidding a certain activity is known as:
    a. specific performance.   c. conversion.
    b. an injunction.   d. a rejoinder.

15. Legal relief through the immediate canceling of most debts can be sought through which form of bankruptcy?
    a. Chapter 1   c. Chapter 11
    b. Chapter 7   d. Chapter 13

16. The debtor who files bankruptcy is allowed to keep:
    a. household furnishings.
    b. income-producing real estate.
    c. a vacation home worth up to $20,000.
    d. all of the above.

17. Bankruptcy proceedings are heard in:
    a. federal court.
    b. small claims court.
    c. surrogate's court.
    d. family court.

18. The personal representative who handles a decedent's estate may be a(n):
    a. referee.   c. plaintiff.
    b. administrator.   d. proxy.

19. Federal tax law provides that one spouse may give another:
    a. any amount without gift or estate taxes due.
    b. up to $100,000 without estate taxes due.
    c. no more than $250,000 tax-free during a lifetime.
    d. up to $20,000 tax-free in any year.

20. New York's estate tax allows a spouse to inherit without any estate tax due:
    a. any amount.
    b. up to $250,000 or one-half the estate.
    c. $100,000.
    d. up to $20,000.

Broker's Practice Examination

The following broker's examination is typical of the type given by the state of New York. Each correct answer is worth one point on this exam. A grade of 70% is passing.

Those who desire additional exam preparation may obtain a copy of *New York Real Estate Exam Guide*, by Judith Deickler, which is available from Real Estate Education Company, Chicago.

1. Those funds left from gross income after commissions have been shared with salespersons, other brokers and franchise networks are referred to as:
   - a. company dollar.
   - b. collateral.
   - c. commission.
   - d. chattel.

2. In a real estate business formed as a sole proprietorship, which of the following would *not* be true?
   - a. The broker may draw a regular salary or take profits as income.
   - b. The broker's salary is taxed twice.
   - c. The broker would enjoy the best tax advantages for a small office.
   - d. The broker has unlimited financial liability.

3. A real estate business organized as a Sub-chapter S corporation:
   - a. carries the same tax disadvantages as a regular corporation.
   - b. may have any desired number of shareholders.
   - c. is automatically dissolved when the principal shareholder dies.
   - d. offers some limit to personal financial liability.

4. Errors and omission insurance covers:
   - a. intentional acts of a broker to deceive.
   - b. punitive damages.
   - c. the defense of "nuisance cases."
   - d. negligence when buying or selling for one's own account.

5. The mixing of client's or customer's funds with an agent's personal funds is known as:
   - a. commingling.
   - b. consideration.
   - c. collateral.
   - d. codicil.

6. The Internal Revenue Service will challenge independent contractor status if the sales associate:
   - a. is licensed as a real estate broker or salesperson.
   - b. receives health and life insurance as an employment benefit.
   - c. has income based on sales output, subject to fluctuation.
   - d. performs services persuant to a written contract specifying independent contractor status.

7. Operating a real estate office in restraint of trade violates the:
   - a. General Obligations Law.
   - b. Sherman Antitrust Act.
   - c. Civil Rights Act.
   - d. Statute of Frauds.

8. As an independent contractor a salesperson:
   - a. has income tax and social security withheld from wages.
   - b. has health and life insurance supplied as a benefit.
   - c. can be told what to do but not how to do it.
   - d. must keep hours as assigned by the broker.

9. It is *not* considered fraudulent when a broker:
   - a. conceals important facts about a property.
   - b. makes false statements about a property.
   - c. makes the unprovable statement that the property "has the best view in the country."
   - d. attempts to close a transaction by not mentioning to the buyer that an amusement park is to be built on the next lot.

10. A real estate broker is most generally a(n):
    a. universal agent.   c. special agent.
    b. general agent.   d. ostensible agent.

11. In real estate advertising which of the following is correct?
    a. The listing salesperson's name must appear in the ad.
    b. The advertisement must indicate that the advertiser is a broker.
    c. A property may be listed as being "in the vicinity of" without stating the exact location.
    d. An ad may indicate only the rate of interest on available financing.

12. ABC Realty may place a For Sale sign on a property only:
    a. if the owner is away and would not be aware of the sign.
    b. if it is an open listing.
    c. with the owner's consent.
    d. if it is an exclusive right to sell.

13. A principal broker is responsible for:
    a. getting listing leads for sales associates.
    b. training sales associates.
    c. sales associates' clothing allowance.
    d. sales associates' business calls placed from a home phone.

14. An affidavit of entitlement to a commission due on the sale of real property:
    a. is a lien.
    b. will prevent transfer of title.
    c. is a public notice, filed and indexed in public records.
    d. prevents the buyer from getting a mortgage.

15. Several brokerage firms may legitimately get together to:
    a. establish reasonable fees for services rendered.
    b. divide up various market areas so as to limit the competition between them.
    c. work toward preventing a "discount broker" from getting business or co-brokerage.
    d. enhance the ethical practices in their area.

16. When two brokers orally agree to share a commission, this agreement is:
    a. void.
    b. voidable.
    c. valid.
    d. subject to the buyer's approval.

17. An associate broker may:
    a. sponsor an applicant for a salesperson's license.
    b. work as a salesperson under the name and supervision of another principal broker.
    c. collect his or her own real estate fees.
    d. act as a principal broker.

18. To practice real estate in New York, a real estate broker need *not:*
    a. display his or her license.
    b. have and maintain a principal place of business.
    c. have a Licensed Real Estate Broker business sign.
    d. have a branch office.

19. When handling funds for others, a broker must:
    a. place all monies in his/her own business account.
    b. use the interest to take care of the expenses he/she incurs.
    c. maintain a separate special bank account exclusively for escrow deposits.
    d. keep the money in a non-interest bearing account.

20. *Not* included in the exemptions to the Federal Fair Housing Act of 1968 would be:
    a. private clubs, not open to the public, restricting the rental of rooms to members, but not operating commercially.
    b. dwelling units, owned by religious institutions, restricted to members of the religion if membership is not discriminatory.
    c. rental of rooms in an owner-occupied two-family house based on national origin.
    d. any sale involving the use of a real estate broker.

21. A New York real estate broker may not:

    a. ever receive payment from both buyer and seller.
    (b.) use the license to act as broker in another state.
    c. hold the license of an associate broker.
    d. share commissions with an out-of-state broker.

22. A salesperson and a broker decide to become partners in a real estate business. They may:

    (a.) not do so.
    b. register as officers of the same corporation.
    c. register the business with broker as principal and salesperson as employee.
    d. register as a joint venture.

23. According to the Code of Ethics of the National Association of REALTORS®, a REALTOR® may:

    (a.) cooperate with other brokers when it is in the best interest of his or her client.
    b. publicly disparage the business practices of a competitor.
    c. engage in activities that constitute the unauthorized practice of law.
    d. accept kickbacks from vendors.

24. The REALTORS® Code for Equal Opportunity provides that REALTORS® may:

    a. volunteer information regarding the racial, creedal or ethnic composition of a neighborhood.
    (b.) not engage in any activity for the purpose of panic selling.
    c. advertise for sale a dwelling in an ethnically dominated neighborhood aimed at that ethnic group.
    d. work the hardest for the customers with the most money.

25. An individual who poses as a customer to check on compliance with fair housing laws is:

    a. always a HUD (Housing and Urban Development) employee.
    b. usually a disgruntled customer.
    (c.) known as a tester.
    d. engaged in unlawful entrapment.

26. Which of the following is a negotiable instrument?

    a. A mortgage   (c.) A check
    b. A stock certificate d. A deed

27. Standards set by the Uniform Commercial Code (UCC) for a negotiable instrument do *not* include that it be:

    a. in writing.
    b. signed by the maker/drawer.
    c. payable to either order or bearer.
    (d.) a conveyance.

28. Stockholders of a corporation are liable:

    (a.) only to the extent of their investment in the firm.
    b. personally for debts and losses.
    c. for the debts of another shareholder.
    d. for the entire debt of the corporation.

29. A Real Estate Investment Trust (REIT):

    a. usually pays out of cash flow.
    b. has a general partner running a project as a fudiciary.
    (c.) can stay in the business indefinitely by investing in further projects.
    d. passes cash and tax losses to partners.

30. A written agreement between two or more parties providing that a certain property will be placed with a third party and will be delivered to a designated person upon the performance of some act or condition is called:

    a. estate.   c. equity.
    (b.) escrow.   d. egress.

31. Anything given to induce entering into a contract, such as money or personal services, is called:

    (a.) consideration.   c. conversion.
    b. condemnation.   d. caveat emptor.

32. Under the Uniform Vendor and Purchaser Risk Act in New York, the party who bears any loss to property that occurs before the title passes, or the buyer takes possession, is the:

    (a.) seller.   c. bank.
    b. buyer.   d. title company.

33. When the seller defaults on a contract of sale, one recourse for the buyer would *not* be to:
    - (a) sue the broker.
    - b. terminate the contract and recover the earnest money.
    - c. sue the seller for specific performance.
    - d. sue the seller for compensatory damages.

34. The executor of an estate may *not:*
    - a. inventory the estate.
    - (b) ignore income taxes of the deceased.
    - c. collect debts and pay claims.
    - d. distribute assets to heirs.

35. A legal proceeding through which a debtor may seek relief from overwhelming financial problems, and have a chance at a fresh start, is called:
    - a. certiorari.
    - (b) bankruptcy.
    - c. capital recapture.
    - d. dispossess proceedings.

36. A real estate limited partnership:
    - a. is often traded on stock exchanges.
    - b. is managed by a board of directors.
    - c. has a reinvestment plan.
    - (d) usually liquidates one project in five to seven years.

37. When a married couple is divorced, their tenancy by the entirety changes to:
    - a. tenancy by sufferage.
    - b. tenancy at will.
    - c. joint tenancy.
    - (d) tenancy in common.

38. Fred Freeman and Apple Annie together own 20 acres. Each has an undivided interest in severalty, without right of survivorship. This form of ownership is known as a:
    - a. tenancy by sufferance.
    - b. tenancy by the entirety.
    - (c) tenancy in common.
    - d. joint tenancy.

39. An example of a unilateral contract would be a(n):
    - a. land contract.
    - b. contract on a house sale.
    - (c) offer of a reward.
    - d. contract to sell a car.

40. The person who delays taking steps to enforce contractual rights within the statutory period risks losing those rights through:
    - a. lis pendens.   c. litigation.
    - (b) laches.   d. lien.

41. When a mortgage instrument states that in the event of mortgagor's default the entire debt is due and payable immediately, this is called the:
    - a. habendum clause.
    - (b) acceleration clause.
    - c. demising clause.
    - d. granting clause.

42. Agreements written into deeds promising performance or nonperformance of certain acts, or stipulating certain uses or nonuses of the property, are known as:
    - (a) covenants.   c. commissions.
    - b. considerations.   d. certioraris.

43. The document in which a mortgagor certifies the amount owed on a mortgage loan and the rate of interest is called a(n):
    - a. satisfaction certificate.
    - (b) estoppel certificate.
    - c. mortgage statement.
    - d. covenant.

44. A transaction in which an owner sells his or her improved property and, as part of the same transaction, signs a long-term lease to remain in possession of the property is called:
    - a. equity of redemption.
    - b. satisfaction piece.
    - (c) sale and leaseback.
    - d. conditional contract of sale.

45. An FHA (Federal Housing Administration) loan is always:
    - a. conventional.   (c) insured.
    - b. guaranteed.   d. prepaid.

46. The right of an owner to reclaim property before it is sold through proceedings is called:
    - (a) equity of redemption.
    - b. escheat.
    - c. depreciation.
    - d. collateral.

47. The amount of a mortgage loan in relation to the value of a house is called:

    a. percentage.
    b. loan-to-value ratio.
    c. negative amortization.
    d. equity loan.

48. Discount charges imposed by lenders to raise the yields on their loans are called:

    a. negative amortization.
    b. points.
    c. laches.
    d. lis pendens.

49. A history of conveyances and encumbrances, affecting a title as far back as records are available, is known as:

    a. color of title.
    b. marketable title.
    c. chain of title.
    d. recorded title.

50. The lender, at the closing, generally does *not* require:

    a. title insurance or abstract of title.
    b. payment of the first three months' mortgage and interest.
    c. fire and hazard insurance policy.
    d. representation by its own attorney.

51. RESPA requirements do not apply when the:

    a. sale of property is paid in cash and in full.
    b. loan is made by a federally insured lender.
    c. loan is insured by FHA or guaranteed by VA.
    d. loan is administered by HUD.

52. The reversion to the state of property in the event the owner abandons it or dies, leaving no will or lawful heirs, is called:

    a. escrow.   c. ejectment.
    b. escheat.   d. eviction.

53. Which of the following is an example of voluntary alienation?

    a. Accretion   c. Erosion
    b. Avulsion   d. Dedication

54. Transfer of title by involuntary alienation is most likely to involve which of the following?

    a. A warranty deed
    b. A bargain and sale deed
    c. A quitclaim deed
    d. Adverse possession

55. Which of the following is considered involuntary alienation?

    a. Transfer of title by will
    b. Transfer of title by sale
    c. Eminent domain
    d. Gift to one's best friend

56. Except for those exempted, successful completion of a continuing education course is required for license renewal how often?

    a. Every year
    b. Every two years
    c. For the first renewal only
    d. Every four years

57. A clause in the lease whereby the landlord (lessor) leases and the tenant (lessee) takes the property is called:

    a. demising clause.
    b. habendum clause.
    c. subletting clause.
    d. defeasance clause.

58. The tenant who remains after the lease period expires is said to have which of the following?

    a. Periodic tenancy
    b. Common tenancy
    c. Holdover tenancy
    d. Fee simple tenancy

59. In a New York residential lease, which would not apply under the implied warrant of habitability?

    a. The landlord must paint the interior every three years.
    b. The leased property must be fit for human habitation.
    c. The common elements must be maintained in good repair.
    d. The tenant cannot be subjected to conditions that could endanger life, health or safety.

60. The Emergency Tenant Protection Act (ETPA) of 1974 was designed to:

    a. freeze rents in controlled apartments.
    b. offer a local option to communities with escalating rents.
    c. increase housing stock.
    d. assure landlords fair return on their investment.

61. Included in the more common types of insurance a property manager would utilize would be:

    a. life insurance.
    b. mortgage insurance.
    c. liability insurance.
    d. disability insurance.

62. Ideally, the property manager should not:

    a. merchandise the property.
    b. control operating expenses.
    c. maintain and modernize the property.
    d. cut corners on maintenance to temporarily increase profits.

63. Where a tenant is removed from possession of a premises, either by force or by process of law, this is known as:

    a. partial eviction.
    b. actual eviction.
    c. constructive eviction.
    d. tentative eviction.

64. A lien on a real estate property:

    a. binds only the current owner.
    b. runs with the land.
    c. prevents the sale of the property.
    d. is renegotiated upon sale.

65. Which type of lien generally holds priority over all others?

    a. Mechanics'   c. Real estate taxes
    b. Mortgage   d. Vendor's

66. An easement may be terminated:

    a. when the property is sold to a third party.
    b. when the owner of the dominant tenement buys the servient tenement.
    c. at any time.
    d. when the owner of the servient tenement desires increased privacy.

67. An easement granted to New York State Electric and Gas Company to put electric service across another's property would be a(n):

    a. easement appurtenant.
    b. easement in gross.
    c. easement by necessity.
    d. easement by prescription.

68. In New York, a special exemption to reduce a real estate tax bill may exist for some:

    a. senior citizens.
    b. welfare recipients.
    c. nonsectarian charities.
    d. parents of children enrolled in private schools.

69. Neighborhood taxes levied on real estate to pay for street lights or sewers would be considered:

    a. ad valorem taxes
    b. in rem.
    c. special assessments.
    d. exclusionary.

70. A legal proceeding against the realty directly, as distinguished from a proceeding against a person, is called:

    a. a tax lien.   c. redemption.
    b. in rem.   d. lis pendens.

71. A home is assessed at 25 percent of its market value of $250,000. The county tax rate is 50 mils. The county tax bill will be:

    a. $3,125.00.   c. $1,250.00.
    b. $312.50.   d. $6,250.00.

72. An investment in real estate:

    a. is highly liquid.
    b. no longer provides any tax shelter.
    c. often utilizes leverage.
    d. requires little expert advice.

73. A statutory accounting concept in real estate investments known as depreciation is also called:

    a. cost recovery.   c. substantiation
    b. appreciation.   d. rehabilitation.

74. An investor sells residential property that was depreciated using an accelerated recovery method. That portion of the gain, the excess of which would have been earned using straight-line recovery, will be taxed as ordinary income. This is known as:

    a. depreciation.   c. recapture.
    b. appreciation.   d. basis.

75. The primary factors that affect appreciation of a real estate investment are:
   a. deflation and obsolescence.
   b. speculation and circulation.
   c. rehabilitation and taxation.
   d. inflation and intrinsic value.

76. Which of the following is *not* one of the three basic land-use classifications in zoning?
   a. Commercial
   b. Residential
   c. Municipal
   d. Industrial

77. In every contract of sale or lease of subdivided lands, if the purchaser or lessee is not represented by an attorney, he or she has:
   a. a 30-day cancellation privilege.
   b. a 90-day cancellation privilege.
   c. a 10-day cancellation privilege.
   d. no cancellation privilege.

78. An offer to sell or lease subdivided lands prior to the filing of both the offering statement and the statement constitutes:
   a. a misdemeanor.
   b. a felony.
   c. escheat.
   d. insubordination.

79. The sale or lease of subdivided lands in New York is primarily governed by:
   a. Article 9A of the Real Property Law.
   b. the Statute of Limitations.
   c. Uniform Commercial Code.
   d. the Civil Rights Act of 1866.

80. Mr. A devises his home to Mrs. A with the provision that at her death, title passes to A., Jr. During Mrs. A's lifetime, A., Jr. has a:
   a. remainder interest.
   b. life estate.
   c. interest pur autre vie.
   d. conditional estate.

81. Which criteria may the government *not* use to condemn private property for public use through the right of eminent domain?
   a. The proposed use is declared by a court to be a public use.
   b. Just compensation is paid the owner.
   c. The property is run down and unsightly.
   d. The property owner's rights are protected by due process.

82. The interest a grantor may retain in a life estate is called:
   a. revocation.
   b. restriction.
   c. reversionary.
   d. remainder.

83. Which of the following is always required for a building certificate of occupancy?
   a. Board of Fire Underwriters Certificate
   b. Variance from the Zoning Board of Appeals
   c. Approval by an Architectural Review Board
   d. Approval by the Department of State

84. Which of the following is not a heating or cooling system?
   a. Oil–hot-water baseboard
   b. Electric hot air
   c. Gas-fired steam
   d. Earth berm

85. Which of the following is *not* an architectural style?
   a. Split-level
   b. Post and beam
   c. Colonial
   d. Ranch

86. A real estate salesperson is not expected to have professional knowledge of:
   a. municipal regulations.
   b. lot lines.
   c. whether a home has a septic tank or is connected to a sewer.
   d. structural or system deficiencies in a building.

87. In terms of real estate appraisal, the present worth of future benefits arising from the ownership of real property is the definition of:
   a. cost.
   b. value.
   c. price.
   d. amenities.

88. Which of the following is *not* a basic approach or technique employed by an appraiser to arrive at an accurate estimate of value?
   a. Direct Sales
   b. Cost
   c. Quantity survey
   d. Income

89. What is the value of a property with an income of $32,000 and a capitalization rate of 12½%?
   a. $256,000
   b. $266,666
   c. $320,000
   d. $400,000

90. The art of analyzing and effectively weighing the findings of value on a property when all the basic approaches to appraisal were used is called:
   a. repudiation.
   b. amortization.
   c. calculation.
   d. reconciliation.

91. Which is *not* a physical characteristic of land?
   a. Scarcity
   b. Immobility
   c. Nonhomogeneity
   d. Indestructibility

92. The leading industry in town has just closed. The resulting real estate situation can be described as:
   a. a sellers' market.
   b. booming.
   c. inflationary.
   d. a buyers' market.

93. Fee simple ownership of an apartment or a housing unit plus an undivided interest in the ownership of the common elements that are jointly owned is called a:
   a. leasehold.
   b. cooperative.
   c. condominium.
   d. dominant tenement.

94. A residential multiunit building with title held by a trust or corporation that is owned and operated for the benefit of persons living within the building, each of whom has a proprietary lease, is called a:
   a. leasehold.
   b. cooperative.
   c. condominium.
   d. dominant tenement.

95. The annual net income on a property is $12,000. The owner wishes to yield an annual 10% rate of return, so this property is worth $120,000 to her. If market conditions change and she now wants a 15% return, what would the value of the property become?
   a. $80,000
   b. $100,000
   c. $150,000
   d. $180,000

96. If a bank charges 10% interest on a loan of $100,000 for 25 years, how much interest must be paid every six months?
   a. $250,000
   b. $10,000
   c. $25,000
   d. $5,000

97. A commercial property, 198' × 175', is listed for sale at $375 per front foot. The commission has been negotiated to 12%. What is the amount of the real estate commission if the property sells for $5 less per front foot than the listing price?
   a. $6,475
   b. $7,875
   c. $8,910
   d. $8,791

98. How many square feet of living area are in a house, if the first floor has a living room, dining room, kitchen, three bedrooms and one bath with dimensions of 24' × 48' and the lower level has the same dimensions, but one-half of it is a two-car garage and the remainder is a family room?
   a. 1,152 sq. ft.
   b. 1,728 sq. ft.
   c. 2,304 sq. ft.
   d. 1,782 sq. ft.

99. A couple has $63,000 cash available for a down payment on a home. Their combined gross income is $98,500. The property taxes are $3,700 and the oil heating cost was $2,500 last year. The bank is offering a 20-year mortgage at 11½% interest, amortizing at $10.66 per month per thousand. The bank has a rule that the combination of the monthly mortgage payment plus the monthly property taxes cannot exceed 29% of the couple's gross income. For what price home can the couple qualify?
   a. $194,000
   b. $257,000
   c. $238,000
   d. $175,000

100. A property valued at $437,000 is assessed at 60% of market value. If the tax rate is $150 per thousand of assessed value, what are the annual taxes?
   a. $39,330
   b. $26,220
   c. $3,933
   d. $2,622

Glossary of Real Estate Terms

Abandonment The voluntary surrender or relinquishment of possession of real property without the vesting of this interest in any other person.

Abstract of title The condensed history of a title to a particular parcel of real estate.

Abstract of title with lawyer's opinion An abstract of title that a lawyer has examined and has certified to be, in his or her opinion, an accurate statement of fact.

Acceleration clause The clause in a note or mortgage that can be enforced to make the entire debt due immediately if the mortgagee defaults.

Accretion The increase or addition of land by the deposit of sand or soil washed up naturally from a river, lake or sea.

Accrued items On a closing statement, items of expense that have been incurred but are not yet payable, such as interest on a mortgage loan.

Acknowledgment A formal declaration made before a duly authorized officer, usually a notary public, by a person who has signed a document.

Acre A measure of land equal to 43,560 square feet; 4,840 square yards; 4,047 square meters; 160 square rods; or 0.4047 hectare.

Actual eviction Action whereby a defaulted tenant is physically ousted from rented property pursuant to a court order. (*See also* Eviction.)

Actual notice Express information or fact; that which is known; actual knowledge.

Adjacent Lying near to but not necessarily in actual contact with.

Adjoining Contiguous; attaching, in actual contact with.

Adjustable rate mortgage A mortgage loan in which the interest rate may increase or decrease to specific intervals, following an economic indicator.

Administrator A person appointed by court to administer the estate of a deceased person who left no will, *i.e.,* who died intestate.

Ad valorem tax A tax levied according to value; generally used to refer to real estate tax. Also called the *general tax*.

Adverse possession The actual, visible, hostile, notorious, exclusive and continuous possession of another's land under a claim of title. Possession for ten years may be a means of acquiring title.

Affidavit A written statement sworn to before an officer who is authorized to administer an oath or affirmation.

Agency That relationship wherein an agent is employed by a principal to do certain acts on the principal's behalf.

Agency coupled with an interest An agency relationship in which the agent is given an estate of interest in the subject of the agency (the property).

Agent One who undertakes to transact some business or to manage some affair for another by authority of the latter.

Air rights The right to use the open space above a property, generally allowing the surface to be used for another purpose.

Alienation The act of transferring property to another.

Alienation clause The clause in a mortgage stating that the balance of the secured debt becomes immediately due and payable at the mortgagee's option if the property is sold.

Amortized loan A loan in which the principal as well as the interest is payable in monthly or other periodic installments over the term of the loan.

Annual percentage rate Rate of interest charged on a loan, calculated to take into account up-front loan fees and points. Usually higher than the *contract interest rate*.

Anti-trust laws Laws designed to preserve the free enterprise of the open marketplace by making illegal certain private conspiracies and combinations formed to minimize competition.

Appeals Complaints made to a higher court requesting the correction of errors in law made by lower courts.

Appellate division Courts of appeal.

Apportionments Adjustment of the income, expenses or carrying charges of real estate usually computed to the date of closing of title so that the seller pays all expenses to that date.

Appraisal An estimate of a property's valuation by an appraiser who is usually presumed to be expert in this work.

Appreciation An increase in the worth or value of a property due to economic or related causes.

Appurtenances Those rights, privileges and improvements that belong to and pass with the transfer of real property but are not necessarily a part of the property such as rights-of-way, easements and property improvements.

APR *See* Annual percentage rate.

ARM *See* Adjustable rate mortgage.

Arm's-length transaction A transaction between relative strangers, each trying to do the best for himself or herself.

Article 9A The section of New York State's Real Property Law relating to subdivision.

Article 12A The section of New York State's Real Property Law relating to real estate licenses.

Assessed valuation A valuation placed upon property by a public officer or a board as a basis for taxation.

Assessment The imposition of a tax, charge or levy, usually according to established rates.

Assignment The transfer in writing of interest in a bond, mortgage, lease or other instrument.

Assumption of mortgage Acquiring title of property on which there is an existing mortgage and agreeing to be personally liable for the terms and conditions of the mortgage, including payments.

Avulsion The removal of land from one owner to another when a stream suddenly changes its channel.

Balloon payment The final payment of a mortgage loan that is considerably larger than the required periodic payments because the loan amount was not fully amortized.

Bargain and sale deed A deed that carries with it no warranties against liens or other encumbrances but that does imply that the grantor has the right to convey title.

Bargain and sale deed with covenant A deed in which the grantor warrants or guarantees the title against defects arising during the period of his or her tenure and ownership of the property but not against defects existing before that time.

Basis The cost that the Internal Revenue Service attributes to an owner of an investment property for the purpose of determining annual depreciation and gain or loss on the sale of the assest.

Benchmark A permanent reference mark or point established for use by surveyors in measuring differences in elevation. *See* Datum.

Beneficiary The person who receives or is to receive benefits resulting from certain acts.

Bequeath To give or hand down by will; to leave by will.

Bequest That which is given by the terms of a will.

Bill of Sale A written instrument given to pass title of personal property from vendor to vendee.

Binder An agreement that may accompany an earnest money deposit for the purchase of real property as evidence of the purchaser's good faith and intent to complete the transaction.

Black book Offering plan for a cooperative or condominium as accepted for filing by the attorney general and used for marketing.

Blanket mortgage A mortgage covering more than one parcel of real estate.

Blockbusting The illegal practice of inducing homeowners to sell their property by making representations regarding the entry or prospective entry of minority persons into the neighborhood.

Blue-sky laws Common name for those state and federal laws that regulate the registration and sale of investment securities.

Board of directors Elected managing body of a corporation, specifically of a cooperative apartment building.

Board of managers Elected managing body of a condominium.

Bond The evidence of a personal debt that is secured by a mortgage or other lien on real estate.

Boot Money or property given to make up any difference in value or equity between two properties in an *exchange*.

Branch office A secondary place of business apart from the principal or main office from which real estate business is conducted.

Breach of contract Violation of any terms or conditions in a contract without legal excuse; for example, failure to make a payment when it is due.

Broker One who buys and sells for another for a fee. *See also* Real estate broker.

Brokerage The business of buying and selling for another for a fee.

Building codes Regulations established by state and local governments stating fully the structural requirements for building.

Building line A line fixed at a certain distance from the front and/or sides of a lot, beyond which no building can project.

Building loan agreement An agreement whereby the lender advances money to an owner with partial payments at certain stages of construction.

Buyer's broker A real estate broker retained by a prospective purchaser, who becomes the broker's principal or client and to whom fiduciary duties are owed.

Bylaws Rules and regulations adopted by an association.

Cap With an adjustable rate mortgage, a limit, usually in percentage points, on how much the interest rate or payment might be raised in each adjustment period. For *lifetime cap, see* Ceiling.

Capital gains Profits realized from the sale of assets like real estate.

Capitalization A mathematical process for estimating the value of a property using a proper rate of return on the investment and the annual net income expected to be produced by the property. The formula is expressed:

$$\frac{\text{Income}}{\text{Rate}} = \text{Value}$$

Capitalization rate The rate of return a property will produce on the owner's investment.

Cash equivalent An appraisal technique that takes into account the influence of concessionary financing.

Cash flow The net spendable income from an investment.

Caveat emptor A Latin phrase meaning "Let the buyer beware."

CC&Rs Covenants, conditions and restrictions of a condominium or cooperative development.

Cease and desist petition A statement filed by a homeowner showing address of premises that notifies the Department of State that such premises are not for sale and the owner does not wish to be solicited.

Ceiling With an adjustable rate mortgage, a limit, usually in percentage points, beyond which the interest rates or monthly payment on a loan may never rise. Sometimes known as a *lifetime cap*.

Certificate of occupancy Document issued by a municipal authority stating that a building complies with building, health and safety codes and may be occupied.

Certificate of title A statement of opinion of title status on a parcel of real property based on an examination of specified public records.

Chain of title The conveyance of real property to one owner from another, reaching back to the original grantor.

Chapter 7, Chapter 11, Chapter 13 Different forms of bankruptcy.

Chattel Personal property such as household goods or fixtures.

Chattel mortgage A mortgage on personal property.

Checkers *See* Testers.

Client The one by whom a broker is employed and by whom the broker will be compensated upon completion of the purpose of the agency.

Closing date The date upon which the buyer takes title to the property.

Closing statement A detailed cash accounting of a real estate transaction showing all cash received, all charges and credits made and all cash paid out in the transaction.

Cloud on the title An outstanding claim or encumbrance that, if valid, would affect or impair the owner's title.

Clustering The grouping of homesites within a subdivision on smaller lots than normal with the remaining land used as common areas.

CMA *See* Comparative market analysis.

C of O *See* Certificate of occupancy.

Coinsurance clause A clause in insurance policies covering real property that requires the policyholder to maintain fire insurance coverage generally equal to at least 80 percent of the property's actual replacement cost.

Collateral Additional security pledged for the payment of an obligation.

Color of title That which appears to be good title but which is not title in fact.

Commingling The illegal act of a real estate broker who mixes other people's money with his or her own.

Commission Payment to a broker for services rendered, such as in the sale or purchase of real property; usually a percentage of the selling price.

Common elements Parts of a property that are necessary or convenient to the existence, maintenance and safety of a condominium or are normally in common use by all of the condominium residents.

Common law The body of law based on custom, usage and court decisions.

Community property A system of property ownership not in effect in New York.

Company dollar A broker's net commission income after cooperating brokers and the firm's own salespersons have been paid.

Comparables Properties listed in an appraisal report that are substantially equivalent to the subject property. Also called *comps*.

Comparative market analysis A study, intended to assist an owner in establishing listing price, of recent comparable sales, properties that failed to sell and parcels presently on the market.

Competent parties Those recognized by law as being able to contract with others; usually those of legal age and sound mind.

Condemnation A judicial or administrative proceeding to exercise the power of eminent domain through which a government agency takes private property for public use and compensates the owner.

Condominium The absolute ownership of an apartment or a unit (generally in a multiunit building) plus an undivided interest in the ownership of the common elements, which are owned jointly with the other condominium unit owners.

Consideration 1. That received by the grantor in exchange for a deed. 2. Something of value that induces a person to enter into a contract. Consideration may be *valuable* (money) or *good* (love and affection).

Constructive eviction Landlord actions that so materially disturb or impair the tenant's enjoyment of the leased premises that the tenant is effectively forced to move out and terminate the lease without liability for any further rent.

Constructive notice Notice given to the world by recorded documents. Possession of property is also considered constructive notice.

Contract An agreement entered into by two or more legally competent parties by the terms of which one or more of the parties, for a consideration, undertakes to do or refrain from doing some legal act or acts.

Contract for deed A contract for the sale of real estate wherein the purchase price is paid in periodic installments by the purchaser, who is in possession of the property even though title is retained by the seller until final payment. Also called an *installment contract* or *land contract*.

Conventional loan A loan not insured or guaranteed by a government.

Conveyance The transfer of title of land from one to another. The means or medium by which title to real estate is transferred.

Cooperative A residential multiunit building whose title is held by a corporation owned by and operated for the benefit of persons living within the building, who are the stockholders of the corporation, each possessing a proprietary lease.

Corporation An entity or organization created by operation of law whose rights of doing business are essentially the same as those of an individual.

Cost approach The process of estimating the value of property by adding to the estimated land value the appraiser's estimate of the reproduction or replacement cost of the building, less depreciation.

Cost basis *See* Basis.

Counteroffer A new offer made as a reply to an offer received.

Covenants Agreement written into deeds and other instruments promising performance or nonperformance of certain acts or stipulating certain uses or nonuses of the property.

CPM Certified Property Manager, a designation awarded by the Institute of Real Estate Management.

Credit On a closing statement, an amount entered in a person's favor.

Criminal law That branch of law defining crimes and providing punishment.

Cubic-foot method A technique for estimating building costs per cubic foot.

Damages The indemnity recoverable by a person who has sustained an injury, either to person, property or rights, through the act or default of another.

Datum Point from which elevations are measured. Mean sea level in New York harbor, or local datum.

DBA "Doing business as"; an assumed business name.

Dealer An IRS classification for a person whose business is buying and selling real estate on his or her own account.

DEC The New York Department of Environmental Conservation.

Decedent A person who has died.

Declaration A formal statement of intention to establish a condominium.

Dedication The voluntary transfer of private property by its owner to the public for some public use such as for streets or schools.

Deed A written instrument that, when executed and delivered, conveys title to or an interest in real estate.

Deed restriction An imposed restriction in a deed for the purpose of limiting the use of the land by future owners.

Default The nonperformance of a duty whether arising under a contract or otherwise; failure to meet an obligation when due.

Deficiency judgment A personal judgement levied against the mortgagor when a foreclosure sale does not produce sufficient funds to pay the mortgage debt in full.

Delinquent taxes Unpaid past due taxes.

Delivery The transfer of the possession of a thing from one person to another.

Demising clause A clause in a lease whereby the landlord (lessor) leases and the tenant (lessee) takes the property.

Department of Housing and Community Renewal The New York State department charged with administering rent regulations.

Deposition Sworn testimony that may be used as evidence in a suit or trial.

Depreciation In appraisal, a loss of value in property due to any cause including physical deterioration, functional obsolescence and locational obsolescence.

Determinable fee estate A fee simple estate in which the property automatically reverts to the grantor upon the occurrence of a specified event or condition.

Developer One who improves land with buildings, usually on a large scale, and sells to homeowners and/or investors.

Devise A gift of real property by will; the act of leaving real property by will.

Devisee One who receives a bequest of real estate made by will.

Devisor One who bequeaths real estate by will.

Direct sales comparison approach The process of estimating the value of a property by examining and comparing actual sales of comparable properties.

Discount points An added loan fee charged by a lender to make the yield on a lower-than-market value loan competitive with higher interest loans.

Documentary evidence Evidence in the form of written or printed papers.

Dominant tenement A property that includes in its ownership the right to use an easement over another person's property for a specific purpose.

DOS New York Department of State; administers license law.

Dual agency Representing both parties to a transaction.

Due-on-sale *See* Alienation clause.

Duress Unlawful constraint or action exercised upon a person who is forced to perform an act against his or her will.

Earnest money deposit Money deposited by a buyer under the terms of a contract, that is to be forfeited if the buyer defaults but applied on the purchase price if the sale is closed.

Easement A right to use the land of another for a specific purpose as for a right-of-way or utilities; an incorporeal interest in land. An *easement appurtenant* passes with the land when conveyed.

Easement by necessity An easement allowed by law as necessary for the full enjoyment of a parcel of real estate; for example, a right of ingress and egress over a grantor's land.

Easement by prescription An easement acquired by continuous, open, uninterrupted, exclusive and adverse use of the property for the period of time prescribed by state law.

Easement in gross An easement that is not created for the benefit of any *land* owned by the owner of the easement but that attaches *personally to the easement owner*.

Economic obsolescence *See* External obsolescence.

Emblements Growing crops, such as grapes and corn, that are produced annually through labor and industry; also called *fructus industriales*.

Eminent domain The right of a government or quasipublic body to acquire property for public use through a court action called *condemnation*.

Encroachment A building or some portion of it—a wall or fence for instance—that extends beyond the land of the owner and illegally intrudes on some land of an adjoining owner or a street or alley.

Encumbrance Any claim by another—such as a mortgage, tax or judgment lien, an easement, encroachment, or a deed restriction on the use of the land—that may diminish the value of a property.

Endorsement An act of signing one's name on the back of a check or note with or without further qualifications.

Equalization The raising or lowering of assessed values for tax purposes in a particular county or taxing district to make them equal to assessments in other counties or districts.

Equitable title The interest held by a vendee under a land contract or an installment contract; the equitable right to obtain absolute ownership to property when legal title is held in another's name.

Equity The interest or value that an owner has in property over and above any mortgage indebtedness and other liens.

Equity of redemption A right of the owner to reclaim property before it is sold through foreclosure by the payment of the debt, interest and costs.

Erosion The gradual wearing away of land by water, wind and general weather conditions; the diminishing of property caused by the elements.

Errors and omissions insurance A form of malpractice insurance for real estate brokers.

Escheat The reversion of property to the state or country, as provided by state law, in cases where a decedent dies intestate without heirs capable of inheriting or when the property is abandoned.

Escrow The closing of a transaction through a third party called an *escrow agent*. Also can refer to earnest money deposits or to mortgagee's trust account for insurance and tax payments.

Estate The degree, quantity, nature and extent of interest that a person has in real property.

Estate at will The occupation of lands and tenements by a tenant for an indefinite period, terminable by one or both parties at will.

Estate for years An interest for a certain, exact period of time in property leased for a specified consideration.

Estate tax Federal tax levied on property transferred upon death.

Estoppel certificate A document in which a borrower certifies the amount he or she owes on a mortgage loan and the rate of interest. Often used incorrectly for *reduction certificate*.

Eviction A legal process to oust a person from possession of real estate.

Evidence of title Proof of ownership of property; commonly a certificate of title, a title insurance policy, an abstract of title with lawyer's opinion, or a Torrens registration certificate.

Exchange A transaction in which all or part of the consideration for the purchase of real property is the transfer of *like kind* property (that is, real estate for real estate).

Exclusive-agency listing A listing contract under which the owner appoints a real estate broker as his or her exclusive agent for a designated period of time to sell the property, on the owner's stated terms, for a commission. The owner reserves the right to sell without paying anyone a commission.

Exclusive right to sell A listing contract under which the owner appoints a real estate broker as his or her exclusive agent for a designated period of time, to sell the property on the owner's stated terms, and agrees to pay the broker a commission when the property is sold, whether by the broker, the owner or another broker.

Executed contract A contract in which all parties have fulfilled their promises and thus performed the contract.

Execution The signing and delivery of an instrument. Also, a legal order directing an official to enforce a judgment against the property of a debtor.

Executor A male person, corporate entity or any other type of organization designated in a will to carry out its provisions.

Executory contract A contract under which something remains to be done by one or more of the parties.

Executrix A woman appointed to perform the duties of an executor.

Express contract An oral or written contract in which the parties state the contract's terms and express their intentions in words.

External obsolescence Reduction in a property's value caused by factors outside the subject property such as social or environmental forces or objectionable neighboring property.

Fee simple estate The maximum possible estate or right of ownership of real property, continuing forever. Sometimes called a *fee* or *fee simple absolute*.

FHA loan A loan insured by the Federal Housing Administration and made by an approved lender in accordance with the FHA's regulations.

Fiduciary relationship A relationship of trust and confidence as between trustee and beneficiary, attorney and client, or principal and agent.

Financing statement *See* Uniform Commercial Code.

Fixture An item of personal property that has been converted to real property by being permanently affixed to the realty.

Foreclosure A procedure whereby property pledged as security for a debt is sold to pay the debt in the event of default in payments or terms.

Franchise An organization that leases a standardized trade name, operating procedures, supplies and referral service to member real estate brokerages.

Fraud Deception that causes a person to give up property or a lawful right.

Freehold estate An estate in land in which ownership is for an indeterminate length of time, in contrast to a leasehold estate.

Front foot A standard measurement, one foot wide, of the width of land, applied at the frontage on its street line. Each front foot extends the depth of the lot.

Functional obsolescence A loss of value to an improvement to real estate due to functional problems, often caused by age or poor design.

Future interest A persons's present right to an interest in real property that will not result in possession or enjoyment until some time in the future.

Gap A defect in the chain of title of a particular parcel of real estate; a missing document or conveyance that raises doubt as to the present ownership of the land.

General agent One authorized to act for his or her principal in a specific range of matters.

General contractor A construction specialist who enters into a formal contract with a landowner or lessee to construct a building or project.

General lien The right of a creditor to have all of a debtor's property—both real and personal—sold to satisfy a debt.

General partnership *See* Partnership.

General tax *See* Ad valorem tax.

Grace period Additional time allowed to perform an act or make a payment before a default occurs.

Graduated lease A lease that provides for a graduated change at stated intervals in the amount of the rent to be paid; used largely in long-term leases.

Grantee A person who receives a conveyance of real property from the grantor.

Granting clause Words in a deed of conveyance that state that grantor's intention to convey the property. This clause is generally worded as ''convey and warrant,'' ''grant,'' ''grant, bargain and sell'' or the like.

Grantor The person transferring title to or an interest in real property to a grantee.

Gross income Total income from property before any expenses are deducted.

Gross lease A lease of property under which a landlord pays all property charges regularly incurred through ownership, such as repairs, taxes and insurance.

Gross rent multiplier A figure used as a multiplier of the gross rental income of a property to produce an estimate of the property's value.

Ground lease A lease of land only, on which the tenant usually owns a building or constructs a building as specified in the lease.

Habendum clause That part of a deed beginning with the words ''to have and to hold'' following the granting clause and defining the extent of ownership the grantor is conveying.

Heir One who might inherit or succeed to an interest in land under the state law of descent when the owner dies without leaving a valid will.

Highest and best use That possible use of land that would produce the greatest net income and thereby develop the highest land value.

Holdover tenancy A tenancy whereby a lessee retains possession of leased property after his or her lease has expired and the landlord, by continuing to accept rent, agrees to the tenant's continued occupancy.

Holographic will A will that is written, dated and signed in the testator's handwriting but is not witnessed.

Homeowner's association A nonprofit group of homeowners in a condominium, cooperative or PUD that administers common elements and enforces covenants, conditions and restrictions.

Homeowner's insurance policy A standardized package insurance policy that covers a residential real estate owner against financial loss from fire, theft, public liability and other commercial risks.

Homestead Land that is owned and occupied as the family home. The right to protect a portion of the value of this land from unsecured judgments for debts.

Hypothecate To give a thing as security without the necessity of giving up possession of it.

Implied contract A contract under which the agreement of the parties is demonstrated by their acts and conduct.

Improvement Any structure erected on a site to enhance the value of the property—buildings, fences, driveways, curbs, sidewalks or sewers.

Imputed interest An IRS concept that treats some concessionary low-interest loans as if they had been paid and collected at a statutory rate.

Income approach The process of estimating the value of an income-producing property by capitalization of the annual net income expected to be produced by the property during its remaining useful life.

Incompetent A person who is unable to manage his or her own affairs by reason of insanity, imbecility or feeble-mindedness.

Independent contractor Someone retained to perform a certain act but is subject to the control and direction of another only as to the end result and not as to the way in which he or she performs the act; contrasted with employee.

Index With an adjustable rate mortgage, a measure of current interest rates, used as a basis for calculating the new rate at time of adjustment.

Infant A person who has not reached 18; a minor.

Informed consent exception A provision in state real estate license law that permits a broker to represent both buyer and seller to a transaction if he or she has their prior mutual consent to do so.

Inheritance tax New York State tax levied on those who inherit property located in the state.

Injunction An order issued by a court to restrain one party from doing an act deemed to be unjust to the rights of some other party.

In rem A proceeding against the realty directly as distinguished from a proceeding against a person.

Installment contact *See* land contract.

Installment sale A method of reporting income received from the sale of real estate when the sale price is paid in two or more installments over two or more years.

Instrument A written legal document, created to effect the rights of the parties.

Interest A charge made by a lender for the use of money.

Interest rate The percentage of a sum of money charged for its use.

Intestate The condition of a property owner who dies without leaving a valid will.

Involuntary alienation *See* Alienation.

Involuntary bankruptcy A bankruptcy proceeding initiated by one or more of the debtor's creditors.

Involuntary lien A lien imposed against property without consent of the owners, *i.e.,* taxes, special assessments.

Irrevocable consent An agreement filed by an out-of-state broker in the state in which he or she wishes to be licensed, stating that suits and actions may be brought against the broker in that state.

Joint tenancy Ownership of real estate between two or more parties who have been named in one conveyance as joint tenants. Upon the death of a joint tenant, his or her interest passes to the surviving joint tenant or tenants.

Joint venture The joining of two or more people to conduct a specific business enterprise.

Judgment The formal decision of a court regarding the respective claims of the parties to an action. After a judgment has been recorded, it usually becomes a general lien on the property of the defendant.

Junior lien An obligation such as a second mortgage that is subordinate in priority to an existing lien on the same realty.

Laches Loss of a legal right through undue delay in asserting it.

Land The earth's surface, extending downward to the center of the earth and upward infinitely into space.

Land contract *See* Contract for deed.

Landlord One who rents property to another.

Law of agency *See* Agent.

Lease A written or oral contract between a landlord (the lessor) and a tenant (the lessee) that transfers the right to exclusive possession and use of the landlord's real property to the lessee for a specified period of time and for a stated consideration (rent).

Leasehold estate A tenant's right to occupy real estate during the term of a lease; generally considered to be personal property.

Legacy A disposition of money or personal property by will.

Legal description A description of a specific parcel of real estate complete enough for an independent surveyor to locate and identify it.

Lessee Tenant.

Lessor Landlord.

Leverage The use of borrowed money to finance the bulk of an investment.

License 1. A privilege or right granted to a person by a state to operate as a real estate broker or salesperson. 2. The revocable permission for a temporary use of land.

Lien A right given by law to certain creditors to have their debt paid out of the property of a defaulting debtor, usually by means of a court sale.

Life estate An interest in real or personal property that is limited in duration to the lifetime of its owner or some other designated person.

Life tenant A person is possession of a life estate.

Like-kind property *See* Exchange.

Limited partnership *See* Partnership.

Liquidity The ability to sell an asset and convert it into cash at a price close to its true value in a short period of time.

Lis pendens A recorded legal document giving constructive notice that an action affecting a particular property has been filed in court.

Listing agreement A contract between a landowner (as principal) and a licensed real estate broker (as agent) by which the broker is employed as agent to sell real estate on the owner's terms within a given time, for which service the landowner agrees to pay a commission or fee.

Listing broker The broker in a multiple-listing situation from whose office a listing agreement is initiated, as opposed to the *selling broker* from whose office negotiations leading up to a sale are initiated.

Litigation The act of carrying on a lawsuit.

Littoral rights 1. A landowner's claim to use water in large navigable lakes and oceans adjacent to his or her property. 2. The ownership rights to land bordering these bodies of water up to the high-water mark.

Locational obsolescence *See* External obsolescence.

Margin With an adjustable rate mortgage, the number of points over an *index* at which the interest rate is set.

Marginal tax rate Percentage at which the last dollar of income is taxed; top tax bracket.

Marketable title Good or clear title reasonably free from the risk of litigation over possible defects.

Market data approach *See* Direct sales comparison approach.

Market price The actual selling price of a property.

Market value The probable price a ready, willing, able and informed buyer would pay and a ready, willing, able and informed seller would accept, neither being under any pressure to act.

Master plan A comprehensive plan to guide the long-term physical development of a particular area.

Mechanic's lien A statutory lien created in favor of contractors, laborers and materialmen who have performed work or furnished materials in the erection or repair of a building.

Meeting of the minds *See* Offer and acceptance.

Metes-and-bounds description A legal description of a parcel of land that begins at a well-marked point and follows the boundaries, using direction and distances around the tract back to the place of beginning.

Mill One-tenth of one cent. A tax rate of 52 mills would be $.052 tax for each dollar of assessed valuation of a property.

Minor A person under 18 years of age.

MIP Mortgage insurance premium.

Month-to-month tenancy A periodic tenancy; that is, the tenant rents for one period at a time. In the absence of a rental agreement (oral or written), a tenancy is generally considered to be month to month.

Monument A fixed natural or artificial object used to establish real estate boundaries for a metes-and-bounds description.

Mortgage A conditional transfer or pledge of real estate as security for the payment of a debt. Also, the document creating a mortgage lien.

Mortgagee A lender in a mortgage loan transaction.

Mortgage lien A lien or charge on the property of a mortgagor that secures the underlying debt obligations.

Mortgage reduction certificate An instrument executed by the mortgagee, setting forth the present status and the balance due on the mortgage as of the date of the execution of the instrument.

Mortgagor A borrower who conveys his or her property as security for a loan.

Multiple listing An exclusive listing with the additional authority and obligation on the part of the listing broker to distribute the listing to other brokers in the multiple-listing organization.

Negative amortization Gradual building up of a large mortgage debt when payments are not sufficient to cover interest due and reduce the principal.

Negligence An unintentional tort caused by failure to exercise reasonable care.

Negotiable instrument A signed promise to pay a sum of money.

Net lease A lease requiring the tenant to pay not only rent but also some or all costs of maintaining the property, including taxes, insurance, utilities and repairs.

Net listing A listing based on the net price the seller will receive if the property is sold. Under a net listing the broker is free to offer the property for sale at the highest price he or she can get in order to increase the commission. This type of listing is outlawed in New York.

Nonconforming use A use of property that is permitted to continue after a zoning ordinance prohibiting it has been established for the area.

Nonhomogeneity A lack of uniformity; dissimilarity. Because no two parcels of land are exactly alike, real estate is said to be nonhomogeneous.

Notary public A public officer who is authorized to take acknowledgments to certain classes of documents such as deeds, contracts and mortgages, and before whom affidavits may be sworn.

Note An instrument of credit given to attest a debt.

Nuisance An act that disturbs another's peaceful enjoyment of property.

NYSAR New York State Association of REALTORS®.

Obsolescence *See* External, Locational and Functional obsolescence.

Offer and acceptance Two essential components of a valid contract; a "meeting of the minds," when all parties agree to the exact terms.

Open-end mortgage A mortgage loan that is expandable to a maximum dollar amount, the loan being secured by the same original mortgage.

Open listing A listing contract under which the broker's commission is contingent upon the broker's producing a ready, willing and able buyer before the property is sold by the owner or another broker.

Option An agreement to keep open for a set period an offer to sell or purchase property.

Package mortgage A method of financing in which the loan that finances the purchase of a home also finances the purchase of certain items of personal property such as a refrigerator, stove and other specified appliances.

Parcel A specific piece of real estate.

Participation financing A mortgage in which the lender participates in the income of the mortgaged venture.

Partition The division that is made of real property between those who own it in undivided shares.

Partnership An association of two or more individuals who carry on a continuing business for profit as co-owners. A *general partnership* is a typical form of joint venture, in which each general partner shares in the administration, profits and losses of the operations. A *limited partnership* is administered by one or more general partners and funded by limited or silent partners who are by law responsible for losses only to the extent of their investments.

Party wall A wall that is located on or at a boundary line between two adjoining parcels of land and is used by the owners of both properties.

Percentage lease A lease commonly used for commercial property whose rental is based on the tenant's gross sales at the premises.

Periodic estate An interest in leased property that continues from period to period—week to week, month to month or year to year.

Personal property Items, called *chattels,* that do not fit into the definition of real property; movable objects.

Personal representative The administrator or executor appointed to handle the estate of a decedent.

Physical deterioration Loss of value due to wear and tear or action of the elements.

PITI Principal, interest, taxes and insurance: components of a regular mortgage payment.

Planned unit development A planned combination of diverse land uses such as housing, recreation and shopping, in one contained development or subdivision.

Planning board Municipal body overseeing orderly development of real estate.

Plat A map of a town, section or subdivision indicating the location and boundaries of individual properties.

PMI Private mortgage insurance.

Point A unit of measurement used for various loan charges; one point equals 1 percent of the amount of the loan. *See also* Discount points.

Point of beginning In a metes-and-bounds legal description, the starting point of the survey, situated in one corner of the parcel. Also called place of beginning.

Police power The government's right to impose laws, statutes and ordinances, including zoning ordinances and building codes, to protect the public health, safety and welfare.

Policy and procedures manual A broker's compilation of guidelines for the conduct of the firm's business.

Power of attorney A written instrument authorizing a person, the *attorney-in-fact,* to act as agent on behalf of another person.

Precedent A court decision that serves as authority for later cases.

Premises Lands and tenements; an estate; the subject matter of a conveyance.

Prepayment clause A clause in a mortgage that gives the mortgagor the privilege of paying the mortgage indebtedness before it becomes due.

Prepayment penalty A charge imposed on a borrower who pays off the loan principal early.

Price-fixing *See* Antitrust laws.

Principal 1. A sum lent or employed as a fund or investment as distinguished from its income or profits. 2. The original amount (as in a loan) of the total due and payable at a certain date. 3. A main party of a transaction—the person for whom the agent works.

Principal broker *See* Supervising broker.

Priority The order of position or time.

Private mortgage insurance Insurance that limits a lender's potential loss in a mortgage default, issued by a private company rather than by the FHA.

Probate To establish the will of a deceased person.

Property manager Someone who manages real estate for another person for compensation.

Proprietary lease A written lease in a cooperative apartment building, held by the tenant/shareholder, giving the right to occupy a particular unit.

Prorations Expenses, either prepaid or paid in arrears, that are divided or distributed between buyer and seller at the closing.

Prospectus A printed statement disclosing all material aspects of a real estate project.

PUD Planned unit development.

Puffing Exaggerated or superlative comments or opinions not made as representations of fact and thus not grounds for misrepresentation.

Pur autre vie For the life of another. A life estate pur autre vie is a life estate that is measured by the life of a person other than the grantee.

Purchase-money mortgage A note secured by a mortgage given by a buyer, as mortgagor, to a seller, as mortgagee. Also any mortgage for purchase rather than refinancing.

Quiet enjoyment The right of an owner or a person legally in possession to the use of property without interference of possession.

Quiet title suit *See* Suit to quiet title.

Quitclaim deed A conveyance by which the grantor transfers whatever interest he or she has in the real estate, if any, without warranties or obligations.

Ready, willing and able buyer One who is prepared to buy property on the seller's terms and is ready to take positive steps to consummate the transaction.

Real estate A portion of the earth's surface extending downward to the center of the earth and upward infinitely into space including all things permanently attached thereto, whether by nature or by a person.

Real estate broker Any person, partnership, association, or corporation who sells (or offers to sell), buys (or offers to buy) or negotiates the purchase, sale or exchange of real estate, or who leases (or offers to lease) or rents (or offers to rent) any real estate or the improvements thereon for others and for a compensation or valuable consideration.

Real estate investment trust (REIT) Trust ownership of real estate by a group of at least 100 individuals who purchase certificates of ownership in the trust.

Real property Real estate plus all the interests, benefits and rights inherent in ownership. Often referred to as *real estate*.

REALTOR® A registered trademark term reserved for the sole use of active members of local REALTOR® boards affiliated with the National Association of REALTORS®.

Reconciliation The final step in the appraisal process, in which the appraiser reconciles the estimates of value received from the direct sales comparison data, cost and income approaches to arrive at a final estimate of value for the subject property.

Recording The act of entering or recording documents affecting or conveying interests in real estate in the recorder's office established in each county.

Rectangular survey system A system established in 1785 by the federal government providing for surveying and describing land by reference to principal meridians and base lines, outside the 13 original colonies.

Redemption period A period of time established by state law during which a property owner has the right to redeem his or her real estate from a tax sale by paying the sales price, interest and costs.

Red herring Preliminary offering plan for a cooperative or condominium project submitted to the attorney general and to tenants and subject to modification.

Redlining The illegal practice of a lending institution denying loans or restricting their number for certain areas of a community.

Regulation Z Law requiring credit institutions and advertisers to inform borrowers of the true cost of obtaining credit; commonly called the *Truth-in-Lending Act*.

Release The act or writing by which some claim or interest is surrendered to another.

Remainder The remnant of an estate that has been conveyed to take effect and be enjoyed after the termination of a prior estate, as when an owner conveys a life estate to one party and the remainder to another.

Remainderman The person who is to receive the property after the death of a life tenant.

Rent A fixed, periodic payment made by a tenant of a property to the owner for possession and use, usually by prior agreement of the parties.

Replacement cost The construction cost at current prices of a property that is not necessarily an exact duplicate of the subject property but serves the same purpose or function as the original.

Reproduction cost The construction cost at current prices of an exact duplicate of the subject property.

Reserves Money set aside to accumulate for future expenses.

Restriction A limitation on the use of real property, generally originated by the owner or subdivider in a deed.

Return The income from a real estate investment, calculated as a percentage of cash invested.

Reverse discrimination *(Benign discrimination)* Housing discrimination, usually based on quotas, designed by a municipality to achieve a racial balance perceived as desirable.

Reversion The remnant of an estate that the grantor holds after he or she has granted a life estate to another person, if the estate will return, or revert, to the grantor; also called a *reverter*.

Reversionary right An owner's right to regain possession of leased property upon termination of the lease agreement.

Revocation An act of recalling a power of authority conferred, as the revocation of a power of attorney, a license or an agency.

Right of survivorship *See* Joint tenancy.

Right-of-way The right to pass over another's land more or less frequently according to the nature of the easement.

Riparian rights An owner's rights in land that borders on or includes a stream, river, lake or sea. These rights include access to and use of the water.

Sale and leaseback A transaction in which an owner sells his or her improved property and, as part of the same transaction, signs a long-term lease to remain in possession of the premises.

Sales contract A contract containing the complete terms of the agreement between buyer and seller for the sale of a particular parcel of real estate.

Salesperson A person who performs real estate activities while employed by or associated with a licensed real estate broker.

Satisfaction piece A document acknowledging the payment of a debt.

S corporation A form of corporation, taxed as a partnership.

Secondary mortgage market A market for the purchase and sale of existing mortgages, designed to provide greater liquidity of mortgages.

Section A portion of a township under the rectangular survey (government survey) system. A section is a square with mile-long sides and an area of one square mile, or 640 acres.

Seisin The possession of land by one who claims to own at least an estate for life therein.

Selling broker *See* Listing broker.

Servient tenement Land on which an easement exists in favor of an adjacent property (called a dominant estate); also called *servient estate*.

Setback The amount of space local zoning regulations require between a lot line and a building line.

Severalty Ownership of real property by one person only; also called *sole ownership*.

Shared appreciation mortgage A mortgage loan in which the lender, in exchange for a loan with a favorable interest rate, participates in the profits (if any) the mortgagor receives when the property is eventually sold.

Situs The location of a property.

Small claims court A special local court for settling disputes without the need for attorneys or expensive court costs.

Special agent One authorized by a principal to perform a single act or transaction.

Special assessment A tax or levy customarily imposed against only those specific parcels of real estate that will benefit from a proposed public improvement like a street or sewer.

Specific lien A lien affecting or attaching only to a certain, specific parcel of land or piece of property.

Specific performance suit A legal action brought in a court of equity in special cases to compel a party to carry out the terms of a contract.

Sponsor The developer or owner organizing and offering for sale a condominium or cooperative development.

Statute of frauds The part of state law requiring certain instruments such as deeds, real estate sales contracts, and certain leases to be in writing in order for them to be legally enforceable.

Statute of limitations That law pertaining to the period of time within which certain actions must be brought to court—in New York, six years for contracts.

Statutory lien A lien imposed on property by statute—a tax lien, for example—in contrast to a voluntary lien such as a mortgage lien that an owner places on his or her own real estate.

Steering The illegal practice of channeling home seekers to particular areas for discriminatory ends.

Straight-line method A method of calculating cost recovery for tax purposes, computed by dividing the adjusted basis of a property by the number of years chosen.

Subagent A broker's sales associate, or cooperating broker in a multiple-listing system, in relationship to the principal who has designated the broker as an agent.

Subchapter S corporation *See* S corporation.

Subcontractor *See* General contractor.

Subdivision A tract of land divided by the owner, known as the *subdivider,* into blocks, building lots, and streets according to a recorded subdivision plat that must comply with local ordinances and regulations.

Subject property The property being appraised.

Subletting The leasing of premises by a tenant to a third party for part of the tenant's remaining term. *See also* Assignment.

Subordination Relegation to a lesser position, usually in respect to a right or security.

Subrogation The substitution of one creditor for another with the substituted person succeeding to the legal rights and claims of the original claimant.

Subscribing witness One who writes his or her name as witness to the execution of an instrument.

Substitution An appraisal principle stating that the maximum value of a property tends to be set by the cost of purchasing an equally desirable and valuable substitute property.

Subsurface rights Ownership rights in a parcel of real estate of any water, minerals, gas, oil and so forth that lie beneath the surface of the property.

Suit to quiet title A court action intended to establish or settle the title to a particular property, especially when there is a cloud on the title.

Supervising broker The one broker registered with the Department of State as in charge of a real estate office, responsible for the actions of salespersons and associate brokers.

Surface rights Ownership rights in a parcel of real estate that are limited to the surface of the property and do not include the air above it (air rights) or the minerals below the surface (subsurface rights).

Surrender The cancellation of a lease by mutual consent of the lessor and the lessee.

Surrogate's court (probate court) A court having jurisdiction over the proof of wills, the settling of estates and adoptions.

Survey The process by which a parcel of land is measured and its area ascertained; also, the map showing the measurements, boundaries and area.

Syndicate A combination of people or firms formed to accomplish a joint venture of mutual interest.

Tacking Adding or combining successive periods of continuous occupation of real property by several different adverse possessors.

Taxation The process by which a government or municipal quasipublic body raises monies to fund its operation.

Tax deed An instrument, similar to a certificate of sale, given to a purchaser at a tax sale.

Tax lien A charge against property created by operation of law. Tax liens and assessments take priority over all other liens.

Tax rate The rate at which real property is taxed in a tax district or county. For example, real property may be taxed at a rate of .056 cents per dollar of assessed valuation (56 mills).

Tax sale A court-ordered sale of real property to raise money to cover delinquent taxes.

Tax shelter An investment yielding paper losses that may be used to shield other income from taxation. In real estate, often the result of *depreciation.*

Tenancy at will An estate that gives the lessee the right to possession until the estate is terminated by either party; the term of this estate is indefinite.

Tenancy by the entirety The joint ownership property acquired by husband and wife during marriage. Upon the death of one spouse, the survivor becomes the owner of the property.

Tenancy in common A form of co-ownership by which each owner holds an undivided interest in real property as if he or she were sole owner. Each individual owner has the right to partition. Tenants in common have no right of survivorship.

Tenant One who holds or possesses lands or tenements by any kind of right or title.

Tenant at sufferance One who comes into possession of lands by lawful title and keeps it afterward without any title at all.

Testate Having made and left a valid will.

Testers Members of civil rights and neighborhood organizations, often volunteers, who observe real estate offices to assess compliance with fair housing laws.

Time is of the essence A phrase in a contract that requires the performance of a certain act within a stated period of time.

Time-sharing Undivided ownership of real estate for only a portion of the year.

Title Evidence that the owner of land is in lawful possession thereof; evidence of ownership.

Title insurance A policy insuring the owner or mortgagee against loss by reason of defects in the title to a parcel of real estate, other than the encumbrances, defects and matters specifically excluded by the policy.

Title search An examination of the public records to determine the ownership and encumbrances affecting real property.

Torrens system A method of evidencing title by registration with the proper public authority, generally called the registrar.

Tort A civil wrong done by one person against another.

Town house A hybrid form of real estate ownership in which the owner has fee simple title to the living unit and land below it, plus a fractional interest in common elements.

Township The principal unit of the rectangular survey (government survey) system, a square with six-mile sides and an area of 36 square miles.

Trade fixtures Articles installed by a tenant under the terms of a lease and removable by the tenant before the lease expires.

Transfer tax Tax stamps required to be affixed to a deed by state and/or local law.

Trespass An unlawful intrusion upon another's property.

Trust A fiduciary arrangement whereby property is conveyed to a person or institution, called a *trustee,* to be held and administered on behalf of another person, called a *beneficiary.*

Trust account Escrow account for money belonging to another.

Trust deed An instrument used to create a mortgage lien by which the mortgagor conveys his or her title to a trustee, who holds it as security for the benefit of the note holder (the lender); also called a *deed of trust.*

Trustee *See* Trust.

Umbrella policy An insurance policy that covers additional risk beyond several underlying policies.

Undivided interest *See* Tenancy in common.

Unenforceable contract A contract that seems on the surface to be valid, yet neither party can sue the other to force performance of it.

Uniform Commercial Code A codification of commercial law, adopted in most states, that attempts to make uniform all laws relating to commercial transactions, including chattel mortgages and bulk transfers.

Unity of ownership The four unities traditionally needed to create a joint tenancy—unity of title, time, interest and possession.

Universal agent One empowered by a principal to represent him or her in all matters that can be delegated.

Useful life In real estate investment, the number of years a property will be useful to the investors.

Usury Charging interest at a rate higher than the maximum established by law.

Valid contract A contract that complies with all the essentials of a contract and is binding and enforceable on all parties to it.

VA loan A mortgage loan on approved property made to a qualified veteran by an authorized lender and guaranteed by the Veterans Administration in order to limit the lender's possible loss.

Valuation Estimated worth or price. The act of valuing by appraisal.

Value The power of a good or service to command other goods in exchange for the present worth of future rights to its income or amenities.

Variance Permission obtained from zoning authorities to build a structure or conduct a use that is expressly prohibited by the current zoning laws; an exception from the zoning ordinances.

Vendee A buyer under a land contract or contract of sale.

Vendor A seller under a land contract or contract of sale.

Voidable contract A contract that seems to be valid on the surface but may be rejected or disaffirmed by one of the parties.

Void contract A contract that has no legal force or effect because it does not meet the essential elements of a contract.

Voluntary transfer *See* Alienation.

Waiver The renunciation, abandonment or surrender of some claim, right or privilege.

Warranty deed A deed in which the grantor fully warrants good clear title to the premises.

Waste An improper use or an abuse of a property by a possessor who holds less than fee ownership, such as a tenant, life tenant, mortgagor or vendee.

Will A written document, properly witnessed, providing for the transfer of title to property owned by the deceased, called the *testator*.

Without recourse Words used in endorsing a note or bill to denote that the future holder is not to look to the endorser in case of nonpayment.

Wraparound mortgage An additional mortgage in which another lender refinances a borrower by lending an amount including the existing first mortgage amount without disturbing the existence of the first mortgage.

Year-to-year tenancy A periodic tenancy in which rent is collected from year to year.

Zone An area set off by the proper authorities for specific use subject to certain restrictions or restraints.

Zoning ordinance An exercise of police power by a municipality to regulate and control the character and use of property.

Answer Key

Chapter 1:
What Is Real Estate?
1. b
2. d
3. b
4. b
5. c
6. c
7. a
8. c
9. c
10. c
11. c
12. a
13. b
14. c
15. c
16. b
17. d
18. b
19. a
20. d

Chapter 2:
Law of Agency
1. a
2. a
3. b
4. b
5. b
6. c
7. c
8. c
9. c
10. d
11. d
12. c
13. b
14. c

15. c
16. d
17. c
18. a
19. a
20. d

Chapter 3:
Real Estate Instruments:
Estates and Interests
1. b
2. a
3. a
4. b
5. d
6. d
7. a
8. d
9. d
10. a
11. c
12. c
13. b
14. b
15. b
16. d
17. b
18. c
19. c
20. b
21. a
22. a
23. a
24. b
25. c

Chapter 4:
Real Estate Instruments:
Deeds and Mortgages
1. c
2. d
3. d
4. b
5. a
6. c
7. b

8. b
9. c
10. b
11. b
12. b
13. d
14. a
15. c
16. b
17. b
18. b
19. a
20. d
21. a
22. b
23. c
24. a
25. c

Chapter 5:
Law of Contracts
1. c
2. b
3. d
4. d
5. b
6. b
7. b
8. d
9. a
10. d
11. d
12. c
13. a
14. d
15. d
16. b
17. b
18. b
19. a
20. d
21. c
22. b
23. d
24. d
25. c

Chapter 6:
Land-Use Regulations

1. c
2. c
3. c
4. b
5. d
6. d
7. c
8. b
9. d
10. d
11. c
12. a
13. b
14. c
15. a
16. c
17. b
18. d
19. c
20. a

Chapter 7:
Real Estate Financing

1. b
2. b
3. c
4. b
5. b
6. b
7. a
8. b
9. d
10. a
11. b
12. b
13. c
14. d
15. d
16. c
17. b
18. b
19. d
20. b
21. b
22. a
23. c
24. b
25. a

Chapter 8:
License Law and Ethics

1. d
2. c
3. b
4. c
5. b
6. d
7. c
8. b
9. d
10. b
11. d
12. b
13. d
14. d
15. d
16. a
17. b
18. a
19. c
20. c
21. c
22. b
23. c
24. a
25. c

Chapter 9:
Valuation and Listing Procedures

1. a
2. a
3. a
4. b
5. d
6. c
7. a
8. c
9. d
10. a
11. b
12. d
13. d
14. d
15. d
16. a
17. b
18. c
19. d
20. d
21. c
22. d

23. b
24. c
25. d

Chapter 10:
Human Rights and Fair Housing

1. c
2. c
3. d
4. b
5. c
6. b
7. c
8. c
9. a
10. a
11. b
12. a
13. c
14. d
15. d
16. b
17. d
18. d
19. a
20. c

Chapter 11:
Closing and Closing Costs

1. a
2. a
3. b
4. d
5. a
6. d
7. d
8. c
9. c
10. d
11. c
12. c
13. c
14. d
15. d
16. b
17. b
18. c
19. c
20. b
21. b
22. d
23. a
24. c
25. a

Chapter 12:
Real Estate Mathematics:

1. 1,200 square yards $\times$ 9 = 10,800 square feet
area = length $\times$ width
10,800 = length $\times$ 60

1. b. 180 feet   10,800 $\div$ 60 = 180 feet

2. $25,000 $\times$ 3% = $25,000 $\times$ .03 = $750
$68,000 – $25,000 = $43,000 remaining purchase price
$43,000 $\times$ 5% = $43,000 $\times$ .05 = $2,150

2. d. $2,900 $750 + $2,150 = $2,900 total down payment

3. 120 feet $\div$ 6 feet per section = 20 sections
One fence post must be added to anchor the other end

3. c. 21   20 + 1 = 21 fence posts

4. $98,000 $\times$ 80% =$98,000 $\times$ .80 = $78,400 insured value
$78,400 $\div$ 100 = 784 hundreds

4. a. $470.40   784 $\times$ $.60 per hundred = $470.40

5. $74,000 + $1,200 = $75,200 sale price less commission
$75,200 = 94% of sale price

5. a. $80,000 $75,200 $\div$ .94 = $80,000 sale price

6. $37,000 $\div$ 12 = $3,083.33 monthly income

6. b. $770.83 $3,083.33 $\times$ .25 = $770.83 permissible mortgage payment

7. $54,000 $\times$ .06 = $3,240 total commission

7. d. $1,620 $3,240 $\times$ .50 = $1,620 Sally's share

8. $1,800 $\div$ 12 = $150 monthly property taxes
$365 $\div$ 12 = $30.42 monthly insurance premium

8. a. $808.54 $150 + $30.42 + $628.12 = $808.54 total monthly payment

9. c. $36,000   9. 120 front feet $\times$ $300 = $36,000 sale price.

10. 43,560 feet per acre $\times$ 5 = 217,800 square feet

10. b. 726 feet   217,800 $\div$ 300 = 726 feet depth

11. $79,500 sale price $\times$ 6½% commission =
$79,500 $\times$ .065 = $5,167.50 Happy Valley's commission
$5,167.50 $\times$ 30% or $5,167.50 $\times$ .30 = $1,550.25 listing salesperson's

11. b. $1,550.25   commission

12.

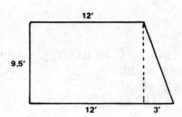

12. c. $277.16

12′ × 9.5′ = 114 square feet, area of rectangle
½ (3′ × 9.5′) = ½ (28.5) = 14.25 square feet, area of triangle
114 + 14.25 = 128.25 square feet
To convert square feet to square yards divide by 9:
128.25 ÷ 9 = 14.25 square yards
$16.95 carpet + $2.50 installation = $19.45 cost per square yard
$19.45 × 14.25 square yards = $277.1625 rounded to $277.16

13. $30,000 Peters + $35,000 Gamble + $35,000 Clooney = $100,000
$125,000 − $100,000 = $25,000 Considine's contribution

$$\frac{part}{whole} = percent$$

13. a. 20%

$25,000 ÷ $125,000 = .20, or 20%

14. 391.42 × 12 = $4,697.04, annual interest

$$\frac{part}{percent} = whole$$

14. b. $40,843.83

$4,697.04 ÷ 11½% or $4,697.04 ÷ .115 = $40,843.826

15. $98,500 × 5% = $98,500 × .05 = $4,925, annual increase in value

15. a. $103,425

$98,500 + $4,925 = $103,425, current market value

16. $95,000 × 60% or $95,000 × .60 = $57,000, assessed value
divided by 100 because tax rate is stated per hundred dollars
$57,000 ÷ 100 = 570
570 × $2.85 = $1,624.50, annual taxes
divide by 12 to get monthly taxes

16. d. $135.38

$1,624.50 ÷ 12 = $135.375

17. 22′ × 15′ = 330 square feet, area of rectangle
½ (4′ × 15′) = ½ (60) = 30 square feet, area of each triangle
30 × 2 = 60 square feet, area of two triangles
330 + 60 = 390 square feet, surface area to be paved
6″ deep = ½ foot

17. d. 195 cubic feet

390 × ½ = 195 cubic feet, cement needed for patio

18. $3,675 − $500 salary = $3,175 commission on sales

18. b. $127,000

$3,175 ÷ 2.5% = $3,175 ÷ .025 = $127,000, value of property sold

19. two sides of 95′ plus one side of 42′6″
    95′ × 2 = 190 feet
    42′6″ = 42.5 feet
    190 + 42.5 = 232.5 linear feet
19. c. $1,615.88   232.5 × $6.95 = $1,615.875

20. $4,500 × 12 = $54,000 annual rental
20. a. $675,000 $54,000 ÷ 8% or $54,000 ÷ .08 = $675,000, original cost of property

21. 100 acres × 43,560 square feet per acre = 4,356,000 total square feet.
    4,356,000 × ⅞ available for lots = 3,811,500 square feet
21. c. 27,225 square feet   3,811,500 ÷ 140 lots = 27,225 square feet per lot

22. $975 ÷ 12 months = $81.25/month's property tax
    $81.25 ÷ 30 days = $2.708 day's property tax
    $81.25 × 2 months = $162.50
    $2.708 × 4 days = $10.832
22. a. $173.33 $162.50 + $10.832 = $173.332 rounded to $173.33, prepaid unused tax

23. $61,550 × 13% = $61,550 × .13 = $8,001.50 annual interest
    $8,001.50 ÷ 12 months = $666.792/month's interest
    $666.792 ÷ 30 days = $22.226/day's interest
    $22.226 × 22 days = $488.972 rounded to $488.97 unpaid back
23. b. $488.97   interest

24. $14,100 commission ÷ 6% commission rate =
24. a. $235,000 $14,100 ÷ .06 = $235,000 sales price

25. 30 years × 12 months = 360 payments
    360 payments × $952.34 = $342,842.40 total payments for principal and interest
    $342,842.40 total payments − $100,000 principal repayment
25. b. $242,842.40   = $242,842.40 total interest paid

26. Two points on a $90,000 loan = $90,000 × .02 or 2 percent = $1,800 paid in points
    $817.85 − $786.35 = $31.50 saved each month with lower payment
    $1,800 ÷ $31.50 = 57.14 months to recoup the payment of points
26. c. 4 years, 9 months   57.14 months = 4 years, 9 months

27. $80,000 × 2 percent or .02 = $2,400 payment for points
    $100,000 − $95,000 = $5,000 received with the higher offer
    $5,000 − $2,400 payment for points = $2,600 realized with the higher
27. a. $2,600   offer after payment of points

Salesperson's Practice License Exam

1. a
2. c
3. c
4. b
5. b
6. c
7. b
8. a
9. b
10. b
11. d
12. b
13. b
14. a
15. b
16. a
17. c
18. b
19. d
20. a
21. d
22. c
23. b
24. b
25. b
26. c
27. c
28. b
29. c
30. a
31. c
32. c
33. a
34. c
35. b
36. c
37. a
38. b
39. b
40. d
41. b
42. b
43. c
44. b
45. a
46. b
47. c
48. c
49. d
50. a

Chapter 13:
Opening a Broker's Office

1. a
2. b
3. d
4. a
5. b
6. a
7. d
8. c
9. c
10. d
11. b
12. c
13. d
14. b
15. b

Chapter 14:
Operation of a Broker's Office

1. b
2. b
3. a
4. c
5. d
6. d
7. d
8. c
9. d
10. b
11. d
12. d
13. b
14. d
15. d
16. c
17. b
18. b
19. b
20. c

Chapter 15:
Advertising

1. b
2. a
3. b
4. b
5. d
6. a
7. c
8. c
9. b
10. d

Chapter 16:
Appraisal

1. c
2. d
3. a
4. d
5. d
6. d
7. b
8. b
9. d
10. a
11. d
12. b
13. a
14. d
15. c
16. c
17. b
18. d
19. a
20. c
21. d
22. d
23. c
24. c
25. a

Chapter 17:
Real Estate Investment

1. c
2. b
3. b
4. b
5. a
6. d
7. b
8. b
9. c
10. c
11. a
12. c
13. c
14. d
15. c
16. d
17. a
18. c
19. a
20. b
21. c
22. d

23. b
24. d
25. b

Chapter 18:
Subdivision and Development
1. d
2. b
3. a
4. d
5. c
6. d
7. c
8. d
9. b
10. b
11. b
12. a
13. b
14. a
15. c
16. c
17. c

Chapter 19:
Construction
1. d
2. d
3. a
4. b
5. c
6. d
7. a
8. b
9. a
10. d
11. a
12. a
13. b
14. b
15. c
16. a
17. c
18. a
19. b
20. c
21. b
22. c
23. b
24. b
25. d

Chapter 20:
Condominiums and Cooperatives
1. a
2. d
3. b
4. d
5. b
6. d
7. d
8. c
9. c
10. b
11. a
12. d
13. b
14. d
15. b

Chapter 21:
Property Management—Rent Regulations
1. d
2. d
3. b
4. d
5. d
6. c
7. a
8. d
9. c
10. b
11. c
12. c
13. c
14. d
15. d
16. b
17. a
18. c
19. d
20. c

Chapter 22:
Leases and Agreements
1. d
2. c
3. b
4. a
5. c
6. d
7. d
8. c
9. c

10. d
11. b
12. a
13. d
14. d
15. c
16. b
17. a
18. d
19. c
20. c

Chapter 23:
Voluntary and Involuntary Alienation
1. c
2. d
3. b
4. d
5. b
6. a
7. c
8. c
9. a
10. d

Chapter 24:
Liens and Easements
1. b
2. b
3. b
4. d
5. c
6. b
7. a
8. c
9. d
10. a
11. c
12. d
13. d
14. c
15. a
16. b
17. d
18. c
19. d
20. b
21. d
22. d
23. b
24. a
25. d

Chapter 25:
Taxes and Assessments
1. d
2. c
3. b
4. b
5. c
6. a
7. c
8. b
9. a
10. a

Chapter 26:
General Business Law
1. d
2. a
3. c
4. b
5. c
6. d
7. a
8. c
9. c
10. d
11. a
12. a
13. c
14. b
15. b
16. a
17. a
18. b
19. a
20. a

Broker's Practice Examination
1. a
2. b
3. d
4. c
5. a
6. b
7. b
8. c

9. c
10. c
11. b
12. c
13. b
14. c
15. d
16. c
17. b
18. d
19. c
20. d
21. b
22. a
23. a
24. b
25. c
26. c
27. d
28. a
29. c
30. b
31. a
32. a
33. a
34. b
35. b
36. d
37. d
38. c
39. c
40. b
41. b
42. a
43. b
44. c
45. c
46. a
47. b
48. b
49. c
50. b
51. a
52. b
53. d
54. d

55. c
56. d
57. a
58. c
59. a
60. b
61. c
62. d
63. b
64. b
65. c
66. b
67. b
68. a
69. c
70. b
71. a
72. c
73. a
74. c
75. d
76. c
77. c
78. b
79. a
80. a
81. c
82. c
83. a
84. d
85. b
86. d
87. b
88. c
89. a
90. d
91. a
92. d
93. c
94. b
95. a
96. d
97. d
98. b
99. b
100. a

Index

More Real Estate Books That Help You Get Ahead...

Mail the completed form to Real Estate Education Company 520 North Dearborn Street Chicago, Illinois 60610-4975

30-Day Money-Back Guarantee
Please send me the book(s) I have indicated. If I return any book within the 30 day period, I'll receive a refund with no further obligation.
(Books must be returned in unused, salable condition).

Payment must accompany all orders (check one)
☐ Check or money order payable to Longman
☐ Credit card charge, circle one: VISA MasterCard AMEX

Name_____

Address _____

City_____ State_____ Zip_____

Telephone No. (   )_____

Account No._____ Exp. Date_____

Signature _____
(All charge orders must be signed.)

Qty.	Order Number	Real Estate Principles/Exam Guides	Price	Total Amount
_____	1. 1510-01	Modern Real Estate Practice, 11th ed.	$32.95	_____
_____	2. 1510-	Supplements for Modern Real Estate Practice are available for many states. Indicate desired state_____	$12.95	_____
_____	3. 1510-02	Modern Real Estate Practice Study Guide, 11th ed.	$13.95	_____
_____	4. 1513-01	Real Estate Fundamentals, 3rd ed.	$22.95	_____
_____	5. 1970-04	Questions & Answers to Help You Pass the Real Estate Exam, 3rd ed.	$21.95	_____
_____	6. 1970-02	Guide to Passing the Real Estate Exam (ACT), 3rd ed.	$21.95	_____
_____	7. 1970-01	The Real Estate Education Company Real Estate Exam Manual, 5th ed. (ETS)	$21.95	_____
_____	8. 1970-06	Real Estate Exam Guide (ASI), 2nd ed.	$21.95	_____
_____	9. 1970-03	How to Prepare for the Texas Real Estate Exam, 4th ed.	$19.95	_____
_____	10. 1970-07	California Real Estate Exam Guide	$19.95	_____

Qty.	Order Number	Advanced Studies/Continuing Education	Price	Total Amount
_____	11. 1556-10	Fundamentals of Real Estate Appraisal, 5th ed.	$38.95	_____
_____	12. 1557-10	Essentials of Real Estate Finance, 5th ed.	$38.95	_____
_____	13. 1559-01	Essentials of Real Estate Investment, 3rd ed.	$38.95	_____
_____	14. 1551-10	Property Management, 3rd ed.	$34.95	_____
_____	15. 1965-01	Real Estate Brokerage: A Success Guide, 2nd ed.	$35.95	_____
_____	16. 1560-01	Real Estate Law, 2nd ed.	$38.95	_____
_____	17. 1512-10	Mastering Real Estate Mathematics, 5th ed.	$25.95	_____
_____	18. 1961-01	The Language of Real Estate, 3rd ed.	$28.95	_____
_____	19. 1560-08	Agency Relationships in Real Estate	$25.95	_____

Qty.	Order Number	Professional Books	Price	Total Amount
_____	20. 1913-01	List for Success	$18.95	_____
_____	21. 1913-04	Close for Success	$18.95	_____
_____	22. 1907-04	Power Real Estate Negotiation	$19.95	_____
_____	23. 1927-03	Fast Start in Real Estate: A Survival Guide for New Agents	$17.95	_____
_____	24. 1926-01	Classified Secrets, 2nd ed.	$29.95	_____
_____	25. 1907-01	Power Real Estate Listing, 2nd ed.	$17.95	_____
_____	26. 1907-02	Power Real Estate Selling, 2nd ed.	$17.95	_____
_____	27. 5606-24	The Mortgage Kit	$14.95	_____
_____	28. 4105-07	How to Profit from Real Estate	$19.95	_____
_____	29. 4105-06	How to Sell Apartment Buildings	$19.95	_____
_____	30. 4105-08	Landlord's Handbook	$21.95	_____
_____	31. 1905-29	A Professional's Guide to Real Estate Finance	$34.95	_____
_____	32. 1909-01	New Home Sales	$24.95	_____
_____	33. 1909-03	New Home Marketing	$34.95	_____
_____	34. 1922-02	Successful Leasing and Selling of Office Property, 3rd ed.	$34.95	_____
_____	35. 1922-03	Successful Industrial Real Estate Brokerage, 4th ed.	$34.95	_____
_____	36. 1978-02	The Recruiting Revolution in Real Estate	$34.95	_____
_____	37. 1922-01	Successful Leasing and Selling of Retail Property, 3rd ed.	$34.95	_____

For Fastest Service, Call Our Toll-Free Order Hotline
1-800-621-9621 x650
(in Illinois, 1-800-654-8596 x650)

Total Book Purchase (inc. tax, if applicable)	Shipping and Handling
$ 00.00-$ 24.99	$ 4.00
$ 25.00-$ 49.99	$ 5.00
$ 50.00-$ 99.99	$ 6.00
$100.00-$249.99	$ 8.00

PRICES SUBJECT TO CHANGE WITHOUT NOTICE.

Book Total _____

Orders shipped to the following states must include applicable sales tax:
AZ, CA, CO, IL, MI, MN, NY, PA, TX, VA and WI.

Add postage and handling (see chart) _____

TOTAL _____

810077

Real Estate Education Company

520 N. Dearborn Chicago, Illinois 60610-4975

PRACTICAL MONEY-MAKERS
FROM REAL ESTATE EDUCATION COMPANY

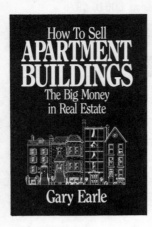

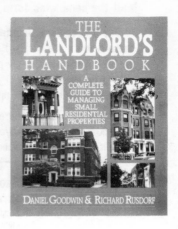

HOW TO SELL APARTMENT BUILDINGS: THE BIG MONEY IN REAL ESTATE,
by Gary Earle

This book provides you with all the details, examples, tables, and illustrations you need to identify the apartment market, understand it and profit. Read this book and you'll discover a practical, remarkably effective sales approach that can help turn your real estate license into a ticket to big commissions.

With *How To Sell Apartment Buildings,* you'll soon reap the rich rewards that go with the territory!

Contents
Sizing Up the Market • Gaining Market Knowledge • How to Price Apartment Buildings • Financing • Tax Aspects of Apartment Ownership • Cataloging Your Territory • Hot Sales Leads from Cold Calls • A Little Letter Can Go a Long Way • Meeting the Seller • Making the Offer • Negotiating the Sale • Closing the Deal • It's All Yours! • Index

6 x 9, hardcover, 200 pages
1988 copyright
Order Number 4105-06
Check box #28 on order form

POWER REAL ESTATE NEGOTIATION,
by William H. Pivar

Negotiating between buyer and seller is the hardest part of any real estate transaction. *Power Real Estate Negotiation* provides hundreds of specific, field-tested tips on negotiating transactions — and how to implement these techniques in direct interpersonal encounters. The unique interactive approach alternates between buyer's and seller's point of view, showing effective strategies and counterploys to each move of the opponent.

Includes:
• Reading the opponent's motivation
• Negotiating price and financing
• Overcoming impasses
• Closing the agreement

Contents
Negotiation Planning • Physical Aspects of Negotiation • General Negotiation Tactics • Negotiating the Price • Negotiating the Financing • Negotiating Other Issues • Impasse • Negotiating Dangers • The Agreement • Index

6 x 9, hardcover, 204 pages
1990 copyright
Order Number 1907-04
Check box #22 on order form

A PROFESSIONAL'S GUIDE TO REAL ESTATE FINANCE: TECHNIQUES FOR THE 1990's,
by Julie Garton-Good

Based on actual real estate practice, this reference provides the real estate professional with immediate answers to the most frequently asked financial questions. When clients call upon you to assist in evaluating financing options, you'll have all the answers in this new comprehensive guide.

Included are complete discussions of mortgage loan types—along with convenient checklists of the major features and pros and cons of each.

A Professional's Guide to Real Estate Finance emphasizes up-to-the-minute information, trend spotting and innovative sales strategies using financing techniques.

Contents
The Mortgage Market • Conventional Fixes-Rate Loans • Adjustable Rate Mortgages • FHA Loans • VA Loans • Special Programs • Buyer Leverage • Index

6 x 9, hardcover, 304 pages
1990 copyright
Order Number 1905-29
Check box #31 on order form

THE LANDLORD'S HANDBOOK: A COMPLETE GUIDE TO MANAGING SMALL RESIDENTIAL PROPERTIES,
by Daniel Goodwin and Richard Rusdorf, CPM

Whether you sell, manage or own small residential income properties, you'll find ideas to save time and headaches and to put money in your pocket. Two Inland Real Estate property management experts share their income-producing secrets.

Over 50 forms and checklists help you establish a smooth, profitable rental operation. Also included are tips on putting "active" self-management techniques to work to maximize tax deductions and profits.

Contents
Self-Management • Resident Relations • Marketing • Applications, Leases & Rental Agreements • Tenant Move-In • Lease Renewals • Tenant Move-Out • Rent Collection • Maintenance • Insurance • Property Taxes • Accounting • Bibliography • Appendix • Index

8-½ x 11, softcover, 236 pages
1989 copyright
Order Number 4105-08
Check box #29 on order form